As Per Latest CBSE Syllabus 2022-23
Issued on 21 April, 2022...

Science

CBSE Class 9

Authors
Heena Sharma (*Physics*)
Shubhankar Vats (*Chemistry*)
Rashmi Gupta (*Biology*)

Arihant Prakashan (School Division Series)

ARIHANT PRAKASHAN (School Division Series)

卐 ADMINISTRATIVE & PRODUCTION OFFICES

Regd. Office

'Ramchhaya' 4577/15, Agarwal Road, Darya Ganj, New Delhi -110002
Tele: 011- 47630600, 43518550; Fax: 011- 23280316

卐 **Head Office**

Kalindi, TP Nagar, Meerut (UP) - 250002, Tel: 0121-7156203, 7156204

卐 SALES & SUPPORT OFFICES

Agra, Ahmedabad, Bengaluru, Bareilly, Chennai, Delhi, Guwahati, Hyderabad, Jaipur, Jhansi, Kolkata, Lucknow, Nagpur & Pune.

PO No : TXT-XX-XXXXXXX-X-XX

Published By Arihant Publications (India) Ltd.

For further information about the books published by Arihant, log on to www.arihantbooks.com or e-mail at info@arihantbooks.com

Follow us on 

PRODUCTION TEAM

Publishing Managers
Mahendra Singh Rawat & Keshav Mohan

Project Coordinator
Yojna Sharma

Cover Designer
Bilal Hashmi

Inner Designer
Ankit Saini

Page Layouting
Rajbhaskar Rana, Subhash Chaprana

Proof Readers
Princi, Ankit

A WORD
WITH THE READERS

All in one Science Class 9th has been written keeping in mind the needs of students studying in Class 9th CBSE. This book has been made in such a way that students will be fully guided to prepare for the exam in the most effective manner, securing higher grades.

The purpose of this book is to equip a CBSE Student with a sound knowledge of Science at Class 9th Level. It covers the whole syllabus of class 9th Science divided into chapters as per the NCERT Textbook. This book will give you support during the course as well as guide you on Revision and Preparation for the exam itself. The material is presented in a Clear & Concise manner and there are questions for you to practice.

KEY FEATURES

- To make the students understand the chapter completely, each chapter has been divided into Individual Topics and each such topic has been treated as a separate chapter. Each topic has easy to understand theory, supported by Solved Examples, Related Figures, Notes, Tables, etc., followed by NCERT Folder having detailed solutions of all the Exercises of NCERT Textbook.
- Exam Practice Section of each chapter contains questions in that format in which these are asked in the examinations. Questions have been divided into Objective Type Questions, Short Answer Type Questions and Long Answer Type Questions.
- All the questions given here having Detailed Answers.
- There are 3 Sample Question Papers to make the students' practice for the examination as well.
- At the end of book, New features like– Statewise NTSE Questions for Stage I and Junior Science Olympiad Questions are added.

All-in-One Science for CBSE Class 9th has all the material required for Learning, Understanding, Practice and Assessment and will surely guide the students on the Path to Success.

We are highly thankful to ARIHANT PRAKASHAN, MEERUT for giving us such an excellent opportunity to write this book. The role of Arihant DTP Unit and Proofreading team is praiseworthy in the making of this book.

Huge efforts have been made from our side to keep this book error free, but inspite of that if any error or whatsoever is skipped in the book then that is purely incidental, apology for the same, please write to us about that so that it can be corrected in the further edition of the book. Suggestions for further improvement of the book will also be welcomed.

In the end, we would like to wish BEST OF LUCK to our readers!

Heena Sharma (Physics)
Shubhankar Vats (Chemistry)
Rashmi Gupta (Biology)

PREVIEW

TOPICAL DIVISION

Contains the necessary study material well supported by Definitions, Facts, Examples, etc. This section is totally in sync with NCERT Textbook and provides all the essentials needed to prepare you for the exam.

NCERT FOLDER

To make the students fully familiar with the NCERT Textbook (the most important books for CBSE examinations), solutions of all the Exercises of NCERT Textbook have been provided with each chapter.

CHAPTER

01

Matter In Our Surroundings

In our surroundings, we see a large variety of objects with different shapes, sizes and textures. All objects infact everything in this universe is made up of material which scientists have named 'matter'. The air we breathe, the food we eat, stones, clouds, stars, plants and animals, even a small drop of water or a particle of sand— everything is matter. Matter can be seen, tasted, smelled or felt.

Matter can neither be created nor destroyed, it can only be changed from one form to another. In modern day, scientists have evolved two types of classification of matter based on their physical and chemical properties. In this chapter, we shall learn about matter based on its physical properties.

Syllabus

- Definition of Matter
  - Solid
  - Liquid
  - Gas
- Characteristics
  - Shape
  - Volume
  - Density
- Change of State
  - Melting (Absorption of Heat)
  - Freezing
  - Evaporation (Cooling by Evaporation)
  - Condensation
  - Sublimation

Matter

Matter is anything that has mass and volume or we can say that anything that has mass, occupies space and can be felt by our one or more sense organs is called **matter**.

Note The SI unit of mass is kilogram (kg), volume is cubic metre (m^3). The common unit of measuring volume is litre (L) and 1 L = 1 dm^3, 1 L = 1000 mL, 1 mL = 1 cm^3

Classification of Matter

(i) Early Indian philosophers classified matter into five basic elements, called the *Panch-Tatva*. These are **air, water, earth, sky** and **fire**. According to them everything living or non-living, was made up of these five basic elements.

(ii) Now a days, matter is classified into groups according to their physical properties and chemical nature.

e.g. **solid, liquid** and **gas** (based on particle arrangement or physical properties) or **elements, compounds** and **mixtures** (based on chemical nature).

(iii) Gases are highly compressible. The **Liquefied Petroleum Gas** (LPG) cylinder used in our homes for cooking or the oxygen supplied to hospitals in cylinders is compressed gas.

Compressed Natural Gas (CNG) is used as a fuel these days in vehicles. Due to its higher compressibility, large volumes of a gas can be compressed into a small cylinder and transported easily.

(iv) In gaseous state, the particles move about randomly at high speed. Due to this random movement, gases exert pressure on the walls of the container, in which they are kept.

Air is the example of gaseous state. It is a mixture of gases like oxygen, nitrogen, carbon dioxide, inert

Check Point 01

1. What was the basic classification of element in ancient time? Name them.
2. (i) As the temperature rises, particles move ....
   (ii) With increase in temperature, the kinetic energy of the particles also ....
   (iii) The rate of diffusion of liquids is .... than that of solids.
3. A piece of chalk can be broken into small particles on hammering, but it is not possible to break a piece of iron in the same fashion. Why?
4. Find the density of a handful of sand having a mass of 208 g and it displaces a volume of 80 mL of water.
5. What is fluid?
6. Why solid ice floats on water?
7. By which physical process the fragrance of burning incense stick spreads all around?

NCERT FOLDER

INTEXT QUESTIONS

1. Which of the following are matter?
Chair, air, love, smell, hate, almonds, thought, cold, cold-drink, smell of perfume. Pg 3

Sol. Anything that occupies space and has mass is called matter. Matter can exist in three physical states-solid, liquid and gas. Chair and almonds are solid states of matter. Cold-drink is a liquid state of matter. Air and smell of perfume are gaseous states of matter.

2. Give reasons for the following observation. The smell of hot sizzling food reaches you several metres away, but to get the smell of cold food, you have to go close. Pg 3

Sol. Particles of matter are continuously moving. They possess kinetic energy. As the temperature rises, particles move faster. The particles of the aroma of hot food mix with the particles of air and reach to us several metres away, but to get an aroma or smell of cold food, we have to go close because the particles that carry smell of cold food move slower as compared to particles that carry smell of hot sizzling food.

3. A diver is able to cut through water in a swimming pool. Which property of matter does this observation show? Pg 3

Sol. This observation shows that the particles of matter have spaces between them.

4. What are the characteristics of the particles of matter? Pg 3

Sol. Characteristics of particles of matter are as follows :
(i) They are very small in size.
(ii) They move faster in gaseous state as compared to solid or liquid state.
(iii) They diffuse faster at higher temperature.

5. The mass per unit volume of a substance is called density (Density = Mass/Volume).
Arrange the following in the order of increasing density.
Air, exhaust from chimneys, honey, water, chalk, cotton and iron. Pg 6

SUMMARY

- Matter is anything that has mass and occupies volume.
- The SI unit of mass and volume is **kilogram** (kg) and **cubic metre** (m^3), respectively.
- Matter is classified into groups based on their physical and chemical properties, i.e. physical properties (solid, liquid and gas) and chemical properties (elements, compounds and mixtures).
- Every matter is made up of certain particles which differ in shape, size and nature.
- The particles of matter have a tendency to diffuse.
- Solids have definite shape, distinct boundaries and fixed volumes.
- Liquids do not have a definite shape.
- Gases have neither definite shape nor volume.
- The state of matter can be interchanged by changing temperature or pressure.
- At specific conditions of temperature and pressure, the conversion of a matter from its solid to its liquid state is called **fusion**.
- The conversion of a matter from its liquid state to vapour (gaseous state) is called **boiling**. It is a bulk phenomenon.
- The conversion of a matter from its liquid to solid state is called **freezing**.
- The conversion of a matter from its liquid to gaseous state is called **vapourisation**.
- The conversion of matter from its gaseous to liquid state is called **condensation**.
- The process of change of solid state directly into gaseous state without passing through the liquid state upon heating and *vice-versa* on cooling is called **sublimation**.
- The heat energy which has to be supplied to change the state of substance is called **latent heat**.
- **Latent heat of vapourisation** is the heat energy required to change 1kg of a liquid to gas at atmospheric pressure at its boiling point.
- **Latent heat of fusion** is the amount of heat energy required to change 1 kg of solid into liquid at its melting point.
- The process of conversion of a liquid into its vapour state at any temperature below its boiling point is called **evaporation**.
- Apart from solid, liquid and gaseous state, scientists have discovered two more states, i.e. **plasma** and **Bose-Einstein condensate**.
- Plasma state consists of super-energetic and super-excited particles.
- The Sun and the stars glow because of the presence of plasma in them.
- The Bose-Einstein condensate is formed by cooling a gas of extremely low density about one hundred thousandth the density of normal air to super low temperature.

NCERT FOLDER

CHECK POINT

To assess your step-by-step learning of chapter, Check Point Questions are incorporated in between the theory.

SUMMARY

For complete revision of each chapter, Summary is given. It contains crux of the chapter theory.

for CBSE Class 9th Examination is a complete book which can give you all; Study & Practice It is hoped that this book will reinforce and extend your ideas about the subject and finally will place you in the ranks of toppers.

Exam Practice

Objective Type Questions [1 Mark each]

Multiple Choice Questions

1. A diver is able to cut through water in a swimming pool. The property shown by the matter is
   (a) the particles are of very small size
   (b) the matter have space between them
   (c) the particles are in solid state
   (d) the particles are running here and there, have no space between them

Sol. (b) A diver is able to cut through water because water is a liquid and have space between the water molecules due to weak force of attraction among the water molecules.

2. Which of the following is found in solid state at room temperature?
   (a) Stone (b) Sand
   (c) Mercury (d) Both (a) and (b)

Sol. (d) Stone and sand are found in solid state at room temperature because of strong attractive force among their particles, (i.e. the particles of stone and sand are held together with strong attractive forces).
Mercury is the only metal which is found in liquid state at room temperature.

Short Answer (SA) Type Questions [3 Marks each]

1. (i) A sponge can be compressed, yet it is a solid? Explain.
   (ii) Name the state of matter that has minimum space between particles.

Sol. (i) A sponge has minute holes, in which air is trapped, when we press it, the air is expelled out and we are able to compress it. Hence, sponge can be compressed, instead of being a solid. (2)
(ii) Solid state has minimum space between their particles. (1)

2. The cover plate is removed from the gas jars shown in the diagram. After several days, the colour of the gas is the same in both jars. Why does this happen? Explain.

Oxygen
Cover plate
Bromine

Sol. Diffusion has occurred in the jars. Bromine molecules move from a region where they are of higher concentration to a region of lower concentration, i.e. they move in the above gas jar. Oxygen molecules move from a region where they are of higher concentration to a region of lower concentration, i.e. they move to the below gas jar. Diffusion continues until both gas jars have uniform distribution of bromine and oxygen molecules. (3)

3. (i) Explain the interconversion of three states of matter in terms of force of attraction and kinetic energy of the molecules.
   (ii) Arrange the three states of matter in the increasing order of rate of diffusion and particle motion.

Sol. (i) During the interconversion of a solid into a liquid and liquid into gas on increasing temperature, the kinetic energy of the molecules increases and force of attraction among molecules decreases and vice-versa. (2)
(ii) (a) Rate of diffusion, Solid < liquid < gas
(b) Particles motion, Solid < liquid < gas. (1)

EXAM PRACTICE

It contains questions in that format in which these are asked in the examinations, i.e., Objective Type Questions, Short Answer Type Questions, Long Answer Type Questions. All the questions are fully explained. The explanations given here teach the students, how to write the explanations in the examinations to get full marks. Students can use these questions for practice and assess their understanding & recall of the chapter.

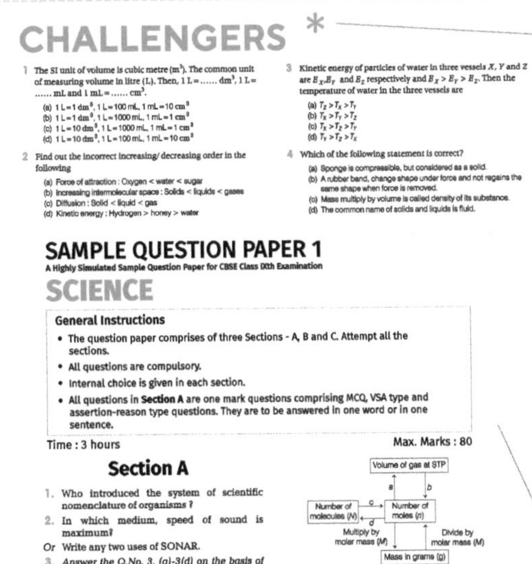

CHAPTER EXERCISE

Objective Type Questions [1 Mark each]

Multiple Type Questions

1. Crystals of $KMnO_4$ in water proves that
   (a) $KMnO_4$ is of red colour
   (b) $KMnO_4$ is acidic in nature
   (c) $KMnO_4$ is made up of millions of tiny particles
   (d) $KMnO_4$ is a reducing agent

2. A few substances are arranged in the increasing order of 'forces of attraction' between their particles. Which one of the following represents a correct arrangement? NCERT Exemplar
   (a) Water, air, wind (b) Air, sugar, oil
   (c) Oxygen, water, sugar (d) Salt, juice, air

Match the Column

10. Match the following column A and B.

Column A	Column B
A. Increase in surface area	(i) Evaporation increase
B. Decrease in temperature	(ii) Evaporation decrease
C. Evaporation	(iii) Bulk phenomenon
D. Boiling	(iv) Surface phenomenon

Assertion-Reason

Direction (Q.Nos. 13-15) *In each of the following questions, a statement of Assertion is given by the corresponding statement of Reason. Of the statements, mark the correct answer as*
(a) If both Assertion and Reason are true and Reason is the correct explanation of Assertion

CHALLENGERS

At the end of the chapter, challenger questions are given. These questions may be or may not be asked in the examination, have been given just for additional practice.

CHAPTER EXERCISE

At the end of the chapter, these unsolved questions are for practice and assessment of students. By practising these questions, students can assess their preparation level for the chapter.

STATEWISE NTSE QUESTIONS

Matter in Our Surroundings

1. Dry ice is (UP)
   (a) freon (b) liquid chlorine
   (c) solid carbon dioxide (d) plaster of Paris

Is Matter Around us Pure?

7. The method used to extract oils which give fragrance to flowers is (Kerala)
   (a) fractional distillation (b) steam distillation
   (c) sublimation (d) crystallisation

Atoms and Molecules

16. Which of the following pairs have the same number of atoms? (Kerala)
    (a) 16 g of O_2 (g) and 4 g of H_2 (g)
    (b) 16 g of O_2 (g) and 44 g of CO_2 (g)
    (c) 28 g of N_2 (g) and 16 g of O_2 (g)
    (d) 12 g of C(s) and 23 g of Na(s)

17. The formulae of an oxide of an element M is MO. The formulae of its phosphate is (UP)
    (a) $M_3(PO_4)_2$ (b) MPO_4
    (c) $M_2(PO_4)_3$ (d) M_3PO_4

Junior Science Olympiad

Chapterwise Questions

Atoms and Molecules

1. An astronaut has to burn 40g of glucose in his body per hour to get the required energy. Find the amount of oxygen that would need to be carried in space to meet his energy requirement for thirty days (2018)
   (a) 10.2 kg (b) 28.8 kg
   (c) 30.7 kg (d) 96.1 kg

The Fundamental Unit of Life

6. Many proteins of the chloroplast are encoded by genes in the nucleus. In these cases, the RNA is transcribed in the nucleus. For such a protein how many membrane(s) does the protein cross to reach the thylakoid space (lumen) of the chloroplast? (2018)
   (a) One (b) Two
   (c) Three (d) Four

SAMPLE QUESTION PAPERS

To make the students practice is real sense, we have provided 3 Sample Question Papers, exactly based on latest pattern and syllabus of CBSE Examination.

NTSE AND JUNIOR SCIENCE OLYMPIAD

At the end of the book, these are Statewise NTSE Questions and Junior Science Olympiad Questions. These Questions will help you to integrate your scheme studies with competitive exams at this level.

CONTENTS

**This chapter will not be assessed in the year end examination.*

LATEST COURSE STRUCTURE

Unit No.	Unit	Marks
I	Matter- Its Nature and Behaviour	25
II	Organisation in the Living World	22
III	Motion, Force and Work	27
IV	Food; Food Production	06
	Total	**80**
	Internal Assessment	20
	Grand Total	**100**

THEME Materials

UNIT I : Matter- Nature and Behaviour

Definition of matter; Solid, Liquid and Gas; Characteristics - Shape, Volume, Density; Change of state-Melting (absorption of heat), Freezing, Evaporation (cooling by evaporation), Condensation, Sublimation.

Nature of Matter Elements, Compounds and Mixtures, Heterogeneous and Homogeneous Mixtures, Colloids and Suspensions. Physical and chemical changes (excluding separating the components of a mixture).

Particle Nature and their Basic Units Atoms and Molecules, Law of Chemical Combination, Chemical formula of common compounds, Atomic and Molecular Masses.

Structure of Atoms Electrons, Protons and Neutrons, Valency, Atomic Number and mass number, Isotopes and Isobars.

THEME The World of the Living

UNIT II : Organisation in the Living World

Cell - Basic Unit of Life Cell as a Basic Unit of Life; Prokaryotic and Eukaryotic Cells, Multicellular Organisms; Cell Membrane and Cell Wall, Cell Organelles and Cell Inclusions; Chloroplast, Mitochondria, Vacuoles, Endoplasmic Reticulum, Golgi Apparatus; Nucleus, Chromosomes - Basic Structure, Number.

Tissues, Organs, Organ System, Organism Structure and Functions of Animal and Plant Tissues (only four types of tissues in animals; Meristematic and permanent tissues in plants).

THEME Moving Things, People and Ideas

UNIT III : Motion, Force and Work

Motion Distance and Displacement, Velocity; Uniform and Non-Uniform Motion Along a Straight Line; Acceleration, Distance-time and Velocity-time Graphs for Uniform Motion and Uniformly Accelerated Motion, Elementary Idea of Uniform Circular Motion.

Force And Newton's Laws Force and Motion, Newton's Laws of Motion, Action and Reaction Forces. Inertia of a Body, Inertia and Mass, Momentum, Force and Acceleration.

Gravitation Gravitation; Universal Law of Gravitation, Force of Gravitation of the Earth (gravity), Acceleration due to Gravity; Mass and Weight; Free Fall.

Floatation Thrust and Pressure, Archimedes Principle, Buoyancy,

Work, Energy and Power Work done by a Force, Energy, Power; Kinetic and Potential Energy; Law of Conservation of Energy (excluding commercial unit of Energy)

Sound Nature of Sound and its Propagation in Various Media, Speed of Sound, Range of Hearing in Humans; Ultrasound; Reflection of Sound; Echo

THEME **Food**

UNIT IV : Food Production

Plant and Animal Breeding and Selection for Quality Improvement and Management; Use of Fertilizers and Manures; Protection from Pests and Diseases; Organic Farming.

NOTE FOR THE TEACHERS

1. The chapter Natural Resources (NCERT Chapter 14) will not be assessed in the year-end examination. However, learners may be assigned to read this chapter and encouraged to prepare a brief write up on any concept of this chapter in their Portfolio. This may be for Internal Assessment and credit may be given for Periodic Assessment/Portfolio.

2. The NCERT text books present information in boxes across the book. These help students to get conceptual clarity. However, the information in these boxes would not be assessed in the year-end examination.

PRACTICALS

Practicals should be conducted alongside the concepts taught in theory classes

LIST OF EXPERIMENTS

1. Preparation of UNIT-I
   a. a true solution of common salt, sugar and alum
   b. a suspension of soil, chalk powder and fine sand in water
   c. a colloidal solution of starch in water and egg albumin/milk in water and distinguish between
      - Transparency
      - Filtration Criterion
      - Stability
2. Preparation of UNIT-I
   a. a mixture
   b. a compound

   using iron filings and sulphur powder and distinguish between these on the basis of

   i. appearance, i.e., homogeneity and heterogeneity

   ii. behaviour towards a magnet

   iii. behaviour towards carbon disulphide as a solvent

   iv. effect of heat
3. Perform the following reactions and classify them as physical or chemical changes
   a. Iron with copper sulphate solution in water
   b. Burning of Magnesium in air
   c. Zinc with dilute sulphuric acid
   d. Heating of copper sulphate crystals
   e. Sodium sulphate with barium chloride in the form of their solutions in water
4. Preparation of prepare stained temporary mounts of (a) onion peel, (b) human cheek epithelial cells and to record observations and draw their labelled diagrams. UNIT-II
5. Identification of parenchyma, Collenchyma and sclerenchyma tissues in plants, striped smooth and cardiac muscle fibers and nerve cells in animals, from prepared slides. Draw their labelled diagrams. UNIT-II
6. Determination of the melting point of ice and the boiling point of water. UNIT-I
7. Verification of the Laws of reflection of sound. UNIT-III
8. Determination of the density of solid (denser than water) by using a spring balance and a measuring cylinder. UNIT-III
9. Establishing the relation between the loss in weight of a solid when fully immersed in UNIT-III
   a. tap water
   b. strongly salty water with the weight of water displaced by it by taking at least two different solids.
10. Determination of the speed of a pulse propagated through a stretched string/slinky (helical spring). UNIT-III
11. Verification of the law of conservation of mass in a chemical reaction. UNIT-III

FACE TO FACE
WITH AllinOne

All-in-One for Science Class 9th has been written by an experienced examiner. specially for students studying in Class 9th with CBSE Curriculum. It provides all the explanation and advise you need to study efficiently and succeed in the exam. This is the only book which strictly follows the Pattern of CBSE.

The purpose of this book is to aid any CBSE student to achieve the best possible grade in the exam. This book will give you support during the course as well as advise on revision and preparation for the exam itself.

Exam Practice

Exam Practice is carried out at the end of a course of learning. It measures or 'sums up' how much a student has learned from the course. It carries 80 Marks out of the 100 Marks of the examination.

All-in-One for Science deals Exam Practice section with chapterwise approach, the whole syllabus has been divided into chapters as per NCERT Textbook. Each chapter starts with detailed Text material in a totally explanatory manner having Key Definitions / Terms. After the theory section there is Exam Practice having questions in that format in which these are asked in the examinations, i.e., Very Short Answer Type Questions, Short Answer Type Questions (3 Marks) & Long Answer Type Questions (5 Marks).

All the questions are explained. To make the students completely compatible with the NCERT Textbook (the most important books for CBSE examinations). Answers of all the Questions of NCERT Textbook has been given with each chapter.

The explanations given in the chapters indicate the students, how to write the explanation in the examinations to get the full marks. Students can use these questions for practise and to assess their understanding & recall of the chapter.

Sample Question Papers

To make the students practise and make them feel the heat of the real examination, we have provided 3 Sample Question Papers, based on the whole syllabus and strictly based on the pattern of CBSE examination.

By attempting these Question Papers, students can make themselves practise for the examination as well as they will be able to learn the Time Management during the examination.

From the above description, it can be concluded that All-in-One Science for CBSE Class 9th has all the material required for Exam Practice and will surely guide the students on the path to success.

How to Attempt the EXAMINATION PAPER

The examination question paper contains different types of questions like Very Short Answer (VSA) Type Questions, Short Answer (SA) Type Questions, Long Answer (LA) Type Questions, etc., but broadly there are two types of questions asked in the examinations, one is Short Answer Type and the other is Long Answer Type.
Both types of questions are dealt with in different ways which are discussed below.

Short Answer (SA) Type Questions

Attempt all the questions, as there are no penalties for incorrect answers. If a calculation is involved, be careful to work logically. Always keep in mind that Very Short Answer (VSA) Type Questions and Short Answer (SA) Type Questions do not involve very lengthy calculations. They generally have a fact hidden behind them. If you find yourself involved in lengthy calculation, then for sure you are going wrong. Always read these types of questions very carefully and understand the demand of the question and answer accordingly.

If you cannot answer a question, or remain uncertain as to what is the correct answer, leave it and return to it when you have completed the other questions.

Long Answer (LA) Type Questions

Once you reach the Long Answer Questions section, go through the section and choose a question you feel confident about. You need not start with the first question. Read the question twice, look at the mark allocation for each part and then decide exactly what is required to secure full marks.

Take reasonable care that your writing is legible-it should be easily read and be marked. Satisfy the Examiner and you can score good Marks.

Writing Examiner Friendly Answers

- Follow the instructions in the question, carefully responding to words and phrases such as describe and give a reason for.
- Try to attempt the questions exactly in the same order as written in the question paper, as it helps the examiner identify the answer immediately and he recognises the set pattern.
- Never attempt a question consisting of two parts at widely different places in the answer book.
- Tie your supplementary sheets in the right order.
- There should be minimum cutting on the paper and it should look neat.
- Structure your answer properly.
- Use capital letters, bullets, and underlining and highlighting as tools to attract attention to important points.
- If you have used any page for rough work, it should be crossed and clearly marked 'Rough Work'.

Be Perfect & Precise

Too many candidates write at length without answering the question properly. Never forget, marks are not awarded for correct subject but for correct subject that answers the question most appropriately.

Time Management During Exam

- As you read through the question paper, plan your strategy. If you have any choice between the questions, then choose carefully, because if you do one option and later decide to attempt the other one, then you would be wasting your time.
- Do not rush, as this is a major cause of mistakes, particularly of misreading the question. The time allocated for the examination is adequate for the students to complete the paper. Leave the hardest questions to be tackled to the end.
- If you finish early, take the opportunity to check through your answers. Ask yourself, have I answered the question and have I made sufficient points to be awarded full marks?

We are sure that using the above tips and advices, you will surely be able to improve your grades in the examination.

CHAPTER

01

Matter In Our Surroundings

In our surroundings, we see a large variety of objects with different shapes, sizes and textures. All objects infact everything in this universe is made up of material which scientists have named 'matter'. The air we breathe, the food we eat, stones, clouds, stars, plants and animals, even a small drop of water or a particle of sand— everything is matter. Matter can be seen, tasted, smelled or felt.

Matter can neither be created nor destroyed, it can only be changed from one form to another. In modern day, scientists have evolved two types of classification of matter based on their physical and chemical properties. In this chapter, we shall learn about matter based on its physical properties.

Chapter Checklist

- Matter
- States of Matter
- Change of States of Matter
- Effect of Change of Temperature
- Effect of Change of Pressure
- Evaporation
- Plasma and Bose-Einstein Condensate

Matter

Matter is anything that has mass and volume or we can say that anything that has mass, occupies space and can be felt by our one or more sense organs is called **matter.**

Note The SI unit of mass is kilogram (kg), volume is cubic metre (m^3). The common unit of measuring volume is litre (L) and $1 L = 1 dm^3$, $1 L = 1000 mL$, $1 mL = 1 cm^3$

Classification of Matter

(*i*) Early Indian philosophers classified matter into five basic elements, called the ***Panch-Tatva.*** These are **air, water, earth, sky** and **fire.** According to them everything living or non-living, was made up of these five basic elements.

(*ii*) Now a days, matter is classified into groups according to their physical properties and chemical nature.

e.g. **solid, liquid** and **gas** (based on particle arrangement or physical properties) or **elements, compounds** and **mixtures** (based on chemical nature).

Physical Nature of Matter

If we study the physical composition of matter, we found that:

(*i*) Every matter is made up of certain particles which differ in shape, size and nature from other type of matter.

(*ii*) The particles of matter are very small or tiny (beyond our imagination).

Characteristics of Particles of Matter

Some important characteristics of particles of matter are as follows:

(*i*) Particles of matter have space between them.

(*ii*) Particles of matter are in a state of continuous movement. This suggests that they possess some energy, called the **kinetic energy**. As the temperature rises, the kinetic energy of the particles increases and hence, particles move faster.

(*iii*) The particles of matter have a tendency to diffuse, i.e. to intermix on their own with each other. They do so by getting into the spaces between the particles. The intermixing of particles of two different types of matter on their own is called **diffusion**.

(*iv*) Particles of matter attract each other. A force of attraction exists between the particles, that is known as **intermolecular force of attraction**. This force keeps the particles together. The strength of this force of attraction varies from one kind of matter to another.

Diffusion and Osmosis

Diffusion is the process in which molecules of a substance move from higher concentration to lower concentration and goes on until a uniform mixture is formed. In osmosis the solvent molecules move from the lower concentration to higher concentration through a semipermeable membrane.

States of Matter

Matter around us exists in three different states which are **solid, liquid** and **gas**. These states of matter arise due to the variation in the characteristics of the particles of matter.

The Solid State

Solid is defined as that form of matter which possesses rigidity, incompressibility and hence, has a definite shape and a definite volume.

Some important properties of solid state are as follows :

(*i*) Solids have definite shape, distinct boundaries and fixed volumes, i.e. have negligible compressibility.

(*ii*) Solids have a tendency to maintain their shape when subjected to outside force. A rubber band, changes shape under force and regains the same shape when the force is removed. If excessive force is applied, it breaks. Sugar and salt also take the shape of the container in which they are placed but are considered as solids. This is because the shape of each individual sugar or salt crystal remains fixed.

(*iii*) Solids either do not diffuse or diffuse at a very slow rate.

Sponge is compressible, but considered as a solid. This is because a sponge has minute holes, in which air is trapped. When it is pressed, the air is expelled out and we are able to compress it.

(*iv*) Solids may break under force, but it is difficult to change their shape, so they are rigid.

(*v*) Generally, solids have higher densities as compared to their liquid or gaseous forms.

Sugar, sand, rocks, stones, metals like iron, copper, aluminium, gold, silver, etc., are the examples of substance which exist in the solid state.

Mass per unit volume of a substance is called its **density**,

i.e. $$\text{Density} = \frac{\text{Mass}}{\text{Volume}} = \frac{m}{V}$$

The Liquid State

Liquid is defined as that form of matter, which possesses a fixed volume, but have no fixed shape.

Some important properties of liquid state are as follows :

(*i*) Liquids do not have a definite shape, i.e. they take up the shape of the container in which they are kept.

(*ii*) Liquids flow and change shape, so they are not rigid, but can be called **fluid**.

Note Fluid In science, the common name of gases and liquids is fluid.

(*iii*) Solids, liquids and gases can diffuse into liquids. The gases from the atmosphere diffuse and dissolve in water. These gases, especially oxygen and carbon dioxide, are essential for the survival of aquatic animals and plants. The aquatic animals can breathe under water due to the presence of dissolved oxygen in water.

(iv) Liquids are almost incompressible.

(v) The attraction force between the particles of liquid is greater than that of gases, but less than that of solids.

(vi) The rate of diffusion of liquids is higher than that of solids. This is due to the fact that in the liquid state, particles move freely and have greater space between each other as compared to particles in the solid state.

(vii) Density of a liquid is generally less than that of its solid form. Some exceptions are also there, e.g. solid ice is lighter than water as it floats on water, i.e. the density of solid form of water (ice) is less as compared to that of the liquid form of water.

Water, milk, juice, oil, kerosene, petrol, alcohol, benzene etc., are the examples of the substance which exist in the liquid state.

The Gaseous State

Gases can be defined as that form of matter which possesses high compressibility and hence, has neither definite shape nor definite volume.

Some important properties of gaseous state are as follows :

(i) Gases have a tendency to flow as liquids do. Therefore, they are also considered as **fluids**.

(ii) Gases show the property of diffusing very fast into other gases due to high speed of particles and large spaces between them.

Due to the high diffusion tendency of gases, the smell of hot cooked food reaches us in seconds. The particles of the aroma of food mix with the particles of air spread, reach us and even farther away.

(iii) Gases are highly compressible. The **Liquefied Petroleum Gas** (LPG) cylinder used in our homes for cooking or the oxygen supplied to hospitals in cylinders is compressed gas.

Compressed Natural Gas (CNG) is used as a fuel these days in vehicles. Due to its higher compressibility, large volumes of a gas can be compressed into a small cylinder and transported easily.

(iv) In gaseous state, the particles move about randomly at high speed. Due to this random movement, gases exert pressure on the walls of the container, in which they are kept.

Air is the example of gaseous state. It is a mixture of gases like oxygen, nitrogen, carbon dioxide, inert gases, etc. Other examples of gases are hydrogen, ammonia, nitrogen dioxide, sulphur dioxide, etc.

(v) All living creatures need to breathe for survival.

So, solids, liquids and gases can diffuse into liquids.

(vi) The density of gases is minimum. A gas is much lighter than the same volume of a solid or a liquid.

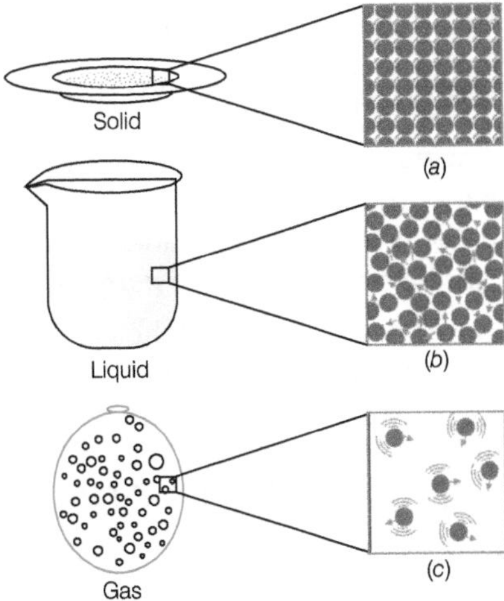

Fig. (a), (b) and (c) show the magnified schematic pictures of the three states of matter. The motion of the particles can be seen and compared in the three states of matter

Rigidity and Fluidity

Rigid means inflexible. A solid is a rigid form of matter, hence it does not require a container to keep it. Fluid is a material which can flow easily and requires a vessel to keep it. A liquid is a fluid form of matter which takes the shape of container, while a gas is a fluid form of matter which fills the container.

Check Point 01

1 What was the basic classification of element in ancient time? Name them.

2 Fill in the blanks.

(i) As the temperature rises, particles move ....

(ii) With increase in temperature, the kinetic energy of the particles also ....

(iii) The rate of diffusion of liquids is .... than that of solids.

3 State True or False for the following statement:
CNG is compressed nitrogen gas.

4 Find the density of a handful of sand having a mass of 208 g and it displaces a volume of 80 mL of water.

5 What is fluid?

6 Why solid ice floats on water?

7 By which physical process the fragrance of burning incense stick spreads all around?

Change of States of Matter

In your daily life, you come across various substances which exist in three states, i.e. solid, liquid and gas, e.g. water, wax, ghee, etc. Water is the most commonly observed example that exists as ice (solid), water (liquid) as well as water vapour (gas).

Interconversion of States of Matter

The states of matter are interconvertible. The phenomenon of change of matter from one state to another and back to the original state by altering the conditions of temperature and pressure is called **interconversion of states of matter.**

Following two factors (or any one of these) make it possible to convert one state of matter into another :

(*i*) Change in temperature (*ii*) Change in pressure

Terms Involved in Change of State

Following terms are involved in change of state:

1. Fusion or Melting and Melting Point

The process of conversion of a matter from its solid state to its liquid state at specific conditions of temperature and pressure, is called **fusion/melting**. And the definite temperature at which a solid starts melting is called the **melting point** of that solid, e.g. melting point of ice is 0°C or 273.16 K. Higher the melting point of a substance, greater will be the force of attraction between its particles.

2. Boiling and Boiling Point

The process of conversion of a matter from its liquid state to vapours (gaseous state) at specific conditions of temperature and pressure is called **boiling**. It is a bulk phenomenon. And the temperature at which a liquid starts boiling at the atmospheric pressure is known as its **boiling point.**

3. Sublimation

The process of change of solid state directly into gaseous state without passing through the liquid state upon heating is known as **sublimation**, and the direct change of gas to solid without changing into liquid is called **deposition.**

e.g. naphthalene, camphor, iodine, ammonium chloride, etc., are the solids that undergo sublimation.

4. Vapourisation

The process of conversion of a matter from its liquid state to gaseous state at specific conditions of temperature and pressure is called **vapourisation.**

5. Freezing and Freezing Point

The process of conversion of matter from its liquid state to solid state at specific conditions of temperature and pressure, is called **freezing.** It is a reverse process of fusion/melting. And the definite temperature at which a liquid changes into solid state by giving out heat energy at 1 atm is called the **freezing point.**

6. Condensation

The process of conversion of matter from its gaseous state to liquid state at specific conditions of temperature and pressure, is called **condensation.** It is a reverse process of vapourisation.

Effect of Change of Temperature

When a solid is heated, the kinetic energy of its particles increases. Due to increase in kinetic energy, the particles start vibrating with greater speed. The energy supplied by the heat overcomes the forces of attraction between the particles.

The particles leave their positions and start moving more freely. At a certain stage (i.e. at melting point), solid melts and is converted into a liquid state.

At a certain temperature, a point is reached when the particles have enough energy to break free from the forces of attraction of each other. At this temperature (i.e. boiling point), the liquid starts changing into gas. In contrast, by decreasing the temperature (by cooling), a gas can be converted into liquid state and a liquid can be converted into solid state.

Effect of change of temperature on the physical state may be summarised as:

So, it can be concluded that the state of matter can be changed into another by changing the temperature.

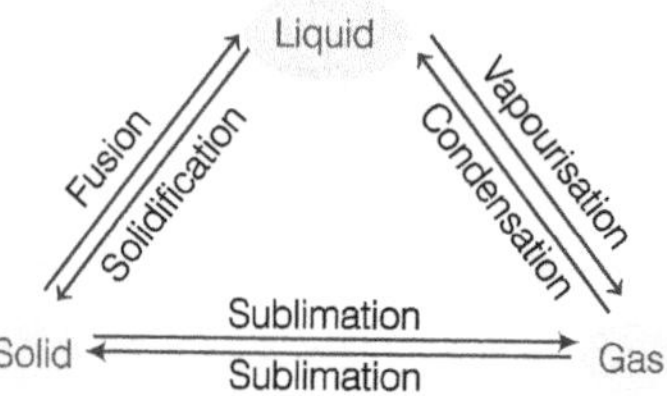

Interconversion of the three states of matter

Difference between Gas and Vapour

A substance is said to be a gas if its boiling point is below room temperature, e.g. O_2, N_2, CO_2, etc. If the normal physical state of a substance is either a solid or a liquid, but gets converted into the gaseous state either on its own or by absorbing energy, the gaseous state is called the vapour state, e.g. vapours of water in air.

Scales of Measuring Temperature

Three scales of measuring temperature are as follows:

(i) Temperature on Kelvin scale

= Temperature on Celsius scale + 273.16;

$T(\text{K}) = t(°\text{C}) + 273.16$

Kelvin is the SI unit of temperature, 0 °C = 273.16 K

For convenience, we take 0°C = 273 K

(ii) Temperature on Celsius scale

= Temperature on Kelvin scale − 273.16;

$t(°\text{C}) = T(\text{K}) - 273.16$

(iii) Temperature on Fahrenheit scale: Celsius and Fahrenheit temperatures are related to each other by the relation, $°\text{F} = \frac{9}{5}(°\text{C}) + 32$

Example 1. *Convert the temperature of 200°C to the Kelvin scale.*

Sol. We know that, temperature on Kelvin scale

= Temperature on Celsius scale + 273.16

= 200 + 273.16 = 473.16 K

Thus, a temperature of 200°C on Celsius scale is equal to 473.16 K on the Kelvin scale.

Example 2. *Convert the temperature of 450 K to the Celsius scale.*

Sol. We know that, temperature on Celsius scale

= Temperature on Kelvin scale − 273.16

= 450 − 273.16 = 176.84°C

Thus, a temperature of 450 K on Kelvin scale is equal to 176.84°C on Celsius scale.

Latent Heat

When a heat is given to a substance, its temperature increases. However, when heat is supplied to change the physical state of a substance, there is no increase in temperature of a substance. Thus, the heat energy which has to be supplied to change the state of substance is called its **latent heat**. In actual, the word 'latent' means 'hidden'. Latent heat does not raise (or increase) the temperature. But latent heat is always supplied to change the state of a substance.

Latent heat is of the following two types :

Latent Heat of Fusion (Solid to Liquid Change)

The amount of heat energy that is required to change 1 kg of a solid into liquid at atmospheric pressure and at its melting point is known as the **latent heat of fusion.** Particles in water at 0°C (273.16 K) have more energy as compared to particles in ice at the same temperature.

Latent Heat of Vapourisation (Liquid to Gas Change)

The amount of heat energy that is required to convert 1 kg of a liquid into gas (at its boiling point) without any rise in temperature is known as the **latent heat of vapourisation.** Particles in steam, i.e. water vapour at 373 K (100°C) have more energy than water at the same temperature.

Note It has been found that burns caused by the steam are much more severe than those caused by boiling water though both of them are at the same temperature of 100°C. As particles in steam have absorbed extra energy in the form of latent heat of vapourisation. Thus, when steam falls on our skin and condense to produce water, it gives more heat than boiling water.

Effect of Change of Pressure

The physical state of a substance can also be changed by changing the pressure. An increase in pressure brings the particles closer and increases the force of attraction between them, that brings about the change. e.g. when high pressure is applied to a gas and its temperature is reduced, the gas is converted to a liquid, i.e. the gas is liquefied. Hence, we can say that pressure and temperature determine the state of a substance, whether it will be solid, liquid or gas.

The pressure exerted by a gas is measured in atmosphere (atm) unit. The pressure of air in atmosphere is called **atmospheric pressure.** Atmospheric pressure at sea level is taken as 1 atm which is also normal atmospheric pressure. As we go higher, atmospheric pressure decreases.

1 atm = 1.01×10^5 Pa (Pa = Pascal, SI unit of pressure)

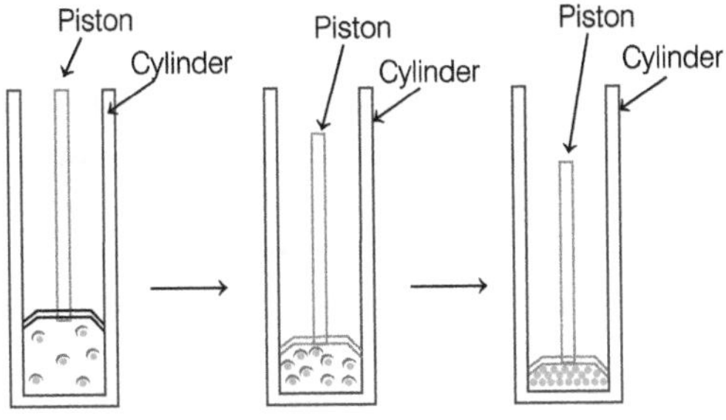

By applying pressure, particles of matter can be brought close together

Check Point 02

1 Fill in the blanks:
   (i) Higher the melting point of a substance,......will be the force of attraction between its particles.
   (ii) Particles from the bulk of the liquid gain energy to change into......state.
   (iii) Naphthalene undergoes the process of......... .
2 Define vapourisation.
3 Why particles start vibrating in solids ?
4 Convert the temperature of 70° C to the Kelvin scale.
5 What is the value of latent heat of fusion of ice?
6 State True or False for the following statement:
   Boiling is a bulk phenomenon.
7 How gases can be liquefy ?
8 What are the factors which are responsible for bringing a change in the physical state of substance.

Evaporation

The process of conversion of a liquid into its vapour state at any temperature below its boiling point is called **evaporation**. The particles of a liquid have different amount of kinetic energies. The particles present at the surface possess comparatively higher kinetic energy as compared to those present in the bulk.

Therefore, particles at the surface with higher kinetic energy is able to break away from the forces of attraction of other particles and get converted into vapour. Water, when left uncovered, slowly changes into vapour. Wet clothes dry up, etc., are happen due to evaporation.

Factors Affecting Evaporation

The rate of evaporation of a liquid depends upon the following factors:

(i) **Surface area** Evaporation is a surface phenomenon, if the surface area is increased, the rate of evaporation increases, e.g. while putting clothes for drying up, we spread them out.

(ii) **Temperature** The rate of evaporation of a liquid increases with a rise in temperature. With the increase of temperature, more number of particles get enough kinetic energy to go into vapour state. That is why, evaporation is faster in a hot summer day than in winter or on a cloudy day.

(iii) **Humidity** It is the amount of water vapour present in air. The air around us cannot hold more than a definite amount of water vapour at a given temperature. If the amount of water in air is already high, the rate of evaporation decreases. That is why, clothes dry up faster on a dry day than on a wet (rainy) day.

(iv) **Wind speed** It is known that clothes dry faster on a windy day. This is because with increase in wind speed, the particles of water vapour move away with the wind, decreasing the amount of water vapour in the surroundings. That is why, the rate of evaporation of a liquid increases with increasing wind speed.

Note The liquids which evaporate fast are called **volatile liquids**.

Evaporation Causes Cooling Effect

In an open vessel, the liquid keeps on evaporating. The particles of liquid absorb energy from the surrounding to regain the energy lost during evaporation. This absorption of energy from the surroundings makes the surroundings cold.

Some daily life examples of cooling effect of evaporation are given below:

(i) When ice cold water is kept in a glass tumbler for some time, water droplets are observed on its outer surface.

Explanation This occurs as the water vapours present in the air come in contact of the glass tumbler, get cooled and condensed to form these small water droplets. The formation of drops of water on the outside surface of a tumbler containing crushed ice, shows the presence of water vapour in air.

(ii) Cotton clothes are used to wear during summer season.

Explanation Cotton is a good absorber of water, so it helps to absorb sweat from our body. As it is obvious, the person perspires more during summer due to auto temperature control mechanism. Hence, wearing of cotton clothes helps in the easy evaporation of sweat. When this sweat evaporates, it takes the latent heat of vapourisation from our body, which in turn, cools the body. Thus, a person feels comfortable.

(iii) People sprinkle water on the roof or open ground on a hot sunny day.

Explanation When water is sprinkled on a hot surface, it gets evaporated very quickly. As evaporated water leaves the surface cool due to the large latent heat of vapourisation of water, this technique is quite effective in summers for cooling the surface.

(iv) Liquids like acetone (nail-polish remover) or alcohol placed on your palm give you feeling of cooling.

Explanation Acetone and alcohol are volatile liquids. When kept on palm, their particles gain energy from the palm or surroundings and evaporate causing the palm to feel cool.

Plasma and Bose-Einstein Condensate (Two More States of Matter)

Now, scientists have also discovered two more states of matter. These are Plasma and Bose-Einstein condensate.

Plasma

This state consists of super-energetic and super-excited particles. These particles are in the form of ionised gases.

Formation of Plasma

In neon sign bulbs, there is neon gas and in fluorescent tube, there is helium gas.

The gas gets ionised, when electrical energy flows through it. This charging up creates a plasma glowing inside the bulb or tube. The plasma glows with a special colour depending on the nature of the gas.

The Sun and the stars glow because of the presence of plasma in them. In stars, plasma is created because of very high temperature.

Bose-Einstein Condensate (BEC)

In 1920, Indian Physicist Satyendra Nath Bose had done some calculations for a fifth state of matter.

Based on his calculation, Albert Einstein predicted a new state of matter—the Bose-Einstein condensate. The BEC is formed by cooling a gas of extremely low density, about one hundred-thousandth the density of normal air to super low temperature. **In 2001, Eric A. Cornell, Wolfgang Ketterle and Carl E. Wieman of USA received the Nobel Prize in Physics for achieving "Bose-Einstein Condensation."**

Some measurable quantities and their units to remember :

Quantity	*Unit*	*Symbol*
Temperature	Kelvin	K
Length	metre	m
Mass	kilogram	kg
Weight	Newton	N
Volume	cubic metre	m^3
Density	kilogram per cubic metre	$kg\ m^{-3}$
Pressure	Pascal	Pa

Check Point 03

1. Fill in the blanks:
   SI unit of weight is ....
2. By which physical process wet clothes dry up?
3. Name the chemical compound contains in nail-polish remover.
4. Which state of matter is responsible for the glow of the sun and the stars?
5. Write the full form of BEC.

To Study NCERT Activities

Visit https://goo.gl/T5szZ7 OR **Scan the Code**

NCERT FOLDER

INTEXT QUESTIONS

1 Which of the following are matter?
Chair, air, love, smell, hate, almonds, thought, cold, cold-drink, smell of perfume. **Pg 3**

Sol. Anything that occupies space and has mass is called matter. Matter can exist in three physical states-solid, liquid and gas. Chair and almonds are solid states of matter. Cold-drink is a liquid state of matter. Air and smell of perfume are gaseous states of matter.

2 Give reasons for the following observation. The smell of hot sizzling food reaches you several metres away, but to get the smell of cold food, you have to go close. **Pg 3**

Sol. Particles of matter are continuously moving. They possess kinetic energy. As the temperature rises, the rate of diffusion increase and the particles of the aroma of hot food mix with the particles of air and reach to us several metres away, but to get an aroma or smell of cold food, we have to go close because the particles that carry smell of cold food diffuses slower as compared to particles that carry smell of hot sizzling food.

3 A diver is able to cut through water in a swimming pool. Which property of matter does this observation show? **Pg 3**

Sol. This observation shows that the particles of matter have spaces between them.

4 What are the characteristics of the particles of matter? **Pg 3**

Sol. Characteristics of particles of matter are as follows :

(*i*) They are very small in size.
(*ii*) They move faster in gaseous state as compared to solid or liquid state.
(*iii*) They diffuse faster at higher temperature.

5 The mass per unit volume of a substance is called density (Density = Mass/Volume).
Arrange the following in the order of increasing density.
Air, exhaust from chimneys, honey, water, chalk, cotton and iron. **Pg 6**

Sol. The increasing order of density is :
Air < exhaust from chimneys < cotton < water <honey < chalk < iron.

6 (*i*) Tabulate the differences in the characteristics of states of matter.
(*ii*) Comment upon the following.
Rigidity, compressibility, fluidity, filling a gas container, shape, kinetic energy and density. **Pg 6**

Sol. (*i*) Refer to Long Ans. 1 on Pg. no. 19.

(*ii*) **Rigidity** The property due to which an object retains its shape and size is known as rigidity. Solids are rigid while liquids and gases are not.

Compressibility The property due to which a substance reduced to its lower volume when force is applied is called compressibility. Gases are the most compressible while solids and liquids are not.

Fluidity The property due to which a substance tends to flow is known as fluidity. Gases and liquids can flow, hence they are known as fluids.

Filling a gas container Particles of a gas move freely in all the directions and occupy all the space available to them. Hence, gas fills the container completely.

Shape The geometry of an object is called its shape. Solids have a definite shape while gases and liquids do not.

Kinetic energy The energy of particles of matter due to their movement is called their kinetic energy. Gases have maximum kinetic energy among the three states of matter. Kinetic energy increases with the rise in temperature and *vice-versa*.

Density The mass per unit volume of a substance is called its density.

$$\text{Density} = \frac{\text{Mass}}{\text{Volume}} \quad \text{or} \quad D = \frac{m}{V}$$

Generally, a substance has maximum density in its solid state as compared to liquid or gaseous state. Units of density are kg m^{-3} or g cm^{-3}.

7 Give reasons.
(*i*) A gas fills completely the vessel in which it is kept.
(*ii*) A gas exerts pressure on the walls of the container.
(*iii*) A wooden table should be called a solid.
(*iv*) We can easily move our hands in air but to do the same through a solid block of wood, we need a karate expert. **Pg 6**

Sol. (*i*) Particles of gas have least forces of attraction between them hence, they move freely in all directions and occupy all the space available to them. Hence, a gas fills the vessel completely in which it is kept.

(*ii*) Due to high kinetic energy possessed by the gas particles, they randomly move at a high speed within the container.

Due to this random movement, the particles hit each other as well as the walls of the container. The force by which these particles strike the container exerts a pressure on its walls.

(*iii*) A wooden table has a definite shape and volume. It is very rigid and cannot be compressed. As wood has all the characteristics of a solid. Hence, a wooden table should be called a solid.

(*iv*) Particles of air are very far apart from each other due to negligible forces of attraction between them. Therefore, our hands get sufficient space to move in air.

We also displace the air particles without much effort. But in a solid block of wood, particles are closely packed with least space between them due to strong intermolecular forces of attraction. So, there is no possibility of moving hands through a block of wood.

8 Liquids generally have lower density as compared to solids. But you must have observed that ice floats on water. Find out why? **Pg 6**

Sol. The mass per unit volume of a substance is called density. As the volume of a substance increases, its density decreases.

Though, ice is a solid, but it has a cage-like structure in which some spaces are present between the particles of water (these spaces are left when water solidifies).

These spaces are trapped by the air particles. In fact these spaces are larger as compared to the spaces present between the particles of water. Thus, the volume of ice is greater than that of water. Hence, the density of ice is less than that of water. A substance with lower density than water can floats on water. Thus, ice floats on water.

9 Convert the following temperatures to Celsius scale.

(*i*) 300 K (*ii*) 573 K **Pg 9**

Sol. For converting Kelvin to Celsius, the formula is

$$\text{K} - 273 = {}^\circ\text{C}$$

(*i*) $300\text{ K} - 273 = 27^\circ\text{C}$

(*ii*) $573\text{ K} - 273 = 300^\circ\text{C}$

10 What is the physical state of water at

(*i*) 250°C? (*ii*) 100°C? **Pg 9**

Sol. (*i*) Water vapour or steam.

(*ii*) Liquid water as well as water vapour, as steam and water co-exist at 100°C.

11 For any substance, why does the temperature remain constant during the change of state? **Pg 9**

Sol. During the change of state, the temperature remains constant because the heat provided is utilised for breaking the attraction forces between the particles of the substance.

This happens at melting point (or boiling point) of the substance and the heat used is called the latent heat of fusion (or vapourisation). During condensation or solidification, the *vice-versa* happens.

12 Suggest a method to liquefy atmospheric gases. **Pg 9**

Sol. Applying high pressure and reducing temperature, helps to liquefy atmospheric (or any other) gases. Because under these conditions, the particles come closer, kinetic energy decreases and the gas is liquefied.

13 Why does a desert cooler cool better on a hot dry day? **Pg 10**

Sol. On a hot dry day, the temperature is high and humidity is low. The rate of evaporation increases with increase in temperature and decrease in humidity. A desert cooler functions on the principle of evaporation. The water takes heat from the hot desert cooler and evaporates. The evaporation of water cools the pads and the circulating water. As a result, the incoming air also gets cooled down.

14 How does the water kept in an earthen pot (matka) become cool during summer? **Pg 10**

Sol. Earthen pots contain tiny pores. During summer, when water is poured into an earthen pot, some of the water seeps through pores to the outer surface.

The water molecules on evaporation escape from the tiny pores of the earthen pot. The heat required for evaporation is taken from the earthen pot and the water in it. This results in lowering of the heat content of the remaining water and the water becomes cool.

15 Why does our palm feel cold when we put some acetone or petrol or perfume on it? **Pg 10**

Sol. Acetone or petrol are volatile liquids which evaporate readily. When these liquids kept on palm, their particles gain energy from the palm or surroundings and evaporate, thus causing the palm to cool.

16 Why are we able to sip hot tea or milk faster from a saucer rather a cup? **Pg 10**

Sol. A saucer or plate has more surface area in comparison to cup. Therefore, evaporation of tea occur more in the saucer rather than cup and more cooling observed in a saucer.

17 What type of clothes should we wear in summer? **Pg 10**

Sol. We should wear cotton clothes in summer because cotton is a good absorber of water and helps in absorbing the sweat and exposing it to the atmosphere for easy evaporation thereby, causing cooling sensation.

Exercises

(On Page 12)

1 Convert the following temperatures to the Celsius scale.

(*i*) 293 K (*ii*) 470 K

Sol. (*i*) 293 K − 273 = 20°C

(*ii*) 470 K − 273 = 197°C

2 Convert the following temperatures to the Kelvin scale.

(*i*) 25°C (*ii*) 373°C

Sol. (*i*) 25°C + 273 = 298 K

(*ii*) 373°C + 273 = 646 K

3 Give reason for the following observations:

(*i*) Naphthalene balls disappear with time without leaving any solid.

(*ii*) We can get the smell of perfume sitting several metres away.

Sol. (*i*) Naphthalene being a sublimable substance converts directly from solid to gaseous state by taking heat from the surroundings through the process, called sublimation. The naphthalene balls keep on forming naphthalene vapours which slowly disappears into the air. Hence, no residue is left after some time.

(*ii*) The smell or aroma of perfume reaches several metres away due to the fast diffusion of the gaseous particles of perfume through air.

4 Arrange the following substances in increasing order of forces of attraction between the particles –water, sugar, oxygen.

Sol. Oxygen(gas) < Water (liquid) < Sugar (solid).

5 What is the physical state of water at

(*i*) 25°C? (*ii*) 0°C? (*iii*) 100° C?

Sol. (*i*) Liquid state

(*ii*) Solid or liquid state (transition state)

(*iii*) Liquid or gaseous state

6 Give two reasons to justify.

(*i*) Water at room temperature is a liquid.

(*ii*) An iron almirah is solid at room temperature.

Sol. (*i*) Water is liquid at room temperature as

(*a*) it has a tendency to flow.

(*b*) it takes the shape of the vessel in which it is filled, but its volume does not change.

(*ii*) An iron almirah is solid at room temperature because

(*a*) it has definite shape and volume.

(*b*) it is hard and rigid.

7 Why is ice at 273 K more effective in cooling than water at the same temperature?

Sol. When ice melts, it absorbs the energy equal to the latent heat of fusion from the surroundings so, it causes cooling more effectively than the water at same temperature (because water does not absorb energy from the surroundings).

8 What produces more severe burns, boiling water or steam?

Sol. Steam causes more severe burns than boiling water. The reason is that it releases the extra amount of heat (latent heat) which it has already taken during vapourisation (when the steam was formed from water).

9 Name *A*, *B*, *C*, *D*, *E* and *F* in the following diagram showing change in its state.

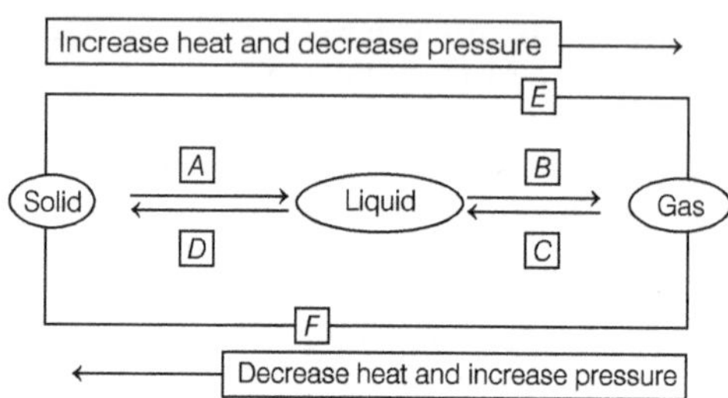

Sol. A = Melting or fusion, here the solid changes into liquid.

B = Evaporation or vapourisation, here the liquid changes into gas.

C = Condensation or liquefication, here the gas changes into liquid.

D = Freezing or solidification, here the liquid changes into solid.

E = Sublimation, here solid directly changes into gas without coming in liquid state.

F = Sublimation, here gas changes into solid without coming in liquid state.

SUMMARY

- Matter is anything that has mass and occupies volume.
- The SI unit of mass and volume is **kilogram** (kg) and **cubic metre** (m^3), respectively.
- Matter is classified into groups based on their physical and chemical properties, i.e. physical properties (solid, liquid and gas) and chemical properties (elements, compounds and mixtures).
- Every matter is made up of certain particles which differ in shape, size and nature.
- The particles of matter have a tendency to diffuse.
- Solids have definite shape, distinct boundaries and fixed volumes.
- Liquids do not have a definite shape.
- Gases have neither definite shape nor volume.
- The state of matter can be interchanged by changing temperature or pressure.
- At specific conditions of temperature and pressure; the conversion of a matter from its solid to its liquid state is called **fusion**.
- The conversion of a matter from its liquid state to vapour (gaseous state) is called **boiling**. It is a bulk phenomenon.
- The conversion of a matter from its liquid to solid state is called **freezing**.
- The conversion of a matter from its liquid to gaseous state is called **vapourisation**.
- The conversion of matter from its gaseous to liquid state is called **condensation**.
- The process of change of solid state directly into gaseous state without passing through the liquid state upon heating and *vice-versa* on cooling is called **sublimation**.
- The heat energy which has to be supplied to change the state of substance is called **latent heat**.
- **Latent heat of vapourisation** is the heat energy required to change 1kg of a liquid to gas at atmospheric pressure at its boiling point.
- **Latent heat of fusion** is the amount of heat energy required to change 1 kg of solid into liquid at its melting point.
- The process of conversion of a liquid into its vapour state at any temperature below its boiling point is called **evaporation**.
- Apart from solid, liquid and gaseous state, scientists have discovered two more states, i.e. **plasma** and **Bose-Einstein condensate**.
- Plasma state consists of super-energetic and super-excited particles.
- The Sun and the stars glow because of the presence of plasma in them.
- The Bose-Einstein condensate is formed by cooling a gas of extremely low density about one hundred thousandth the density of normal air to super low temperature.

For Mind Map

Visit https://goo.gl/mFKV9g OR **Scan the Code**

Exam Practice

Objective Type Questions

Multiple Choice Questions

1 A diver is able to cut through water in a swimming pool. The property shown by the matter is

(a) the particles are of very small size
(b) the matter have space between them
(c) the particles are in solid state
(d) the particles are running here and there, have no space between them

Sol. (*b*) A diver is able to cut through water because water is a liquid and have space between the water molecules due to weak force of attraction among the water molecules.

2 Which of the following is found in solid state at room temperature ?

(a) Stone (b) Sand
(c) Mercury (d) Both (a) and (b)

Sol. (*d*) Stone and sand are found in solid state at room temperature because of strong attractive force among their particles, (i.e. the particles of stone and sand are held together with strong attractive forces).
Mercury is the only metal which is found in liquid state at room temperature.

3 Gases show faster rate of diffusion because

(a) of higher boiling point
(b) of low intermolecular space
(c) of high melting point
(d) of large intermolecular space

Sol. (*d*) Gases show faster rate of diffusion because these have weak intermolecular forces between them and move with higher speed. As a result, these have large intermolecular space between the molecules.

4 The similarity between a liquid and a gas is

(a) both do not show definite shape
(b) both have definite volume
(c) both have same boiling point
(d) both have same nature

Sol. (*a*) Liquids and gases both are considered as fluids but due to weak intermolecular force of attraction, gases occupy the shape and volume of container in which they are placed. Liquids have slightly more force of attraction than gases, thus they have definite volume but not the definite shape.

5 The property to flow is unique to fluids. Which one of the following statements is correct?

(a) Only gases behave like fluids
(b) Gases and solids behave like fluids
(c) Gases and liquids behave like fluids
(d) Only liquids are fluids **NCERT Exemplar**

Sol. (c) Gases and liquids behave like fluids. Both gases and liquids tend to flow due to less force of attraction between their particles.

6 Choose the correct statement of the following.

(a) Conversion of solid into vapours without passing through the liquid state is called vaporisation.
(b) Conversion of vapours into solid without passing through the liquid state is called sublimation.
(c) Conversion of vapours into solid without passing through the liquid state is called freezing.
(d) Conversion of solid into liquid is called sublimation. **NCERT Exemplar**

Sol. (*b*) Conversion of solid into vapours on heating or vapours into solid on cooling without undergoing in liquid state is called **sublimation.**

7 The boiling points of diethyl ether, acetone and *n*-butyl alcohol are 35°C, 56°C and 118°C, respectively. Which one of the following correctly represents their boiling points in kelvin scale?

(a) 306 K, 329 K, 391 K (b) 308 K, 329 K, 392 K
(c) 308 K, 329 K, 391 K (d) 329 K, 392 K, 308 K
NCERT Exemplar

Sol. (*c*) The correct order of boiling points of diethyl ether, acetone and *n*-butyl alcohol in Kelvin scale is 308 K, 329 K and 391 K, which can be explained as $(\because T^\circ C + 273 = T K)$.

Boiling point of diethyl ether

$$= 35^\circ C + 273 = 308 \text{ K}$$

Boiling point of acetone $= 56^\circ C + 273 = 329$ K

Boiling point of *n*-butyl alcohol

$$= 118^\circ C + 273 = 391 \text{ K}$$

8 Temperature 200° C equals nearly to

(a) 300 K (b) 373 K (c) 473 K (d) −73 K

Sol. (*c*) Celsius scale ($^\circ$C) and Kelvin scale are related as follows :

Temperature on Kelvin scale

$$= \text{Temperature on } ^\circ C + 273.$$

Hence, temperature on Kelvin scale

$$= 200 + 273 = 473 \text{ K}$$

9 Which condition out of the following will increase the evaporation of water?

(a) Increase in temperature of water
(b) Decrease in temperature of water
(c) Less exposed surface area of water
(d) Adding common salt to water

NCERT Exemplar

Sol. (*a*) Increase in temperature of water will increase the evaporation of water. It is because, on increasing the temperature, kinetic energy of water molecules increases and more particles get enough kinetic energy to go into the vapour state. This increases the rate of evaporation.

10 During summer, water kept in an earthen pot becomes cool because of the phenomenon of **NCERT Exemplar**

(a) diffusion
(b) transpiration
(c) osmosis
(d) evaporation

Sol. (*d*) During summer, water kept in an earthen pot becomes cool because of the phenomenon of evaporation. Earthen pot has a large number of tiny pores in its walls and some of the water molecules continuously keep seeping through these pores to outside the pot.

Fill in the Blanks

11 The arrangement of particles is less ordered in the ....state. However, there is no order in the ....state.

Sol. liquid, gaseous.

In liquid state, there is more force of attraction between particles as compared to gaseous state.

12 Liquids and .... states are fluid states.

Sol. gaseous

Because they have a tendency to flow.

13 Density is measured in.........

Sol. kg/m^3

14 In solid state, particles are packed ...... and are unable to ......

Sol. tightly, move.

Force of attraction between particles is highest so they are packed closely.

15 Matter is made up of small......... .

Sol. particles.

Atom is the smallest particle in nature which are indestructible.

True and False

16 We may find plasma in a star.

Sol. True

The sun and stars glow because of the presence of plasma in them.

17 Evaporation and boiling are the same processes because molecules move from liquid to gaseous state.

Sol. False

Evaporation is surface phenomenon and boiling is a bulk phenomenon.

18 Water at room temperature is a liquid.

Sol. True

At room temperature, water has no shape but has a fixed volume and at room temperature water flows easily.

19 Compressibility of both gas and liquid is same.

Sol. False

Compressibility of gas is more than liquid because in gaseous state, there is large space between particles as compared to liquid.

20 Conversion of gas directly into solid is called combination.

Sol. False

Conversion of gas directly into solid is called deposition.

21 Two gases cannot diffuse into each other.

Sol. False

Gaseous particles are easily diffuse into each other because of large intermolecular space between them.

Match the Columns

22 Match the following columns.

	Column A		Column B
A.	In liquids particles are held together.	(i)	Slightly
B.	Liquids can be compressed.	(ii)	Less firmly
C.	In gases particles are held together.	(iii)	Most firmly
D.	In solids, particles are held together.	(iv)	Least firmly

Sol A→(ii), B→(i), C→(iv), D→(iii)

In solids, intermolecular force of attraction between particles are maximum. This force keep the particles together. The strength of this force is less in liquid as compared to solid and least in gaseous state.

Assertion-Reason

Direction (Q.Nos. 23-27) *In each of the following questions, a statement of Assertion is given by the corresponding statement of Reason. Of the statements, mark the correct answer as*

(a) If both Assertion and Reason are true and Reason is the correct explanation of Assertion.
(b) If both Assertion and Reason are true but Reason is not the correct explanation of Assertion.
(c) If Assertion is true but Reason is false.
(d) If Assertion is false, Reason is true.

23 **Assertion** Smell of burning incense stick spreads all around due to the diffusion of its fumes into air.

Reason Increased temperature results in increased kinetic energy of the molecules.

Sol. (*a*) As the temperature increases, velocity of particles increases, so rate of diffusion as well as kinetic energy increases.

24 **Assertion** The smell of hot cooked food reaches us in seconds.

Reason Rate of diffusion of solids is greater than that of gases.

Sol. (*c*) The smell of hot cooked food reaches us in seconds. This is because, gases show the property of diffusing into other gases very fast. Which is due to high speed of particles and large intermolecular spaces between their particles.

25 **Assertion** Naphthalene does not leave a residue when kept open for sometime.

Reason The conversion of a gas directly into solid is called condensation.

Sol. (*c*) Naphthalene being a sublimate sublimes and hence, does not leave a residue when kept open for sometime. Conversion of a gas directly into solid (without coming into liquid state) is called sublimation while condensation is the process of conversion of a gas into its liquid form.

26 **Assertion** There is no change in the temperature of a substance when it undergoes a change of state though it is still being heated.

Reason The heat supplied is absorbed either as latent heat of fusion or as latent heat of vaporisation.

Sol. (*a*) Latent heat means hidden form of heat and, thus it does not result in increase of temperature of a substance.

27 **Assertion** During evaporation of liquids the temperature remains unaffected.

Reason Kinetic energy of the molecules is directly proportional to temperature.

Sol. (*d*) During evaporation of liquids the temperature increases and, thus kinetic energy of the molecules also increases.

Case Based Questions

Direction (Q.Nos. 28-31) *Answer the questions on the basis of your understanding of the following passage and related studied concepts:*

A student of a class performed an experiment in a chemistry laboratory. He took a conical flask containing ice cubes and placed the flask on a burner with a thermometer suspended in it. Student recorded the following observations in his note book. The observations are:

Time (min)	0	2	4	6	10	15	20	25	30	35
Temp (°C)	– 3	0	0	12	22	30	50	73	100	100

Based on the above observations, answer the following:

28 State the change(s) observed between 2-4 minutes.

Sol. Between 2-4 minutes, ice converts into water.

29 Name the process involved during the reading 2-4 minutes.

Sol. During 2-4 minutes, the process take place is called fusion.

30 Between 30-35 minutes, the temperature remains constant. Why?

Sol. Between 30-35 minutes, the temperature remain constant because the heat supplied is used up in over coming the intermolecular forces of liquid to change into vapours.

31 Define the heat involved during 30-35 min and its SI unit.

Sol. The heat involved during the process of 30-35 minutes is called latent heat of vaporisation. Latent heat of vaporisation define as the amount of heat or energy required to change 1 kg of liquid into gas at its boiling point. SI unit is 1 kg^{-1}.

Direction (Q.Nos. 32-35) *Answer the questions on the basis of your understanding of the following passage and related studied concepts:*

The phenomenon of change of liquid into vapours at any temperature below its boiling point is called **evaporation**.

The rate of evaporation increases with increase in surface area, temperature, speed of wind and decrease in humidity. Evaporation causes cooling due to decrease in average kinetic energy of the remaining liquid after the surface molecules leave. Lower the boiling point of the liquid, higher is the rate of evaporation.

32. Synthetic clothes are uncomfortable in summer because
    (a) they absorb kinetic energy from the air molecules
    (b) they do not let the sweat to evaporate
    (c) they are highly porous
    (d) they are very thick

Sol. (*b*) Synthetic clothes are not porous hence they do not absorb sweat from our body. As sweat from our skin does not evaporate, the body does not lose heat energy and hence we have an uncomfortable feeling.

33. Liquids like ether and acetone are kept in cool places because
    (a) ether and acetone have high boiling point
    (b) the rate of evaporation increases with surface area
    (c) ether and acetone are volatile liquids with low boiling point
    (d) ether and acetone have lower density than water.

Sol. (*c*) Ether and acetone have low boiling points hence they evaporate fast. If they are not kept at lower temperature, their rate of evaporation becomes faster.

34. The water spilled on the floor evaporates faster than the water in a glass. Explain?

Sol. When the water is spilled on the floor the surface area of water increases, hence the rate of evaporation also increases.

35 You want to wear a favourite shirt to a party, but the problems is that it is still wet after a wash. Mention three steps with reason that you would take to dry it faster.

Sol. (i) Squeeze the shirt with force. By doing so, some of the moisture get removed.
(ii) Spread the shirt on a stand. It provides greater surface area for evaporation.
(iii) Iron the shirt . Increase in temperature helps in drying the shirt.

Very Short Answer Type Questions

36 A substance has no mass. Can we consider it as matter?

Sol. No, because matter has definite mass.

37 A given substance X has definite volume, but no definite shape and can diffuse easily. What is the physical state of a substance X?

Sol. The physical state of a substance X is liquid because liquids do not have definite shape, but have a definite volume and can diffuse easily.

38 Rubber band changes its shape. Is it solid?

Sol. Rubber band changes its shape under force and regains its shape after removing the force. Thus, it is a solid.

39 Why do liquids take up the shape of the container in which they are kept?

Sol. Forces of attraction are not very strong in liquids which is necessary to maintain their shape. Therefore, they acquire the shape of the container in which they are kept.

40 What would be the effect of
(*i*) temperature and (*ii*) density of liquids
on the rate of diffusion of liquids?

Sol. (*i*) On increasing temperature, the rate of diffusion of liquids increases.
(*ii*) Rate of diffusion is more for a liquid having lower density.

41 Why do gases exert more pressure on the walls of the container than the solids?

Sol. In gases, the particles move randomly at high speed and they collide with each other and also with the walls of the container. Thus, they exert more pressure on the walls of the container than solids.

42 Which characteristic of a gas is used in supplying oxygen cylinders to hospitals?

Sol. Gases are highly compressible in nature and can be liquefied. Due to these properties, gases are used in supplying oxygen cylinders to hospitals.

43 Why is boiling called a bulk phenomenon?

Sol. Since, boiling starts from the bulk, i.e. inside the liquid, therefore it is a bulk phenomenon.

44 Why the temperature remains constant during sublimation?

Sol. During the process of sublimation, heat given to the system is used up to evaporate solid into vapour at constant temperature.

45 What is meant by latent heat of vapourisation?

Sol. It is the amount of heat required to convert 1 kg of liquid into vapours at its boiling point.

46 Benzene is a liquid at 80°C, liquid benzene is in equilibrium with its vapours. It is found that particles of benzene vapours are more energetic than particles of liquid benzene. Explain the observation.

Sol. Particles of benzene vapours are more energetic because these have absorbed extra energy in the form of latent heat of vapourisation.

47 What happens to the melting point of solids with the decrease in pressure?

Sol. Generally, for solids like ice, melting point increases with the decrease in pressure.

48 Why should wet clothes are spread while drying?

Sol. On spreading wet clothes, the surface area exposed to air increases and evaporation becomes faster. Thus, they dry quickly.

49 What is the effect of sprinkling of water on the roof or open ground on a hot sunny day?

Sol. The water evaporates by absorbing heat from the ground and the surrounding air. By losing heat, the roof or open ground becomes cool and people feel comfortable.

50. When a solid melts, its temperature remain constant, so where does the heat energy go?

Sol. When a solid melts, the heat energy given is used up to convent solid into liquid. This is called latent heat of fusion.

51. Why do we sweat more in a humid day ?

Sol. In a humid day, the air around us has already contain high percentage of water vapours. Therefore, the water coming from the skin gets less opportunity to change into vapours and remain sticking to our body. We therefore sweat more on a humid day.

Short Answer (SA) Type Questions

1 (*i*) A sponge can be compressed, yet it is a solid? Explain.

(*ii*) Name the state of matter that has minimum space between particles.

Sol. (*i*) A sponge has minute holes, in which air is trapped, when we press it, the air is expelled out and we are able to compress it. Hence, sponge can be compressed, instead of being a solid.

(*ii*) Solid state has minimum space between their particles.

2 The cover plate is removed from the gas jars shown in the diagram. After several days, the colour of the gas is the same in both jars. Why does this happen? Explain.

Oxygen
Cover plate
Bromine

Sol. Diffusion has occurred in the jars. Bromine molecules move from a region where they are of higher concentration to a region of lower concentration, i.e. they move in the above gas jar. Oxygen molecules move from a region where they are of higher concentration to a region of lower concentration, i.e. they move to the below gas jar. Diffusion continues until both gas jars have uniform distribution of bromine and oxygen molecules.

3 (*i*) Explain the interconversion of three states of matter in terms of force of attraction and kinetic energy of the molecules.

(*ii*) Arrange the three states of matter in the increasing order of rate of diffusion and particle motion.

Sol. (*i*) During the interconversion of a solid into a liquid and liquid into gas on increasing temperature, the kinetic energy of the molecules increases and force of attraction among molecules decreases and *vice-versa*.

(*ii*) (*a*) Rate of diffusion, Solid $<$ liquid $<$ gas

(*b*) Particles motion, Solid $<$ liquid $<$ gas.

4 How do you differentiate between solids, liquids and gases on the basis of their melting and boiling points?

Sol. Solids have melting and boiling points above room temperature.

Liquids have melting point below room temperature and boiling point above room temperature.

Gases have both melting and boiling points below room temperature.

5 (*i*) Dry ice is compressed under high pressure. What happens to it when the pressure is released?

(*ii*) Define

(*a*) Melting point (*b*) Fusion.

Sol. (*i*) On releasing the pressure, dry ice sublimes to vapour state without undergoing liquid state.

(*ii*) (*a*) **Melting point** The definite temperature at which a solid starts melting is called the melting point of that solid, e.g. melting point of ice is 0°C or 273.16 K.

(*b*) **Fusion** The process of conversion of a solid into liquid state on heating is called fusion or melting.

6 What is dry ice? How is it formed?

Sol. Dry ice is solid carbon dioxide which sublimes to form carbon dioxide gas without undergoing into liquid state. Term dry is used to denote sublimation. On sublimation, vapours of carbon dioxide create a foggy dense appearance denoted by term ice. Hence, solid carbon dioxide is also termed as dry ice.

Dry ice is formed when gaseous carbon dioxide is compressed and stored under high pressure. On decreasing pressure to 1 atm, it again changes to the gaseous form without coming into liquid state.

7 Draw a well-labelled diagram showing sublimation of ammonium chloride.

Sol. Take some ammonium chloride in a China dish and place the China dish on a tripod stand. Cover the China dish with an inverted glass funnel.

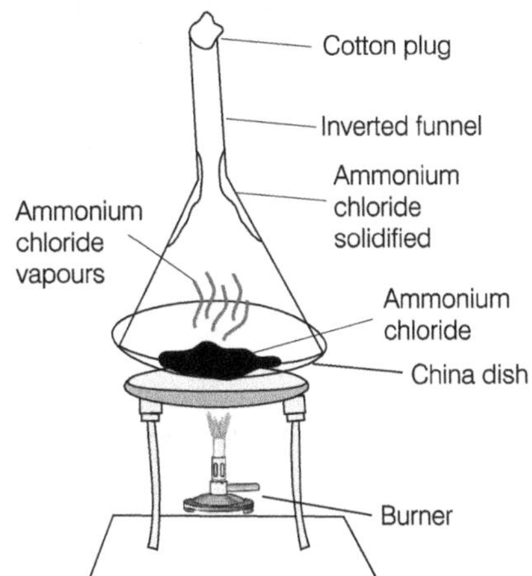

Sublimation of ammonium chloride

Put a loose cotton plug in the upper open end of the funnel to prevent the ammonium chloride vapour from escaping into the atmosphere.

The China dish is heated by using a burner. On heating, ammonium chloride changes into white vapours.

These vapours rise up and get converted into solid ammonium chloride on coming in contact with the cold, inner walls of the funnel.

8 From the graph given below:

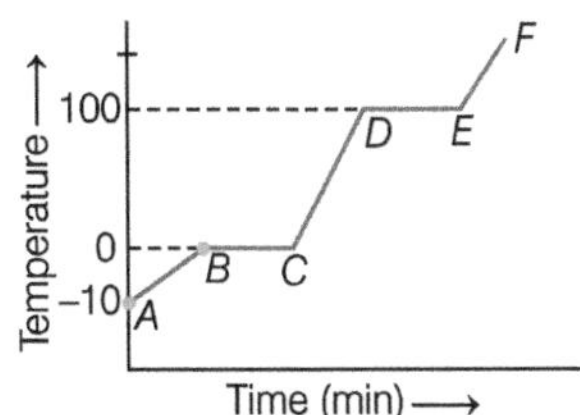

(*i*) Which region contains only solid?

(*ii*) Which region contains all liquids?

(*iii*) Which region shows latent heat of vapourisation?

Sol. (*i*) *AB* is the region that contains only solid.

(*ii*) *CD* is the region that contains all liquids.

(*iii*) DE is the region that shows latent heat of vapourisation.

9 Comment on the following statements:

(*i*) Evaporation produces cooling.

(*ii*) Rate of evaporation of an aqueous solution decreases with increase in humidity.

(*iii*) Sponge though compressible is a solid.

NCERT Exemplar

Sol. (*i*) Evaporation of liquid produces cooling because liquid takes away the heat from the surroundings, thereby producing a cooling effect.

(*ii*) If humidity is high, then air is already saturated with water vapour, i.e. it has a lot of water vapour. Therefore, it will not take more water vapour easily. Hence, rate of evaporation decreases.

(*iii*) Sponge has minute holes in which air is trapped. The material is also not so rigid. On pressing this, air is expelled out, that is why, it can be compressed, but it is solid as it has a definite shape and volume and does not change its shape unless compressed.

10 (*i*) How will you show that the process of evaporation depends on the nature of the liquid?

(*ii*) Why a drop of dettol is evenly distributed in a bucket of water without the need of stirring?

Sol. (*i*) Take 10 mL of ether (a low boiling point liquid with boiling point 34°C) in a test tube and 10 mL of water (boiling point 100°C) in another test tube. Keep both the test tubes near the window for some time. It is observed that ether evaporates in a shorter time. Thus, lower the boiling point of the liquid, higher is its rate of evaporation.

(*ii*) A drop of dettol is diffused in water and can be distributed throughout the water, since there is enough space between the particles of water.

11 Look at the following figures and suggest in which of the vessels *A*, *B*, *C* or *D*, the rate of evaporation will be the highest? Explain.

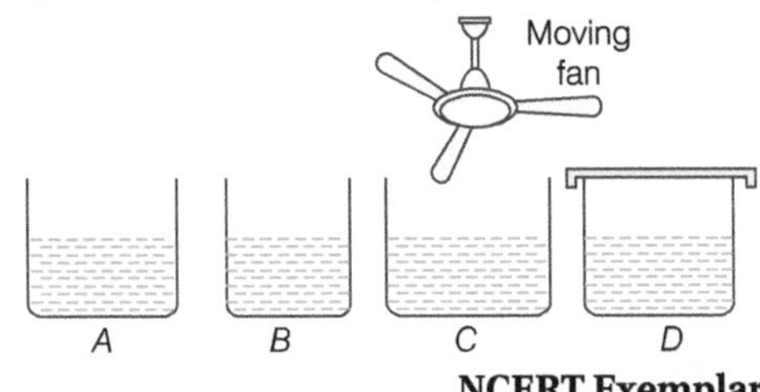

NCERT Exemplar

Sol. The rate of evaporation will be highest in vessel *C* as the surface area exposed for evaporation is larger than *B* (smaller size) . The moving fan increases the wind speed which also increases the rate of evaporation. Although, *A* and *D* are also equal in size to that of *C*, but *A* is at a greater distance from the fan and *D* is covered with a lid.

12 How will you change water from gaseous state to liquid state? Suggest a simple activity.

Sol. Water can be changed from gaseous state to liquid state by passing the water vapour through a water condenser as used in case of simple distillation.

Activity Take ice cold water in a glass. Observe the outer surface of the glass. You find small droplets of water on it. These water droplets are formed as a result of condensation of water vapour present in the air to form liquid water.

13 How does the change in temperature and humidity affect the rate of evaporation?

Sol. The rate of evaporation increases on increasing the temperature of the liquid. When the temperature of a liquid is increased by heating, more particles of the liquid get enough kinetic energy to go into vapour state. This increases the rate of evaporation.

When the humidity of air is low, then the rate of evaporation is high and water evaporates rapidly. When the humidity of air is high then the rate of evaporation is low and water evaporates very slowly.

14 (*i*) Which factors determine the state of a substance?

(*ii*) Convert 30°C into Kelvin.

(*iii*) Water droplets are observed on the outer surface of a glass tumbler containing ice cold water. Give reason.

Sol. (*i*) Temperature and pressure determine the state of a substance.

(*ii*) $30°C = 273 + 30 = 303$ K

(*iii*) Water droplets are observed on glass tumbler because water vapours present in the air get condensed on the cold surface of the glass which appears as water droplets.

15 It is a hot summer day. Priyanshi and Ali are wearing cotton and nylon clothes, respectively. Who do you think would be more comfortable and why?

NCERT Exemplar

Sol. Priyanshi would be more comfortable. The reason is that cotton absorbs sweat from the body and provides a larger surface area for evaporation which causes more cooling effect.

Nylon being a bad absorber of water does not absorb sweat. Thus, the sweat does not evaporate from the body and Ali would feel uncomfortable.

16. (*i*) Ghee freezes at room temperature and mustard oil does not during winter time.

(*ii*) You are given a mixture of sand, sodium chloride and ammonium chloride. Write the names of two methods used to separate the components of the mixture.

Sol. (*i*) Since, ghee freezes at room temperature and mustard oil does not during winter time, it shows that intermolecular forces between particles of ghee are stronger compared to those of mustard oil.

(*ii*) (*a*) Ammonium chloride is separated from its mixture, with sand and sodium chloride by the process of sublimation.

(*b*) Sodium chloride and sand are separated by the process of evaporation.

17. Give reason for the following:

(*i*) Butter is generally wrapped in wet cloth during summer if no refrigeration is available?

(*ii*) When sugar crystals dissolve in water, the level of water does not rise appreciably.

Sol. (*i*) In summer, the weather is quite high (hot). As a result, water present in wet cloth readily evaporates. Since, cooling is caused during evaporation, the temperature of butter gets lowered and it does not give any foul odour.

(*ii*) Since, water is a liquid, there are intermolecular space. Sugar particles occupy these spaces. As a result, water level does not rise appreciably.

Long Answer (LA) Type Questions

1 What are the differences between solid, liquid and gaseous states?

Sol. Differences between solid, liquid and gaseous states are as follows

Solid state	*Liquid State*	*Gaseous State*
Solids have definite shape and volume.	Liquids have definite volume, but indefinite shape.	Gases neither have a definite shape nor definite volume.
Solids are rigid and non- compressible.	Liquids are non rigid as well as non-compressible.	Gases are not rigid, but they are compressible.
Solids have high density (except ice).	Liquids have less density than solid.	Gases have least density.
Solids do not diffuse easily.	Liquids diffuse very slowly.	Diffusion of gases is very fast.
Solids do not tend to flow.	Liquids tend to flow.	Gases also tend to flow.
Intermolecular spaces are small and intermolecular forces of attraction are maximum.	Intermolecular space is more than solids, while intermolecular force of attraction is less than solids.	Intermolecular space is maximum, while intermolecular force of attraction is minimum.

2 (*i*) Explain the term density. Arrange different states of matter in increasing order of density.

(*ii*) Explain how ice floats on water?

Sol. (*i*) The mass per unit volume of a substance is called density. Density depends upon the volume of the substance. Substance with small intermolecular spaces have small volumes and high densities. The increasing order of intermolecular spaces between the different states of matter are solid < liquid < gas. Thus, the increasing order for their density would be gas <liquid<solid.

(*ii*) Ice is a solid, but it has a cage-like structure in which some spaces are present between the particles of water. These spaces are trapped by the air particles.

These spaces are larger as compared to the spaces present between the particles of water. Thus, the volume of ice is greater than that of water. Hence, the density of ice is less than water and it floats on water.

3 Benzoic acid is used as a food preservative. The given graph shows the heating curve for benzoic acid. Study the graph and answer the following questions :

(*i*) At what time does benzoic acid begin to

(*a*) melt? (*b*) boil?

(*ii*) What is the melting point of benzoic acid?

(*iii*) What happens to the temperature while benzoic acid melts?

(*iv*) What is the physical state of benzoic acid during time interval of 35-45 mins?

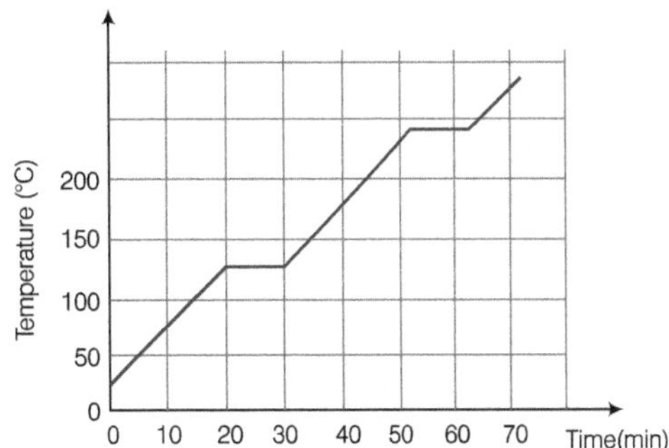

Sol. (*i*) (*a*) Benzoic acid begins to melt at 20 min.

(*b*) Benzoic acid begins to boil at 52 min.

(*ii*) The melting point of benzoic acid is 120° C.

(*iii*) The temperature remains constant at 120°C until all the benzoic acid has melted.

(*iv*) The physical state of benzoic acid is liquid during the time interval of 35-45 min.

4 (*i*) What is matter? Write two properties of solids and two properties of liquids.

(*ii*) Give reasons for the following:

(*a*) Ice at 0°C appears colder in the mouth than water at 0°C.

(*b*) Doctors advise to put the strips of wet cloth on the forehead of a person having high temperature.

Sol. (*i*) Matter is a substance which has mass and occupies space.

(*a*) In solids, force of attraction between particles is strongest and intermolecular space is very less.

(*b*) In liquids, force of attraction is relatively less and intermolecular space is more in comparison to solids.

(*ii*) (*a*) As ice absorbs the latent heat of fusion too from the mouth so, it feels colder than the water at the same temperature, i.e. 0°C.

(*b*) As the temperature of the patient's body is high, the water from the wet strips evaporates by absorbing the heat from the body.

This lowers 1the body temperature of the patient. That is why, doctors advised to put the strips of wet cloth on the forehead of a person suffering from high fever.

5 The temperature-time graph given below shows the heating curve for pure wax.

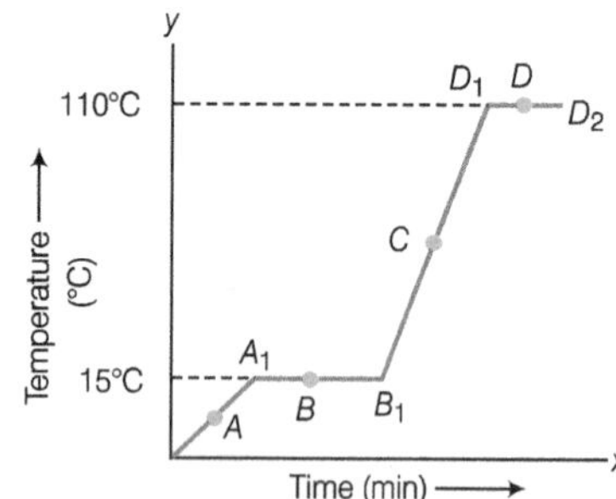

From the graph, answer the following:

(i) What is the physical state of the substance at the points A,B,C, and D?

(ii) What is the melting point of the wax?

(iii) What is its boiling point?

(iv) Which portions of the graph indicate that change of state is taking place?

(v) Name the terms used for heat absorbed during change of states involved in the above processes.

Sol. (i) At point A = Solid wax

At point B = Solid as well as liquid wax (Melting continues)

At point C = Liquid wax

At point D = Liquid as well as vapour state (Boiling continues)

(ii) Melting point of wax = 15°C

(iii) Boiling point of wax = 110°C

(iv) Straight lines in the curve parallel to time-axis (x-axis) indicates the change of state. These portions are A_1 to B_1 (solid to liquid) and D_1 to D_2 (liquid to vapour state).

(v) During melting, at melting point, the heat absorbed is called **latent heat of fusion.** During boiling, at boiling point, the heat absorbed is called **latent heat of vapourisation.**

6 (i) What temperature in Kelvin scale is equal to 50°C?

(ii) Describe an activity to show that rate of evaporation increases with surface area.

(iii) Describe the method of formation of plasma and Bose-Einstein condensate.

Sol. (i) 50 + 273 = 323 K

(ii) **Activity** Take little amount of water in three containers which have different surface areas. Keep them in sunlight for 2 h. Measure the volume of water left in all three containers.

Observation The amount of water left will be least in container having largest surface area among them.

Conclusion Greater the surface area, more will be the rate of evaporation.

(iii) **Formation of plasma** In neon sign bulbs, there is neon gas and in fluorescent tube, there is helium gas. The gas get ionised, when electrical energy flow through it. This charging up creates a plasma glowing inside the bulb or tube.

Formation of Bose-Einstein condesate The Bose-Einstein condesate is formed by cooling a gas of extremely low density, about one hundred-thousandth the density on normal air to super low temperature.

7. With the help of a labelled diagram describe an activity to show that particles of matter are very small.

Sol. Take 2-3 crystals of potassium permanganate and dissolve them in 100 mL of water.

Take out approximately 10 mL of this solution and put it into 90 mL of clear water.

Take out 10 mL of this solution and put it into another 90 mL of clear water.

Keep diluting the solution like this 5 to 8 times.

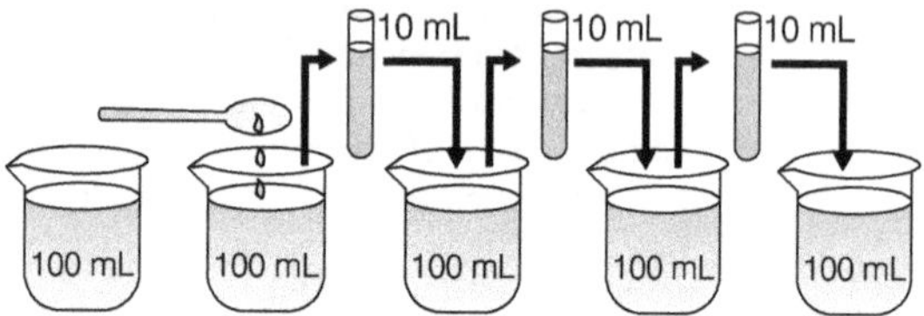

Estimating how small are the particles of matter. With every dilution through the colour becomes light, it is still visible.

This experiment shows that just a few crystals of potassium permanganate can colour a large volume of water (about 1000 L).

So, we conclude that there must be millions of tiny particles in just one crystal of potassium permanganate. Which keep on dividing themselves into smaller and smaller particles.

CHAPTER EXERCISE

Multiple Type Questions

1 Crystals of $KMnO_4$ in water proves that

(a) $KMnO_4$ is of red colour

(b) $KMnO_4$ is acidic in nature

(c) $KMnO_4$ is made up of millions of tiny particles

(d) $KMnO_4$ is a reducing agent

2 A few substances are arranged in the increasing order of 'forces of attraction' between their particles. Which one of the following represents a correct arrangement? **NCERT Exemplar**

(a) Water, air, wind

(b) Air, sugar, oil

(c) Oxygen, water, sugar

(d) Salt, juice, air

3 A solid substance possess

(a) rigidity, fluidity and weak force of attraction

(b) rigidity, fluidity and fixed volume

(c) rigidity, fixed volume and high attractive forces of attraction

(d) rigidity, fixed shape and large intermolecular space between particles

4 A gas fills completely the vessel in which it is kept, because

(a) of weak intermolecular attractive forces

(b) of strong intermolecular attractive forces

(c) of very weak intermolecular repulsive forces

(d) of rigidity

5 On converting 25°C, 38°C and 66°C to Kelvin scale, the correct sequence of temperature will be

(a) 298 K, 311 K and 339 K **NCERT Exemplar**

(b) 298 K, 300 K and 338 K

(c) 273 K, 278 K and 543 K

(d) 298 K, 310 K and 338 K

Fill in the Blanks

6 The energy supplied by heat......the force of attraction between the particles.

7 ....and.........determine the state of a substance.

True and False

8 We perspire more on a humid day than on a dry day.

9 Cooling is caused during evaporation and boiling.

Match the Columns

10 Match the following column A and B.

Column A	Column B
A. Increase in surface area.	(i) Evaporation increase
B. Decrease in temperature.	(ii) Evaporation decrease
C. Evaporation	(iii) Bulk phenomenon
D. Boiling	(iv) Surface phenomenon

Assertion-Reason

Direction (Q.Nos. 11-13) *In each of the following questions, a statement of Assertion is given by the corresponding statement of Reason. Of the statements, mark the correct answer as*

(a) If both Assertion and Reason are true and Reason is the correct explanation of Assertion

(b) If both Assertion and Reason are true but Reason is not the correct explanationi of Assertion

(c) If Assertion is true but Reason is false

(d) If Assertion is false, but Reason is true.

11 **Assertion** Camphor disappears without leaving any residue.
Reason Camphor undergoes sublimation.

12 **Assertion** The process of diffusion is always followed by effusion.
Reason Both diffusion and effusion deal with spreading of gas.

13 **Assertion** Liquids diffuse less easily as compared to gases.
Reason Intermolecular forces are greater in gases.

Case Based Questions

Direction (Q.Nos. 14-17) *Answer the questions on the basis of your understanding of the following paragraph and related studied concepts:*

Gases are highly compressible as compared to solids and liquids. The Liquified Petroleum Gas (LPG) cylinder that we get in our home for cooking or the oxygen supplied to hospital in cylinder is compressed gas. Compressed Natural Gas (CNG) is used as fuel these clays in vehicles. Due to its high compressibility, large volumes of gas can be compressed into a small cylinder and transported easily.

The smell of cooked food in our home easily reaches to our nostrils even without entering in kitchen. It happens so because the particles of the air spread from kitchen and reaches us.

14 Name the process by which smell of perfume spreads out

(a) evaporation (b) diffusion

(c) condensation (d) fusion

15 A gas fills completely the vessel in which it is kept because of

(a) weak intermolecular attractive forces

(b) strong intermolecular attractive forces

(c) very weak intermolecular repulsion forces

(d) rigidity

16 Dry ice is compressed under high pressure, what happen to it when the pressure is released?

17 Name the process, when different substances mix as a result of random motion of their molecules.

Answers

1. (c) 2. (c) 3. (c) 4. (a) 5. (a)
6. Overcomes
7. Pressure and temperature
8. True 9. False
10. A→(i), B→(ii), C→(iv), D→(iii)
11. (a) 12. (b) 13. (c) 14. (b)
15. (d)

Very Short Answer Type Questions

18 When a drop of blue ink is put in water, the blue colour spreads and the whole solution becomes blue. Name the phenomenon due to which this happens.

19 Out of dry and wet air which one is heavier?

20 Which property of gases helps us in detecting the leakage of LPG gas?

21 What is humidity?

22 Give examples in which matter is present in the plasma state.

23 Name some substance that can be separated by sublimation.

Short Answer (SA) Type Questions

24 Why do solids are generally denser than liquids and gases?

25 With the help of an example, explain how diffusion of gases in water is essential?

26 How is high compressibility property of gas is useful to us?

27 The melting point of ice is 273.16 K. What does this mean? Explain in detail.

28 How are particles of matter affected with increasing or reducing pressure at a given temperature?

29 Why is it advisable to use pressure cooker at higher altitudes for cooking food?

30 On a hot sunny day, why do we feel pleasant sitting under a tree?

31 (*i*) Give reason.

(*a*) Plasma is found in the stars.

(*b*) The molecules of a solid have the strongest intermolecular forces.

(*ii*) Out of four gases Cl_2, CO_2, CH_4, N_2, which gas would diffuse most rapidly and why?

32 When ice at −10°C is slowly heated, temperature of ice gradually increases till 0°C, the temperature of the system remains constant when the ice changes into water and then further rises. Explain the observation.

Long Answer (LA) Type Questions

33 Write an activity to show that the rate of diffusion of liquids decreases with increase in density of the liquids.

34 Show by an activity that the gases are highly compressible as compared to liquids.

35 Describe an activity to determine the boiling point of water and melting point of ice.

36 Pressure and temperature determine the state of a substance. Explain this in detail.

Challengers*

1 The SI unit of volume is cubic metre (m^3). The common unit of measuring volume in litre (L). Then, 1 L = ... dm^3, 1 L = ... mL and 1 mL = ... cm^3.

(a) 1 L = 1 dm^3, 1 L = 100 mL, 1 mL = 10 cm^3
(b) 1 L = 1 dm^3, 1 L = 1000 mL, 1 mL = 1 cm^3
(c) 1 L = 10 dm^3, 1 L = 1000 mL, 1 mL = 1 cm^3
(d) 1 L = 10 dm^3, 1 L = 100 mL, 1 mL = 10 cm^3

2 Find out the incorrect increasing/ decreasing order in the following

(a) Force of attraction : Oxygen < water < sugar
(b) Increasing intermolecular space : Solids < liquids < gases
(c) Diffusion : Solid < liquid < gas
(d) Kinetic energy : Hydrogen > honey > water

3 Kinetic energy of particles of water in three vessels X, Y and Z are E_X,E_Y and E_Z respectively and $E_X > E_Y > E_Z$. Then the temperature of water in the three vessels are

(a) $T_Z > T_X > T_Y$
(b) $T_X > T_Y > T_Z$
(c) $T_X > T_Z > T_Y$
(d) $T_Y > T_Z > T_X$

4 Which of the following statement is correct?

(a) Sponge is compressible, but considered as a solid.
(b) A rubber band, change shape under force and not regains the same shape when force is removed.
(c) Mass multiply by volume is called density of its substance.
(d) The common name of solids and liquids is fluid.

5 Match the column I (hypothesis) with column (II) (evidence that supports it)

Column I (Hypothesis)	Column II (Evidence)
P. Particles in a solid move farther apart on heating.	I. You can smell dinner cooking in the kitchen when you are in your bedroom.
Q. Different particles of different elements have different masses.	II. It is easier to squash a ballon filled with air than a ballon filled with water.
R. Gas particles always spread out to fill the space available to them.	III. A metal rod expands on heating.
S. Gas particles are farther apart than liquid particles.	IV. A gold bracelet is much heavier than an identical silver bracelet.

Codes

	P	Q	R	S		P	Q	R	S
(a)	III	IV	II	I	(b)	IV	I	II	III
(c)	I	II	III	IV	(d)	IV	III	II	I

6 You are given the following substances with their boiling and melting points.

Substance	Boiling point (°C)	Melting point (°C)
A	–183	–219
B	445	119
C	78	–15

Point out the physical states of A, B and C at room temperature (30 °C).

	A	B	C
(a)	Gas	Solid	Liquid
(b)	Gas	Liquid	Solid
(c)	Liquid	Solid	Gas
(d)	Solid	Liquid	Gas

7 Among the following, which one is the false statement?

(a) Sublimation is the process of conversion of a matter from its liquid state to gaseous state at specific conditions of temperature and pressure.
(b) Naphthalene, camphor, iodine, ammonium chloride are undergo sublimation.
(c) The melting point of ice is 0°C or 273.16 K
(d) Condensation is the process of conversion of matter from its gaseous state to liquid state at specific conditions of temperature and pressure.

8 Effect of change of temperature on the physical state may be represented as

$$X \underset{\text{Cool}}{\overset{\text{Heat}}{\rightleftharpoons}} Y \underset{\text{Cool}}{\overset{\text{Heat}}{\rightleftharpoons}} Z$$

What is X, Y and Z?

(a) X = Liquid state, Y = Gaseous state, Z = Solid state
(b) X = Solid state, Y = Gaseous state, Z = Liquid state
(c) X = Liquid state, Y = Solid state, Z = Gaseous state
(d) X = Solid state, Y = Liquid state, Z = Gaseous state

9 What will be the correct sequence of temperature when 25°C and 45°C are converted to Kelvin scale and Fahrenheit scale?

(a) 278.16 K, 308.16 K, 74°F, 103° F
(b) 298.16 K, 318.16 K, 74° F, 103° F
(c) 298.16 K, 318.16 K, 77° F, 113° F
(d) 318.16 K, 298.16 K, 77° F, 113° F

10 The non-SI units and SI units of some physical quantities are given in Column I and Column II respectively. Match the units belonging to the same physical quantity.

	Column I		Column II
A.	Degree celsius	I.	Kilogram
B.	Centimetre	II.	Pascal
C.	Bar	III.	Metre
D.	Milligram	IV.	Kelvin

Codes

	P	Q	R	S		P	Q	R	S
(a)	IV	III	II	I	(b)	III	IV	I	II
(c)	II	III	IV	I	(d)	I	II	III	IV

Answer Key

1.	(b)	**2.**	(d)	**3.**	(b)	**4.**	(a)	**5.**	(a)
6.	(a)	**7.**	(a)	**8.**	(d)	**9.**	(c)	**10.**	(a)

RELATED ONLINE VIDEOS

Visit https://www.youtube.com/watch?v=wclY8F-UoTE
OR **Scan the Code**

Visit https://www.youtube.com/watch?v=uYYEX5v5a9A
OR **Scan the Code**

Visit https://www.youtube.com/watch?v=94tReSbyPYc
OR **Scan the Code**

Visit 4.https://www.youtube.com/watch?v=shdLjIkRaS8
OR **Scan the Code**

These questions may or may not be asked in the examination, have been given just for additional practice.

CHAPTER

02

Is Matter Around Us Pure?

In chemistry, when we say a substance is pure, it means that the substance is made up of only one type of constituent particles. In other words, a substance is a pure single form of matter.

Depending upon the chemical composition, matter is classified into elements, compounds, (i.e. pure substances that are non-separable by physical methods) and mixtures (separable by physical methods like sublimation, etc).

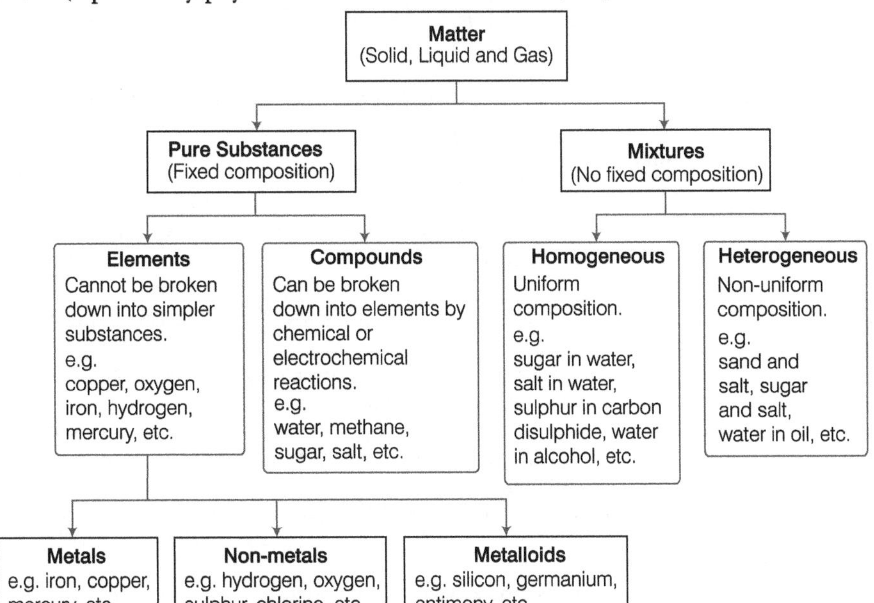

Chapter Checklist

- Pure Substance
- Mixtures
- Solution
- Suspension
- Colloidal Solution
- Separating the Components of a Mixture
- Physical and Chemical Changes

Pure Substance

A substance that consists of only a single type of constituent particles is called **pure substance**, e.g. gold, water, etc. Based upon the nature of the constituent particles, a pure substance is of two types, i.e. elements and compounds.

1. Elements

The term element was first used by **Robert Boyle** in 1661. According to **Antoine Laurent Lavoisier,** a French chemist, (1743-94), 'an element is a basic form of matter that cannot be broken down into simpler substances by chemical reactions'. An element is a pure substance.

Till now 118 elements have been discovered, out of these 92 are natural elements and others are man-made. On the basis of variation in properties, elements can be broadly classified as **metals, non-metals** and **metalloids.**

(i) Metals

A metal is an element that is malleable (i.e. can be hammered into thin sheets), ductile (i.e. can be drawn into wires), sonorous (i.e. make a ringing sound when hit), and conduct heat and electricity. They are lustrous (shine) and have silvery-grey or golden- yellow colour, e.g. gold, silver, copper, iron, sodium, potassium, etc. Mercury is the only metal that is liquid at room temperature.

Gallium and caesium because of their very low melting points remain in liquid state at a temperature slightly above room temperature (303K).

(ii) Non-metals

A non-metal is an element that is neither malleable nor ductile and does not conduct heat and electricity. They display a variety of colours, e.g. hydrogen, oxygen, iodine, carbon (coal, coke), bromine, chlorine, etc. Bromine is the only non-metallic element that exists in liquid state at normal conditions of temperature and pressure.

(iii) Metalloids

Elements having intermediate properties between those of metals and non-metals are called metalloids, e.g. boron, silicon, germanium, etc.

2. Compounds

A compound is a substance composed of two or more elements, chemically combined with one another in a fixed proportion, e.g. water (H_2O), methane (CH_4), carbon dioxide (CO_2), ammonia (NH_3), sodium chloride ($NaCl$), etc.

Mixtures

Mixtures are constituted by more than one kind of pure form, known as a substance. Most of the matter around us exist as mixtures of two or more pure components, e.g. sea water, minerals, soil, etc, are all mixtures.

Types of Mixtures

Depending upon the nature of the components that form a mixture, we have two types of mixtures:

(i) Homogeneous Mixture

A mixture in which the constituents are uniformly distributed throughout i.e. without any clear boundary of separation, is called **homogeneous mixture**. Here, the constituents cannot be seen with naked eyes or under a microscope. Some of the examples of homogeneous mixtures are salt solution, sugar solution, air, soft drinks, petroleum, biogas, alloys, etc.

Note Air is a homogeneous mixture of gas. Its two major constituents are oxygen (21 %) and nitrogen (78 %) and other gases in small quantities.

(ii) Heterogeneous Mixture

A mixture that does not have uniform composition, i.e. has visible boundaries of separation between its constituents is called **heterogeneous mixture.** Here, the constituents of a heterogeneous mixture can be seen by naked eyes or under a microscope. Examples of heterogeneous mixtures are sugar and sand mixture, salt and sand mixture, polluted air, muddy water, etc.

Differences between Compounds and Mixtures

Compound	*Mixture*
Definite elements are present in a definite ratio.	Substances mix in any ratio.
Elements combine chemically to form a compound.	Chemical reaction does not take place during its formation.
Constituents lose their properties.	Constituents retain their properties.
Constituents cannot be separated by simple physical methods.	Constituents can be separated by simple physical methods.
Considerable energy changes take place during the formation or decomposition of a compound.	Energy changes do not take place (or negligible) during the formation or decomposition of a mixture.
A compound is always homogeneous in nature.	A mixture may be homogeneous or heterogeneous in nature.

Check Point 01

1 Name one metal that is liquid at room temperature.
2 State True or False for the following statement:
Soft drinks and soil are not single pure substance.
3 Give two examples of heterogeneous mixtures.
4 Fill in the blank:
Mixture contains more than one ....

Solution

A homogeneous mixture of two or more substances is called solution. A solution is sometimes also called a **true solution.** Lemonade, soda water, salt solution, sugar solution, etc., all are the examples of solutions. In a solution, there is homogeneity at the particle level, i.e. the particles of dissolved substances are evenly distributed in the solution and are indistinguishable from one another.

There are two main components of a solution:

(*i*) **Solvent** (Dissolving Phase) The component (usually present in larger amount) of the solution that dissolves the other component in it, is called the **solvent.**

(*ii*) **Solute** (Dissolved Phase) The component (usually present in lesser quantity) of the solution that is dissolved in the solvent is called the **solute.**

Some common examples of solution:

(*i*) In sugar solution, sugar is the solute and water is the solvent.

(*ii*) A solution of iodine in alcohol known as **tincture of iodine,** has iodine (solid) as the solute and alcohol (liquid) as the solvent.

(*iii*) Aerated drinks like soda water, etc., are gas in liquid solutions. CO_2 (gas) as solute and water (liquid) as solvent.

(*iv*) Solid solutions (alloys) and gaseous solutions (air).

Alloys

Alloys are mixtures of two or more metals or a metal and a non-metal and cannot be separated into their components by physical methods. But still, an alloy is considered as a mixture because it shows the properties of its constituents and can have variable composition, e.g. brass is a mixture of approximately 30% zinc and 70% copper.

Properties of a Solution

Some important properties of a solution are as follows:

(*i*) A solution is a homogeneous mixture.

(*ii*) The particles of a solution are smaller than 1 nm (10^{-9} m) in diameter. Therefore, they cannot be seen by naked eyes.

(*iii*) Due to very small particles, they do not scatter a beam of light passing through the solution. So, the path of light is not visible in a solution.

(*iv*) A solution is stable, i.e. the solute particles do not settle down when left undisturbed. The solute particles cannot be separated from the mixture by the process of filtration.

Concentration of a Solution

The concentration of a solution is the amount of solute present in a given amount (mass or volume) of solution, or the amount of solute dissolved in a given mass or volume of the solvent. In a solution, the relative proportion of the solute and solvent can be varied. Depending upon the amount of solute present in a given amount of solvent, it can be classified as under :

(*i*) **Saturated solution** A solution in which no more amount of solute can be dissolved at a given temperature, is called **saturated solution.** The amount of the solute present in the saturated solution at this temperature is called **solubility.**

$$\text{Solubility} = \frac{\text{Mass of solute}}{\text{Mass of solvent}} \times 100$$

(*ii*) **Unsaturated solution** If the amount of solute contained in a solution is less than the saturation level, it is called an **unsaturated solution.**

$$\text{Concentration of solution} = \frac{\text{Amount of solute}}{\text{Amount of solution}} \times 100$$

Expressing the Concentration of a Solution

The methods by which the concentration of a solution can be expressed are:

(*i*) Mass by mass percentage of a solution

$$= \frac{\text{Mass of solute}}{\text{Mass of solution}} \times 100$$

(*ii*) Mass by volume percentage of a solution

$$= \frac{\text{Mass of solute}}{\text{Volume of solution}} \times 100$$

(iii) Volume by volume percentage of a solution

$$= \frac{\text{Volume of solute}}{\text{Volume of solution}} \times 100$$

Example 1. *A solution contains* 50 g *of common salt in* 450 g *of water. Calculate the concentration of the solution.*

Sol. Concentration of solution $= \frac{\text{Mass of solute}}{\text{Mass of solution}} \times 100$

Mass of common salt (solute) = 50 g

Mass of water = 450 g

Mass of solution = 50 + 450 = 500 g

Concentration of solution $= \frac{50}{500} \times 100 = 10\%$

Example 2. 4 g *of a solute is dissolved in* 40 g *of water to form a saturated solution at* 25° C. *Calculate the solubility of the solute at* 25° C.

Sol. Solubility $= \frac{\text{Mass of solute}}{\text{Mass of solvent}} \times 100$

Mass of solute = 4 g, Mass of solvent = 40 g,

Solubility $= \frac{4\ (g)}{40\ (g)} \times 100 = 10$ g

Check Point 02

1 State True or False for the following statement:
The particles of solution can be seen by naked eye.

2 Fill in the blank:
A solution is a ...... mixture.

3 A solution of alcohol in water has been prepared by mixing 100 mL of alcohol in 300 mL of water. Calculate the volume percentage of the solution. [**Ans.** 25%]

4 Calculate the mass of water and mass of glucose required to make 250 g of 40% solution of glucose. [**Ans.** 150 g, 100 g]

Suspension

A suspension is a heterogeneous mixture in which the solute particles do not dissolve, but remain suspended throughout the bulk of the medium, e.g. a mixture of chalk powder in water, a mixture of sand in water, smoke coming out of a chimney of a factory.

Properties of Suspension

Some important properties of suspension are as follows:

(*i*) Suspension is a heterogeneous mixture.
(*ii*) Its particles can be seen by naked eyes.
(*iii*) Its particles scatter a beam of light passing through it and make its path visible (Tyndall effect).
(*iv*) It is unstable, i.e. the solute particles settle down when suspension is left undisturbed. They can be separated by the process of filtration. When the particles settle down, the suspension breaks and it does not scatter light any more.

Note The insoluble particles in a suspension are called 'suspended particles', whereas the solvent is referred to as 'medium'.

Colloidal Solution

A colloid (or colloidal solution) is a mixture that is actually heterogeneous but appears to be homogeneous as the particles are uniformly spread throughout the solution, e.g. milk, shaving cream, cheese, etc. Colloidal solutions are also called **colloidal sols.**

Properties of a Colloid

Some important properties of a colloid are as follows :

(*i*) A colloid is a heterogeneous mixture.
(*ii*) The size of particles of a colloid is too small to be individually seen by naked eyes.
(*iii*) Colloids are big enough to scatter a beam of light passing through it and make its path visible.
(*iv*) The colloids are quite stable. Particles do not settle down when a colloid is left undisturbed.
(*v*) Particles of colloid can pass through filter paper, therefore a colloid cannot be separated by filtration. However, they get separated by a special technique called **centrifugation.**

Common Examples of Colloids

Colloids are classified according to the state (solid, liquid or gas) of the dispersion medium and the dispersed phase.

Types of Colloids

Type of Colloid	*Dispersed Phase*	*Dispersion Medium*	*Examples*
Aerosol	Liquid	Gas	Fog, cloud, mist
Aerosol	Solid	Gas	Smoke, automobile exhaust
Foam	Gas	Liquid	Shaving cream
Emulsion	Liquid	Liquid	Milk, face cream
Sol	Solid	Liquid	Milk of magnesia, mud
Foam	Gas	Solid	Foam, rubber, sponge, pumice
Gel	Liquid	Solid	Jelly, cheese, butter
Solid sol	Solid	Solid	Milky glass, coloured gemstone

Tyndall Effect

The scattering of light by colloidal particles is known as Tyndall effect. In a true solution, the solute particles are so small that they cannot scatter light falling on them. In a colloidal solution, the particles are big enough to scatter light. Tyndall effect can also be observed in the following situations:

(*i*) When a fine beam of light enters a room through a small hole (due to scattering of beam of light by the particles of dust and smoke in air).
(*ii*) When sunlight passes through the canopy of a dense forest (as the mist containing tiny droplets of water scatter it).

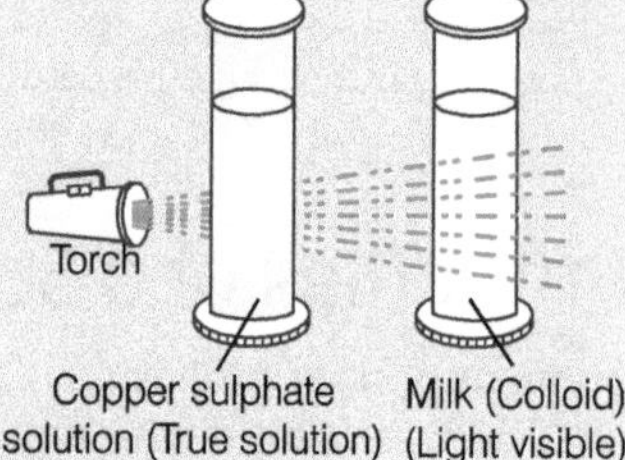

Demonstration of Tyndall effect

- The components of a colloidal solution are the dispersed phase and the dispersion medium.
- The solute-like component or the dispersed particles in a colloid form is the dispersed phase and the component in which the dispersed phase is suspended, is known as the dispersion medium.

Check Point 03

1 State True or False for the following statement:
Particles of colloids is two small, they cannot be seen by naked eye.
2 What are 'suspended particles?
3 By which technique of separation, colloidal particles being separated?
4 Fill in the blank:
Gel is a colloidal sol of ......in...... .
5 Define dispersion medium.
6 Write the dispersed phase and dispersion medium present in foam. Give an example.

Separating the Components of a Mixture

Most of the natural substances are not chemically pure. Different methods of separation are used to get individual components from a mixture. In order to separate components of a mixture, single or a combination of methods are used. Selection of method depends upon the nature of the components present in the mixture.

Heterogeneous mixtures can be separated into their respective constituents by simple physical methods like handpicking, sieving, filtration, etc., that we use in our day-to-day life. Sometimes, special techniques are adopted for the separation of components of a mixture, e.g. separation of coloured component (dye) from ink.

Evaporation (Separation of Volatile Component from Non-Volatile Component)

The process of conversion of a substance from a liquid state to a gaseous state is called **evaporation** and the substance is said to be **volatile**.

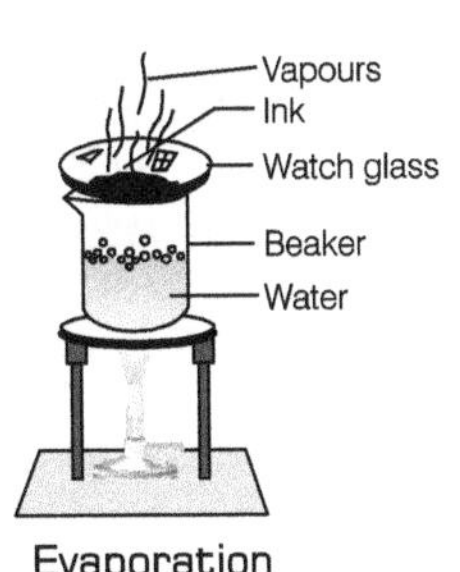

Evaporation

This method can be used to separate a volatile component (solvent) from a non-volatile component (solute) of a mixture. On heating the mixture, the volatile component evaporates leaving behind the non-volatile component, e.g. common salt from sea water can be separated by this method. The heat of sun gradually evaporates water in the shallow lakes and common salt is left behind as a solid.

Note Separation of dye (ink) from water is done via evaporation. Direct heating of ink is avoided because the blue or the black dye may decompose on direct heating.

Centrifugation (Separation of Colloidal Particles from Solution)

Two components having difference in densities can be separated by centrifugation. This method is based on the principle that, the denser particles are forced to the bottom and the lighter particles stay at the top when spun rapidly. A device used to separate liquids from solids by spinning is called **centrifuge.**

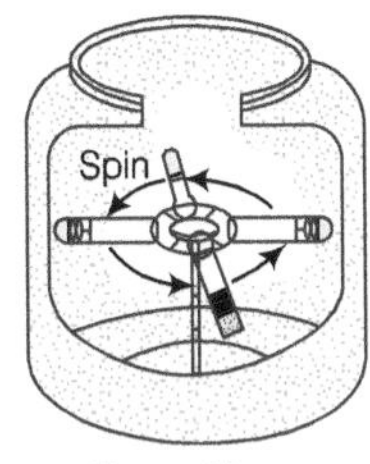

Centrifuge

Centrifugal machines are commonly used for this method. The machine can be rotated either by hand, i.e. manually or electrically.

Applications Centrifugation technique is used in

- diagnostic laboratories for blood and urine tests.
- washing machines to squeeze out water from wet clothes.
- dairies and homes to separate butter from cream.

Separation by using Separating Funnel (Separation of Mixture of Two Immiscible Liquids)

This method is used to separate a mixture of two immiscible liquids. This method is based upon the principle that immiscible liquids separate out in layers depending on their densities.

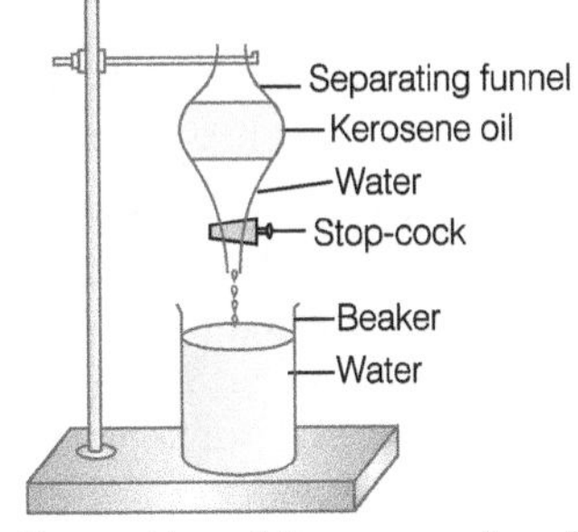

Separation of kerosene oil and water by separating funnel

Applications
Separating funnel is used in

- separation of mixture of oil and water.
- during extraction of iron from its ore, the lighter slag is removed from molten iron.

Sublimation (Separation of a Solid Volatile Component from Mixture)

Some solids have a tendency to sublime on heating, i.e. they convert directly from solid to gaseous/ vapour phase on heating without passing through the liquid phase. A mixture containing such solid with any other (normal) solid can be separated by sublimation. Examples of solids that sublime are camphor, ammonium chloride, naphthalene, iodine, anthracene, etc.

Hence, sublimation is used to separate such mixtures that contain a sublimable volatile component from a non-sublimable impurity, e.g. a mixture of common salt and ammonium chloride can be separated by sublimation.

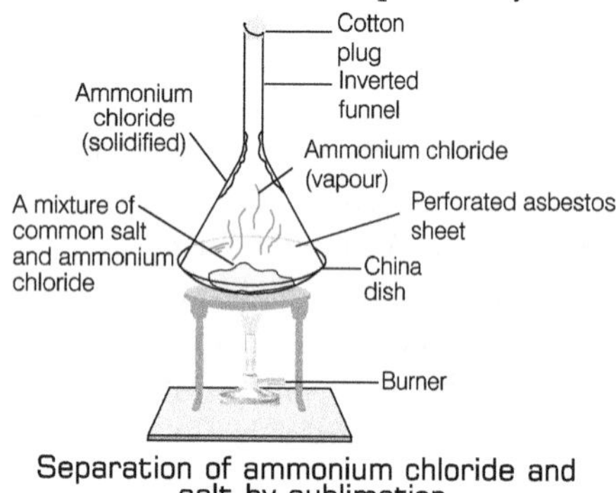

Separation of ammonium chloride and salt by sublimation

Chromatography (Separation of Components with the Help of Same Solvent)

The term chromatography is based on Greek word, *kroma* means colour. This technique was first used for the separation of colour.

Chromatography is the technique used for the separation of those solutes that dissolve in the same solvent. The separation of different components of a mixture is depend upon their different solubilities in the same solvent, e.g. separation of dyes present in ink by paper chromatography.

The ink that we use has water as the solvent and the dye is soluble in it. As the water rises on the filter paper it takes along with it the dye particles. Usually, a dye is a mixture of two or more colours. The coloured component that is more soluble in water, rises faster and in this way the colours get separated.

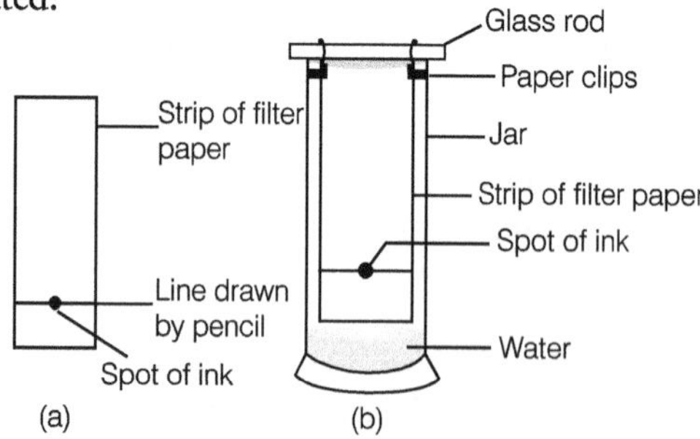

Separation of dyes in black ink using chromatography

Applications Chromatography is used to separate

(*i*) drugs from blood.

(*ii*) pigments from natural colours.

(*iii*) colours in a dye.

Distillation (Separation of Two Miscible Liquids)

If liquids in a mixture are miscible, boil without decomposition and possess different boiling points, then they can be separated by distillation. Distillation involves the conversion of a liquid into vapour followed by the condensation of vapour back into the liquid. Distillation is used only if the liquids have a difference in boiling points of more than 25 K.

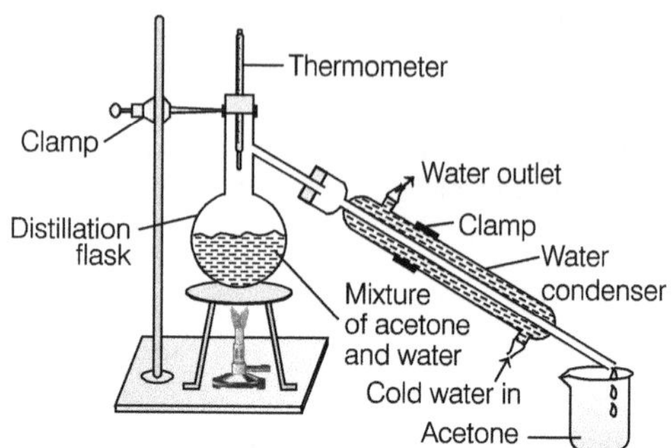

Separation of two miscible liquids by distillation

Fractional Distillation

To separate a mixture of two or more miscible liquids for which the differences in boiling points is less than 25 K, fractional distillation process is used, e.g. separation of different gases from air, different fraction from petroleum products, etc.

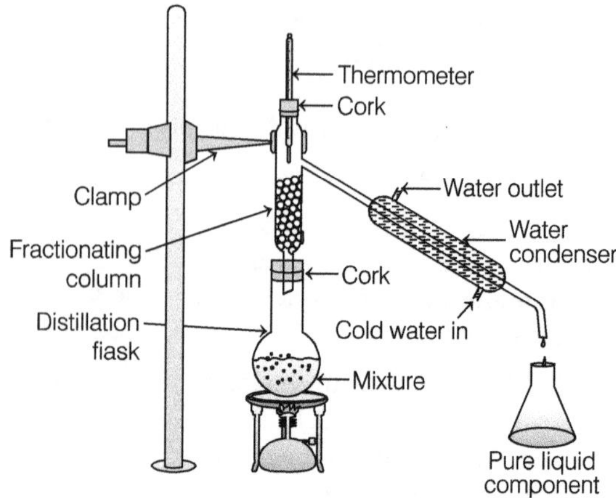

Fractional distillation

- The apparatus is similar to that for simple distillation, except that a fractionating column is fitted in between the distillation flask and the condenser.
- A simple fractionating column is a tube packed with glass beads. The beads provide surface for the vapours to cool and condense repeatedly.

Separation of Different Gases Present in Air

Air is a homogeneous mixture and can be separated into its components by fractional distillation. For this purpose, the air is compressed by increasing the pressure and cooled to a very low temperature. Thus, liquid air is obtained. This liquid air is allowed to warm up slowly in a fractional distillation column, where gases get separated at different heights depending upon their boiling points.

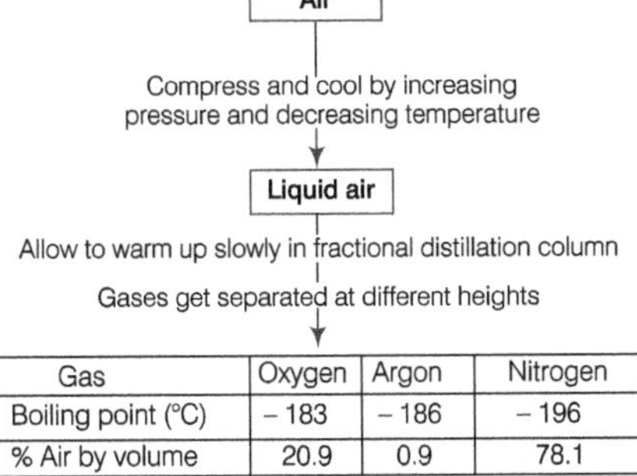

Gas	Oxygen	Argon	Nitrogen
Boiling point (°C)	– 183	– 186	– 196
% Air by volume	20.9	0.9	78.1

Flow diagram showing the separation of gases from air

The actual apparatus used for the separation of gases is shown in the following figure:

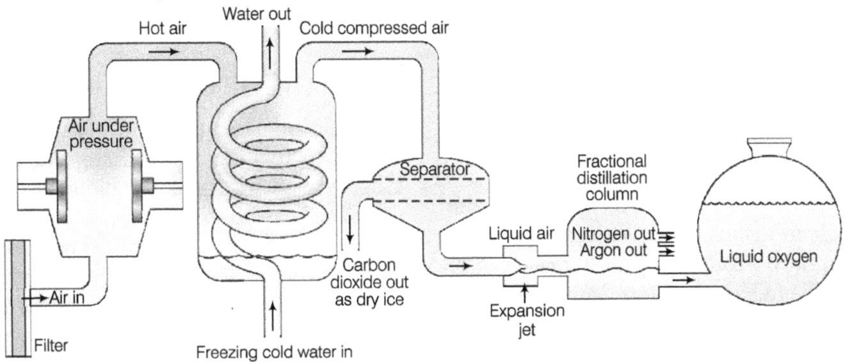

Separation of components of air

Check Point 04

1. By which method of separation the volatile component from its non-volatile solute can be separated?
2. Why direct heating of ink is avoided, during separation of ink?
3. State True or False for the following statement:
   Sublimation is the technique used to separate non-volatile component from mixture.
4. Give two examples of solids which sublimes.
5. What should be the boiling point (°C) for the separation of two miscible liquids by fractional distillation?
6. Fill in the blank:
   Oxygen is separated from air by......... .

Crystallisation (Separation of Pure Substance from its Impure Form)

Crystallisation is a process that separates a pure solid in the form of its crystals from a solution. This method is used to purify solids, e.g. the salt we get from sea water can have many impurities in it. To remove these impurities, the process of crystallisation is used.Crystallisation technique is better than simple evaporation technique as

- some solids decompose or some, like sugar, may get charred during heating to dryness.
- some impurities may remain dissolved in the solution even after filtration. On evaporation these contaminate the solid.

Applications Crystallisation technique is used in

- purification of salt obtained from sea water.
- separation of crystals of alum (*phitkari*) from impure samples.

Purification of Drinking Water

In cities, drinking water is supplied from water works. A number of dissolved and suspended impurities are to be removed before making it fit for drinking purposes.

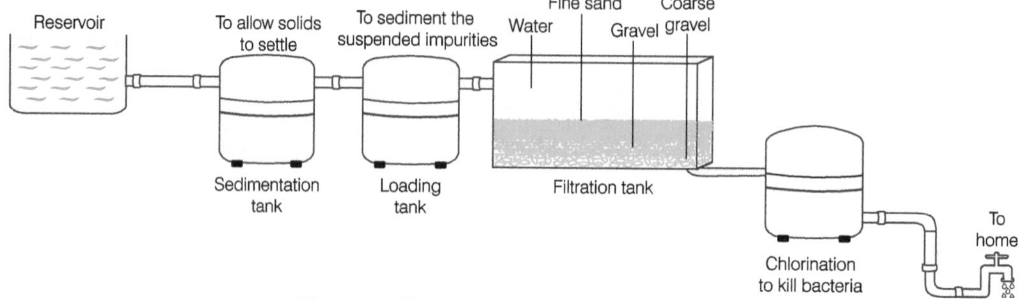

Water purification system in water works

The various processes used in water works for purification are:

(*i*) **Sedimentation** to remove suspended solids (water is allowed to stand for sometime so that suspended impurities settle down).

(*ii*) **Loading** with alum to remove small particles like clay present in the colloidal state. Particles like clay being negatively charged are neutralised by alum and are coagulated at the bottom of tank.

(*iii*) **Filtration** to remove dissolved solids by passing the water through filtration tank which possess three layers. Coarse gravel at the bottom, fine gravel in the centre and fine sand at the top acts as filters. Impure water is introduced from the bottom such that impurities are retained in three layers of gravel and pure water goes to the top and sent to chlorination tank.

(*iv*) **Chlorination** to kill bacteria. Filtered water is treated with bleaching powder to kill bacteria. The pure water is now supplied to homes for drinking purpose.

Physical and Chemical Changes

Physical Changes

The properties that can be observed and specified like colour, hardness, rigidity, fluidity, density, melting point, boiling point, etc., are physical properties.

The changes which occur without a change in composition and in chemical nature of the substance are called **physical changes**. The interconversion of states is a physical change, e.g. change of water in ice is a physical change because chemically, ice and liquid water both are same. Although ice, water and water vapour all look different and display different physical properties but chemically they are same.

Chemical Changes

In chemical changes, one substance reacts with another substance to undergo a change in chemical composition. Chemical changes bring a change in the chemical properties of matter and a new substance is obtained. A chemical change is also called a **chemical reaction**, e.g. both water and cooking oil are liquid, but their chemical characteristics are different. They differ in odour and inflammability.

Oil burns in air whereas water extinguishes fire, i.e. it is the chemical property of oil that makes it different from water.

Note
- Burning is a chemical change.
- During burning of a candle, both physical and chemical changes take place.

Check Point 05

1. What is chlorination?
2. What is a physical change? Give an example of physical change.
3. In which type of change a new substance is formed?
4. Give an example in which physical and chemical changes take place together.
5. Fill in the blanks:
   (*i*) Chemical changes bring a change in the .... properties of matter.
   (*ii*) Physical changes are generally......... .
6. State True or False for the following statement:
   Loading is the process used to remove suspended particles from water.

To Study NCERT Activities
Visit https://goo.gl/8U1Nos OR **Scan the Code**

NCERT FOLDER

INTEXT QUESTIONS

1 What is meant by a substance? **Pg 15**

Sol. The substance which is made up of single type of particles is called pure substance, e.g. hydrogen, oxygen, sulphur, etc.

2 List the points of differences between homogeneous and heterogeneous mixtures. **Pg 15**

Or Differentiate between homogeneous and heterogeneous mixtures with examples. **Pg 18**

Sol. The main points of differences between the homogeneous and heterogeneous mixtures are as follows:

Homogeneous Mixture	*Heterogeneous Mixture*
Its constituents are uniformly distributed all over the mixture.	Its constituents are not distributed uniformly.
There are no visible boundaries of separation.	There are distinct and visible boundaries of separation in most of the cases.
Its constituents cannot be easily separated. Special methods are required for this purpose.	Its constituents can be easily separated by simple methods.
e.g. alloys, air, soft drinks, vinegar, etc.	e.g. mixture of sand and common salt, mixture of chalk powder and water, etc.

3 How are sol, solution and suspension different from each other? **Pg 18**

Sol. Refer to text on Pg 27 and 28.

4 To make a saturated solution, 36 g of sodium chloride is dissolved in 100 g of water at 293 K. Find its concentration at this temperature **Pg 18**

Sol. Mass of solute (NaCl) $= 36$ g

Mass of solvent (H_2O) $= 100$ g

Mass of solution $= 36 + 100 = 136$ g

Concentration (by mass) of the solution

$$= \frac{\text{Mass of solute}}{\text{Mass of solution}} \times 100 = \frac{36}{136} \times 100 = 26.47\%$$

5 How will you separate a mixture containing kerosene and petrol (difference in their boiling points is more than 25°C), which are miscible with each other? **Pg 24**

Sol. A mixture of kerosene and petrol can be separated by simple distillation, as their boiling points differ by more than 25°C. In a distillation flask, the given mixture is half-filled and heated slowly (over a sand bath). As petrol is more volatile than kerosene, it vaporises first.

Its vapours are condensed and collected in a receiver. The kerosene remains in the distillation flask.

Boiling point range of petrol is $70°$ C to $120°$ C. When temperature becomes constant, vapours of petrol start passing through the condenser and collect in the receiver. As soon as the temperature starts rising again, heating is stopped and kerosene is obtained from the distillation flask.

6 Name the technique to separate

(*i*) butter from curd

(*ii*) salt from sea water

(*iii*) camphor from salt **Pg 24**

Sol. (*i*) Centrifugation

(*ii*) Evaporation and crystallisation

(*iii*) Sublimation

7 What type of mixtures are separated by the technique of crystallisation? **Pg 24**

Sol. Crystallisation method can be used to purify those mixtures which

(*i*) contain insoluble and/or soluble impurities.

(*ii*) are crystalline in nature.

(*iii*) either decompose or get charred (e.g. sugar) on heating to dryness, i.e. which cannot be separated by evaporation.

(*iv*) cannot be separated by filtration as some impurities are soluble.

8 Classify the following as chemical or physical changes: **Pg 24**

- cutting of trees,
- melting of butter in a pan,
- rusting of almirah,
- boiling of water to form steam,
- passing of electric current through water and the water breaking down into hydrogen and oxygen gases,
- dissolving common salt in water,
- making a fruit salad with raw fruits, and
- burning of paper and wood.

Sol. **Physical changes**

- cutting of trees,
- melting of butter in a pan,
- boiling of water to form steam,
- dissolving common salt in water, and
- making a fruit salad with raw fruits

Chemical changes

- rusting of almirah
- passing of electric current through water and breaking down of water into hydrogen and oxygen gases.
- burning of paper and wood.

9 Try segregating the things around you as pure substances or mixtures.

Sol. **Pure substance**- Sugar, common salt, rubber.

Mixture- Wood, coal, milk, soap, soil.

*The soap that we use in our daily life is a mixture.

Exercises
(On Pages 28 and 30)

1 Which separation techniques will you apply for the separation of the following?

(*i*) Sodium chloride from its solution in water.
(*ii*) Ammonium chloride from a mixture containing sodium chloride and ammonium chloride.
(*iii*) Small pieces of metal in the engine oil of a car.
(*iv*) Different pigments from an extract of flower petals.
(*v*) Butter from curd.
(*vi*) Oil from water.
(*vii*) Tea leaves from tea.
(*viii*) Iron pins from sand.
(*ix*) Fine mud particles suspended in water.

Sol. (*i*) Evaporation and crystallisation
(*ii*) Sublimation
(*iii*) Filtration
(*iv*) Chromatography
(*v*) Centrifugation
(*vi*) By using separating funnel
(*vii*) Filtration
(*viii*) Magnetic separation
(*ix*) Loading and decantation

Loading Alum is added to muddy water so that the fine soil particles become heavy and settle down.

2 Write the steps you would use for making tea. Use the words solution, solvent, solute, dissolve, soluble, insoluble, filtrate and residue.

Sol. **Method of preparation of tea**

(*i*) Take some water (solvent) in a pan and heat it.
(*ii*) Add some sugar (solute) and boil to dissolve the sugar completely, the obtained homogeneous mixture is called solution.
(*iii*) Add tea leaves (or tea) in the solution and boil the mixture.
(*iv*) Now add milk and boil again.
(*v*) Filter the mixture through the tea stainer and collect the filtrate or soluble substances, i.e. tea in a cup. The insoluble tea leaves left behind as residue in the strainer.

3 Pragya tested the solubility of three different substances at different temperatures and collected the data as given below (results are given in the following table, as grams of substance dissolved in 100 g of water to form a saturated solution).

Substance Dissolved	***Temperature*** (in K)				
	283	293	313	333	353
	Solubility				
Potassium nitrate	21	32	62	106	167
Sodium chloride	36	36	36	37	37
Potassium chloride	35	35	40	46	54
Ammonium chloride	24	37	41	55	66

(*i*) What mass of potassium nitrate would be needed to produce a saturated solution of potassium nitrate in 50 g of water at 313 K?
(*ii*) Pragya makes a saturated solution of potassium chloride in water at 353 K and leaves the solution to cool at room temperature. What would she observe as the solution cools? Explain.
(*iii*) Find the solubility of each salt at 293 K. Which salt has the highest solubility at this temperature?
(*iv*) What is the effect of change of temperature on the solubility of a salt?

Sol. (*i*) At 313 K, solubility of potassium nitrate in 100 g of water = 62

$$\text{Solubility} = \frac{\text{Mass of solute}}{\text{Mass of solvent}} \times 100$$

$$\Rightarrow \text{Mass of solute} = \frac{\text{Solubility} \times \text{Mass of solvent}}{100}$$

$$\therefore \text{Mass of potassium nitrate} = \frac{62 \times 50}{100} = 31\text{ g}$$

Hence, 31g of potassium nitrate would be needed to produce a saturated solution of potassium nitrate in 50 g of water at 313 K.

(*ii*) The amount of potassium chloride that should be dissolved in water to make a saturated solution increases with temperature. Thus, as the solution cools, some of the potassium chloride will precipitate out of the solution and form crystals.

(*iii*) The solubility of the salts at 293 K are:
Potassium nitrate 32 ; Sodium chloride 36,
Potassium chloride 35 ; Ammonium chloride 37
Thus, ammonium chloride has the maximum solubility (37) at 293 K.

(*iv*) The solubility of a solid (salt) decreases with fall in temperature, while it increases with rise in temperature.

4 Explain the following giving examples :

(*i*) Saturated solution
(*ii*) Pure substance
(*iii*) Colloid
(*iv*) Suspension

Sol. (*i*) **Saturated solution** Refer to text on Pg 27.
(*ii*) **Pure substance** Refer to text on Pg. 26.
(*iii*) **Colloid** Refer to text on Pg 28.
(*iv*) **Suspension** Refer to text on Pg 28.

5 Classify each of the following as a homogeneous or heterogeneous mixture. Soda water, wood, air, soil, vinegar, filtered tea.

Sol. **Homogeneous mixtures** Air, soda water, vinegar, filtered tea.
Heterogeneous mixtures Wood, soil.

Note Homogeneous mixtures have same composition throughout, while the composition of heterogeneous mixture is not uniform.

6 How would you confirm that a colourless liquid given to you is pure water?

Sol. Take a given colourless liquid in a beaker and suspend a thermometer into it. Place beaker on a wire gauze and start heating with the help of burner.
Note down the temperature at which water begins to boil. If the given liquid boils at 100°C, the liquid will be a pure water as the boiling point of pure water is 100°C.

7 Which of the following materials fall in the category of pure substance?

(*i*) Ice (*ii*) Milk
(*iii*) Iron (*iv*) Hydrochloric acid
(*v*) Calcium oxide (*vi*) Mercury
(*vii*) Brick (*viii*) Wood
(*ix*) Air

Sol. Ice, iron, calcium oxide and mercury are pure substances as they have definite composition. Hydrochloric acid is a mixture of hydrogen chloride gas and water, so it is a mixture and not a pure substance.

8 Identify the solutions among the following mixtures.

(*i*) Soil (*ii*) Sea water
(*iii*) Air (*iv*) Coal
(*v*) Soda water

Sol. Sea water, air and soda water, as these are the homogeneous mixtures of two or more substances.

Note Sea water is also considered as heterogeneous solution.

9 Which of the following will show Tyndall effect?

(*i*) Salt solution
(*ii*) Milk
(*iii*) Copper sulphate solution
(*iv*) Starch solution

Sol. Milk and starch solution being a colloid will show Tyndall effect, while salt solution and copper sulphate solution are true solutions that will not show Tyndall effect due to small size of their particles.

10 Classify the following into elements, compounds and mixtures.

(*i*) Sodium (*ii*) Soil
(*iii*) Sugar solution (*iv*) Silver
(*v*) Calcium carbonate (*vi*) Tin
(*vii*) Silicon (*viii*) Coal
(*ix*) Air (*x*) Soap
(*xi*) Methane (*xii*) Carbon dioxide
(*xiii*) Blood

Sol. **Elements** Sodium, silver, tin and silicon.
Compounds Calcium carbonate, methane, carbon dioxide and soap.
Mixtures Soil, sugar solution, coal, air, blood and soap. Soap is a compound, but to make it suitable for specific purpose, various substances are added to it. Then, it becomes a mixture.

11 Which of the following are chemical changes?

(*i*) Growth of a plant
(*ii*) Rusting of iron
(*iii*) Mixing of iron filings and sand
(*iv*) Cooking of food
(*v*) Digestion of food
(*vi*) Freezing of water
(*vii*) Burning of a candle

Sol. Growth of a plant, rusting of iron, cooking of food, digestion of food and burning of a candle are chemical changes.

SUMMARY

- A substance that consists of only a single type of constituent particles is called **pure substance.**
- An **element** is a basic form of matter that cannot be broken down into simpler substances by chemical reactions.
- A **metal** is an element that is malleable, ductile, sonorous and conduct heat and electricity.
- A **non-metal** is an element that is neither malleable nor ductile and does not conduct heat and electricity.
- **Metalloids** are intermediate properties between those of metals and non-metals.
- **Compound** can be defined as a substance composed of two or more elements, chemically combined with one another in a fixed proportion.
- **Mixtures** are constituted by more than one substance mixed in any proportion.
- Depending upon the nature of the components that form a mixture, we have two types of mixtures:
  (*i*) **Homogeneous Mixture** A mixture in which the constituents are uniformly distributed throughout i.e. without any clear boundary of separation is called homogeneous mixture.
  (*ii*) **Heterogeneous Mixture** A mixture that does not have uniform composition, i.e. has visible boundaries of separation between its constituents is called heterogeneous mixture.
- A solution is a homogeneous mixture of two or more substances. There are two main components of a solution; **solvent** and **solute.**
- The concentration of a solution is the amount of solute present in a given amount (mass or volume) of solution, or the amount of the solute dissolved in a given mass or volume of the solvent. Depending upon the amount of solute present in a given amount of solvent, it can be classified as under:
  (*i*) **Saturated Solution** A solution in which no more amount of solute can be dissolved at a given temperature, is called saturated solution.
  (*ii*) **Unsaturated Solution** If the amount of solute contained in a solution is less than the saturation level, it is called an unsaturated solution.
- Concentration of solution $= \frac{\text{Amount of solute}}{\text{Amount of solution}} \times 100$
- A **suspension** is a heterogeneous mixture in which the solute particles do not dissolve, but remain suspended throughout the bulk of the medium.
- A **colloid** is a mixture that is actually heterogeneous, but appears to be homogeneous as the particles are uniformly spread throughout the solution.
- The scattering of light by colloidal particles is known as **Tyndall effect.**
- Special techniques have to be used for the separation of components of a mixture, i.e. evaporation, centrifugation, separation by using separating funnel, sublimation, chromatography, distillation and crystallisation, etc.
- **Evaporation** method can be used to separate a volatile component (solvent) from a non-volatile component (solute) of a mixture.
- **Centrifugation** method is used where two components having difference in densities.
- **Separation by using separating funnel** based upon the principle that immiscible liquids separate out in layers depending on their densities.
- Mixture of common salt and ammonium chloride can be separated by **sublimation.**
- **Chromatography** is the technique used for the separation of those solutes dissolve in the same solvent.
- If liquids in a mixture are miscible, boil without decomposition and possess different boiling points, then they can be separated by **distillation.**
- **Distillation** is used only if the liquids have a difference in boiling points of more than 25 K.
- **Crystallisation** is a process that separates a pure solid in the form of its crystals from a solution.
- In **physical changes**, only physical properties of the substance changes.
- In **chemical changes**, one substance reacts with another substance to undergo a change in chemical composition.

For Mind Map

Visit https://goo.gl/fTNH7n OR **Scan the Code**

Exam Practice

Objective Type Questions

Multiple Choice Questions

1 Which of following is a pure substance?

(a) Air (b) Distilled water
(c) Steel (d) Brass

Sol. (*b*) Any substance that contain only one type of particles (e.g. molecules/atoms etc.)are said to be a pure substance. Among the given options, only distilled water has one type of particles (i.e. H_2O molecules).

2 Which of the following statements are true for pure substances?

(*i*) Pure substances contain only one kind of particles.
(*ii*) Pure substances may be compounds or mixtures.
(*iii*) Pure substances have the same composition throughout.
(*iv*) Pure substances can be exemplified by all elements other than nickel.

(a) (i) and (ii) (b) (i) and (iii)
(c) (iii) and (iv) (d) (ii) and (iii)

NCERT Exemplar

Sol. (*b*) A pure substance is one which is made up of only one kind of atoms or molecules. They have the same composition throughout.

3 Which of the following property does not prove that water is a compound?

(a) Water is made up of two different elements (H and O). Which chemically combined with one another in a fixed proportion.
(b) Water has fixed boiling point (b.p.).
(c) The constituents of water cannot be separated by simple physical methods
(d) Distilled water and tap water have same taste and constituents.

Sol. (*d*) Distilled water and tap water have different taste and different constituents. Distilled water has pure H_2O molecules while tap water may contain others molecules also.

4 Two elements X and Y combine to give a product Z. The correct statement about Z is

(a) Z has more mass than that of X
(b) Z has less mass than that of X
(c) Z has less mass than that of Y
(d) Z show same properties as that of X and Y

Sol. (*a*) $\because$ Product Z is formed by the combination of X and Y, thus has more mass than of X and Y separately. Also Z is entirely a new product, thus cannot show same properties, as of X and Y.

5 Two substances, A and B were made to react to form a third substance, A_2B according to the following reaction $2A + B \rightarrow A_2B$. Which of the following statements concerning this reaction are incorrect?

(*i*) The product A_2B shows the properties of substances A and B.
(*ii*) The product will always have a fixed composition.
(*iii*) The product so formed cannot be classified as a compound.
(*iv*) The product so formed is an element.

(a) (i), (ii) and (iii) (b) (ii), (iii) and (iv)
(c) (i), (iii) and (iv) (d) (ii), (iii) and (iv)

NCERT Exemplar

Sol. (*c*) A_2B is a compound made up of two elements A and B in a fixed ratio. The properties of a compound (e.g., A_2B) are entirely different from those of its constituent elements (e.g., A and B). The composition of a compound is fixed.

6 Which of the following substances are homogeneous in nature?

(*i*) Ice (*ii*) Wood
(*iii*) Soil (*iv*) Air

(a) (i) and (iii) (b) (ii) and (iv)
(c) (i) and (iv) (d) (iii) and (iv)

NCERT Exemplar

Sol. (*c*) Ice and air are homogeneous in nature as their particles are not distinctly visible. A homogeneous mixture has a uniform composition throughout its mass.

7 Which of the following will not show Tyndall effect ?

(a) Smoke (b) Foam
(c) Jelly (d) Salt solution

Sol. (*d*) Salt solution will not show Tyndall effect as it is a true solution and particles of salt solution are very small (size < 1 nm). So, these cannot scatter a beam of light, hence do not show Tyndall Effect.

8 The method used to separate a dye from blue ink is

(a) evaporation (b) sedimentation
(c) crystallisation (d) filteration

Sol. (*a*) Blue ink is a mixture of blue-dye (non-volatile solute) and water (volatile solvent). On evaporation, water is separated from the blue-dye (∵ water becomes volatile at 100°C, while blue-dye is left in the container). Hence, (a) is the correct option.

9 The most suitable technique used to separate mixture of different gases from bulk of air, can be

(a) chromatography (b) sublimation
(c) fractional distillation (d) centrifugation

Sol. (*c*) Fractional distillation method is used to separate different gases present in air.

10 Which of the following are chemical changes?

(i) Decaying of wood (ii) Burning of wood
(iii) Sawing of wood
(iv) Hammering of a nail into a piece of wood

(a) (i) and (ii) (b) (ii) and (iii)
(c) (iii) and (iv) (d) (i) and (iv)

NCERT Exemplar

Sol. (a) Decaying of wood and burning of wood are chemical changes, because in these processes, the chemical composition of wood is changed and new substances are formed, which cannot be converted back into their original form.

Fill in the Blanks

11 Distillation method is applied for the separation of a mixture of liquid components having difference in......... .

Sol. boiling point;

Distillation method is used only if the liquids have a difference in boiling points of more than 25K.

12 ....is used when a mixture contains two components, out of which one is soluble.

Sol. Filtration;

In filtration, filtrate contains soluble component and insoluble component remains in filter paper as a residue.

13 Miscible liquids are separated by......... .

Sol. fractional distillation;

To separate a mixture of two or more miscible liquids for which the difference in boiling point is less than 25 K.

True and False

14 Mixture of sand and sulphur can be separated by dissolving the mixture in water and filtering it.

Sol. False;

Sulphur and sand are insoluble in water. Sulphur dissolves in carbon disulphide (CS_2).

15 Making of wine from grapes is a chemical change.

Sol. True;

Fermentation of grapes is a chemical change as the yeast which are responsible for fermentation digest the sugar in grapes in order to produce alcohol.

16 During burning of candle, both physical and chemical changes takes place.

Sol. True;

During burning of candle, both physical and chemical changes take place. The melting of wax changes the state of wax from solid to liquid and energy is absorbed. Which is a physical change. The wax vapours form CO_2, H_2O and energy is evolved, which is a chemical change.

17 The particles of colloid can pass through filter paper.

Sol. True;

Because the size of particles is two small between (1nm-1000 nm) and can easily pass through filter paper.

18 The coloured components from blue or black ink are separated by centrifugation.

Sol. False;

The coloured component from blue or black ink are separated by chromatography.

19 When zinc and copper are mixed we get heterogeneous mixture.

Sol. False;
Alloys are homogeneous mixture.

Match the Columns

20 Match the column *A* and *B*

	Column A		Column B
A.	Miscible liquids	(i)	Distillation
B.	Immiscible liquids	(ii)	Crystallisation
C.	Pure copper sulphate from an impure sample.	(iii)	Sublimation
D.	Salt and ammonium chloride	(iv)	Separating funnel

Sol. A→(i), B→(iv), C→(ii), D→(iii)

A→(i) Miscible liquids have different boiling point so they get separated at their respective boiling point. This is called distillation.

B→(iv) Liquid which have higher density form different layer and settled down at bottom. This is done by using separating funnel.

C→(ii) Impurities are soluble in solvent and crystals get separated out.

D→(iii) NH_4Cl is sublimable volatile component and get separated from salt by sublimation.

Assertion-Reason

Direction (Q.Nos. 21-25) *In each of the following questions, a statement of Assertion is given by the corresponding statement of Reason. Of the statements, mark the correct answer as*

(a) Both Assertion and Reason are true and Reason is the correct explanation of Assertion.
(b) Both Assertion and Reason are true but Reason is not the correct explanation of Assertion.
(c) Assertion is true but Reason is false.
(d) Assertion is false, but Reason is true.

21 **Assertion** A solution of table salt in a glass of water is homogeneous.

Reason A solution having different composition throughout is homogeneous.

Sol. (c) A solution having same composition throughout is homogeneous.

22 **Assertion** A mixture of sugar and benzoic acid can be separated by shaking with ether.

Reason Sugar is insoluble in water.

Sol. (c) Sugar is soluble in water and insoluble in ether.

23 **Assertion** True solutions exhibins Tyndall effect.

Reason Particles are very small in size.

Sol. (d) True solutions do not exhibit Tyndall effect, since the particle size is very small.

24 **Assertion** Impure benzoic acid can be purified by sublimation.

Reason Benzoic acid sublimes on heating.

Sol. (a) Benzoic acid sublimes on heating while impurities do not.

25 **Assertion** Chromatography can be used to separate a mixture of plant pigments.

Reason Chromatography is a process of separation of components of a mixture.

Sol. (a) Chromatography can be used to separate constituents of any coloured mixture.

Case Based Questions

Direction (Q.Nos. 26-29) *Answer the questions on the basis of your understanding of the following passage, table and related studied concepts:*

Abhinav tested the solubility of four different salts i.e. Potassium nitrate, sodium chloride. Potassium chloride and ammonium chloride at different temperature. He took four beakens and marked as (I) Potassium nitrate, (II) Sodium chloride, (III) Potassium chloride, (IV) Ammonium chloride and then he dissolved each salt in 100 g of water and placed a thermometer in it. Heat the contents of the beaker and recored the following observations.

Substance dissolved		Temperature (in K)				
		283	293	313	333	353
		Solubility				
I.	Potassium nitrate	21	32	62	106	167
II.	Sodium chloride	36	36	36	37	37
III.	Potassium chloride	35	35	40	46	54
IV.	Ammonium chloride	24	37	41	55	66

26 Solubility of which substance is highest at 283 K?

(a) I (b) III (c) IV (d) II

Sol. (d) Solubility is the maximum amount of solute (in g) dissolved in a solvent. Sodium chloride have highest solubility (36 g) at 283 K.

27 Which substance show maximum change in its solubility, when the temperature is raised from 313 K to 333 K.

(a) I (b) II (c) III (d) IV

Sol. (a) Potassium nitrate (106 – 62) = 44 g in 100 g of water.

28 In the above question, if the amount of water taken is reduced by 20 per cent, what amount of ammonium chloride would be required to prepare its saturated solution at 353 K?

Sol. (d) Amount of water available = 100 – 20 = 80 g

In 100 g, the amount of NH_4Cl at 353 K = 66 g

80 g, the amount of NH_4Cl at 353 K $= \frac{66}{100} \times 80$

$= 52.8 \text{ g} = 53 \text{ g}$

29 What is the effect of temperature on the solubility of a salt?

Sol. From the above data, it is clear that the solubility of salt in water increases with rise in temperature.

Direction (Q.Nos. 30-33) *Answer the questions on the basis of your understanding of the following passage and related studied concepts:*

Different methods of separation are used to get individual components from a mixture. Separation make it possible to study and use the individual components of a mixture. Heterogeneous mixtures can be separated into their respective constitutents by simple physical methods like hand picking, sieving filtration that we use in our day-to-day life. Sometimes special techniques have to be used for the separation of the components of a mixture for examples, distillation, centrifugation, chromatography etc.

30 Why is the separation of a mixture done? Write any two reasons.

Sol. Separation of components of a mixture is done for the following reasons or purpose:

(*i*) To obtain a pure sample of a substance.

(*ii*) To remove an undesirable or harmful components.

31 What is the principle of separation?

Sol. Principle of separation based on the difference in physical or chemical properties of constituents of a mixture. Depending upon the kind of constituents and their respective properties, different techniques are used.

32 How will you separate a mixture of ethyl alcohol (boiling point 78°C) and water (boiling point 100°C)? Describe the process.

Sol. Ethyl alcohol and water are completely miscible liquids and these have sufficient difference in their boiling point. So these can be separated by the process of simple distillation.

33 What are the commonly used techniques used by farmers in villages to purify food grains?

Sol. Farmers generally use the following techniques.

(*i*) Hand picking (*ii*) Winnowing

(*iii*) Sieving

Very Short Answer Type Questions

34 Is ice water homogeneous or heterogeneous substance? Is it pure or impure substance?

Sol. Ice water is a heterogeneous, but pure substance as ice is made up of water only, which contain only one kind of particle.

35 The 'sea water' can be classified as a homogeneous as well as heterogeneous mixture. Comment. **NCERT Exemplar**

Sol. Sea water is called homogeneous mixture as it contains dissolved salts in it. It may be called heterogeneous mixture as it contains various insoluble components too such as sand, microbes, shells made up of calcium carbonate and so many other things.

36 Is fresh air free of dust particles and impurities of all other kind, a pure substance?

Sol. No, only elements and compounds are pure substances. Air is a mixture of gases and so, not a pure substance.

37 What is meant by concentration of a solution?

Sol. The amount of solute present in a given amount (mass or volume) of solution (or solvent) is known as concentration of solution.

38 Why particles in a true solution cannot be seen with naked eyes?

Sol. Particles of a true solution are very small in size (less than 1nm), hence they are not visible.

39 Do suspension show the property of Tyndall effect?

Sol. Yes, suspensions show the property of Tyndall effect because their particles are too large and scatter the light.

40 State which of the following solutions exhibit Tyndall effect?

Starch solution, sodium chloride solution, tincture of iodine, smoke.

Sol. Starch solution and smoke.

41 How can you separate particles of colloidal solution? Name the process.

Sol. By high speed rotation of colloidal solution, we can separate the particles of colloidal solution. This technique is known as centrifugation.

42 How can we obtain coloured component (dye) from blue/black ink?

Sol. By method of evaporation, we can separate dye (solid) from liquid (solvent) and by chromatography method, we can separate components of the dye.

43 List the two conditions essential for using distillation as a method for separation of the components from a mixture.

Sol. (*i*) The components (liquids) must be miscible with each other.

(*ii*) The components must differ in their boiling points by less than 25K.

44 What are the favourable qualities given to gold when it is alloyed with copper or silver for the purpose of making ornaments? **NCERT Exemplar**

Sol. When alloyed with copper or silver, the gold becomes harder and stronger and its brittleness decreases and become suitable for making ornaments.

45 Which of the tubes in Figures (a) and (b) will be more effective as a condenser in the distillation apparatus?

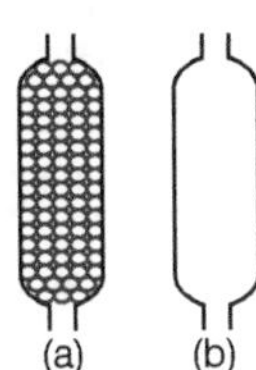

NCERT Exemplar

Sol. Condenser (a) will be more effective in the distillation apparatus because beads present will provide more surface area for cooling and condensation of the vapour occurs repeatedly by passing through it.

46 Salt can be recovered from its solution by evaporation. Suggest some other technique for the same. **NCERT Exemplar**

Sol. Crystallisation method.

47 How will you justify that rusting of iron is a chemical change?

Sol. In a chemical change, new substance is formed and rust is totally different from iron.

Iron is an element while rust is hydrated oxide of iron ($Fe_2O_3 \cdot xH_2O$). Thus, formation of rust from iron is a chemical change.

Short Answer (SA) Type Questions

1 Non-metals are usually poor conductors of heat and electricity. They are non-lustrous, non-sonorous, non-malleable and are coloured.

(*i*) Name a lustrous non-metal.

(*ii*) The allotropic form of a non-metal is a good conductor of electricity. Name the allotrope.

(*iii*) Name a non-metal which is known to form the largest number of compounds.

(*iv*) Name a non-metal other than carbon which shows allotropy.

(*v*) Name a non-metal which is required for combustion.

(*vi*) Name a non-metal that form common salt with sodium. **NCERT Exemplar**

Sol. (*i*) Iodine (*ii*) Graphite (Carbon)
(*iii*) Carbon (*iv*) Phosphorus
(*v*) Oxygen (*vi*) Chlorine

2 Classify the substances given below into elements and compounds.

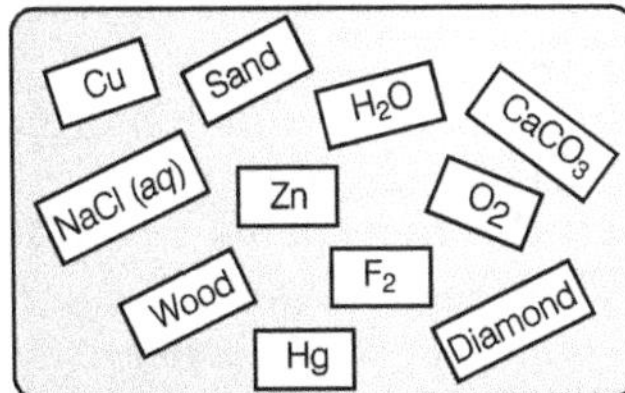

NCERT Exemplar

Sol. The given substances are classified as follows:

Elements	Compounds
Cu	Sand
O_2	H_2O
Zn	$CaCO_3$
F_2	NaCl(*aq*)
Hg	
Diamond (carbon)	

Wood is neither an element nor a compound. It is a mixture. An element is made up of the same type of atoms and compound is a mixture of different elements and but in fixed ratio. O_2 and F_2 are molecular elements.

3 Which of the following are not compounds?

(*i*) Chlorine gas (*ii*) Potassium
(*iii*) Iron (*iv*) Iron sulphide
(*v*) Aluminium (*vi*) Iodine
(*vii*) Carbon
(*viii*) Carbon monoxide
(*ix*) Sulphur powder **NCERT Exemplar**

Sol. (*i*) Chlorine gas (*ii*) Potassium
(*iii*) Iron (*v*) Aluminium
(*vi*) Iodine (*vii*) Carbon
(*ix*) Sulphur powder

Substances mentioned above are the elements, not compounds. Cl_2 gas is molecular element.

4 (*i*) Give the difference between mixture and compound.

(*ii*) Classify the following mixtures as homogeneous and heterogeneous.

(*a*) Tincture of iodine
(*b*) Smoke
(*c*) Brass
(*d*) Sugar solution

Sol. (*i*) Refer to text on Pg 26.

(*ii*) (*a*) Homogeneous (*b*) Heterogeneous
(*c*) Homogeneous (*d*) Homogeneous

5 Tell whether each of the following properties describes a homogeneous mixture, a solution, a heterogeneous mixture, a compound or an element.

(*i*) A homogeneous liquid which leaves a solid residue on boiling.

(*ii*) A cloudy liquid which after some time appears more cloudy towards the bottom.

(*iii*) A colourless liquid which boils at a definite temperature and can be decomposed into simpler substances.

Sol. (*i*) A solution (a solid like salt dissolved in water from which water evaporates on boiling, leaving a solid residue, salt).

(*ii*) A heterogeneous mixture in which suspended particles start settling down at the bottom (muddy water).

(*iii*) A compound.

6 Define solute and solvent. Is it possible to separate them?

Sol. Refer to text on Pg 27. Yes, we can separate solute from solvent by using evaporation method.

7 What would you observe when

(*i*) a saturated solution of potassium chloride prepared at 60°C is allowed to cool to room temperature?

(*ii*) an aqueous sugar solution is heated to dryness?

(*iii*) a mixture of iron filings and sulphur powder is heated strongly?

NCERT Exemplar

Sol. (*i*) Crystals of potassium chloride are formed because solubility decreases with decrease in temperature.(1)

(*ii*) As water evaporates completely, sugar gets charred and turns black.

(*iii*) The compound iron sulphide is formed.

$$Fe + S \xrightarrow{\Delta} FeS$$

8 Why copper sulphate solution in water does not show Tyndall effect, but mixture of water and milk shows?

Sol. The solution of copper sulphate in water is a true solution. In a true solution, the solute particles are so small that they cannot scatter light falling on them. Hence, copper sulphate solution in water does not show Tyndall effect. Mixture of water and milk is a colloid and in colloidal solution, the particles are big enough to scatter light. So, the mixture of water and milk shows Tyndall effect.

9 Explain the term 'Centrifugation'. Give its two applications.

Sol. Centrifugation is the process of separation of two components having difference in densities. This method is based on principle that, when the mixture is agitated rapidly, the lighter particles come at the top and the heavier (or denser) remain at the bottom.

Applications

(*a*) Washing machines to squeeze out water from wet clothes.

(*b*) Dairies and homes to separate butter from cream.

10 A mixture containing two liquids is placed in separating funnel. Answer the following questions.

(*i*) What type of liquids form the mixture?

(*ii*) Which of the liquids will form the lower layer?

(*iii*) What is the basis of this method?

Sol. (*i*) Two liquids which are immiscible with each other form the mixture.

(*ii*) The liquid having higher density will form the lower layer.

(*iii*) The method is based on the difference in the densities of the two liquids.

11 Name the process associated with the following:

(*i*) Dry ice is kept at room temperature and at one atmospheric pressure.

(*ii*) A drop of ink placed on the surface of water contained in a glass spreads throughout the water.

(*iii*) A potassium permanganate crystal is in a beaker and water is poured into the beaker with stirring.

(*iv*) An acetone bottle is left open and the bottle becomes empty.

(*v*) Milk is churned to separate cream from it.

(*vi*) Settling of sand when a mixture of sand and water is left undisturbed for some time.

(*vii*) Fine beam of light entering through a small hole in a dark room, illuminates the particles in its paths. **NCERT Exemplar**

Sol. (*i*) Sublimation (*ii*) Diffusion
(*iii*) Dissolution (*iv*) Evaporation/Vapourisation
(*v*) Centrifugation (*vi*) Sedimentation
(*vii*) Tyndall effect

12 (*i*) Name the technique used for the separation of those solutes that dissolve in the same solvent.

(*ii*) Explain the technique used.

(*iii*) Give any two applications of this technique.

Sol.(*i*) Chromatography

(*ii*) Refer to text on Pg 30.

(*iii*) (*a*) To separate amino acids from proteins.

(*b*) To separate colours from dye.

13 While diluting a solution of salt in water, a student by mistake added acetone (boiling point 56°C).What technique can be employed to get back the acetone? Justify your choice. **NCERT Exemplar**

Sol. Acetone can be obtained back from the solution by the process of simple distillation. When the difference in the boiling point of the two liquids is 25 K or more, we use simple distillation. However, when the difference in the boiling points of the components of a mixture is less than 25 K, fractional distillation is employed.

The boiling point of water is 100°C (373 K), while the boiling point of acetone is 56°C. The difference between the boiling points of two compounds is 44 K, which is much greater than 25 K. Hence simple distillation can be used to easily separate the mixture of acetone and water.

14 (*i*) Name the separation technique you would follow to separate the following mixtures.

(*a*) Clear water from muddy water

(*b*) Kerosene and water

(*c*) Iron filings and sand

(*ii*) What is the advantage of fractional distillation over simple distillation?

Sol. (*i*) (*a*) Filtration

(*b*) By using separating funnel

(*c*) Magnetic separation

(*ii*) In fractional distillation, liquids having difference in their boiling points less than 25°C can be separated and more than two components can be separated while in simple distillation, only two components can be separated.

15 With the help of a flow diagram, show the process of obtaining different gases from air. If the boiling points of oxygen, argon and nitrogen are −183°C, −186°C and −196°C, respectively, then which gas forms the liquid first as the air is cooled?

Sol. Refer to text on Pg 31.

16 Write the role of following in water purification system.

(*i*) Sedimentation tank

(*ii*) Loading tank

(*iii*) Chlorination tank

Sol. Refer to text on Pg 32.

17 Determine whether each of the following change is physical or chemical. Give reason for your answer.

(*i*) A balloon filled with hydrogen gas explodes upon contact with a spark.

(*ii*) Copper turns green on exposure to air and water.

(*iii*) A metal surface becomes dull because of continued abrasion.

Sol.(*i*) **Chemical change** Hydrogen gas burns to form water.

(*ii*) **Chemical change** Copper combines with oxygen of air and water to form copper oxide which has green colour.

(*iii*) **Physical change** Some of the particles of metal from the surface are removed. As a result, only physical appearance changes.

18 Can physical and chemical changes occur together? Illustrate your answer.

Sol. In some cases, physical and chemical changes occur together. One such example is burning of candle. The solid wax present in the candle first changes into liquid state and then into the vapour state. Both these changes are physical changes.

The wax vapours then combine with oxygen of the air to form a mixture of carbon dioxide and water. This involves a chemical change.

The unburnt wax vapours again change first to the liquid state and finally to the solid state. This interconversion of states is a physical change. Thus, burning of candle involves both physical and chemical changes.

19 Calculate the mass of sodium sulphate required to prepare its 20% (mass per cent) solution in 100 g of water? **NCERT Exemplar**

Sol. Mass % of sodium sulphate solution = 20%

Mass of the solvent = 100 g

Let the mass of solute (sodium sulphate) = x g

Applying the formula,

$$\text{Mass \%} = \frac{\text{Mass of solute}}{\text{Mass of solution}} \times 100$$

$$20 = \frac{x \text{ g}}{(x + 100) \text{ g}} \times 100$$

$\Rightarrow \quad 20(x+100) = 100x$

$\Rightarrow \quad 20x + 2000 = 100x$

$\Rightarrow \quad 100x - 20x = 2000$

$\Rightarrow \quad 80x = 2000$

$\therefore \quad x = \frac{2000}{80} = 25 \text{ g}$

Mass of sodium sulphate = 25 g

20 110 g of salt is present in 550 g of solution. Calculate the mass percentage of the solution.

Sol. Mass percentage of solution

$$= \frac{\text{Mass of solute}}{\text{Mass of solution}} \times 100$$

Mass of solute = 110 g [given]
Mass of solution = 550 g [given]

$$\text{Mass percentage} = \frac{110}{550} \times 100 = 20\%$$

21 A solution contains 40 g of common salt in 320 g of water. Calculate the concentration in terms of mass by mass percentage of the solution.

Sol. Mass of solute (salt) = 40 g
Mass of solvent (water) = 320 g
Mass of solution = mass of solute + mass of solvent
= 40g + 320 g = 360g

$$\text{Mass \% of solution} = \frac{\text{mass of solute}}{\text{mass of solution}} \times 100 = \frac{40}{360} \times 100 = 11.1\%$$

Long Answer (LA) Type Questions

1 (*i*) What are elements?
(*ii*) What are the three main types of elements?
(*iii*) Write a property of each type of element.

Sol. (*i*) An element consists of only one type of atoms. It is a basic form of matter that cannot be broken down into simpler substances by chemical reactions.
(*ii*) Metals, non-metals and metalloids.
(*iii*) Metals—Malleable and ductile
Non-metals—Brittle
Metalloids—Semiconductors

2 (*i*) Distinguish among the true solution, suspension and colloid in a tabular form under the following heads:
(a) Stability (b) Filterability
(c) Type of mixture
(*ii*) Give expression for the concentration of a solution. How will you prepare a 10% solution of glucose by mass in water?

Sol.(*i*) Distinctions between true solution, suspension and colloid are:

Property	Solution	Suspension	Colloid
Stability	It is stable. Constituting particles do not settle down on keeping undisturbed.	It is unstable. Constituting particles settle down on keeping undisturbed.	It is stable. Constituting particles do not settle down on keeping undisturbed.
Filterability	Particles cannot be separated by filtration.	Particles are large, so they can be easily separated by ordinary filtration.	Cannot be separated by ordinary filter paper, but can be separated by ultrafiltration.
Type of mixture	Homogeneous	Heterogeneous	Heterogeneous

(*ii*) The methods by which the concentration of a solution can be expressed are:
(a) Mass by mass% of solution

$$= \frac{\text{Mass of solute}}{\text{Mass of solution}} \times 100$$

(b) Mass by volume% of solution

$$= \frac{\text{Mass of solute}}{\text{Mass of solution}} \times 100$$

(c) Volume by volume percentage of a solution

$$= \frac{\text{Volume of solute}}{\text{Volume of solution}} \times 100$$

10 per cent solution of glucose can be prepared by dissolving 10 g of glucose in 90 g of water.

3 Write your observations when the following processes take place:
(*i*) An aqueous solution of sugar is heated to dryness.

(*ii*) A saturated solution of potassium chloride prepared at 608°C is allowed to cool at room temperature.

(*iii*) A mixture of iron filings and sulphur powder is heated strongly.

(*iv*) A beam of light is passed through a colloidal solution.

(*v*) Dilute HCl is added to the mixture of iron and sulphur.

Sol.(*i*) Sugar remains as residue in the form of a solid mass.

(*ii*) Potassium chloride crystallises out.

(*iii*) A black coloured compound is formed.

(*iv*) The path of the light becomes visible.

(*v*) A colourless gas is evolved.

4 (*i*) Pond water contains sand grains, clay particles, salt, pieces of paper and some air bubbles. Select from amongst these, an example each of a solvent, solute, colloid and suspension.

(*ii*) Give one example of each of the following:

(*a*) A solution of gas in liquid

(*b*) A solution of two solids

(*c*) A solution of two gases

Sol.(*i*) Solvent–Water

Solute–Salt, pieces of paper, air bubbles

Colloid–Mixture of air bubbles and water

Suspension–

(*a*) Mixture of water and sand grains

(*b*) Mixture of water and clay particles

(*ii*) (*a*) Aerated drinks, (*b*) Brass, (*c*) Air

5 You are provided with a mixture of naphthalene and sodium chloride by your teacher. Suggest an activity to separate them with well-labelled diagram. **NCERT Exemplar**

Sol. Mixture of naphthalene and sodium chloride is separated by the process of sublimation as naphthalene is a sublimable substance, but sodium chloride does not.

For separating the mixture, take it in a China dish over which an inverted funnel is placed and stem of the funnel is closed with cotton.

Set the apparatus as shown in the figure below:

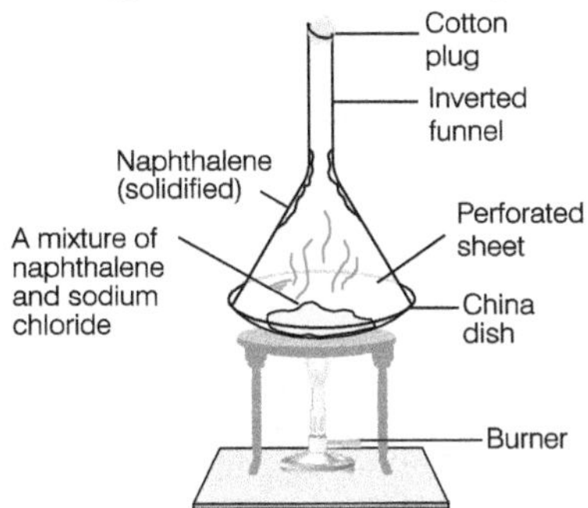

Now, heat the mixture, naphthalene being a sublimable, sublimes and when its vapours reach at the funnel they get condensed there to give solid naphthalene. Sodium chloride remains as a residue in the China dish.

6 Give an example each for the mixture having following characteristics. Suggest a suitable method to separate the components of these mixtures. **NCERT Exemplar**

(*i*) A volatile and non-volatile component.

(*ii*) Two volatile components with appreciable difference in boiling points.

(*iii*) Two immiscible liquids.

(*iv*) One of the components changes directly from solid to gaseous state.

(*v*) Two or more coloured constituents soluble in same solvent.

Sol. (*i*) Mixture of acetone and water–Simple distillation.

(*ii*) Mixture of kerosene and petrol–Simple distillation.

(*iii*) Mixture of mustard oil and water–Separating funnel.

(*iv*) Mixture of ammonium chloride and common salt–Sublimation.

(*v*) A mixture of different pigments from an extract of flower petals–Chromatography.

7 Fractional distillation is suitable for separation of miscible liquids with a boiling point difference of about 25 K or less. What part of fractional distillation apparatus makes it efficient and possess an advantage over a simple distillation process? Explain using a diagram. **NCERT Exemplar**

Sol. Refer to text on Pg 30.

Advantages

(*i*) This method can separate the liquids with a boiling point difference about or less than 25 K.

(*ii*) During the process, both evaporation and condensation take place simultaneously.

(*iii*) A mixture (like petroleum) can also be separated by fractional distillation process which contains several components.

8 (*i*) You are given a mixture of sand, water and mustard oil. How will you separate the components of this mixture? Explain it with the help of different separation methods involved in it.

(*ii*) Give flow diagram showing the process of obtaining gases from air.

Sol.(*i*) Filter the mixture. Filtrate will contain mustard oil and water, while sand will left as a residue. To separate mustard oil and water, take this mixture in separating funnel. Shake the funnel containing the mixture and left it undisturbed for a few minutes.

A layer of water and oil forms, upper layer consists of oil while lower layer is of water. On opening the stopcock, water will come out first. Collect the water in beaker, mustard oil will be left in separating funnel.

(*ii*) Refer to text on Pg 31.

9 (*i*) Write the steps involved in the process of obtaining pure copper sulphate from an impure sample.

(*ii*) Give any one application of this method.

(*iii*) Why is this technique better than simple evaporation to purify solids?

Sol.(*i*) The steps involved in the process of obtaining pure copper sulphate from an impure sample are as follows:

- Dissolve copper sulphate in water.
- Add few drops of dil. H_2SO_4 to get clear solution.
- Heat the solution in China dish till crystallisation point is reached.
- Cool this saturated solution.
- Crystals of pure copper sulphate are formed. Impurities remain behind in the solution.
- Separate these crystals from solution by filtration and dry them.

(*ii*) The method is crystallisation. It is used for the purification of common salt from water.

(*iii*) Soluble impurities can be removed by this technique which are not removed by evaporation.

10 Show diagrammatically how water is purified in the water works system and list the processes involved.

Sol. Refer to text on Pg 32.

11 (*i*) Draw a neat and labelled diagram of the apparatus used to separate components of blue-black ink. Name the process and state the principle involved.

(*ii*) Identify the physical and chemical changes from the following.

(*a*) Burning of magnesium in air.
(*b*) Tarnishing of silver spoon.
(*c*) Sublimation of iodine.
(*d*) Electrolysis of water.

Sol. (*i*)

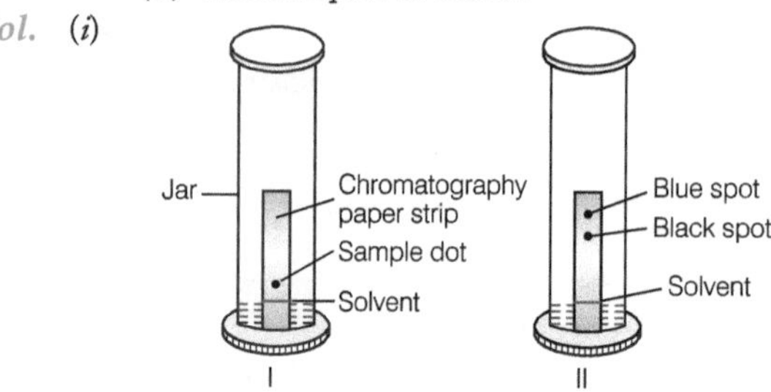

Separation of blue and black dyes from blue-black ink by paper chromatography

Name of the process Paper chromatography.

Principle of paper chromatography Different components of a mixture move with different speeds in a solvent, so they separate at different heights. Here blue ink and black ink rise with the help of solvent at different speeds to form two spots at different heights.

(*ii*) (*a*) Chemical change (*b*) Chemical change
(*c*) Physical change (*d*) Chemical change

12 Classify each of the following as a physical or a chemical change. Give reasons.

(*i*) Drying of a shirt in the sun.
(*ii*) Rising of hot air over a radiator.
(*iii*) Burning of kerosene in a lantern.
(*iv*) Change in the colour of black tea on adding lemon juice to it.
(*v*) Churning of milk cream to get butter.

NCERT Exemplar

Sol. (*i*) **Physical change** Because evaporation of water takes place, but no change occurs in the composition of the substance.

(*ii*) **Physical change** It is also involving only movement of air, no change in the composition of air.

(*iii*) **Physical as well as chemical change** Physical change occurs when kerosene vapourises. After that, burning of kerosene is a chemical change because during burning, kerosene oil gets converted into carbon dioxide and water both of which are new compounds.

(*iv*) **Chemical change** The acid present in lemon juice will react with the constituent (e.g. caffeine) present in black tea.

(v) **Physical change** As there is no change in composition. Only the separation of components takes place by the physical phenomenon of centrifugation. However, butter will not change to milk easily.

13 Iron filings and sulphur were mixed together and divided into two parts, *A* and *B*. Part *A* was heated strongly while part *B* was not heated. Dilute hydrochloric acid was added to both the parts and evolution of gas was seen in both the cases. How will you identify the gases evolved? **NCERT Exemplar**

Sol. **Part *A***

$$\underbrace{Fe + S}_{\text{Part } A} \xrightarrow{\Delta} FeS$$

$$\underset{(A)}{FeS} + 2HCl\,(dil.) \longrightarrow FeCl_2 + H_2S\uparrow$$

Part *B* is not heated, so the reaction will be as such

$$\underset{(\text{In Part } B)}{Fe} + 2HCl\,(dil.) \longrightarrow FeCl_2 + H_2\uparrow$$

In part *A*, H_2S gas is produced, which is identified by its characteristic smell of rotten eggs. In part *B*, H_2 gas is produced.

Hydrogen gas is tested by bringing a burning matchstick near the mouth of the test tube. It burns with a pop sound and water is formed.

14 Rama tested the solubility of four substances at different temperatures and found gram of each substance dissolved in 100 g of water to form a saturated solution.

Substance Dissolved (in gram)	Temperature (K)		
	293	**313**	**333**
Ammonium chloride	37 g	41g	55 g
Potassium chloride	35 g	40 g	46 g
Sodium chloride	36 g	36 g	37 g
Potassium nitrate	32 g	62 g	106 g

(i) Which solution is least soluble at 293 K?

(ii) Which substance shows maximum change in its solubility when the temperature is raised from 293 K to 313 K?

(iii) Find the amount of ammonium chloride that will separate out when 55 g of its solution at 333 K is cooled to 293 K.

(iv) What is the effect of temperature on the solubility of a salt?

(v) What mass of sodium chloride would be needed to make a saturated solution in 10 g of water at 293 K?

Sol. (i) Potassium nitrate.

(ii) Potassium nitrate.

(iii) At 333 K, ammonium chloride dissolved per 100 g = 55 g

At 293 K, ammonium chloride dissolved per 100 g = 37 g

When solution is cooled from 333 K to 293 K, amount of ammonium chloride that will separate out = 55 − 37 = 18 g

(iv) Solubility of a salt (soild) increases with rise in temperature and *vice-versa.*

(v) At 293K, amount of NaCl dissolved in 100 g of water = 36 g,

∴ At 293 K, amount of NaCl dissolved in 10 g

$$\text{of water} = \frac{36}{100} \times 10 = 3.6\text{ g}$$

15 During an experiment, the students were asked to prepare a 10% (mass/mass) solution of sugar in water. Ramesh dissolved 10 g of sugar in 100 g of water while Sarika prepared it by dissolving 10 g of sugar in water to make 100 g of the solution. **NCERT Exemplar**

(i) Are the two solutions of the same concentration?

(ii) Compare the mass % of the two solutions.

Sol. (i) No.

(ii) Ramesh's solution concentration

$$\text{Mass \%} = \frac{\text{Mass of solute}}{\text{Mass of solution}} \times 100$$

$$= \frac{10\text{ g}}{(10 + 100)\text{g}} \times 100$$

$$= \frac{10}{110} \times 100 = \frac{100}{11} = 9.09\% = 9.1\%$$

Sarika's solution concentration

$$\text{Mass \%} = \frac{10}{100} \times 100 = 10\%$$

The solution prepared by Ramesh has less percentage by mass than that of Sarika.

16 (i) Under which category of mixtures will you classify alloys and why?

(ii) Whether a solution is always liquid or not. Comment.

(iii) Can a solution be heterogeneous?

Sol. (i) Alloys are homogeneous mixture of metals, or non-metals because

(a) it shows the properties of its constituents, and

(b) it has variable composition, e.g. brass is considered a mixture, because it shows the properties of its constituents, copper and zinc; and it has a variable composition.

(ii) A solution is generally a liquid, not always, e.g. alloys are known to be solid solutions.

(iii) The term solution is generally used for 'true solution'. In this case, the solution is always homogeneous.

In case of 'colloidal solution', that is not a true solution, the solution is heterogeneous.

CHAPTER EXERCISE

Multiple Choice Questions

1 A mixture of sulphur and carbon disulphide is **NCERT Exemplar**

(a) heterogeneous and shows Tyndall effect
(b) homogeneous and shows Tyndall effect
(c) heterogeneous and does not show Tyndall effect
(d) homogeneous and does not show Tyndall effect

2 The pair of substance (*s*) that can be separated by sublimation is/are

(a) NH_4Cl and salt
(b) sugar solution in water
(c) salt solution in water
(d) kerosene oil and water

3 Which of the following substance cannot be broken down by a chemical method?

(a) Ammonia (NH_3) (b) Helium (He)
(c) Methane (CH_4) (d) Water (H_2O)

4 During purification of water, which of the following step(s) is incorrect ?

(a) Sedimentation of water
(b) Loading of water with alum
(c) Electrolysis of water
(d) Chlorination of water

5 Which of the following are physical changes?

(i) Melting of iron metal **NCERT Exemplar**
(ii) Rusting of iron
(iii) Bending of an iron rod
(iv) Drawing a wire of iron metal

(a) (i), (ii) and (iii)
(b) (i), (ii) and (iv)
(c) (i), (iii) and (iv)
(d) (ii), (iii) and (iv)

Fill in the Blanks

6 A colloid is a ....mixture and its components can be separated by the technique known as......... .

7 Milk is an emulsion in which the dispersed phase is...........and the dispersion medium is......... .

True and False

8 Evaporation is a chemical change while decantation is physical process.

9 Whipped cream is example of foam.

Match the Columns

10 Match the following columns.

Column A	Column B
A. Alcohol water	P. Gas in liquid
B. Amalgamated zinc	Q. Solid in liquid
C. Aqueous solution of sodium chloride	R. Liquid in liquid
D. Aerated water	S. Liquid in solid

Assertion-Reason

Direction (Q. Nos. 11-13) *In each of the following questions, a statement of Assertion is given by the corresponding statement of Reason. Of the statements, mark the correct answer as*

(a) Both Assertion and Reason are true and Reason is the correct explanation of Assertion.
(b) Both Assertion and Reason are true but Reason is not the correct explanation of Assertion.
(c) Assertion is true but Reason is false.
(d) Assertion is false and Reason is true.

11 **Assertion** Colloidal particles do not show Tyndall effect.
Reason Colloidal solutions are stable and the colloidal particles do not settle down.

12 **Assertion** Tyndall effect is an optical property.
Reason Scattering of beam of light by the colloidal particles is known as Tyndall effect.

13 **Assertion** A mixture of acetone and methanol can be separated by fractional distillation.
Reason The difference between boiling point of acetone and methanol is very less.

Case Based Questions

Direction (Q.Nos. 14-17) *Answer the questions on the basis of your understanding of the following paragraph and related studied concepts:*

Ravi took some amount of substance *X* and add it into a transparent beaker containing water. He mixed the solution very well and then passed light through this solution by using a torch. The result observed by him is shown below :

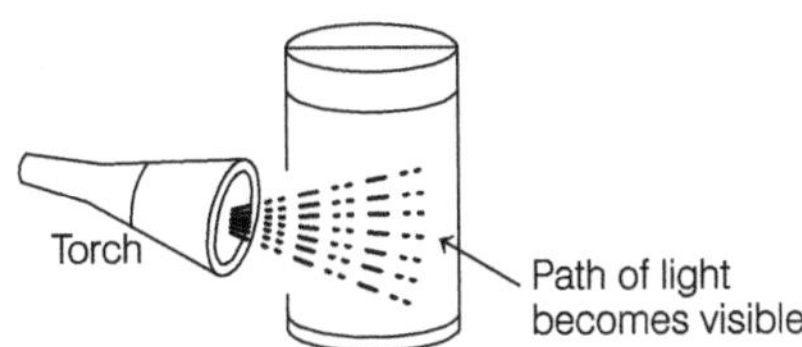

Ravi wants to show this experiment to his younger brother. He kept the solution for 10 minutes and calls his brother and further repeat the experiment, but results are different at this time. The path is not visible.

14 What was the reason for change in result ?
(a) In first case, the path is visible because of the presence of impurities.
(b) In second case, the particles settle down.
(c) In second case, the concentration increases.
(d) In second case, the impurities dissolve in the solution.

15 What is the nature of solution obtained, when *X* is added to water?
(a) Colloid (b) True solution
(c) Suspension (d) Data insufficient

16 What observation(s) was made when the light passed through the solution in this experiment?

17 What are the suspended particles and medium in this experiment?

Answers

1. (a) 2. (a) 3. (b) 4. (c) 5. (c)
6. heterogeneous, centrifugation
7. liquid, liquid 8. False 9. True
10. A-R, B-S, C-Q, D-P 11. d
12. (a) 13. (a) 14. (b) 15. (c)

Very Short Answer Type Questions

18 What are solute and solvent in aerated drinks?

19 Name the two components of a colloid.

20 What is the particle size of a colloidal solution?

21 Define the term colloidal solution.

22 What is the process called in which pigments of natural colours can be separated?

23 To obtain a solid from its solution, which technique is better, evaporation or crystallisation?

Short Answer (SA) Type Questions

24 What is the difference between a pure substance and a mixture? Give one example in each case.

25 Mention the three characteristics of a mixture.

26 How can a saturated solution be made unsaturated?

27 Define solubility. How does solubility of a solid in water change with temperature?

28 Identify colloids and true solutions from the following.
(*i*) Vinegar (*ii*) Muddy water
(*iii*) Mist (*iv*) Aluminium paint

29 What happens, when
(*i*) light is passed through a colloidal solution?
(*ii*) electricity is passed through a colloidal solution?
(*iii*) sugar solution is kept undisturbed.

30 Give one example each of the following :
(*i*) Solution of a gas in liquid
(*ii*) Solution of a liquid in solid
(*iii*) Solution of a solid in solid

31 State the principle of centrifugation. Give its two applications.

32 Define distillation. What types of liquids (substances) can be separated by this process?

33 The boiling points of two liquids *A* and *B* are 61°C and 111° C respectively. How will you separate this mixture?

34 (*i*) Differentiate between physical and chemical change.
(*ii*) 'All mixtures are homogeneous', comment upon this statement.

35 A solution contains 16 g of urea in 120 g of the solution. What is mass by mass percentage of solution?

36 A solution of alcohol in water has been prepared by mixing 150 mL of alcohol with 600 mL of water. Calculate the volume percentage of the solution.

37 A solution contains 50 mL of alcohol mixed with 150 mL of water. Calculate the concentration of this solution.

38 The solubility of potassium nitrate at 20°C is 32 g per 100 g of water. How much salt is required to prepare 66 g of its saturated solution?

39 How many litres of 15% (mass/volume) sugar solution would it take to get 75 g of sugar?

40 Consider the following figure :

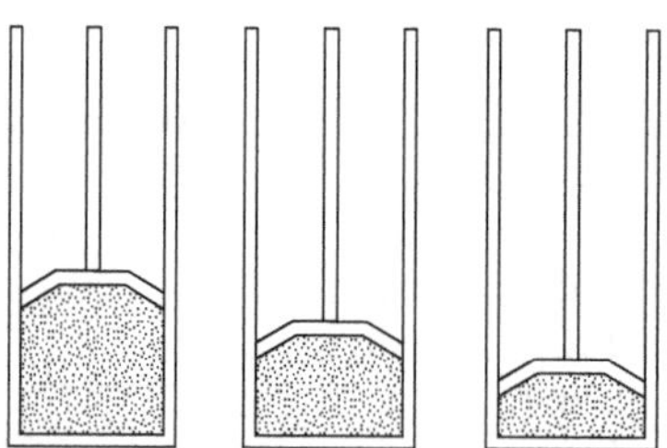

The above figure is showing the effect of change of pressure on gaseous particles. By applying pressure, the physical state of substance can be changed. Explain this by process in your words.

41 Consider the following figures :

The above experimental set up shows that the particles of matter have spaces between them. Analyse the above experimental set up and describe it in your own words.

Long Answer (LA) Type Questions

42 Draw a flow sheet diagram showing the separation of various components of a mixture containing camphor, sand and iron filings.

43 Describe the process to show that the dye used in blue/black ink is a mixture of two or more components with diagram.

44 How will you separate the components of a mixture containing two miscible liquids? Give experimental details.

45 What is crystallisation? How can this technique be used to purify impure copper sulphate?

46 Describe the various steps involved in the purification of water for city water supply.

RELATED ONLINE VIDEOS	
Visit https://www.youtube.com/watch?v=LhFRsGq6KjY OR **Scan the Code**	**Visit** https://www.youtube.com/watch?v=KEXWd3_fM94 OR **Scan the Code**
Visit https://www.youtube.com/watch?v=mP4Hgui-g6U OR **Scan the Code**	**Visit** https://www.youtube.com/watch?v=9z14l51ISwg OR **Scan the Code**

Challengers*

1 Two chemical species X and Y combine together to form a product P which contains both X and Y, $X + Y \rightarrow P$, X and Y cannot be broken down into simpler substances by simple chemical reactions. Which of the following concerning the species X, Y and P are correct?

(i) P is a compound
(ii) X and Y are compounds
(iii) X and Y are elements
(iv) P has a fixed composition **NCERT Exemplar**

(a) (i), (ii) and (iii)
(b) (i), (ii) and (iv)
(c) ii), (iii) and (iv)
(d) (i), (iii) and (iv)

2 The purpose of separating the components of a mixture is

(a) Separation makes it possible to study and use the individual components of a mixture
(b) It is helpful in removing any harmful or undesirable constituents
(c) It is helpful in removing the pure form from impure form.
(d) It is helpful in separation of all solids.

3 Which flow chart correctly describes a homogeneous material?

(a) Unknown-density-three layers
(b) Unknown-filtration-two substances
(c) Unknown-magnet-two substances
(d) Unknown-boiling-one temperature

4. Match Column I with the Column II.

Column I	Column II
A. Solution	I. Chalk in water
B. Colloid	II. Tincture of iodine
C. Suspension	III. Starch in water
D. Homogeneous	IV. A mixture of chalk and sand
E. Heterogeneous	V. Air

Codes

	A	B	C	D	E		A	B	C	D	E
(a)	II	III	I	V	IV	(b)	I	II	III	IV	V
(c)	II	III	I	IV	V	(d)	III	II	IV	V	I

5 Tyndall effect can be observed in a colloidal solution. Consider light scattering in the following:

I. When sunlight passes through the canopy of a dense forest.
II. When normal light passes through copper sulphate solution.
III. When normal light passes through milk.
IV. When a fine beam of light enters a room through a small hole.

Tyndall effect is observed in

(a) I and IV
(b) I, III and IV
(c) II and III
(d) III and IV

6 Colloid consist of dispersed phase and dispered medium. Aerosol is one type of colloid. Aerosol is made up of which of the following combination?

I. Gas in liquid
II. Liquid in gas
III. Solid in gas
IV. Gas in solid

(a) Only II
(b) I, II and III
(c) I and II
(d) II, III and IV

7 Match the Column I (Type of colloid) with Column II (Examples).

Column I	Column II
A. Gel	I. Rubber
B. Foam	II. Face cream
C. Emulsion	III. Coloured gemstone
D. Solid sol	IV. Butter
E. Aerosol	V. Cloud

Point out the correct option.

	A	B	C	D	E		A	B	C	D	E
(a)	I	II	IV	V	III	(b)	II	I	III	IV	V
(c)	IV	I	II	III	V	(d)	III	IV	V	I	II

Answer Key

1.	(d)	2.	(a)	3.	(d)	4.	(a)	5.	(b)
6.	(c)	7.	(c)						

*These questions may be or may not be asked in the examination, have been given just for additional practice.

CHAPTER

03

Atoms and Molecules

In the present chapter, we shall discuss about the various laws (which explains how atoms combine to form molecule), symbols and formulae of atoms and molecules and various ways of expressing their masses.

Chapter Checklist

- Laws of Chemical Combination
- Atoms
- Molecules
- Ions
- Valency
- Writing Chemical Formulae
- Molecular Mass

Laws of Chemical Combination

Whenever reactants react together to form the products or the elements combine together to form a compound, they do this according to certain laws. These laws are called **laws of chemical combination.**

Antoine L. Lavoisier laid the foundation of chemical sciences by establishing two important laws of chemical combination which are as follows:

1. Law of Conservation of Mass

It states that, 'mass can neither be created nor be destroyed during a chemical reaction.' This means that in any chemical reaction, the total mass of the reactants is equal to the total mass of the products and there is no change in mass during the chemical reaction.

Example 1. *If 4.0 g of sodium carbonate reacts with 10 g of hydrochloric acid, it results in the formation of 2.5 g of carbon dioxide and 11.5 g of sodium chloride solution. Show that these results are in accordance with the law of conservation of mass.*

Sol. $\underset{(4.0\text{ g})}{\text{Sodium carbonate}} + \underset{(10.0\text{ g})}{\text{Hydrochloric acid}} \longrightarrow \underset{(2.5\text{ g})}{\text{Carbon dioxide}} + \underset{(11.5\text{ g})}{\text{Sodium chloride}}$

Here, total mass of reactants $= 4.0 + 10 = 14$ g

Total mass of products $= 2.5 + 11.5 = 14$ g

Since, the reactants and products have the same mass, this means that there was no loss or gain of mass after the reaction. Hence, the data is in agreement with the law of conservation of mass.

2. Law of Constant Proportions/ Law of Definite Proportions

According to this law, in a chemical substance (or compound), the elements are always present in definite proportions (or ratios) by mass.

e.g. In a compound such as water, the ratio of the mass of hydrogen to the mass of oxygen is always 1 : 8, whatever the source of water. Thus, if 9 g of water is decomposed, 1 g of hydrogen and 8 g of oxygen are always obtained.

Similarly, carbon dioxide (CO_2) always contains carbon and oxygen in the ratio of 3 : 8. If a sample of CO_2 contains 36 g of carbon then it is compulsory that the sample has 96 g oxygen.

This is calculated as $\frac{3}{8} = \frac{36}{x}$;

$\therefore \quad x = \frac{36 \times 8}{3} = 96\text{ g}$

Example 2. *Copper oxide was prepared by two different methods. In one case, 1.75 g of the metal gave 2.19 g of oxide. In the second case, 1.14 g of the metal gave 1.43 g of the oxide. Show that the given data illustrate the law of constant proportions.*

Sol. *Case* I Mass of copper = 1.75 g

And mass of copper oxide = 2.19 g

So, mass of oxygen = Mass of copper oxide − Mass of copper $= 2.19 - 1.75 = 0.44\text{ g}$

Now, in first sample of copper oxide compound.

Mass of copper : Mass of oxygen = 1.75 : 0.44

$= \frac{1.75}{0.44} : 1$

$= 3.98 : 1 \approx 4 : 1$

Case II Mass of copper = 1.14 g

And, mass of copper oxide = 1.43 g

So, mass of oxygen = Mass of copper oxide − Mass of copper $= 1.43 - 1.14 = 0.29\text{ g}$

Now, in second sample of copper oxide compound.

Mass of copper : Mass of oxygen = 1.14 : 0.29

$= \frac{1.14}{0.29} : 1$

$= 3.93 : 1 \approx 4 : 1$

From the above calculations we can see that the ratio (or proportion) of copper and oxygen elements in the two samples of copper oxide compound is the same, i.e. 4 : 1. So, the given data verify the law of constant proportions.

Explanation of Laws of Chemical Combination : Dalton's Atomic Theory

Dalton's atomic theory provided an explanation for the law of chemical combination. According to Dalton's atomic theory, all matter (whether an element, a compound or a mixture), is composed of small particles, called **atoms.**

The main postulates of Dalton's atomic theory:

- Every matter is made up of very small particles, called the atoms.
- Atoms are indivisible particles which can neither be created nor be destroyed in a chemical reaction.
- Atoms of a given element are identical in mass as well as in chemical properties.
- Atoms of different elements have different masses and chemical properties.
- Atoms combine in the ratio of small whole numbers to form compounds.
- The relative numbers and kinds of atoms are constant in a given compound.

Check Point 01

1. If 100 g of calcium carbonate on heating produces 44 g of carbon dioxide, how much quicklime will be formed? Which law is followed for solving this problem?
[**Ans.** 56 g; law of conservation of mass]
2. Which law states, that in a chemical compound, elements always combine in a fixed proportion?
3. 20 g silver nitrate solution is added to 20 g of sodium chloride solution. What change in mass do you expect after the reaction and why?
4. In a given sample of ammonia, 9 g hydrogen and 42 g nitrogen are present. In another sample, 5 g hydrogen is present alongwith nitrogen. Calculate the amount of nitrogen in the second sample.
[**Ans.** 23.33 g]
5. Fill in the blank:
Atoms are............particles, which cannot be created or destroyed in achemical reaction.

Atoms

Atoms are the smallest particles of an element which may or may not have independent existence but take part in a chemical reaction. These are the building blocks of all matter.

e.g. atoms of hydrogen, oxygen, nitrogen etc., are not capable of independent existence whereas atoms of helium, neon etc., are capable of existing independently.

Size of Atoms

Atoms are very small and their radius is measured in **nanometres.**

$$1/10^9 \text{ m} = 1\text{ nm}$$

or

$$1\text{m} = 10^9 \text{ nm}$$

Hydrogen atom is the smallest atom and its radius is 0.1 nm.

Modern Day Symbols of Atoms of Different Elements

In chemistry, symbols are the representation of an element. It is simple to use the symbol of an element rather writing a whole word of an element. Dalton was the scientist who introduced symbols for representing elements for the first time.

⊙ Hydrogen	○ Carbon	○ Oxygen
⊗ Phosphorus	⊕ Sulphur	Ⓘ Iron
Ⓒ Copper	Ⓛ Lead	Ⓢ Silver
Ⓖ Gold	Ⓟ Platina	○ Mercury

Symbols for some elements as proposed by Dalton

As Dalton's symbol for elements were difficult to draw and inconvenient to use, modern symbols for the elements were introduced by **J J Berzelius.** These are defined as "a short hand representation of the name of an element".

In the beginning, the names of elements were derived from the name of the place where they were found for the first time. Now a days, it is the IUPAC (International Union of Pure and Applied Chemistry) who approves the names and symbols of the elements. Many of the symbols are the first one or two letters of the element's name in English.

The first letter of a symbol is always written in capital letter and the second letter as a small letter.

e.g. chlorine (Cl), zinc (Zn) and aluminium (Al).

Symbols of some elements have been taken from their names in different languages such as Latin, German, Greek etc.

e.g. Iron — Fe from *Ferrum* (Latin name)
Gold — Au from *Aurum* (Latin name)
Potassium — K from *Kalium* (Latin name)
Chlorine — Cl from *Chloros* (Greek name)
Cobalt — Co from *Kobold* (German name)
Sodium — Na from *Natrium* (Latin name)

Symbols for Some Elements

Elements	*Symbols*	*Elements*	*Symbols*	*Elements*	*Symbols*
Aluminium	Al	Copper	Cu	Nitrogen	N
Argon	Ar	Fluorine	F	Oxygen	O
Barium	Ba	Gold	Au	Phosphorus	P
Boron	B	Hydrogen	H	Potassium	K
Bromine	Br	Iodine	I	Silicon	Si
Calcium	Ca	Iron	Fe	Silver	Ag
Carbon	C	Lead	Pb	Sodium	Na
Chlorine	Cl	Magnesium	Mg	Sulphur	S
Chromium	Cr	Mercury	Hg	Uranium	U
Cobalt	Co	Neon	Ne	Zinc	Zn

Atomic Mass

According to Dalton's, each element has a characteristic atomic mass. But determining the mass of an individual atom was a relatively difficult task due to its very small size. Hence, their relative atomic masses were determined using the laws of chemical combinations and the compounds formed.

For this purpose, initially 1/16 of the mass of an atom of naturally occurring oxygen was taken as standard unit because of the following two reasons:

(*i*) Oxygen reacted with a large number of elements and formed compounds.

(*ii*) This unit gave masses of most of the elements as whole numbers.

However in 1961, carbon (C-12 isotope) was chosen as standard reference for measuring atomic masses universally.

Relative Atomic Mass

It is defined as the number of times a given atom is heavier than 1/12th of mass of 1 atom of carbon-12 (C-12) or it is the average mass of the atom as compared to 1/12th the mass of one carbon-12 atom.

Atomic Mass Unit

It is defined as the mass unit equal to exactly 1/12th of the mass of one atom of C-12 isotope. Earlier, it was abbreviated as **amu** but according to latest recommendations of IUPAC, it is now written as **'u'- unified mass.**

Atomic Masses of Few Elements

Element	*Atomic Mass* (u)
Hydrogen	1
Carbon	12
Nitrogen	14
Oxygen	16
Sodium	23
Magnesium	24
Sulphur	32
Chlorine	35.5
Calcium	40

Note Atoms of most of the elements are not able to exist independently. Atoms form molecules and ions. These molecules or ions aggregate in large numbers to form the matter that we can see, feel or touch.

Molecules

The smallest particle of an element or compound which is capable of independent existence and shows all the properties of that substance is called a molecule. In general, molecule is a group of two or more atoms that are chemically bonded together. Atoms of the same element or of different elements can join together to form molecules.

Molecules can be divided into two categories:

1. Molecules of Elements

The molecules of an element contains same type of atoms. Molecules of many elements are made up of only one atom of that element. e.g. noble gases like argon (Ar), helium (He) etc. The molecules of most of the non-metals are made up of more than one atom.

e.g. a molecule of oxygen (O_2) consists of two atoms of oxygen and is known as diatomic molecule, ozone (O_3) consists of three atoms of oxygen is known as triatomic molecules.

Atomicity

It is defined as the number of atoms present in a molecule. On the basis of atomicity, molecules can be classified as:

(*i*) **Monoatomic molecules** They consist of only one atom.
e.g. He, Ne, Ar, Xe, Fe, Al etc.

(*ii*) **Diatomic molecules** They consist of two atoms.
e.g. $H_2, O_2, N_2, I_2, Br_2, Cl_2$, HCl, NaCl etc.

(*iii*) **Triatomic molecules** They consist of three atoms.
e.g. O_3, CO_2, NO_2 etc.

(*iv*) **Tetra-atomic molecules** They consist of four atoms.
e.g. P_4, H_2O_2 etc.

(*v*) **Polyatomic molecules** They consist of more than four atoms.
e.g. CH_4 (penta-atomic), S_8 (octa-atomic) etc.

Atomicity of Some Elements (Non-metals)

Name	*Atomicity*	*Name*	*Atomicity*
Argon	Monoatomic	Chlorine	Diatomic
Helium	Monoatomic	Ozone	Triatomic
Oxygen	Diatomic	Phosphorus	Tetra-atomic
Hydrogen	Diatomic	Sulphur	Poly-atomic (octa-atomic)
Nitrogen	Diatomic		

2. Molecules of Compounds

Atoms of different elements join together in definite proportions to form molecules of compounds.

Molecules of Some Compounds

Compound	*Combining Elements*	*Ratio by Mass*
Water (H_2O)	Hydrogen and oxygen	1 : 8
Ammonia (NH_3)	Nitrogen and hydrogen	14 : 3
Carbon dioxide (CO_2)	Carbon and oxygen	3 : 8
Hydrogen sulphide (H_2S)	Hydrogen and sulphur	1 : 16
Sulphuric acid (H_2SO_4)	Hydrogen, sulphur and oxygen	1 : 16 : 32
Glucose ($C_6H_{12}O_6$)	Carbon, hydrogen and oxygen	6 : 1 : 8
Baking powder ($NaHCO_3$)	Sodium, hydrogen, carbon and oxygen	23 : 1 : 12 : 48
Common salt (NaCl)	Sodium, chlorine	23 : 35.5
Limestone ($CaCO_3$) or calcium carbonate	Calcium, carbon and oxygen	40 : 12 : 48 or 10 : 3 : 12
Caustic soda (NaOH)	Sodium, oxygen and hydrogen	23 : 16 : 1
Caustic potash (KOH)	Potassium, oxygen and hydrogen	39 : 16 : 1
Ethanol (C_2H_5OH)	Carbon, hydrogen and oxygen	24 : 6 : 16 or 12 : 3 : 8
Methanol (CH_3OH)	Carbon, hydrogen and oxygen	12 : 4 : 16 or 3 : 1 : 4
Ethyne (C_2H_2)	Carbon and hydrogen	24 : 2 or 12 : 1

Prediction of Number of Atoms from Mass Ratio

In order to predict the number of atoms from mass ratio, divide the given mass of each element by the atomic mass of the element and calculate the simplest ratio between the obtained moles, e.g. we know that mass ratio of nitrogen and hydrogen in ammonia molecule is $14:3$. The number of atoms of nitrogen and hydrogen present in the molecule of ammonia can be calculated as,

Element	Mass Ratio (x)	Atomic Mass (y)	Mole Ratio (x/y)	Simplest Ratio
N	14	14	$\frac{14}{14}=1$	1
H	3	1	$\frac{3}{1}=3$	3

Thus, in ammonia molecule, one N and three H-atoms are present hence, the formula of ammonia is NH_3.

Check Point 02

1 State True or False for the following statement:
Symbols are the representation of an element.

2 What is wrong in the following symbols?
Give the correct symbol in each case:
(i) Sodium (So)
(ii) Hydrogen (Hg)
(iii) Copper (Co)
(iv) Sulphur (s)
(v) Calcium (CA)

3 Name any two elements whose symbols do not start with the same letter as that of the name of the element.

4 Why the symbols of few elements, like sodium, do not start with the initial letter of the name?

5 What is the difference between 2Cl and Cl_2? Which one of these two forms exists in nature? Also, give the atomic mass of this element.

6 The atomicity of I_2 and Na_2SO_4 respectively are......and......... .

7 An oxide of nitrogen is found to contain nitrogen and oxygen combined together in the ratio of 7 : 16 by mass.
Derive the formula of the oxide and name it.

Ions

When atoms, groups of atoms or molecules lose or gain electron(s) they become charged. These charged species are known as **ions.** Atoms in solution generally exist in the form of ions. These can be negatively or positively charged, thus can be categorised into two groups.

Cations

The positively charged ions are known as cations.
e.g. Na^+, K^+, Ca^{2+}, Al^{3+} etc. These are formed when elements loses electrons. Usually, metals form cations.

Anions

The negatively charged ions are known as anions.
e.g. Cl^-, Br^-, O^{2-}, N^{3-} etc. These are formed when elements gain electrons. Usually, non-metals form anions.

Polyatomic Ion

A group of atoms carrying charge and act as a single entity is known as a polyatomic ion. It carries a fixed charge. e.g. NO_3^- (nitrate ion), CO_3^{2-} (carbonate ion) and SO_4^{2-} (sulphate ion) etc.

Some Ionic Compounds

Ionic Compounds	Constituting Elements	Ratio by Mass
Calcium oxide	Calcium and oxygen	5:2
Magnesium sulphide	Magnesium and sulphur	3:4
Sodium chloride	Sodium and chlorine	23:35.5

Note Ionic compounds are formed by cations and anions, e.g. sodium chloride or common salt (NaCl) consists of a positively charged sodium ion (Na^+ cation) and negatively charged chloride ion (Cl^- anion).

Valency

The combining power (or capacity) of an element is called its **valency.** Valency can be used to find out how the atoms of an element will combine with the atom(s) of another element to form a chemical compound. The valency of an ion is equal to the charge on the ion.

Names, Symbols and Valency of Some Ions

Valency	Ion of Metallic Element	Symbol	Ion of Non-Metallic Element	Symbol	Polyatomic Ions	Symbol
1	Sodium	Na^+	Hydrogen	H^+	Ammonium	NH_4^+
	Potassium	K^+	Hydride	H^-	Hydroxide	OH^-
	Silver	Ag^+	Chloride	Cl^-	Nitrate	NO_3^-
	Copper (I)*	Cu^+	Bromide	Br^-	Hydrogen carbonate (bicarbonate)	HCO_3^-
			Iodide	I^-		
2	Magnesium	Mg^{2+}	Oxide	O^{2-}	Carbonate	CO_3^{2-}
	Calcium	Ca^{2+}	Sulphide	S^{2-}	Sulphite	SO_3^{2-}
	Zinc	Zn^{2+}			Sulphate	SO_4^{2-}
	Iron (II)*	Fe^{2+}				
	Copper (II)*	Cu^{2+}				
3	Aluminium	Al^{3+}	Nitride	N^{3-}	Phosphate	PO_4^{3-}
	Iron (III)*	Fe^{3+}	Phosphide	P^{3-}		

Note These elements show more than one valency. Here, the Roman numeral written in brackets shows their valency.

Writing Chemical Formulae

The shortest way to represent a compound with the help of symbols and valency of elements is known as **chemical formula.** Chemical formula of a compound shows its constituent elements and the number of atoms of each combining element. In ionic compounds, the charge on each ion is used to determine the chemical formula of a compound.

There are some rules for writing the chemical formula:

(*i*) The valencies or charges on the ion must be balanced.

(*ii*) When a compound consists of a metal and a non-metal, the symbol of the metal is written first and on the left whereas of non-metal on its right. e.g. calcium oxide (CaO), sodium chloride (NaCl), iron sulphide (FeS), copper oxide (CuO) etc., where oxygen, chlorine, sulphur are non-metals and are written on the right, whereas calcium, sodium, iron and copper are metals and are written on left.

(*iii*) When compound is formed with polyatomic ions, the ion is enclosed in a bracket before writing the number to indicate the ratio. e.g. $Ca(OH)_2$. In case if the number of polyatomic ion is one, the bracket is not required. e.g. NaOH.

Formulae of Simple Compounds

To write the chemical formula for simple compounds :

(*i*) write the symbols of constituent elements and their valencies as shown below.

(*ii*) write the symbol of cation first followed by the symbol of anion.

(*iii*) then criss-cross their charges or valencies to get the formula.

(*iv*) the positive and negative charges must balance each other and the overall structure must be neutral.

Note The simplest compounds made up of two different elements are also called binary compounds.

e.g.

Hydrogen sulphide

Symbol	H	S
Charge	+1	−2
Formula	H_2S	

Note When the subscript is number 1, subscript is not written.

Carbon tetrachloride

Symbol	C	Cl
Charge	+4	−1
Formula	CCl_4	

Magnesium chloride

Symbol	Mg	Cl
Charge	+2	−1
Formula	$MgCl_2$	

Calcium oxide

Symbol	Ca	O
Charge	+2	−2
Formula	Ca_2O_2 or CaO	

Note When the valency of both elements are numerically equal, the subscripts are not written.

Aluminium oxide

Symbol	Al	O
Charge	+3	−2
Formula	Al_2O_3	

Sodium nitrate

Symbol	Na	NO_3
Charge	+1	−1
Formula	$NaNO_3$	

Potassium carbonate

Symbol	K	CO_3
Charge	+1	−2
Formula	K_2CO_3	

Sodium carbonate

Symbol	Na	CO_3
Charge	+1	−2
Formula	Na_2CO_3	

We use brackets when we have two or more of the same polyatomic ions in the formulae. e.g.

Aluminium hydroxide

Symbol	Al	OH
Charge	+3	−1
Formula	$Al(OH)_3$	

Ammonium sulphate

Symbol	NH_4	SO_4
Charge	+1	−2
Formula	$(NH_4)_2SO_4$	

All subscripts must be reduced to lowest term (except for molecule or covalent compound), e.g.

Tin (IV) oxide

Symbol	Sn	O
Charge	+4	−2
Formula	Sn_2O_4 or SnO_2	

Molecular Mass

The molecular mass of a substance is the sum of the atomic masses of all the atoms in a molecule of the substance. It is therefore, the relative mass of a molecule expressed in atomic mass units (u). e.g. the relative molecular mass of water (H_2O) is 18 u, which can be calculated as,

atomic mass of hydrogen = 1 u

atomic mass of oxygen = 16 u

H_2O contains two hydrogen atoms and one oxygen atom. Therefore, molecular mass of water is $= 2 \times 1 + 1 \times 16 = 18$ u

Example 3. *Calculate the molecular mass of the following substances.*

(i) Ammonia *(ii) Hydrochloric acid*
(iii) Phosphorus molecule *(iv) Hydrogen molecule*
(v) Oxygen molecule *(vi) Sulphur dioxide*

Sol. (i) Molecular mass of ammonia (NH_3) $= 1 \times 14 + 3 \times 1 = 17$ u

(ii) Molecular mass of hydrochloric acid (HCl)
$= 1 \times 1 + 1 \times 35.5 = 36.5$ u

(iii) Molecular mass of phosphorus molecule (P_4)
$= 4 \times 31 = 124$ u

(iv) Molecular mass of hydrogen molecule (H_2)
$= 2 \times 1 = 2$ u

(v) Molecular mass of oxygen molecule (O_2)
$= 2 \times 16 = 32$ u

(vi) Molecular mass of sulphur dioxide (SO_2)
$= 32 + 2 \times 16 = 64$ u

Formula Unit Mass

It is the sum of the atomic masses of all atoms present in a formula unit of a compound. Formula unit mass is calculated in the same manner as we calculate the molecular mass. The difference is that, here the word formula unit is used for the substance whose constituent particles are ions. e.g. formula unit mass for sodium chloride (NaCl)

$$= 1 \times 23 + 1 \times 35.5 = 58.5 \text{ u}$$

Check Point 03

1. How an ion is different from an atom? How cation is different from anion?
2. Fill in the blanks:
   The total number of atoms in aluminium hydroxide and sodium oxide respectively.........and......... .
3. Give symbol and valency of the following ions:
   Hydroxide ion, carbonate ion.
4. What is the role of valency in the combination of atoms?
5. An element *X* forms $X_2(CO_3)_3$ type compound.
   What is the formula of its phosphate and chloride?
6. Write the formula of the following compounds :
   (i) Magnesium sulphate (ii) Sodium bromide
   (iii) Calcium chloride (iv) Potassium nitrate
   (v) Sodium phosphate

To Study NCERT Activities
Visit https://goo.gl/afyXbM OR **Scan the Code**

NCERT FOLDER

INTEXT QUESTIONS

1 In a reaction, 5.3 g of sodium carbonate reacted with 6 g of ethanoic acid. The products were 2.2 g of carbon dioxide, 0.9 g of water and 8.2 g of sodium ethanoate. Show that these observations are in agreement with the law of conservation of mass.

Sodium carbonate + Ethanoic acid $\longrightarrow$

Sodium ethanoate + Carbon dioxide + Water **Pg 32**

Sol. Total mass of reactants = Mass of sodium carbonate + Mass of ethanoic acid

$= 5.3 + 6.0 = 11.3$ g

Total mass of products = Mass of sodium ethanoate + Mass of carbon dioxide + Mass of water

$= 8.2 + 2.2 + 0.9 = 11.3$ g

Since, the sum of masses of reactants is equal to the sum of masses of products, therefore, the observation made is in agreement with the law of conservation of mass.

2 Hydrogen and oxygen combine in the ratio of 1:8 by mass to form water. What mass of oxygen gas would be required to react completely with 3 g of hydrogen gas? **Pg 33**

Sol. Since, H and O combine in the ratio of 1 : 8 by mass.

Therefore, $\frac{\text{Mass of H}}{\text{Mass of O}} = \frac{1}{8}$

Let the mass of oxygen required to react completely with 3 g of hydrogen gas be x.

$\therefore \quad \frac{3}{x} = \frac{1}{8}$ or $x = 24$ g

Therefore, 24 g of oxygen is required to react with 3 g of hydrogen to form water.

3 Which postulate of Dalton's atomic theory is the result of the law of conservation of mass? **Pg 33**

Sol. The postulate which is the result of law of conservation of mass is "atoms are indivisible particles, which can neither be created nor be destroyed in a chemical reaction".

4 Which postulate of Dalton's atomic theory can explain the law of definite proportions? **Pg 33**

Sol. 'The relative number and kinds of atoms are constant in a given compound'. This postulate explains law of definite proportions.

5 Define atomic mass unit. **Pg 35**

Sol. One atomic mass unit (u) is the mass unit equal to exactly 1/12th of the mass of one atom of C-12 isotope.

6 Why is it not possible to see an atom with naked eyes? **Pg 35**

Sol. Atoms are very small, they are smaller than anything we can imagine. More than millions of atoms when stacked would make a layer barely as thick as the sheet of paper. These are very small in radii and measured in terms of nanometers ($1 \text{nm} = 10^{-9}$m). Hence, it is not possible to see an atom with naked eyes.

7 Write down the formulae of

(i) sodium oxide

(ii) aluminium chloride

(iii) sodium sulphide

(iv) magnesium hydroxide **Pg 39**

Sol. (i) **Sodium oxide**

Symbol	Na	O
Charge	+1	−2
Formula	Na_2O	

(ii) **Aluminium chloride**

Symbol	Al	Cl
Charge	+3	−1
Formula	$AlCl_3$	

(iii) **Sodium sulphide**

Symbol	Na	S
Charge	+1	−2
Formula	Na_2S	

(iv) **Magnesium hydroxide**

Symbol	Mg	(OH)
Charge	+2	−1
Formula	$Mg(OH)_2$	

8 Write down the names of compounds represented by the following formulae. **Pg 39**

(i) $Al_2(SO_4)_3$ (ii) $CaCl_2$ (iii) K_2SO_4

(iv) KNO_3 (v) $CaCO_3$

Sol. (i) Aluminium sulphate [$Al_2(SO_4)_3$]

(ii) Calcium chloride ($CaCl_2$)

(iii) Potassium sulphate (K_2SO_4)

(iv) Potassium nitrate (KNO_3)

(v) Calcium carbonate ($CaCO_3$)

9 What is meant by the term chemical formula ? **Pg 39**

Sol. It is the shortest way to represent a compound with the help of symbols and valency (charge) of elements.

e.g. Element Ca Cl
Charge +2 −1
Formula $CaCl_2$

10 How many atoms are present in a (*i*) H_2S molecule and (*ii*) PO_4^{3-} ion ? **Pg 39**

Sol. (*i*) In H_2S molecule, three atoms [i.e. 2 atoms of H + 1 atom of S] are present.

(*ii*) In PO_4^{3-} ion, five atoms [i.e. 1 atom of P + 4 atoms of O] are present.

11 Calculate the molecular masses of H_2, O_2, Cl_2, CO_2, CH_4, C_2H_6, C_2H_4, NH_3, CH_3OH **Pg 40**

Sol. (*i*) Molecular mass of H_2 (hydrogen)
= Atomic mass of hydrogen × 2 = 1 × 2 = 2 u

(*ii*) Molecular mass of O_2 (oxygen)
= Atomic mass of oxygen × 2 = 16 × 2 = 32 u

(*iii*) Molecular mass of Cl_2 (chlorine)
= Atomic mass of chlorine × 2 = 35.5 × 2 = 71 u

(*iv*) Molecular mass of CO_2 (carbon dioxide)
= (Atomic mass of carbon × 1) + (Atomic mass of oxygen × 2)
$= 12 \times 1 + (16 \times 2) = 12 + 32 = 44$ u

(*v*) Molecular mass of CH_4 (methane)
= (Atomic mass of carbon × 1) + (Atomic mass of hydrogen × 4)
$= 12 \times 1 + (1 \times 4) = 12 + 4 = 16$ u

(*vi*) Molecular mass of C_2H_6 (ethane)
= (Atomic mass of carbon × 2) + (Atomic mass of hydrogen × 6)
$= (12 \times 2) + (1 \times 6) = 24 + 6 = 30$ u

(*vii*) Molecular mass of C_2H_4 (ethene)
= (Atomic mass of carbon × 2) + (Atomic mass of hydrogen × 4)
$= (12 \times 2) + (1 \times 4) = 24 + 4 = 28$ u

(*viii*) Molecular mass of NH_3 (ammonia)
= (Atomic mass of nitrogen × 1) + (Atomic mass of hydrogen × 3)
$= (14 \times 1) + (1 \times 3) = 14 + 3 = 17$ u

(*ix*) Molecular mass of CH_3OH (methanol or methyl alcohol) = (Atomic mass of carbon × 1) + (Atomic mass of hydrogen × 3) + (Atomic mass of oxygen × 1) + (Atomic mass of hydrogen × 1)
$= (12 \times 1) + (1 \times 3) + (16 \times 1) + (1 \times 1)$
$= 12 + 3 + 16 + 1 = 32$ u

12 Calculate the formula unit masses of ZnO, Na_2O, K_2CO_3.
[Given, atomic mass of Zn = 65 u, Na = 23u, K = 39 u, C = 12u and O = 16u] **Pg 40**

Sol. (*i*) Formula unit mass of ZnO (zinc oxide)
= 65 + 16 = 81 u

(*ii*) Formula unit mass of Na_2O (sodium oxide)
$= (23 \times 2) + (16 \times 1)$
= 46 + 16 = 62 u

(*iii*) Formula unit mass of K_2CO_3 (potassium carbonate) $= (39 \times 2) + (12 \times 1) + (16 \times 3)$
= 78 + 12 + 48 = 138 u

EXERCISES
(On Pages 43 and 44)

1 A 0.24 g sample of compound of oxygen and boron was found by analysis to contain 0.096 g of boron and 0.144 g of oxygen. Calculate the percentage composition of the compound by weight.

Sol. Mass of the compound = 0.24 g,
Mass of boron = 0.096g
Mass of oxygen = 0.144g

$$\text{Percentage of boron} = \frac{\text{Mass of boron}}{\text{Mass of compound}} \times 100 = \frac{0.096\text{ g}}{0.240\text{ g}} \times 100 = 40\%$$

$$\text{Percentage of oxygen} = \frac{\text{Mass of oxygen}}{\text{Mass of compound}} \times 100 = \frac{0.144\text{ g}}{0.240\text{ g}} \times 100 = 60\%$$

Alternative method
Percentage of oxygen = 100 − percentage of boron
= 100 − 40 = 60%

2 When 3.0 g of carbon is burnt in 8.00 g oxygen, 11.00 g of carbon dioxide is produced. What mass of carbon dioxide will be formed when 3.00 g of carbon is burnt in 50.00 g of oxygen? Which law of chemical combination will govern your answer?

Sol. First we find the proportion of mass of carbon and oxygen in carbon dioxide.
In CO_2, C : O = 12 : 32 or 3 : 8
In other words, we can say that
∵ 12.00 g carbon reacts with oxygen = 32.00 g
∴ 3.00 g carbon will react with oxygen = 8 g

$$C + O_2 \longrightarrow CO_2$$
2 g 32 g 12 + 16 × 2 = 44 g
3 g 8 g 3 + 8 = 11 g

Therefore, 3.00 g of carbon will always react with 8.00 g of oxygen to form 11 g of carbon dioxide, even if large amount (50.00 g) of oxygen is present.

This means when 3.00 g of carbon is burnt in 50.00 g of oxygen, only 8.00 g of oxygen will be used to produce 11.00 g of carbon dioxide. The remaining 42.00 g of oxygen will remain as it is. This reaction will be governed by the law of constant proportions.

3 What are polyatomic ions? Give examples.

Sol. A group of atoms carrying a charge and behaving like one entity is known as polyatomic ion.
e.g. oxygen atom and hydrogen atom combine to form hydroxide ion ($\overline{O}H$) and one C-atom and three O-atoms combine to form carbonate ion (CO_3^{2-}).

4 Write the chemical formulae of the following :
(*i*) Magnesium chloride (*ii*) Calcium oxide
(*iii*) Copper nitrate (*iv*) Aluminium chloride
(*v*) Calcium carbonate

Sol. For (i), (ii) Refer to text on Pg. 52.
(iii) $Cu(NO_3)_2$ (iv) $AlCl_3$ (v) $CaCO_3$

5 Give the names of the elements present in the following compounds :
(*i*) Quicklime (*ii*) Hydrogen bromide
(*iii*) Baking powder (*iv*) Potassium sulphate

Sol. (*i*) **Quicklime** Calcium oxide — CaO
Elements Calcium and oxygen

(*ii*) **Hydrogen bromide** — HBr
Elements Hydrogen and bromine

(*iii*) **Baking powder** Sodium hydrogen carbonate — $NaHCO_3$
Elements Sodium, hydrogen, carbon and oxygen

(*iv*) **Potassium sulphate** — K_2SO_4
Elements Potassium, sulphur and oxygen

6 Calculate the molar mass of the following substances :
(*i*) Ethyne, C_2H_2
(*ii*) Sulphur molecule, S_8
(*iii*) Phosphorus molecule, P_4
(Atomic mass of phosphorus = 31)
(*iv*) Hydrochloric acid, HCl
(*v*) Nitric acid, HNO_3

Sol. (*i*) Molar mass of C_2H_2 = (2 × Atomic mass of C) + (2 × Atomic mass of H)
$= (2 \times 12) + (2 \times 1) = 26$ g/mol

(*ii*) Molar mass of S_8 = 8 × Atomic mass of S
$= 8 \times 32 = 256$ g/mol

(*iii*) Molar mass of P_4 = 4 × Atomic mass of P
$= 4 \times 31 = 124$ g/mol

(*iv*) Molar mass of HCl = (Atomic mass of H) + (Atomic mass of Cl)
$= 1 + 35.5 = 36.5$ g/mol

(*v*) Molar mass of HNO_3 = (Atomic mass of H) + (Atomic mass of N) + (3 × Atomic mass of O)
$= 1 + 14 + (3 \times 16) = 15 + 48 = 63$ g/mol

SUMMARY

- Antoine L Lavoisier laid the foundation of chemical sciences by establishing two important laws of chemical combination which are:
  (i) **Law of Conservation of Mass** It states that, "mass can neither be created nor destroyed in a chemical reaction".
  (ii) **Law of Constant Proportion** It states that, "in a pure chemical substance, the elements are always present in definite proportions by mass". It was given by J Proust and is also known as law of definite proportions.
- **Dalton's Atomic Theory**
  (i) It states that matter is made up of very small indivisible particles called **atoms**.
  (ii) Atoms of a given element are identical but those of different elements have different masses and chemical properties.
  (iii) The major draw back of this theory is that atoms are no longer considered indivisible. Discoveries show that atoms are made up of electron, proton and neutron.
- **Atom** It is the smallest particle of matter which takes part in a chemical reaction.
- **Symbols** of elements are derived from one or two letters of names of the elements in English, Greek, Latin, German etc. First letter is written in capital and the second one in small. e.g. iron: Fe (from ferrum).
- **Relative Atomic Mass** It is defined as the number of times a given atom is heavier than 1/12th of mass of 1 atom of carbon-12.
- **Atomic mass unit** (amu) now called unified mass (u) is defined as the mass of 1/12th of the mass of one atom C-12 isotope.
- **Molecule** It is atom or groups of bonded atoms that exist independently.
  (i) **Molecules of Elements** These are made up of atoms of only one kind. e.g. Ar, He, O_2, O_3, etc.
  (ii) **Molecules of Compounds** These are made up of atoms of different elements, join together in fixed ratio. e.g. H_2O, CH_4, etc.
- **Atomicity** It is defined as the number of atoms present in a molecule of an element or a compound. Monoatomic (He, Ne etc.) diatomic (H_2, HCl etc.) triatomic (O_3, H_2O etc.) and polyatomic (P_4, S_8 etc.) molecules consist one, two, three and more than three atoms respectively.
- **Ions** are the charged species and can be positively or negatively charged. Positive charged ions are called cations (e.g. Na^+, K^+ etc) and negative charged ions are called anions (e.g. Cl^-, O^{2-} etc). Polyatomic ions consists of group of atoms that carries a net charge on them. (e.g. OH^-, SO_4^{2-} etc).
- **Ionic Compounds** These compounds are made up of cations and anions. e.g. NaCl (Na^+, Cl^-).
- **Valency** It is the combining capacity of an element and it is equal to charge in case of ions.
- **Molecular Mass** It is the sum of atomic masses of all the atoms present in a molecule. It is expressed in atomic mass unit (u). e.g. $H_2O = 2 \times 1 + 16 = 18$ u

For Mind Map

Visit https://goo.gl/zLGFri OR **Scan the Code**

Exam Practice

Objective Type Questions

Multiple Choice Questions

1 If 12 g of C is burnt in the presence of 32 g of O_2, how much CO_2 will be formed ?

(a) 40 g CO_2 (b) 44 g CO_2
(c) 30 g CO_2 (d) 22 g CO_2

Sol. (*b*) CO_2 is formed by the following reaction :

$$\underset{12g}{C} + \underset{32g}{O_2} \longrightarrow CO_2$$

By the law of conservation of mass,

Mass of reactants = Mass of products

Mass of C+ Mass of O_2 = Mass of CO_2

12 g + 32 g = 44 g

Therefore, 44 g of CO_2 will be formed.

2 Which of the following statement is not true about an atom?

(a) Atoms are not able to exist independently
(b) Atoms are the basic units from which molecules and ions are formed
(c) Atoms are always neutral in nature
(d) Atoms aggregate in large numbers to form the matter that we can see, feel or touch

NCERT Exemplar

Sol. (*d*) Statement (d) is not true.

The correct statement is as The molecules and ions aggregate together in large number to form the matter. We cannot see the individual molecules/ions with our eyes, only we can see the various substances which are a big collection of molecules/ions.

3 The chemical symbol for sodium is

(a) So (b) Sd (c) NA (d) Na

NCERT Exemplar

Sol. (*d*) The chemical symbol for sodium is derived from its Latin name 'Natrium'. In a 'two letter' symbol, the first letter is the 'capital letter' but the second letter is the 'small letter'. Therefore, its symbol is 'Na'.

4 Which of the following represent 1 amu ?

(a) Mass of hydrogen molecule
(b) $\frac{1}{12}$th of mass of C-12 atom
(c) Mass of O-12 atom
(d) Mass of C-12 atom

Sol. (*b*) 1 amu = $\frac{1}{12}$th of mass of C-12 atom.

5 Which of the following represents a correct chemical formula ?

(a) CaCl (b) $BiPO_4$ (c) $NaSO_4$ (d) NaS

NCERT Exemplar

Sol. (*b*) $BiPO_4$, is the correct formula, its name is bismuth phosphate.

6 The formula of chloride of a metal *M* is MCl_3, then the formula of the phosphate of metal *M* will be

(a) M_2PO_4 (b) MPO_4 (c) $M_2(PO_4)_3$ (d) M_3PO_4

Sol. (b) Valency of *M* is +3

Symbol	M	PO_4
Charge	3	3
Formula	MPO_4	

∴ The formula of phosphate of metal *M* will be MPO_4.

Fill in the Blanks

7 Law of conservation of mass was established by......... .

Sol. Antoine L.Lavoisier;

Antoine L.Lavoisier established two important laws of chemical combinations, i.e. law of conservation of mass and law of constant proportions.

8 Atoms combine in the ratio of small .... to form compounds.

Sol. whole numbers;

According to Dalton atomic theory, atoms combine in the ratio of small whole numbers to form compounds.

9 The chemical name of the compound with formula $CaCO_3$ is............ .

Sol. calcium carbonate;

The chemical name of $CaCO_3$ is calcium carbonate.

10 The chemical formula of potassium carbonate is ....

Sol. K_2CO_3;

The chemical formula of potassium carbonate is K_2CO_3.

True and False

11 Formation of 56 g of calcium oxide and 44 g of carbon dioxide, when 100 g of chalk is decomposed is in accordance with law of definite proportions.

Sol. False;

The given statement is in accordance with law of conservation of mass.

12 Different proportions of oxygen in various oxides of nitrogen provide law of multiple proportions.

Sol. True;

13 Dalton suggested that all, whether an element, a compound or a mixture, is composed of small particles, called atoms which take part in chemical reactions.

Sol. True;

14 The symbol of silver is Si.

Sol. False;

The symbol of silver is Ag.

Match the Columns

15 Match the formula units given in Column I with their masses given in Column II.

Column I		*Column II*
A. Calcium oxide	1.	56 u
B. Magnesium chloride	2.	95 u
C. Aluminium phosphide	3.	58 u
D. Calcium carbonate	4.	100 u
D. Aluminium oxide	5.	102 u

Sol. A→(1), B→(2), C→(3), D→(4)

A. Calcium oxide, CaO

$40+16=56$ u.

B. Magnesium chloride, $MgCl_2$

$24+2\times35.5=95$ u

C. Aluminium phosphide, AlP

$27+31=58$ u

D. Calcium carbonate, $CaCO_3$

$40+12+3\times16=100$ u

E. Aluminium oxide, Al_2O_3

$2\times27+3\times16=102$ u

Assertion-Reason

Direction (Q.Nos. 16-19) *In each of the following questions, a statement of Assertion is given by the corresponding statement of Reason. Of the statements, mark the correct answer as*

(a) Both Assertion and Reason are correct and Reason is the correct explanation of Assertion.

(b) Both Assertion and Reason are correct but Reason is not the correct explanation of Assertion.

(c) Assertion is correct but Reason is incorrect.

(d) Assertion is correct and Reason is incorrect.

16 **Assertion** Pure water obtained from different sources such as river, well, spring, sea, etc. always contains hydrogen and oxygen in the ratio of 1 : 8 by mass.

Reason A chemical compound always contains elements combined in a fixed proportions by mass.

Sol. (*a*) The law of constant proportion states that in a chemical substance, the elements are always present in definite proportion by mass. So, pure water obtained from different sources such as river, well, spning, etc. contain H and O in the ratio 1 : 8. Hence, both Assertion and Reason are correct and Reason is the correct explanation of Assertion.

17 **Assertion** Atomic mass of aluminium is 27.

Reason An atom of aluminium is 27 times heavier than 1/12th of the mass of carbon-12 atom.

Sol. (*a*) Atomic mass of aluminium is 27. It shows how many times an atom of that element is heavier than 1/12th of the mass of C-12 atom. Hence, both Assertion and Reason are correct and Reason is the correct explanation of Assertion.

18 **Assertion** Atomic mass has no unit but expressed in amu.

Reason It is the average mass of an atom taking care of relative abundance of its all isotopes.

Sol. (*a*) $\text{Atomic mass} = \dfrac{\text{Average mass of an atom}}{\frac{1}{12}\times \text{mass of an atom } ^{12}C}$

Average mass of an atom

$$= \frac{(RA)_1 \times z_1 + (RA)_2 \times z_2}{(RA)_1 + (RA)_2}$$

Here, RA = relative abundance and z = mass number.

As atomic mass is a ratio, so it is a unitless quantity. Hence, both Assertion and Reason are correct and Reason is the correct explanation of Assertion.

19 **Assertion** Magnesium ion and chloride ion combine to form a compound having chemical formula $MgCl_2$.

Reason Magnesium ion and chloride ion contain +1 and −2 charges respectively.

Sol. (*c*) Assertion is correct but Reason is incorrect. The correct reason is as follows :
Magnesium and chloride ions contain +2 and −1 charges respectively.

Case Based Question

Direction (Q.Nos. 20-23) *Answer the questions on the basis of your understanding of the following passage and related studied concepts:*

The molecular mass of a substance is the sum of the atomic masses of all the atoms in a molecule of the substance. It is therefore, the relative mass of a molecule expressed in atomic mass units (u). Depending upon the number of atoms of same or different elements present in the molecule, it can be monoatomic, diatomic, triatomic, tetra-atomic or plyatomic molecule. The formula unit mass is calculated in the same manner as the molecular mass calculated. It is a sum of the atomic masses of all atoms in a formula unit of compound.

20 Which of the following is an example of polyatomic molecule ?
(a) H_2 (b) O_3 (c) S_8 (d) Cl_2

Sol. (*c*) S_8 has more than 4 atoms. Therefore, it is an example of polyatomic molecule (octa-atomic).

21 The relative molecular mass of H_2O is
(a) 23 u (b) 18 u (c) 10 u (d) 40 u

Sol. (b) The relative molecular mass of water (H_2O) is $= 2\times1+1\times16 = 18\,u$

22 How many kinds of atoms are present in a molecule of copper carbonate ($CuCO_3$)?

Sol. Copper carbonate ($CuCO_3$) is a triatomic molecule, contains three type of atoms, i.e. one copper atom, one carbon atom and three oxygen atoms.

23 Calculate the ratio by mass of the combing elements in the compound : Methanol.

Sol. Methanol$(CH_3OH) \rightarrow C:H:O = 12:4:16 = 3:1:4$.

Direction (Q.Nos. 24-27) *Answer the questions on the basis of your understanding of the following passage and related studied concepts:*

Ravi was performing some experiments related to the laws of chemical combination in his science laboratory under the guidance of his chemitry teacher Mr. John. Mr. John gave him different samples of reacting species having different masses. Ravi performed the experiments and collected data as:

S. No.	Compounds	Reactant species	Masses of reactant species (in gram)
1.	H_2O	H	1
		O	8
2.	CO_2	C	12
		O	32
3.	NH_3	N	14
		H	3

24 Calculate the mass of carbon dioxide gas formed.

Sol. Mass of reactants = Mass of products
Mass of carbon dioxide
$= \text{Mass of carbon} + \text{Mass of oxygen}$
$= 12 + 32\text{ g} = 44\text{g}$

25 In a given sample ammonia coutains 3 g of hydrogen and 14 g of nitrogen. If another sample contains 5g of hydrogen then how much amount of nitrogen present in second sample?

Sol. The ratio of mass of hydrogen and nitrogen = 3 : 14
If 5g of hydrogen, then nitrogen $= \frac{5\times14}{3}$
Mass of nitrogen = 23.3g

26 Which law of chemical combination govern these experiments?

Sol. These experiments governed by law of conservation of mass. In this, the total mass of the reactants is equal to the total mass of the product and there is no change in mass during chemical reactions.

27 Write the balanced chemical reaction for the reaction between nitrogen and hydrogen.

Sol. The chemical reaction for the reaction between nitrogen and hydrogen follows as:

$$\underset{\text{Nitrogen}}{N_2} + \underset{\text{Hydrogen}}{3H_2} \longrightarrow \underset{\text{Ammonia}}{2NH_3}$$

Very Short Answer Type Questions

28 How did Berzelius assign symbols to the elements ?

Sol. Berzelius assigned symbols to the elements by taking first one or two letters of the element's name in english and in some cases the symbols have been taken from the names of elements in different languages such as Latin, German, Greek etc.

29 Write one example of each.

(i) tetra-atomic molecule

(ii) diatomic molecule

Sol. (i) Phosphorus (P_4)

(ii) Nitrogen (N_2)

30 Is argon monoatomic or diatomic?

Sol. Argon is monoatomic because its atom can exist independently.

31 Give the difference between a cation and an anion.

Sol. **Cation** It is the positively charged ion. e.g. Na^+, K^+, Ca^{2+}, Mg^{2+} etc.

Anion It is the negatively charged ion. e.g. Cl^-, Br^-, F^-, O^{2-}, N^{3-} etc.

32 Choose an ionic compound among S_8, $Cu(NO_3)_2$, P_4, H_2 and O_2?

Sol. $Cu(NO_3)_2$ is an ionic compound because it has Cu^{2+} and NO_3^- ions.

33 What is the chemical formula of ammonium phosphate?

Sol. $\underset{+1}{NH_4} \times \underset{-3}{PO_4} = (NH_4)_3PO_4$

34 If an element X has its valency equal to 3, what will be its formula with carbonate ion?

Sol. $\underset{+3}{X} \times \underset{-2}{CO_3} = X_2(CO_3)_3$

35 Calculate the formula unit mass of $NaHCO_3$.
[Atomic mass of Na = 23 u, H = 1 u, C = 12 u, O = 16 u]

Sol. $NaHCO_3$ = (Atomic mass of Na) + (Atomic mass of H) + (Atomic mass of C) + (3× Atomic mass of O) = (23 + 1 + 12 + 3 × 16) = 84 u

36 Calculate the molar mass of sugar ($C_{12}H_{22}O_{11}$).

[Atomic mass of C = 12u, O = 16u, H = 1u]

Sol. $C_{12}H_{22}O_{11} = 12 \times 12 + 22 \times 1 + 11 \times 16 = 342$ g/mol

Short Answer (SA) Type Questions

1 (i) State the law of constant proportion.

(ii) In a compound carbon and oxygen react in a ratio 3 : 8 by mass to form carbon dioxide. What mass of oxygen is required to react completely with 9 g carbon?

Sol. (i) Law of constant proportion states that, "a pure chemical compound always consists of the same elements that are combined together in a fixed (or definite) proportion by mass".

(ii) Carbon : oxygen (by mass) = 3 : 8, i.e. 3 g of carbon requires 8 g of oxygen to form carbon dioxide.

∴ 9 g of carbon require (3 × 8) 24 g of oxygen to form carbon dioxide.

2 (i) (a) What mass of silver nitrate will react with 5.85 g of sodium chloride to produce 14.35 g of silver chloride and 8.5 g of sodium nitrate?

(b) On what law is the above reaction based and state the law?

Sol. (i) (a) Silver nitrate + Sodium chloride (5.85 g) ⟶ Silver chloride (14.35 g) + Sodium nitrate (8.5 g)

Total mass of reactants = Total mass of products

$x + 5.85 = 14.35 + 8.5 \Rightarrow x + 5.85 = 22.85$

$\Rightarrow \quad x = 22.85 - 5.85 \Rightarrow x = 17$ g

Therefore, silver nitrate is 17 g.

(b) It is based on law of conservation of mass which states that matter can neither be created nor be destroyed in a chemical reaction.

3 State three points of differences between an atom and a molecule.

Sol.

	Atom	Molecule
(i)	An atom is the smallest particle of an element that can take part in a chemical reaction.	A molecule is the smallest particle of an element or compound which has the properties of that element or compound.
(ii)	An atom may or may not exist independently.	A molecule is capable of independent existence.
(iii)	Examples : hydrogen (H), oxygen (O).	Examples: hydrogen molecule (H_2), oxygen molecule (O_2), water molecule (H_2O).

4 Calcium carbonate decomposes on heating to form calcium oxide and carbon dioxide. When 10 g of calcium carbonate is decomposed completely then 5.6 g of calcium oxide is formed? Calculate the mass of carbon dioxide formed. Which law of chemical combination will you use in solving this problem? State the law.

Sol. The reaction occurs as follows:

$$CaCO_3 \xrightarrow{\Delta} CaO + CO_2$$

According to the law of conservation of mass,
Total mass of reactant(s) = Total mass of products(s)

$\Rightarrow \quad 10\ g = 5.6\ g + \text{Mass of } CO_2$

$\Rightarrow$ Mass of $CO_2 = 10 - 5.6 = 4.4\ g$

This problem is solved using law of conservation of mass according to which mass can neither be created nor be destroyed during a chemical reaction.

5 Classify each of the following on the basis of their atomicity. **NCERT Exemplar**

(i) F_2 (ii) NO_2
(iii) N_2O (iv) C_2H_6
(v) P_4 (vi) H_2O_2
(vii) P_4O_{10} (viii) O_3
(ix) HCl (x) CH_4
(xi) He (xii) Ag

Sol.

Monoatomic	:	Ag, He
Diatomic	:	HCl, F_2
Triatomic	:	NO_2, N_2O, O_3
Tetra-atomic	:	P_4, H_2O_2
Polyatomic	:	C_2H_6, P_4O_{10}, CH_4

6 Give the formulae of the compounds formed from the following sets of elements.

(i) Calcium and fluorine **NCERT Exemplar**
(ii) Hydrogen and sulphur
(iii) Nitrogen and hydrogen
(iv) Carbon and chlorine
(v) Sodium and oxygen
(vi) Carbon and oxygen

Sol.

(i)	Calcium and fluorine	$Ca^{2+} \times F^{1-} = CaF_2$
(ii)	Hydrogen and sulphur	$H^{1+} \times S^{2-} = H_2S$
(iii)	Nitrogen and hydrogen	$N^{3-} \times H^{1+} = NH_3$
(iv)	Carbon and chlorine	$C^{4+} \times Cl^{1-} = CCl_4$
(v)	Sodium and oxygen	$Na^{1+} \times O^{2-} = Na_2O$
(vi)	Carbon and oxygen	$C^{4+} \times O^{2-} = C_2O_4$ or CO_2

7 Write the molecular formulae for the following compounds : **NCERT Exemplar**

(i) Copper (II) bromide
(ii) Aluminium (III) nitrate
(iii) Calcium (II) phosphate
(iv) Iron (III) sulphide
(v) Mercury (II) chloride
(vi) Magnesium (II) acetate

Sol. (i) $Cu^{2+} \times Br^{1-} = CuBr_2$ [Copper (II) bromide]

(ii) $Al^{3+} \times NO_3^{1-} = Al(NO_3)_3$ [Aluminium (III) nitrate]

(iii) $Ca^{2+} \times PO_4^{3-} = Ca_3(PO_4)_2$ [Calcium (II) phosphate]

(iv) $Fe^{3+} \times S^{2-} = Fe_2S_3$ [Iron (III) sulphide]

(v) $Hg^{2+} \times Cl^{1-} = HgCl_2$ [Mercury (II) chloride]

(vi) $CH_3COO^{1-} \times Mg^{2+} = (CH_3COO)_2Mg$ [Magnesium (II) acetate]

8 (i) An element X has a valency of 2. Write the chemical formula for
(a) bromide of the element
(b) oxide of the element.
(ii) Define formula unit mass of a substance.

Sol. (i) (a) Valency of $X = 2$
Valency of bromine = 1
$\therefore$ The formula of compound

$$= \begin{matrix} X & \times & Br \\ +2 & & -1 \end{matrix}$$

$$= XBr_2$$

(b) Valency of $X = 2$
Valency of oxygen = 2
$\therefore$ The formula of compound

$$= \begin{matrix} X & \times & O \\ +2 & & -2 \end{matrix}$$

$$= X_2O_2 \text{ or } XO$$

(ii) Formula unit mass is the sum of atomic masses of all atoms present in a formula unit of compound. It is calculated by adding the atomic masses of all the atoms present in one formula unit.

9 Write the chemical formulae of following compound, using criss-cross method.

(i) Magnesium bicarbonate
(ii) Barium nitrate
(iii) Potassium nitrate

Sol. (i) **Charge** $\begin{matrix} Mg & \times & HCO_3 \\ +2 & & -1 \end{matrix}$

Formula $Mg(HCO_3)_2$.

(ii) **Charge** $\begin{matrix} Ba & \times & NO_3 \\ +2 & & -1 \end{matrix}$

Formula $Ba(NO_3)_2$.

(iii) **Charge** $\begin{matrix} K & \times & NO_3 \\ +1 & & -1 \end{matrix}$

Formula KNO_3.)

10 Find the ratio by mass of the combining elements in the following compounds : **NCERT Exemplar**

(i) $CaCO_3$ (ii) $MgCl_2$
(iii) H_2SO_4 (iv) C_2H_5OH
(v) NH_3 (vi) $Ca(OH)_2$

Sol. (i) $CaCO_3 \rightarrow Ca : C : O = 40 : 12 : 48$
$= 10 : 3 : 12$

(ii) $MgCl_2 \rightarrow Mg : Cl = 24 : 2 \times 35.5 = 24 : 71$

(iii) $H_2SO_4 \rightarrow H : S : O = 2 \times 1 : 32 : 4 \times 16$
$= 2 : 32 : 64 = 1 : 16 : 32$

(iv) $C_2H_5OH \rightarrow C : H : O = 2 \times 12 : 6 \times 1 : 16$
$= 24 : 6 : 16 = 12 : 3 : 8$

(v) $NH_3 \rightarrow N : H = 14 : 3 \times 1 = 14 : 3$

(vi) $Ca(OH)_2 \rightarrow Ca : O : H = 40 : 2 \times 16 : 2 \times 1$
$= 40 : 32 : 2 = 20 : 16 : 1$

11 Nitrogen and hydrogen atoms combine in the ratio 14 : 3 by mass to form ammonia molecule. Find the formula of ammonia molecule by calculating the molar ratio. [Given atomic mass of N = 14 u and H = 1 u]

Sol. Number of nitrogen atom present in the molecule

$$= \frac{\text{Proportion by mass}}{\text{Atomic mass}} = \frac{14}{14} = 1$$

Number of hydrogen atom present in the molecule

$$= \frac{\text{Proportion by mass}}{\text{Atomic mass}} = \frac{3}{1} = 3$$

This means number of nitrogen and hydrogen atoms combine in ratio = 1 : 3

Thus, the formula of molecule of ammonia is NH_3.

12 Give the chemical formulae for the following compounds and compute the ratio by mass of the combining elements in each one of them. **NCERT Exemplar**

(i) Ammonia
(ii) Carbon monoxide
(iii) Hydrogen chloride
(iv) Aluminium fluoride
(v) Magnesium sulphide

Sol.

S.No.	Compound	Chemical Formula	Ratio by Mass of the Combining Elements
(i)	Ammonia	NH_3	N : H = 14 : 3
(ii)	Carbon monoxide	CO	C : O = 12 : 16 = 3 : 4
(iii)	Hydrogen chloride	HCl	H : Cl = 1 : 35. 5
(iv)	Aluminium fluoride	AlF_3	Al : F = 27 : 57 = 9 : 19
(v)	Magnesium sulphide	MgS	Mg : S = 24 : 32 = 3 : 4

13 I. An element $^{14}_{7}A$ exists as diatomic gas in nature which is relatively inert and forms 78% of earth's atmosphere.

(i) Identify the gas and write its molecular formula. Write the formulae of nitrite and nitrate ions.

(ii) Calculate the molecular mass of
(a) NH_4NO_3 and (b) HNO_3
[Given atomic masses N = 14 u, O = 16 u, H = 1 u]

II. Calculate the formula unit mass of Na_2SO_3.
[Atomic mass of Na = 23 u, S = 32 u, O = 16u, H = 1 u and $N_A = 6.022 \times 10^{23}\ mol^{-1}$]

Sol. I. (i) Nitrogen gas (N_2), nitrite ion (NO_2^-), nitrate ion (NO_3^-)

(ii) (a) Molecular mass of NH_4NO_3
$= 14 + 1 \times 4 + 14 + 3 \times 16 = 80$ u

(b) Molecular mass of HNO_3
$= 1 + 14 + 3 \times 16 = 63$ u

II. Formula unit mass of Na_2SO_3
$= 2 \times 23 + 32 + 3 \times 16$
$= 46 + 32 + 48 = 126$ u

14 (a) 'SO_2 is an air pollutant released during burning of fossil fuels and from automobile exhaust'.

(i) Write the names of elements present in this gas.

(ii) What are the valencies of sulphur in SO_2 and SO_3?

(b) Define the term molecular mass.

(c) Determine the molecular mass of $ZnSO_4$ [Atomic mass of Zn = 65 u, S = 32 u and O = 16 u].

Sol. (a) (i) Sulphur and oxygen

(ii) Valency of sulphur in $SO_2 = 4$
Valency of sulphur in $SO_3 = 6$

(b) **Molecular mass** It is the sum of the atomic masses of all the atoms present in a molecule of the substance.

(c) $ZnSO_4 = 65 + 32 + 4 \times 16 = 161$ u

Long Answer (LA) Type Questions

1 (i) Explain, why the number of atoms in one mole of hydrogen gas is double the number of atoms in one mole of helium gas?

(ii) Explain atomic mass unit.

(iii) How many atoms are present in

(a) MnO_2 molecule (b) CO molecule?

Sol. (i) Hydrogen gas exist as diatomic molecule, i.e. each hydrogen gas molecule (H_2) has two atoms. While helium gas exist as monoatomic particle that is its atoms exist individually. Thus, one mole of hydrogen gas has double number of atoms as compare to one mole of helium gas.

(ii) The unit of mass equivalent to the twelfth part of the mass of C-12 isotope of carbon is called atomic mass unit (amu) or unified mass (u).

(iii) (a) In MnO_2 molecule, three atoms are present: one manganese atom and two oxygen atom.

(b) In CO molecule, two atoms are present: one carbon atom and one oxygen atom.

2 Fill in the blanks.

(i) In a chemical reaction, the sum of the masses of the reactants and products remains unchanged. This is called .... .

(ii) A group of atoms carrying a fixed charge on them is called .... .

(iii) The formula unit mass of $Ca_3(PO_4)_2$ is

(iv) Formula of sodium carbonate is ... and that of ammonium sulphate is .... .

NCERT Exemplar

Sol. (i) law of conservation of mass

(ii) polyatomic ion

(iii) 310 u

$[Ca_3(PO_4)_2 = 3 \times 40 + 2 \times 31 + 8 \times 16 = 310 u]$

(iv) Na_2CO_3; $(NH_4)_2SO_4$

3 Write the molecular formulae of all the compounds that can be formed by the combination of following ions :

$Cu^{2+}, Na^+, Fe^{3+}, Cl^-, SO_4^{2-}, PO_4^{3-}$

NCERT Exemplar

Sol. Compounds of Cu^{2+}

(i) with $Cl^- \rightarrow Cu^{2+} \times Cl^{1-} = CuCl_2$

(ii) with $SO_4^{2-} \rightarrow Cu^{2+} \times SO_4^{2-} = CuSO_4$

(iii) with $PO_4^{3-} \rightarrow Cu^{2-} \times PO_4^{3-} = Cu_3(PO_4)_2$

Compounds of Na^+

(i) with $Cl^- \rightarrow Na^{1+} \times Cl^{1-} = NaCl$

(ii) with $SO_4^{2-} \rightarrow Na^{1+} \times SO_4^{2-} = Na_2SO_4$

(iii) with $PO_4^{3-} \rightarrow Na^{1+} \times PO_4^{3-} = Na_3PO_4$

Compounds of Fe^{3+}

(i) with $Cl^- \rightarrow Fe^{3+} \times Cl^{1-} = FeCl_3$

(ii) with $SO_4^{2-} \rightarrow Fe^{3+} \times SO_4^{2-} = Fe_2(SO_4)_3$

(iii) with $PO_4^{3-} \rightarrow Fe^{3+} \times PO_4^{3-} = FePO_4$

4 Write the formulae for the following and calculate the molecular mass for each one of them :

(i) Caustic potash (ii) Baking soda

(iii) Limestone (iv) Caustic soda

(v) Ethanol (vi) Common salt

NCERT Exemplar

Sol. (i) KOH

Molecular mass of KOH $= 39 + 16 + 1 = 56$ u

(ii) $NaHCO_3$

Molecular mass of $NaHCO_3$

$= 23 + 1 + 12 + 3 \times 16 = 23 + 1 + 12 + 48 = 84$ u

(iii) $CaCO_3$

Molecular mass of $CaCO_3$

$= 40 + 12 + 3 \times 16$

$= 100$ u

(iv) NaOH

Molecular mass of NaOH $= 23 + 16 + 1 = 40$u

(v) C_2H_5OH

Molecular mass of C_2H_5OH or C_2H_6O

$= 2 \times 12 + 6 \times 1 + 16$

$= 24 + 6 + 16 = 46$ u

(vi) NaCl

Molecular mass of NaCl $= 23 + 35.5 = 58.5$ u

CHAPTER EXERCISE

Objective Type Questions

1 A sample of pure water, irrespective of its source, contain 11.1% hydrogen and 88.9% oxygen. The data supports
(a) law of multiple proportions
(b) law of reciprocal proportions
(c) law of constant proportions
(d) law of conservation of mass

2 In which of the following, the valency of each of the constituent elements is equal to the total number of atoms in one molecule of the compound?
(a) HCl (b) H_2S
(c) $MgCl_2$ (d) CaO

3 The chemical symbol for nitrogen gas is **NCERT Exemplar**
(a) Ni (b) N_2
(c) N^+ (d) N

4 The simplest compound made up of two different elements are also called......... .

5 Molecular mass of ethyne (C_2H_2) is 28 g/mol.

6 Particles having more or less electrons than the normal atoms are called ions.

7 Match the elements given in Column I with their symbols given in Column II.

Column I	Column II
A. Phosphorus	1. C
B. Carbon	2. P
C. Gold	3. Co
D. Neon	4. Au
E. Cobalt	5. Ne

Assertion–Reason

Direction (Q. Nos. 8-10) *In each of the following questions, a statement of Assertion is given by the corresponding statement of Reason. Of the statements, mark the correct answer as*
(a) Both Assertion and Reason are true and Reason is the correct explanation of Assertion.
(b) Both Assertion and Reason are true but Reason is not the correct explanation of Assertion.
(c) Assertion is true but Reason is false.
(d) Assertion is false and Reason is true.

8 **Assertion** When 10 g of $CaCO_3$ is decomposed, 5.6 g of residue is left and 4.4 g of CO_2 escapes.
Reason Law of conservation of mass is followed.

9 **Assertion** SI unit of atomic mass and molecular mass is u.
Reason It is equal to the mass of 6.023×10^{23} atoms.

10 **Assertion** Atomicity of O_3 is 3.
Reason 1 mole of an element contains 6.023×10^{23} atoms.

Case Based Questions

Direction (Q.Nos. 11-14) *Answer the questions on the basis of your understanding of the following passage and related studied concepts:*

The combining capacities of different elements are compared with that of hydrogen. The valency of hydrogen is taken as 1 and the valencies of all other elements are measured against this standard. An atom of calcium always combines with two atoms of hydrogen to form calcium hydride, a compound of calcium and hydrogen. Hence, the combining capacity or valency of calcium is twice that of hydrogen.

But, there are elements which do not combine with hydrogen at all. However, they can combine with chlorine. For example, gold does not combine with hydrogen but it combines with chlorine to form a compound ($AuCl_3$), in which one atom of gold is united with three atoms of chlorine.

Since, the valency of chlorine is one, we conclude that the valency of gold must be three. Hence, valency is measured by the number of hydrogen or chlorine atoms which combine with or are displaced by one atom of the element. There are some elements which show different valencies in different compounds. Copper shows two valencies, one and two.

In the red oxide of copper, its valency is one, while in the black oxide, its valency is two. Similarly, iron shows valency two and three.

11 The element B shows valencies of 4 and 6. The formulae of its two oxides respectively are
(a) BO_3, BO_2 (b) B_2O_6, BO_4
(c) BO_2, BO_3 (d) BO_4, B_2O_6

12 The formula of the sulphate of an element X is $X_2(SO_4)_3$. The formula of nitride of the element X is

(a) X_2N (b) XN_2 (c) XN (d) X_2N_3

13 Write the formula of the compound formed by the ions Al^{3+} and SO_4^{2-}.

14 The formula of oxide of an element Z is Z_2O_3. What is the valency of element Z?

Answers

1. (c) 2. (d) 3. (b) 4. binary compounds
5. False 6. True
7. A→(2); B→(1); C→(4); D→(5); E→(3)
8. (a) 9. (c) 10. (b) 11. (c) 12. (c)

Very Short Answer Type Questions

15 In which form do atoms exist in aqueous solutions? Give example.

16 Give the symbols of the following elements.

(i) Aluminium (ii) Cobalt
(iii) Arsenic (iv) Radon

17 Write the ions present in

(i) $Al_2(CO_3)_3$ (ii) $AlBr_3$

18 An element has a valency of 3. Write the simplest formula for sulphide of the element.

19 Name the compound represented by formula K_2SO_4.

20 The formula of carbonate of a metal M is M_2CO_3. What is the formula for phosphate of M?

Short Answer (SA) Type Questions

21 Name any two monovalent cations, divalent cations and trivalent cations. Also name any one compound each one of them make.

22 The symbols of some of the ions are given below

$$Na^+, Mg^{2+}, H^+, CO_3^{2-}, Cl^-, S^{2-}$$

Using this information, find out the formulae of

(i) sodium carbonate
(ii) magnesium chloride
(iii) hydrogen sulphide

23 Write the chemical formulae of nitrates (NO_3^-) of $Na^+, K^+, Al^{3+}, Mg^{2+}, Ca^{2+}, Zn^{2+}$.

24 Write the chemical formulae and names of the compounds formed by the following ions:

(i) Cr^{3+} and SO_4^{2-} (ii) Pb^{2+} and NO_3^-
(iii) Mg^{2+} and CO_3^{2-}

25 In a chemical compound calcium sulphate:

(i) Identify the two ions.
(ii) Write the chemical formula of compound formed when positive ion is replaced by sodium ion.
(iii) Name the resulting compound.

26 (i) Name a greenhouse gas with molar mass 44 g mol^{-1} and is known to extinguish fire.
(ii) Name the elements present in this gas and write their valency.
(iii) Calculate the formula unit mass of Na_2CO_3.
[Given atomic mass of Na = 23 u, C = 12 u and O = 16 u]

27 An element X has a valency 1.

(i) Write the chemical formula of its phosphide.
(ii) Write the chemical formula of its chloride.
(iii) Is element X a metal or a non-metal?

Long Answer (LA) Type Questions

28 State the two important laws of chemical combination. How Dalton's atomic theory explains the two Laws?

29 Give a brief description about the following:

(i) Relative atomic mass (ii) Atomic mass unit
(iii) Ions
(iv) Ionic compound
(v) Atomicity

30 Give the formulae of the compounds formed from the following set of elements.

(i) Carbon and hydrogen
(ii) Nitrogen and magnesium
(iii) Sodium and phosphorus
(iv) Potassium and oxygen
(v) Boron and oxygen

Challengers*

1 Antacid are prescribed during acidity. Commercially available antacids consist of magnesium hydroxide [$Mg(OH)_2$], sugar and flavouring agents. The magnesium hydroxide act as base and form salt and water on reaction with hydrochloric acid of the stomach. The mass of salt and water formed is equal to the combined mass of

(a) $Mg(OH)_2$ and HCl
(b) $Mg(OH)_2$, flavouring agent and HCl
(c) $Mg(OH)_2$, sugar and HCl
(d) $Mg(OH)_2$, sugar, flavouring agent and HCl

2 In order to verify the law of conservation of mass, we carry out chemical reactions in a closed container, so that

(a) gaseous products do not escape
(b) heat transfer does not occur
(c) reactants do not mix with the products
(d) None of the above

3 Four students *A*, *B*, *C* and *D* verified the law of conservation of mass by performing chemical reaction between barium chloride and sodium sulphate. All of them took 107.2 g barium chloride solution and 116.1g of sodium sulphate solution and mixed them in the beaker of mass 150 g. They reported their results as follows:

Student	***Colour of reaction mixture after mixing***	***Mass of reaction mixture in the beaker including mass of beaker***
A	White precipitate	383.3g
B	Brown precipitate	393.3g
C	White precipitate	373.3g
D	Brown precipitate	363.3g

The correct observation is that of student

(a) *A* (b) *B*
(c) *C* (d) *D*

4 In a chemical reaction 10.6 g of sodium carbonate reacted with 12 g of ethanoic acid. The products were 4.4 g carbon dioxide, 1.8 g of water and sodium ethanoate. The mass of sodium ethanoate formed is

(a) 16.4 g (b) 0.16 g
(c) 24 g (d) 8.2 g

5. During an experiment hydrogen (H_2) and oxygen (O_2) gases reacted in an electric arc to produce water as follows: $2H + O_2 \xrightarrow{\text{Electricity}} 2H_2O$

The experiment is repeated three times and data tabulated as shown below:

Experiment number	***Mass of H_2 reacted***	***Mass of O_2 reacted***	***Mass of H_2O produced***
1	2g	16 g	18 g
2	4g	32 g	36 g
3	-	-	9 g

During 3rd experiment the researcher forgot to list masses of H_2 and O_2 used. So, if the law of constant proportion is correct then find mass of O_2 used during 3rd experiment.

(a) 4 g (b) 8 g (c) 16 g (d) 32 g

6. Nitrogen and hydrogen combine together to form ammonia. $N_2 + 3H_2 \rightarrow 2NH_3$
[Relative atomic masses of N = 14 u, H = 1 u]
The mass of nitrogen and hydrogen which combine together to form 6.8 g ammonia is

(a) $N_2 = 2.8g$, $H_2 = 4.0g$ (b) $N_2 = 5.6g$, $H_2 = 12g$
(c) $N_2 = 4.0g$, $H_2 = 2.8g$ (d) $N_2 = 12g$, $H_2 = 5.6g$

Answer Key

1.	(a)	2.	(a)	3.	(c)	4.	(a)	5.	(b)
6.	(b)								

*These questions may be or may not be asked in the examination, have been given just for additional practice.

CHAPTER

04

Structure of the Atom

Chapter Checklist

- Charged Particles in Matter
- Structure of an Atom
- Atomic Number and Mass Number
- Different Atomic Species

We have learnt that atoms and molecules are the fundamental building blocks of matter. The existence of different kinds of matter around us is due to different types of atoms and molecules present in them. Dalton assumed that atom is indivisible, i.e. it has no constituent particles. But, a series of experimental evidences revealed that an atom is not the smallest particle. Some other particles smaller than the atom are also present which are called sub-atomic particles, i.e. electrons, protons and neutrons. The atoms of different elements differ in the number of electrons, protons and neutrons.

In this chapter, we will describe how electrons, protons and neutrons were discovered and the various models that have been proposed to explain how these particles are arranged within the atom.

Charged Particles in Matter

The particles that carry an electric charge are called **charged particles**. Generally, on rubbing two objects together, they become electrically charged. It means that some charged particles are present within the atom or atom is made up of some charged particles. Two such particles are electrons and protons.

Discovery of Electrons

It was known by 1900, that the atom was not a simple, indivisible particle but contained atleast one sub-atomic particle—the electron, which was identified by **J. J. Thomson,** when he performed cathode ray experiment using a discharge tube.

In the experiment, a gas at low pressure was taken in a discharge tube made up of glass. At the ends of the discharge tube two electrodes (metal plates) were placed, connected to a battery for high voltage supply. The electrode connected to the negative end was known as cathode and that to the positive as anode.

During this experiment, he found a beam of negatively charged particles, called **cathode rays,** as they were originated from the cathode. These negatively charged particles were called **electrons.**

Electrons are negatively charged particles and are denoted by 'e^-'. The charge present on an electron is equal to -1.6×10^{-19} Coulomb. Since, this charge is considered to be the smallest, therefore, charge on e^- is taken as -1. The mass of an electron is equal to 9.1×10^{-31} kg.

Discovery of Protons

An atom is electrically neutral but the formation of cathode rays has shown that all the atoms contain negatively charged electrons. So, atoms must also contain some positively charged particles to balance the negative charge of electrons. This was the basis of the discovery of protons.

Before the identification of electron, **E. Goldstein** in 1886, discovered the presence of new radiations known as **canal rays** or **anode rays.** These rays were positively charged radiations which are seen moving from the anode towards cathode in a specially designed discharge tube (with a porous cathode), when a high voltage is applied across the electrodes. Porous cathode is used to provide the path for passing anode rays. It led to the discovery of another sub-atomic particle, the **proton.**

Protons are positively charged particles and are denoted by 'p^+'. The charge present on proton is equal to $+1.6 \times 10^{-19}$ Coulomb and it is considered as $+1$. The mass of a proton is equal to 1.6×10^{-27} kg. The mass of proton is approximately 2000 times as that of the electron.

Conclusion

The mass of a proton is taken as one unit and its charge is (+1), whereas the mass of an electron is considered to be negligible and its charge is (−1). It seems that an atom is composed of protons and electrons, mutually balancing their charges.

Structure of an Atom

According to **Dalton's atomic theory**, atom was indivisible and indestructible. Now, the discovery of two fundamental particles (electrons and protons) inside the atom, led to the failure of this aspect of Dalton's theory. To know the arrangement of electrons and protons within an atom, many scientists proposed various atomic models.

Thomson's Model of an Atom

J.J. Thomson was the first scientist to propose a model for the structure of an atom. Thomson's model of an atom was similar to Christmas pudding. The electrons in a sphere of positive charge, were like currants (dry fruits) in a spherical Christmas pudding.

It can also be compared to a watermelon, in which, the positive charge in an atom is spread all over like the red edible part, while the electrons studded in the positively charged sphere, like the seeds in the watermelon.

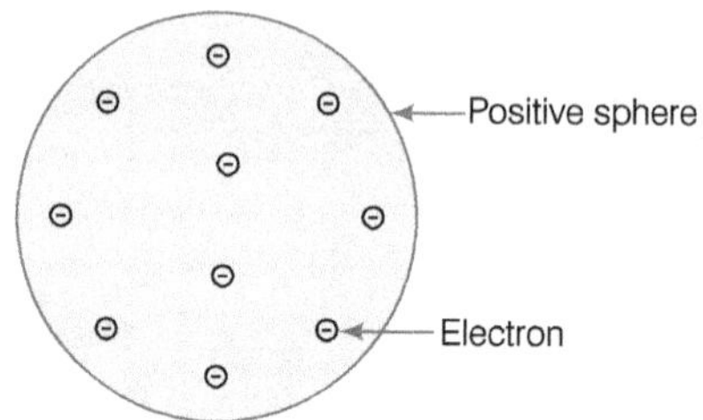

Thomson's model of an atom

Following are the postulates of this model:

(*i*) Electrons are embedded in the sphere of positive charge.

(*ii*) The negative and positive charges are equal in magnitude. Therefore, the atom as a whole is electrically neutral.

(*iii*) The mass of an atom is assumed to be uniformly distributed throughout the atom.

Limitations of Thomson's Model of an Atom

Limitations of J.J. Thomson's model of an atom are:

(*i*) J.J. Thomson's model could not explain the experimental results of other scientists such as Rutherford, as there is no nucleus in the atomic model proposed by Thomson.

(*ii*) It could not explain the stability of an atom, i.e. how positive and negative charges could remain, so close together.

Rutherford's Model of an Atom

Ernest Rutherford designed an experiment to know how the electrons are arranged within an atom. He bombarded fast moving α-particles (these are doubly charged helium ions having a mass of 4 u) on thin sheet of gold foil. He selected a gold foil because he wanted a layer as thin as possible. This gold foil was about 1000 atoms thick.

The following observations were made by Rutherford:

(*i*) Most of the fast moving α-particles passed straight through the gold foil.

(*ii*) Some of the α-particles were deflected by the foil by small angles.

(*iii*) Very few α-particles (one out of 12000) appeared to rebound.

On the basis of his experiment, Rutherford concluded that:

(i) Most of the space inside the atom is empty because most of the α-particles passed through the gold foil without getting deflected.

(ii) Very few particles were deflected from their path, indicating that the positive charge of the atom occupies very little space.

(iii) A very small fraction of α-particles were deflected by 180° (i.e. they rebound), indicating that all the positive charge and mass of atom were concentrated in a very small volume within the atom.

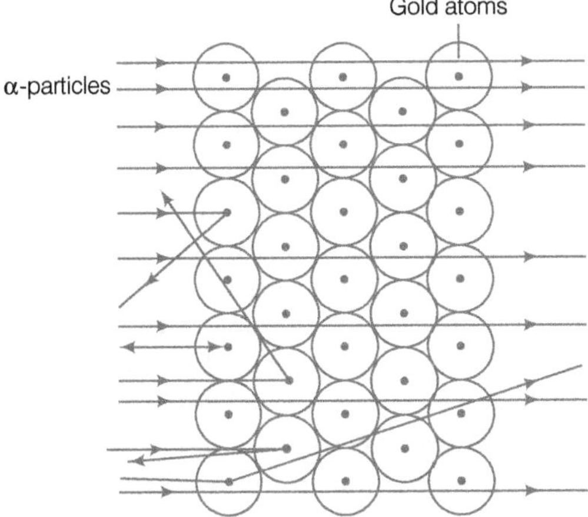

Scattering of α-particles by gold foil

On the basis of his experiment, Rutherford put forward the nuclear model of an atom, having the following features:

(i) There is a positively charged, highly densed centre in an atom, called **nucleus**. Nearly, the whole mass of the atom resides in the nucleus.

(ii) The electrons revolve around the nucleus in circular path.

(iii) The size of the nucleus (10^{-15} m) is very small as compared to the size of the atom (10^{-10} m).

Note Rutherford suggested that his model of atom was similar to that of solar system. In the solar system, the different planets are revolving around the Sun. Similarly, in an atom the electrons are revolving around the nucleus. So, these electrons are also called planetary electrons.

Limitations of Rutherford's Model of an Atom

Limitations of Rutherford's model of an atom are:

(i) Any charged particle when accelerated is expected to radiate energy. To remain in a circular orbit, the electron would need to undergo acceleration. Therefore, it would radiate energy. Thus, the revolving electron would lose energy and finally fall into the nucleus. If this were so, the atom should be highly unstable. Therefore, matter would not exist, but we know matter exists. It means that atoms are quite stable. Thus, it could not explain the stability of an atom when charged electrons are moving under the attractive force of positively charged nucleus.

(ii) Rutherford's model could not explain the distribution of electrons in the extra nuclear portion of the atom.

Bohr's Model of an Atom

To overcome the objections raised against Rutherford's model of the atom, **Neils Bohr** put forward the following postulates about the model of an atom:

(i) Atom consists of positively charged nucleus around which electrons revolve in **discrete orbits,** i.e. electrons revolve in certain permissible orbits and not just in any orbit.

(ii) Each of these orbits are associated with certain value of energy. Hence, these orbits are called **energy shells** or **energy levels**. As the energy of an orbit is fixed (stationary), orbit is also called **stationary state**.

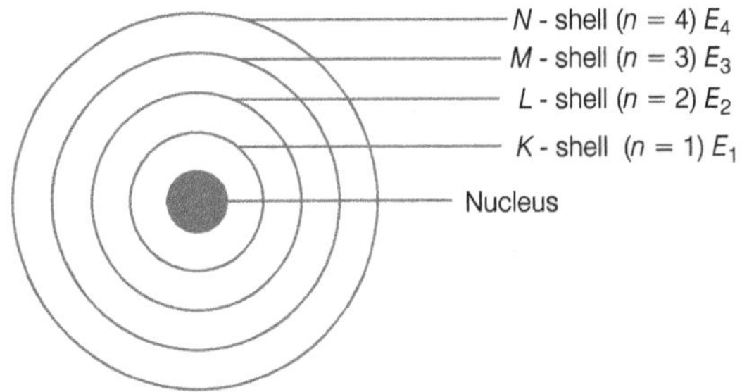

A few energy levels in an atom

(iii) Starting from nucleus, energy levels (orbits) are represented by numbers (1, 2, 3, 4 etc.) or by alphabets (K, L, M, N etc.).

(iv) The electrons present in first energy level (E_1) have lowest energy. Energies increases on moving towards outer energy levels.

(v) Energy of an electron remains same as long as it remains in discrete orbit and it does not radiate energy while revolving.

(vi) When energy is supplied to an electron, it can go to higher energy levels. While an electron falls to lower energy level, when it radiate energy.

Neutrons (n)

Neutron is another sub-atomic particle, discovered by **J. Chadwick** in 1932. It is represented by n. Neutrons are electrically neutral particles and are as heavy as protons (i.e. their mass is 1.67493×10^{-27} kg) which is equal to that of proton.

Neutrons are present in the nucleus of all atoms except hydrogen. The mass of an atom is given by the sum of the masses of protons and neutrons present in the nucleus.

Check Point 01

1 When we rub two objects together they become electrically charged. Where did this electric charge come from?
2 How cathode rays are different from anode rays?
3 Name the discoveror of electrons, protons and neutrons.
4 What conclusion would be drawn by Rutherford when he observed that most of the fast moving α-particles passed straight through the gold foil?
5 State True or False for the following statement:
Canal rays is positively charged radiation.
6 What do you understand by the term 'discrete orbit'?
7 Fill in the blank:
.........was the first one to propose a model for the structure of an atom.

Distribution of Electrons in Different Orbits (Shells)

The distribution of electrons into different orbits of an atom was suggested by **Bohr** and **Bury**. For writing the number of electrons in different energy levels or shells, some rules are followed.

These are:

(*i*) The maximum number of electrons present in a shell is given by the formula $2n^2$, where, n is the orbit number or energy level, 1, 2, 3, ...

Therefore, the maximum number of electrons in different shells are as follows :

First orbit or K-shell $= 2 \times (1)^2 = 2$

Second orbit or L-shell $= 2 \times (2)^2 = 8$

Third orbit or M-shell $= 2 \times (3)^2 = 18$

Fourth orbit or N-shell $= 2 \times (4)^2 = 32$ and so on.

(*ii*) The maximum number of electrons that can be accommodated in the outermost orbit is 8.

(*iii*) Electrons are not accommodated in a given shell, unless the inner shells are filled (i.e. the shells are filled in a stepwise manner).

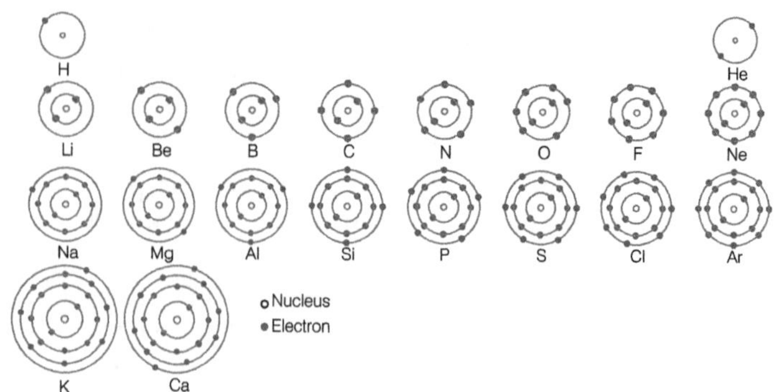

Schematic atomic structure of the first twenty elements

Valency

The electrons present in the outermost shell of an atom are known as the **valence electrons.** They govern the chemical properties of atoms. The atoms of elements having completely filled outermost shell means which has eight electrons show little chemical activity, i.e. they are highly stable. Such elements are called **inert elements.** It means, their valency is zero. Of these inert elements, the helium atom has two electrons in its outermost shell and all other elements have atoms with eight electrons in the outermost shell.

The tendency to react with atoms of the same or different elements to form molecules is an attempt to attain fully-filled outermost shell. It means, atoms react with other atoms in order to attain fully-filled outermost shell. An outermost shell, which had eight electrons is called an **octet.** Atoms would thus react, so as to achieve an octet in the outermost shell. This was done by sharing, gaining or the loss of electrons. The number of electrons lost or gained or shared by an atom to become stable or to achieve an octet in the outermost shell is known as **valency of that element.**

In other words, it is the combining capacity of the atom of an element with the atom(s) of other element(s) in order to complete its octet.

The valencies of elements of some groups are described below:

(*i*) Hydrogen (H), lithium (Li), sodium (Na) and potassium (K) atoms contain one electron each in their outermost shell, therefore, each one of them can lose one electron to become stable. Hence, their valency is 1.

(*ii*) The valency of each of Mg, Ca and Be is 2 because all of these have 2 valence electrons and they can lose these 2 electrons to make the octet of electrons in the outermost shell or to become stable.

(*iii*) The valency of boron and aluminium is 3 because each has 3 valence electrons.

(*iv*) The valency of carbon and silicon is 4 because each has 4 valence electrons.

(*v*) Nitrogen and phosphorus each has 5 valence electrons, so their valency is 3 because they can gain 3 electrons (instead of losing five electrons) to become stable. Hence, their valency is determined by subtracting five electrons from the octet, i.e. $8 - 5 = 3$. However, P can also share 5 electrons, hence it shows a valency of 5 alongwith 3.

(*vi*) Oxygen and sulphur each has 6 valence electrons, therefore, their valency is 2 because they can gain 2 electrons or share 2 electrons to complete their octet.

(*vii*) Similarly, fluorine and chlorine each has 7 valence electrons, their valency is 1 because they can gain 1 electron or share 1 electron to complete their octet.

(*viii*) All the inert elements, i.e. He, Ne, Ar etc., have completely filled outermost shells. Therefore, their valency is zero.

Note For metals, valency = Number of valence electrons and for non-metals, valency = 8 – number of valence electrons.

Composition of Atoms of the First Twenty Elements with Electron Distribution in Various Shells

Name of element	*Symbol*	*Atomic number*	*Number of protons*	*Number of neutrons*	*Number of electrons*	*Distribution of electrons*				*Valency*
						K	*L*	*M*	*N*	
Hydrogen	H	1	1	—	1	1	—	—	—	1
Helium	He	2	2	2	2	2	—	—	—	0
Lithium	Li	3	3	4	3	2	1	—	—	1
Beryllium	Be	4	4	5	4	2	2	—	—	2
Boron	B	5	5	6	5	2	3	—	—	3
Carbon	C	6	6	6	6	2	4	—	—	4
Nitrogen	N	7	7	7	7	2	5	—	—	3
Oxygen	O	8	8	8	8	2	6	—	—	2
Fluorine	F	9	9	10	9	2	7	—	—	1
Neon	Ne	10	10	10	10	2	8	—	—	0
Sodium	Na	11	11	12	11	2	8	1	—	1
Magnesium	Mg	12	12	12	12	2	8	2	—	2
Aluminium	Al	13	13	14	13	2	8	3	—	3
Silicon	Si	14	14	14	14	2	8	4	—	4
Phosphorus	P	15	15	16	15	2	8	5	—	3, 5
Sulphur	S	16	16	16	16	2	8	6	—	2
Chlorine	Cl	17	17	18	17	2	8	7	—	1
Argon	Ar	18	18	22	18	2	8	8	—	0
Potassium	K	19	19	20	19	2	8	8	1	1
Calcium	Ca	20	20	20	20	2	8	8	2	2

Check Point 02

1 What can be the maximum number of electrons in the outermost orbit?

2 Find out the number of electrons present in last shell of an atom having atomic number 15. **[Ans. 5]**

3 In an atom first four shells (*K*, *L*, *M* and *N*) are completely filled. Then what is the total number of electrons in that atom? **[Ans. 36]**

4 Why helium and neon do not take part in chemical reactions?

5 Fill in the blank:
K-shell of any atom cannot have more than.........electrons.

6 State True or False for the following statement:
Elements with valency 1 are always metals.

Atomic Number and Mass Number

Atomic Number

It is defined as the number of protons present in the nucleus of an atom. All the atoms of the same element have the same number of protons in their nuclei and hence, they have the same atomic number. It is denoted by Z and written as a subscript to the left of the symbol. e.g. $^4_2\text{He}, ^7_3\text{Li}$, $Z = 2$ and 3 for He and Li respectively.

Note In neutral atom, atomic number = number of protons = number of electrons

Mass Number

It is defined as the sum of number of protons and neutrons present in the nucleus of an atom. Protons and neutrons together are called as **nucleons**. Mass number is denoted by A. Mass number (A) = Number of protons + number of neutrons. e.g. ${}_{2}^{4}\text{He}$, ${}_{3}^{7}\text{Li}$, $A=4$ and 7 for He and Li respectively.

Number of neutrons = Mass number – atomic number

($\because$ Atomic number = Number of protons)

Mass number is written as a superscript to the left of the symbol. In the notation for an atom, the atomic number, mass number and symbol of the element are to be written as:

Mass number
$${}_{7}^{14}\text{N}$$
Symbol of element
Atomic number

Example 1. *An atom of an element A may be written as ${}_{12}^{24}A$.*

(i) What does the superscript 24 indicate?

(ii) What does the subscript 12 indicate?

(iii) What are the number of protons, neutrons and electrons in an atom A ?

(iv) Write the symbol of ion formed by an atom of element A.

Sol. (*i*) 24 is the mass number of atom A.

(*ii*) 12 is the atomic number of atom A.

(*iii*) Number of protons = 12

Number of neutrons = 12

Number of electrons = 12

(*iv*) Electronic configuzration of given atom = $\begin{matrix} K & L & M \\ 2, & 8, & 2 \end{matrix}$.

It can lose two electrons (and attain stable configuration), therefore its symbol of its ion is A^{2+}.

Different Atomic Species

Isotopes

These are defined as the atoms of the same element, having same atomic number but different mass numbers.

e.g. there are 3 isotopes of hydrogen atom, namely protium (${}_{1}^{1}\text{H}$), deuterium (${}_{1}^{2}\text{H}$) and tritium (${}_{1}^{3}\text{H}$) and 2 isotopes of carbon, ${}_{6}^{12}\text{C}$, ${}_{6}^{14}\text{C}$.

In other words, it can be said that isotopes have same number of protons but differ in the number of neutrons. Each isotope of an element is a pure substance.

Since, chemical properties of elements largely depend on their electronic configuration or outermost electrons and as the isotopes of an element have similar electronic configuration, therefore, isotopes of an element have same chemical properties.

We know that, masses of isotopes of elements are different. Since, physical properties such as density, light scattering etc., depend on mass therefore, these are different for isotopes of an element.

Average Atomic Mass

If an element has no isotopes, the mass of its atom would be the same as the sum of masses of protons and neutrons in it. But if an element occurs in isotopic forms, then from the percentage of each isotopic form, the average mass is calculated as:

Average atomic mass of an element

[(Atomic mass of isotope I × percentage of isotope I) + (Atomic mass of isotope II × percentage of isotope II) + ...]

e.g. the two isotopic forms of chlorine atom with masses 35u and 37u occur in the ratio of 3 : 1. Therefore, the average atomic mass of chlorine atom, can be calculated as:

The average atomic mass of chlorine atom

$$= \left(35 \times \frac{75}{100} + 37 \times \frac{25}{100}\right) = \left(\frac{105}{4} + \frac{37}{4}\right) = \frac{142}{4} = 35.5 \text{ u}$$

Here, 35.5 u is not the atomic mass of any one atom of chlorine but it shows that its given amount contains both the isotopes and their average atomic mass is 35.5 u.

Note The fractional atomic masses of elements are due to the existence of their isotopes having different masses.

Applications of Isotopes

(*i*) An isotope of uranium (U-235) is used as a fuel for the production of electricity in nuclear reactors.

(*ii*) U-238 is used to determine the age of very old rocks and even the age of the earth.

(*iii*) An isotope of cobalt (Co-60) is used in the treatment of cancer.

(*iv*) An isotope of carbon (C-14) is used to determine the age of old specimens of wood or old bones of living organisms.

(*v*) An isotope of iodine (I-131) is used in the treatment of goitre.

Isobars

Atoms of different elements with different atomic numbers but same mass number are known as **isobars.** In other words, isobars are the atoms of different elements that have same number of nucleons (protons + neutrons) but differ in the number of protons. e.g. ${}_{18}^{40}\text{Ar}$ and ${}_{20}^{40}\text{Ca}$ are **isobars.**

Since, isobars have different atomic number as well as different electronic configuration. Thus, they also have different chemical properties.

Example 2. *Consider the following pairs,*

(i) $^{58}_{26}A$, $^{58}_{28}B$

(ii) $^{79}_{35}X$, $^{80}_{35}Y$

(a) *Which of the above pairs are isotopes and isobars?*

(b) *What factors are responsible for the change in superscripts, 79, 80 (in case II), though the element is the same?*

(c) *Give the nuclear composition of* $^{58}_{26}A$.

Sol. (a) **Isobars :** $^{58}_{26}A$ and $^{58}_{28}B$ **Isotopes :** $^{79}_{35}X$ and $^{80}_{35}Y$

(b) X and Y are pair of isotopes. Isotopes have same number of protons but differ in the number of neutrons (hence, their mass number differs, from each other because mass number is the sum of number of protons and neutrons).

(c) Number of protons = 26, Number of electrons = 26
Number of neutrons = 58 − 26 = 32

Check Point 03

1 What are the number of protons, neutrons and electrons in $^{16}_{8}O$ and $^{40}_{18}Ar$? What are their atomic number and mass number?

2 The atomic number of Al and Cl are 13 and 17 respectively. What will be the number of electrons in Al^{3+} and Cl^{-}?
[**Ans.** Al^{3+} = 10, Cl^{-} = 18]

3 Lithium atom has an atomic mass of 6u and three protons in its nucleus. How many neutrons does it have?

4 State True or False for the following statement:
The number of proton in Na^{+} is 10. It means that it contains more electrons as compared to protons.

5 Fill in the blanks:
.........have same electronic configuration but.........do not.

6 Identify the isotopic pair(s) out of the following species ?
$_{8}C^{16}$, $_{6}C^{14}$, $_{7}N^{14}$, $_{8}O^{18}$, $_{7}N^{16}$

7 (i) Name the isotope used as a fuel in nuclear reactors.
(ii) What is the number of sub-atomic particles in this isotope ?

To Study NCERT Activities
Visit https://goo.gl/9ytyZH OR **Scan the Code**

NCERT FOLDER

INTEXT QUESTIONS

1 What are canal rays? **Pg 47**

Sol. Canal rays or anode rays are the positively charged rays which are seen moving from the anode towards cathode in a specially designed discharge tube, when a high voltage is applied across the electrodes.

2 If an atom contains one electron and one proton, will it carry any charge or not? **Pg 47**

Sol. An electron is a negatively charged particle, whereas a proton is a positively charged particle and the magnitude of their charges is equal. Therefore, an atom containing one electron and one proton will not carry any charge. Thus, it will be a neutral atom.

3 On the basis of Thomson's model of an atom, explain how the atom is neutral as a whole? **Pg 49**

Sol. According to Thomson model, an atom consists of a positively charged sphere and the electrons are embedded in it. The negative and positive charges are equal in magnitude. So, the atom as a whole is electrically neutral.

4 On the basis of Rutherford's model of an atom, which sub-atomic particle is present in the nucleus of an atom? **Pg 49**

Sol. According to Rutherford's model of an atom nucleus is positively charged, therefore, protons are present inside the nucleus.

5 Draw a sketch of Bohr's model of an atom with three shells. **Pg 49**

Sol. Three shells or orbits are presented by the letters K, L, M (or the numbers, $n = 1, 2, 3$)

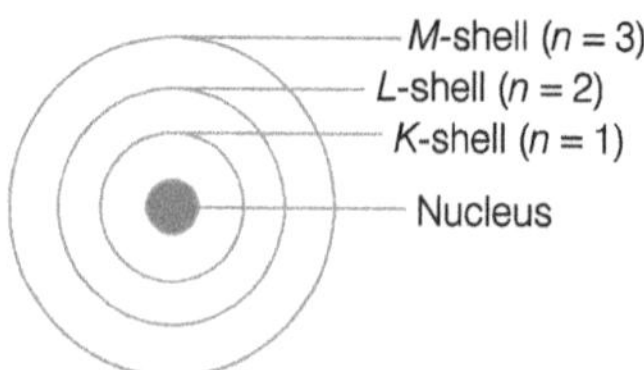

Bohr's model of an atom with three shells

6 What do you think would be the observation if the α-particle scattering experiment is carried out using a foil of a metal other than gold? **Pg 49**

Or Why did Rutherford select a gold foil in his α-rays scattering experiment? **NCERT Exemplar**

Sol. If α-particle scattering experiment is carried out using a foil of any other metal by Rutherford, there would be no change in observations. Since other metals are not so malleable. So such a thin foil is difficult to obtain.

If we use a thick foil, more α-particles would bounce back and no idea about the location of positive mass in the atom would be available with such a correctness. This means as the thickness of the foil increases, the possibility of correctness for the experiment decreases. So, use of gold in this case is preferred.

7 Name the three sub-atomic particles in an atom. **Pg 49**

Sol. The sub-atomic particles present in an atom are electrons, protons and neutrons.

8 Helium atom has an atomic mass of 4u and two protons in its nucleus. How many neutrons does it have? **Pg 49**

Sol. Atomic mass of helium = 4 u

Number of protons = 2

Let the number of neutrons = x

Number of protons + number of neutrons = Atomic mass

$$2 + x = 4$$

$$\Rightarrow \quad x = 4 - 2 = 2$$

9 Write the distribution of electrons in carbon and sodium atoms. **Pg 50**

Sol. Refer to text on Pg 76.

10 If K and L-shells of an atom are full then what would be the total number of electrons in the atom? **Pg 50**

Sol. The maximum number of electrons that can occupy K and L-shells of an atom are 2 and 8 respectively. Therefore, if K and L-shells of an atom are fully filled, then the total number of electrons in the atom would be $(2 + 8) = 10$ electrons.

11 How will you find the valency of chlorine, sulphur and magnesium? **Pg 52**

Sol. Magnesium is a metal while chlorine and sulphur are non-metals.

Valency of a metal = Number of valence electrons (i.e. number of electrons present in outermost shell)
Valency of a non-metal
= 8 – number of valence electrons

(*i*) $_{12}Mg$ = 2, 8, 2 ; Valency of magnesium = 2
(*ii*) $_{16}S$ = 2, 8, 6 ; Valency of sulphur = 8 – 6 = 2
(*iii*) $_{17}Cl$ = 2, 8, 7 ; Valency of chlorine = 8 – 7 = 1

12 If the number of electrons in an atom is 8 and the number of protons is also 8, then
(*i*) what is the atomic number of the atom?
(*ii*) what is the charge on the atom? **Pg 52**

Sol. (*i*) Atomic number = Number of protons = 8
(*ii*) The charge on the atom is zero because number of electrons and number of protons are equal.

13 With the help of table given on page 92, find out the mass number of oxygen and sulphur atoms. **Pg 52**

Sol. Mass number = Number of protons + number of neutrons
∴ Mass number of oxygen = 8 + 8 = 16
and mass number of sulphur = 16 + 16 = 32

14 For the symbol H, D and T, tabulate three sub-atomic particles found in each of them. **Pg 53**

Sol.

Symbol	Proton	Neutron	Electron
$_1H^1$	1	0	1
$_1D^2$	1	1	1
$_1T^3$	1	2	1

15 Write the electronic configuration of any one pair of isotopes and isobars. **Pg 53**

Sol. **Isotopes,** e.g. $^{35}_{17}Cl$ and $^{37}_{17}Cl$

Electronic configuration of both the isotopes of chlorine is same as their atomic number is same.

$$\begin{matrix} & K & L & M \\ _{17}Cl = & 2, & 8, & 7 \end{matrix}$$

Isobars, e.g. $^{40}_{20}Ca$ and $^{40}_{18}Ar$.

Electronic configuration of both isobars would be different as both have different atomic numbers but have same mass number.

$$\begin{matrix} & K & L & M & N \\ _{20}Ca = & 2, & 8, & 8, & 2 \\ _{18}Ar = & 2, & 8, & 8 & \end{matrix}$$

EXERCISES
(On Pages 54, 55 and 56)

1 Compare the properties of electrons, protons and neutrons.

Sol. Properties of electrons, protons and neutrons are as follows:

Property	*Electron*	*Proton*	*Neutron*
Location	Outside the nucleus i.e. they are present in orbits	Inside nucleus	Inside nucleus
Absolute charge	$(-)1.6\times10^{-19}C$	$(+)1.6 \times10^{-19}$ C	Nil
Relative charge	– 1	+ 1	Nil
Absolute mass	9.1×10^{-31} kg	1.67×10^{-27} kg	1.675×10^{-27} kg
Relative mass	1/2000	1	1

2 What are the limitations of J.J. Thomson's model of the atom?

Sol. Limitations of J.J. Thomson's model of the atom are:
(*i*) It could not explain the experimental results of other scientists such as Rutherford, as there is no nucleus in the atomic model proposed by Thomson.
(*ii*) It could not explain the stability of an atom, i.e. how positive and negative charges could remain so close together.

3 What are the limitations of Rutherford's model of the atom?

Sol. Limitations of Rutherford's model of the atom are:
(*i*) Rutherford's model could not explain why a moving charge (electrons) does not lose energy and fall into the nucleus.
(*ii*) It could not explain the stability of an atom when charged electrons are moving under the attractive force of positively charged nucleus.
(*iii*) The model could not explain as to how the electrons are distributed in the extra nuclear portion of an atom.

4 Describe Bohr's model of the atom.

Sol. The main postulates of Bohr's model of an atom are as follows:
(*i*) Electrons revolve around the nucleus in special orbits called **discrete orbits** (energy levels).
(*ii*) While revolving in discrete orbits, the electrons do not radiate energy.
(*iii*) These orbits are represented by the letters, *K, L, M, N* or the numbers *n* = 1, 2, 3 ,4 .

5 Compare all the proposed models of an atom given in the chapter.

Sol.

Thomson	*Rutherford*	*Bohr*
Atoms consists of a positively charged sphere.	A positively charged centre in an atom called nucleus. All mass of an atom resides in the nucleus.	The positive charge in centre of an atom called nucleus.
Electrons are embedded in the sphere of + ve charge.	Electrons revolve around the nucleus.	Electrons revolve in discrete orbits and do not radiate energy.
An atom is electrically neutral, as positive charge = negative charge	Size of nucleus is very small as compared to size of atom.	The orbits were termed as energy shells labelled as *K*, *L*, *M*, *N* or *n* = 1, 2, 3, 4.

6 Summarise the rules for writing of distribution of electrons in various shells for the first eighteen elements.

Sol. Refer to text on Pg 76.

7 Define valency by taking examples of silicon and oxygen.

Sol. The combining capacity of the atom of an element with the atom(s) of same or other element(s) in order to complete its octet is called the valency of that element. The valency of an element is determined by the number of valence electrons present in the atom of that element. If the number of valence electrons of the atom of an element is less than or equal to four then the valency of that element is equal to the number of valence electrons. e.g. the atom of silicon has four valence electrons [∵ atomic no of silicon is 14, therefore its electronic configuration is $\overset{K}{2}, \overset{L}{8}, \overset{M}{4}$].

Thus, the valency of silicon is four.

On the other hand, if the number of valence electrons of the atom of an element is greater than four, the valency of that element is obtained by subtracting the number of valence electrons from eight. e.g. the atom of oxygen has six valence electrons [∵ atomic no. of oxygen is 6, therefore, its electronic configuration is $2(K), 6(L)$]. Thus, the valency of oxygen is two $[8-6=2]$.

8 Explain with examples.

(*i*) Atomic number (*ii*) Mass number
(*iii*) Isotopes (*iv*) Isobars

Give any two uses of isotopes

Sol. (*i*) **Atomic number** The number of protons present in the nucleus of the atom of an element is called its atomic number.

Atomic number = Number of protons

e.g. sodium atom has 11 protons. Thus, its atomic number is 11. It is represented as $_{11}Na$.

(*ii*) **Mass number** The sum of number of protons and neutrons (together called nucleons) present in the nucleus of an atom is called its mass number.

Mass number = Number of protons + number of neutrons

e.g. sodium atom has 11 protons and 12 neutrons. Its mass number is 23. It is represented as ^{23}Na.

(*iii*) **Isotopes** Atoms of an element having same atomic number but different mass numbers are called isotopes of that element.

e.g. hydrogen has 3 isotopes $_1H^1, _1H^2$ and $_1H^3$.

(*iv*) **Isobars** Atoms of different elements with different atomic numbers but same mass number are known as isobars.

e.g. $^{40}_{18}Ar$ and $^{40}_{20}Ca$ are isobars.

Uses of isotopes are:

(*i*) An isotope of uranium (U-235) is used as a fuel for the production of electricity in nuclear reactors.

(*ii*) An isotope of cobalt is used in the treatment of cancer.

9 Na^+ has completely filled *K* and *L*-shells. Explain.

Sol. Electronic configuration of Na (atom) = $\overset{K}{2}, \overset{L}{8}, \overset{M}{1}$.

When an atom loses one electron, it acquires a positive charge. Thus, when Na-atom lose one electron from its *M*-shell it gets converted into Na^+ ion.

Electronic configuration of Na^+(ion) = $\overset{K}{2}, \overset{L}{8}$.

As the maximum capacity of *K*-shell to occupy electrons is 2 and that of *L*-shell is 8 electrons, so, Na^+ has completely filled *K* and *L*-shells.

10 If bromine atom is available in the form of, say, two isotopes $^{79}_{35}Br$ (49.7%) and $^{81}_{35}Br$ (50.3%), calculate the average atomic mass of bromine atom.

Sol. Average atomic mass of an element

$$= \left[\left(\text{Atomic mass of isotope I} \times \frac{\text{percentage of isotope I}}{100}\right) + \left(\text{Atomic mass of isotope II} \times \frac{\text{percentage of isotope II}}{100}\right)\right]$$

Average atomic mass of bromine

$$= \left[\left(79 \times \frac{49.7}{100}\right) + \left(81 \times \frac{50.3}{100}\right)\right]$$

$= 39.263 + 40.743$

$= 80.006$ u.

11 The average atomic mass of a sample of an element X is 16.2 u. What are the percentages of isotopes ${}^{16}_{8}X$ and ${}^{18}_{8}X$ in the sample?

Sol. Let, the percentage of ${}^{16}_{8}X = x\,\%$

Then, the percentage of ${}^{18}_{8}X = (100 - x)\,\%$ ...(i)

Average atomic mass of $X = 16.2$ u

According to the given data,

$$16 \times \frac{x}{100} + 18 \times \frac{(100-x)}{100} = 16.2 \quad \text{... (ii)}$$

$$\frac{16x}{100} + \frac{1800 - 18x}{100} = 16.2$$

$$16x + 1800 - 18x = 1620 – 2x = - 1800 + 1620$$

$$\Rightarrow \quad x = \frac{180}{2} = 90\,\%$$

Placing the value of x in Eq. (i)

Percentage of ${}^{18}_{8}X = 100 - 90 = 10\%$

$\therefore$ Isotope ${}^{16}_{8}X = 90\%$, isotope ${}^{18}_{8}X = 10\%$

12 If $Z = 3$, what would be the valency of the element? Also, name the element.

Sol. Electronic configuration of element,

$$(Z = 3) = \overset{K}{2}, \ \overset{L}{1}$$

Valency of the element = Number of valence electrons = 1

Name of the element = Lithium (Li)

13 Composition of the nuclei of two atomic species X and Y are given as under.

	X	Y
Protons	6	6
Neutrons	6	8

Give the mass numbers of X and Y. What is the relation between the two species?

Sol. Mass number = Number of protons + number of neutrons

Mass number of $X = 6 + 6 = 12$

Mass number of $Y = 6 + 8 = 14$

To find the relation between X and Y.

Atomic number of X = Number of protons = 6

Atomic number of Y = Number of protons = 6

It can be that the atomic numbers of both the elements X and Y are same (6) but their mass number is different, so, X and Y are isotopes of the same element (carbon). Hence, X and Y are ${}^{12}_{6}C$ and ${}^{14}_{6}C$ respectively.

14 For the following statements, write T for True and F for False.

(*i*) J.J. Thomson's proposed that the nucleus of an atom contains only nucleons.

(*ii*) A neutron is formed by an electron and a proton combining together. Therefore, it is neutral.

(*iii*) The mass of an electron is about $\frac{1}{2000}$ times that of proton.

(*iv*) An isotope of iodine is used for making tincture of iodine, which is used as a medicine.

Sol. (*i*) (F) Because in J.J. Thomson's model, nucleus was not present.

(*ii*) (F) Neutron is a fundamental particle (a subatomic particle) of the atom of an element, thus cannot be made by combining an electron and a proton. It is neutral, as it carries no charge.

(*iii*) (T) Mass of electron is $\frac{1}{1840}$ times, which is nearly about $\frac{1}{2000}$ times that of proton.

(*iv*) (T) Tincture of iodine is made by dissolving an isotope of iodine in alcohol (I-131).

15 Rutherford's α-particle scattering experiment was responsible for the discovery of

(a) atomic nucleus
(b) electron
(c) proton
(d) neutron

Sol. (*a*) On the basis of his experiment, Rutherford predicted that centre part of the atom is positively charged and is responsible for the mass of the atom. He called these protons as atomic nucleus.

16 Isotopes of an element have

(a) the same physical properties
(b) different chemical properties
(c) different number of neutrons
(d) different atomic numbers

Sol. (*c*) Isotopes have different physical properties, similar chemical properties, same atomic number but different mass numbers. Hence, isotopes of an element have different number of neutrons.

17 Number of valence electrons in Cl^- ion are

(a) 16 (b) 8
(c) 17 (d) 18

Sol. (*b*) Valence electrons are the electrons present in outermost shell of an atom. Cl^- ion is formed when Cl atom gains an electron. The atomic number of Cl is 17, it has $17e^-$, when it gains one e^-, it becomes Cl^- ion and has $18e^-$.

Thus, electronic configuration of Cl^- atom and Cl^- ion are as follows:

Cl (atom) = 2, 8 7; Valence electrons = 7

Cl^- (ion) = 2, 8, 8 Valence electrons = 8

Hence Cl^- ion has 8 valence electrons.

18 Which of the following is a correct electronic configuration of sodium?

(a) 2, 8 (b) 8, 2, 1 (c) 2, 1, 8 (d) 2, 8, 1

Sol. (*d*) The atomic number of sodium atom is 11, therefore, its electronic configuration is $\overset{K}{2}, \overset{L}{8}, \overset{M}{1}$.

19 Complete the following table.

Atomic Number	Mass Number	Number of Neutrons	Number of Protons	Number of Electrons	Name of the Atomic Species
9	—	10	—	—	—
16	32	—	—	—	Sulphur
—	24	—	12	—	—
—	2	—	1	—	—
—	1	0	1	0	—

Sol.

Atomic Number	Mass Number	Number of Neutrons	Number of Protons	Number of Electrons	Name of the Atomic Species
9	19	10	9	9	Fluorine
16	32	16	16	16	Sulphur
12	24	12	12	12	Magnesium
1	2	1	1	1	Deuterium
1	1	0	1	0	Hydrogen ion

Explanation

(*i*) **Fluorine** ($^{19}_{9}F$) Given, atomic number = 9 and number of neutrons = 10

Mass number = Atomic number + number of neutrons = 9 + 10 = 19

Number of protons = Atomic number = Number of electrons = 9

(*ii*) **Sulphur** ($^{32}_{16}S$) Given, atomic number = 16

Number of protons = Number of electrons = 16

Number of neutrons = Mass number − atomic number = 32 − 16 = 16.

(*iii*) **Magnesium** ($^{24}_{12}Mg$) Number of protons = 12

Atomic number = Number of protons = 12

Number of electrons = Number of protons = 12

Number of neutrons = Mass number − atomic number = 24 − 12 = 12

(*iv*) **Deuterium** ($^{2}_{1}D$) Number of protons = 1 and Number of electrons = 1

∴ Atomic number = 1, mass number = 2

Number of neutrons = 2 − 1 = 1

(*v*) **Hydrogen ion** ($_1H^+$) Mass number = 1

Number of protons = 1

Number of neutrons = 0

Number of electrons = 0

Atomic number = Number of protons = 1

Because number of electrons is zero, i.e. not equal to that of protons, so the species is hydrogen ion, not hydrogen atom.

SUMMARY

Discovery of Electrons

- **J.J. Thomson** in 1990 discovered **cathode rays** (or electrons) originating or emitting from the cathode in a gas discharge tube. Electrons are the fundamental particles of all atoms.
- Cathode rays travel in a straight line. In the presence of electric field, these get deflected towards the positive electrode. They produce fluorescence when strike on the walls of discharge tube.
- Charge and mass of electron are 1.6×10^{-19} C and 9.11×10^{-31} kg respectively.

Discovery of Protons

- **E. Goldstein** in 1886, discovered the presence of new radiations known as canal rays or anode rays passing through holes or 'canals' of cathode and moving towards cathode in a discharge tube.
- Anode rays consist of positively charged particles, known as protons.
- Protons have a charge, equal in magnitude but opposite in sign to that of electron. Its mass is about 2000 times as that of the electron.

Thomson's Model of an Atom: Postulates are:

- The mass of an atom is assumed to be uniformly distributed throughout atom.
- An atom is considered to be a sphere of uniformly distributed positive charge in which electrons are embedded.
- The negative and positive charge balance each other therefore, atom as a whole is neutral.

Rutherford's Model of an Atom After performing α-particle experiment, he suggested that:

- There is a positively charged, highly densed centre in an atom, called the nucleus. Nearly the whole mass of atom resides in it.
- The electrons revolve around the nucleus in circular paths.
- The size of the nucleus is very small as compared to the size of the atom.

Bohr's Model of an Atom: Postulates are:

- Only certain special orbits called discrete orbits or energy levels of electrons are allowed inside the atom.
- While revolving in discrete orbits, the electrons do not radiate energy.
- The orbits are represented by letters *K, L, M, N* or the numbers 1, 2, 3, 4.

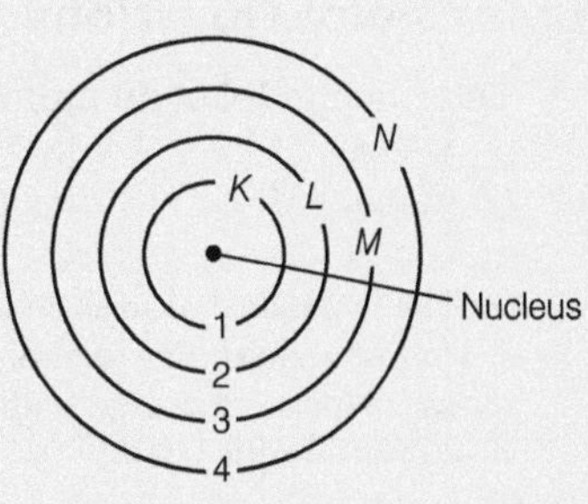

Bohr's model

Neutrons

In 1932, J. Chadwick discovered another sub-atomic particle called neutrons. They are electrically neutral and are as heavy as protons. They are present in the nucleus of all atoms, except hydrogen.

- **Bohr and Bury Scheme for Distribution of Electrons in Different energy Levels**
  The maximum number of electrons in an energy level is equal to $2n^2$ where, 'n' is the energy level or orbits or shells.
- **Valency** It is the combining capacity of an element with the atom(s) of other element(s) in order to complete its octet.
- **Atomic Number** It is defined as the number of protons present in a nucleus of an atom. It is also equal to the number of electrons in case of neutral atom. It is denoted by Z and written as subscript. e.g. $_6C$.
- **Mass Number** It is defined as the sum of numbers of protons and neutrons in the nucleus. It is denoted by A.
- **Isotopes** They have same atomic number but different mass number or same number of protons but different number of neutrons. e.g. $_1H^1$, $_1H^2$, $_1H^3$. Their chemical properties are same due to same atomic number.
- **Isobars** They have different atomic number but same mass number. Their physical and chemical properties are different. e.g. $^{40}_{18}Ar$, $^{40}_{20}Ca$.

For Mind Map

Visit https://goo.gl/ZGX3zn OR **Scan the Code**

Exam Practice

Objective Type Questions

Multiple Choice Questions

1 The first model of an atom was given by

(a) N Bohr (b) E Goldstein
(c) Rutherford (d) JJ Thomson

NCERT Exemplar

Sol. (*d*) The first model of an atom was given by JJ Thomson. According to him, an atom consists of a sphere of positive charge with negatively charged electrons embedded in it.

2 Which of the following statements about Rutherford's model of an atom are correct?

(i) Considered the nucleus as positively charged.
(ii) Established that the α-particles are four times as heavy as a hydrogen atom.
(iii) Can be compared to solar system.
(iv) Was in agreement with Thomson's model.

(a) (i) and (iii) (b) (ii) and (iii)
(c) (i) and (iv) (d) Only (i)

NCERT Exemplar

Sol. (*a*) According to Rutherford model, a central positively charged nucleus is present in the atom and electrons revolve around it. This model is similar to solar system so also called planetary model.

3 Which class is nearest to the nucleus of an atom?

(a) *K*-class (shell) (b) *L*-class (shell)
(c) *M*-class (shell) (d) *N*-class (shell)

Sol. (*a*) *K*-class (shell) is the nearest to the nucleus of an atom.

4 Who discovered neutron?

(a) J. Chadwick (b) Dalton
(c) Bohr (d) Rutherford

Sol. (*a*) Neutron is another sub-atomic particle, discovered by J. Chadwick in 1932, it is represented by *n*. Neutrons are electrically neutral particles.

5 The electron distribution in an aluminium atom is **NCERT Exemplar**

(a) 2, 8, 3 (b) 2, 8, 2
(c) 8, 2, 3 (d) 2, 3, 8

Sol. (*a*) Aluminium atom has 13 protons and 13 electrons.

$$\text{Therefore, electronic configuration of } {}_{13}\text{Al} = \overset{K}{2}\ \overset{L}{8}\ \overset{M}{3}$$

6 Which one of the following element has 2, 8, 8, 2 electronic configuration?

(a) Calcium (b) Copper
(c) Silver (d) Palladium

Sol. (*a*) The given electronic configuration contains 20 electrons. Therefore, it is the electronic configuration of calcium ($Z = 20$).

7 Identify the Mg^{2+} ion from the figure where, *n* and *p* represent the number of neutrons and protons respectively.

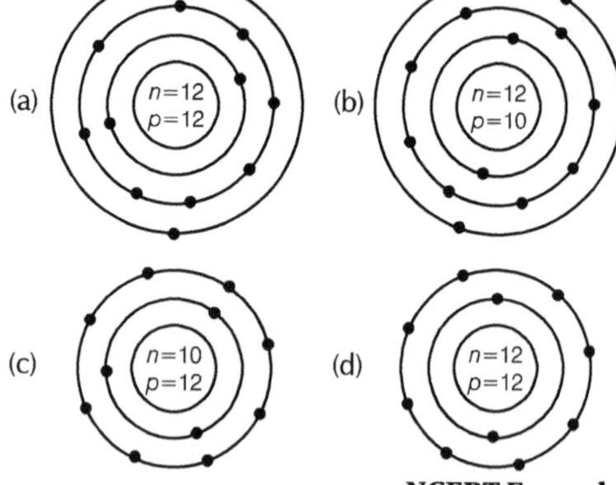

NCERT Exemplar

Sol. (*d*) *K L M*

Electronic configuration ${}_{12}Mg$ atom = 2, 8, 2 and that of Mg^{2+} ion = 2, 8

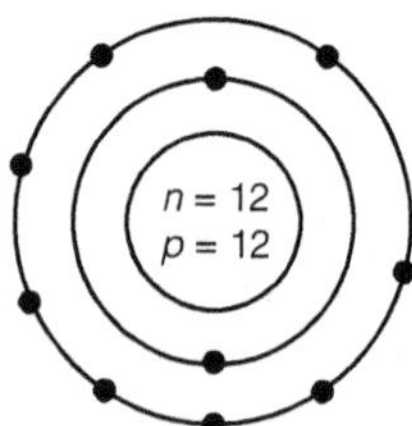

Number of protons in Mg atom = 2 + 8 + 2 = 12
Number of neutrons in Mg atom = 24 − 12 = 12
[as mass number of Mg atom = 24 and number of neutrons = mass number − number of protons]
Therefore, option (d) is the correct answer.

8 Which of the following is the valency of an element, if it has 2, 8, 2 electronic configuration?

(a) 2 (b) 4 (c) 6 (d) 0

Sol. (*a*) Valency of an element is 2 because two electrons are present in outer most shell.

9 An atom with 3 protons and 4 neutrons will have a valency of **NCERT Exemplar**

(a) 3 (b) 7 (c) 1 (d) 4

Sol. (*c*) Given that, number of protons in an atom = 3 and number of neutrons = 4

Electronic configuration of $_3Li = \overset{K}{2}, \overset{L}{1}$

As, it has one valence electron, therefore its valency is also 1.

10 $_1H^1$ is named as

(a) protium (b) deuterium
(c) tritium (d) proton

Sol. (*a*) The name of the $_1H^1$ is the protium.

Fill in the Blanks

11 The radius of nucleus is about.........times less than the radius of the atom.

Sol. 10^5;

The size of nucleus (10^{-15} m) is very small as compared to the size of the atom (10^{-10} m).

12 Elements are defined by the number of ....they possess.

Sol. protons;

Elements are identified by their atomic number.

The atomic number is defined as the total number of protons present in the nucleus of an atom.

13 Neutrons have a mass equal to........., but have no electric charge.

Sol. 1 amu;

The mass of proton and neutron is taken as one unit each.

14 The valency of nitrogen in N_2 molecule is.........

Sol. Three N : $\overset{K}{2}\ \overset{L}{5}$;

Valency in case of non-metal = 8 − 5 = 3

15 Atoms are not indivisible, comes from studying ....

Sol. Static electricity;

On rubbing two objects together they become electrically charged. So, atom is divisible and consists charged particles.

True and False

16 An isotope of iodine is used for making tincture of iodine, which is used as medicine?

Sol. False;

Tincture of iodine is the solution of ordinary iodine in alcohol.

17 Isobars because of the presence of same number of nucleons have same chemical properties.

Sol. False;

Isobars always have different chemical properties because of their different atomic number.

18 Helium is a noble gas with 2 electrons in its outermost shell. Its valency is 0.

Sol. True;

$He(Z) = 2, \overset{K}{2}$

Valency = 0. It is inert or noble gas.

19 An α-particle contains a unit positive charge.

Sol. False;

α-particles are doubly-charged helium ions.

20 Valence electrons are responsible for the chemical properties of an atom.

Sol. True;

Elements having the same number of valence electrons in their atom possess similar chemical properties and different valence electron possess different chemical properties.

21 In Thomson's model of atom, an atom consist of negatively charged sphere and positive charge embedded in it.

Sol. False;

In an atom the electrons are uniformly distributed in the positively charged sphere.

Match the Columns

22 Match the following Columns.

Column A	Column B
A. J. J. Thomson	(i) The distribution of electrons into different orbit of an atom.
B. E. Goldstein	(ii) The stability of atom could not be explained by him.
C. Neils Bohr	(iii) Discovered the presence of new radiation called canal rays.
D. E. Rutherford	(iv) Proposed that electrons are embedded in a positive sphere.

Sol. A→(iv), B→(iii), C→(i), D→(ii)

A→(iv) Thomson proposed the model in which the positive charge in the atom spread all over like the red edible part of watermelon in which electrons are studded like seeds in watermelon.

B→(iii) E. Goldstein discovered that canal rays are positively charged rays and leads to the discovery of another subatomic particle proton.

C→(i) The distribution of electrons into different orbit of an atom was suggested by Bohr and Bury.

D →(ii) The major drawback of Rutherford's model was that it could not explain the stability of atom.

Assertion-Reason

Direction (Q.Nos. 23-27) *In each of the following questions, a statement of Assertion is given by the corresponding statement of Reason. Of the statements, mark the correct answer as*

(a) Both Assertion and Reason are true and Reason is the correct explanation of Assertion.
(b) Both Assertion and Reason are true but Reason is not the correct explanation of Assertion.
(c) Assertion is true but Reason is false.
(d) Assertion is false and Reason is true.

23. Assertion Atom is electrically neutral.

Reason A neutral particle, neutron is present in the nucleus of atom.

Sol. (*b*) Because of the presence of equal number of protons and electrons the atom is neutral. Proton and neutron collectively called nucleons present in the nucleus of the atom.

24 Assertion Cathode rays get deflected towards the positive plate of electric field.

Reason Cathode rays consist of negatively charged particles known as electrons.

Sol. (a) Being made up of negatively charged particles, the cathode rays get deflected towards the positive plate of electric field.

25 Assertion In Rutherford's gold foil experiment, very few α-particles are deflected back.

Reason Nucleus present inside the atom is heavy.

Sol. (*b*) Because nucleus present inside the atom is heavy but small.

26 Assertion Electronic configuration of neon is 2, 8.

Reason Atomic number of neon is 8.

Sol. (*c*) The atomic number of neon is 10. Therefore, its electronic configuration is

$$\begin{matrix} & K & L \\ = & 2 & 8 \end{matrix}$$

27 Assertion The atoms of different elements having same mass number but different atomic number are known as isobars.

Reason The sum of protons and neutrons, in the isobars is always different.

Sol. (*c*) Mass number = Number of p^+ + number of n^0.

It remains same in case of isobars.

Case Based Questions

Direction (Q.Nos. 28-31) *Answer the questions on the basis of your understanding of the following passage and related studied concepts:*

Protons are present in the nucleus of an atom. It is equal to the number of protons in an atom, which determines its atomic number. It is denoted by '*Z*'. All atoms of an element have the same atomic number, *Z*. Therefore, the atomic number is defined as the total number of protons present in the nucleus of an atom. The mass of an atom is practically due to the protons and neutrons alone. These are present in the nucleus of an atom. Hence, protons and neutrons are called nucleus. The mass number is equal to the sum of total number of protons and neutrons present in the nucleus of an atom.

Information about 6 elements is given below.

Element	**Lithium**	**Beryllium**	**Carbon**
Symbol	Li	Be	C
Atomic number	3	4	6
Relative atomic mass	7	9	12
Element	**Oxygen**	**Aluminium**	**Chlorine**
Symbol	O	Al	Cl
Atomic number	8	13	17
Relative atomic mass	16	27	35.5

28. The electronic structure of the oxygen [O] atom may be written as : 2, 6. Show in a similar way the electronic structures of the other five elements in the table.

Sol. Li : 2, 1
Be : 2, 2
C : 2, 4
Al : 2, 8, 3
Cl : 2, 8, 7

29. Which compound is liquid at room temperature ?

(a) LiO_2 (b) CCl_4 (c) BeO (d) $AlCl_3$

Sol. (*b*) CCl_4 (Carbon tetrachloride) is liquid at room temperature.

30. Which elements are good conductors of electricity ?

Sol. Li, Be, Al

31. How many neutrons are there in beryllium ?

(a) 0 (b) 2 (c) 5 (d) 4

Sol. (*c*) Mass number of Be = 9

Atomic no. = 4

Atomic no. = No. of protons = 4

Mass no. = No. of protons + No. of neutrons

9 = 4 + No. of neutrons

No. of neutrons = 9 − 4 = 5

Direction (Q.Nos. 32-35) *Answer the questions on the basis of your understanding of the following passage and related studied concepts:*

In nature, some elements have been identified, which have the same atomic number but different mass number. These are called isotopes. Many elements consist of a mixture of isotopes. Each isotope of an element is a pure substance. The chemical properties of isotopes are similar but their physical properties are different. The mass of an atom of any natural element is taken as the average mass of all the naturally occuring atoms of that element. If an element have no isotopes, then the mass of its atom would be same as the sum of protons and neutrons in it. But, if an element occurs in isotopic forms, then we have to know the percentage of each isotopic form and then average mass is calculated. These have special properties which find them useful in various fields.

32 Hydrogen has three isotopes : ^1_1H, ^2_1H, ^3_1H. Why are these electrically neutral?

Sol. Isotopes of hydrogen are electrically neutral because all these have only one electron and one proton.

33 The relative atomic mass of a sample of an element X is 16.2. Calculate percentage of isotopes $^{16}_8X$ and $^{18}_8X$ present in the sample.

Sol. Atomic masses of $^{16}_8X$ and $^{18}_8X$ are 16 and 18.

$$\left[16 \times \frac{A}{100} + 18\frac{(100-A)}{100}\right] = 16.2$$

$\therefore A = 90\%$ and $B = 100 - A$

$\therefore B = 10\%$

34 Chlorine have two isotopes, $^{35}_{17}Cl$ and $^{37}_{17}Cl$. If the abundance of $^{17}_{35}Cl$ is 75% and $^{17}_{37}Cl$ is 25%, what is the average atomic mass of chlorine?

Sol. Average mass of chlorine $= \left[35 \times \frac{75}{100} + 37 \times \frac{25}{100}\right]$

$= 35.5$

35 Why is that certain atoms are radioactive while many others are not?

Sol. In certain atoms, the number of neutrons exceeds the number of protons and became unstable.

Very Short Answer Type Questions

36 Which scientist concluded that size of nucleus is very small as compared to size of an atom?

Sol. Ernest Rutherford.

37 One electron is present in the outermost shell of the atom of an element X. What would be the nature and value of charge on the ion formed if this electron is removed from the outermost shell? **NCERT Exemplar**

Sol. An element X is a metal because one electron is present in the outermost shell, i.e. 1 valence electron. When this valence electron is removed from the outermost shell, a cation (positive ion) will be formed with a charge of +1.

38 In the atom of an element X, 6 electrons are present in the outermost shell. If it acquires noble gas configuration by accepting requisite number of electrons, then what would be the charge on the ion so formed? **NCERT Exemplar**

Sol. Element X has 6 electrons in the outermost shell. In order to acquire noble gas configuration, element X require 2 electrons. Therefore, when it gains electrons it acquires negative charge i.e. −2. The charge on the anion (X^{2-}), so formed is −2.

39 What is the atomic number of the atom of an element X, which has 2 shells, K and L having 2 and 6 electrons respectively?

Sol. $K = 2, L = 6$

Atomic number = Number of protons

= Number of electrons in neutral atom

Atomic number = 2 + 6 = 8

40 What is the difference between Na and Na^+ in terms of number of electrons?

Sol. Number of electrons in Na = 11

Number of electrons in $Na^+ = 11 - 1 = 10$

[∵ In case of positive ion, number of electrons = Number of protons − total positive charge]

41 Write the mass number of neon and argon from the data given below.

Element	Number of Protons	Number of Neutrons
Neon	10	10
Argon	18	22

Sol. Mass number = Number of protons + number of neutrons

For neon, mass number = 10 + 10 = 20

For argon, mass number = 18 + 22 = 40

42 Calculate the number of neutrons present in the nucleus of an element X which is represented as $^{31}_{15}X$.

Sol. Atomic number, Z of ${}^{31}_{15}X = 15$

Mass number, A of ${}^{31}_{15}X = 31$

$\therefore$ Number of neutrons $= A - Z = 31 - 15 = 16$

43 Identify the pair of isotopes from the following:

$${}^{16}_{8}X, \; {}^{16}_{7}X, \; {}^{17}_{8}X$$

Sol. ${}^{16}_{8}X$ and ${}^{17}_{8}X$ are isotopes as they have same atomic number, but different mass number.

44 The atomic number of calcium and argon are 20 and 18 respectively but the mass number of both these elements is 40. What is the name given to such a pair of elements? **NCERT Exemplar**

Sol. Mass number of calcium = 40, i.e. ${}^{40}_{20}Ca$.

Mass number of argon = 40, i.e. ${}^{40}_{18}Ar$.

A pair of elements having same mass number but different atomic number is called isobars.

45 Which of the two would be chemically more reactive: element A with atomic number 18 or element D with atomic number 16 and why?

Sol. Electronic configuration of ${}_{18}A = 2, 8, 8$

It would be chemically inert due to its complete octet.

Electronic configuration of ${}_{16}D = 2, 8, 6$

To complete its octet, it will gain 2 electrons, therefore it will be more reactive.

46 Which isotope of hydrogen contain same number of electrons, protons and neutrons?

Sol. Deuterium (${}^{2}_{1}D$),

Number of electron (1), Number of proton (1),

Number of neutron $= 2 - 1 = 1$

Short Answer (SA) Type Questions

1 How can you justify that cathode-rays originate from the cathode whereas anode rays do not?

Sol. On applying high potential on discharge tube, any metal used as cathode-electrode emits beam of electrons having (–)ve charge, move towards the oppositely charged (+)ve plate (anode electrode) are known as cathode-rays.

Anode rays are gaseous (+)ve-ions (kept in discharge tube) produced due to knock out of electrons from gaseous atoms that move towards (–)ve plate.

This shows that cathode-rays originate from the cathode where as anode rays do not.

2 Write the conclusions drawn by Rutherford when he observed the following.

(*i*) Most of the α-particles passing straight through the gold foil.

(*ii*) Some α-particles getting deflected from their path.

(*iii*) Very small fraction of α-particles getting deflected by 180°.

Sol. (*i*) Most of the space inside the atom is empty.

(*ii*) It indicates that the positive charge of the atom occupies a very little space.

(*iii*) All the positive charge and mass of the atom were concentrated in a very small volume called nucleus.

3 List down three different names given to the path in which electrons revolve around the nucleus. Also, explain why are they called so?

Sol. The three different names are:

(*i*) **Discrete orbit** It is called so because electrons revolve in certain distinct path and not just in any orbit.

(*ii*) **Energy level** (energy shell) The energy associated with different orbits (with which electron revolves) is distinct for each orbit, hence it is called so.

(*iii*) **Stationary state** Since, the energy associated with an orbit is fixed. Hence, the electron revolving in a particular orbit have stationary energy. That's why, orbit is also called stationary state.

4 (*i*) What will be the maximum number of electrons which can be filled in Z-shell of an imaginary atomic model?

(*ii*) Why is it almost impossible to find such an atom in nature?

Sol. (*i*) According to Bohr and Bury rule, the maximum number of electrons in Z-shell (16th shell, starting from K)

$$= 2n^2 = 2 \times 16 \times 16 = 512$$

(*ii*) Atom with greater number of electrons have greater number of protons and neutrons therefore they have unstable nucleus which radiates energy or divide itself into smaller stable nucleus. Hence, elements with atomic number greater than 100 are rarely found in nature.

5 Atomic number of aluminium is 13 and mass number is 27. Calculate the number of electrons, protons and neutrons in its atom. Represent the ion of this element.

Sol. Number of electrons = 13
Number of protons = 13
Number of neutrons = 27 − 13 = 14

Its electronic configuration is $\overset{K}{2}, \overset{L}{8}, \overset{M}{3}$

'Al' may lose 3 electrons easily to achieve completely filled outermost shell and hence become stable, it acquires a positive charge of +3. Therefore, its ion is represented as Al^{3+}.

6 (i) Write the name of an element whose atom has same number of sub-atomic particles. Draw the atomic structure of the atom.
(ii) Draw atomic structure of an atom with same number of electrons in *L* and *M*-shells.

Sol. (i) Name of element: Oxygen ($^{16}_{8}O$)

Atomic number (8) = $\overset{K}{2}\ \overset{L}{6}$

Number of electrons = 8
Number of protons = 8
Number of neutrons = 16 − 8 = 8

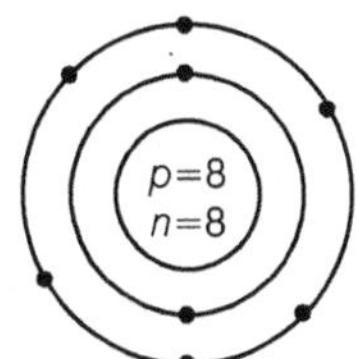

(ii) Name of element : Argon

Atomic number (18) = $\overset{K}{2}, \overset{L}{8}, \overset{M}{8}$

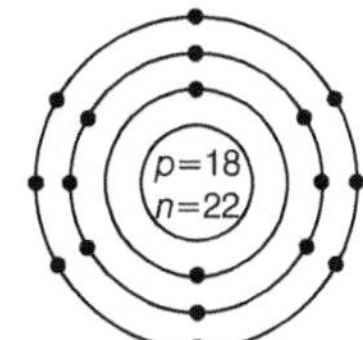

Number of electrons in *L*-shell = 8
Number of electrons in *M*-shell = 8

7 Given below is the atomic structure of an atom of element $^{23}_{11}A$, according to Bohr's model of atom.

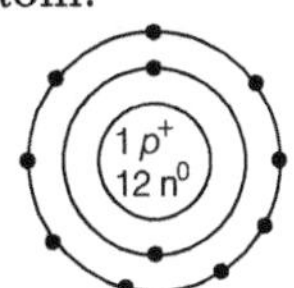

(i) What is wrong with this structure of atom?
(ii) Draw a correct representation of this atom.
(iii) Write the chemical formula of the chloride of this element.

Sol. (i) The element *A* is Na has three shells *K*, *L* and *M* but here only 2 shells are given. Further, *L*-shell cannot have more than 8 electrons but here 9 electrons are given.

(ii) The correct structure is

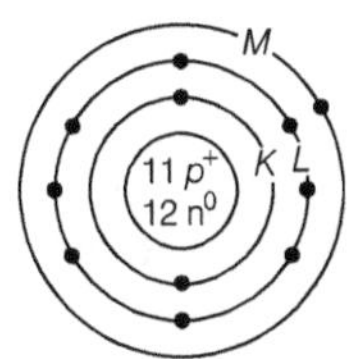

(iii) As Na has 1 valence electron, thus it has a valency of +1 and chlorine has a valency of −1. Hence, the formula of its chloride is *A*Cl, i.e. NaCl.

8 Write the electronic configuration and valency of the following.
(i) Chlorine (ii) Sodium (iii) Silicon

Sol.
(i) Chlorine ($_{17}Cl$): $\overset{K}{2}, \overset{L}{8}, \overset{M}{7} \Rightarrow$ Valency = 1
(ii) Sodium ($_{11}Na$): $\overset{K}{2}, \overset{L}{8}, \overset{M}{1} \Rightarrow$ Valency = 1
(iii) Silicon ($_{14}Si$): $\overset{K}{2}, \overset{L}{8}, \overset{M}{4} \Rightarrow$ Valency = 4

9 Write the electronic configurations for the following elements and deduce their valencies.
(i) Magnesium (ii) Neon
(iii) Sulphur

Sol.
(i) Magnesium (12) = $\overset{K}{2}, \overset{L}{8}, \overset{M}{2}$
$\Rightarrow$ Valency = 2
(ii) Neon (10) = $\overset{K}{2}, \overset{L}{8}$
$\Rightarrow$ Valency = 0
(iii) Sulphur (16) = $\overset{K}{2}, \overset{L}{8}, \overset{M}{6}$
$\Rightarrow$ Valency = 8 − 6 = 2

10 Find out the valency of atoms represented by the following figures.

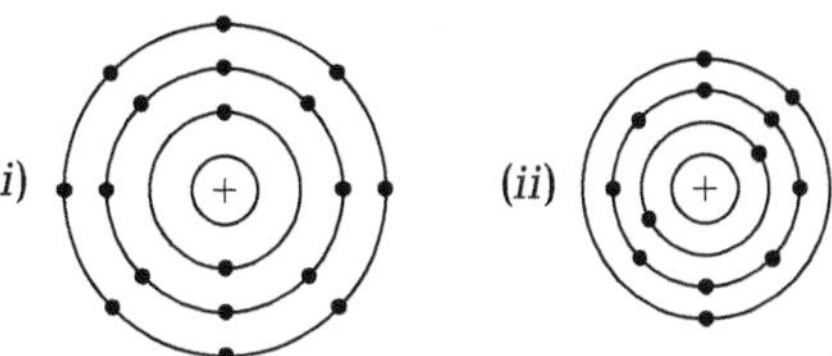

(iii) 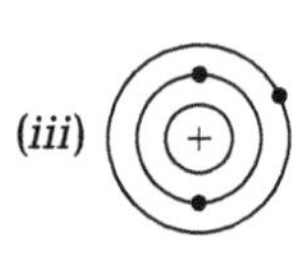

(iv) 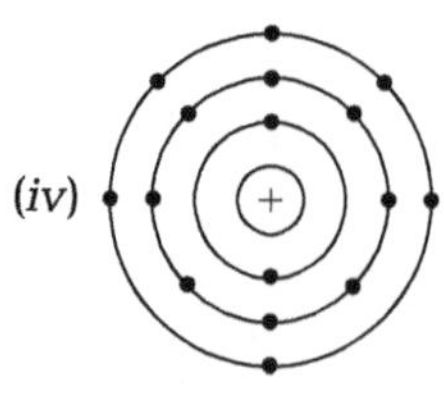

Sol. (i) Valency = 0 [$\because$ number of valence electrons = 8]

(ii) Valency = 3 [$\because$ number of valence electrons = 3]

(iii) Valency = 1 [$\because$ number of valence electron = 1]

(iv) Valency = 2 [$\because$ number of valence electrons = 6]

[valency = 8 − 6 = 2]

11 The following data represents the distribution of electrons, protons and neutrons in atoms of four elements *A*, *B*, *C*, *D*.

Element	Protons	Neutrons	Electrons
A	10	10	10
B	11	12	11
C	12	12	12
D	13	14	13

Solve the following questions.

(i) Write the electronic distribution of atoms of element *A* and *D*.

(ii) Element *A* is an inert gas. Why?

(iii) What is the valency of element *C*?

Sol. (i) Electronic distribution of element *A* and *D*.

$$\begin{array}{ll} & K\ L\ M \\ A = & 2, 8 \\ D = & 2, 8, 3 \end{array}$$

(ii) The number of electrons in the outermost shell of element *A* is 8.

The outermost shell of this element is complete and the element does not need to gain or lose electrons to complete its outermost shell. Hence, *A* is an inert gas

(iii) Valency of element *C* (2, 8, 2) is 2.

12 You are given the atom of an element $^{16}_{8}X$. Find out the

(i) number of protons, electrons and neutrons in X.

(ii) valency of X.

(iii) chemical formula of the compound formed when X reacts with

(a) hydrogen (b) carbon.

Sol. (i) Number of protons = 8

Number of electrons = 8

Number of neutrons = 16 − 8 = 8

(ii) Valency = 8 − 6 = 2

$$\because \quad \begin{bmatrix} K & L \\ 2, & 6 \end{bmatrix}$$

(iii) (a) H_2X (b) CX_2

13 An atom of an element has 5 electrons in L-shell.

(i) What is the atomic number of the element?

(ii) State its valency.

(iii) Identify the element and write its name.

Sol. (i) Since, there are 5 electrons in *L*-shell, so there must be 2 electrons in *K*-shell. Thus, the element has a total of 7 electrons, which is equal to the number of protons, hence the atomic number of the element is 7.

(ii) As *L*-shell is outermost shell and it contains 5 electrons. Therefore, it has 5 valence electron. Thus, its valency is 3 [8 − 5 = 3].

(iii) Element having atomic number 7 is nitrogen (N).

14 (i) Answer the following questions :

(a) Name the scientist who discovered protons.

(b) What is the charge and mass on a proton?

(c) Where is proton located in an atom?

(ii) An atom of an element has mass number 28 u and its atomic number is 14. How many neutrons does it have? Also, name the element.

Sol. (i)(a) Protons were discovered by E.Goldstein.

(b) The charge on a proton is $+1.6 \times 10^{-19}$ C and its mass is 1.67×10^{-27} kg.

(c) Proton is located in the nucleus of an atom.

(ii) Number of neutrons

= Mass number − atomic number = 28 − 14 = 14

The element is silicon ($^{28}_{14}Si$).

15 Show diagramatically the electron distributions in a sodium atom and a sodium ion and also give their atomic number. **NCERT Exemplar**

Sol. Atomic number of sodium (*Z*) = 11

Mass number of sodium (*A*) = 23

$\therefore$ Number of protons in the nucleus = 11

Number of neutrons in the nucleus = 23 − 11 = 12

Number of electrons = 11

$\therefore$ Electronic configuration of Na-atom $= \overset{K}{2}, \overset{L}{8}, \overset{M}{1}$

Na^+ ion is formed from sodium atom by loss of an electron (present in the outermost shell). Hence, its electronic configuration is $\overset{K}{2}, \overset{L}{8}$. However, number of protons and neutrons remain the same.

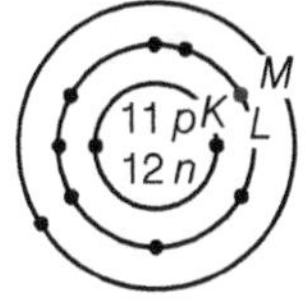

Sodium atom

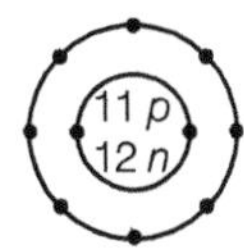

Sodium ion

16 An atom of an element has two electrons in the outermost M-shell. State

(i) electronic configuration
(ii) atomic number
(iii) number of protons
(iv) valency of this element

Sol. (i) Atom of an element has two electrons in M-shell. Therefore, its electronic configuration $= \overset{K}{2}, \overset{L}{8}, \overset{M}{2}$

(ii) Atomic number $= 2 + 8 + 2 = 12$

(iii) Number of protons $= 12$

(iv) 2, because there are 2 valence electrons, which it can lose easily to achieve stable outermost electronic configuration.

17 What information do you get from the figure about the atomic number, mass number and valency of atoms X, Y and Z? Give your answer in a tabular form.

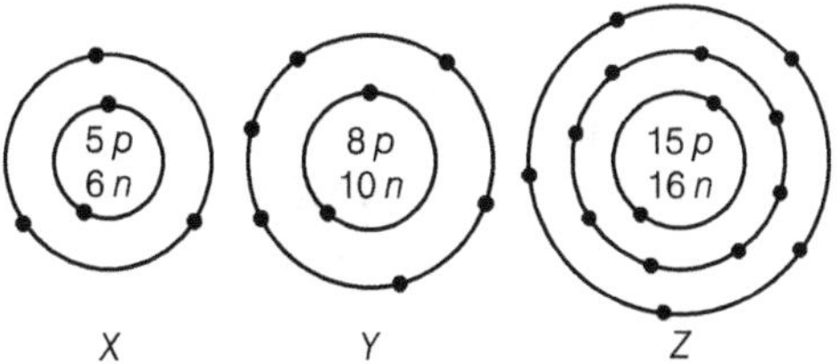

NCERT Exemplar

Sol. The tabular form is as below:

Element	Atomic Number (= no. of p)	Mass Number {= no. of (p + n)}	Number of Electrons (= no. of p)	Electronic Configuration	Valency
X	5	5 + 6 = 11	5	2, 3	3
Y	8	8 + 10 = 18	8	2, 6	2
Z	15	15 + 16 = 31	15	2, 8, 5	3, 5

18 Complete the table on the basis of information available in the symbols given below. **NCERT Exemplar**

(i) $^{35}_{17}Cl$ (ii) $^{12}_{6}C$ (iii) $^{81}_{35}Br$

Element	n_p	n_n

Sol. Atomic number is written on the lower left side of the symbol of element whereas mass number is written on the upper left side of the symbol of element.
Number of protons (n_p) = Atomic number of atoms and number of neutrons (n_n) = Mass number − atomic number.

	Element	n_p	n_n
(i)	$^{35}_{17}Cl$	17	35 − 17 = 18
(ii)	$^{12}_{6}C$	6	12 − 6 = 6
(iii)	$^{81}_{35}Br$	35	81 − 35 = 46

19 Complete the following table.

Element	Atomic Number	Protons	Electrons	Neutrons	Mass Number
A	17		17	18	
B		14	14	14	
C		9	9		19

Sol. A: Atomic number = Number of protons = 17;
Mass number = Number of protons + number of neutrons
$= 17 + 18 = 35$

B: Atomic number = Number of protons = 14;
Mass number = Number of protons + number of neutrons
$= 14 + 14 = 28$

C: Atomic number = Number of protons = 9;
Number of neutrons =
Mass number − number of protons $= 19 - 9 = 10$

Element	Atomic Number	Protons	Electrons	Neutrons	Mass Number
A	17	17	17	18	17 + 18 = 35
B	14	14	14	14	14 + 14 = 28
C	9	9	9	19 − 9 = 10	19

20 In the following table the mass numbers and the atomic numbers of certain elements are given.

Element	A	B	C	D	E
Mass no.	1	7	14	40	40
At. no.	1	3	7	18	20

(i) Select a pair of isobars from the above table.

(ii) What would be the valency of element C listed in the above table?

(ii) Which two sub-atomic particles are equal in number in a neutral atom?

Sol. (i) D and E have same mass number but different atomic numbers. Hence, they are a pair of isobars.

(ii) Electronic configuration of C is $2(K), 5(L)$. Hence, its valency is three because it gains three electrons to attain stable electronic configuration.
[or valency can be find as, $8-5=3$]

(iii) For a neutral atom,
Number of electrons = Number of protons

Thus, electrons and protons are equal in numbers in a neutral atom.

21 Two elements are represented as ${}_{17}X^{35}$ and ${}_{12}Y^{24}$.

(i) Which of these elements will lose and gain electrons?

(ii) What is the number of electrons an atom loses, gains or shares called?

(iii) Write the electronic configurations of X and Y.

Sol. (i) Y will lose (2) electrons and X will gain (1) electron.

(ii) The number of electrons lost, gained or shared by an atom is called its valency.

(iii) Electronic configuration of X
(atomic number = 17) = 2, 8, 7
Electronic configuration of Y
(atomic number = 12) = 2, 8, 2

22 A metal (mass number = 40) having same number of protons and neutrons, combines with two chlorine atoms. Identify the element with which electronic configuration of this metal matches in combined state.

Sol. As mass number = Number of protons + number of neutrons

$\Rightarrow$ $40 = 2 \times$ number of protons

$\Rightarrow$ Number of protons = 20

Hence, the metal is calcium (Ca).

Since, it combines with 2 Cl-atoms (total valency = 2)

Hence, it will acquire 2 positive charge, after losing 2 electrons.

Electronic configuration of Ca^{2+} ion = 2, 8, 8 (K, L, M)

This electronic configuration matches to that of argon (Ar).

23 In response to a question, a student stated that in an atom, the number of protons is greater than the number of neutrons, which in turn is greater than the number of electrons. Do you agree with the statement? Justify your answer.

NCERT Exemplar

Sol. The given statement is incorrect.

According to this statement:

$$p > n > e$$

But actually, number of protons can never be greater than the number of neutrons (except protium). Number of neutrons can be equal to or greater than the number of protons because mass number is equal to double the atomic number or greater than double the atomic number.

Of course, number of neutrons can be greater than the number of electrons because number of electrons are equal to number of protons in the neutral atom.

24 An ion M^{3-} contains 10 electrons and 7 neutrons. What is the atomic number and mass number of the element M? Name the element.

Sol. The number of protons in M^{3-} ion $= 10 - 3 = 7$

$\therefore$ The atomic number is 7.

Mass number = Number of protons + number of neutrons
$= 7 + 7 = 14$

As the atomic number is 7.

$\therefore$ The element is nitrogen.

25 Sulphur dioxide (SO_2) is a colourless pungent smelling gas and is a major air pollutant.

(i) Write the electronic configuration of its constituent elements 'sulphur and oxygen' (Given, ${}^{32}_{16}S, {}^{16}_{8}O$).

(ii) Write the valency of sulphur and oxygen.

(iii) Are sulphur and oxygen isotopes of same element? Explain your answer.

Sol. (i) Electronic configuration of sulphur (S) : 2, 8, 6 (K L M)

Electronic configuration of oxygen (O) : 2, 6

(ii) Valency of both sulphur and oxygen is 2, as they have the tendency to gain two electrons to achieve stable outer shell electronic configuration.

(iii) Isotopes are the elements having the same atomic number but different mass number. Therefore, they are not isotopes as their atomic numbers are different.

26 Study the data given below and answer the questions which follow:

Particle	Electrons	Protons	Neutrons
A	2	3	4
B	10	9	8
C	8	8	8
D	8	8	10

(i) Write the mass number and atomic number of particles A, B, C, D.

(ii) Which particles represent a pair of isotopes? Explain.

Sol. (i)

Particle	Atomic number	Mass number
A	3	$3+4=7$
B	9	$9+8=17$
C	8	$8+8=16$
D	8	$8+10=18$

(ii) Particles C and D as they have same number of protons, i.e. same atomic number but different mass number.

27 The two isotopes of chlorine have mass number 35 and 37 and number of neutrons 18 and 20 respectively. Which one will have higher valency? Do they have same physical or chemical properties?

Sol. Number of protons in $^{35}Cl = 35-18 = 17$

$\Rightarrow$ Number of electrons = Number of protons = 17

Similarly, number of protons in $^{37}Cl = 37-20 = 17$

$\Rightarrow$ Number of electrons = Number of protons = 17

Since, both have same number of electrons (i.e. 17). Hence, they will have same valency (i.e. 1).

Isotopes having same number of electrons show same chemical properties but may show some different physical properties.

28 (i) What is the number of electrons in Cl^- ion (Cl = 17)?

(ii) What is the electronic configuration of phosphorus (P = 15)?

(iii) Which isotope of uranium is used in nuclear fuel?

Sol. (i) $17+1$ (gained) $=18$ electrons [because negative charge shows gain of electrons].

(ii) Atomic number of phosphorus = 15

$$\text{Electronic configuration} = \begin{matrix} K & L & M \\ 2, & 8, & 5 \end{matrix}$$

(iii) Uranium-235 isotope.

29 An element M forms the compound MH_3 when it reacts with hydrogen.

(i) Find the valency of element M.

(ii) Write the valency of chlorine and sulphur.

(iii) Name three isotopes of hydrogen.

Sol. (i) Valency of $M = 3$ because it combines with three atoms of hydrogen.

(ii) Valency of chlorine, Cl (2, 8, 7) $= 8-7 = 1$

Valency of sulphur, S (2, 8, 6) $= 8-6 = 2$

(iii) Protium $_1H^1$, deuterium $_1H^2$ and tritium $_1H^3$

30 (i) Identify which of the following pairs are isotopes and which are isobars? Give reasons for your choice.

$$^{58}A_{26},\ ^{58}B_{28},\ ^{79}X_{35},\ ^{80}Y_{35}$$

(ii) Do isobars also have identical chemical properties like isotopes? State reason.

Sol. (i) A and B are isobars as they are atoms of different elements having the same mass number.

X and Y are isotopes as they are atoms of same element (same atomic number) having different mass numbers.

(ii) No, isobars do not have identical chemical properties because they have different atomic numbers as well as electronic configurations.

31 (i) Chlorine occurs in nature in two isotopic forms with masses 35 u and 37 u. The percentage of ^{35}Cl is 75%. Find the average atomic mass of chlorine atom.

(ii) Give any three applications of isotopes.

Sol. (i) % of $^{37}Cl = 100-75 = 25\%$

$$\text{Average atomic mass} = \left(\frac{35\times 75}{100}+\frac{37\times 25}{100}\right)$$

$$= \left(\frac{105}{4}+\frac{37}{4}\right) = \frac{142}{4}$$

$$= 35.50\text{ u}$$

(ii) **Applications of isotopes**

(a) An isotope of iodine is used in the treatment of goitre.

(b) An isotope of uranium is used as a fuel in nuclear reactors.

(c) An isotope of cobalt is used in the treatment of cancer.

32 On the basis of the number of protons, neutrons and electrons in the samples given below identify

(i) the cation.

(ii) the pair of isobars, and

(iii) the pair of isotopes.

Sample	Protons	Neutrons	Electrons
A	17	18	16
B	18	19	18
C	17	20	17
D	17	17	17

Sol. (i) Sample *A* has more protons than the electrons. Hence, it is a cation.

(ii) Sample *B* and *C* have same mass number (Mass number = Number of protons + number of neutrons = 37) but different atomic numbers (i.e. 18 and 17 respectively). Hence, they are a pair of isobars.

(iii) Samples *C* and *D* have same atomic number but different mass numbers. Hence, they are a pair of isotopes.

33 In the gold foil experiment of Geiger and Marsden, that paved the way for Rutherford's model of an atom, ~ 1.00% of the α-particles were found to deflect at angles greater than 50°. If one mole of α-particles were bombarded on the gold foil, compute the number of α-particles that would deflect at angles less than 50°. **NCERT Exemplar**

Sol. From mole concept

1 mole $= 6.022 \times 10^{23}$ particles

(mole concept was discussed in previous chapter)

Number of α-particles deflected at angles greater than 50° = 1% (Given)

∴ Number of α-particles deflected at the angles less than 50° = 100 − 1 = 99%.

∴ Actual number of α-particles deflected at the angles less than $50° = \frac{99}{100} \times 6.022 \times 10^{23} = 5.96 \times 10^{23}$

Hence, number of α-particles deflect at angle less than $50° = 5.96 \times 10^{23}$.

34 If the mass of a proton is 1.67×10^{-27} kg and if electron is found to be 1840 times lighter than hydrogen ion. Then find the charge to mass ratio of cathode rays. [Given, charge on 1 electron $= 1.6 \times 10^{-19}$ C]

Sol. $\text{Mass of electron} = \frac{\text{Mass of H}^+}{1840}$

$= \frac{\text{Mass of proton}}{1840}$

$= \frac{1.67 \times 10^{-27}\text{ kg}}{1840}$

$= 9.1 \times 10^{-31}$ kg

Since, cathode rays are composed of electrons only. Hence, *e/m* ratio of cathode rays = *e/m* ratio of electron

$$= \frac{1.6 \times 10^{-19}\text{ C}}{9.1 \times 10^{-31}\text{ kg}} = 1.76 \times 10^{11}\text{C kg}^{-1}$$

35 Two ions having 3 negative and 3 positive charges are found to have 7 and 14 neutrons respectively. If electronic configuration of these ions are similar to that of neon (Ne), then find the mass number of both the ions.

Sol. The electronic configuration of Ne = 2, 8 (K, L)

Atom, which forms ion similar to neon with 3 negative charges, will have electronic configuration as = 2, 5 (K, L)

Hence, the given atom is nitrogen.

Mass number = Number of protons + number of neutrons

= 7 + 7 = 14

Similarly, atom which forms ion similar to neon with 3 positive charges, will have electronic configuration as = 2, 8, 3 (K, L, M)

Hence, the given atom is aluminium.

Mass number = Number of protons + number of neutrons

= 13 + 14 = 27

36 (i) Why do isotopes of an element show similar chemical properties?

(ii) How did Rutherford come to the conclusion that most of the space in an atom is empty?

Sol. (i) Chemical properties depend on the electronic configuration of an atom. Since, isotopes of an element have same atomic number and number of electrons or more precisely same electronic configuration hence, isotopes of an element show similar chemical properties.

(ii) When Rutherford bombarded fast moving α-particles on gold foil he observed that few α-rays were deflected and very few α-rays re-bounded completely and most of the α-particles passed straight. Then, he concluded that nearly all mass of an atom is concentrated within the nucleus and most of the space in an atom is empty.

Long Answer (LA) Type Questions

1. (i) Which popular experiment is shown in the figure?
   (ii) List three observations of this experiment.
   (iii) State conclusions drawn from each observation of this experiment.
   (iv) State the model of the atom suggested on the basis of the experiment.

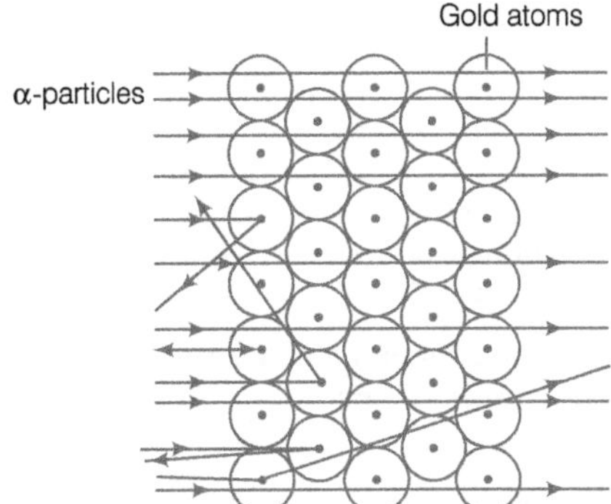

Sol. (i) This figure shows scattering of α-particles by a gold foil which is known as Rutherford's experiment or α-particle scattering experiment.
(ii) Refer to text on Pg 74.
(iii) Refer to text on Pg 75.
(iv) **Rutherford's atomic model** Refer to text on Pg 74-75.

2 (i) Describe Bohr's model of an atom. Draw a sketch of Bohr's model of an atom with three shells.
(ii) What was the drawback of Rutherford's model of an atom?

Sol. (i) Refer to text on Pg 75 and Ans. 5 on NCERT Folder on Pg 80.
(ii) Refer to text on Pg 75.

3 (i) What is an octet? How do elements attain an octet?
(ii) Make a schematic atomic structure of magnesium and phosphorus.
[Given number of protons of magnesium =12 and that of phosphorus = 15]

Sol. (i) An outermost shell, which has eight electrons is said to possess an octet. Elements attain their octet by sharing, gaining or losing electrons.
(ii) **Atomic structure of Mg**

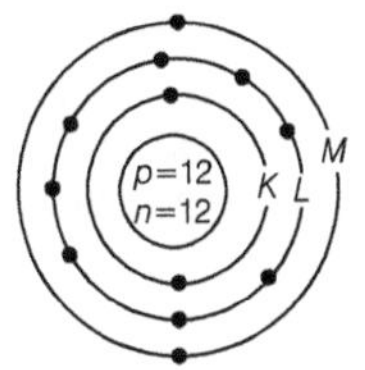

$$\begin{array}{l} \quad\;\; K\ L\ M \\ {}_{12}Mg = 2,\ 8,\ 2 \end{array}$$

Atomic structure of P

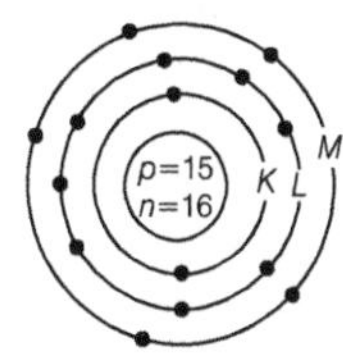

$$\begin{array}{l} \quad\;\; K\ L\ M \\ {}_{15}P = 2,\ 8,\ 5 \end{array}$$

4 (i) An element X has an atomic number = 12 and mass number = 26. Draw a diagram showing the distribution of electrons in the orbits and the nuclear composition of the neutral atom of the element. What is the valency of the element and why?
(ii) If this element X combines with another element Y whose electronic configuration is 2, 8, 7. What will be the formula of the compound thus formed? State how did you arrive at this formula.

Sol. (i) Atomic number = 12
Mass number = 26
Atomic structure of X

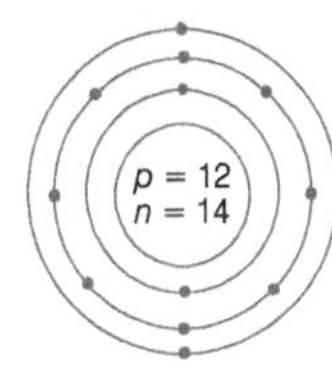

Electronic configuration = 2, 8, 2

Nuclear composition

Number of protons = 12

Number of neutrons = 26 − 12 = 14

Valency = 2

Because it can donate 2 electrons easily to complete its octet and become stable.

(ii) Valency of the element Y would be 1, i.e. it can gain 1 electron to become stable. When it combines with the element X of valency 2, the compound formed will be XY_2.

Element X Y

Valency +2 1

Formula of the compound would be XY_2.

5 (i) From Rutherford's α-particle scattering experiment, give the experimental evidence for deriving the conclusion that

(a) most of the space inside the atom is empty.

(b) the nucleus of an atom is positively charged.

(ii) An element has mass number = 32 and atomic number = 16, find

(a) the number of neutrons in the atom of the element.

(b) the number of electrons in the outermost shell of the atom.

(iii) On the basis of Rutherford's model of an atom, which subatomic particle is present in the nucleus of an atom?

Sol. (i) (a) As most of the α-particles passed straight through the gold foil.

(b) A few of the α-particles which are positively charged, deflected due to the positive charge of nucleus.

(ii) (a) Number of neutrons = Mass number − atomic number = 32 − 16 = 16

(b) The electronic configuration of the element will be as follows:

K	L	M
2	8	6

Hence, the number of electrons in outermost shell is 6.

(iii) According to Rutherford's model of an atom, positively charge protons are present in the nucleus of an atom.

6 (i) Write two differences between isotopes and isobars.

(ii) Write uses of Co-60 and U-235.

Sol. (i) Difference between isobars and isotopes:

Isotopes	Isobars
These are the atoms of the same element having same atomic number but different mass numbers.	These are the atoms of the different elements having same mass number but different atomic numbers.
They have identical chemical properties and different physical properties. e.g. ${}^1_1H$, ${}^2_1H$, ${}^3_1H$	They have different chemical properties and different physical properties because these are the atoms of different elements. e.g. ${}^{40}_{18}Ar$ and ${}^{40}_{20}Ca$

(ii) Isotope of cobalt (Co-60) is used in the treatment of cancer.

Isotope of uranium (U-235) is used as a fuel in nuclear reactor.

7 Number of electrons, protons and neutrons in chemical species A, B, C and D is given below.

Chemical species	Electrons	Protons	Neutrons
A	2	3	4
B	10	9	8
C	8	8	8
D	8	8	10

Now answer the following questions.

(i) What is the mass number of A and B?

(ii) What is the atomic number of B?

(iii) Which two chemical species represent a pair of isotopes and why?

(iv) What is the valency of element C?

Also justify your answers.

Sol. (i) Mass number of $A = 3 + 4 = 7$

Mass number of $B = 9 + 8 = 17$

(ii) Atomic number of B = Number of protons = 9

(iii) C and D are isotopes as they have same atomic numbers but different mass numbers.

(iv) Electronic configuration of C : K 2, L 6

It needs two electrons to complete its octet. Hence, its valency is 2.

CHAPTER EXERCISE

Multiple Choice Questions

1. The cathode ray experiment was done for the first time by
   (a) Goldstein (b) J. J. Thomson
   (c) Dalton (d) Rutherford

2. How many neutrons are present in the nucleus of hydrogen atom?
   (a) 1 (b) 2 (c) 3 (d) 0

3. Which of the following correctly represent the electronic distribution in the Mg atom ?
   (a) 3, 8, 1 (b) 2, 8, 2
   (c) 1, 8, 3 (d) 8, 2, 2

4. Number of valence electrons present in N^{3-} ion is
   (a) 16 (b) 10 (c) 7 (d) 4

5. The number of electrons in an element X is 15 and the number of neutrons is 16. Which of the following is the correct representation of the element?
   (a) ${}^{31}_{15}X$ (b) ${}^{31}_{16}X$ (c) ${}^{16}_{15}X$ (d) ${}^{15}_{16}X$

Fill in the Blanks

6. The orbits or shells are called ....
7. The mass number of an atom is equal to the number of......in its nucleus.

True and False

8. If the atomic shells are complete, then the atoms will be stable and less reactive.
9. Electrons could easily be removed off but not protons.

Match the Columns

10. Match the following Columns.

	Column A		Column B
P.	Protons	(i)	Number of positively charged particles in nucleus
Q.	Carbon-dating	(ii)	Positively charged particles
R.	Valence electrons	(iii)	Technique to know age of fossils.
S.	Atomic number	(iv)	Number of electrons in outermost shell.

	P	Q	R	S
(a)	(i)	(iii)	(iv)	(ii)
(b)	(ii)	(iv)	(iii)	(i)
(c)	(ii)	(iii)	(iv)	(i)
(d)	(iii)	(ii)	(i)	(iv)

Assertion-Reason

Direction (Q. Nos. 11-13) *In each of the following questions, a statement of Assertion is given by the corresponding statement of Reason. Of the statements, mark the correct answer as*

(a) Both Assertion and Reason are true and Reason is the correct explanation of Assertion.
(b) Both Assertion and Reason are true but Reason is not the correct explanationi of Assertion.
(c) Assertion is true but Reason is false.
(d) Assertion is false but Reason is true.

11. **Assertion** The valency of an atom of flourine is 7.
    Reason The number of electrons present in the outermost shell of an atom are known as the valence electrons.

12. **Assertion** Bohr's orbits are called stationary orbits.
    Reason Electrons remain stationary in these orbits for some time.

13. **Assertion** According to Bohr's model, the orbits of an atom are also called energy levels.
    Reason Orbits are the spheres containing definite value of energy.

Case Based Questions

Direction (Q. Nos. 14-17) *Answer the questions on the basis of your understanding of the following passage and related studied concepts:*

The maximum number of the electrons which are permitted to be assigned to an energy shell of an atom is called the electron capacity of that shell. The distribution of electrons in different orbits or shell is governed by a scheme known as Bohr-Bury scheme.

According to this scheme,

(*i*) the maximum number of electrons that can be present in any shell is given by the formula $2n^2$ where, n is the number of energy level.
(*ii*) the maximum number of electrons that can be accommodated in the outermost shell is 8.
Electrons are filled in the shells in a stepwise manner in increasing order of energy of the energy shell.

14 What is the maximum electron capacity of N-shell?
(a) 24 (b) 8
(c) 18 (d) 32

15 Which of the following have same valency $A(2,8,2), B(2,8,4), C(2,6), D(2,8)$?
(a) A and B
(b) B and C
(c) A and C
(d) C and D

16 Arrange the following shells in increasing order of their energy : K, L, M, N

17 Identify the element with following configuration:
$$K\text{-}2, L\text{-}8, M\text{-}3$$

Answers

1. (b)	2. (d)	3. (b)	4. (b)
5. (a)	6. Energy level		
7. Nucleons	8. True	9. True	10. (c)

Very Short Answer Type Questions

18 Does the nucleus contain neutrons also?

19 An element X has 5 electrons in its M-shell. What is its atomic number?

20 Give the number of neutrons in an atom of the element $^{107}_{47}Ag$.

21 If an atom of an element has atomic number = 15 and mass number = 31, find the number of protons, electrons, neutrons in its atoms.

22 How are the following pairs of atoms related?
$$_8X^{16}, {}_8X^{17}, {}_{18}Y^{40}, {}_{20}Z^{40}$$

Short Answer (SA) Type Questions

23 Describe the essential properties of the atomic nucleus. Compare these with the properties of electron.

24 The electronic configurations of some elements are given below. Name the elements.
(i) 2, 8, 5 (ii) 2, 8, 8, 2
(iii) 2, 8, 1

25 An atom X has 4 protons and 5 neutrons with electronic configuration 2, 2.
Give information about its
(i) atomic number (ii) mass number
(iii) valency

26 The number of neutrons and protons present in the nuclei of two atomic species A and B are given below.

Atomic Species	A	B
Protons	8	8
Neutrons	8	10

(i) Write the mass numbers of A and B.
(ii) What is the relation between two species?
(iii) Write the electronic configuration of atoms A and B.

27 What information do you get from the figure given below about the atomic number, mass number and valency of atom X?

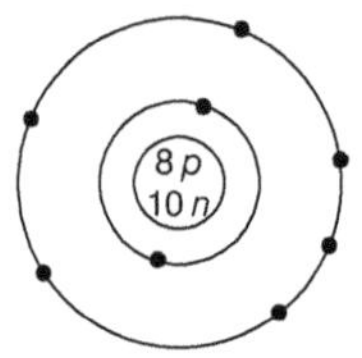

28 The atomic number and the mass number of certain elements are given below in the table.

Element	A	B	C	D	E	F
Atomic number	1	3	8	18	20	1
Mass number	2	7	16	40	40	1

(i) Select a pair of isobar and isotope from the above table.
(ii) What would be the valency of elements B and E?

Long Answer (LA) Type Questions

29 What are the features and drawbacks of Rutherford's nuclear model of an atom?

30 (i) How did discovery of protons take place?
(ii) Why do helium, neon and argon have zero valency?

31 (i) What are inert elements? Why are they called so?
(ii) What is the valency of these elements and why?
(iii) How many electrons can be accommodated in a M and N-shell?

32 Explain Bohr and Bury rules for distribution of electrons into different shells.

RELATED ONLINE VIDEOS

Visit https://www.youtube.com/watch?v=kBgIMRV895w OR **Scan the Code**
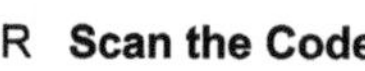

Visit https://www.youtube.com/watch?v=u7xrDhpY-oA OR **Scan the Code**

Visit https://www.youtube.com/watch?v=fm2C0ovz-3M OR **Scan the Code**

Visit https://www.youtube.com/watch?v=Awxcl-RwWsk OR **Scan the Code**

Challengers*

1 In the Thomson's model of atom, which of the following statements are correct?

(i) The mass of the atom is assumed to be uniformly distributed over the atom.

(ii) The positive charge is assumed to be uniformly distributed over the atom.

(iii) The electrons are uniformly distributed in the positively charged sphere.

(iv) The electrons attract each other to stabilise the atom. NCERT Exemplar

(a) (i), (ii) and (iii)
(b) (i) and (iii)
(c) (i) and (iv)
(d) (i), (iii) and (iv)

2 The atomic number of an element is 13 and its mass, mass number is 27. The correct order representing the number of electrons, protons and neutrons respectively in this atom is

(a) 13, 13, 14 (b) 14, 13, 13
(c) 27, 13, 13 (d) 27, 14, 13

3 The following diagram depicts the Rutherford's experiment.

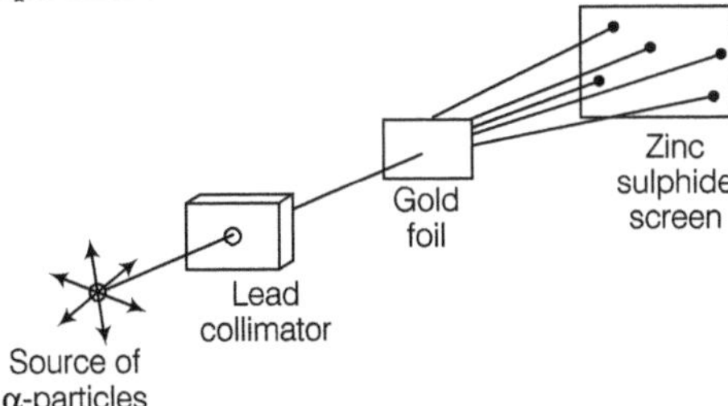

Why was zinc sulphide screen is used in the experiment?

(a) To block α-particles from going straight.
(b) To detect deflection of α-particles.
(c) To further deflect α-particles as the gold foil did.
(d) To absorb α-particles and utilise it again.

4 Atomic models have been improved over the years. Arrange the following atomic models in the order of their chronological order.

(i) Rutherford's atomic model
(ii) Thomson's atomic model
(iii) Bohr's atomic model NCERT Exemplar

(a) (i), (ii) and (iii) (b) (ii), (iii) and (i)
(c) (ii), (i) and (iii) (d) (iii), (ii) and (i)

5 Which of the following are true for an element?

(i) Atomic number = Number of protons + number of electrons

(ii) Mass number = Number of protons + number of neutrons

(iii) Atomic mass = Number of protons = Number of neutrons

(iv) Atomic number = Number of protons = Number of electrons

NCERT Exemplar

(a) (i) and (ii) (b) (i) and (iii)
(c) (ii) and (iii) (d) (ii) and (iv)

6 The number of electrons in an element *X* is 18 and the number of neutrons is 22. Which of the following is the correct representation of the element? NCERT Exemplar

(a) ${}^{22}_{18}X$ (b) ${}^{40}_{22}X$
(c) ${}^{22}_{40}X$ (d) ${}^{18}_{22}X$

7 Different isotopes are matched with their uses as

(i) Co-60-To treat cancer
(ii) U-238-To produce electricity
(iii) I-131-To treat goitre
(iv) Na-24-In agricultural research

Which of the above matches are correct?

(a) (i) and (ii) (b) (ii) and (iii)
(c) (iii) and (iv) (d) (i) and (iii)

8 In a sample of ethyl ethanoate ($CH_3COOC_2H_5$) the two oxygen atoms have the same number of electrons but different number of neutrons. Which of the following is the correct reason for it? NCERT Exemplar

(a) One of the oxygen atoms has gained electrons.
(b) One of the oxygen atoms has gained two neutrons.
(c) The two oxygen atoms are isotopes.
(d) The two oxygen atoms are isobars.

Answer Key

1.	(a)	2.	(a)	3.	(b)	4.	(c)	5.	(d)
6.	(a)	7.	(d)	8.	(c)				

These questions may be or may not be asked in the examination, have been given just for additional practice.

CHAPTER

05

The Fundamental Unit of Life

All organisms including plants and animals are composed of cells. Each and every cell arises from pre-existing cell. These cells become specialised to perform different specialised functions after division. Cell is the basic fundamental, structural and functional unit of living organisms. In this chapter, we will study about the complex structure of a cell, its various cell organelles and their functioning inside the cell.

Chapter Checklist

- Discovery of Cell
- Cellular Composition in Different Organisms
- Structural Organisation of a Cell
- Cell Organelles

Discovery of Cell

Robert Hooke (in 1665), examined a thin slice of cork under the primitive microscope. He observed that cork consists of small box-like structures resembling honeycomb. He called these boxes **cells.** The substance called **cork** comes from the bark of a tree. Cell is a Latin word for 'a little room'. Basic characteristics of cells are as follows:

(*i*) They have the ability to replicate independently.

(*ii*) They contain hereditary information.

(*iii*) They can perform all the life sustaining activities on their own.

(*iv*) They show similar chemical composition and metabolic activities.

Major Landmarks Related to Cell Discovery

Scientist	Year	Work
Robert Hooke	1665	Discovered cells for first time in cork slice with the help of a primitive microscope.
Leeuwenhoek	1674	Discovered free-living cells in pond water using an improved microscope.
Robert Brown	1831	Discovered nucleus in cell.
Schleiden and Schwann	1838-1839	Presented cell theory, which states that all plants and animals are composed of cells and they are the basic unit of life.
Purkinje	1839	Coined the term 'protoplasm' for the fluid substance of cell.
Virchow	1855	Expanded the cell theory by suggesting that all cells arise from pre-existing cells.

Cellular Composition in Different Organisms

On the basis of the number of cells present in different organisms, they are classified into two types:

(*i*) Unicellular organisms (having single cell)

(*ii*) Multicellular organisms (having many cells).

Every multicellular organism starts its life as a single cell (i.e. zygote), which divides and forms many cells. All cells thus, come from pre-existing cells.

The invention of magnifying lenses made the discovery of single-celled microscopic organisms possible.

Differences between Unicellular and Multicellular Organisms

Unicellular Organism	Multicellular Organism
A single cell constitutes the whole organism.	Multiple cells are grouped together in a single body which assume different functions in the body to form various body parts.
There is no division of labour in prokaryotic unicellular organism, but it may be seen within the cell of eukaryotic organism.	All cells are specialised to perform different functions of the multicellular body so that there is a division of labour within a single cell as well as in group of cells.
e.g. *Amoeba*, *Chlamydomonas*, *Paramecium*, bacteria etc.	e.g. fungi, plants, animals including humans etc.

Microscopes

- These are high resolution instruments. They are used for observing the fine details of very minute objects, e.g. cells. With the help of a microscope, the size of a small cell can be magnified upto 300-1500 times. A simple microscope, which is often used in schools is compound microscope. It uses sunlight for illumination of objects to be seen, so it is called as light microscope.
- An electron microscope is used to observe complex internal structures of the cell.

Shape and Size of Cells

- Some cells have fixed shape (e.g. most plant and animal cells), while some cells like WBCs and *Amoeba* keep changing their shapes. Fixed shaped cells may be of various types like elliptical (e.g. fat cell), spherical (e.g. ovum), spindle-shaped (e.g. smooth muscle cell), knobbed thread (e.g. sperm), discoidal (e.g. RBC), elongated (e.g. nerve cell), etc.

Following figures depict some cells from the human body:

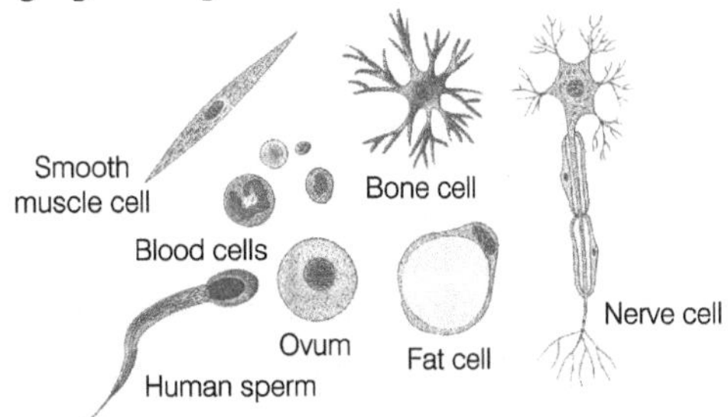

Various cells from the human body

- The size of cell varies significantly from the smallest cell of *Mycoplasma* (0.1-0.5 μm) to very large egg cells of the Ostrich (18 cm). Longest cells of human body are the nerve cells, which may reach upto a length of 90 cm. (motor neurons)

Functions of Cells

Each living cell has the capacity to perform some basic functions that characterise the living organisms.

(*i*) The shape and size of cells are related to the specific function they perform.

(*ii*) Multicellular organisms like human beings perform these functions by division of labour. Different parts of human body are specialised to perform different functions. For example, heart is made to pump blood, stomach to digest food, kidney to filter blood to make urine etc.

(*iii*) Division of labour is also seen within a single cell. Every cell possesses certain specific components known as **cell organelles**. These enable it to survive and perform special functions.

(*iv*) Cell organelles together along with protoplasm constitute the basic unit of life called the cell. Each kind of cell organelle performs a specific function. For example, obtaining nutrition, respiration, clearing waste material or forming new progeny. Mitochondria is the organelle responsible for providing energy to the cell.

Note Some cellular organelles are found in all the cells regardless of their function and the type of organism in which they are found.

Check Point 01

1. The free-living cells were first observed by ....
2. Give name of two organisms each that are
   (*i*) Unicellular (*ii*) Multicellular
3. Name the two cells which can change their shape.
4. Which is the longest cell in human body?
5. State True or False for the following statement:
   In unicellular organisms a single cell gets specialised to perform all body functions.

Structural Organisation of a Cell

Microscopic studies revealed that every cell possesses three basic features in common, i.e. plasma membrane, nucleus and cytoplasm. Due to the presence of these features, all activities inside the cell and interaction of the cell with its environment are possible.

Plasma Membrane or Cell Membrane

This is the outermost living, thin and delicate covering of cell. It separates the contents of the cell from its external environment.

Presence of lipids (as phospholipids) and proteins provides flexibility to plasma membrane. It enables cell to engulf food and other materials from external environment. This process is called **endocytosis,** e.g. *Amoeba* acquires food through this process, with the help of finger-like projections called **pseudopodia.**

Functions of Plasma Membrane

(*i*) It allows the entry and exit of some selective materials in and out of the cell. The cell membrane therefore, acts as semipermeable, selectively permeable, partially permeable and differentially permeable membrane.

(*ii*) It helps to maintain the shape of the cell.

(*iii*) It acts as a mechanical barrier and protects the internal contents of the cell from leaking out.

(*iv*) It provides protection against microbes and foreign substances.

(*v*) It gets modified to perform different functions, e.g. microvilli in intestine of human beings for absorption.

(*vi*) Its semipermeability enables the cell to maintain cellular homeostasis.

Amongst all the functions listed above, the transport of substances is the most important function.

It may take place with expenditure of energy (active transport) and without the expenditure of energy (passive transport).

Transport Across the Membrane

Plasma membrane perform certain physical activities such as diffusion and osmosis for the intake of some substance.

These are discussed below

1. Transport Across the Membrane by Diffusion

The spontaneous movement of a substance (solid, liquid or gas) from a region of its higher concentration to a region of its lower concentration is called **diffusion.**

For example, CO_2 (cellular waste, which needs to be excreted out) accumulates in higher concentration inside the cell. In the cell's external environment, the concentration of CO_2 is lowered compared to inside of the cell.

Due to this difference in the concentration, CO_2 moves out of the cell by the process of diffusion. Similarly, O_2 enters the cell by the process of diffusion, when the level or concentration of O_2 inside the cell decreases.

Diffusion is faster in the gases than in liquids and solids. It plays an important role in gaseous exchange between the cells and also between the cell and its external environment.

In addition to gaseous exchange, diffusion also helps an organism in obtaining nutrition from the environment.

2. Transport Across the Membrane by Osmosis

The movement of water molecules through a selectively permeable membrane along the concentration gradient is called **osmosis.** The movement of water across the plasma membrane is also affected by the amount of substance dissolved in water.

Osmosis is thus, also defined as the movement of water molecules from a region of its higher concentration to a region of lower concentration through a semipermeable membrane. Unicellular freshwater organisms and most plant cells tend to gain water through osmosis.

Absorption of water by plant roots is also an example of osmosis. The process of osmosis can be seen in a cell placed in solution of different concentrations (such as hypotonic, isotonic and hypertonic).

(*i*) **Hypotonic Solution** The medium or solution surrounding the cell has high water concentration as compared to inside of the cell (or the outside solution is very diluted).

The cell gain water and swell up *via* endosmosis. This happens because the water molecules are free to pass through the cell membrane in both directions. More water however enters the cell than that leaving it.

(*ii*) **Isotonic Solution** The medium surrounding a cell has same concentration of water as that present inside the cell.

Water crosses the cell membrane in both directions, but the amount moving in remains the same as the amount moving out. So, there is no overall movement of water. As a result, no overall change is observed and the cell size remains the same.

(*iii*) **Hypertonic Solution** The medium surrounding a cell has a lower concentration of water than the cell (i.e. outside solution is very concentrated).

Water crosses the cell membrane in both directions, but this time more water leaves the cell than enters it. As a result, the cell protoplasm gets shrinked (exosmosis).

Cell Wall

It is a tough, non-living covering outside the plasma membrane. It is found in plant and fungal cells. It is freely permeable. It is mainly made up of cellulose, a complex carbohydrate that provides structural strength to plants.

Functions of Cell Wall

(*i*) Cell wall permits the cells of plants, fungi and bacteria to withstand hypotonic conditions without bursting.

In hypotonic media, the cells tend to take up water by osmosis. The cell swells up, building up pressure against the cell wall. The wall exerts an equal pressure against the swollen cell. Cell wall help plant cells to tolerate greater changes in surrounding medium. It is absent in animal cells.

(*ii*) It has narrow pores, called **pits**. Through them, fine strands of cytoplasm (or cytoplasmic bridges) called **plasmodesmata** are able to cross the cell walls. Plant cells interact with each other through these cytoplasmic channels.

Plasmolysis

It is the phenomenon, in which a living plant cell losses water through osmosis when kept in hypertonic solution. In this process there is either the shrinkage or contraction of protoplasm away from the cell wall.

Check Point 02

1 Fill in the blank:

.... molecules contribute to the flexibility exhibited by the plasma membrane.

2 State True or False for the following statement:

Plasma membrane is a permeable membrane.

3 Name the process by which CO_2 is removed from the cell.

4 Apart from gaseous exchange, how is diffusion important for organisms?

5 Which component of plant cell provides the structural strength to it?

Nucleus

It is popularly called as the **brain of cell**. It is composed of a double layered covering called **head nuclear membrane**. It has numerous pores called **nuclear pores**. They transfer the materials from inside the nucleus to cytoplasm.

The nucleus contains **chromosomes**. When they are visible as rod-shaped structures only when the cell is about to divide. It encloses a liquid ground substance called **nucleoplasm**. It contains nucleolus and chromatin material.

Nucleolus is a more or less round structure found inside the nucleus. It does not have covering of membranes. It is known as factory of ribosomes.

Chromatin is an entangled network of long, thread-like structures. It condenses to form chromosomes during cell division.

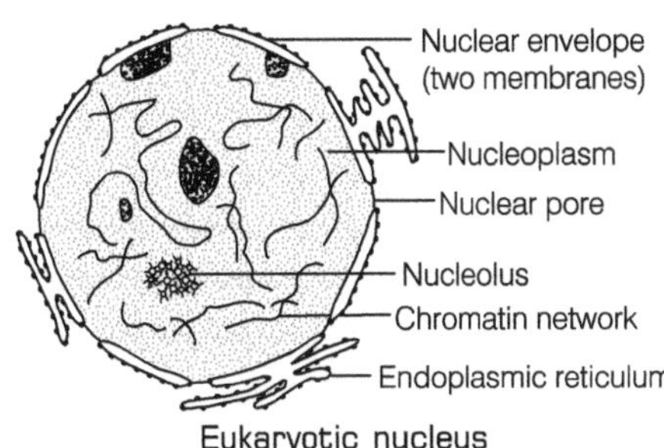

Eukaryotic nucleus

Chromosomes contain information for the inheritance of features from parents to next generation in the form of **DNA** (Deoxyribonucleic Acid). Chromosomes are composed of two components, i.e. DNA and protein. The DNA molecules contain information necessary for constructing and organising cells. The functional segments of DNA are called **genes**.

Nucleus also contains RNA that directs protein synthesis.

In some organisms like bacteria, the nuclear region of the cell is poorly defined because of the absence of nuclear membrane. The nuclear region in these organisms contains only nucleic acid. Such an undefined nuclear region is called **nucleoid**.

Functions of Nucleus

(*i*) Nucleus plays an important role in cellular reproduction. In this process, a cell divides to form two new cells.

(*ii*) It determines the cell development and maturity by directing the chemical activities of the cell.

(*iii*) It helps in the transmission of hereditary traits from parents to offsprings.

(*iv*) It controls all metabolic activities of cell. If it is removed, the protoplasm dries up.

Prokaryotic and Eukaryotic Cell

Organisms whose cells lack a nuclear membrane are called **prokaryotes** (*pro* = primitive, *karyote* ≈ karyon = nucleus).

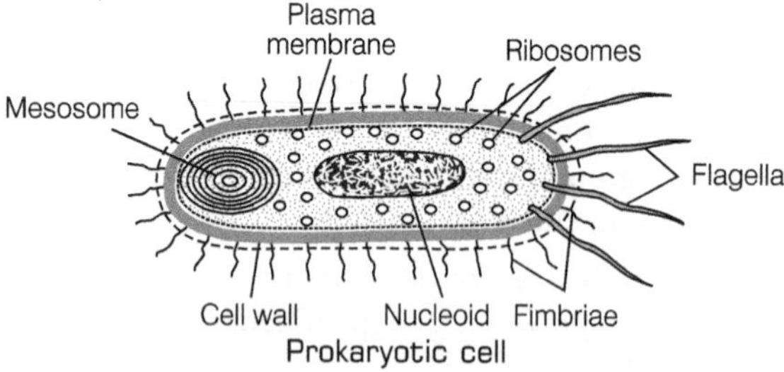

Prokaryotic cell

Prokaryotes also lack cytoplasmic organelles. Most functions are thus performed by poorly developed parts of cytoplasm. For example, the chlorophyll in photosynthetic prokaryotic bacteria is associated with membrane vesicles or lamellar structures. Plastids are not observed in it as in photosynthetic eukaryotes. The organisms with cells having a well-defined nucleus enclosed in nuclear membrane are called **eukaryotes.** Eukaryotic cells are further categorised into plant and animal cells. These are also different from each other in many ways.

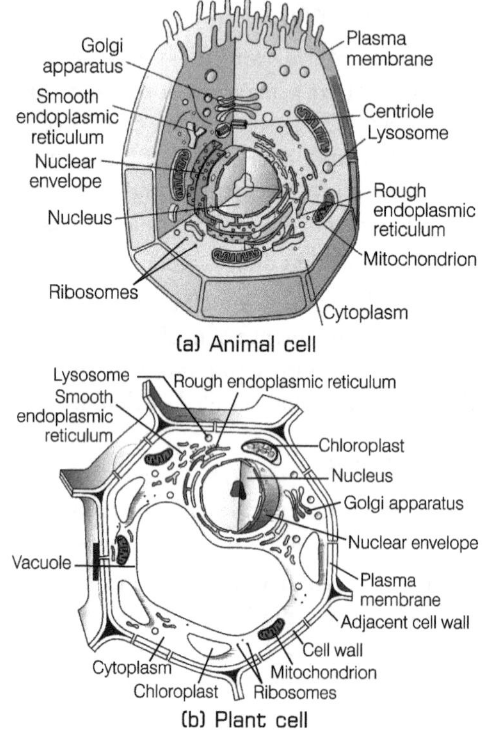

(a) Animal cell

(b) Plant cell

Differences between Prokaryotic and Eukaryotic Cells

Feature	Prokaryotic cell	Eukaryotic cell
Size	Generally small (1-10 μm).	Generally large (5-100 μm).
Nuclear region	Poorly developed, no nuclear membrane and called as nucleoid.	Well-defined, surrounded by nuclear membrane.
Chromosome	Single	More than one
Nucleolus	Absent	Present
Membrane-bound cell organelles	Absent	Present, e.g. mitochondria, plastids, endoplasmic reticulum etc.
Centriole	Absent	Present in animal cells.
Organisms	Found in bacteria, blue-green algae etc.	Found in fungi, plants and animals.
Cell division	Takes place by binary fission and budding.	Takes place by mitotic and meiotic cell division.

Cytoplasm

The large region of each cell enclosed by cell membrane is called **cytoplasm.** It is the fluid content present inside the plasma membrane. It contains many specialised cell organelles, each of which performs a specific function for the cell.

Functions of Cytoplasm

(*i*) It helps in the exchange of material between cell organelles.

(*ii*) It acts as a storehouse of vital molecules such as amino acid, glucose, vitamin, iron etc.

(*iii*) It acts as the site for certain metabolic pathways such as glycolysis etc.

Note **Protoplasm** It is the living content of a cell. It consists of the cytoplasm and nucleoplasm.

Check Point 03

1 State True or False for the following statement:
The role of nuclear pores in a cell is to maintain continuity with cytoplasm.

2 What are genes? Where are they located?

3 Fill in the blank:
The ……… present in nucleus directs the synthesis of cellular proteins.

4 How do prokaryotic cells reproduce? Name two prokaryotes.

5 Give one significance of cytoplasm in a eukaryotic cell.

Cell Organelles

Large and complex cells need a lot of chemical activities to support their complicated structure and function. To keep these activities separated from each other, these cells use membrane-bound structures. These structures perform specialised functions within themselves and called **cell organelles**. This is the main characteristic feature that differentiates eukaryotic cells from prokaryotic cells.

Endoplasmic Reticulum (ER)

It is a large network of membrane-bound tubes and sheets. It extends from outer nuclear membrane into the cytoplasm. It looks like long tubules round and oblong bags (vesicles). The ER membrane is similar in structure to the plasma membrane.It occurs in three forms, i.e. cisternae, vesicles and tubules. Depending upon nature of its membrane, ER is of two types:

(*i*) **Rough Endoplasmic Reticulum** (RER) It contains ribosomal particles on its surfaces due to which its surface is rough. The ribosomes are the site of protein synthesis. RER is mainly formed of cisternae.

(*ii*) **Smooth Endoplasmic Reticulum** (SER) It's surface is smooth due to the absence of ribosomes. It helps in manufacture of fat molecules or lipids. It is formed of vesicles and tubules. ER appears in varying forms in different cells. It always form a network system of vesicles and tubules and forms is cytoskeleton in cytoplasm.

Functions of Endoplasmic Reticulum

(*i*) Ribosomes present in all active cells act as sites for protein synthesis. Proteins manufactured here are transported throughout the cell by endoplasmic reticulum.

(*ii*) Fat and lipid molecules manufactured by SER helps in building cell membrane and other cell components. This process is called **membrane biogenesis.**

(*iii*) Some other proteins and lipids synthesised by ER function as enzymes and hormones.

(*iv*) SER plays a crucial role in **detoxification** of poisons and drugs in liver cells of vertebrates (group of animals).

(*v*) It forms a network system, providing channels for the transport of materials especially proteins. It transports between various regions of the cytoplasm or between the cytoplasm and the nucleus mainly.

(*vi*) It functions as cytoplasmic framework. It provide a surface for some of the biochemical activities of the cell.

(*vii*) It gives mechanical support to the cells.

Golgi Apparatus

It consists of a system of membrane-bound, fluid-filled **vesicles**, large spherical **vacuoles** and smooth, flattened **cisternae.** These are stacked parallel to each other. Each of these stacks is called a **cistern.** The Golgi apparatus (or dictyosomes) arises from the membrane of smooth ER. Therefore, it constitutes another portion of a complex cellular membrane system. The material that is synthesised near Endoplasmic Reticulum (ER) is packaged and dispatched to various parts of the cell through Golgi apparatus.

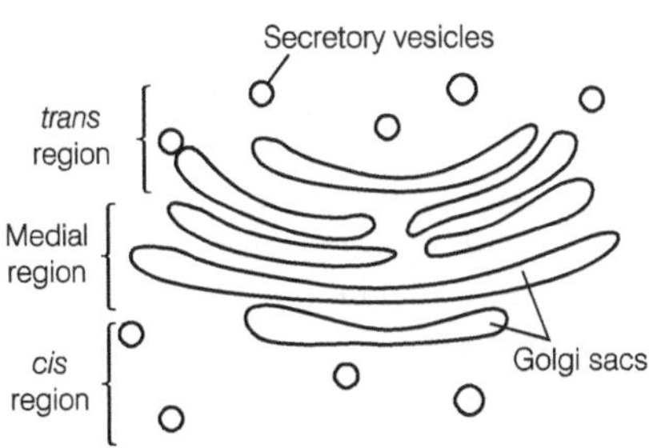

Ultrastructure of Golgi apparatus

Functions of Golgi Apparatus

(*i*) Golgi apparatus stores, modifies and packs products in vesicles.

(*ii*) It is involved in the formation of **lysosomes.**

(*iii*) It forms complex sugars from simple sugars in some cases.

(*iv*) It is involved in the synthesis of cell wall and plasma membrane.

Note
- The scientist, who described Golgi apparatus for the first time was Camillo Golgi. Most of his investigations were concerned with the nervous system. His greatest work was a revolutionary method of staining individual nerve and cell structures. This method is called 'black reaction'.
- It uses silver nitrate solution to trace most delicate ramification of cells. He shared the Nobel Prize in 1906 with Santiago Ramón y Cajal for their work on the structure of nervous system.

Lysosomes

These are a kind of waste disposal system of the cell. Lysosomes are membrane-bound sacs that are filled with digestive enzymes. These enzymes are made by rough endoplasmic reticulum. Lysosomes are also called the **suicidal bags** of a cell. During the disturbance in cellular metabolism or when the cell gets damaged, lysosomes may burst and the enzymes can digest their own cell. They are absent in RBCs.

Functions of Lysosomes

(*i*) They help to keep the cell clean by digesting any foreign material that enters the cell as well as worn out cellular organelles. Hence, called **scavengers** and **cellular housekeepers.**

(*ii*) They remove foreign material by breaking it into small pieces through its powerful digestive enzymes.These enzymes can breakdown all organic materials.

(*iii*) During starvation, the lysosomes digest stored food contents by autophagy and supply energy to the cell.

Mitochondria

These were first observed by **Kölliker** in 1880. It is a **double membrane** bounded cell organelle. The outer membrane is very porous. The inner membrane is deeply folded into finger-like projections called **cristae.** It creates large surface area for ATP generating chemical reactions.

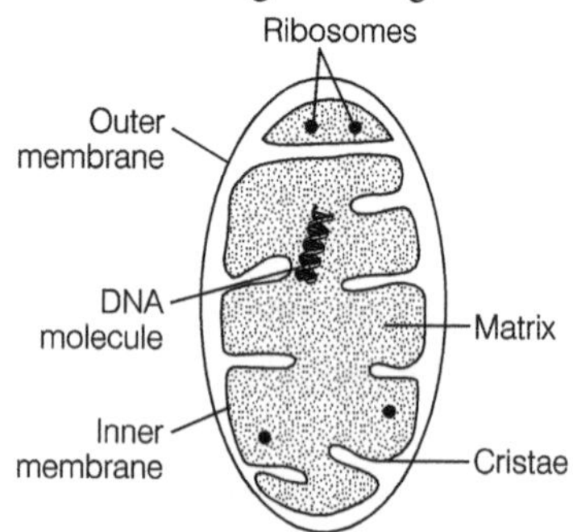

Internal structure of mitochondria

Space between outer and inner membrane is called **intermembranous space.** Mitochondrion is self-replicating (**semiautonomous**) organelle. It is the largest organelle in animal cells.

Functions of Mitochondria

(*i*) It generates energy for various activities of cell. It is known as the **power house of the cell.** Mitochondria are sites of cellular respiration. They release energy required by the cell in the form of ATP (Adenosine Triphosphate). This ATP is known as **energy currency** of the cell.

(*ii*) Whenever, the cell requires energy, ATP molecule breaks down. It generate energy to be used for metabolic activities of the body.

(*iii*) Mitochondria are strange organelles in the sense that they have their own DNA and ribosomes. Hence, they are able to make some of their own proteins.

(*iv*) They provide intermediates for the synthesis of various chemicals like fatty acids, steroids, amino acids etc.

Plastids

These are found only in plant cells. The internal organisation of plastids contains numerous membrane layers embedded in a material called the **stroma.** Plastids are similar to mitochondria in external structure. They are double layered. They contain their own DNA and ribosomes.

Types of Plastids

Plastids are of three types

(*i*) **Chloroplasts** These are the plastids containing chlorophyll (a green pigment). They give green colour to the plant. Chloroplasts also contain various yellow or orange pigments in addition to chlorophyll. It is a semiautonomous organelle. Chloroplasts are also known as the **kitchen of cells.**

Function These are important for photosynthesis in plants.

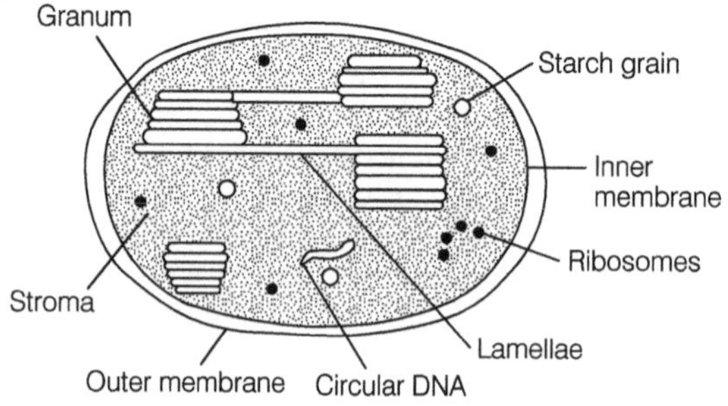

Internal structure of chloroplast

Note Photosynthetic bacteria do not contain chloroplasts. They contain light absorbing pigments and reaction centres, which make them capable of converting light energy into chemical energy.

(*ii*) **Leucoplasts** These are the white or colourless plastids. They can change into other types of plastids.

Function Leucoplasts store materials such as starch (amyloplasts), oils (elaioplasts) and protein granules (aleuroplasts).

(*iii*) **Chromoplasts** These are coloured plastids (except green).

Function Chromoplasts impart colour to flowers and fruits. They are rich in **carotenoid pigments** and **lipids.**

Vacuoles

These are the storage sacs for solid or liquid contents. In animal cells, vacuoles are small-sized, but in plants, the vacuoles are large-sized. Some may occupy 50-90% of the total cell volume. The vacuole is bounded by a membrane called **tonoplast.**

Functions of Vacuoles

(*i*) Vacuoles are full of cell sap and provide turgidity and rigidity to cells in plants.

(*ii*) Many substances like amino acids, sugars, organic acids and proteins are stored in vacuoles.

(*iii*) In *Amoeba*, consumed food items are stored in food vacuoles.

(*iv*) In some unicellular organisms, vacuoles also play an important role in expelling excess water and some wastes from the cell.

Cell Division

New cells are formed in an organism in order to grow, replace cells (old, dead, injured) and form gametes during sexual reproduction.

Cell division is a process of formation of new cells from the pre-existing cells. These are of two types

1. Mitosis or Mitotic Cell Division

This occurs for growth of organisms and to replace old, dead or injured cells. The dividing cells are called mother cells which form two identical daughter cells.

Each daughter cell has same chromosome number as that of mother cell.

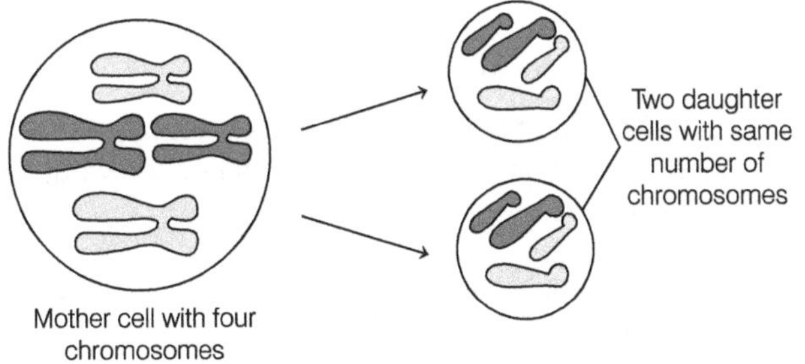

2. Meiosis or Meiotic cell division

This occurs in the sex organs of sexually reproducing cells. The gametes are formed by this kind of cell division. The male and female gamete unit to form zygote after fertilisation give rise to offspring.

When a cell divides by meiosis, it produces four new cells instead of just two.

The process of meiosis occurs in two stages, i.e. meiosis-I and meiosis-II. In meiosis-I, the germ cells divide into two daughter cells which have only half number of chromosomes in comparison to mother germ cells. In contrast to meiosis-I, meiosis-II resembles a normal mitosis.

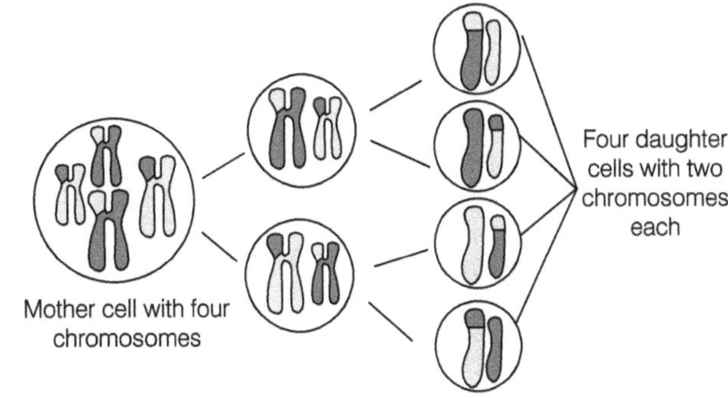

Check Point 04

1. Identify the site for protein synthesis in a cell.
2. What is the role of SER in liver cells of vertebrates?
3. Which organelle constitutes the network of complex cellular membrane system in living cells?
4. Fill in the blank:

   Lysosomes are known to digest stored food during starnation through process called ....
5. Comment on the similarity between mitochondria and plastids? Any two.
6. Name the organelle, which acts as storage sacs of the cell.

To Study NCERT Activities

Visit https://goo.gl/qAy6hm OR **Scan the Code**

NCERT FOLDER

Intext Questions

1 Who discovered cells and how? **Pg 59**

Sol. Cells were discovered by Robert Hooke in 1665. He observed cells in a cork slice with the help of a primitive microscope. The cork slice resembled the structure of a honeycomb consisting of many small compartments or box like structures. Hooke called these boxes as cells.

2 Why is the cell called the structural and functional unit of life? **Pg 59**

Sol. All living organisms are made up of cells, which perform various functions essential for survival of the organisms, e.g. respiration, digestion, excretion etc. Thus, cell is the functional unit of life.

In unicellular organisms, a single cell carries out all the functions, while in multicellular organisms, group of cells carry out different functions. Thus, cell is the structural and functional unit of all living organisms.

3 How do substances like CO_2 and water move in and out of the cell? Discuss. **Pg 61**

Sol. CO_2 and other gases move in and out of the cell by the process of diffusion. When the concentration of carbon dioxide is more inside the cell than outside, CO_2 diffuses out of the cell. If CO_2 concentration inside the cell is less, CO_2 moves inside the cell from outside.

The water moves in and out of the cell by the process of osmosis. Osmosis is the diffusion of water from a region of its high concentration to low concentration through a semipermeable membrane.

4 Why is the plasma membrane called a selectively permeable membrane? **Pg 61**

Sol. The plasma membrane is called a selectively permeable membrane because it allows entry and exit of some selected molecules only through the cells. It also prevents movement of some other materials.

5 How is a prokaryotic cell different from a eukaryotic cell? **Pg 66**

Or

Fill in the gaps in the following table illustrating differences between prokaryotic and eukaryotic cells. **Pg 63**

Sol.

Prokaryotic Cell	Eukaryotic Cell
Size: generally small (1-10 μm) 1 μm = 10^{-6}m	Size : generally large (5-100 μm)
Nuclear region: poorly defined and known as nucleoid	Nuclear region: well-defined and surrounded by a nuclear membrane.
Chromosome: single.	More than one chromosome.
Membrane bound cell organelles are absent.	Membrane bound cell organelles are present.

6 Can you name two organelles we have studied that contain their own genetic material? **Pg 65**

Sol. Mitochondria and plastids are the two cell organelles that contain their own genetic material.

7 If the organisation of a cell is destroyed due to some physical or chemical influence, what will happen? **Pg 65**

Sol. Living cells are capable of performing certain basic functions due to the presence of cell organelles present in it. If these are destroyed then cell will not be able to work properly and will die after sometime.

8 Why are lysosomes known as suicidal bags? **Pg 65**

Sol. Lysosomes contain powerful digestive enzymes. During the disturbance in cellular metabolism, lysosomes may burst and digest their own cell. Therefore, they are called suicidal bags of the cell.

9 Where are proteins synthesised inside the cell? **Pg 65**

Sol. Ribosomes are the site of protein synthesis inside the cell.

Exercises (On Pages 66 and 67)

1 Make a comparison and write down ways, in which plant cells are different from animal cells.

Sol. **Comparison of Plant Cell and Animal Cell**

Plant Cell	Animal Cell
Cell wall is present outside the plasma membrane.	Cell wall is absent.
Generally regular in shape.	Generally irregular in shape.
Larger in size than animal cells.	Smaller in size than plant cells.
Plastids are present.	Plastids are absent in all except *Euglena*.
A permanent and large vacuole is present.	Vacuoles are many, small and temporary.
Many simple units of Golgi apparatus called dictyosome are present.	A single, highly complex and prominent Golgi apparatus is present.

2 What would happen if the plasma membrane ruptures or breaks down?

Sol. In case plasma membrane ruptures or breaks down,

(*i*) all the useful substances will move out of the cell because membrane is selectively permeable.

(*ii*) the transportation of materials will be disturbed.

(*iii*) the cell will loose its normal shape.

(*iv*) this may lead ultimately to the death of the cell.

3 What would happen to the life of a cell if there was no Golgi apparatus?

Sol. Effects of the absence of Golgi apparatus on life of a cell are as follows:

(*i*) The packaging and dispatching of different types of proteins to various targets inside and outside the cell will be influenced.

(*ii*) The products of cell cannot be stored and modified later.

(*iii*) This will affect the lysosomes formation. This will cause accumulation of worn out and dead cell organelles within the cell, which may cause cell death.

4 Which organelle is known as the powerhouse of the cell? Why?

Sol. Mitochondria are called powerhouse of the cell. It contains oxidative enzymes, which oxidise the food and convert it into energy currency of the cell in the form of ATP (Adenosine Triphosphate). This energy is used by body for making new chemical compounds and for doing other works. This is the reason, mitochondria are called powerhouse of the cell.

5 Where do the lipids and proteins constituting the cell membrane get synthesised?

Sol. The synthesis of lipids occurs in Smooth Endoplasmic Reticulum (SER). The proteins are synthesised in the ribosomes, which are attached to the Rough Endoplasmic Reticulum (RER).

6 How does *Amoeba* obtain its food?

Sol. *Amoeba* obtains its food through endocytosis. It is the process of ingestion of food through the plasma membrane. This occurs due to flexibility of plasma membrane, which enables the *Amoeba* to engulf food and other materials from surroundings.

7 What is osmosis?

Sol. Osmosis is a process of diffusion of water from a region of its higher concentration to a region of lower concentration through a semipermeable membrane.

8 Carry out the following osmosis experiment: Take four peeled potato halves and scoop each one out to make potato cups. One of these potato cups should be made from a boiled potato. Put each potato cup in a trough containing water. Now,

(*i*) keep cup *A* empty

(*ii*) put one tea spoon sugar in cup *B*.

(*iii*) put one tea spoon salt in cup *C*.

(*iv*) put one tea spoon sugar in the boiled potato cup *D*.

Keep them for two hours. Then observe the four potato cups and answer the following:

(*i*) Explain, why water gathers in the hollowed portion of *B* and *C*?

(*ii*) Why is potato *A* necessary for experiment?

(*iii*) Explain, why water does not gather in the hollowed out portion of *A* and D?

Sol. (*i*) The water gathers in the hollowed portion of *B* and *C* due to the process of osmosis. Concentration of solute (sugar in cup *B* and salt in cup *C*) is higher inside the cup than water. Hence, water flows from a region of its higher concentration to the region of lower concentration.

(*ii*) Potato *A* acts as reference of control for the experiment, which helps in comparing results.

(*iii*) Water does not gather in the hollow portion of *A* and *D* because of the following reasons:

(a) Hollow portion of potato *A* is empty and there is no concentration difference so, no osmosis occurs.

(b) The hollowed portion of potato *D* contains sugar, but the potato cup is boiled. Osmosis cannot occur as semipermeable membrane is destroyed by boiling.

9 Which type of cell division is required for growth and repair of body and which type is involved in formation of gametes.

Sol. The mitotic cell division is required for growth and repair of the body. The meiotic cell division is involved in the formation of gametes.

SUMMARY

- **Cell** is the basic structural and functional unit of all living organisms. It was discovered by Robert Hooke in the year 1665.
- **Unicellular organisms** are those organisms which are made up of a single cell only, e.g. *Amoeba, Chlamydomonas*, bacteria, etc.
- **Multicellular organisms** are organisms made up of many cells. These cells group together and assume different functions in the body to form various body parts, e.g. plants and animals.
- **Prokaryotic cells** are cells lacking a well-defined nucleus enclosed by nuclear membrane, e.g. bacteria and cyanobacteria.
- **Eukaryotic cells** are those having a well-defined nucleus enclosed in nuclear membrane, e.g. plant cell and animal cell.
- **Plant cells** possess a cell wall and a vacuole that occupies most of the space. It lacks centrosome and centrioles.
- **Animal cells** do not have cell wall, these possess highly complex Golgi bodies, centrioles, etc.
- Structurally, a cell mainly consists of plasma membrane, cytoplasm and nucleus. Cell organelles such as Golgi bodies, mitochondria, etc, are also present in cytoplasm.
- **Plasma membrane** is the outermost covering of the cell that is composed of proteins and lipids. It permits the entry and exit of some materials. It maintains the shape of the cell, acts as mechanical barrier and protects the internal contents of cell.
- **Transport of substances** across plasma membrane may take place by diffusion, i.e. process of movement of solutes or osmosis, i.e. process of movement of water.
- **Nucleus** is properly called as brain of the cells. It controls all functions of a cell. It also determines the development of cell by directing the chemical activities of cell.
- **Cytoplasm** is the fluid content present inside the plasma membrane that contains many specialised cell organelles and acts as a site for metabolic pathways such as glycolysis.
- **Endoplasmic reticulum** is a large network of membrane bound tubules and sheets. It plays an important role in protein and lipid synthesis.
- **Mitochondria** is known as the powerhouse of cell that releases energy required by the cell in the form of ATP.
- **Golgi apparatus** consists of a system of membrane-bound vesicles called cisternae. It helps in the formation of lysosomes and in storing and packaging of various molecules in a cell.
- **Lysosomes** are waste disposal system of a cell also called as suicidal bags of cell.
- **Plastids** are found in plant cells as chloroplasts, chromoplasts and leucoplasts.
- **Vacuoles** are storage sacs of solids and liquids.
- **Cell division** The process by which cell increase in their number is called cell division. It is of two types
- **Mitotic cell division** It occurs in somatic cells of body for growth and for repairing of old/injured cells. The chromosomes number is the newly formed cells remain same as in mother or dividing cell.
- **Meiotic cell division** It occurs germ cells of sexually reproducing organisms to form male gametes and female gametes. These have halps number of chromosomes as compared to mother cell.

For Mind Map

Visit https://goo.gl/U3NXJ2 OR **Scan the Code** 

Exam Practice

Objective Type Questions

Multiple Choice Questions

1 The term 'protoplasm' was coined by
(a) Purkinje (b) Robert Hooke
(c) Virchow (d) Robert Brown

Sol. (*a*) Purkinje in 1839 coined the term 'protoplasm' for the fluid substance of the cell.

2 Choose the incorrect statement from the following options
(a) All cells arise from pre-existing cells only
(b) Rudolf Virchow proposed the cell theory
(c) Nucleus was discovered by Robert Brown in 1831
(d) The nucleus and cytoplasm of a living cell, altogether form the protoplasm

Sol. (*b*) The cell theory was proposed by Schleiden and Schwann in 1839, postulating that all living beings are composed of cells and their products. In 1855, Rudolf Virchow modified the cell theory with his postulate, *'Omnis cellula-e-cellula'*, which means, a new cell is derived from a pre-existing cell only.

3 The flexibility of plasma membrane can be contributed to the presence of
(a) proteins (b) lipids
(c) nucleic acids (d) Both (a) and (b)

Sol. (*d*) Presence of lipids and proteins as phospholipids provides flexibility to plasma membrane. This helps cell in engulfing food and other materials from external environment.

4 A cell will swell up if the
(a) concentration of water molecules in the cell is higher than the concentration of water molecules in surrounding medium
(b) concentration of water molecules in surrounding medium is higher than concentration of water molecules in the cell
(c) concentration of water molecules is same in the cell and in the surrounding medium
(d) concentration of water molecules does not matter **NCERT Exemplar**

Sol. (*b*) Osmosis is a spontaneous process where movement of water molecules occurs from a region of higher its concentration to a region of lower solute concentration through a selectively permeable membrane, so as to tend to equalise its concentration on the both two sides in a biological system.

When movement of the solvent takes place from outside to inside the cell (inward movement) the process is endosmosis. It occurs in hypotonic solution and causes the swelling of cell.

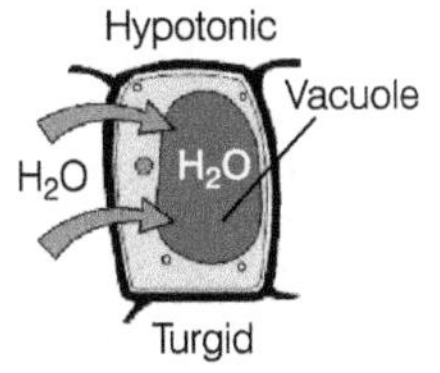

5 The cell wall of which out of these is not made up of cellulose?
(a) Bacteria (b) *Hydrilla*
(c) Mango tree (d) Cactus
NCERT Exemplar

Sol. (*a*) Plant cells, in addition to the plasma membrane, have another rigid outer covering called the cell wall. Bacteria is not a plant therefore, its cell wall is made up of a heteropolysaccharide named peptidoglycan.

6 Which one of the following terms describes 'a nucleus without nuclear membrane'?
(a) Nucleolus (b) Primitive nucleus
(c) Nucleoid (d) All of these

Sol. (*c*) The primitive type of undeveloped nucleus which lacks a nuclear membrane is called nucleoid. A nucleoid is found in prokaryotic cell, e.g. bacteria, mycoplasma.

7 Which one of the following cellular functions is performed by endoplasmic reticulum ?
(a) Production of hydrolytic enzymes
(b) Supply of energy to cell
(c) Formation of lysosomes
(d) Production of vacuoles

Sol. (*a*) The digestive or hydrolytic enzymes (proteins) are produced by rough endoplasmic reticulum for the synthesis of lysosomes.

8 Organelle other than nucleus, containing DNA is
(a) endoplasmic reticulum
(b) Golgi apparatus
(c) mitochondria
(d) lysosome **NCERT Exemplar**

Sol. (*c*) Other than nucleus, mitochondria contain DNA and are able to synthesise their own proteins. They are regarded as semiautonomous organelles.

9 Kitchen of the cell is

(a) mitochondria (b) endoplasmic reticulum
(c) chloroplast
(d) Golgi apparatus **NCERT Exemplar**

Sol. (*c*) Chloroplasts have a green pigment called chlorophyll and they are involved in the photosynthesis of food. Therefore, they are also known as the 'kitchen of the cell'.

10 Select the correct functional role of vacuole in a cell.

(a) Vacuoles do not help in maintaining rigidity of cell
(b) Vacuoles form thread-like tail in sperms of many mammals
(c) Vacuoles expell excess water and waste products from the cell
(d) Vacuoles store only excretory products of a cell

Sol. (*c*) In unicellular organisms, vacuoles carry out the role of expelling excess water (osmoregulation) and wastes from the cell (excretion). They also store food and water in cell and help in maintaining rigidity of cell by controlling osmosis.

11 At root tip, the number of divisions to produce 100 cell would be

(a) 25 (b) 50 (c) 99 (d) 100

Sol. (*b*) The cells of root tip divide by mitotic cell divisions so to make 100 cell, 50 divisions in 50 mother cells will take place. This way the root tip will keep growing are ovary daughter cell will again divide to form new cells.

12 The meiotic cell division in plants occurs in

(a) leaves and stem (b) stem and branches
(c) in anther and ovary (d) None of the above

Sol. (*c*) The meiotic cell division occurs in anthers and ovary to form pollen grain (male gamete) and egg cell female gamete.

Fill in the Blanks

13 An additional protective layer in plants present outside the plasma membrane is called ....

Sol. cell wall

14 The cell theory was refined by ....

Sol. Virchow

15 The cell organelle involved in cellular respiration is ......

Sol. Mitochondria

16 Ribosomes are concerned with the synthesis of ....

Sol. proteins

True or False

17 Plant cell vacuoles occupies 10–20% of plant cell volume.

Sol. False; Plant cell vacuoles occupy more than 10–20% plant cell volume.

18 Chromosones is condensed form of chromation.

Sol. True.

19 Oxidation of food takes place in mitochondria.

Sol. True

20 All kinds of plastids have pigments.

Sol. False; Leucoplast is a kind of plastid that do not have pigments.

Match the Columns

21 Match the following columns.

Column I		Column II
A. Robert Hooke	(i)	Discovery of nucleus
B. Schleiden and Schwann	(ii)	Protoplasm
C. Robert Brown	(iii)	Cell theory
D. Purkinje	(iv)	Discovered cell

Sol. A→(iv), B→(iii), C→(i), D→(ii)

Assertion-Reason

Direction (Q.Nos. 22-26) *In each of the following questions, a statement of Assertion is given by the corresponding statement of Reason. Of the statements, mark the correct answer as*

(a) If both Assertion and Reason are true and Reason is the correct explanation of Assertion
(b) If both Assertion and Reason are true, but Reason is not the correct explanation of Assertion
(c) If Assertion is true, but Reason is false
(d) If Assertion is false, but Reason is true

22 **Assertion** Rudolf Virchow proposed cell theory.

Reason His cell theory states that all plants and animals are composed of cells.

Sol. (*b*) 'All plants and animals are composed of cells' was presented as cell theory by Schleiden and Schwann (1838-39). Rudolf Virchow modified and expanded this earlier theory by suggesting that 'all cells arise from pre-existing cells'.

23 **Assertion** Chromosomes are constituted by DNA and protein.

Reason These are thread-like structures present in nucleus.

Sol. (*b*) Chromosomes are made up of DNA and proteins (i.e. histones). These are thread- like structures present in nucleus of the cell and contain genetic information that is transferred from parents to next generation.

24 **Assertion** Prokaryotic cells are primitive and larger than eukaryotic cells.

Reason Prokaryotic cells lack cytoplasmic organelles.

Sol. (*d*) Prokaryotic cells are smaller in size as compared to eukaryotic cells. These cells also lack cytoplasmic membrane bound organelles. Thus, most functions are performed by poorly developed parts of cytoplasm.

25 **Assertion** Golgi bodies store, modify and pack products in vesicles.

Reason They are involved in the formation of lysosomes.

Sol. (*b*) Golgi bodies store, modify and pack products (proteins) in vesicles, which are distributed to various parts of the cell. These Golgi bodies are also involved in the formation of lysosomes (waste disposal system of the cell).

26 **Assertion** Mitochondria are known as the powerhouse of a cell.

Reason These generate energy (as ATP) for various cellular activities.

Sol. (*a*) Mitochondria are the sites of cellular respiration. These generate energy required by the cell in the form of ATP which gets utilised in cellular functions. That is why mitochondria are also known as power house of the cell.

Case Based Questions

Direction (Q.Nos. 27-30) *Answer the questions on the basis of your understanding of the following passage and related studied concepts:*

The cytoplasm is the liquid part of the cell. It contains several simple and complex materials of the following elements. Study the table given and answer the questions.

Chemical constituents of the cytoplasm or cytosol.

Chemical	Percentage
Oxygen	64.00
Carbon	18.00
Hydrogen	10.00
Nitrogen	0.3.00
Trace elements (Ca, P, Cl, S, K, Na, Mg, I, Fe)	0.5.00

27 Which amongst the following is not a trace element?

(a) Calcium (b) Chloride
(c) Iodine (d) Carbon

Sol. Carbon

28 Cytoplasm acts as the site of metabolic pathways like

(a) Glycolysis (b) Ultrafilteration
(c) Photolysis (d) None of these

Sol. Glycolysis is a metabolic reaction that occurs in cytoplasm of a cell.

29 Is cytoplasm living content of the cell?

Sol. Yes, Cytoplasm is a living content of the cell.

30 What will happen if the cytoplasm of a cell is removed ?

Sol. In the absence of cytoplasm there would only be nucleus, so cell won't be able to perform its functions at all.

Direction (Q.Nos. 31-34) *Answer the questions on the basis of your understanding of the following passage and related studied concepts:*

To keep metabolic activities of different types separate from each other, eukaryotic cells have membrane bound organelles within themselves.

Cell organelles are "small organs" of the cell and are found embedded in the cytosol. They form living part of the cell. Each of them has a definite shape, structure and function. Examples of such organelles are nucleus, mitochondria, chloroplasts, endoplasmic reticulum,

31 Name the organisms in which plasma membrane and cell wall both are found.

Sol. Plant cell/Plant

32 State the function of ribosomes.

Sol. These are the site for protein synthesis.

33 Much of the DNA is localised in chromosomes of the nucleus. What is the other major constituent of the chromosomes?

Sol. Apart from DNA, the other major constituent of chromosomes are proteins (basic in nature).

34 Which of the following organelle in a eukaryotic cell is concerned with synthesis and transport of lipid molecules within a cell?

Sol. Lipid molecules are synthesised and transported within a cell by smooth endoplasmic reticulum.

Very Short Answer Type Questions

35 Name two unicellular organisms.

Sol. *Paramecium* and *Chlamydomonas* are the two unicellular organisms of the kingdom-Protozoa and kingdom plantae, respectively.

36 Name the process in which diffusion takes place through a semipermeable membrane.

Sol. Osmosis takes place through a semipermeable membrane.

37 What will happen if the already swollen raisin is kept in salt solution?

Sol. The water flows out from the raisin and goes into the solution medium. Consequently, the raisin shrinks in size.

38 Name the process by which unicellular freshwater organisms and most plant cells tend to gain water.

Sol. Endosmosis, i.e. inward movement of water into the cell from surrounding medium.

39 What is the function of cellulose in plant cell?

Sol. The plant cell wall is mainly composed of cellulose. Cellulose is a complex substance, which provides structural strength to plants.

40 Why is nucleus called controller or brain of the cell?

Sol. The nucleus coordinates and directs all the metabolic functions of the cell, that is why it is called controller or brain of the cell.

41 State two important functions of the nucleus of the cell.

Sol. (*i*) Nucleus is the control centre of a cell.

(*ii*) It consists of cell's DNA (genetic information) in the form of genes which carries hereditary characters from one generation to another.

42 What is DNA? Where is it present?

Sol. DNA is Deoxyribonucleic Acid. It is the genetic map of an organism, present in nucleus.

43 How DNA is present in a cell which is (*i*) dividing? (*ii*) not dividing?

Sol. (*i*) Chromosomes

(*ii*) Part of chromatin material.

44 Which organelle is called factory of ribosomes?

Sol. Nucleolus is called factory of ribosomes.

45 What are dictyosomes?

Sol. In plants, Golgi bodies are called as dictyosomes.

46 Is there any animal cell that lacks lysosomes?

Sol. Mammalian RBCs (Red Blood Corpuscles) lack lysosomes.

47 In which cell organelle, the complete breakdown of glucose in the presence of oxygen takes place?

Sol. The complete breakdown of glucose in the presence of oxygen in a cell is called aerobic respiration. It takes place in mitochondria.

48 Name the energy currency of cell.

Sol. **Adenosine Triphosphate** (ATP) is considered by biologists to be the energy currency of cell.

49 Which organelles are present only in plants cells and possess their own genome and ribosomes?

Sol. Plastids are found in plant cells only and contain DNA, RNA and ribosomes.

50 Name two structures, which are found in plant cell, but not in animal cell.

Sol. Chloroplast and cell wall are found in plant cell, but not in animal cell.

51 Name the type of plastid that helps in the process of photosynthesis.

Sol. Chloroplast helps in the process of photosynthesis.

52 Plant cells have large vacuoles each surrounded by a membrane. What is the name of this membrane?

Sol. The membrane that surrounds the vacuole is called tonoplast.

53 Mitotic cell division can be observed in which part of the organisms?

Sol. It occurs in somatic cells of the body of organisms.

54 How are gametes formed in sexually reproducing organisms?

Sol. Gametes are formed by meioic cell division in sexually reproducing organisms.

Short Answer (SA) Type Questions

1 List the contributions of the scientists given below in context of the study of cells
(*i*) Antony van Leeuwenhoek
(*ii*) Robert Brown
(*iii*) Camillo Golgi

Sol. (*i*) Antony van Leeuwenhoek discovered free-living cells in pondwater using an improved version of microscope.
(*ii*) Robert Brown discovered the brain of the cell, i.e. nucleus, which controls all the physiological activities of cell.
(*iii*) Golgi bodies were discovered by Camillo Golgi using a weak solution of silver nitrate to stain individual nerve and cell structures.

2 What are the consequences of the following conditions? **NCERT Exemplar**
(*i*) Cell having higher water concentration than surrounding medium.
(*ii*) A cell having lower water concentration than surrounding medium.
(*iii*) A cell having equal concentration to its surrounding medium.

Sol. (*i*) A cell having higher water concentration than surrounding medium will undergo exosmosis and will lose water.
(*ii*) A cell having lower water concentration than surrounding medium will undergo endosmosis and absorb water from outside.
(*iii*) A cell having equal concentration to its surrounding medium will neither gain nor lose water to the external medium.

3 State in brief, what happens when
(*i*) Dry apricots are left for some time in pure water and later transferred to sugar solution.
(*ii*) Rheo leaves are boiled in water first and then a drop of sugar syrup is pour on it.
(*iii*) Golgi apparatus are removed from the cell. **NCERT Exemplar**

Sol. (*i*) Dry apricots will swell up due to endosmosis when placed in pure water. On being transferred to sugar solution, they shrink due to exosmosis.
(*ii*) Cells of Rhoe leaves are killed due to boiling, so they will not undergo plasmolysis.
(*iii*) Formation of lysosome and secretory vesicles will stop and biosynthesis of proteins and lipids will not occur.

4 (*i*) Explain how do cell walls permit the cells of fungi to withstand very dilute external media without bursting.
(*ii*) Why does the skin of your fingers shrink when you wash clothes for a long time? **NCERT Exemplar**

Sol. (*i*) Fungi withstand very dilute/hypotonic external media without bursting because of their cell walls. In such media, the cells swell up by taking up water through osmosis and hence, building up pressure against the cell wall. The wall exerts an equal pressure against the swollen cell, thus preventing it from bursting.
(*ii*) The solution of soaps and detergents are hypertonic as compared to the osmotic concentration of our skin.

Therefore, washing of clothes results in exosmosis in skin cells that come in contact with the soap solution. Due to this reason, the skin of the fingers shrinks while washing clothes for a long time.

5 Describe the structural features of cell membrane and cell wall. Why is cell membrane called selectively permeable membrane?

Sol. Cell membrane is flexible, semipermeable and living portion of cell, which is made up of lipids and proteins. On the other hand, cell wall is tough, rigid and non-living portion of plant cell, which is made up of cellulose.

The plasma or cell membrane permits the entry and exit of selected materials in and out of the cell. It also prevents the movement of cell content outside the cell. Hence, it is called selectively permeable membrane.

6 Explain in detail what do you know about the structure of nucleus.

Sol. Robert Brown discovered nucleus in the cell in 1831. The nucleus is the control centre of a cell.

Structure of nucleus is composed of:
(*i*) **Nuclear membrane** It encloses the nucleus in eukaryotes. The nuclear membrane is penetrated by large nuclear pore complexes, which selectively transport molecules into or out of the nucleus.
(*ii*) **Nucleoplasm** It is a kind of protoplasm found in the nucleus containing genetic material (DNA), chromosomes and nucleolus.
(*iii*) **Chromatin** The chromatin material inside the nucleus is an organisation of DNA and protein. As a cell prepares itself to divide, the chromatin condenses and becomes thick enough to form specialised structures called chromosomes.

(iv) **Nucleolus** It acts as the most important site of RNA synthesis. It was first recognised by Fontana in 1874.

7 (i) Where are chromosomes located? What is chromatin material and how does it change just before the cell divides?

(ii) 'The functional segments of DNA are genes.' Give reason.

Sol. (i) Chromosomes are located in the nucleus of the cells. Chromatin is a mass of thread-like structures. It condenses to form chromosomes just before the cell divides.

(ii) Genes present on DNA segments carry the hereditary information in them, which is transferred from one generation to next. They determine the structural and functional aspects of next generation.

8 State three differences between plasma membrane and cell wall.

Sol.

Plasma Membrane	Cell Wall
It provides support and shape to the cell.	It gives strength and rigidity to the plant cell.
It is semipermeable in nature allowing the entry of selected molecules into the cell.	It is completely permeable in nature.
It is elastic, living and thin.	It is rigid, non-living and thick.

9 What do you mean by the following terms?

(i) Protoplasm (ii) Cytoplasm

(iii) Nucleoplasm

Sol. (i) **Protoplasm** It is the living substance present in the cell containing both cytoplasm and nucleoplasm.

(ii) **Cytoplasm** It is a part of protoplasm filled within the space between the nuclear membrane and cell membrane. It is homogeneous in nature containing water, amino acids, oxygen etc.

(iii) **Nucleoplasm** It is a transparent, semi-fluid substance filled within the space between nuclear membrane and nucleolus. It consists of nucleic acids, basic and acidic proteins, lipids and minerals.

10 State some differences between cytoplasm and nucleoplasm.

Sol. Differences between cytoplasm and nucleoplasm are as follows:

Cytoplasm	Nucleoplasm
It is enclosed by plasma membrane.	It is enclosed by nuclear membrane.
Cytoplasm contains the organelles, vitamins, enzymes, sugars etc.	It contains nucleolus, chromosomes etc.
It is general mass of protoplasm excluding nucleus.	It is semi-fluid ground substance found in nucleus.

11 Differentiate between Rough Endoplasmic Reticulum (RER) and Smooth Endoplasmic Reticulum (SER). How endoplasmic reticulum is important for membrane biosynthesis?

Sol. Differences between RER and SER are as follows:

Rough Endoplasmic Reticulum (RER)	Smooth Endoplasmic Reticulum (SER)
In RER, ribosomes are attached to the surface.	In SER, ribosomes are not attached to the surface.
It helps in protein synthesis.	It helps in lipid synthesis.
It is formed of tubules and is situated near the nucleus.	It is formed of cisternae and is situated near the plasma membrane.

Importance of ER in membrane biosynthesis are as follows:

(i) RER synthesises proteins, which are passed on to Golgi apparatus.

(ii) The SER helps in the manufacturing of fats and lipids, which along with protein help in building of cell membrane.

(iii) It also helps in transporting proteins to various places.

12 Describe the phenomenon of membrane biogenesis. Give one function of ER.

Sol. The smooth endoplasmic reticulum helps in the manufacture of lipid or fat molecules, important for cell function. Some of these lipids and proteins manufactured in RER help in building the cell membrane. This process is known as membrane biogenesis.

ER functions as a cytoplasmic framework providing surface for some of the biochemical activities of the cells.

13 Name the organelle of the cell, which is involved in the formation of lysosomes. Write its functions in the cell.

Sol. Golgi apparatus is the organelle involved in the formation of lysosomes.

Functions of Golgi apparatus are:

(i) Storage, modification and packaging of products in vesicles.

(ii) Helps to make complex sugars from simple sugars.

(*iii*) Material synthesised near the ER is packaged and dispatched to various targets inside and outside the cell through Golgi apparatus.

14 Name the organelle of the cell, which has membrane-bound sac filled with powerful digestive enzymes. Write any four common functions it performs inside the cell.

Sol. Lysosome is membrane-bound sac filled with powerful digestive enzymes.
For functions of lysosomes, refer to Pg 118.

15 (*i*) Why lysosomes are known as 'scavengers of the cell'? **NCERT Exemplar**
(*ii*) Lysosomes are self-destructive. True/ false. Give reason.

Sol. (*i*) Lysosomes are called scavengers of the cell because they remove dead and worn out cells by digesting them and act as a kind of waste disposal system of a cell.
(*ii*) Lysosomes are self-destructive. This is true as during breakdown of cell structure, lysosomes may burst and the enzymes contained in it may eat up their own cells.

16 How many membranes are present in mitochondria? Give the characteristic features of these membranes. What is the advantage of such features?

Sol. Mitochondria have two plasma-membranes.
The outer membrane is very porous, while the inner membrane is deeply folded and is selectively permeabl(e.)
Porous membrane helps in getting oxygen and food, while the folds create a large surface area for ATP generating chemical reactions.

17 Name a cell organelle found only in a plant cell and mention its various types along with their functions and location.

Sol. Plastids are found only in plant cells.
Types of plastids are:

Name of the plastid	*Pigment present*	*Function*	*Location*
Chloroplast	Green (called chlorophyll)	Involved in the photosynthesis of food.	Leaves
Chromoplast	Any colour other than green	Impart attractive colours to flowers and fruits.	coloured parts of plant
Leucoplast	No pigment (colourless)	Stores starch, oils and protein granules.	Underground/ storage parts of plant

18 Give the differences between leucoplasts and chromoplasts.

Sol. Refer to solution of Q. 17.

19 Which type of plastid stores starch, oil and proteins?

Sol. Leucoplasts are the plastids that function to store starch, oil and proteins and hence, it is of three types:
(*i*) Amyloplasts – Store starch
(*ii*) Elaioplasts – Store oil
(*iii*) Aleuroplasts – Store proteins

20 Write the name of different plant parts in which chloroplast, chromoplast and leucoplast are present. **NCERT Exemplar**

Sol. Refer to solution of Q. 17.

21 Why does plant cell possess large-sized vacuoles?

Sol. Plant cell possesses large-sized vacuole because
(*i*) it stores salt, sugar, amino acid, organic acid and some proteins.
(*ii*) the vacuole contains cell sap and helps in maintaining turgidity of cell.
(*iii*) they store some metabolic byproducts or end products of plant metabolism.
(iv) lysosomal enzymes occur in vacuole of plant cell.

22 State reason for the following:
(*i*) Mitochondria is known as powerhouse of the cell.
(*ii*) Plastids are able to make their own protein.
(*iii*) Plant cell shrinks when kept in hypertonic solution.

Sol. (*i*) Oxidation of food takes place in mitochondria, that result in the release of energy in the form of ATP. This energy helps in various chemical activities needed for life. Hence, mitochondria is known as powerhouse of the cell.
(*ii*) Plastids have their own DNA and ribosomes. Therefore, they are able to make their own proteins.
(*iii*) Hypertonic solution has lower concentration of water than the cell. When a plant cell is kept in it, water present in the cell leaves the cell due to exosmosis. Therefore, cell shrinks.

23 Name the organelles, which show analogy written as under.

(i) Transporting channels of the cell.
(ii) Powerhouse of the cell.
(iii) Packaging and dispatching unit of the cell.
(iv) Digestive bag of cell.
(v) Storage sac of the cell.
(vi) Control room of the cell.

NCERT Exemplar

Sol. (i) Endoplasmic reticulum (ii) Mitochondria
(iii) Golgi apparatus (iv) Lysosome
(v) Vacuole (vi) Nucleus

24 Enlist any three functions of vacuoles.

Sol. The three functions of vacuoles are as follows

(i) Vacuoles are full of cell soap and provide turgidity and rigidity to cells in plants.
(ii) Many substances like amino acids, sugars, organic acids and proteins are stored in vacuoles.
(iii) In *Amoeba*, consumed food items are stored in food vacuoles.

25 Differentiate between the mitosis and meiosis.

Sol. The difference between mitosis and meiosis is tabulated below

Mitosis	Meiosis
It occurs in somatic cells of body of the organisms.	It occurs in germ cells of the body of organisms.
Two daughter cells are formed.	Four daughter cells are formed.
The number of chromosome remains same in daughter cells as found in mother cell.	The number of chromosomes is reduced to half in daughter cells in comparison to mother cells.
It is helpful in growth, repair of body of organisms.	It is helpful in sexual reproduction by forming male and female gametes.

Long Answer (LA) Type Questions

1 Describe an activity to demonstrate endosmosis and exosmosis. Draw the diagram also.

Sol. **Activity to show endosmosis and exosmosis** Put dried raisins in plain water and leave them for some time. Then place them into a concentrated solution of salt.

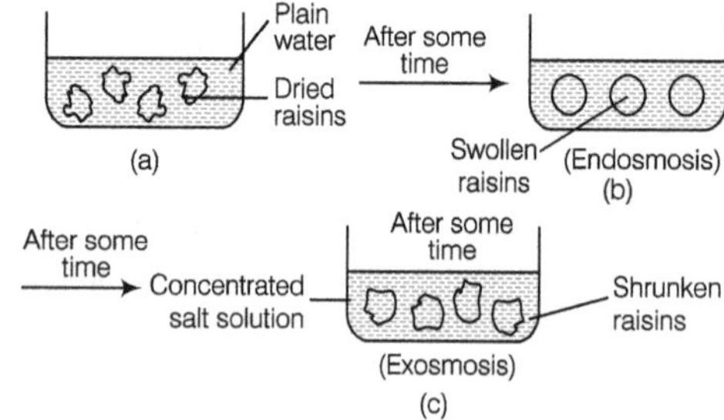

Observation

(i) When dried raisins are placed in plain water, raisins swell up due to osmotic entry of water into raisins. Plain water is hypotonic medium for raisins. Thus, endosmosis occurs.
(ii) When swollen raisins are transferred to a concentrated solution, raisins shrink. Concentrated solution is a hypertonic medium for swollen raisins. Thus, exosmosis occurs.

2 Explain main functional regions of a cell with the help of a diagram.

Sol. Plasma membrane, cytoplasm and nucleus are three main functional regions of a cell.

(i) **Plasma membrane** It is a thin, selectively permeable membrane, covering the cell and is made up of lipids and proteins.

(*ii*) **Cytoplasm** It is aqueous material containing a variety of cell organelles along with non-living inclusions.

(*iii*) **Nucleus** It is the control centre of a cell. It contains the cell's hereditary information (DNA).

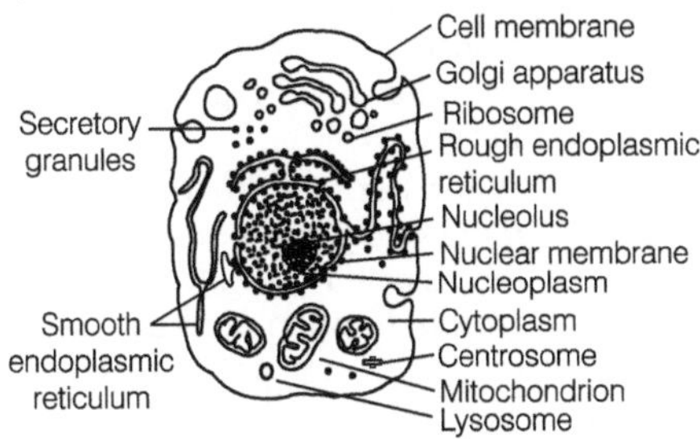

A eukaryotic cell

3 Given below statements have underlined words which may be incorrect. Rewrite these words and state one function for each of them other than those (if) given.

(*i*) The fundamental organisational unit of life is an organ.

(*ii*) The cell wall is an active part of the cell, and is selectively permeable.

(*iii*) The presence of plasma membrane enables the cells of plants and fungi to exist in hypotonic media without bursting.

(*iv*) The Golgi body functions both as a passageway for intracellular transport and as a manufacturing surface.

(*v*) Leucoplasts contain carotenoides and their primary function is to provide colours to flowers and fruits.

Sol. (*i*) **A Cell** They perform many important physiological functions in living organisms essential for life.

(*ii*) **Plasma membrane** It acts as a mechanical barrier, preventing the leakage of cellular contents to the outside environment.

(*iii*) **Cell wall** It helps in interaction among plant cells through cytoplasmic channels called plasmodesmata.

(*iv*) **Endoplasmic reticulum** It functions as cytoplasmic framework providing surface for some biochemical activities of the cell.

(*v*) **Chromoplasts** They impart colour to the parts of plants like flowers and fruits.

4 (*i*) Draw a neat labelled diagram of animal cell.

(*ii*) Name the structure, which helps in

(*a*) energy production

(*b*) exchange of materials between cytoplasm and nucleoplasm.

(*c*) lipid synthesis

Sol. (*i*) For the diagram of an animal cell. Refer to the fig. on Pg 106.

(*ii*) (*a*) Mitochondria (*b*) Nuclear pore
(*c*) Smooth endoplasmic reticulum

5 Why are mitochondria called powerhouse of the cell? Give three similarities and one difference between mitochondria and plastid.

Sol. Mitochondria are often associated with cellular respiration and energy generation of the cell.

The energy required for various chemical activities is released by the mitochondria in the form of ATP molecules. For this reason, mitochondria are known as the powerhouse of the cell.

Three similarities between mitochondria and plastids are as follows:

(*i*) Both have their own DNA and ribosomes.

(*ii*) External structures of mitochondria and plastids are similar.

(*iii*) Both have more than one membrane layer.

One major difference between mitochondria and plastids is that mitochondria are present in both plant and animal cells, whereas plastids are present only in plant cells.

6 Write the main functions of atleast ten cell components.

Sol. (*i*) **Plasma membrane** It acts as a semipermeable membrane and allows only selective substances to pass through it.

(*ii*) **Chromosomes** To carry hereditary characters of an organism from one generation to another.

(*iii*) **Lysosomes** Breakdown of unwanted macromolecules is the main function of these organelles.

(*iv*) **Ribosomes** These help in protein synthesis.

(*v*) **Nucleus** Control centre of the cell. Contains cellular DNA (genetic information) in the form of genes.

(*vi*) **Mitochondria** The main function of mitochondria in aerobic cells is the production of energy by synthesis of ATP.

(*vii*) **Nucleolus** Biosynthesis of ribosomal RNA (*r*RNA) and acts as a platform for protein synthesis.

(*viii*) **Cell wall** It provides protection and rigidity to the plant cell.

(*ix*) **Chloroplasts** These are the sites of photosynthesis within plant cells.

(*x*) **Endoplasmic reticulum** Serves as channels for transport of materials.

7. Grass looks green, papaya appears yellow. Which cell organelle is responsible for this? **CBSE 2016**

Sol. **Plastids** These are found in plant cells only. Plastids are the major cell organelles in plants. On the basis of pigments present in plastids, they are divided into two types; (*i*) the colourless **leucoplasts** and (*ii*) the pigmented **chromoplasts**. The colourless **leucoplasts** store starch, oil and protein granules whereas the pigmented chroloplasts have different colours and can be of several types.

The most important ones are those containing the pigment **chlorophyll**, known as **chloroplasts**, which is responsible for the preparation of food by photosynthesis. Other chromoplasts contain non-green pigments, which are responsible for the characteristic colours of fruits and flowers, e.g. anthocyanin.

8 How are the following related to each other?

(*i*) Chromatin network and chromosomes

(*ii*) Chloroplast and chlorophyll

(*iii*) Genes and DNA **CBSE 2016**

Sol. (*i*) The cell contains nuclear material which can be seen as entangled mass of thread-like structure when it is not dividing. The chromatin material gets organised into rod-like structures called chromosomes when the cell is about to divide.

(*ii*) Chloroplasts are green-coloured plastids which contain green coloured pigment called chlorophyll.

(*iii*) Genes are the functional segments of DNA (present on DNA) which control a specific trait by making specific protein.

9 (*i*) Describe the role played by the lysosomes. Why are they termed as suicidal bags? How do they perform their function?

(*ii*) What happens to the dry raisins, when placed in plain water for some time? State the reason for whatever is observed. What would happen if these raisins are then placed in concentrated salt solution?

Sol. (*i*)
- Lysosomes are membrane-bound sacs filled with hydrolytic digestive enzymes.These enzymes are made by rough endoplasmic reticulum.
- Lysosomes are a kind of waste disposal system of the cell.
- During the disturbance in cellular metabolism, e.g. when a cell gets damaged, lysosomes present in the cell may burst and the enzymes digest the damaged cell. Hence, lysosomes are also called as 'suicidal bags' of a cell.
- Lysosomes break up the foreign materials entering into the cell, such as bacteria or food into small pieces.

(*ii*) The raisins will swell up due to endosmosis. If these raisins are again placed in concentrated salt solution, they will shrink, due to exosmosis.

10. Discuss in detail the importance of mitotic and meiotic cell division. **CBSE 2016**

Sol. Refer to text on Pg 109.

CHAPTER EXERCISE

Multiple Choice Questions

1 The smallest known cell is
(a) yeast (b) ovum
(c) *Mycoplasma* (d) nerve cell

2 Identify the organelle present only in animal cells
(a) Chloroplast (b) Nucleus
(c) Centrioles (d) Vacuoles

3 Which of these is not related to endoplasmic reticulum? **NCERT Exemplar**
(a) It behaves as transport channel for proteins between nucleus and cytoplasm
(b) It transports materials between various regions in cytoplasm
(c) It can be the site of energy generation
(d) It can be the site for some biochemical activities of the cell

4 The best material for the study of mitosis in laboratory is
(a) anther (b) root tip
(c) leaf tip (d) ovary

Fill in the Blanks

5 Nerve cell is the .... cell in human body.

6 A spindle shaped cell found in human body is ....

7 Transport of oxygen in unicellular organisms occurs by the process of ....

8 Absorption of water by plant roots demonstrate the process of ....

True or False

9 *Amoeba* is a unicellular organism with a definite shape.

10 A cell kept in .... solution will swell up due to encreased turgidity.

11 Phospholipids present in cell increase the toxicity of the cell membrane.

12 Lysosomes are also referred to as suicidal bags.

Match the Columns

13 Match the following columns.

	Column I		Column II
A.	Central vacuole in plant cell	1.	Cell wall
B.	Cellulose	2.	Glucose synthesis
C.	Chloroplast	3.	Cell sap
D.	Chromosome	4.	Inheritance

Assertion–Reason

Direction (Q.Nos. 14-15) *In each of the following questions, a statement of Assertion is given by the corresponding statement of Reason. Of the statements, mark the correct answer as*
(a) If both Assertion and Reason are true and Reason is the correct explanation of Assertion
(b) If both Assertion and Reason are true but Reason is not the correct explanation of Assertion
(c) If Assertion is true, but Reason is false
(d) If Assertion is false, but Reason is true

14 **Assertion** Robert Brown discovered nucleus.
Reason Nucleoplasm and cytoplasm of a living cell together form the protoplasm.

15 **Assertion** Lysosomes are often called as 'suicidal bags' of a cell.
Reason Lysosomes contain hydrolytic enzymes capable of digesting cellular waste.

Case Based Questions

Direction (Q. Nos. 16-19) *Answer the questions on the basis of your understanding of the following passage and related studied concepts:*

Meiosis is a type of cell division where the number of chromosomes becomes half in the daughter nuclei compound to the parental nuclei. It involves two successive cell divisions, i.e. meiosis-I and II. Meiosis-I is often called as reductional division while II is called as equational division.

16 How is meiosis different from mitotic cell division?

17 How can meiosis cell division help in the process of reproduction?

18 Do you think meiosis cell division contributes to evolutionary process ?

19 Mitosis or meiosis, which cell division helps in maintaining the specific chromosome number of each species across generations in sexually reproducing organisms?

Very Short Answer Type Questions

20 From where do new cells arise?

21 Give two examples of organisms in which a single cell performs all the functions.

22 In which form is the DNA present in a cell when the cell is not dividing?

23 What would happen to the life of a cell, if there are no vacuoles?

Answers

1. (c) 2. (c) 3. (c) 4. (b) 5. *Chlamydomonas* or *Amoeba* or *Paramecium*
6. longest 7. *Mycoplasma* 8. diffusion
9. False 10. True 11. False 12. True
13. (A) → (3), (B) → (1), (C) → (2), (D) → (4)
14. (b) 15. (a)

Short Answer (SA) Type Questions

24 Name the fluid content of a cell. Write its function(s).

25 Why is it said that 'a cell without nucleus is without any future'?

26 Write the function of leucoplast and chromoplast.

27 How do vacuoles perform differently in plant cell and a unicellular organism like *Amoeba*?

Long Answer (LA) Type Questions

28 What will happen if
(*i*) excess amount of fertilisers is added to a green lawn?
(*ii*) salt is added to cut pieces of raw mango?

29 Draw a well-labelled diagram of a eukaryotic nucleus. How is it different from nucleoid?

30 Given along side is a diagrammatic sketch of a certain generalised cell.

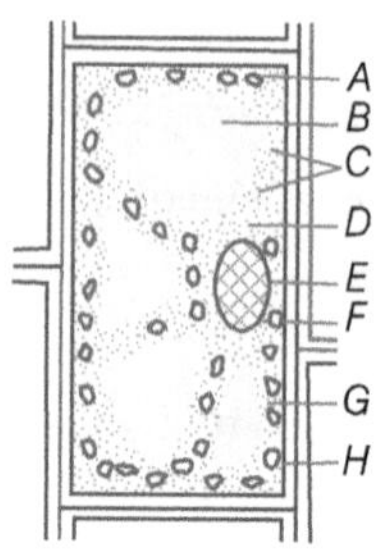

(*i*) Name the parts labelled as *A-H*.
(*ii*) Is it a plant cell or an animal cell? Give two reasons in support of your answer.
(*iii*) List the functions of parts marked as *A*, *F* and *H*.

31 Discuss the importance of meiotic cell division.

RELATED ONLINE VIDEOS

Visit https://www.youtube.com/watch?v=he_Qw4_vOJk
OR **Scan the Code**

Visit https://www.youtube.com/watch?v=9-_nQHukz94
OR **Scan the Code**

Visit https://www.youtube.com/watch?v=cA-Ou_t2sag
OR **Scan the Code**

Visit https://www.youtube.com/watch?v=39HTpUG1MwQ
OR **Scan the Code**

Challengers*

1 Which among the following cells is involved in continuity of life?

(a) 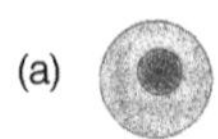 (b) 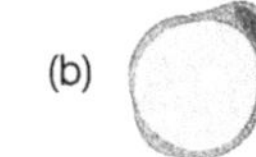

(c) 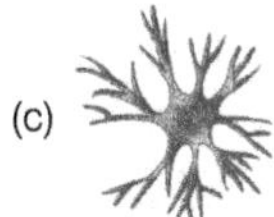 (d) 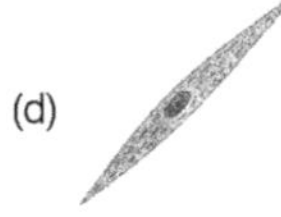

2 Swollen feet and ankle can be naturally cured by dipping them in salt water. Suggest the mechanism involved in this treatment.

(a) Diffusion (b) Osmosis
(c) Plasmolysis (d) Deplasmolysis

3 The cell organelle found in prokaryotes as well as eukaryotes is

(a) centrioles (b) plastids
(c) endoplasmic reticulum (d) ribosomes

4 Which of these options are not a function of ribosomes?

I. It helps in manufacture of protein molecules
II. It helps in manufacture of enzymes
III. It helps in manufacture of hormones
IV. It helps in manufacture of starch molecules

(a) Only II (b) Only III
(c) Only IV (d) Only I

5 Cell wall of fungi is made up of

(a) cellulose (b) chitin
(c) pectins (d) All of these

6 DNA stands for

(a) Deoxyribonucleic acid (b) Dihydroribonucleate acetate
(c) Diribonucleate acetate (d) Decarboribonucleic acid

7 Pick out the incorrect statement.

(a) Leucoplast is a colourless plastid.
(b) Cell wall is a non-living structure, mainly composed of cellulose.
(c) Golgi apparatus acts as the site of protein synthesis.
(d) Protoplasm is a life giving substance of a cell.

8 Choose the incorrectly matched pair from the options given below.

(a) Director of the cell – Nucleus
(b) Protein factories – Ribosomes
(c) Semiautonomous organelle – Mitochondria
(d) Cytoplasmic bridges – Nucleolus

9 Which of the following plastids imparts red colour to pomegranate?

(a) Chloroplast (b) Chromoplast
(c) Amyloplast (d) Leucoplast

10 Vacuoles

(a) disrupt water balance in animals
(b) provide flexibility to plant cells
(c) are small-sized in animal cell and large-sized in plant cell
(d) All of the above

Answers

1.	(a)	2.	(c)	3.	(d)	4.	(c)	5.	(b)
6.	(a)	7.	(c)	8.	(d)	9.	(b)	10.	(c)

These questions may be or may not be asked in the examination, have been given just for additional practice.

CHAPTER

06

Tissues

Chapter Checklist

- Plant Tissues
  - Meristematic Tissue
  - Permanent Tissue
- Animal Tissues
  - Epithelial Tissue
  - Connective Tissue
  - Muscular Tissue
  - Nervous Tissue

All living organisms are composed of cells. In unicellular organism, a single cell performs all the basic functions, but in multicellular organisms, different functions are performed by different cells.

A group of cells similar in structure which work together to achieve a particular function forms a tissue. These cells are arranged and designed, so as to give the highest possible efficiency of the function they perform. All cells of a tissue have a common origin. A tissue may be simple or complex type. Blood, phloem and muscles are all examples of tissues.

The structural and functional organisation of cells in plants and animals is different. Plants remain stationary, while animals move as per their needs. In this chapter, we will study various types of tissues found in plants and animals alongwith their respective functions.

Plant Tissues

On the basis of dividing capacity, plant tissues can be classified into two fundamental types are as follows:

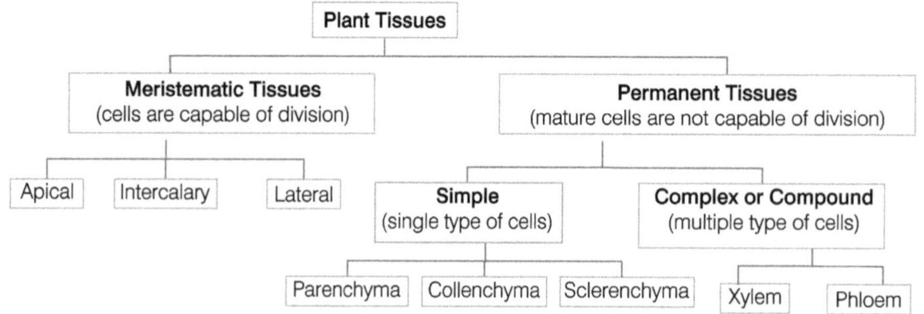

1. Meristematic Tissue

The tissues in which cells always keep dividing giving rise to new cells are called meristematic tissues. These tissues are responsible for the growth of plants. Plants grow only in those regions where meristematic tissues are present, e.g. root and shoot tip. It is also called as **growth tissue.**

Cells forming this tissue are very active, have dense cytoplasm, thin cellulose walls and prominent nuclei. They lack vacuoles because vacuoles are full of cell sap and provide turgidity and rigidity to the cell. These all cause hindrence in cell division.

The new cells produced by meristem are initially like those of meristem. Their characteristics change once they grow and become differentiated as components of other tissues.

Meristematic tissue is classified on the basis of their position in the plant body. These are as follows

(i) Apical Meristem

It is present at growing tips of stems and roots. Thus, helpful in increasing the length of the stems and the roots. It acts as pro-meristem having actively dividing cells, giving rise to other meristems.

(ii) Intercalary Meristem

It is present at the base of the leaves or internodes (on either side of the node) of twigs. It helps in longitudinal growth (elongation) of plants.

(iii) Lateral Meristem (Cambium)

It is present on the lateral sides of stems and roots. It helps in increasing the girth of stem and root.

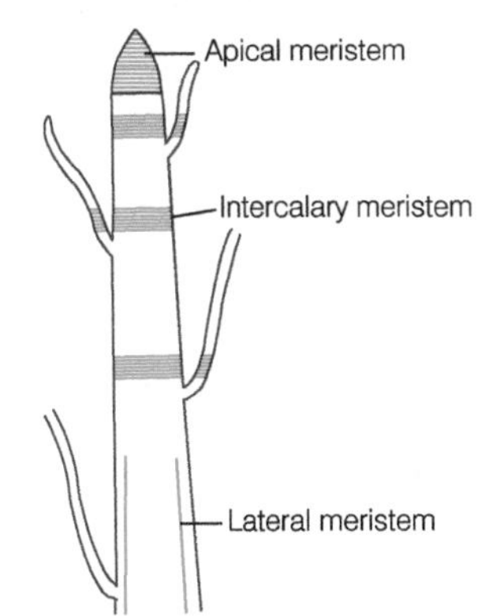

Location of meristematic tissues in plant body

2. Permanent Tissue

These tissue is formed from the cells of meristematic tissue when they loose their ability to divide. The cells of this tissue have attained a permanent shape, size and function by the process called **differentiation**.

As a result of differentiation, the meristematic tissues tend to form different types of permanent tissues which are as follows:

(i) Simple Permanent Tissue

It is made up of only one type of cells, i.e. the cells forming these tissues are similar in structure and function. These tissue is further classified into three types are as follows

(a) Parenchyma

A few layers of cells form the basic tissue found in plants. These are present in cortex and pith of stems and roots and in the mesophyll of leaves.

- These are simple living cells with little specialisation and thin cell walls.
- Cells are usually loosely packed with large spaces between them (intercellular spaces).
  The transverse section and longitudinal section of parenchyma are shown below

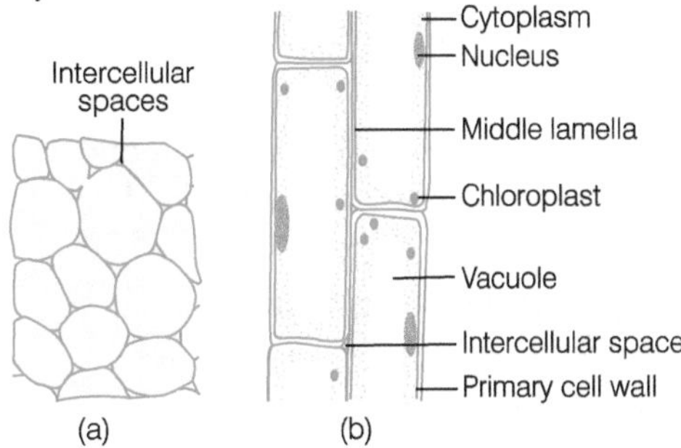

Parenchyma tissue: (a) Transverse section (b) Longitudinal section

Functions of parenchyma are

- It serves as a food storage tissue.
- This tissue provides support to plants.
- When the parenchyma cell contains chlorophyll in some situations, it performs photosynthesis. Such type of parenchyma tissue is called chlorenchyma.
- In aquatic plants, large air cavities are present in parenchyma cells in order to give buoyancy to plants, which help them to float. Such type of parenchyma tissue is called **aerenchyma.**
- Parenchyma of stems and roots also stores nutrients and water.

(b) Collenchyma

These tissues are generally found in leaf stalks below the epidermis and leaf midribs.

- Cells are living, elongated and irregularly thickened at the corners due to the deposition of pectin.
- These have very little intercellular spaces.

The transverse section and longitudinal section of collenchyma are shown below

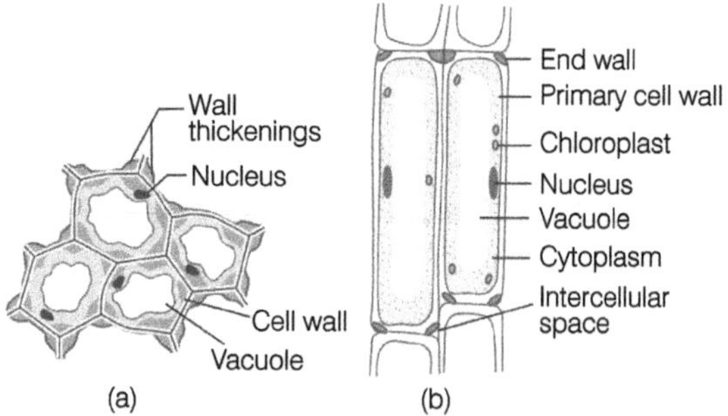

Collenchyma tissue; (a) Transverse section (b) Longitudinal section

Functions of collenchyma are

- It provides mechanical support and elasticity (flexibility) to plants.
- It also allows easy bending in various parts of a plant (tendrils and stems of climbers) without breaking.

(c) Sclerenchyma

This type of tissue is present in stems, around vascular bundles, in the veins of leaves and in the hard covering of seeds and nuts.

- The cells of sclerenchymatous tissue are dead.
- The cells are long and narrow in appearance.
- Cell walls are thickened due to lignin (a chemical substance) deposition, which acts as cement and hardens them.
- Due to the presence of thick walls, there is no internal space between the cells.
- The transverse section and longitudinal section of sclerenchyma are as follows:

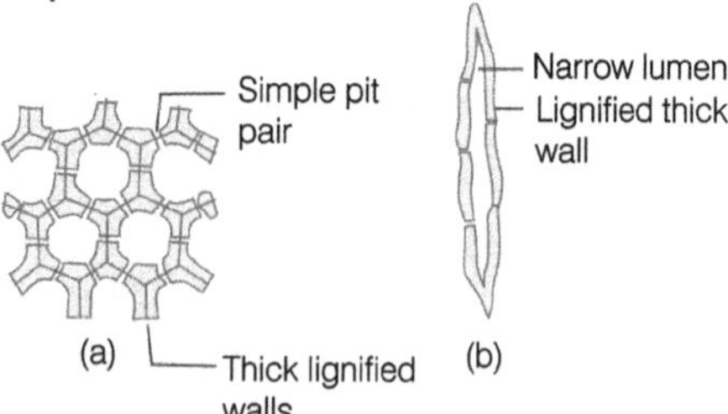

Sclerenchyma; (a) Transverse section (b) Longitudinal section

Functions of sclerenchyma are

- It is known to be the chief mechanical tissue, which makes plant hard and stiff, e.g. husk of coconut is made up of sclerenchymatous tissue.
- It forms protective covering around seeds and nuts. It gives rigidity, flexibility and elasticity to the plant body.

Protective Tissues

These meant to provide protection to the plants from undue loss of water. The two types of protective tissues present in plants are:
(i) Epidermis (*ii*) Cork (or phellem)

(i) Epidermis

The outermost layer, i.e. epidermis in plants is made up of a single layer of cells. It protects all parts of the plant.

On the aerial parts of the plant, epidermal cells often secrete a waxy, water-resistant layer on their outer surface. It provides protection against loss of water, mechanical injury and invasion by microbes.

Cells of epidermal tissue form a continuous layer. They have no intercellular spaces due to its protective role. Most epidermal cells are relatively flat. The outer wall and side walls are thicker than the inner wall. Epidermal cells of leaf bear small pores known as stomata. These are enclosed by two kidney-shaped cells called guard cells.

Guard cells and epidermal cells are shown below:

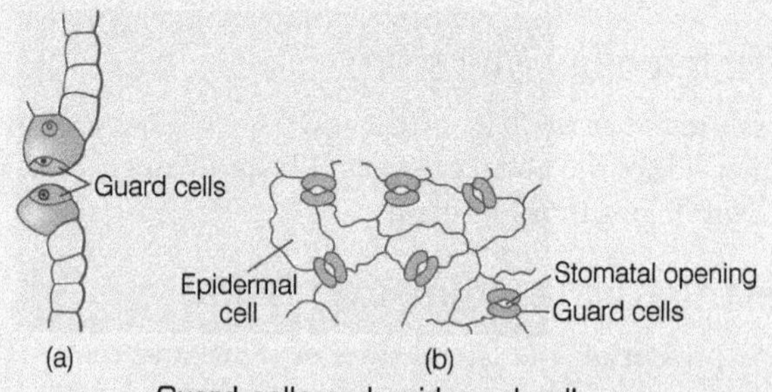

Guard cells and epidermal cells : (a) Lateral view (b) Surface view

Stomata are responsible for the exchange of gases with the atmosphere and for the process of transpiration (loss of water in the form of water vapours).

Epidermal cells of the roots bear long hair-like outgrowths called root hairs. They greatly increases the total absorptive surface area and help the roots to absorb water and nutrients from the soil.

In case of desert plants, epidermis of the aerial parts has a thick waxy coating of cutin (chemical substance with waterproof quality) on its outer surface. It prevent water loss.

(ii) Cork

It is the strip of secondary meristem, which replaces the epidermis of older stems. Cells of cork are dead, compactly arranged and have no intercellular spaces. It forms bark of the tree (several layer thick). A chemical called suberin is present in their walls. It makes them impervious to gases and water.

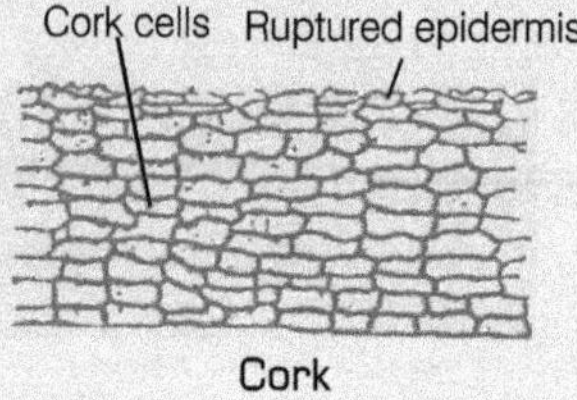

Cork

Check Point 01

1 What forms the basis of classification of tissues present in plants and animals?

2 Why the growth of plants occurs only in certain specific regions?

3 Fill in the blanks:

(i) .... cell lack vacuoles and intercellular spaces.

(ii) .... tissue helps in easy bending of plants.

4 State True or False for the following statement:

Lateral meristem seen in some plants is located near the node.

5 Aerenchyma tissue contains chlorophyll and performs photosynthesis. True or False.

(ii) Complex Permanent Tissue

It is made up of more than one type of cells having a common origin. Regardless of different appearances, all the cells coordinate to perform a common function.

There are two types of complex permanent tissue, i.e.

(*a*) xylem (*b*) phloem

Both of them are **conducting tissues** and constitute a vascular bundle. This is a distinctive feature of complex plants. It has made possible their survival in the terrestrial environment.

(a) Xylem

Xylem

It is responsible for the transport of water and minerals from roots to other parts of the plant. The cells of xylem have thick walls and many of them are dead.

Xylem consists of various types of elements, which are as follows :

I. Tracheids

Pits

- These are dead, long, tubular structures with tapering ends.
- They transport water and minerals vertically.

II. Vessels

Pits

- These are long, tube-like structures, formed by a row of cells, placed end to end.
- These are also dead cells with lignified walls.
- They also help in conduction of water.

III. Xylem parenchyma

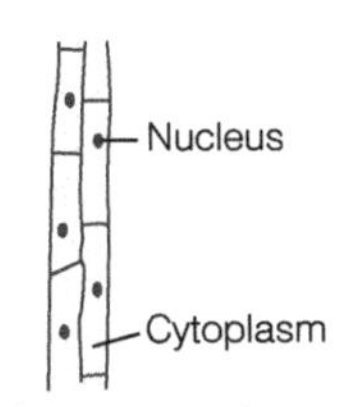

Xylem parenchyma

- These are only living cells of xylem with thin cell walls.
- These store food and helps in the sideways conduction of water.

IV. Xylem fibres

- These are elongated dead cells with tapering ends and thick cell walls.
- These are fibres associated with xylem and supportive in functioning of xylem.

(b) Phloem

It transports food from leaves to other parts of the plant. Materials can move in both directions in it. All phloem cells are living except phloem fibres.

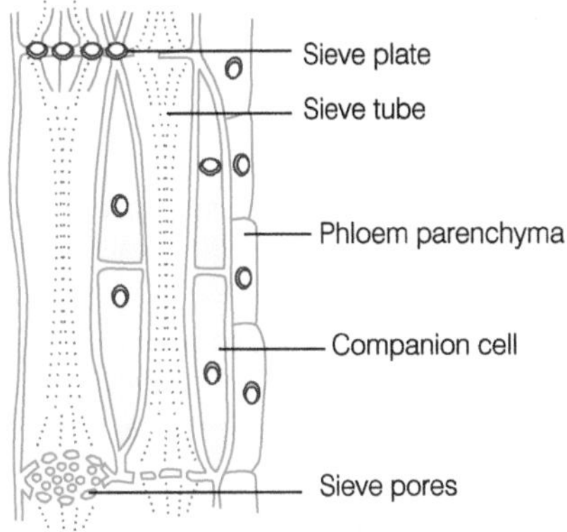

Section of phloem

Phloem is made up of following five types of elements:

I. Sieve tubes

- These are tubular cells with perforated walls.
- These have thin layer of cytoplasm.

II. Sieve cells

- These are long, conducting cells in the phloem that do not form sieve tubes.
- The major difference between sieve cells and sieve tube members is the lack of sieve plates in sieve cells.

III. Companion cells

- These are small elongated cells having thin walls which are not perforated and have active cytoplasm. These help sieve tubes in the translocation of food.

IV. Phloem fibres

- These are thick walled sclerenchyma cells which provide mechanical strength to the tissue.

V. Phloem parenchyma

- These are thin-walled cells which help in storage and slow lateral conduction of food.

Differences between Meristematic and Permanent Tissues

Meristematic Tissue	*Permanent Tissue*
Cells divide repeatedly.	Cells are differentiated from the meristematic tissue and normally do not divide.
Cells are undifferentiated and intercellular spaces are absent.	Cells are fully differentiated and intercellular spaces are present.
Vacuoles are absent.	Vacuoles are present.
Cells have dense cytoplasm.	Cells have thin-layered cytoplasm around the vacuoles.
Cells are always living.	Cells may be living or dead.
Cell walls of its cells are thin.	Cell walls of its cells can be thick or thin.

Check Point 02

1. How are complex permanent tissues different from simple permanent tissues?
2. Fill in the blanks:
   (*i*) The distinctive feature of complex plants that helped in their survival on the earth is the presence of .... in them.
   (*ii*) The component of xylem responsible for the transport of minerals is ....
3. State True or False for the following statement:
   The only living constituent of xylem tracheid.
4. Identify the phloem component which provides mechanical strength to this tissue.

Animal Tissues

On the basis of the functions they perform, animal tissues are classified into four basic types are as follows:

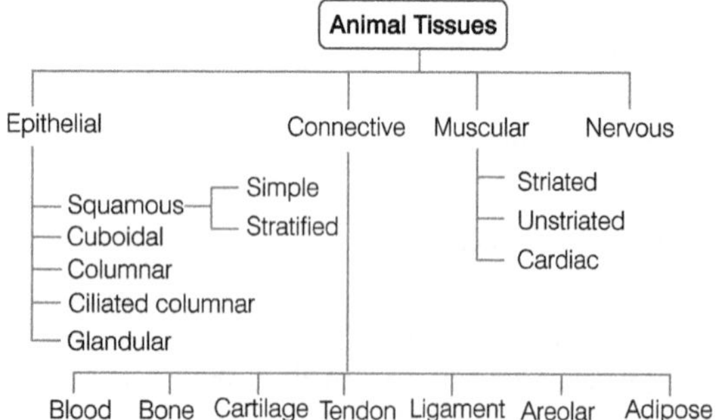

1. Epithelial Tissue

The covering or protective tissue in the animal body is epithelial tissue. It is the simplest protective tissue of the animal body. It covers most organs and cavities of the body.

- It forms a barrier to keep different body systems separated from each other. In this tissue, cells are tightly packed and form a continuous sheet. There is almost no intercellular space between them. They have a very small amount of cementing material between them.
- The epithelium is separated from underlying tissue by an extracellular fibrous basement membrane containing collagen.

On the basis of shape of the cells and their arrangement, epithelial tissues are further classified as follows:

(i) Squamous Epithelium

It constitutes the skin which protects the body. It is further categorised into two types:

(a) Simple Squamous Epithelium

- It is single-layered and closely fitted epithelium. The cells are very thin and flat and appear as tiles over a floor.
- It forms a delicate lining of blood vessels and lung alveoli, where substance transport occurs through a selectively permeable membrane.
- It also covers the oesophagus and the lining of mouth.

(b) Stratified Squamous Epithelium

- It is found in the outer side of skin as it is highly resistant to mechanical injury and is water-proof.
- Cells are arranged in many layers to prevent their wear and tear.

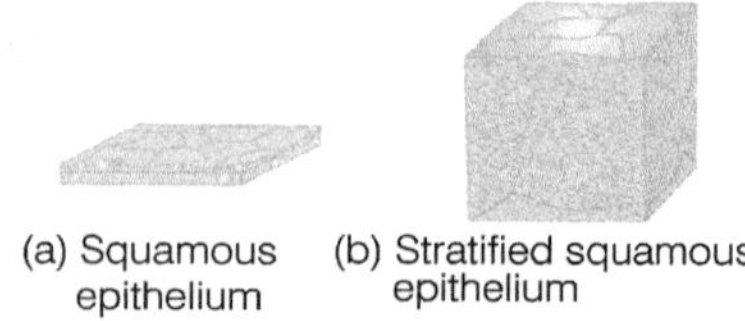

(a) Squamous epithelium (b) Stratified squamous epithelium

(ii) Cuboidal Epithelium

- It is made up of cube-shaped cells, which have round nuclei.
- It forms the lining of kidney tubules and the ducts of salivary glands where it provides mechanical support. It also forms the germinal epithelium of gonads.
- It also helps in absorption, excretion and secretion of materials.

Cuboidal epithelium

(iii) Columnar Epithelium

- It is made up of tall, pillar-like cells, with elongated nuclei.
- It is usually found in the inner lining of intestine where absorption and secretion occur.
- It facilitates the movement across epithelial barrier.

(iv) Ciliated Columnar Epithelium

- When columnar epithelial cells possess cilia (hair-like projections), it is called ciliated columnar epithelium.
- The cilia have the ability to move. Their movement pushes substances like mucus forward.

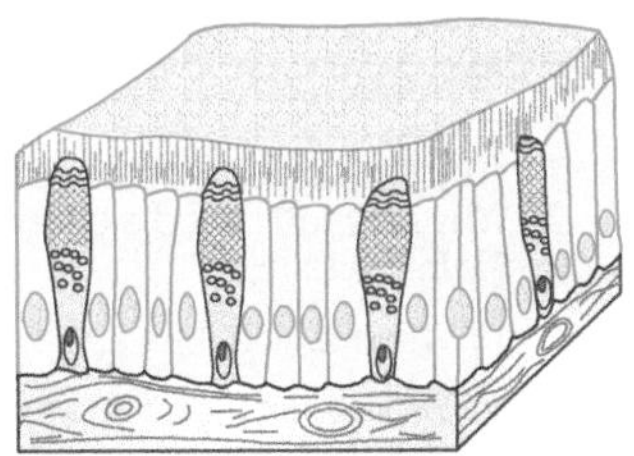

Columnar (Ciliated)

- It is found in the respiratory tract and also lines oviducts, sperm ducts, kidney tubules, etc.

(v) Glandular Epithelium

- Gland cells secrete substances at the epithelial surface.
- Sometimes, portion of epithelial tissue folds inward. This results in the formation of a multicellular gland. This is called **glandular epithelium.**

Functions of Epithelial Tissue

(*i*) It protects the underlying cells from drying, injury, infections and also from harmful effects of chemicals.

(*ii*) It plays a vital role in regulating the exchange of materials between the body and external environment and between different body parts.

(*iii*) It helps in absorption of water and nutrients and in diffusion of gases.

(*iv*) It helps in elimination of waste products from the body.

Check Point 03

1 How are epithelial tissue classified on the basis of cell shape and arrangement?

2 Fill in the blanks:

(*i*) The tissue which facilitates transportation of substances through a thin, selectively permeable membrane is ....

(*ii*) The sites where cuboidal epithelium is present, will be specialised in ....

3 State True or False for the following statement:

The cells of stratified squamous epithelium are arranged in many layers.

4 In which type of epithelium, cilia are present? What is their role in this epithelium?

5 How glandular epithelium is formed?

6 Epithelial tissue helps in elimination of waste products from the body. True or False.

2. Connective Tissue

These tissue is specialised to connect various body organs with each other. For example, it connects two or more bones to each other, muscles to bones, binds different tissues together and also gives support to various parts of the body.

The cells of connective tissue are loosely packed, living and embedded in an intercellular matrix that may either be jelly-like, fluid, dense or rigid in nature. The nature of matrix differs in concordance with the function of the particular connective tissue.

Various types of connective tissues are as follows:

(i) Blood

It is a fluid connective tissue that links different parts of the body. It helps to maintain the continuity of body. It contains fluid matrix called **plasma** and **blood cells** such as **RBCs** (Red Blood Corpuscles or Cells), **WBCs** (White Blood Corpuscles) and **platelets** suspended in it.

Plasma also contains proteins, salts and hormones. Blood transports nutrients, gases, hormones and vitamins to various tissues of the body. It carries excretory products from tissues to excretory organs. It also conducts heat and regulates body temperature.

The properties shown by different blood cells in the body are as follows:

- **RBCs** help in transport of respiratory gases, oxygen and carbon dioxide with the help of haemoglobin to and from the various parts of our body. The average lifespan of RBCs is about 120 days.
- **WBCs** are also called leucocytes, fight with diseases by producing antibodies.
- **Blood platelets** are also called thrombocytes, help in the clotting of blood.

  Different types of blood cells are shown below

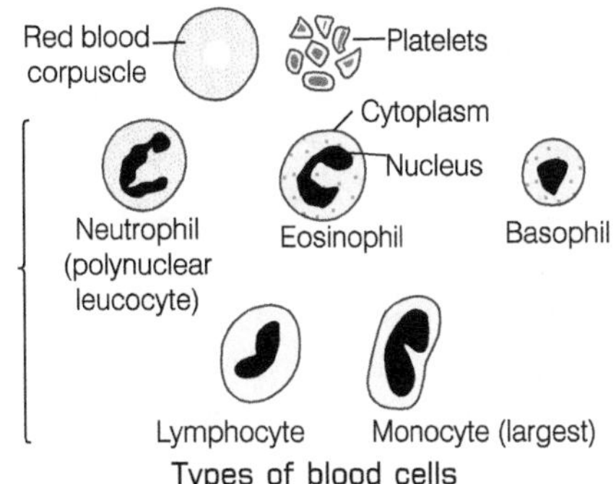

Types of blood cells

(ii) Bone

It is very strong and non-flexible tissue. It is porous, highly vascular, mineralised, hard and rigid. Its matrix is made up of proteins and is rich in salts of calcium and phosphorus. It forms the framework that supports the body. It also anchors the muscles and supports the main organs. The Haversian canal and canaliculus in a compact bone are shown below:

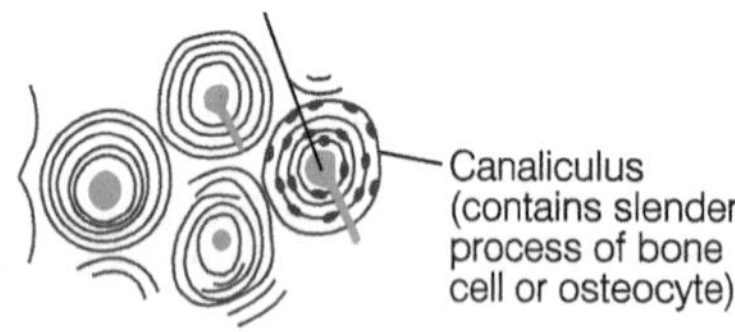

(iii) Ligaments

These connect one bone to other bone. A ligament is very elastic and has considerable strength. It contains very little matrix. Ligaments strengthen joints and permit normal movement. Their overstretching leads to sprain.

(iv) Tendons

These are strong and inelastic structures, which join skeletal muscles to bones. These are composed of white fibrous tissues with limited flexibility, but great strength.

(v) Cartilage

It is a specialised connective tissue having widely spaced cells. It has solid matrix called **chondrin** which is composed of proteins and sugars. Cartilage provides smoothness to the bone surfaces at the joints. It is present in nose, ear, trachea and larynx. We can fold the cartilage of the ears, but we cannot bend the bones in our arms.

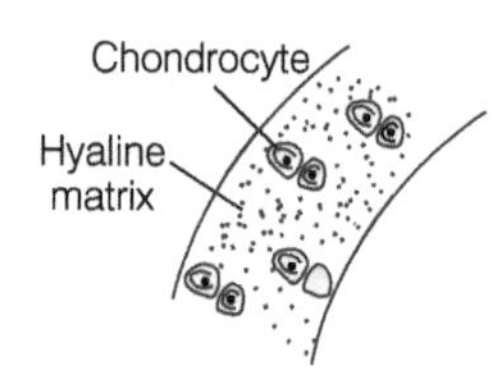

(vi) Areolar Tissue

It is a supporting and packing tissue found between the organs lying in body cavity. It is located between skin and muscles, around blood vessels and nerves and in the bone marrow. It is a loose and cellular tissue. It fills the space inside the organs, supports internal organs. It helps in the repair of tissues.

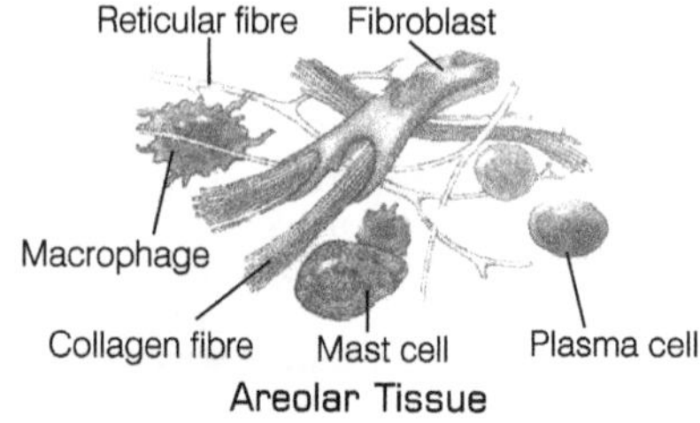

Areolar Tissue

(vii) Adipose Tissue

It serves as a fat reservoir, keeps visceral organs in position. It acts as an insulator due to the storage of fats. It is located below the skin in between the internal organs.

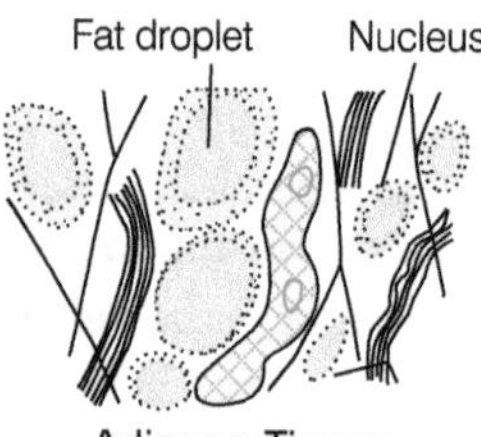

Adipose Tissue

Check Point 04

1. Why are connective tissue named so?
2. Why is blood called a connective tissue?
3. Fill in the blanks:
   (*i*) The main constituents of blood are .... and ....
   (*ii*) Two bones attach to each other by ....
4. What type of tissue is present in bone marrow?
5. Name the tissue found between the organs. What is its function?
6. State True or False for the following statement:
   Adipose tissue acts as insulator in the body.

3. Muscular Tissue

It consists of elongated cells, called **muscle fibres**. These tissue is responsible for the movement in our body. It contains special type of proteins called **contractile proteins** which causes movement of muscles by contraction and relaxation.
Different types of muscular tissues are given below:

(i) Striated Muscles

The muscles present in our limbs which move or stop as per our will, are called striated muscles. These are also called as **voluntary muscles** as we can move them by conscious will. Mostly these are attached to bones and help in body movement, e.g. muscles of limbs. Hence, these are also called as **skeletal muscles.**

The cells of such muscles are long, cylindrical, unbranched and multinucleate (having many nuclei). Under microscope, striated muscles show alternate **light** and **dark bands** or striations. Thus, these are also known as **striated muscles** which are as shown below:

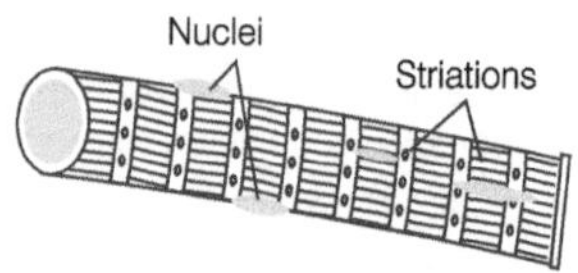

Striated muscle

(ii) Smooth Muscles

The muscles which we cannot move as per our will are called smooth muscles. These are also called **involuntary muscles.** The movement of food in the alimentary canal, contraction and relaxation of blood vessels are involuntary movements.

These muscles are found in the iris of eye, in ureters and in bronchi of lungs.

The cells constituting these muscles are long, with pointed ends (spindle-shaped) and uninucleate (single nucleus). These muscles do not show any dark or light band. Hence, these are also called **unstriated muscles.**

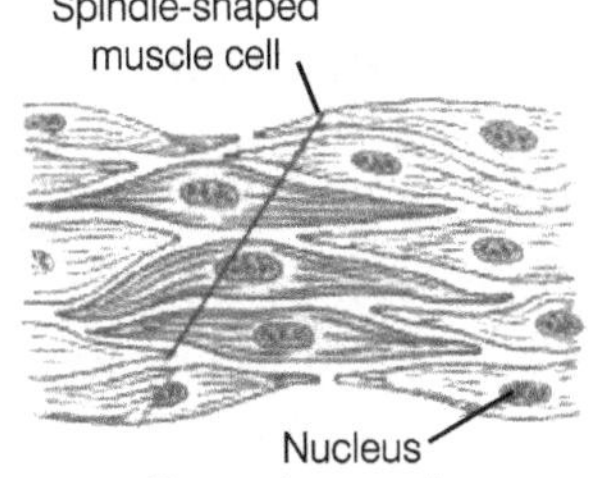

Smooth muscle

(iii) Cardiac Muscles

These are involuntary muscles present only in our **heart**. These perform rhythmic contraction and relaxation throughout the life. The cells constituting cardiac muscles are cylindrical, uninucleate and branched. Cardiac muscles have stripes of light and dark bands.

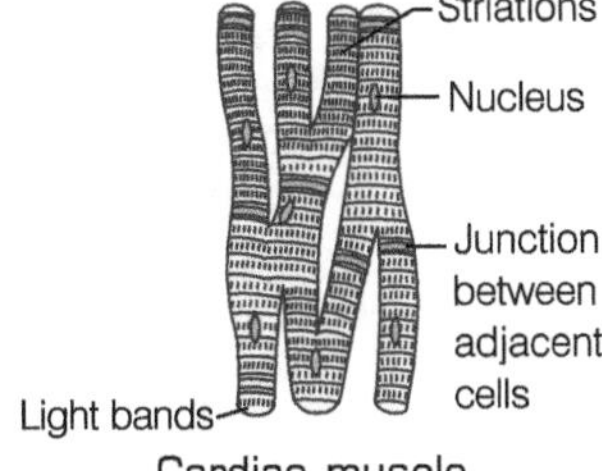

Cardiac muscle

4. Nervous Tissue

The tissue that receives stimulus and transmits it from one part of the tissue to other are called nervous tissues.The cells that constitute nervous tissue are called nerve cells or neurons. These are highly specialised for receiving stimulus and then transmitting it very rapidly from one place to another within the body itself. Brain, spinal cord and nerves are composed of nervous tissue.

An individual nerve cell or a neuron may be upto a metre long and is composed of three major parts:

(*i*) **Cell body** It consists of cytoplasm, nucleus and cell membrane.

(*ii*) **Axon** It is a single long conducting fibre extending from neuron. It transmits impulse away from the cell body.

(*iii*) **Dendrites** These are short branched fibres of neuron, which receive nerve impulses.

The well-labelled diagram of neuron is shown below:

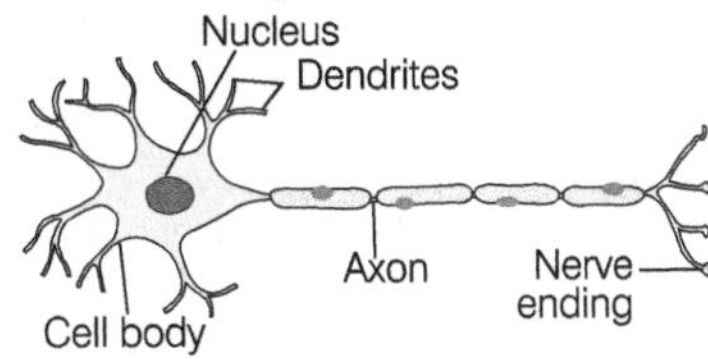

Note Synapse is a region of union of axon of one neuron with the dendrite of next neuron. This allows the transfer of nerve impulse generated to and fro in the body.

Many nerve fibres bound together by connective tissue make up a nerve. Nerve impulse allows us to move our muscles according to our will. Combination of nerve and muscle tissue in animals is of fundamental importance as causes rapid movement in response to stimuli.

Differences between Plant Tissues and Animal Tissues

Plant Tissues	*Animal Tissues*
In plants, dead supportive tissues are more abundant as compared to living tissues.	In multicellular animals, living tissues are more common as compared to dead tissues.
They require less maintenance energy as they are autotrophic and can make their own food.	They require more maintenance energy as they are heterotrophic and have to move in search of food.
There is a differentiation of tissues into meristematic and permanent tissues, which are localised in certain regions of plant based on their dividing capacity.	Such differentiation is absent in animals as their growth is uniform.
Due to activity of meristematic tissue, plants continue to grow throughout life.	Animals do not show growth after reaching maturity. Reparative growth is however, present.
Organisation of plant tissues is simple.	Organisation of animal tissues is complex with the development of more specialised and localised organs and organ systems.
Tissue organisation is meant for stationary habit of plants.	Tissue organisation is targeted towards high mobility of animals.

Check Point 05

1 State True or False for the following statement:
Striated muscles are called skeletal muscles.

2 Name the type of muscles present in
(*i*) iris of eye (*ii*) alimentary canal
(*iii*) bronchi of lungs

3 Smooth muscles are also called as unstriated muscles. Why?

4 Where are cardiac muscles present?

5 Fill in the blanls:
(*i*) The type of cells, which form nervous tissue is ....
(*ii*) The conducting part of a neuron is ....

6 A person carrying a heavy weight gets tired and removes the weight to relax his muscles. Which tissues will be involved in this action?

To Study NCERT Activities
Visit https://goo.gl/Z717Q8
OR **Scan the Code**

NCERT FOLDER

Intext Questions

1 What is a tissue? **Pg 69**

Sol. The group of cells combined together to perform a common function is called tissue, e.g. blood, muscle.

2 What is the utility of tissue in multicellular organisms? **Pg 69**

Sol. Multicellular organisms show division of labour because a particular function is carried out by a cluster of cells (tissue) at a definite place in the body. The tissue is arranged and designed so as to give the highest possible efficiency of function.

3 Name the types of simple tissue. **Pg 73**

Sol. The three main types of simple tissues in plants are:
(*i*) Parenchyma (*ii*) Collenchyma (*iii*) Sclerenchyma

4 Where is apical meristem found? **Pg 73**

Sol. Apical meristem is present in growing tips of stems and roots of plants.

5 Which tissue makes up the husk of coconut? **Pg 73**

Sol. Sclerenchymatous tissue makes up the husk of coconut.

6 What are the constituents of phloem? **Pg 73**

Sol. The main constituents of phloem are:
(*i*) Sieve cells (*ii*) Sieve tubes (*iii*) Companion cells
(*iv*) Phloem parenchyma (*v*) Phloem fibres

7 Name the tissue responsible for movement in our body. **Pg 77**

Sol. Muscular tissue is responsible for movement in our body.

8 What does a neuron look like? **Pg 77**

Sol. A neuron possesses a cell body and various processes emerging from it. These processes include a long axon and short dendrites.

9 Give three features of cardiac muscles. **Pg 77**

Sol. Features of cardiac muscles are listed below:

(*i*) These are involuntary muscles.
(*ii*) Cells of these muscles are cylindrical, branched and uninucleate.
(*iii*) These muscles show rhythmic contraction and relaxation throughout the life.

10 What are the functions of areolar tissue? **Pg 77**

Sol. Functions of areolar tissue are as follows:

(*i*) It fills the space inside the organs and supports internal organs.
(*ii*) It helps in repair of the tissues.

Exercises (On Page 78 & 79)

1 Define the term 'tissue'.

Sol. Refer to Ans. no. 1 of intext questions.

2 How many types of elements together make up the xylem tissue? Name them.

Sol. Four elements makeup xylem tissue which include:

(*i*) Tracheids
(*ii*) Vessels
(*iii*) Xylem parenchyma
(*iv*) Xylem fibres

3 How are simple tissues different from complex tissues in plants?

Sol. Differences between simple tissues and complex tissues are as follows

Simple Tissue	*Complex Tissue*
These are made up of one type of cells.	These are made up of multiple type of cells.
These are mainly responsible for storage and mechanical support.	These are mainly responsible for transportation.
e.g. parenchyma, collenchyma.	e.g. xylem, phloem.

4 Differentiate between parenchyma, collenchyma and sclerenchyma on the basis of their cell wall.

Sol. Differences between parenchyma, collenchyma and sclerenchyma are as follows:

Parenchyma	*Collenchyma*	*Sclerenchyma*
These are living cells with thin walls.	These are living cells with slightly thick walls.	These are dead cells with thick cell walls.
Cells are uniformly thin.	Cells are elongated.	Cells are long and narrow.
The cells are loosely packed with large intercellular spaces.	The cells are irregularly thickened at the corners with very little intercellular spaces.	The cells are thickened due to lignin and there is no internal space inside the cell.

5 What are the functions of the stomata?

Sol. The main functions of stomata are:

(*i*) They help in exchange of gases (CO_2 and O_2) with atmosphere.
(*ii*) They help in transpiration (loss of water in the form of water vapour).

6 Diagrammatically show the difference between the three types of muscle fibres.

Sol. The differences between the three types of muscle fiberes are shown below diagrammatically:

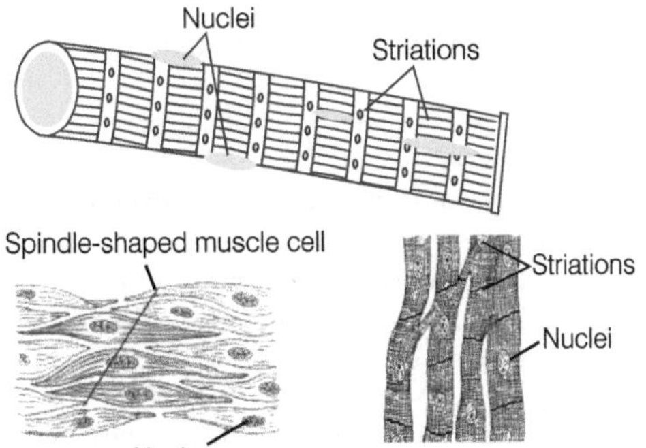

7 What is the specific function of cardiac muscle?

Sol. Cardiac muscles contract and relax rhythmically throughout the life.

8 Differentiate between striated, smooth and cardiac muscles on the basis of their structure and site/location in the body.

Sol. The differences between striated, smooth and cardiac muscles are as follows:

Types	*Striated Muscles*	*Smooth Muscles*	*Cardiac Muscles*
Structure	These are made up of long, cylindrical, unbranched and multinucleate cells.	These muscles are made up of long uninucleate cells with pointed ends.	These are made up of cylindrical, branched and uninucleate cells.
	These show alternate light and dark striations.	These do not show striations.	These muscles show faint striations.
Site/ Location	These are located in limbs and are mostly attached to bones to help in body movement.	These are mostly present in walls of alimentary canal, blood vessels, ureters, bronchi of the lungs and in the iris of eyes.	These are present only in the walls of heart.

9 Draw a labelled diagram of a neuron.

Sol. The well-labelled diagram of a neuron is as follows:

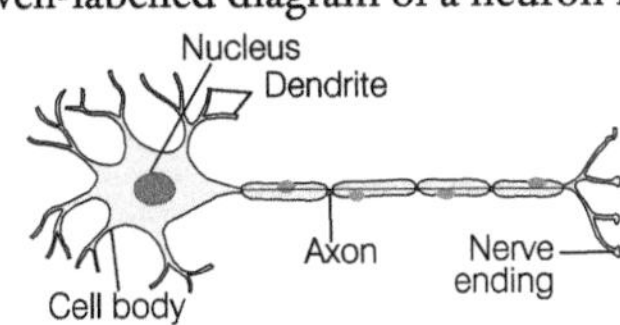

10 Name the following.

(*i*) Tissue that forms the inner lining of the mouth.
(*ii*) Tissue that connects muscle to bone in humans.
(*iii*) Tissue that transports food in plants.
(*iv*) Tissue that stores fat in our body.
(*v*) Connective tissue with a fluid matrix.
(*vi*) Tissue present in the brain.

Sol. (*i*) Squamous epithelium (*ii*) Tendons (*iii*) Phloem (*iv*) Adipose tissue (*v*) Blood (*vi*) Nervous tissue.

11 Identify the type of tissue in following: Skin, bark of tree, bone, lining of kidney tubule, vascular bundle.

Sol. **Skin** Squamous epithelium
Bark of tree Epidermal tissue
Bone Connective tissue
Lining of kidney tubule Cuboidal epithelium
Vascular bundle Conductive tissue (xylem and phloem).

12 Name the regions in which parenchyma tissue is present.

Sol. Parenchyma tissue is mainly found in soft parts of the plant such as roots, stem, leaves and also present in ground tissue of petioles.

13 What is the role of epidermis in plants?

Sol. Role of epidermis in plants:

(*i*) It helps in protection of internal parts of plant.
(*ii*) It becomes thick and prevents water loss in plants living in very dry habitats.
(*iii*) Its cells secrete a waxy, water resistant layer on the outer surface, which protects against loss of water, mechanical injury and infections.
(*iv*) Leaf epidermis have stomata to help in gas exchange and transpiration.
(*v*) In old plants, epidermal layer becomes thick and forms cork. Cork cells contain a chemical called suberin in their walls, which makes them impervious to gases and water.

14 How does the cork act as a protective tissue?

Sol. Cork is made up of several layers of epidermal cells. These cells of cork are dead and compactly arranged without intercellular spaces. They also have a chemical called suberin in their walls, which makes cork impervious to gases and water.

15 Complete the table.

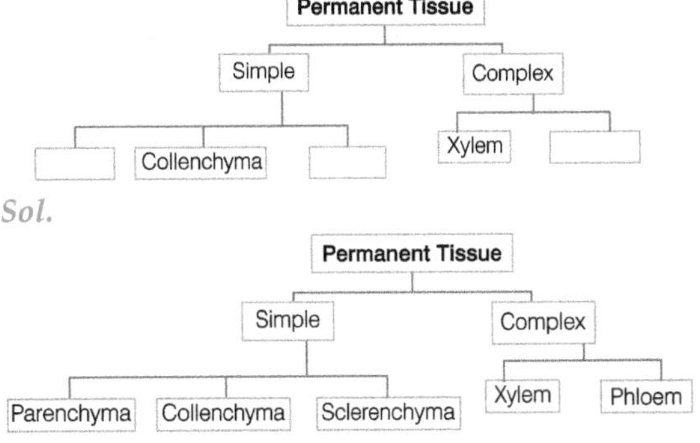

SUMMARY

- **Tissues** are group of cells that are similar in structure and work together to achieve a particular function, e.g., blood, phloem and muscles. Tissues are broadly classified into plant and animal tissues.
- On the basis of dividing capacity, plant tissues can be classified into two fundamental types, i.e., meristematic tissue and permanent tissue.
- **Meristematic tissues** divide actively throughout the life. These are found in growing regions of plant like root and shoot tip. These tissues are mainly of three types, i.e. apical meristem, intercalary meristem and lateral meristem.
- **Apical meristems** are present at growing tips of stems and roots. These are helpful in increasing the length of the stems and the roots.
- **Intercalary meristems** are present at the base of the leaves or internodes of the twigs.
- **Lateral meristems** are present on the lateral sides of stems and roots. It helps in increasing the girth of the stem or root.
- **Permanent tissue** is formed from the cells of meristematic tissue when they loose their ability to divide and have attained a permanent shape, size and function by the process called **differentiation**. These are mainly of two types, i.e. simple and complex permanent tissue.
- **Parenchyma tissue** form the basic packing tissue. These tissues are present in cortex, pith of stem, roots and also in mesophyll of leaves.
- **Collenchyma cells** are living, elongated and irregularly thickened at the corners, generally found in leaf stocks below the epidermis. These provide mechanical support and elasticity to plants tissues.
- **Sclerenchyma tissue** is present in stems around vascular bundles, in veins of leaves and in hard covering of seeds and nuts. These provide strength and enable the plant to bear various stresses.
- **Complex permanent tissues** are made up of more than one types of cells.
- **Xylem** is a vascular and mechanical conducting tissue. It is responsible for transport of food from roots to other parts of a plant.
- **Phloem** is a vascular tissue, responsible for transport of food from leaves to other parts of the plant.
- **Animal tissues** are classified on the basis of the functions they perform, i.e. epithelial, connective, muscular and nervous tissue.
- **Epithelial tissue** is a protective tissue. It is tightly packed and is present in skin and lining of mouth.
- **Squamous epithelium** cells are flat, it forms the delicate lining of oesophagus and mouth. It may be several layers thick as in skin, known as stratified squamous epithelium.
- **Columnar epithelium** cells are tall, pillar-like and have elongated nuclei. It is usually found in inner lining of intestine, where absorption and secretion occur.
- **Ciliated columnar epithelium** cells have cilia, hair-like projections found on the outer surface of columnar epithelial cells found in trachea, bronchi, etc.
  Glandular epithelium cells acquire additional specialisation known as gland cells that can secrete substances at the epithelial surface.
- **Connective tissue** connects various body organs, i.e. blood, bone, tendon, areolar, adipose, cartilage etc.
- **Muscular tissue** consists of elongated cells and is responsible for movement. Striated muscles mostly attached to bones and help in body movement. Unstriated muscles cannot be moved according to will. Cardiac muscles present in heart, show rhythmic contraction and relaxation throughout the life.
- **Nervous tissue** enables body to response to stimulus. They transmit stimuli from one place to another within body, through neurons.
- **Neuron** forms the functional unit of nervous tissue

For Mind Map

Visit https://goo.gl/cGGYxH OR **Scan the Code** 

Exam Practice

Objective Type Questions

Multiple Choice Questions

1 Meristematic tissues in plants are

(a) localised and permanent
(b) not limited to certain regions
(c) localised and dividing cells
(d) growing in volume **NCERT Exemplar**

Sol. (c) Meristematic tissues consist of actively dividing cells and are present in the growing regions of plants, e.g., the tips of roots and stems. The cells of meristematic tissue are round, oval, polygonal or rectangular.

2 Parenchyma cells are

(a) relatively unspecified and thin-walled
(b) thick-walled and specialised
(c) lignified
(d) None of the above **NCERT Exemplar**

Sol. (a) Parenchyma cells form the bulk of the plant body. The cells are rounded or isodiametric, i.e. equally expanded on all sides, relatively unspecified and thin-walled. Its cells are living and they possess the power of division.

3 Flexibility in plants is due to

(a) collenchyma
(b) sclerenchyma
(c) parenchyma
(d) chlorenchyma **NCERT Exemplar**

Sol. (a) Collenchyma is a mechanical tissue in young dicotyledonous stems and provides mechanical support and flexibility to plant organs. It allows easy bending in various parts of a plant mainly young growing stem without breaking them.

4 Which of the following is true?

(a) Vessels are multicellular tube-like structures with wide lumen
(b) Tracheids are multicellular tube-like structures with wide narrow lumen
(c) Vessels are unicellular tube-like structures with wide lumen
(d) Tracheids are unicellular tube-like structures with wide lumen

Sol. (a) Vessels are multicellular tube-like structures with wide lumen found in xylem of plants and help in the conduction of water and minerals.

5 A long tree has several branches. The tissue that helps in the sideways conduction of water in the branches is

(a) collenchyma
(b) xylem parenchyma
(c) parenchyma
(d) xylem vessels **NCERT Exemplar**

Sol. (d) Xylem vessels are very long tube-like structures formed by a row of cells placed end to end. The transverse walls between these cells are partially or completely dissolved to form continuous water channels.

6 Choose the wrong statement.

(a) The nature of matrix differs according to the function of the tissue
(b) Fats are stored below the skin and in between the internal organs
(c) Epithelial tissues have intercellular spaces between them
(d) Cells of striated muscles are multinucleate and unbranched **NCERT Exemplar**

Sol. (c) Statement is option (c) is incorrect. In the epithelial tissues, cells are tightly packaged and form a continuous sheet. There is almost no intercellular space between them. Rest statements are correct.

7 Lining of kidney tubules is made up of

(a) stratified columnar epithelium
(b) simple cuboidal epithelium
(c) stratified squamous epithelium
(d) simple columnar epithelium

Sol. (b) Lining of kidney tubules and ducts of salivary glands are made up of cuboidal epithelium (cube-shaped cells having round nuclei).

It provides mechanical support and also helps in absorption, excretion and secretion.

8 Choose the correctly matched pair.

(a) Inner lining of salivary ducts– Ciliated epithelium
(b) Moist surface of buccal cavity– Glandular epithelium
(c) Tubular parts of nephrons– Cuboidal epithelium
(d) Inner surface of bronchioles– Squamous epithelium

Sol. (c) Cuboidal epithelium is present in the tubular parts of nephron. These cells often form microvilli to increase the absorptive surface area of cell.

9 Connective tissue is

(a) ectodermal in origin with intercellular spaces
(b) ectodermal in origin without intercellular spaces
(c) mesodermal in origin without intercellular spaces
(d) mesodermal in origin with intercellular spaces

Sol. (d) Connective tissue is mesodermal in origin with intercellular spaces, connective tissue cells and fibres. Major functions of the connective tissue are binding, support, protection, transport, insulation, fat storage and body defence, etc.

10 Which of the following helps in repair of tissue and fills up the space inside the organ?

(a) Tendon
(b) Adipose tissue
(c) Areolar
(d) Cartilage **NCERT Exemplar**

Sol. (c) Areolar tissue is a loose and cellular connective tissue. It fills the space inside the organs and supports internal organs. It helps in the repair of tissues.

11 While doing work and running, you move your organs like hands, legs, etc. Which among the following is correct?

(a) Smooth muscles contract and pull the ligament to move the bones
(b) Smooth muscles contract and pull the tendons to move the bones
(c) Skeletal muscles contract and pull the ligament to move the bones
(d) Skeletal muscles contract and pull the tendon to move the bones **NCERT Exemplar**

Sol. (d) While doing work and running, skeletal muscles contract and pull the tendon (which connects muscles to bones) to move the bone.

12 Select the incorrect sentence.

(a) Blood has matrix containing proteins, salts and hormones
(b) Two bones are connected with ligament
(c) Tendons are non-fibrous tissue and fragile
(d) Cartilage is a form of connective tissue **NCERT Exemplar**

Sol. (c) A tendon is a white fibrous tissue which has great strength, but limited flexibility. Tendons are cord-like, strong, inelastic structures that join skeletal muscles to bones.

Fill in the Blanks

13 The movement of food in phloem from leaves to other parts is ....

Sol. bidirectional

14 Xylem transports water and .... from soil.

Sol. minerals

15 the tissue constituting the husk of coconut is. ....

Sol. sclerenchyma

16 The outer layer of the skin has .... cells .

Sol. squamous

17 The cells that drive the mucus in the respiratory tract are ....

Sol. ciliated

True and False

18 The division and differentiation of the cells of meristematic tissue give rise to permanent tissues.

Sol. True

19 Tracheids and vessels do not transport sap.

Sol. False, Tracheids and vessels transport water and minerals vertically.

20 Cork cambium is the example of lateral meristem.

Sol. True

21 Parenchyma gives rigidity, flexibility and elasticity to the plant body.

Sol. False; Sclerenchyma gives ridigit flexibility and elasticity to the plant body.

22 Phloem fibres are living sclerenchyma cells.

Sol. False, Phloem fibres are dead, sclerenchyma cells.

Match the Columns

23 Match the following columns.

	Column I		*Column II*
1.	Cambium	A.	Air cavities
2.	Suberin	B.	Round nuclei
3.	Columnar epithelium	C.	Elongater nuclei
4.	Cuboidal epithelium	D.	Cork
5.	Aerenchyma	E.	Lateral meristem

Sol. $1 \rightarrow E, 2 \rightarrow D, 3 \rightarrow C, 4 \rightarrow B, 5 \rightarrow A$.

23 Match the following columns.

Column I		Column II	
1.	Chondrin	A.	heart
2.	Cardiac muscles	B.	Fat
3.	Adipose tissue	C.	Chlorophyll
4.	Chlorenchyma	D.	Waxy coating
5.	Cutin	E.	Cartilage

Sol. 1 → E, 2 → A, 3 → B, 4 → C, 5 → D.

Assertion-Reason

Direction (Q.Nos. 24-28) *In each of the following questions, a statement of Assertion is given by the corresponding statement of Reason. Of the statements, mark the correct answer as*

(a) If both Assertion and Reason are true and Reason is the correct explanation of Assertion
(b) If both Assertion and Reason are true but Reason is not the correct explanation of Assertion
(c) If Assertion is true but Reason is false
(d) If Assertion is false, but Reason is true

24 **Assertion** Lateral meristems are present along the side of various organs in plants.

Reason These help in the healing of wounds in plants.

Sol. (b) Lateral meristems are present along the side of the organs, e.g. vascular cambium in the plants. These are responsible for healing wounds of plants by its their meristematic activity. Both Assertion and Reason are correct but Reason is not the correct explanation of Assertion.

25 **Assertion** Cork is a protective tissue present in plants.

Reason It aids in protection against water loss, mechanical injury and microbial infestation.

Sol. (a) Cork is a waxy layer impervious to gases and water. This is due to a chemical called suberin in its walls. This layer protects the plants from physical (water loss) and biological stresses (mirobial infection). Both Assertion and Reason are correct and Reason is the correct explanation of Assertion.

26 **Assertion** Blood is a fluid connective tissue.

Reason It is a motile connecting tissue which connects all the tissues, organs with each other.

Sol. (a) Blood consists of fluid matrix along with suspended cells. It performs many functions like gaseous transport, nutrient exchange, waste collection, etc., involving all the tissues and organs of the body. Both Assertion and Reason are correct and Reason is the correct explanation of Assertion.

27 **Assertion** The movements of alimentary canal, iris of the eye and bronchi of lungs are not under our will.

Reason These are controlled voluntary muscles.

Sol. (c) Voluntary muscles are the muscles, which are under our complete control, e.g. the working and movement of limbs. On the other hand, involuntary muscles are controlled by hypothalamus, i.e. they are regulated rhythmically, e.g. alimentary canal, iris of the eye and bronchi of lungs. Thus, Assertion is true, but Reason is false.

28 **Assertion** Axon and dendrites are special feature of neurons.

Reason They help in the rapid conduction of nerve impulses.

Sol. (a) Axon and dendrites are parts of neuron or a nerve cell. In a neuron, dendrites may be one to several, but axon is always one. They help in the rapid conduction of impulse.

Both Assertion and Reason are correct and Reason is the correct explanation of Assertion.

Case Based Questions

Direction (Q.Nos. 29-32) *Answer the questions on the basis of your understanding of the following table and related studied concepts:*

Types of Muscular Tissue

Features	Skeletal	Smooth	Cardiac
Shape	Long, cylindrical and unbranched	Long, spindle shaped with pointed ends	Cylindrical and branched
Number of nuclei	Many	Single	One or two
Position of nuclei	Near the periphery	In the centre	In the centre

29 Refer to the information given in the table Among these types of muscular tissue, which one do not show striations?

Sol. Smooth muscles are called unstriated muscles because they do not show striations (alternate light and dark bands).

30 Smooth muscles are also known as visceral muscles. They have the capacity to increase in size and bulk whenever the need arise. Based on the above information, identify which of the following cannot be a function of these muscles

(a) contraction of blood vessels
(b) movement of food in alimentary canal
(c) movement of skeleton and body
(d) relaxation of blood vessels

Sol. Movement of skeletion and thus the body is a function of striated or skeletal muscles. Rest other are functions of smooth muscles.

31 Multinucleated muscle fibres are

(a) skeletal muscle (b) smooth muscles
(c) cardiac muscles (d) Both (a) and (c)

Sol. (d) Skeletal and cardiac muscles have more than one nuclei, thus they are known as multinucleate muscle fibres.

32 The muscle tissues are one of the most active tissues of the body. Which organelle would you expect to be more in number in cells of this tissue and why ?

Sol. The organelle which should be present in more members in muscle tissue is mitochondria. This tissue is responsible for performing movement of the body and its various parts which requires a lot of energy. This demand of energy can be net by mitochondria which is the power house of the cells.

Direction (Q.Nos. 33-36) *Answer the questions on the basis of your understanding of the following passage and related studied concepts:*

Plants have a transport system to move things around the xylem moves water and solutes from roots to leaves through transpiration. The phloem moves glucose and amino acids from the leaves all evelnd the plant through translocation. In modern plants, the xylem and phloem are arranged in groups called vascular bundles. The xylem is constituted by 4 elements, i.e. tracheids, vessels, parenchyma and fibres while phloem is constituted by sieve tubes, companion cells, phloem fibres and parenchyama.

33 Why are xylem and phloem classified as complex permanent tissues?

Sol. Xylem and phloem are classified as complex permanent tissue because they are made up of more then one type of cells that differ from one another in structure.

34 All phloem cells are living with one exception. Which component is this exception?

Sol. Phloem fibres are the non-living or dead component of phloem tissue. Rest all are living.

35 What is the function of companion cells of phloem tissue?

Sol. Companion cells help sieve tubes in translocation of food to all parts of a plant.

36 What is the advantage of presence of vascular bundles in higher plants?

Sol. Vasculer bundle (i.e. Xylem and phloem) make the survival of higher plants possible in terrestrial habitats.

Very Short Answer Type Questions

37 Which process in meristematic tissue converts it to permanent tissue?

Sol. Differentiation is the process by which meristematic tissue takes up a permanent shape, size and function.

38 Which feature of meristematic tissue helps aquatic plants to maintain buoyancy in water?

Sol. Large air cavities present in parenchyma (aerenchyma) of aquatic plants help the plant to maintain buoyancy in water.

39 Why epidermis of plants living in dry habitats is thicker?

Sol. Epidermis of plants living in dry habitats is thicker in order to prevent loss of water.

40 Identify the following.

(*i*) Living component of xylem
(*ii*) Dead element of phloem

Sol. (*i*) Xylem parenchyma consists of living cells having thin cell walls.
(*ii*) Phloem fibres are the dead elements of phloem.

41 Which type of conducting tissues conduct water and minerals vertically?

Sol. Tracheids and vessels of xylem are the two conducting tissues, which conduct water and minerals vertically.

42 Stratified squamous epithelium is abundantly found in the outer side of skin. What is the advantage of this arrangement in living body?

Sol. Stratified squamous epithelium is highly resistant to mechanical injury and is also waterproof. It is multilayered, thus capable of preventing the wear and tear occurring in living body.

43 Blood, bone, ligaments, cartilages., etc, are all types of connective tissue present in body with different nature of matrix. Why?

Sol. The nature of matrix of different connective tissues differs in concordance with their specific function e.g. Blood transports nutrient, gases, etc., hence, it is a fluid tissue.

44 Which body cell provides resistance against infection?

Sol. WBCs provide resistance against infection by producing antibodies in the body.

45 What is the function of ligament?

Sol. It connects bone to bone.

46 The matrix of cartilage is made up of a different compound than that of bone. Give its name.

Sol. Chondrin.

47 Name the connective tissue, which provides smoothness to the bone surfaces at the joints.

Sol. Cartilage provides smoothness to the bone surfaces at the joints.

48 What is the prominent function of adipose tissue?

Sol. It serves as a fat reservoir, keeps visceral organs in position and acts as an insulator.

49 What will happen if the cardiac muscles stop performing the rhythmic contraction and relaxation in living body?

Sol. The heart will stop beating and the organism will die.

50 Name the following:

(*i*) Multinucleate muscle.

(*ii*) Muscle with intercalated discs.

Sol. (*i*) Skeletal muscle.

(*ii*) Cardiac muscle.

51 Which type of tissue contracts, when it is stimulated by nerve impulse?

Sol. Striated muscle fibres contract, when stimulated by nerve cells.

Short Answer (SA) Type Questions

1 Draw a diagrammatic labelled sketch of stem tip to show the location of meristematic tissue. Mention the functions of different types of meristematic tissue.

Sol. Refer to fig. "Location of meristematic tissues in plant body" on Pg 127.

Functions of meristematic tissue are:

(*i*) **Apical meristem** It increases the length of stem and root.

(*ii*) **Lateral meristem** It increases the girth of stem and root.

(*iii*) **Intercalary meristem** It increases horizontal growth of plant.

2 Explain the basic criteria for classification of permanent tissue in plants.

Sol. The following points form the basis of criteria for classification of permanent tissue in plants:

(*i*) Whether the tissue is made up of one type of cell (simple) or more than one type of cells (complex).

(*ii*) Whether the function is supportive (parenchyma), protective (epidermis) or conducting (xylem and phloem).

(*iii*) Whether the cell wall is thick or thin.

(*iv*) Whether the cells are living or dead.

3 (*i*) A plant tissue is observed under a microscope, as shown in the figure below. Identify the tissue.

(*ii*) State the characteristic features of these cells.

(*iii*) Name any two parts of the plant, where such cells are present.

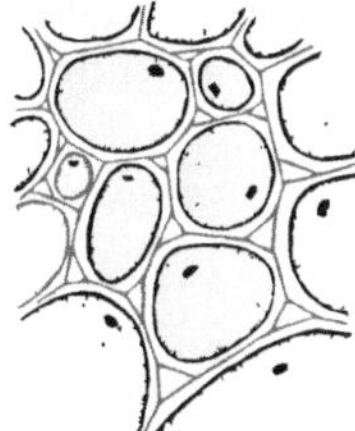

Sol. (*i*) The tissue given in the figure is parenchyma.

(*ii*) It consists of thin-walled unspecialised cells, which are loosely packed, i.e. having intercellular spaces. Each cell has a prominent nucleus.

(*iii*) (*a*) Pith (*b*) Cortex

4 List any six characteristics of parenchyma.

Sol. Major characteristics of parenchyma are as follows:

(*i*) The cells of parenchyma are living and possess the power of division.

(*ii*) Each parenchyma cell is isodiametric in shape with thin cell wall and encloses dense cytoplasm and small nucleus.

(iii) The cells are loosely packed with large intercellular spaces between them.
(iv) It is found in soft parts of plant such as cortex of roots, ground tissue in stem and mesophyll cells of leaves.
(v) It serves as a packing tissue to fill the spaces between other tissues and maintains the shape of plant.
(vi) It stores waste products of plant such as tannin, gum, crystals, etc.

5 (i) Identify the tissue given in the following figure.
(ii) Mention the characteristic features of the cells.
(iii) Specify the function of this tissue.
(iv) Name any one part of the plant, where these cells are present.

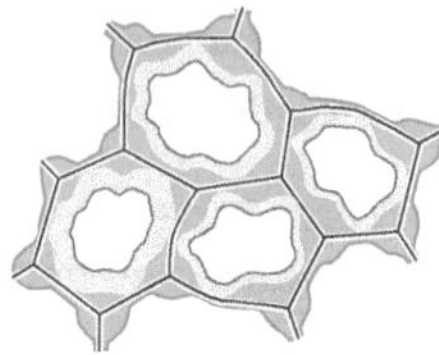

Sol. (i) The tissue given in the figure is collenchyma.
(ii) The cells of collenchyma are living, elongated, thickened at the corners and have very little intercellular space.
(iii) It provides mechanical support and flexibility to the plant.
(iv) It is present in leaf stalks, below the epidermis.

6 Name the tissue responsible for the flexibility in plants. How would you differentiate it from other permanent tissues?

Sol. Collenchyma tissue is responsible for providing flexibility in plants.

Differences between collenchyma tissue and other permanent tissues (parenchyma and sclerenchyma) are as follows:

Parenchyma	Collenchyma	Sclerenchyma
Cell wall is primary.	Cell wall is primary.	Cell wall is secondary.
Cell wall is very thin and made up of cellulose.	Cell wall has irregular thickenings of cellulose and pectin.	Cell wall is uniformly thick due to the deposition of lignin.
It provides turgidity to plant.	It provides mechanical strength as well as flexibility to plant.	It provides mechanical strength to plant.
These are formed of living cells.	These are formed of living cells.	They are composed of dead cells.
They have isodiametric cells.	They have elongated or oval cells.	Some of the cells are spindle-shaped, long and narrow.

7 Answer the following:
(i) How is the epidermis of the plants living in very dry habitats adapted?
(ii) Write functions of guard cells of stomata in the leaf.
(iii) Epidermal cells help in the absorption of water and nutrients from soil. How?

Sol. (i) The epidermis of the plants living in very dry habitats has a thick waxy coating of waterproof cutin over it. This prevents the loss of water.
(ii) They help in exchange of gases with atmosphere, due to opening and closing of stomatal pore.
(iii) Epidermal cells in roots bear long hair-like outgrowth. i.e., root hairs that greatly increase the total absorptive surface area and help in increased absorption of water and nutrients from soil.

8 Describe three functions of protective tissue in plants.

Sol. Two types of protective tissue present in plants are epidermis and cork. The three common functions of these protective tissues are :
(i) Cork protects plants from invasion of parasitic microorganisms and from excessive heat and cold.
(ii) The cuticle of epidermis checks the excessive evaporation of water.
(iii) Epidermis allows transpiration and gaseous exchange through stomata.

9 (i) Identify the given figures.

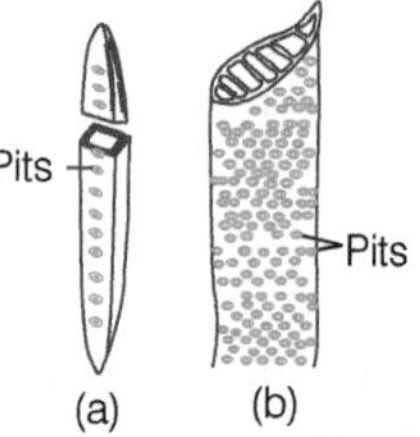

(ii) Give any two major differences between the structures identified.
(iii) Describe the role performed by these two in the plant body.

Sol. (i) The given figures are of tracheids (a) and vessels (b) of xylem tissue.

(*ii*) The differences between tracheids (*a*) and vessels (*b*) are as follows:

Tracheids	*Vessels*
They are unicellular and small-sized with tapering ends.	They are multicellular and large-sized.
More lignified, so have narrow lumen.	Less lignified, so have wide lumen.

(*iii*) Tracheids and vessels are lignified tissues that provide mechanical strength to the plant body. They also function in carrying water and mineral salts from roots to different parts of plant body vertically.

10 List the constituents of phloem. What will happen if the phloem at the base of a branch is removed?

Sol. Major constituents of phloem include sieve cells, sieve tubes, companion cells, phloem fibres and phloem parenchyma.

If the phloem at the base of branch is removed, then lower area of the branch will not receive food from the leaves. But the plant will not die, as it will continue to receive food from other branches as food can move through phloem in both the directions.

11 Give the name of the following:

(*i*) Tissue concerned with the conduction of food materials.
(*ii*) Tissue capable of cell division.
(*iii*) Multiple pores present in epidermis of leaf.

Sol. (*i*) Complex tissue (phloem)
(*ii*) Meristematic tissue
(*iii*) Stomata (Singular stoma)

12 Which is the simplest protective tissue present in animal body? State its two functions.

Sol. The most simple protective tissue present in animal body is epithelial tissue.

Its major functions are:

(*i*) It protects underlying cells from drying, injury and infections.
(*ii*) It helps in elimination of waste products from the body.

13 Name the type of epithelium present in respiratory tract. What is its specialisation?

Sol. Ciliated columnar epithelium is present in respiratory tract of humans.

It has specialised hair-like projections called cilia which help in the movement of substances and mucus forward.

14 Give three differences between epithelial tissue and connective tissue.

Sol. Differences between epithelial and connective tissues are as follows:

Epithelial Tissue	*Connective Tissue*
It is the covering tissue and protects body from infections, injury, etc.	It is connecting tissue as it connects various body organs.
Cells are tightly packed.	Cells are loosely packed.
Cells contain very little or no intercellular matrix.	Space between cells is filled with non-living matrix (solid or fluid).

15 Mention three different types of blood cells with their functions. Draw diagrams also.

Sol. Three different types of blood cells with their function are as follow

(*i*) **Red Blood Cells** (RBCs) Contains haemoglobin, help in the transportation of gases, digested food, hormones, etc.
(*ii*) **White Blood Cells** (WBCs) Integral part of immune system, help in fighting diseases by producing antibodies and engulfing the germs and pathogens.
(*iii*) **Platelets** Help in the clotting of blood.
For diagram, Refer to fig. on Pg 131.

16 Name the tissue that smoothens bones surfaces at joints. Describe its structure with the help of a diagram.

Sol. Cartilage is the tissue that smoothens bones surfaces at joints.

Structure It is a specialised connective tissue, which is compact and less vascular.

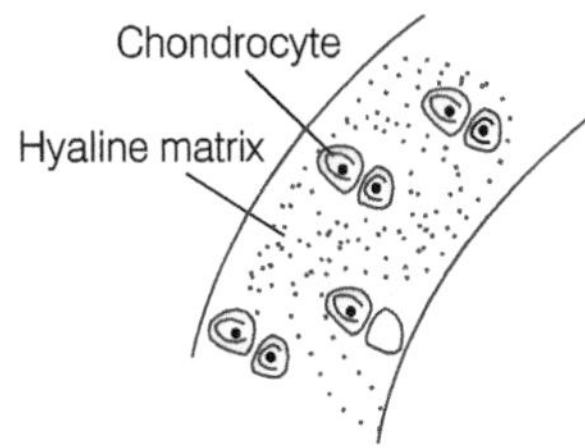

Hyaline cartilage

Its extensive matrix is composed of proteins and slightly hardened by calcium salts and also has delicate network of collagen fibres, living cells and chondrocytes.

The chondrocytes are present in lacunae. Cartilage provides support and flexibility to body parts. It is present in nose, trachea, ear and larynx.

17 Give the differences between tendon and ligament.

Sol. The differences between tendon and ligament are as follows:

Tendon	Ligament
It is strong and non-flexible in nature.	It is elastic and flexible in nature.
It joins muscles to bones.	It joins bones to bones.
It is formed of white fibrous connective tissue.	It is formed of yellow fibrous connective tissue.

18 State the functions of skeletal connective tissue.

Sol. The functions of skeletal connective tissue are:

(*i*) It gives definite shape to the body.

(*ii*) It protects the vital organs of the body, e.g. brain.

(*iii*) It provides surface for attachment of muscles to increase their efficiency.

19 Write a note about structure and significance of striated muscles with diagram.

Sol. Striated muscles are voluntary muscles, i.e., we can move these muscles according to our conscious will.

These are mostly attached to bones and help in body movement. They show alternate light and dark bands or striations (when stained appropriately).

Cells of striated muscles are long, cylindrical, unbranched and multinucleate, e.g., muscle of limbs. The striated muscles is shown below.

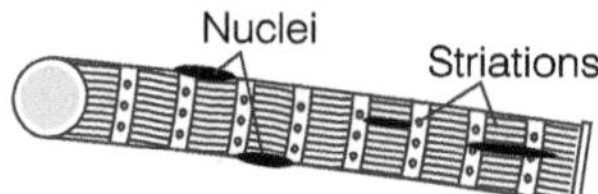

Striated muscle

20 Name the kinds of muscles found in your limbs and lungs. How do they differ from each other structurally and functionally?

Sol. (*i*) The striated muscles are found in our limbs.

Structure Cells are long and cylindrical in shape, presence of dark and light bands, multinucleate and unbranched.

Function Responsible for voluntary movements.

(*ii*) The smooth or non-striated muscles are found in our lungs.

Structure Cells are spindle-shaped, absence of striation, uninucleate and unbranched.

Function Responsible for involuntary movements.

21 Which type of muscle, smooth or striated is found in the iris of eye? Why are smooth muscles called involuntary muscles? In what way are they different from striated muscles with respect to number of nuclei?

Sol. Smooth muscles are found in the iris of eye. Smooth muscles are the muscles that cannot be moved or stopped according to our will. So, they are known as involuntary muscles. Smooth muscles are uninucleate, whereas striated muscles are multinucleate.

22 Draw a labelled diagram of unstriated muscle tissue and mention its occurrence, features and functions.

Sol. The diagram of unstriated muscle tissue (Refer to fig. on Pg. no. 133)

Occurrence These tissues are found in the walls of alimentary canal, urinary bladder, oesophagus, iris, bronchi, etc.

Features

(*i*) They are unbranched and non-striated.

(*ii*) Cells are long, thin and spindle-shaped.

(*iii*) Each cell has a single central nucleus.

Functions

(*i*) These muscles do not work as per our will.

(*ii*) They carry out the movement in urinary bladder and gall bladder.

23 Draw a well-labelled diagram of cardiac muscle found in the human body. Write two differences between striated and smooth muscles.

Sol. Refer to fig. "Cardiac muscle" on Pg 133.

Differences between striated muscles and smooth muscles are as follows:

Striated Muscles	Smooth Muscles
They are known as voluntary muscles, and are attached to bones. Responsible for body movements.	They are known as involuntary muscles and help in movement of food, opening and closing of tubes, etc.
These are present in limbs and tongue.	These are present in visceral organs like alimentary canal.

24 What are neurons? Where are they found in the body? What function do they perform in the body of an organism?

Sol. Neurons are structural and functional units of nervous system. These are found in brain, spinal cord and nerves.

Functions

(i) They coordinate various body parts during any body function.

(ii) They control all the activities of the body.

(iii) They transmit message in the form of nerve impulses to brain and spinal cord.

25 Differentiate between axon and dendrite.

Sol. Differences between axon and dendrite are as follows:

Axon	Dendrite
It carries impulses away from the cell body.	It carries impulses towards the cell body.
It is long and may or may not be branched.	It is short and always branched.
It is covered with sheath.	Sheath is absent.

26 Give one function of each of the following.

(i) Stomata

(ii) Contractile proteins in muscles

(iii) Cardiac muscle fibres

Sol. (i) **Stomata** These help in the gaseous exchange between the plant and atmosphere. Transpiration also takes place through stomata.

(ii) **Contractile proteins in muscles** These muscles contract and relax to cause movement in the body parts.

(iii) **Cardiac muscle fibres** These help in rhythmic contraction and relaxation of heart throughout the life.

27 Write functions of the following:

(i) Areolar connective tissues

(ii) Neurons

(iii) Adipose connective tissues

Sol. (i) **Areolar connective tissues** These fill the space inside the organs and supports internal organs of the body. They also help in repair of tissues.

(ii) **Neurons** These are the fundamental cells of nervous tissue. They are highly specialised for being stimulated and then transmitting the stimulus very rapidly from one place to another within the body.

(iii) **Adipose connective tissues** These are fat storing tissue found below the skin between internal organs. The cells of this tissue are filled with fat globules. Due to storage of fats, these act as an insulators.

28 What happens, when

(i) formation of cork in older stem does not occur.

(ii) blood platelets are removed from blood.

(iii) apical meristem is damaged in plants.

Sol. (i) If the formation of cork does not occur in older stem, then the outer tissue will rupture due to the increase in girth and plant will get infected by the diseases.

(ii) Blood clotting will not occur at the site of injury. Bleeding will continue and a significant loss of blood may lead to death.

(iii) If apical meristem get damaged in plants, the growth of plant will not occur.

Long Answer (LA) Type Questions

1 Give reasons for the following:

(i) Meristematic cells have prominent nucleus and dense cytoplasm, but they lack vacuole.

(ii) Intercellular spaces are absent in sclerenchymatous tissue.

(iii) We get crunchy and granular feeling, when we chew pear fruit.

(iv) Branches of tree move and bend freely in high wind velocity. **NCERT Exemplar**

(v) It is difficult to pull out husk of coconut

Sol. (i) Meristematic cells undergo division and do not store food, thus lack vacuole.

(ii) Because their walls are lignified and form bundles for mechanical functions.

(iii) Due to the presence of sclerenchymatous tissue (stone cell) or sclereids, we get a crunchy feeling, when we chew pear fruit.

(iv) The presence of collenchyma tissue provides flexibility to the branches of tree.

(v) Husk of coconut is made up of sclerenchymatous fibres, which are closely packed.

2 Write a note on the protective tissue in plants. (Give appropriate diagram also)

Sol. The protective tissue or the outermost covering of cells in plants is known as epidermis, which performs protective function (protecting plants from adverse conditions). It is usually made up of a single layer of cells. In dry habitats, epidermis gets thicker to protect the plant from undue loss of water.

On aerial parts of plant, epidermal cells often secrete a waxy, water-resistant layer on their outer surface. This waxy covering aids in protecting the plant against loss of water, mechanical injury and invasion by disease causing microbes. The cells of epidermal tissue are present in a continuous layer without intercellular spaces.

Small pores are present on the epidermis of leaf. These pores are called **stomata.** They are enclosed by two kidney-shaped cells called guard cells. They help in gaseous exchange and transpiration.

Protective tissue and surface view of epidermal cell showing stomata (Refer to fig. on Pg. no. 128.)

As plant grows older, a strip of secondary meristem replaces the epidermis of stem. This forms a several layer thick **cork** or bark of the tree in which cells are dead and compactly arranged without intercellular spaces.

3 List the characteristics of cork. How is it formed? Mention its role. **NCERT Exemplar**

Sol. The common characteristics of a cork are:

(*i*) It is the outer protective tissue of older stem and roots.
(*ii*) It is formed by secondary lateral meristem called cork cambium.
(*iii*) The mature cork becomes dead and filled with tannin, resin.
(*iv*) The cells are arranged compactly without intercellular spaces and several layers become thick, which are impermeable due to the deposition of suberin in their wall.

Formation of Cork

As plant grows older, the outer protective tissue undergoes certain changes. A strip of secondary meristem replaces the epidermis of stem.

Cells on the outside are cut-off from this epidermal layer. This forms several layer thick cork or bark with no intercellular spaces.

Role of Cork

(*i*) It prevents loss of water by evaporation.
(*ii*) It protects plant from the invasion of parasites and other harmful microorganisms.

4 The transportation system of plants is composed of complex permanent tissue. They have their transportation system within themselves. Justify in detail with appropriate diagrams.

Sol. The transportation system of plants is composed of complex permanent tissue. These tissues are made up of more than one type of cells, and all these cells coordinate to perform a common specific function.

These cells may appear structurally different, but they perform the same function.

The permanent tissues are of two types:

(*i*) **Xylem** It helps in the transportation of water and minerals from roots to other parts of the plant.

(Tracheid, vessel and xylem paranchyma (Refer to fig. on Pg. no. 129).

Elements of Xylem

(*a*) **Tracheids and Vessels** Tubular structure, transport water and minerals vertically.
(*b*) **Parenchyma** Stores food, helps in sideways conduction of water.
(*c*) **Fibres** Supportive in function.

(*ii*) **Phloem** It transports food from leaves to other parts of the plant. Food is prepared in leaves by the process of photosynthesis.

Elements of Phloem

(*a*) **Sieve cells** Long, conducting cells in the phloem that do not form sieve tubes.
(*b*) **Sieve tubes** Tubular cells with perforated walls. These consist of living cells.
(*c*) **Companion cells** Small elongated cells with dense cytoplasm.
(*d*) **Phloem parenchyma** Thin-walled cells. Mainly function in storage and transportation of food.
(*e*) **Phloem fibres** Composed of thick-walled cells. Which are dead cells. Provide mechanical strength to tissue.

Both xylem and phloem maintain a transportation system within the plants. There is continuous transportation of food, water and minerals within the plant.

This transportation is necessary for the proper growth and maintenance of the plant.

Section of phloem (Refer to fig. on Pg. no 129).

5 Explain the significance of the following:

(*i*) Hair-like structures on epidermal cells.
(*ii*) Epidermis has a thick waxy coating of cutin in desert plants.
(*iii*) Small pores in epidermis of leaf.
(*iv*) Numerous layers of epidermis in cactus.
(*v*) Presence of a chemical suberin in cork cells.

Sol. (*i*) Hair-like structures called root hairs on epidermal cells increase the total absorptive surface area and help in absorption.

(*ii*) Cutin has a waterproof quality and helps in preventing water loss due to transpiration. It also protects plants from entry of pathogens, etc.

(*iii*) Stomata help in gaseous exchange and transpiration process.

(*iv*) Numerous layers of epidermis in cactus prevent water loss.

(*v*) Suberin makes cork cells impervious to gases and water.

6 (i) What will happen if cells are not properly organised in tissue?
(ii) Under certain circumstances squamous epithelium is known as stratified squamous epithelium. Justify.

Sol. (i) Different organisms whether unicellular or multicellular need to perform many functions in the body such as respiration, digestion, locomotion.

In multicellular organisms, cells present in a group and specialised in one particular function form a tissue. Some tissues help in growth, while others in locomotion and some in body movement. So, if cells are not organised in these tissues, then highly organised and specialised process will become disorganised. There will be no coordination in the functioning of the cells and body.

(ii) When simple squamous epithelium is arranged in a pattern of multilayers to prevent wear and tear, the epithelium is called stratified squamous epithelium, e.g. skin.

7 Differentiate between bone and cartilage with respect to structure, function and location.

Sol. Differences between bone and cartilage are as follows:

Point of Difference	Bone	Cartilage
Structure	It is strong and non-flexible tissue, whose cells are embedded in a hard matrix, which is composed of calcium and phosphorus compounds.	It is soft and flexible tissue, whose solid matrix is composed of proteins and sugars. Also, it has widely spaced cells.
Function	It forms the framework that supports the body. It anchors the muscles that support the main organs of the body.	It smoothens bone surfaces at joints.
Location	It is present in skeletal system of vertebrates.	It is present in nose, ear, trachea and larynx.

8 (i) Describe adipose tissue with the help of diagram.
(ii) How is adipose tissue different from blood tissue?

Sol. (i) For diagram refer to fig on Pg. no. 132.

Adipose tissue is a fat storing connective tissue. Its matrix is packed with large oval fat cells or adipocytes. The fat cells are arranged into globules separated by collagen and elastin fibres. It mainly stores reserve fat. It acts as an insulator and works as a shock absorber for visceral organs. (3)

(ii) Differences between adipose and blood tissue are as follows:

Adipose Tissue	Blood Tissue
It is a loose connective tissue.	It is a fluid connective tissue.
The matrix contains fibres.	The matrix does not contain fibres.
It stores and metabolises fats.	It helps in the transport of substances and respiratory gases.

9 Differentiate between various types of muscular tissues. Draw appropriate diagrams.

Sol. Refer to Ans. 6 and 8 of NCERT Folder on Pg. no. 135.

10 'We can control some of the actions of our body, but some are not in our control'. Comment on this statement.

Sol. Some of the actions like moving our limbs, fingers, neck, etc., can be controlled by our will. We can move these parts of our body whenever we want to, but some actions of our body like contraction and relaxation of heart, blinking of eye etc., are not under our will, i.e. we cannot stop functioning of heart, if we want to do so.

The actions, which can be manipulated by our wishes are known as voluntary actions. The muscles, which can perform voluntary actions are voluntary muscles. These muscles are also called skeletal muscles or striated muscles.

These muscles are mostly attached to bones and help in body movement. Their cells are long, cylindrical, unbranched and multinucleate (having many nuclei). The actions, which are not under our control are known as involuntary actions. These actions are performed by smooth muscles or involuntary muscles. Their cells are long with pointed ends (spindle-shaped) and uninucleate (single nucleus).

Striated and smooth muscles (Refer to fig. on Pg. no. 132 and 133).

11 Define nervous tissue. Describe the structure of a typical neuron and also draw a well labelled diagram of it. Write the functions of nervous tissue.

Sol. Refer to text, 'Nervous tissue' on Pg. no. 133.

12 Write differences between plant tissue and animal tissue.

Sol. Refer to text "Differences between plant tissues and animal tissues" on Pg. no. 133.

CHAPTER EXERCISE

Multiple Type Questions

1 The living simple tissue that provides support to the growing parts of a plant is
(a) sclerenchyma (b) collenchyama
(c) parenchyma (d) fibres

2 Which of the following is not a part of epidermal tissue system?
(a) Companion cells
(b) Guard cells
(c) Root hairs
(d) Subsidiary cells

3 Find out correct sentence **NCERT Exemplar**
(a) Parenchymatous tissues have not intercellular spaces
(b) Collenchymatous tissues are irregularly thickened at corners
(c) Apical and intercalary meristems are permanent tissues
(d) All are correct statement

4 The number of nuclei present in striped muscle fibre is
(a) one (b) many
(c) two (d) None of these

5 Intestine absorbs the digested food materials. What type of epithelial cells are responsible for that? **NCERT Exemplar**
(a) Stratified squamous epithelium
(b) Columnar epithelium
(c) Spindle fibres
(d) Cuboidal epithelium

Fill in the Blanks

6 Longitudinal growth of a plant is mediated by ....

7 A tendon attaches a ...... to a ....

8 The cell wall in sclerenchyma is evenly thickened with ....

True and False

9 Intercellular spaces are common in epithelial cells.

10 An epithelium made of cube-shaped cells with round nuclei that performs absorption, excretion and secretion will be found in the lining of kidney tubules.

11 Areolar connective tissue acts as insulator.

Match the Columns

12 Match the following

Column I	Column II
A. Apical meristem	(i) Sclerenchyma
B. Lignin	(ii) Guard cells
C. Skeletal muscles	(iii) Involuntary
D. Cardiac muscles	(iv) multinucleate
E. Stomata	(v) Primary meristem

Assertion–Reason

Direction (Q.Nos. 13-15) *In each of the following questions, a statement of Assertion is given by the corresponding statement of Reason. Of the statements, mark the correct answer as*

(a) If both Assertion and Reason are true and Reason is the correct explanation of Assertion
(b) If both Assertion and Reason are true but Reason is not the correct explanation of Assertion
(c) If Assertion is true, but Reason is false
(d) If Assertion is false, but Reason is true

13 **Assertion** Apical meristem is present at shoot and root tips.
Reason It helps in the longitudinal growth of plants.

14 **Assertion** Water hyacinth can float on water surface.
Reason Aerenchyma tissue is present in water hyacinth.

15 **Assertion** Heart can pump blood throughout the body.
Reason It is made up of cardiac muscles.

Case Based Question

Direction (Q.Nos. 16-19) *Answer the questions on the basis of your understanding of the following paragraph and related studied concepts:*

The cells that produce the bone are called osteoblasts. They secrete the matrix of calcium phosphate and collagen fibres that forms the rigid bone. Once mature and embedded within the matrix, the bone cells are called osteocytes.

Dense bone has a very regular structure, composed of repeating units called Haversian systems. Each Haversian system has concentric rings of hard material enclosing the bone cells. Haversian canals running through the bone contain blood vessels and nerves.

16 Why is a bone classified as connective tissue?

17 Bone is a strong and non-flexible tissue. What would be the advantage of these properties for bone functions.

18 Bone is a connective tissue where two bones can be connected to each other by which type of connective tissue.

(a) tendon (b) bone
(c) ligament (d) blood

19 Which of the following is / are function of bone

(a) It forms the frame work that supports the body
(b) It anchors the muscles and supports the main organs of the body
(c) It acts as an insulator
(d) Both (a) and (b)

Answers

1. (b) 2. (a) 3. (b) 4. (b) 5. (b)
6. Intercalary meristem 7. Skeletal muscle, bone
8. lignin 9. False 10. True 11. False
12. A→(v), B→(i), C→(iv), D→(iii), E→(ii)
13. (c) 14. (a) 15. (b)
18. (c) 19. (d)

Very Short Answer Type Questions

20 Give one similarity between permanent and meristematic tissue.

21 Name a component of phloem formed by end to end fusion of cells with perforated transverse walls.

22 What is the function of thin, hair-like projections present on the cuboidal epithelium?

23 Which part of neuron receives and transmits impulses?

Short Answer (SA) Type Questions

24 Bark of a tree is impervious to gases and water. Give reasons.

25 Where are companion cells located in plants? Mention their functions.

26 Name the tissue, which helps in transportation of oxygen that we inhale to various parts of the body. Write the composition of this tissue.

27 The functional combination of nerve and muscle tissue is fundamental to most animals. Comment.

28 Mention the location of the following tissues.

(i) Tendon
(ii) Areolar tissues
(iii) Cuboidal epithelium

Long Answer (LA) Type Questions

29 (i) Identify the structures marked below as *A*, *B* and *C*.
(ii) Complete the labelling of each structure.
(iii) Write the function of each structure.

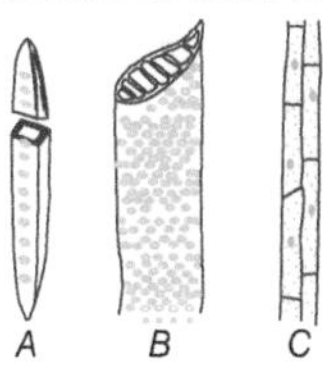

30 (i) Identify *A*, *B*, *C* and *D*.
(ii) Write the functions of *A*, *B*, *C* and *D*.
(iii) Write the difference between *A* and *D*.

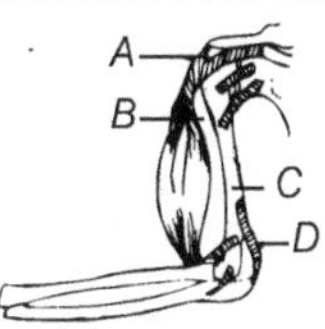

31 Write important functional differences between striated and smooth muscle tissues. Draw a labelled diagram of the muscle tissue that shows rhythmic contraction and relaxation throughout the life.

32 Name the tissue and write characteristic feature of following.

(i) Connects bone to bone in humans.
(ii) Forms inner lining of alveoli.
(iii) Has prominent middle lamella.
(iv) Transports water and minerals in plants.

33 (i) You can very easily bend the stem of a plant without breaking it. Name the tissue in the plant, which makes it possible. Where is it located? State any two characteristics of the cells of this tissue.
(ii) Draw a labelled diagram of the transverse section of this tissue.

RELATED ONLINE VIDEOS

Visit https://www.youtube.com/watch?v=xWUuDM1g4Rg
OR **Scan the Code**

Visit https://www.youtube.com/watch?v=e1tBr80uO-Q
OR **Scan the Code**

Challengers*

1 Contractile proteins are found in
(a) bones (b) blood
(c) cartilage (d) muscles

2 Which among the following is not a leucocyte?

(a) 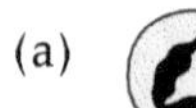 (b)  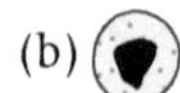 (c) 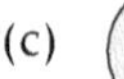 (d) 

3 Find out incorrect sentence
(a) Parenchymatous tissues have intercellular spaces
(b) Collenchymatous tissues are irregularly thickened at corners
(c) Apical and intercalary meristems are permanent tissues
(d) Meristematic tissues in its early stage lack vacuoles

4 Presence of which tissue made it possible for survival of plants in terrestrial environment?
(a) Protective tissue
(b) Parenchymatous tissue
(c) Permanent tissue
(d) Conducting tissue

5 Which among the following statements is true?
(a) All xylem cells are living except tracheids
(b) All phloem cells are living except sieve tubes
(c) All xylem cells are dead cells except xylem parenchyma
(d) All phloem cells are living cells except phloem fibres

6 A person met with an accident in which two long bones of hand were dislocated. Which among the following may be the possible reason?
(a) Tendon break
(b) Break of skeletal muscle
(c) Ligament break
(d) Areolar tissue break

7 Walls of collenchyma are irregularly thickened due to the deposition of
(a) pectin (b) lignin
(c) suberin (d) All of these

8 In the given figure, which of the following parts transmits impulse away from the cell body?

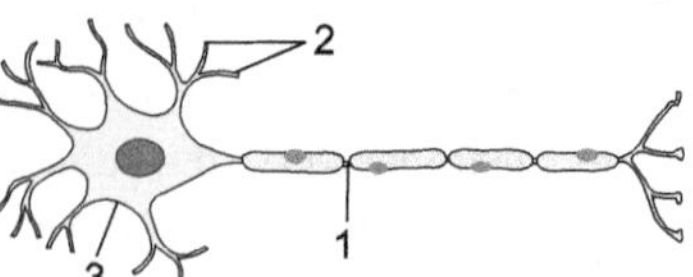

(a) 1 (b) 2
(c) 1 and 2 (d) 3

9 Complete the analogy given below and choose the correct option.

Cutin : Epidermis ; Suberin : ....

(a) Cambium
(b) Apical meristem
(c) Sieve tube
(d) Cork cells

10 A fat person is less affected by the cold wheather because of the presence of more
(a) areolar tissue
(b) striated muscles
(c) adipose tissue
(d) platelets

11 Choose the incorrectly matched pair from the options given below
(a) Salivary gland — Glandular epithelium
(b) Companion cells — Perforated walls
(c) Collenchyma — Flexibility
(d) Axon — Nerve cell

12 Nucleus is located at the periphery in
(a) cardiac muscles (b) smooth muscles
(c) striated muscles (d) Both (a) and (c)

Answer Key

1.	(d)	2.	(c)	3.	(c)	4.	(d)	5.	(d)
6.	(c)	7.	(a)	8.	(a)	9.	(d)	10.	(c)
11.	(b)	12.	(c)						

These questions may be or may not be asked in the examination, have been given just for additional practice.

CHAPTER

07

Motion

In everyday life, we observe several types of motions like vehicles moving on a road, flying birds, movement of needles of a watch, movement of blades of a fan, circulation of blood through veins and arteries, etc. Atoms molecules, planets, stars and galaxies are all in motion. If a body change its position with respect to time and its surroundings, it is said to be in motion. Motion and rest are always relative but never absolute.

Chapter Checklist

- Various Terms Related to Motion
- Uniform and Non-uniform Motion
- Rate of Motion
- Graphical Representation of Motion
- Equations of Motion
- Uniform Circular Motion

Various Terms Related to Motion

Position

The location of an object with respect to a particular point, is known as the **position** of the object. The particular point about which the position of the object is defined, is called **reference point** or **origin.**

Scalar and Vector Quantities

Physical quantities with which we can associate only magnitude, i.e. numbers are called **scalar quantities**. e.g. mass, time, distance, speed, etc.
Physical quantities with which we can associate magnitude, i.e. numbers as well as direction are called **vector quantities.** e.g. weight, displacement, velocity, etc.

Distance

The distance travelled by a moving body is the actual length of the path covered by it, irrespective of the direction in which the body travels. It is a **scalar quantity**. Its SI unit is **metre.** e.g. Consider the motion of an object moving along a straight path.

8 m
B
C
10 m
20 m
5 m
O
A
D

Let the object start its motion from point O and move through point A, B, C and reach upto point D.

Then, total distance covered to the object = actual length upto D of the path travelled

$$= OA + AB + BC + CD = 5\text{ m} + 10\text{ m} + 8\text{ m} + 20\text{ m} = 43\text{ m}$$

Displacement

The displacement of an object is the change in the position of the object when it moves from a given position to another position.

It is equal to the length of the shortest path measured in the direction from the initial position to the final position of the object. It is a **vector quantity**. Its SI unit is **metre** (m).

Suppose an object starts to move from point O and reaches to point B, passing through A.

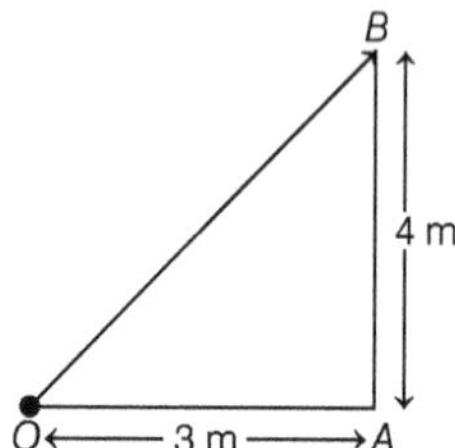

Here, initial position of the object is O and final position is B.

So, displacement of the object

= length of the shortest path between initial position (O) and final position (B)

$= OB = \sqrt{OA^2 + AB^2}$ [from pythagoras theorem]

$= \sqrt{(3)^2 + (4)^2} = \sqrt{9+16}$

$= \sqrt{25} = 5$ m

But, distance in this case = length of actual path

$= OA + AB$

$= 3\text{ m} + 4\text{ m} = 7\text{ m}$

Distance *versus* Displacement

(*i*) Displacement of a moving object can never be greater than the distance travelled by it.

$\therefore$ Displacement $\leq$ Distance

$\Rightarrow \dfrac{\text{Displacement}}{\text{Distance}} \leq 1$

i.e. Ratio of displacement and distance is always less than or equal to 1.

(*ii*) If a body moves along a straight line (only in one direction), then distance and displacement will be equal.

(*iii*) Displacement of the object can be positive, negative or zero but distance can never be negative or zero.

Example 1. *A Jogger jogs along one length and breadth of a rectangular park. If the dimensions of park are 150 m × 120 m, then find the distance travelled and displacement of the Jogger.*

Sol. According to question, the Jogger starts from point A and after covering one breadth and one length reaches at point C.

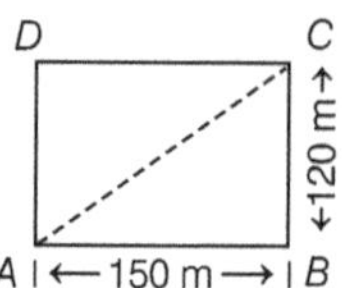

Length, $AB = l = 150$ m,

Breadth, $BC = b = 120$ m

Distance travelled, s = ?

Displacement of the Jogger = ?

Distance, s = Length of the total path covered

$= AB + BC$

$= 150 + 120$

$= 270$ m

Displacement = Minimum distance between initial and final position = AC

From Pythagoras theorem, $AC = \sqrt{(AB)^2 + (BC)^2}$

i.e. Displacement $= \sqrt{(150)^2 + (120)^2} = 30\sqrt{41}$ m

Thus, the Jogger travels a distance of 270 m and his displacement is $30\sqrt{41}$ m.

Example 2. *A body moves in a circular path of radius 20 cm. If it completes two and half revolution along the circular path, then find distance and displacement of the body.*

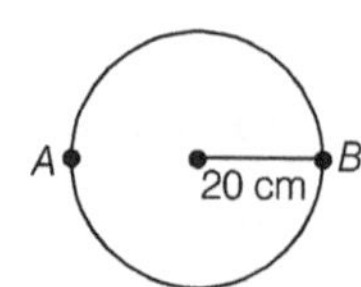

Sol. According to question, body moves in a circular path of radius 20 cm. So, during one complete revolution the distance (s) moved by the body is equal to the circumference of the circular path, i.e. $2\pi r$.

where, r = radius of circular path

So, for two and half revolution, body covers two complete revolutions, i.e. $2 \times 2\pi r$ distance and half revolution,

i.e. $\dfrac{2\pi r}{2} = \pi r$ distance.

Total distance (s) covered by the body

$= (2 \times 2\pi r) + \pi r = 5\pi r$

$= 5 \times 3.14 \times 20$ [$\because \pi = 3.14$]

$= 314$ cm

Now, as we know displacement (d) is the straight line distance between initial and final position of the body. So, after two and half revolution, total displacement (d) of the body will be $2r$, i.e. displacement (d) $= 2 \times 20 = 40$ cm.

Check Point 01

1 SI unit of both distance and displacement is metre (m). Is this true or false?

2 Fill in the blank:
Displacement is a .... quantity.

3 What is the displacement of a satellite when it makes a complete round along its circular path?

4 In which one of the following cases will the distance covered and the magnitude of the displacement are not the same? Justify.
(i) A passenger in a train travels from Delhi to Kolkata.
(ii) A raindrop falling in still air.
(iii) An athlete completes one lap in a race.

5 After studying the motion of a ball rolling on a straight line as shown in figure:

|← 2 m →|
P R Q
|← 10 m →|

Find its distance and displacement covered
(i) when it rolls from P to Q and then to R (i.e. P to Q to R) and
(ii) finally comes back to P (i.e. P to P) (take, P as reference point).
[**Ans.** (i) 12 m, 8 m, (ii) 20 m, zero]

Uniform and Non-uniform Motion

Uniform Motion A body is said to have a uniform motion, if it travels equal distances in equal intervals of time, no matter how small these intervals may be. The distance travelled by an object in uniform motion increases **linearly**.

e.g. If a car moving along a straight line path, it covers equal distances in equal intervals of time, it is said to be in uniform motion.

Non-uniform Motion A body is said to have a non-uniform motion, if it travels unequal distances in equal intervals of time, no matter how small these intervals may be.

e.g. A car moving through a crowded market has non-uniform motion.

Rate of Motion

The ratio of distance travelled by an object to the time taken is called rate of motion. The various terms required to measure the rate of motion are as given below:

Speed

Speed of an object is defined as the distance travelled by it per unit time.

$$\text{Speed of an object } (v) = \frac{\text{Distance}(s)}{\text{Time}(t)}$$

Speed is a **scalar quantity**. The SI unit of speed is **metre per second** (m/s). The distance travelled by an object is either positive or zero, so the speed may be positive or zero but never negative.

Speed can be classified as:

(i) **Uniform speed** If a moving body covers equal distances in equal intervals of time, then the speed of the body is said to be uniform, i.e. constant speed.

(ii) **Non-uniform speed** If a moving body covers unequal distances in equal intervals of time, then the speed of the body is said to be non-uniform, i.e. variable speed.

(iii) **Average speed** It is defined as the ratio of the total distance travelled by a body to the total time taken. It is expressed as

$$\text{Average speed} = \frac{\text{Total distance travelled}}{\text{Total time taken}} = \frac{s_1 + s_2 + s_3 + \dots}{t_1 + t_2 + t_3 + \dots}$$

(iv) **Instantaneous speed** The speed of an object at any particular instant of time or at a particular point of its path is called the instantaneous speed of the object.

Example 3. *The odometer of a bike reads* 1600 km *at the start of the trip and* 2000 km *at the end of the trip. If the bike took* 16 h, *calculate the average speed of the bike in* km/h *and* m/s.

Sol. Distance covered by bike, $s = 2000 \text{ km} - 1600 \text{ km} = 400 \text{ km}$
Time taken, $t = 16 \text{ h}$

$$\therefore \text{ Average speed, } v_{av} = \frac{s}{t} = \frac{400}{16} = 25 \text{ km/h}$$

$$v_{av} = 25 \times \frac{5}{18} = 6.9 \text{ m/s}$$

Therefore, the average speed of the bike is 6.9 m/s.

Example 4. *An object travels* 14 m *in* 4 s *and then another* 16 m *in* 2 s. *What is the average speed of an object?*

Sol. According to question,
First distance, $s_1 = 14 \text{ m}$
Second distance, $s_2 = 16 \text{ m}$, Times, $t_1 = 4 \text{ s}$, $t_2 = 2 \text{ s}$

$$\therefore \text{ Average speed} = \frac{\text{Total distance}}{\text{Total time}} = \frac{s_1 + s_2}{t_1 + t_2} = \frac{14+16}{4+2} = \frac{30}{6} = 5 \text{ m/s}$$

Therefore, the average speed of an object is 5 m/s.

Speed with Direction : Velocity

Velocity of an object is defined as the displacement of the body per unit time. i.e. velocity is the speed of an object moving in a definite direction.

It is expressed as

$$\text{Velocity of an object } (v) = \frac{\text{Displacement}(d)}{\text{Time}(t)}$$

Velocity is a **vector quantity**. The SI unit of velocity is **metre per second** (m/s). Velocity of an object can be **positive**, **zero** or **negative**. Velocity of an object can be changed by changing the object's speed, direction of motion or both.

Velocity can be classified as:

(*i*) **Uniform velocity** If an object covers equal displacements in equal intervals of time without changing direction, then its velocity is known as uniform velocity, i.e. constant velocity.

(*ii*) **Non-uniform velocity** If an object covers unequal displacements in equal intervals of time, then its velocity is known as non-uniform velocity, i.e. variable velocity.

(*iii*) **Average velocity** It is defined as the ratio of total displacement of the object to the total time taken.

It is expressed as $v_{av} = \dfrac{\text{Total displacement}}{\text{Total time taken}}$

If the velocity of an object changes at a uniform rate, then average velocity,

$$(v_{av}) = \frac{\text{Initial velocity }(u) + \text{ Final velocity}(v)}{2}$$

(*iv*) **Instantaneous velocity** The velocity of an object at a particular instant of time or at a particular point of its path is called its instantaneous velocity.

Note (*i*) Speedometer is a device which is used to measure instantaneous speed of a moving body.

(ii) If a body is moving in a straight line, then the magnitude of its speed and velocity will be equal.

(*ii*) Average speed of an object can never be zero but the average velocity of a moving object can be zero.

Example 5. *Rajeev went from Delhi to Chandigarh and returned to Delhi on his motorbike. The odometer of that read* 4200 km *at the start of trip and* 4460 km *at the end of his trip. If Rajeev took* 4 h 20 min *to complete his trip, then find the average speed and average velocity in* km/h *as well as in* m/s.

Sol. As we know that, the total distance covered,

s = final reading of odometer – initial reading of odometer

$= (4460 - 4200)\text{ km} = 260\text{ km}$

Total time taken, $t = 4\text{ h }20\text{ min} = 4.33\text{ h}$

$$\therefore \text{Average speed} = \frac{\text{Total distance covered }(s)}{\text{Total time taken }(t)}$$

$$= \frac{260\text{ km}}{4.33\text{ h}} = 60\text{ km/h} = \frac{60 \times 5}{18} = 16.67\text{ m/s}$$

$$\therefore \text{Average velocity} = \frac{\text{Total displacement}(d)}{\text{Total time taken}(t)}$$

$$= \frac{0}{4.33} = 0\text{ m/s or }0\text{ km/h}$$

Average speed of Rajeev is 16.67 m/s and average velocity is 0.

Rate of Change of Velocity : Acceleration

Acceleration is defined as the rate of change of velocity with respect to time.

Mathematically, it is expressed as

$$\text{Acceleration }(a) = \frac{\text{Change in velocity}(\Delta v)}{\text{Change in time}(\Delta t)}$$

If in a given time interval t, the velocity of a body changes from u to v, then acceleration a is expressed as

$$a = \frac{\text{Final velocity}(v) - \text{Initial velocity}(u)}{\text{time interval}(t)}$$

$$a = \frac{v - u}{t}$$

This kind of motion is known as **accelerated motion**. The SI unit of acceleration is m/s^2. It is a **vector quantity.**

The acceleration is taken to be **positive**, if it is in the direction of velocity, **negative** if it is opposite to the direction of velocity and **zero** when a body is moving with a constant velocity.

If velocity of an object decreases with time, then it is said to have **negative acceleration.** Negative acceleration is also called **deceleration** or **retardation.**

Acceleration can be classified as:

(*i*) **Uniform acceleration** If an object travels in a straight line and its velocity increases or decreases by equal amounts in equal intervals of time, then the object is said to be in a uniform acceleration.

e.g. (*a*) The motion of a freely falling body.

(*b*) The motion of a ball rolling down on an inclined plane.

(*ii*) **Non-uniform acceleration** If the velocity of an object increases or decreases by unequal amounts in equal intervals of time, then the object is said to be in a non-uniform acceleration.

e.g. (*a*) The movement of a car on a crowded city road.

(*b*) The motion of the train leaving or entering the platform.

Example 6. *Starting from a stationary position, a car attains a velocity of 5 m/s in 20 s. Then, the driver of the car applies a brake such that the velocity of the car comes down to 3 m/s in the next 6 s. Calculate the acceleration of the car in both the cases.*

Sol. *Case* I Initial velocity of the car, $u = 0$

[$\because$ it starts from stationary position]

Final velocity, $v = 5$ m/s, Time taken, $t = 20$ s

$$\therefore \text{Acceleration, } a = \frac{\text{Change in velocity}}{\text{Time}}$$

$$= \frac{\text{Final velocity} - \text{Initial velocity}}{\text{Time}}$$

$$= \frac{v-u}{t} = \frac{5-0}{20} = 0.25 \text{ m/s}^2$$

Case II Initial velocity, $u = 5$ m/s

Final velocity, $v = 3$ m/s,

Time taken, $t = 6$ s

$$\therefore \text{Acceleration, } a = \frac{v-u}{t} = \frac{3-5}{6} = -0.33 \text{ m/s}^2$$

Thus, the acceleration in both the cases are 0.25 m/s^2 and -0.33 m/s^2.

Check Point 02

1. Define average speed, write any one point of difference between average speed and average velocity.
2. The maximum speed of a train is 80 km/h. It takes 10 h to cover a distance of 400 km. Find the ratio of its maximum speed to its average speed. [**Ans.** 2 : 1]
3. Which of the two can be zero under certain conditions : average speed of a moving body or average velocity of a moving body?
4. (*i*) Give two factors on which acceleration depends.
   (*ii*) Mention the formula and SI unit of acceleration.
5. Fill in the blanks.
   (*i*) .... is the term used for negative acceleration.
   (*ii*) A bus starting from rest attains a velocity of 54 km/h in 60 s, its acceleration is ....

Graphical Representation of Motion

In order to describe the motion of an object, we can use line graphs.

In this case, line graphs show dependence of one physical quantity, such as distance or velocity, on another quantity, such as time.

Note For graphical description of a motion, it is convenient to take time along *X*-axis, whereas distance, speed or velocity is taken along *Y*-axis.

Types of Graph

There are two main types of graph which we will be studying as given below:

1. Distance-Time Graph

The change in the position of an object with time can be represented on the distance-time graph adopting a convenient scale of choice.

To draw distance-time graph, time is plotted along *X*-axis distance of the body is plotted along *Y*-axis.

In this case, the slope of the distance-time graph is equal to the speed of the object.

Distance-time graphs under various conditions are explained below:

(i) Distance-Time Graph for Uniform Motion

If an object travels equal distances in equal intervals of time, then it moves with uniform speed.

For uniform speed, a graph of distance travelled against time is a straight line as shown in figure given below:

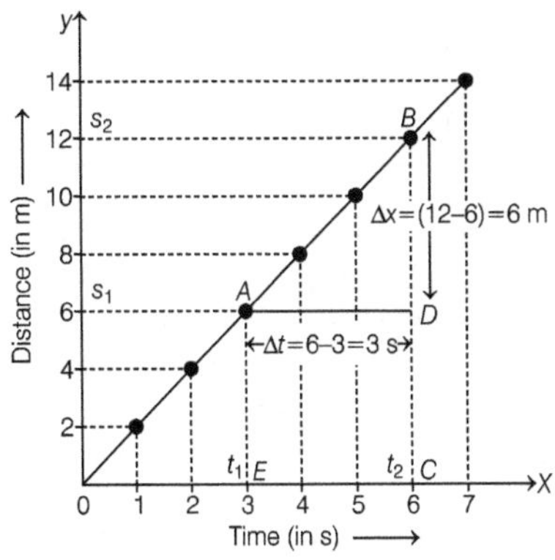

Distance-time graph for uniform motion

Interpretation

From the graph, it is clear that in equal interval of time, i.e. 2s, the object covers equal distance 4m, so the motion is uniform and graph is a straight line.

Calculation of speed To calculate the speed of the object from a distance-time graph, choose any two points say A and B on the straight line. From points A and B, draw perpendiculars AE and BC respectively, on time axis. Now, draw a perpendicular AD on BC.

The distance travelled by the object from point A to B is given by

$$\Delta x = BC - CD = s_2 - s_1$$

Time taken by the object to cover this distance

$$= \Delta t = t_2 - t_1.$$

$\therefore$ Speed, $v = \Delta x/\Delta t = (s_2 - s_1)/(t_2 - t_1)$

i.e. $\Delta x/\Delta t =$ Slope of distance-time graph.

(ii) Distance-Time Graph for Non-uniform Motion

If a body travels unequal distances in equal intervals of time, then the motion of the body is known as **non-uniform motion.** Non-uniform motion is of two types such as:

(a) When the speed of the body increases with passage of time, then the distance-time graph will be a curve with positive slope as shown below:

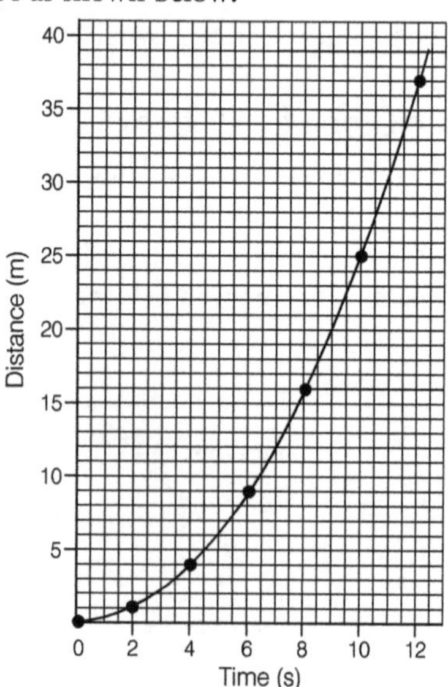

Interpretation

From the graph, it is clear that in equal intervals of time of two seconds, the body is covering unequal distances and this distance goes on increasing. That means, with the passage of time, the body is covering more and more distance in equal time, i.e. the speed of the body is increasing.

(b) When the speed of the body decreases with passage of time, then the distance-time graph will be a curve with negative slope as shown below:

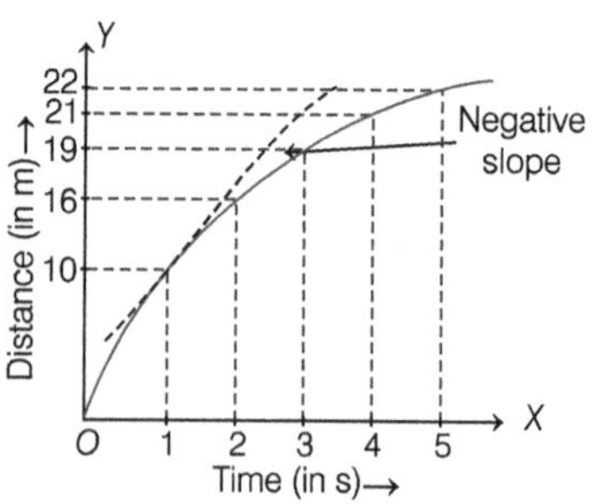

Interpretation

From the graph, it is clear that in equal intervals of time of one second, the body is covering unequal distances and this distance goes on decreasing. That means, with the passage of time, the body is covering lesser and lesser distance in equal time, i.e. the speed of the body is decreasing.

Example 7. *The graph shows below the positions of a body at different times. Calculate the speed of the body as it moves from (i) A to B, (ii) B to C and (iii) C to D.*

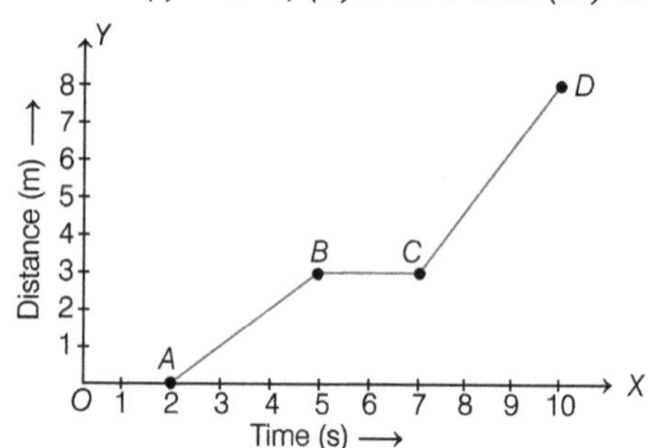

Sol.

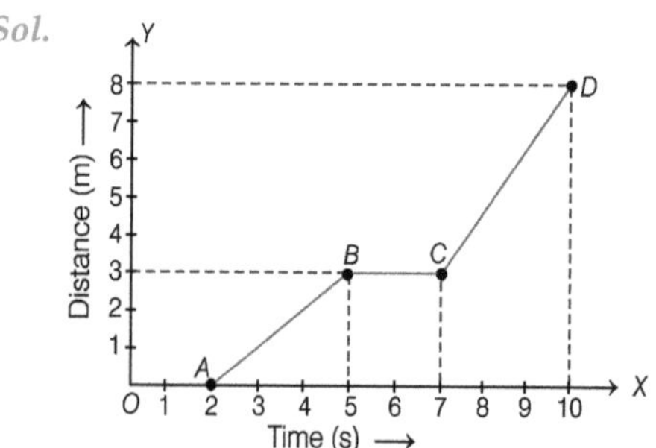

(i) For the motion from point A to B,

time taken, $t = 5 - 2 = 3$ s

Distance covered $= 3 - 0 = 3$ m

$\therefore$ Speed during the motion from point A to B

$$= \frac{\text{Distance}}{\text{Time}}$$

$$= \frac{3}{3} = 1 \text{ m/s}$$

(*ii*) For the motion from point B to C,
time taken, $t = 7 - 5 = 2$ s
Distance covered $= 3 - 3 = 0$ m
[$\because$ body does not change its position from point B to C]
$\therefore$ Speed during the motion from point B to C

$$= \frac{\text{Distance}}{\text{Time}}$$

$$= \frac{0}{2} = 0 \text{ m/s} = 0$$

(*iii*) For the motion from point C to D,
time taken, $t = 10 - 7 = 3$ s
Distance covered $= 8 - 3 = 5$ m
$\therefore$ Speed during the motion from point C to D

$$= \frac{\text{Distance}}{\text{Time}} = \frac{5}{3} \text{ m/s}$$

Example 8. *The following table gives the data about motion of a car:*

Time (h)	11:00	11:30	12:00	12:30	1:00
Distance (km)	0	20	30	65	100

Plot the graph and
(*i*) find the speed of the car between 12:00 h and 12:30 h.
(*ii*) what is the average speed of the car?
(*iii*) is the car's motion is an example of uniform motion? Justify.

Sol. According to given data about motion of a car, graph of Distance-Time will be plotted as

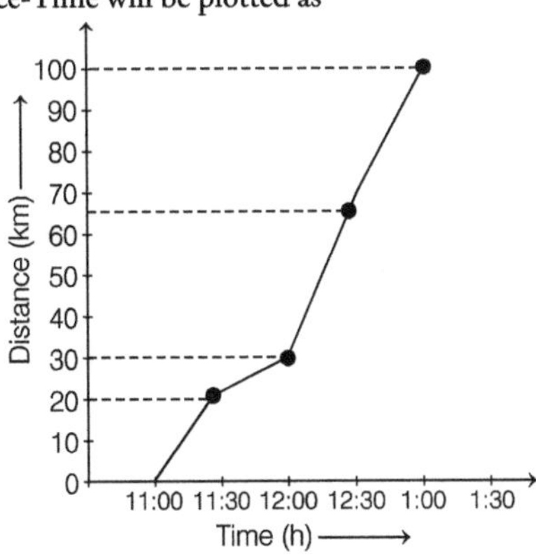

(*i*) Speed of the car between 12:00 h and 12:30 h is given by

$$v = \frac{65 - 30}{\frac{30}{60}} = \frac{35}{\left(\frac{1}{2}\right)} = 70 \text{ km/h}$$

(*ii*) Average speed, $v_{av} = \frac{100}{2} = 50$ km/h

(*iii*) No, because the car covered unequal distances in equal intervals of time.

2. Velocity-Time Graph

Velocity-time graph shows how the velocity of a body changes with passage of time. To draw velocity-time graph, velocity of the body is plotted along *Y*-axis and the time taken by the body is plotted along *X*-axis.

The area under velocity-time graph gives displacement. Velocity-time graphs under various conditions are explained as below:

(i) Velocity-Time Graph for a Body Moving with Constant Velocity

When a body moves with constant velocity, i.e. its motion is uniform, then its velocity does not change with time.

The graph will be a straight line parallel to the time axis.

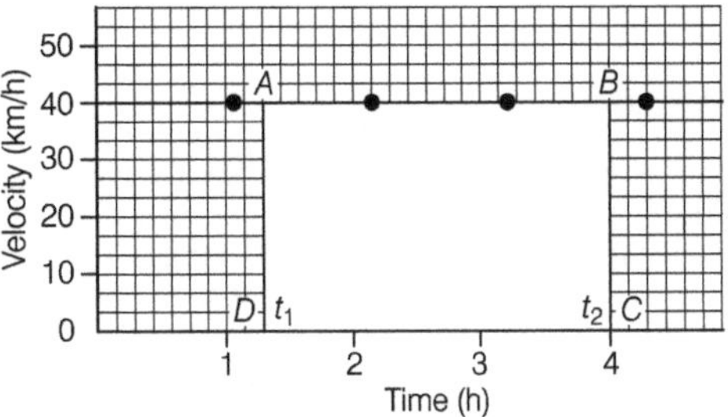

Interpretation

From the graph, it is clear that with the passage of time, there is no change in the velocity, i.e. the body is moving with constant velocity.

Calculation of distance or magnitude of displacement
Let us calculate the distance or magnitude of the displacement of a body between time t_1 and time t_2.

Draw perpendiculars AC and BD from the points corresponding to time t_1 and time t_2 on the graph.

Now, $AD = BC$ = velocity of the body
$CD = (t_2 - t_1)$ = time interval

Thus, $AD \times CD$ = area of rectangle $ABCD$
Also, $AD \times CD$ = velocity $\times$ time
= distance or magnitude of displacement

Thus, magnitude of displacement
= area under velocity-time graph

(ii) Velocity-Time Graph for Uniform Accelerated Motion

In uniform accelerated motion, the velocity changes by equal amount in equal interval of time. In this case the velocity-time graph is a straight line passing through the origin.

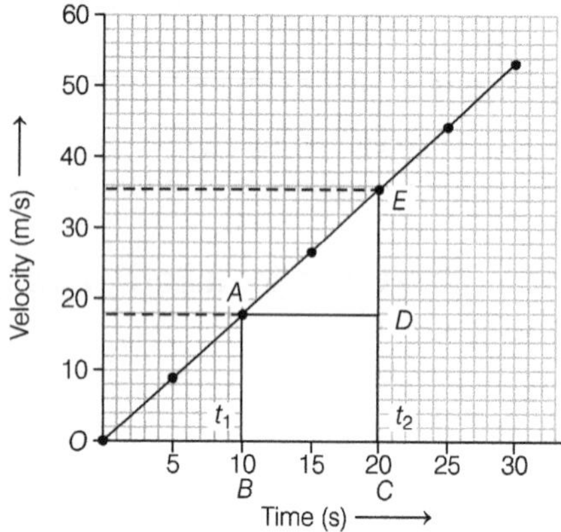

Interpretation

The nature of the graph shows that velocity changes by equal amounts in equal intervals of time. In equal interval of time, i.e. 10 s, the change in velocity is 18 m/s, which remains same, that means the acceleration of the body is constant. Thus, for all uniformly accelerated motion, the velocity-time graph is a straight line.

Calculation of distance or magnitude of displacement To determine the distance moved by the car from its velocity-time graph. The area under the velocity-time graph gives the distance (magnitude of displacement) moved by the car in a given interval of time.

Therefore, $S =$ Area of $ABCDE$

$$= \text{Area of the rectangle } ABCD + \text{Area of triangle } ADE$$

$$= AB \times BC + \frac{1}{2}(AD \times DE)$$

(iii) Velocity-Time Graph for Non-uniform Accelerated Motion

Velocity-time graph for non-uniform accelerated motion is given below:

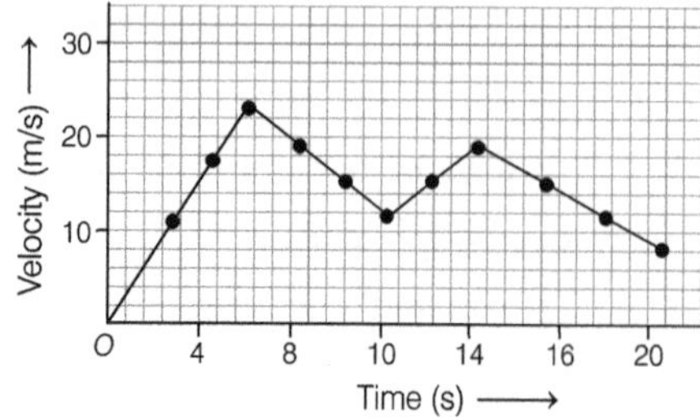

It shows that the velocity of a body (or object) varies non-uniformly with time.

Example 9. *The velocity-time graph of an ascending passenger lift is shown in figure below.*

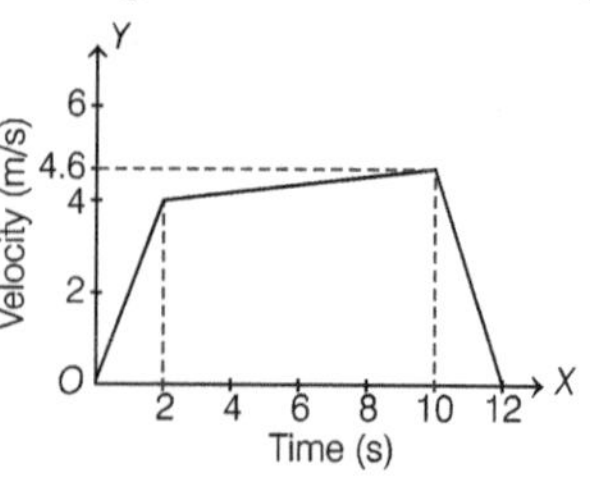

What is the acceleration of the lift

(i) during the first two seconds?

(ii) between 2nd and 10th second?

(iii) during the last two seconds?

Sol. *(i)* *Case* I From given graph, we have

Change in velocity, $\Delta v = 4 - 0 = 4 \text{m/s}$,

Time, $\Delta t = 2 - 0 = 2\text{s}$, $a_1 = ?$

$\therefore$ Acceleration, $a_1 = \frac{\Delta v}{\Delta t} = \frac{4}{2} = 2 \text{ m/s}^2$

(ii) *Case* II Change in velocity, $\Delta v = 4.6 - 4 = 0.6 \text{ m/s}$,

Time, $\Delta t = 10 - 2 = 8\text{ s}$, $a_2 = ?$

$\because$ Acceleration, $a_2 = \frac{\Delta v}{\Delta t} = \frac{0.6}{8} = 0.075 \text{ m/s}^2$

(iii) *Case* III Change in velocity, $\Delta v = 0 - 4.6 = -4.6 \text{ m/s}$,

Time, $\Delta t = 12 - 10 = 2\text{ s}$, $a_3 = ?$

$\therefore$ Acceleration, $a_3 = \frac{\Delta v}{\Delta t} = \frac{-4.6}{2} = -2.3 \text{ m/s}^2$

Negative sign shows retardation.

Example 10. *A body moves with a velocity of* 2 m/s *for* 5 s, *then its velocity increases uniformly to* 10 m/s *in next* 5 s. *Thereafter, its velocity begins to decrease at a uniform rate until it comes to rest after* 5 s.

(i) Plot a velocity-time graph for the motion of the body.

(ii) From the graph, find the total distance covered by the body after 2 s and 12 s.

Sol. *(i)* Velocity-time graph for the motion of the body is

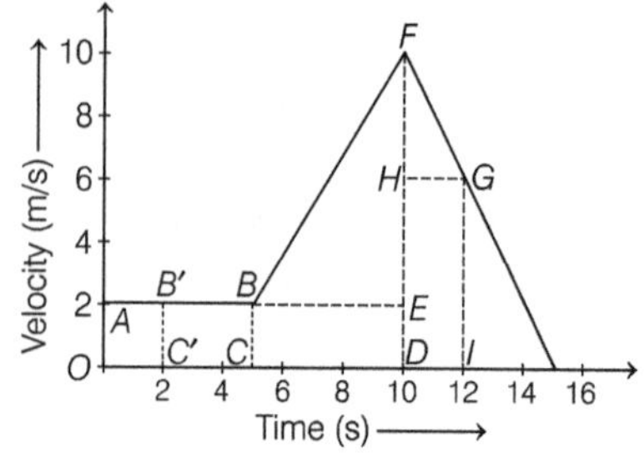

(ii) As we know, the distance moved by the body after 2 s

$= \text{Area } OAB'C'$

$= 2 \text{ m/s} \times 2 \text{ s}$

$= 4 \text{ m}$

Again distance covered by the body after 12 s

$= \text{Area } OAED + \text{Area of } \Delta BEF + \text{Area of } DHGI + \text{Area of } \Delta FHG$

$= 2 \text{ m/s} \times 10 \text{ s} + \frac{1}{2} \times 5 \text{ s} \times 8 \text{ m/s} + 6 \text{ m/s} \times 2 \text{ s} + \frac{1}{2} \times 2 \text{ s} \times 4 \text{ m/s}$

$= 20 \text{ m} + 20 \text{ m} + 12 \text{ m} + 4 \text{ m} = 56 \text{ m}$

Check Point 03

1 If the distance-time graph of a particle is parallel to time axis, then how much is the velocity of the particle?

2 The time-distance graph of cyclist is shown in the figure below

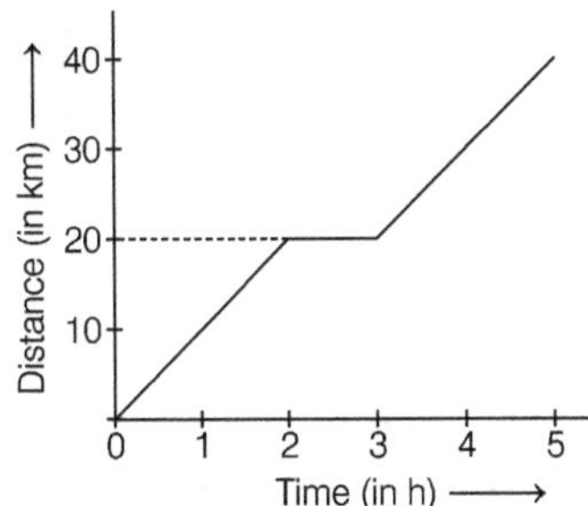

From the graph, find out average speed in the whole journey.

[**Ans.** 7 km/h]

3 Give one similarity and one dissimilarity between the two graphs:

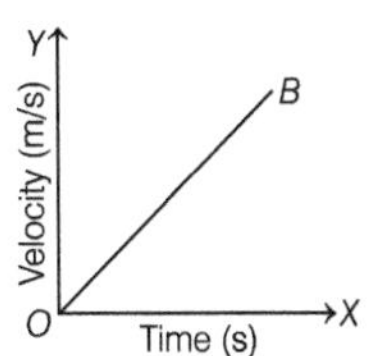

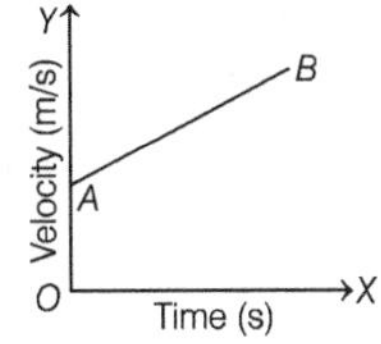

[**Ans.** Both have uniform acceleration]

4 The value of acceleration in the following graph is ....

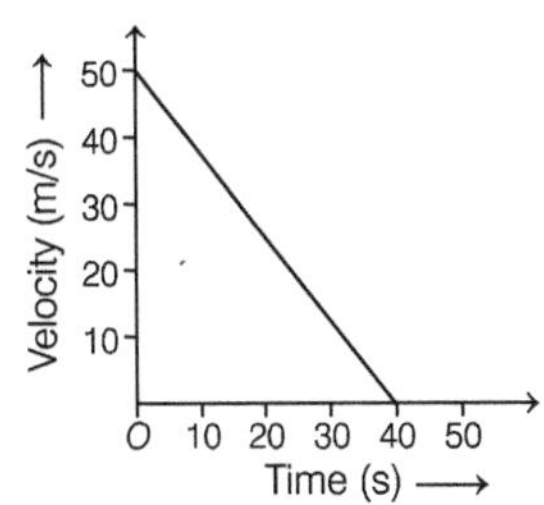

[**Ans.** -1.25 m/s^2, negative sign for retardation]

5 Given graphs represent the motion of two objects *P* and *Q*. Which of the objects has positive acceleration and which one has negative acceleration?

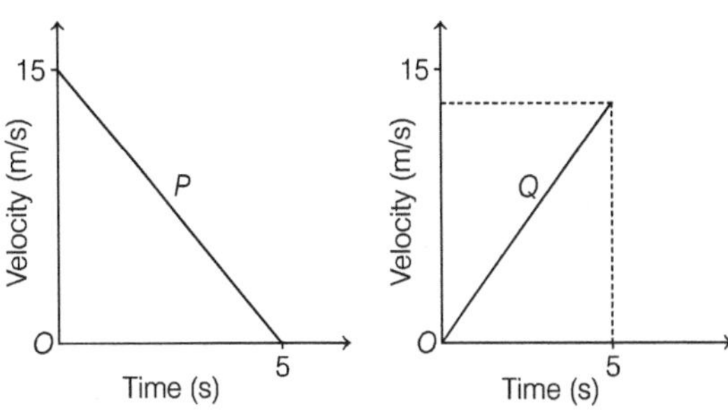

[**Ans.** *P* has negative acceleration, *Q* has positive acceleration]

6 Velocity-time graphs of two objects *P* and *Q* are as given below:

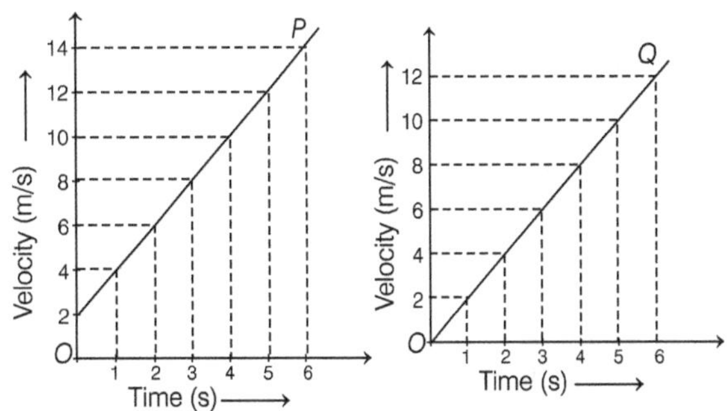

(i) Object *Q* starts from rest.

(a) True (b) False

(ii) Object *Q* has more velocity after 5 s.

(a) True (b) False

[**Ans.** (a) True, (b) False]

Equations of Motion

Relation between velocity of the body, acceleration of the body and the distance travelled by the body in a particular time interval are known as equation of motion.

The three equations of motion are as given below:

1. $v = u + at$
2. $s = ut + \frac{1}{2} at^2$
3. $v^2 - u^2 = 2as$

where, u is the initial velocity of the body, a is the uniform acceleration of the body, v is the final velocity of the body after t second and s is the distance travelled in this time.

Example 11. *The brakes applied to a car produce an acceleration of 4 m/s^2 in the opposite direction to the motion. If the car takes 3 s to stop after the application of brakes, calculate the distance it travels during this time.*

Sol. Given, final velocity, $v = 0$; Time, $t = 3$ s;

Acceleration, $a = -4\ m/s^2$

From first equation of motion, $v = u + at$

Substituting given values, we get

$$0 = u + (-4) \times 3$$

$$\Rightarrow \quad u = 12\ m/s$$

From second equation of motion, $s = ut + \frac{1}{2}at^2$

$$= (12) \times (3) + \frac{1}{2} \times (-4) \times (3)^2$$

$$= 36 - 18 = 18\ m$$

Thus, car covers the distance during time, $t = 3$ s is 18 m.

Example 12. *A motorbike accelerates uniformly from 54 km/h to 72 km/h in 2s. Calculate (i) the acceleration and (ii) the distance covered by the motorbike in that time.*

Sol. (*i*) Initial velocity, $u = 54\ km/h = 54 \times \frac{5}{18} = 15\ m/s$

Final velocity, $v = 72\ km/h = 72 \times \frac{5}{18} = 20\ m/s$

From the first equation of motion

$$v = u + at$$

$$a = \frac{v-u}{t} = \frac{20-15}{2}$$

Acceleration of motorbike, $a = \frac{5}{2} = 2.5\ m/s^2$

(*ii*) The distance covered by the motorbike

$$s = ut + \frac{1}{2}at^2 = 15 \times 2 + \frac{1}{2} \times (2.5) \times (2)^2$$

$$= 30 + 5 = 35\ m$$

The acceleration of the motorbike is 2.5 m/s^2 and the distance covered is 35 m.

Example 13. *A train starting from rest attains a velocity of 90 km/h in 3 min. Assuming that the acceleration is uniform, find (i) the acceleration and (ii) the distance travelled by the train for attaining this velocity.*

Sol. Given, final velocity, $v = 90\ km/h = 90 \times 5/18 = 25\ m/s$

Initial velocity, $u = 0$, Time, $t = 3\ min = 3 \times 60 = 180$ s

(*i*) Acceleration, $a = ?$

$a = (v - u)/t$ [from first equation of motion]

$a = (25 - 0)/180 = 5/36\ m/s^2$

(*ii*) From the third equation of motion

$$v^2 = u^2 + 2as$$

$$v^2 = 0 + 2as \qquad [\because u = 0]$$

$$\text{Distance, } s = \frac{v^2}{2a} = \frac{(25)^2}{2 \times 5/36} = 2250\ m$$

Uniform Circular Motion

If an object moves in a circular path with uniform speed, then its motion is called uniform circular motion.

- When an object moves along a circular path, its direction of motion keeps changing continuously. The velocity changes due to continuous change in direction and thus motion along a circular path is said to be accelerated.
- When a body takes one round of a circular path, then it travels a distance equal to its circumference which is $2\pi r$, where r is the radius of the circular path.
- Then, speed of the body moving in a circular path, $v = 2\pi r/t$, where t is the time taken for one round of circular path and π is constant having value 22/7.

Some of the examples of uniform circular motion are as follows:

(*i*) A piece of stone tied to a thread and rotated in a circle with a uniform speed.

(*ii*) The motion of blades of an electric fan around the axle.

(*iii*) The motion of the moon and the earth.

(*iv*) A satellite in a circular orbit around the earth.

(*v*) A car is moving on a circular path with constant speed.

Example 14. *The minute hand of a wall clock is 10 cm long. Find its displacement and the distance covered from 10:00 am to 10:30 am.*

Sol. Given, length of the minute hand, $l = 10$ cm

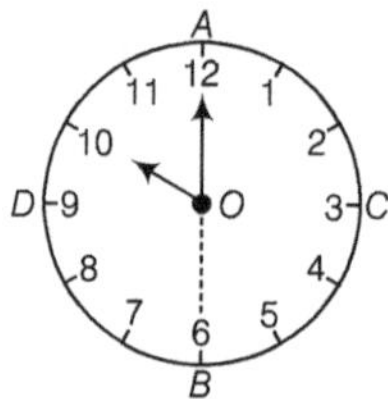

$\therefore$ Displacement from 10:00 am to 10:30 am is given by diameter $= AOB = 2l = 20$ cm

Total distance covered by the minute hand

$$= ACB = \pi l = \frac{22}{7} \times 10\ cm = \frac{220}{7} = 31.43\ cm$$

The displacement of the minute hand is 20 cm and distance is 31.43 cm.

Check Point 04

1 A body is moving with a velocity of 10 m/s. If it starts accelerating with the rate of 2.5 m/s^2. Find out its velocity after 10 s. [Ans. 35 m/s]

2 Fill in the blank:
If a car travels 50 m distance in 4 s with a acceleration of 5 m/s^2, then its initial speed is .... m/s.

3 A cyclist is moving with a speed of 14 m/s. He starts accelerating with a rate of 6 m/s^2 and acquired the speed of 18 m/s. Calculate, what distance did he move in acquiring that speed? [Ans. 10.67 m]

4 A bus is moving with a speed 72 km/h can be stopped by brakes after atleast 10 m. What will be the minimum stopping distance, if the same bus is moving at a speed of 144 km/h? [Ans. 40 m]

5 If the acceleration of the particle is constant in magnitude but not in direction, then what type of path does the particle follow? [Ans. Circular path]

To Study NCERT Activities
Visit https://goo.gl/FmVrrg
OR Scan the Code

NCERT FOLDER

INTEXT QUESTIONS

1 An object has moved through a distance. Can it have zero displacement? If yes, support your answer with an example. **Pg 100**

Sol. Yes, the displacement can be zero even, if the object has moved through a distance, e.g. a boy starts from his home to market and comes back. He has covered a distance but his displacement is zero.

2 A farmer moves along the boundary of a square field of side 10 m in 40 s. What will be the magnitude of displacement of the farmer at the end of 2 min 20 s from his initial position? **Pg 100**

Sol. Farmer takes 40 s to move along the boundary of the square field of side 10 m, i.e. after 40 s farmer is again at his initial position, so his displacement is zero.

Time given = 2 min 20 s = (2 × 60 + 20) s = 140 s

Displacement of farmer after 2 min 20 s, i.e. after 140 s

= Displacement after (3 × 40 + 20) s

= 0 + displacement after 20 s

[∵ after each 40 s displacement is zero]

Farmer completes one round in 40 s, so he will complete 1/2 round in 20 s, i.e. after 20 s final position of farmer is C.

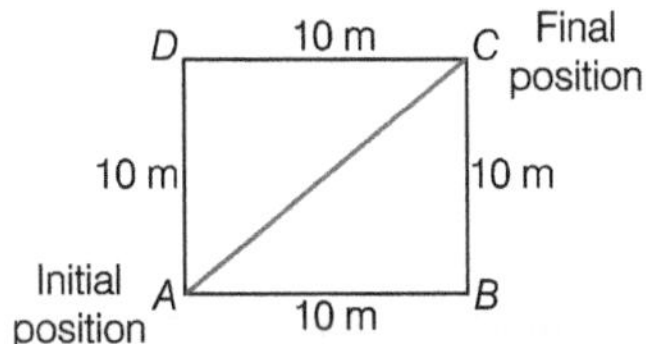

Displacement of farmer,

$$AC = \sqrt{AB^2 + BC^2} = \sqrt{10^2 + 10^2}$$
$$= 10\sqrt{2} = 10 \times 1.414$$
$$= 14.14 \text{ m}$$

3 Which of the following is true for displacement?
(i) It cannot be zero.
(ii) Its magnitude is greater than the distance travelled by the object. **Pg 100**

Sol. (i) The displacement can be zero, so the first statement is false.

(ii) The magnitude of displacement can never be greater than the distance travelled by the object. So, the second statement is also false.

4 Distinguish between speed and velocity. **Pg 102**

Sol. Difference between speed and velocity are as given below:

Speed	Velocity
Distance travelled per unit time.	Displacement per unit time.
It is a scalar quantity.	It is a vector quantity.
Speed is always positive.	Velocity can be negative, positive or zero.

5 Under what condition(s) is the magnitude of average velocity of an object equal to its average speed? **Pg 102**

Sol. When the object travels in one direction along a straight line path then its average velocity will be equal to average speed.

6 What does the odometer of an automobile measure? **Pg 102**

Sol. It measures the distance travelled by an automobile.

7 What does the path of an object look like when it is in a uniform motion? **Pg 102**

Sol. An object having uniform motion has a straight line path.

8 During an experiment, a signal from a spaceship reached the ground station in five minutes. What was the distance of the spaceship from the ground station? The signal travels at the speed of light, i.e. 3×10^8 m/s. **Pg 102**

Sol. Given, speed of signal $= 3 \times 10^8$ m/s

Time taken by the signal in reaching the earth

$= 5 \text{ min} = 5 \times 60 = 300$ s

Distance of spaceship from ground station

= Distance travelled by the signal in 5 min

$= \text{Speed} \times \text{Time} = 3 \times 10^8 \times 300 = 9 \times 10^{10}$ m

9 When will you say a body is in (*i*) uniform acceleration? (*ii*) non-uniform acceleration? **Pg 103**

Sol. (*i*) A body is in uniform acceleration, if it travels in a straight path when its velocity increases or decreases by equal amount in equal time intervals.

(*ii*) A body is in non-uniform acceleration, if it travels in a straight path when its velocity increases or decreases by unequal amount in equal time intervals.

10 A bus decreases its speed from 80 km/h to 60 km/h in 5 s. Find the acceleration of the bus. **Pg 103**

Sol. Given, initial speed of the bus,

$$u = 80 \text{ km/h} = 80 \times \frac{5}{18} = 22.22 \text{ m/s}$$

Final speed of the bus,

$$v = 60 \text{ km/h} = 60 \times \frac{5}{18} = 16.67 \text{m/s}$$

Time taken to decrease the speed, $t = 5$ s

$$\therefore \text{ Acceleration of the bus, } a = \frac{v-u}{t}$$

[$\because$ first equation of motion]

$$= \frac{16.67 - 22.22}{5} = -1.11 \text{ m/s}^2$$

The negative sign of acceleration indicates that the velocity of the bus is decreasing, i.e. the bus retards.

11 A train starting from a railway station and moving with uniform acceleration attains a speed of 40 km/h in 10 min. Find its acceleration. **Pg 103**

Sol. Initial velocity of train, $u = 0$

Final velocity of train, $v = 40 \text{ km/h} = 40 \times \frac{5}{18}$

$= 11.11$ m/s

Time taken, $t = 10 \text{ min} = 10 \times 60 = 600$ s

$$\therefore \text{ Acceleration, } a = \frac{v-u}{t}$$

$$= \frac{11.11 - 0}{600}$$

$$= 0.0185 \text{ m/s}^2$$

$$= 1.85 \times 10^{-2} \text{ m/s}^2$$

Hence, acceleration of the train is $= 1.85 \times 10^{-2}$ m/s^2.

12 What is the nature of distance-time graphs for uniform and non-uniform motion of an object? **Pg 107**

Sol. The distance-time graph for uniform motion of an object is a straight line.

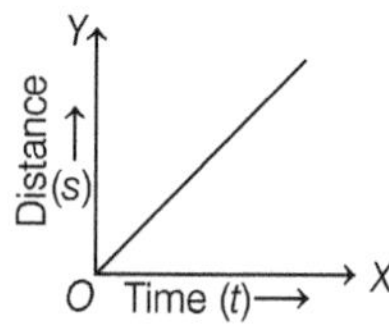

Uniform motion

The distance-time graph for non-uniform motion of an object is a curved line.

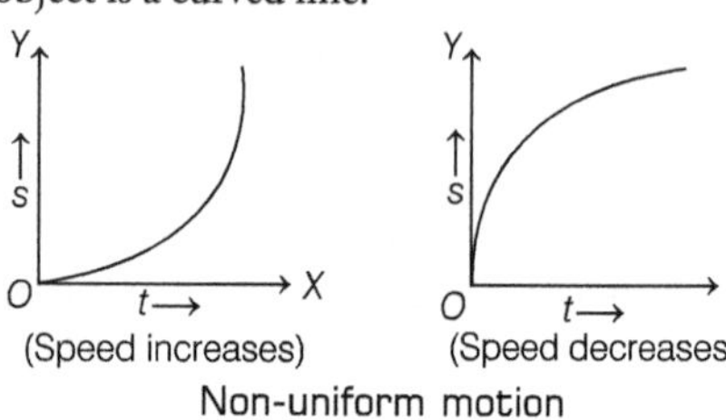

Non-uniform motion

13 What can you say about the motion of an object whose distance-time graph is a straight line parallel to the time axis? **Pg 107**

Sol. When an object is at rest, then its distance-time graph is a straight line parallel to the time axis. Thus, it indicates that with a change in time, there is no change in the position of the object, i.e. the object is at rest.

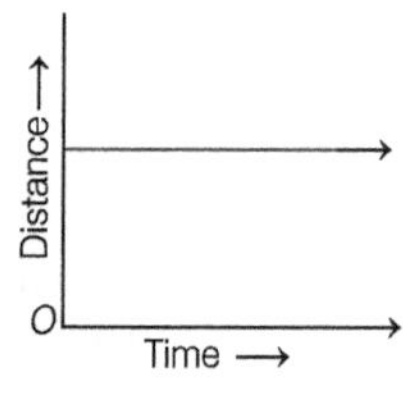

14 What can you say about the motion of an object, if its speed-time graph is a straight line parallel to time axis? **Pg 107**

Sol. A straight line parallel to the time axis in a speed-time graph indicates that a change in time, there is no change in the speed of the object. This indicates the speed of the object is constant.

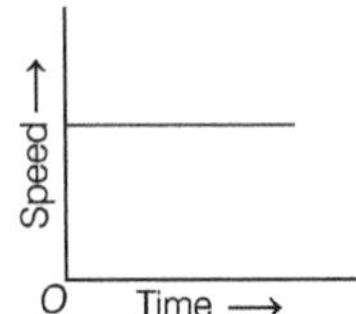

15 What is the quantity which is measured by the area occupied below the velocity-time graph? **Pg 107**

Sol. The displacement is measured by the area occupied below the velocity-time graph.

16 A bus starting from rest moves with a uniform acceleration of 0.1 m/s^2 for 2 min. Find
(*i*) the speed acquired.
(*ii*) the distance travelled. **Pg 109**

Sol. Given, acceleration, $a = 0.1\text{ m/s}^2$

Time, $t = 2\text{ min} = 2 \times 60 = 120\text{ s}$, initial speed, $u = 0$

(*i*) From first equation of motion, speed acquired by the bus,

$$v = u + at = 0 + 0.1 \times 120 = 12\text{ m/s}$$

(*ii*) From second equation of motion,

$$\text{distance travelled, } s = ut + \frac{1}{2}at^2$$
$$= 0 \times 120 + \frac{1}{2} \times 0.1 \times 120 \times 120$$
$$= 0.1 \times 60 \times 120 = 720\text{ m}$$

The distance travelled by the bus is 720 m.

17 A train is travelling at a speed of 90 km/h. Brakes are applied, so as to produce a uniform acceleration of – 0.5 m/s^2. Find how far the train will go before it is brought to rest? **Pg 110**

Sol. Given, initial speed, $u = 90\text{ km/h} = 90 \times \frac{5}{18} = 25\text{ m/s}$

Acceleration, $a = -0.5\text{ m/s}^2$

Train brought to rest, so final speed, $v = 0$

From third equation of motion,

$$v^2 = u^2 + 2as$$
$$\Rightarrow \quad 0 = (25)^2 - 2 \times 0.5 \times s$$
$$0 = 625 - s \Rightarrow s = 625\text{ m}$$

The train will travel a distance of 625 m before it is brought to rest.

18 A trolley while going down an inclined plane has an acceleration of 2 cm/s^2. What will be its velocity 3 s after the start? **Pg 110**

Sol. Given, initial velocity of trolley, $u = 0$

Acceleration, $a = 2\text{ cm/s}^2 = 0.02\text{ m/s}^2$,

Time taken, $t = 3\text{ s}$

From first equation of motion,

$$v = u + at = 0 + 0.02 \times 3 = 0.06\text{ m/s}$$

Hence, the velocity of the trolley after 3 s of start is 0.06 m/s.

19 A racing car has a uniform acceleration of 4 m/s^2. What distance will it cover in 10 s after the start? **Pg 110**

Sol. Given, acceleration, $a = 4\text{ m/s}^2$

Time taken, $t = 10\text{ s}$,

Initial velocity of the racing car, $u = 0$

From second equation of motion,

$$s = ut + \frac{1}{2}at^2 = 0 + \frac{1}{2} \times 4 \times (10)^2 = 200\text{ m}$$

The distance travelled by the racing car in 10 s is 200 m.

20 A stone is thrown in a vertically upward direction with a velocity of 5 m/s. If the acceleration of the stone during its motion is 10 m/s^2 in the downward direction, then what will be the height attained by the stone and what time will it take to reach there? **Pg 110**

Sol. Given, initial velocity, $u = 5\text{ m/s}$,

Acceleration, $a = -10\text{ m/s}^2$,

[negative sign is due to downward direction]

Final velocity, $v = 0$

[at maximum height velocity is zero]

Height attained, $s = ?$

Time taken, $t = ?$

(*i*) From third equation of motion,

$$v^2 = u^2 + 2as$$
$$0 = (5)^2 + 2 \times (-10) \times s$$
$$s = \frac{25}{20} = 1.25\text{ m}$$

Height attained by the stone is 1.25 m.

(*ii*) From first equation of motion,

$$v = u + at$$
$$0 = 5 + (-10)\,t$$
$$t = \frac{5}{10} = 0.5\text{ s}$$

The time taken by the stone to reach at the top will be 0.5 s.

EXERCISES *(On Pages 112 and 113)*

1 An athlete completes one round of a circular track of diameter 200 m in 40 s. What will be the distance covered and the displacement at the end of 2 min 20 s?

Sol. According to the question,

diameter of the circular track = 200 m

Hence, radius, $r = 100\text{ m}$

In 40 s, an athlete completes 1 round.

In 140 s, an athlete completes $\frac{140}{40} = 3\frac{1}{2}$ rounds.

Hence, the distance covered by the athlete

$$= 3 \times 2\pi r + \frac{1}{2} \times 2\pi r$$

$$= 3 \times 2 \times \frac{22}{7} \times 100 + \frac{1}{2} \times 2 \times \frac{22}{7} \times 100 = 2200 \text{ m}$$

Displacement = Shortest path between the initial position and the final position = $2r$

$$= 2 \times 100 = 200 \text{ m}$$

2 **Joseph jogs from one end *A* to the other end *B* of a straight 300 m road in 2 min 30 s and then turns around and jogs 100 m back to point *C* in another 1 min. What are Joseph's average speeds and velocities in jogging (*i*) from *A* to *B* and (*ii*) from *A* to *C*?**

Sol. Joseph jogs from one end *A* to other end *B* of a straight 300 m road in 2 min 30 s and then turns around and jogs 100 m back to point *C* in another 1 min, as shown in figure

300 m

A — C — B

100 m

(*i*) From *A* to *B*, Joseph covers distance = 300 m

Time = 2 min 30 s = $2 \times 60 + 30$

$= 120 + 30 = 150$ s

Hence, average speed = $\frac{\text{Total distance}}{\text{Total time}}$

$= \frac{300}{150} = 2$ m/s

$\therefore$ Average velocity = $\frac{\text{Total displacement}}{\text{Total time}} = \frac{300}{150}$

= 2 m/s

As in both cases, distance covered and direction are same.

(*ii*) From *A* to *C*, Joseph covers distance = 400 m

Time = 150 + 60 = 210 s

Hence, average speed = $\frac{400}{210} = 1.9$ m/s

Displacement = 200 m

Time = 150 + 60 = 210 s

Hence, average velocity = $\frac{200}{210} = 0.952$ m/s

3 **Abdul, while driving to school, computes the average speed for his trip to be 20 km/h. On his return trip along the same route, there is less traffic and the average speed is 30 km/h. What is the average speed for Abdul's trip?**

Sol. Let the distance covered by Abdul while driving to school = x

While going $v_1 = 20 = \frac{x}{t_1}$

[where, t_1 = time taken to cover distance x]

While returning $v_2 = 30 = \frac{x}{t_2}$

[where, t_2 = time taken to cover x while returning]

Hence, $t_1 = \frac{x}{20}$, $t_2 = \frac{x}{30}$

$$\therefore \text{Average speed} = \frac{\text{Total distance}}{\text{Total time}} = \frac{2x}{\frac{x}{20} + \frac{x}{30}} = \frac{2x}{\frac{5x}{60}}$$

$$= \frac{2x \times 60}{5x} = 24 \text{ km/h}$$

4 **A motorboat starting from rest on a lake accelerates in a straight line at a constant rate of 3 m/s^2 for 8 s. How far does the boat travel during this time?**

Sol. The motorboat starts from rest, so initial velocity, $u = 0$

Time taken, $t = 8$ s, Acceleration, $a = 3$ m/s^2

$\therefore$ Distance covered during the given time,

$s = ut + \frac{1}{2}at^2$ [from second equation of motion]

$$= 0 \times 8 + \frac{1}{2} \times 3 \times (8)^2 = \frac{1}{2} \times 3 \times 64 = 96 \text{ m}$$

5 **A driver of a car travelling at 52 km/h applies the brakes and accelerates uniformly in the opposite direction. The car stops in 5 s. Another driver going at 3 km/h in another car applies his brakes slowly and stops in 10 s. On the same graph paper, plot the speed *versus* time graphs for the two cars. Which of the two cars travelled farther after the brakes were applied?**

Sol. $\therefore$ Initial speed of car A = 52 km/h = $52 \times \frac{5}{18}$

= 14.44 m/s

The car stops in 5 s, i.e. final speed of car, $v = 0$, time, $t = 5$ s. For speed-time graph of car A,

Speed (s)	14.44 m/s	0
Time (t)	0	5

Initial speed of car B = 3 km/h = $3 \times \frac{5}{18} = 0.83$ m/s

The car stops in 10 s, i.e. final speed of car, $v = 0$, time, $t = 10$ s.

For speed-time graph of car B,

Speed (s)	0.83 m/s	0
Time (t)	0	10 s

The speed-time graph of both cars A and B is shown as below:

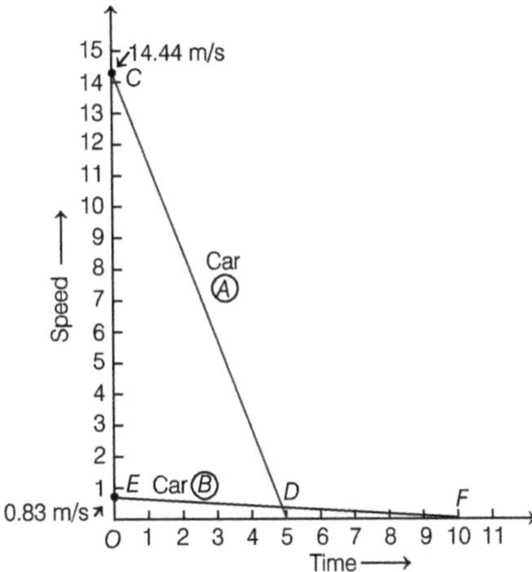

Distance travelled by car A = Area of ΔOCD

$$= \frac{1}{2} OC \times OD = \frac{1}{2} \times 14.44 \times 5 = 36.1 \text{ m}$$

Distance travelled by car B = Area of ΔOEF

$$= \frac{1}{2} OE \times EF = \frac{1}{2} \times 0.83 \times 10 = 4.15 \text{ m}$$

Thus, the car A travelled farther than car B after the brakes are applied.

6 **Figure shows the distance-time graph of three objects *A*, *B* and *C*. Study the graph and answer the following questions:**

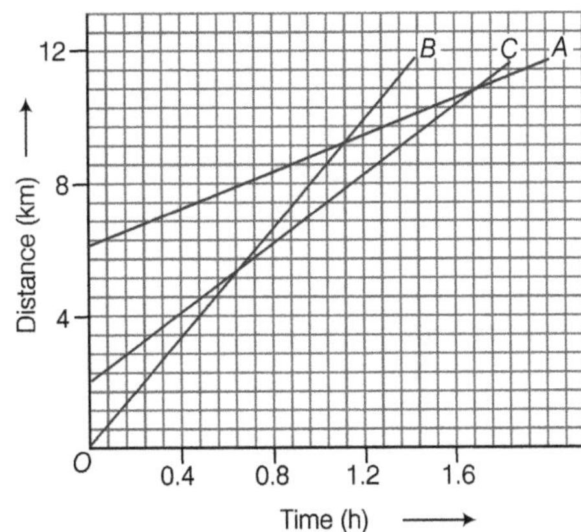

(*i*) Which of the three is travelling the fastest?
(*ii*) Are all three ever at same point on the road?
(*iii*) How far has *C* travelled when *B* passes *A*?
(*iv*) How far has *B* travelled by the time it passes *C*?

Sol. Scale Along distance Axis 1 div = 0.4 km

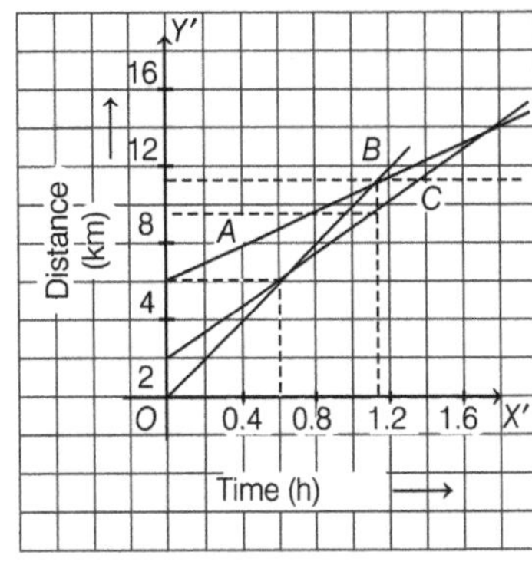

(*i*) The object for which slope of distance-time graph is maximum will have maximum speed, i.e. will travel the fastest. Here, for object B, slope is maximum, so it is travelling the fastest.

(*ii*) All the three objects will be at the same point on the road, if the speed-time graph intersect each other at any point. Here, all the three graphs do not intersect each other, so these three will never be at the same point on the road.

(*iii*) When B passes A, then distance travelled by

$$C = 9.6 - 2 = 7.6 \text{ km}$$

(*iv*) Distance travelled by B when it passes $C = 6$ km.

7 **A ball is gently dropped from a height of 20 m. If its velocity increases uniformly at the rate of 10 m/s², then with what velocity will it strike the ground? After what time will it strike the ground?**

Sol. Initial velocity of the ball, $u = 0$

Acceleration, $a = 10 \text{ m/s}^2$

Distance, $s = 20$ m

From the equation of motion, $v^2 - u^2 = 2as$

$$v^2 - 0 = 2 \times 10 \times 20$$

$$v^2 = 400 \Rightarrow v = 20 \text{ m/s}$$

Again from the first equation of motion

$$v = u + at$$

$$20 = 0 + 10 \times t$$

$$t = 2 \text{ s}$$

After time t = 2s, it will strike the ground.

8 **The speed-time graph for a car is shown in the below figure:**

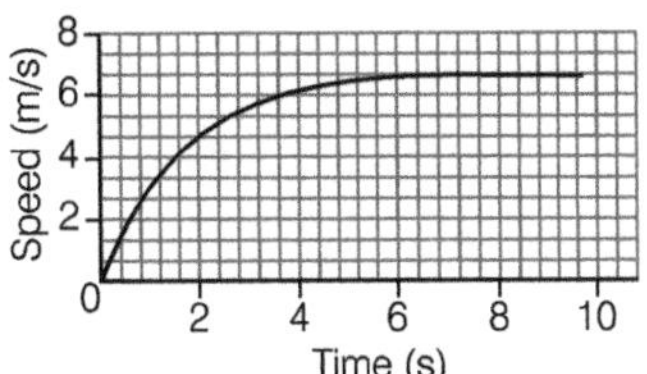

(*i*) Find how far does the car travel in the first 4 s. Shade the area on the graph that represents the distance travelled by the car during the period.

(*ii*) Which part of the graph represents uniform motion of the car?

Sol. The area under the slope of the speed-time graph gives the distance travelled by an object.

(*i*) We will calculate the distance represented by 1 square of the graph. This can be done as follow. If 5 square on *X*-axis = 2 s,

1 square on *X*-axis = 2/5 s,

3 square on *Y*-axis = 2 m/s,

1 square on *Y*-axis = 2/3 m/s

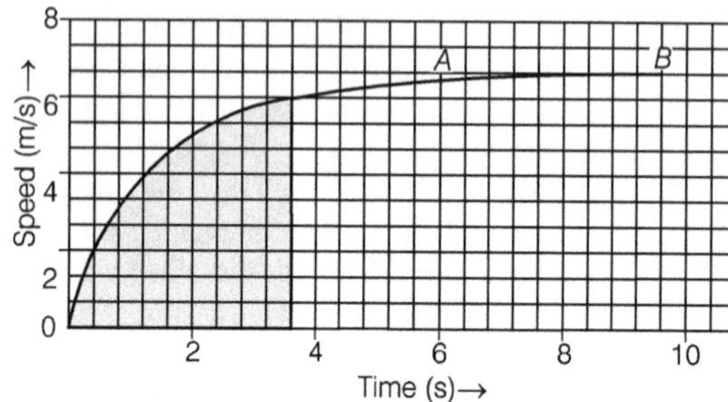

So, area of 1 square on graph $= \frac{2}{5} \times \frac{2}{3} = \frac{4}{15}$ m

1 square represents distance $= \frac{4}{15}$ m

Since, approximately 62 squares come under the area of slope for the time of 4 s.

So, distance travelled in 4 s $= \frac{4}{15} \times 62 = 16.53$ m

(*ii*) For uniform motion, the speed-time graph is a straight line parallel to the time axis. So, the straight part of the curve parallel to the time axis represents the uniform motion of the car.

9 State which of the following situations are possible and give an example for each.

(*i*) An object with a constant acceleration but with zero velocity.

(*ii*) An object moving in a certain direction with an acceleration in the perpendicular direction.

Sol. (*i*) When an object is thrown vertically upward, then at highest point its velocity is zero but it has constant acceleration 9.8 m/s^2 (acceleration due to gravity).

(*ii*) An aeroplane flies in horizontal direction but the acceleration due to gravity acts on it in vertically downward direction, i.e. along the direction perpendicular to the direction of motion.

10 An artificial satellite is moving in a circular orbit of radius 42250 km. Calculate its speed, if it takes 24 h to revolve around the earth.

Sol. Given, radius of the orbit, r = 42250 km

Distance covered in one revolution,

$d = 2\pi r$ [circumference of the orbit]

$= 2 \times \frac{22}{7} \times 42250 = 265571.43$ km

Time taken in one revolution, t = 24 h

$\therefore$ Speed of satellite $= \frac{\text{Distance}}{\text{Time}} = \frac{265571.43}{24}$

$= 11065.48$ km/h

SUMMARY

- An object is said to be in **motion** if its position changes with time.
- The **distance** travelled by a body is the actual length of the path covered by it, irrespective of the direction in which the body travels.
  It is a **scalar quantity**. Its SI unit is **metre**.
- The shortest distance between the initial and final position of the moving object is called the **displacement** of the object.
  It is a **vector quantity**. Its SI unit is **metre**.
- The ratio of distance travelled by an object to the time taken is called **rate of motion**.
- **Speed** of an object is defined as the distance travelled by it in unit time.
  Speed of an object $(v) = \dfrac{\text{Distance } (s)}{\text{Time } (t)}$
  It is a **scalar quantity**. Its SI unit is **metre per second** (m/s).
- **Velocity** of an object is defined as the displacement of the body per unit time.
  Velocity of an object $(v) = \dfrac{\text{Displacement } (d)}{\text{Time } (t)}$
  It is a **vector quantity**. Its SI unit is **metre per second** (m/s).
- **Acceleration** is defined as the rate of change of velocity with respect to time.
- Acceleration $(a) = \dfrac{\text{Change in velocity } (\Delta v)}{\text{Change in time } (\Delta t)}$
  It is a **vector quantity**. Its SI unit is m/s^2.
- Types of acceleration
  (i) **Uniform acceleration** If the velocity of an object changes by an equal amount in equal intervals of time, then the acceleration of the object is known as uniform acceleration.
  (ii) **Non-uniform acceleration** If the velocity of an object changes by an unequal amount in equal intervals of time, then the acceleration of the object is known as non-uniform acceleration.
- **Equations of motion** Let u be the initial velocity of the object, a the uniform acceleration, v its velocity after time t and s is the distance travelled in time t, then the following equations hold good:
  (i) $v = u + at$
  (ii) $s = ut + \frac{1}{2}at^2$
  (iii) $v^2 - u^2 = 2as$
  These equations are known as equations of motion.
- When an object moves in a circular path with uniform speed, its motion is called uniform circular motion.

For Mind Map
Visit https://goo.gl/wQASYz
OR Scan the Code

Exam Practice

Objective Type Questions

Multiple Choice Questions

1 The numerical ratio of displacement and distance for a moving object is

(a) always less than 1
(b) always equal to 1
(c) always more than 1
(d) equal or less than 1 **NCERT Exemplar**

Sol. (d) Displacement of an object can be less than or equal to the distance covered by the object, because the magnitude of displacement is not equal to distance. However, it can be so if the motion is along a straight line without any change in direction.

So, the numerical ratio of displacement to distance is always equal to or less than 1.

2 A particle is moving in a circular path of radius r. The displacement after half a circle would be **NCERT Exemplar**

(a) zero (b) πr (c) $2r$ (d) $2\pi r$

Sol. (c) Given, after half the circle, the particle will reach the diametrically opposite point *i.e.,* from point A to point B as shown in figure below. We know displacement is shortest path between initial and final point.

$\therefore$ Displacement after half circle $= AB = OA + OB$

$= r + r = 2r$ [$\because$ Given, OA and $OB = r$]

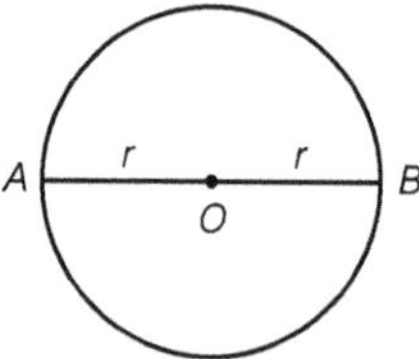

Hence, the displacement after half circle is $2r$.

3 Speedometer is a device which is used to measure

(a) average speed
(b) average acceleration
(c) instantaneous speed
(d) instantaneous acceleration

Sol. (c) Speedometer is used to measure instantaneous speed.

4 If velocity of an object decreases with time, then it is called

(a) retardation (b) deceleration
(c) negative acceleration (d) All of these

Sol. (d) When velocity of an object decreases with time, then it is said to be retardation, deceleration or negative acceleration.

5 Four cars A, B, C and D are moving on a levelled road. Their distance *versus* time graphs are shown in figure. Choose the correct statement. **NCERT Exemplar**

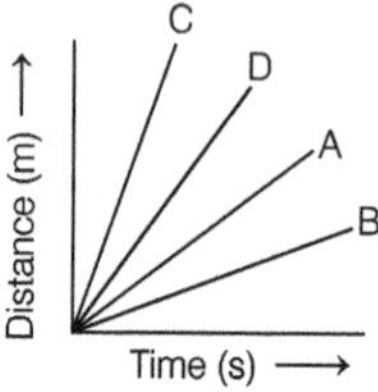

(a) Car A is faster than car D
(b) Car B is the slowest
(c) Car D is faster than car C
(d) Car C is the slowest

Sol. (b) The slope of distance-time graph represents the speed. From the given graph, it is clear that the slope of distance-time graph for car B is less than all other cars. So, the slope is minimum for car B. Hence, car B is the slowest.

6 Which of the following figures represents uniform motion of a moving object correctly?

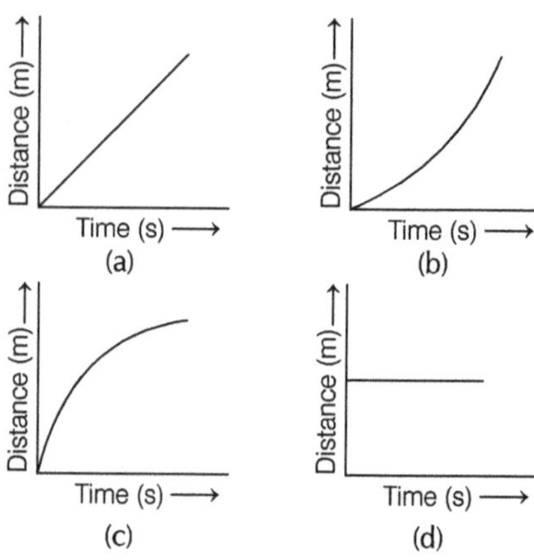

NCERT Exemplar

Sol. (a) For uniform motion, the distance-time graph is a straight line (because in uniform motion object covers equal distance in equal interval of time).

7 Velocity-time graph for a moving object is found to be curved line, then its acceleration is

(a) constant (b) variable
(c) zero (d) None of these

Sol. (b) Since, velocity-time graph for a moving object is curved line, this means that object is moving with non-uniform accelerated motion, therefore body is moving with variable acceleration.

8 Slope of a velocity-time graph gives

(a) the distance (b) the displacement
(c) the acceleration (d) the speed

NCERT Exemplar

Sol. (c) Slope of velocity-time graph gives acceleration.

Because slope of the curve $= \frac{\text{Velocity}}{\text{Time}} = \frac{v}{t}$

where, $\frac{v}{t} =$ acceleration.

9 In the following figure of velocity-time graph for the motion of the body, the total distance covered by the body from 3 s to 7 s is

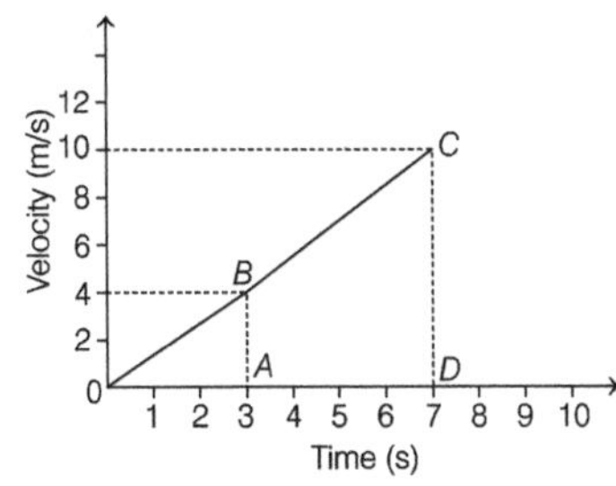

(a) 28 m (b) 56 m (c) 14 m (d) 35 m

Sol. (a) Total distance moved by the body from 3 s to 7 s

$$= \text{Area of shape } ABCD = \frac{(AB + DC) \times AD}{2}$$

From given graph, we have

$AB = 4$ m/s

$DC = 10$ m/s

$AD = (7 - 3) = 4$ s

$$= \frac{(4 + 10)(7 - 3)}{2} = \frac{14 \times 4}{2} = 28 \text{ m}$$

10 A train starting from rest attains a velocity of 90 km/h in 2 min, then the distance travelled by the train for attaining this velocity is

(a) 1.5 km (b) 2 km (c) 2.5 km (d) 1.2 km

Sol. (a) Given, initial velocity, $u = 0$,

Final velocity, $v = 90 \text{ km/h} = 90 \times \frac{5}{18} = 25$ m/s

Time, $t = 2 \text{ min} = 2 \times 60 = 120$ s

From the equation of motion,

$$v = u + at$$

$$\Rightarrow \quad a = \frac{v}{t} \qquad [\because u = 0]$$

$$= \frac{25}{2 \times 60} = \frac{5}{24} \text{ m/s}^2$$

Distance (s) covered is,

$$s = ut + \frac{1}{2}at^2 = 0 + \frac{1}{2} \times \frac{5}{24} \times (120)^2$$

$$= \frac{1}{2} \times \frac{5}{24} \times 120 \times 120$$

$$= 1500 \text{ m} = 1.5 \text{ km}$$

11 If the displacement of an object is proportional to square of time, then the object moves with **NCERT Exemplar**

(a) uniform velocity
(b) uniform acceleration
(c) increasing acceleration
(d) decreasing acceleration

Sol. (b) Let object starts from rest *i.e.*, initial velocity (u) = 0 and an acceleration (a) in time (t).

From second equation of motion,

$$s = ut + \frac{1}{2}at^2$$

Then, $s = 0 \times t + \frac{1}{2}at^2 \Rightarrow s = \frac{1}{2}at^2$

$$s \propto t^2, \text{ if } a = \text{constant}$$

Thus, displacement (s) of an object is proportional to square of time t, then the object moves with constant or uniform acceleration.

12 A car moves towards South with a speed of 20 ms^{-1}. It changes its direction to East and moves with speed of 20 ms^{-1}. What is its velocity now?

(a) 20 ms^{-1} South-East
(b) $20\sqrt{2}$ ms^{-1} South-East
(c) 10 ms^{-1} South-East
(d) 40 ms^{-1} South-East

Sol. (b) A car moves towards South with speed 20 ms^{-1} then it changes its direction to East with speed 20 ms^{-1} as shown in figure below

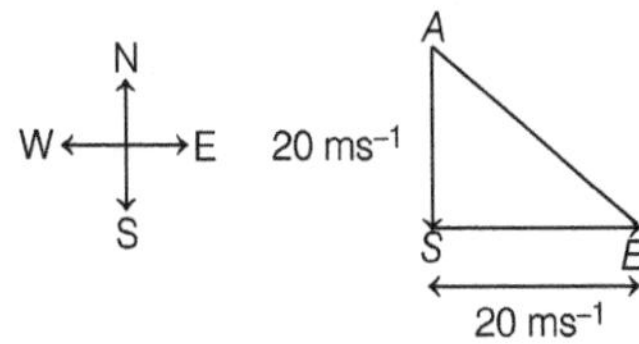

$AE = ?$

Now, $AE^2 = AS^2 + SE^2$

$$AE = \sqrt{AS^2 + SE^2} = \sqrt{(20)^2 + (20)^2} = 20\sqrt{2}$$

$AE = 20\sqrt{2}$ m/s South-East

Thus, its velocity is $20\sqrt{2}$ m/s South-East.

Fill in the Blanks

13 Odometer measures .... covered by the vehicles.

Sol. Distance

14 The area under the velocity-time graph gives the value of ....

Sol. Distance travelled

15 A particle cannot be accelerated if its .... is constant.

Sol. Velocity

16 The motion of blades of an electric fan around the axle is an example of ....

Sol. Uniform circular motion.

True and False

17 Acceleration is defined as the rate of change of velocity with respect to time.

Sol. True

18 When a moving body comes to rest, then its initial velocity is taken as zero.

Sol. False

19 Motion of particle on a wheel is an example of uniform circular motion.

Sol. True

20 Magnitude of displacement is greater than the distance travelled by the object.

Sol. False

Match the Columns

21 Match the following columns.

Column I Acceleration is		Column II Example	
A.	in the direction of motion	p.	Motion of freely falling body
B.	against the direction of motion	q.	Car moves through congested market
C.	uniform	r.	Brakes applied to moving car
D.	Non-uniform	s.	Train start moving from a station

Sol. (A)→(s), (B)→(r), (C)→(p), (D)→(q)

Assertion-Reason

Direction (Q.Nos. 22-26) *In each of the following questions, a statement of Assertion is given by the corresponding statement of Reason. Of the given statements, mark the correct answer as*

(a) If both Assertion and Reason are true and Reason is the correct explanation of Assertion.
(b) If both Assertion and Reason are true, but Reason is not the correct explanation of Assertion.
(c) If Assertion is true, but Reason is false.
(d) If Assertion is false, but Reason is true.

22 **Assertion** Displacement of body may be zero, when distance travelled by it is not zero.

Reason The displacement is the longer distance between initial and final positions.

Sol. (c) The shortest distance between two point is called displacement. Displacement may be positive, negative or zero, while distance is always positive. Hence, Assertion is true but Reason is false.

23 **Assertion** Speedometer is a device used to measure instantaneous speed.

Reason Speedometer is used for measuring various speeds in each time interval.

Sol. (c) Speedometer is a device used to measure instantaneous speed. Hence, Assertion is true but Reason is false.

24 **Assertion** Acceleration of a moving body is always positive.

Reason Acceleration of a moving body is the rate of change in velocity with respect to time.

Sol. (d) Assertion is false because acceleration may be positive, negative or zero.
Hence, Assertion is false but Reason is true.

25 **Assertion** A body can have acceleration even its speed is constant.

Reason In uniform circular motion, speed of body is constant but its velocity continuously changes.

Sol. (a) In uniform circular motion, speed of body remains same while its velocity continuously changes due to change in its direction at each point. Hence, body moves with acceleration. Therefore, Assertion and Reason both are true and Reason is the correct explanation of Assertion.

26 **Assertion** Acceleration and displacement are in the opposite direction during retardation.

Reason Acceleration is given as the change in velocity per unit time.

Sol. (a) Acceleration is defined as the rate of change of velocity with respect to time and negative acceleration is called retardation. Displacement is length of the shortest path measured in direction from initial position to final position of the object. Both Assertion and Reason are true and reason is the correct explanation of assertion.

Case Based Questions

Direction (Q.Nos. 27-30) *Answer the questions on the basis of your understanding of the following table and related studied concepts:*

Distance travelled by a train and time taken by it is shown in the following table:

Time	*Distance* (in km)
10:00 am	0
10:30 am	25
10:40 am	28
11:00 am	40
11:15 am	42
11:30 am	50

27 Plot distance-time graph.

Sol. Distance-time graph is shown as:

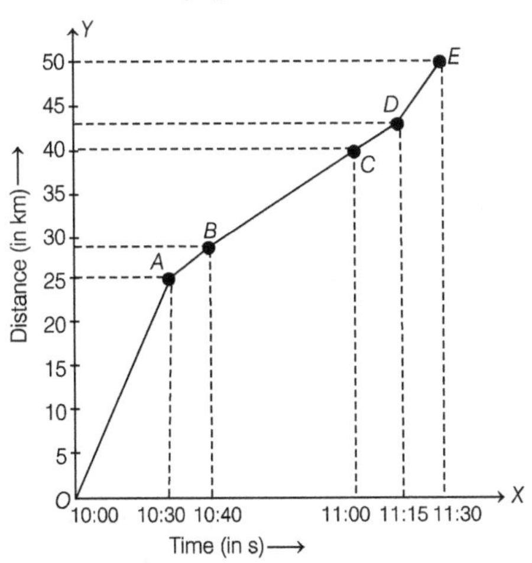

28 When is the train travelling at the highest speed?

Sol. We know that, speed = slope of distance-time graph. The greater the slope, greater is the speed. From the graph, it is clear that slope of distance-time graph is maximum between 10:00 am to 10:30 am, so the train was travelling at the highest speed during this interval of time.

29 What is the average speed of the train?

(a) 33.33 km/h (b) 3.33 km/h
(c) 33.33 m/s (d) 3.33 m/s

Sol. (a) $\therefore$ Average speed $= \dfrac{\text{Total distance travelled}}{\text{Total time taken}}$

From the given table, total distance travelled $= 50$ km

Total time taken 10:00 am to 11:30 am

$$= 1\text{ h } 30\text{ min} = 1\frac{1}{2}\text{ h} = \frac{3}{2}\text{ h}$$

Now, average speed $= \dfrac{50\text{ km}}{3/2\text{ h}} = \dfrac{100}{3} = 33.33$ km/h

30 At what distance does the train slow down?

(a) Between 30 km and 32 km
(b) Between 40 km and 42 km
(c) Between 38 km and 40 km
(d) Between 50 km and 52 km

Sol. (b) The part *CD* of the graph has minimum slope, so the train had minimum speed between 11:00 am and 11:15 am. Thus, the train had slowed down between 40 km and 42 km.

Direction (Q.Nos. 31-34) *Answer the questions on the basis of your understanding of the following passage and related studied concepts:*

A train travels from one station to the next. The driver of train *A* starts from rest at time $t = 0$ and accelerates uniformly for the first 20s. At time $t = 20$s, train reaches its top speed of 25 m/s, then travels at this speed for further 30s before decelerating uniformly to rest. Total time for the journey of train *A* is 60s. Another train *B* is travelling on the parallel of train *A* with zero initial speed at $t = 0$ and then accelerates uniformly for first 10s. At time $t = 10$s it reaches its top speed of 30 m/s, then travels at this speed for further 20s before decelerating uniformly to rest. Total time for the journey of train *B* is 80s.

31 Sketch a speed-time graph for the motion of train *A*.

Sol. Speed-time graph for the motion of train *A* is

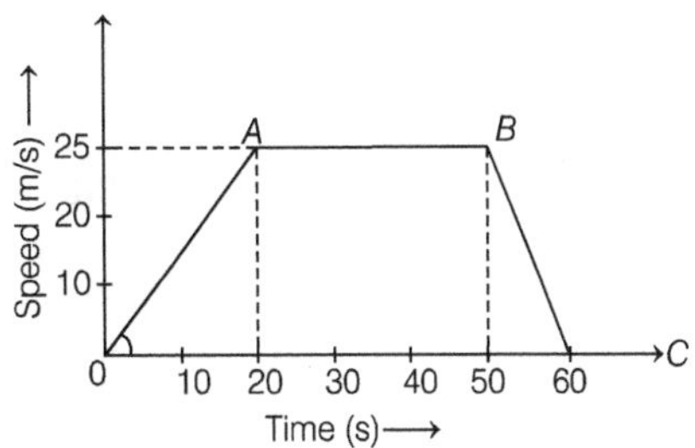

32 Calculate the deceleration of train A, as it comes to rest.

Sol. $$\text{Deceleration} = \frac{\text{Change in velocity}}{\text{Time interval}} \quad \ldots\text{(i)}$$

Given, change in velocity = 25m/s

Time interval (for deceleration) = 10 s

Substituting above values in Eq. (i), we get

$$= 2.5 \text{ m/s}^2$$

Thus, deceleration of train A is 2.5 m/s^2.

33 In which time interval, speed of train B is constant?

Sol. Speed of train B is constant during time interval 10s to 30s, i.e. 20s.

34 What is the initial speed of trains A and B?

Sol. Initial speed of trains A and B is zero as both trains start from rest.

Very Short Answer Type Questions

35 What is the importance of reference point?

Sol. Reference point is important because it states the position of object correctly, as motion is a relative in nature.

36 Is it possible that the train in which you are sitting appears to move while it is at rest?

Sol. Yes, if other train is moving in adjacent line to the train we are sitting, then it seems that our train is moving in opposite direction.

37 Odometer measures displacement of the vehicle. Correct this statement.

Sol. No, Odometer measures distance covered by a vehicle.

38 A particle is moving in a circular path of radius r. What will be the displacement after half a circle?

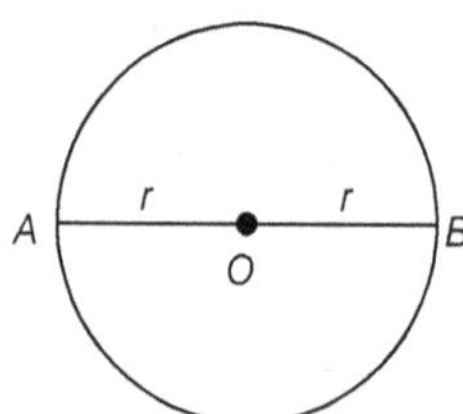

NCERT Exemplar

Sol. After half the circle, the particle will reach the diametrically opposite point, i.e. from point A to B.

$\therefore$ Displacement after half circle = AB

$$= OA + OB = r + r = 2r$$

39 In which condition, will the magnitude of the displacement be equal to the distance travelled by an object?

Sol. If an object moves in a straight line from one point to another, then the magnitude of displacement and distance will be equal.

40 What is the numerical ratio of average velocity to average speed of an object when it is moving along a straight path?

Sol. The numerical ratio of average velocity and average speed of an object when it is moving along a straight path is 1 : 1.

41 The distance-time graph for motion of Ram and Shyam is shown alongside.

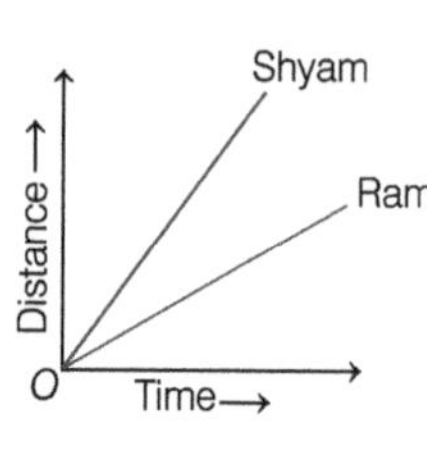

Which of them has greater acceleration? Justify your answer.

Sol. Both Ram and Shyam have zero acceleration as they are moving with constant velocity. Since, distance-time graph is a straight line.

42 If the displacement-time graph for a particle is parallel to time axis, what is the velocity of the particle?

Sol. Zero

43 From the given v-t graph (see figure), what can be inferred?

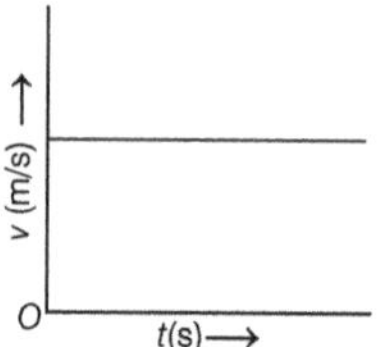

NCERT Exemplar

Sol. From the given v-t graph, it is clear that the velocity of an object is not changing with time, i.e. the object is in a uniform motion.

44 Is the motion of a body uniform or accelerated, if it goes round the sun with constant speed in a circular orbit?

Sol. In this case, the motion of a body is accelerated as its velocity changes due to the change in direction.

45 Find the angular velocity of satellite which revolves in a circular orbit of radius 35000 km and completes one round in 12 h.

Sol. Given, time taken to complete one round = 12 h

Angle subtended at centre = 2π

$\therefore$ Angular velocity $= \dfrac{\text{Angle subtended at centre}}{\text{Time taken}}$

$= \dfrac{2\pi}{12} = \dfrac{\pi}{6}$ rad/h

46 If the displacement of an object is proportional to square of time, then predict the motion of an object. **NCERT Exemplar**

Sol. From second equation of motion,

$$s = ut + \frac{1}{2}at^2$$

If object starts from rest, i.e. $u = 0$, then

$$s = \frac{1}{2}at^2$$

If a = constant, $s \propto t^2$

So, the object moves with constant or a uniform acceleration.

Short Answer (SA) Type Questions

1 (i) What is motion?

(ii) State the types of motion.

(iii) Write the unit of acceleration.

Sol. (i) If a body changes its position with respect to time and its surroundings, then it is said to be in motion.

(ii) Generally, there are two types of motion:
(a) Uniform motion (b) Non-uniform motion

(iii) The SI unit of acceleration is m/s^2.

2 A cow and a bird both travelled from point A to point B. The cow travelled in a straight line but the bird travelled along the curved path as shown alongside:

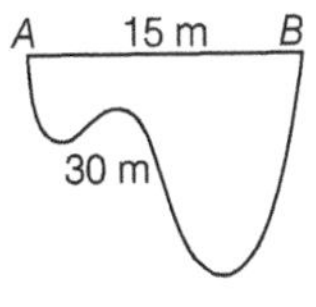

(i) What is the distance travelled by the cow?

(ii) What is the distance travelled by the bird?

(iii) Which one of them has more displacement?

Sol. (i) Distance travelled by the cow = 15 m

(ii) Distance travelled by the bird = 30 m

(iii) Displacement of the cow = 15 m

Displacement of the bird = 15 m

So, cow and bird have same displacement.

3 Express average velocity when the velocity of a body changes at a non-uniform rate and a uniform rate.

Sol. When the velocity of a body changes at a non-uniform rate, then its average velocity is calculated by dividing the net displacement covered with the total time taken.

i.e. Average velocity $= \dfrac{\text{Net displacement}}{\text{Total time taken}}$

In case, the velocity of a body changes at a uniform rate, the average velocity is given by the arithmetic mean of initial velocity and final velocity for a given period of time, i.e.

Average velocity

$$= \frac{\text{Initial velocity} + \text{Final velocity}}{2}$$

4 Give one example each of the type of motion when

(i) acceleration is in the direction of motion.

(ii) acceleration is against the direction of motion.

(iii) acceleration is uniform.

Sol. (i) A train starts moving from a station.

(ii) Brakes applied to a moving car.

(iii) A car travelling in such a way that its velocity changes at constant rate.

5 Draw a velocity *versus* time graph of a stone thrown vertically upwards and then coming downwards after attaining the maximum height. **NCERT Exemplar**

Sol. When a stone is thrown vertically upwards, then it has some initial velocity (u). As the stone goes up its velocity decreases (since, it is moving against the gravity) and at the highest point, i.e. maximum height,) its velocity becomes zero.

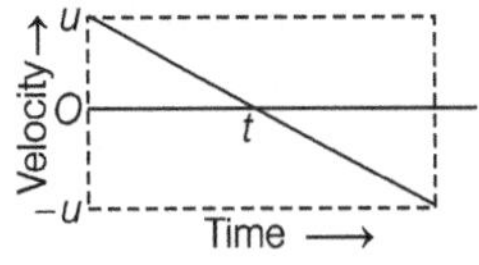

Let the stone takes time the t second to reach at the highest point. After that stone begins to fall (with zero initial velocity) and its velocity goes on increasing (since, it is moving with the gravity) and it reaches its initial point of projection with the velocity ($-u$) in the same time (with which it was thrown). So,

Velocity	u	0	$-u$
Time	0	t	$2t$

6 How will the equations of motion for an object moving with a uniform velocity change? **NCERT Exemplar**

Sol. We know that, the equations of uniformly accelerated motion are:

(i) $v = u + at$

(ii) $s = ut + \frac{1}{2}at^2$

(iii) $v^2 = u^2 + 2as$

where, u = initial velocity, v = final velocity, a = acceleration, t = time and s = distance

For an object moving with uniform velocity (velocity which is not changing with time), then acceleration $a = 0$.

So, equations of motion will become (putting $a = 0$ in above equations)

(i) $v = u$ (ii) $s = ut$

(iii) $v^2 = u^2$

7 State the three equations of motion. Which of them describes

(i) velocity-time relation?

(ii) position-time relation?

Sol. For a body moving along a straight line at velocity u and accelerating uniformly at a for time t to attain a velocity v and cover displacement s. Thus, the three equations of motion are as:

First equation, $v = u + at$ ...(i)

Second equation, $s = ut + 1/2at^2$ ...(ii)

Third equation, $v^2 = u^2 + 2as$ ...(iii)

(i) First equation represents velocity-time relation.

(ii) Second equation represents position-time relation.

8 A car moves with a speed of 30 km/h for half an hour, 25 km/h for one hour and 40 km/h for two hours. Calculate average speed of the car.

Sol. Time taken to travel, $t_1 = 0.5$ h,

$t_2 = 1$ h, $t_3 = 2$ h

$\therefore$ Total time, $t = t_1 + t_2 + t_3$

$= 0.5 + 1 + 2 = 3.5$ h

Speeds, $v_1 = 30$ km/h, $v_2 = 25$ km/h,

$v_3 = 40$ km/h

$\therefore$ Distances, $s_1 = v_1 t_1 = 30 \times 0.5 = 15$ km

$s_2 = v_2 t_2 = 25 \times 1 = 25$ km

and $s_3 = v_3 t_3 = 40 \times 2 = 80$ km

$\therefore$ Total distance, $s = s_1 + s_2 + s_3$

$= 15 + 25 + 80$

$= 120$ km

$$\text{Average speed} = \frac{\text{Total distance}}{\text{Total time}}$$

$$= \frac{s}{t} = \frac{120}{3.5} = 34.3 \text{ km/h}$$

9 The graph given below is the distance-time graph of an object.

(i) Find the speed of the object during first four seconds of its journey.

(ii) How long was it stationary?

(iii) Does it represent a real situation? Justify your answer.

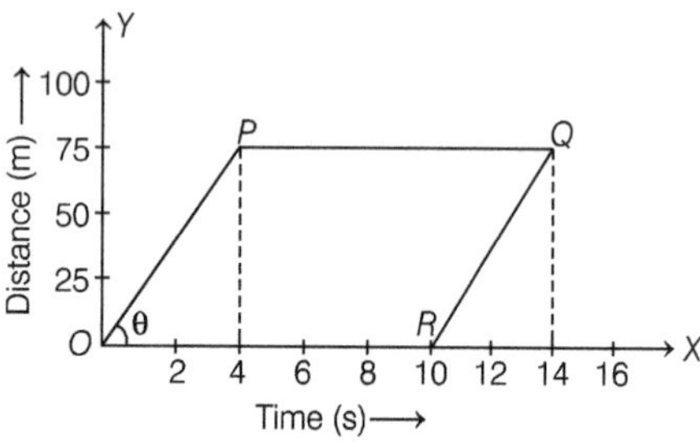

Sol. (i) Speed during first 4 s = Slope of OP

From the given graph, we have

$$\tan\theta = \frac{75}{4} = 18.75 \text{ m/s}$$

(ii) From 4 s to 14 s, distance is not changing with time, so it is stationary for 10 s.

(iii) No, it is not a real situation because distance travelled cannot decrease with time. Moreover, time cannot flow backward as shown by QR part of the graph.

10 The velocity-time graph (see figure) shows the motion of a cyclist. Find, (i) its acceleration, (ii) its velocity and (iii) the distance covered by the cyclist in 15 s. **NCERT Exemplar**

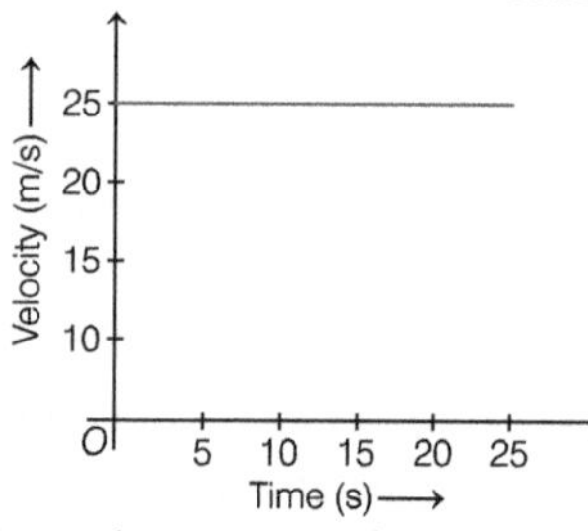

Sol. (i) From the given graph, it is clear that velocity is not changing with time, i.e. acceleration is zero.

(ii) Again from the graph, we can see that there is no change in the velocity with time, so velocity is after 15 s will remain same as 20 m/s.

(iii) Distance covered in 15 s = Velocity × Time

$= 20 \times 15 = 300$ m

11 Find the total displacement of the body from the following graph.

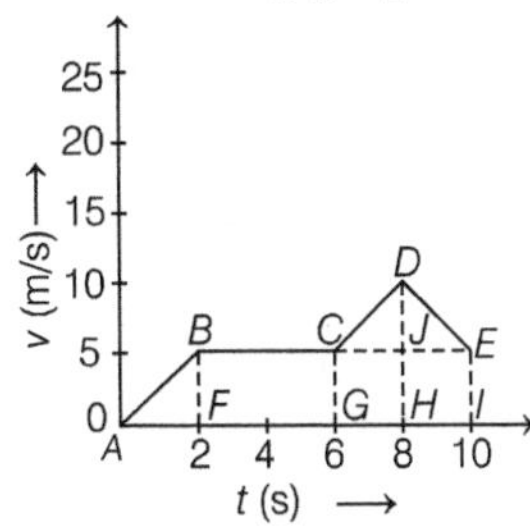

Sol. Total displacement = Sum of areas of

$(\Delta ABF + \text{Rectangle } BCGF + \Delta CDE + \text{Rectangle } CEIG)$

$$= \left[\frac{1}{2}(AF \times FB) + (BC \times CG) + \frac{1}{2}(CE \times DJ) + (CE \times EI)\right]$$

From given graph, we will substitute the values, we get

$$= \left[\frac{1}{2}(2 \times 5) + (4 \times 5) + \frac{1}{2}(4 \times 5) + (5 \times 4)\right] = 55 \text{ m}$$

12 The speed-time graphs of two cars are represented by P and Q as shown below:

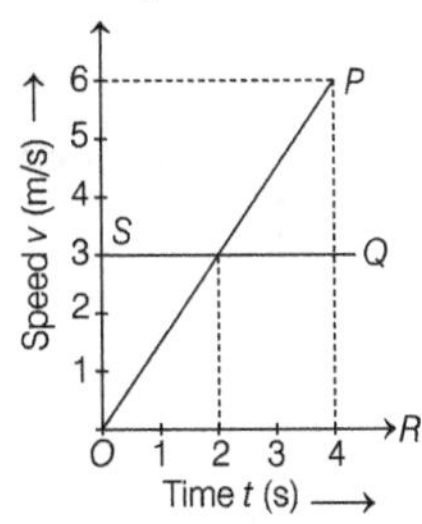

(*i*) Find the difference in the distance travelled by the two cars (in m) after 4 s.

(*ii*) Do they ever move with the same speed? If, so when?

(*iii*) What type of motion of car P and car Q are undergoing?

Sol. (*i*) Total distance travelled by P (area of ΔPOR)

$$= \frac{1}{2} \times 4 \times 6 = 12 \text{ m}$$

Total distance travelled by Q (area of $RQSO$)

$$= 4 \times 3 = 12 \text{ m}$$

Difference in the distance travelled by two cars (P and Q) $= 12 - 12 = 0$

(*ii*) Yes, they move with same velocity equal to 3 m/s at time 2 s. It can be determined by viewing the intersection point of two v-t graphs.

(*iii*) P is moving with constant acceleration while Q is moving with constant velocity, i.e. zero acceleration.

13 Study the v-t table and answer the following:

Velocity (m/s)	0	10	15	20	15	10	0
Time (s)	0	5	10	15	20	25	30

(*i*) What is the value of a in 0 to 15 s.

(*ii*) Predict the nature of acceleration in different part of the graph.

Sol. (*i*) $\therefore a = \dfrac{\text{Change in velocity}}{\text{Time interval}}$

From the given v-t table

$$a = \frac{20-0}{15-0} = \frac{20}{15} = \frac{4}{3} = 1.33 \text{ m/s}^2$$

(*ii*) Body is in uniform motion from 0 to 15 s, then non-uniform related motion from 15 s to 30 s.

Here, OA = uniformly accelerated

AB, BC, CD = non-uniformly accelerated

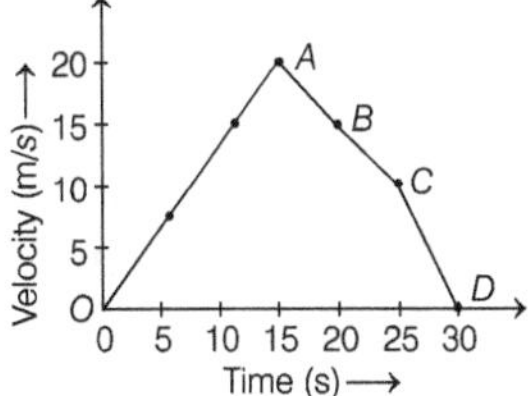

14 Brakes applied to a car produce an acceleration of 6 m/s^2 in opposite direction to motion. If the car takes 2 s to stop after application of brakes, then calculate the distance it travels during this time.

Sol. Given, final velocity, $v = 0$,

[since, car stops after applying the brakes]

Acceleration, $a = -6 \text{ m/s}^2$, Time, $t = 2$ s

From first equation of motion, $v = u + at$

or $u = v - at = 0 - (-6)(2) = 12$ m/s

From the second equation of motion,

$$s = ut + \frac{1}{2}at^2 = (12)(2) + \frac{1}{2}(-6)(2)^2 = 12 \text{ m}$$

Distance travelled in 2 s is 12 m.

15 A train accelerates uniformly from 36 km/h to 72 km/h in 20 s. Find the distance travelled.

Sol. Given, initial velocity, $u = 36$ km/h

$$= 36 \times \frac{5}{18} = 10 \text{ m/s}$$

Final velocity, $v = 72 \text{ km/h} = 72 \times \frac{5}{18} = 20$ m/s

Time, $t = 20$ s

From first equation of motion,

$$a = \frac{v - u}{t} = \frac{20 - 10}{20} = 0.5 \text{ m/s}^2$$

From third equation of motion, $s = \frac{v^2 - u^2}{2a}$

$= \frac{(20)^2 - (10)^2}{2 \times 0.5} = 300 \text{ m}$

Thus, distance travelled by train = 300 m

16 The speedometer readings of a car are shown below. Find the acceleration of the car and its displacement.

Time	Speedometer
9:25 am	36 km/h
9:45 am	72 km/h

Sol. Initial velocity, $u = 36 \text{ km/h} = 36 \times \frac{5}{18} = 10 \text{ m/s}$

Final velocity, $v = 72 \text{ km/h} = 72 \times \frac{5}{18} = 20 \text{ m/s}$

$t = 9:45 - 9:25 = 20 \text{ min} = 20 \times 60 = 1200 \text{ s}$

From first equation of motion,

$$a = \frac{v-u}{t} = \frac{20-10}{1200} = \frac{10}{1200} = \frac{1}{120} \text{ m/s}^2$$

From third equation of motion,

$$s = \frac{v^2 - u^2}{2a} = \frac{(20)^2 - (10)^2}{2 \times \frac{1}{120}} = \frac{400-100}{1/60}$$

$$= 300 \times 60 = 18000 \text{ m} = 18 \text{ km}$$

17 A car starts from rest and moves along the X-axis with constant acceleration 5 m/s^2 for 8 s. If it then continues with constant velocity, then what distance will the car cover in 12 s, since it started from rest? **NCERT Exemplar**

Sol. Given, the car starts from rest, so its initial velocity, $u = 0$

Acceleration, $a = 5 \text{ m/s}^2$ and time, $t = 8$ s

From first equation of motion,

$$v = u + at$$
$$v = 0 + 5 \times 8 = 40 \text{ m/s}$$

So, final velocity v is 40 m/s.

Again, from second equation of motion,

$$s = ut + \frac{1}{2}at^2$$
$$s = 0 \times 8 + \frac{1}{2} \times 5 \times (8)^2 = \frac{1}{2} \times 5 \times 64$$
$$s = 5 \times 32 = 160 \text{ m}$$

So, the distance covered in 8 s is 160 m.

Given, total time, $t = 12$ s

After 8 s, the car continues with constant velocity, i.e. the car will move with a velocity of 40 m/s.

The distance covered in the last 4 s = $40 \times 4 = 160$ m

[$\because$ distance = velocity × time]

We have used the direct formula because after 8 s, car is moving with constant velocity, i.e. zero acceleration.

$\therefore$ Total distance travelled in 12 s = 160 + 160 = 320 m

18 An object is moving with a uniform speed in a circle of radius r. Calculate the distance and displacement, (*i*) when it completes half the circle, (*ii*) when it completes full circle, (*iii*) what type of motion does the object possess?

Sol. (*i*) When an object completes half the circle, then the distance travelled by an object

$= \frac{1}{2} \times$ circumference of a circle

$= \frac{1}{2} \times 2\pi r = \pi r$

$\therefore$ Displacement of an object = $2r$

(*ii*) When an object completes full circle, then distance travelled by an object = $2\pi r$

Displacement travelled by an object = 0

[since, initial and final position are same]

(*iii*) Direction of motion of an object changes continuously in the circle, hence its velocity changes and its motion is accelerated motion.

Long Answer (LA) Type Questions

1 Give one example of each of the following situations:

(*i*) Uniformly accelerated motion.

(*ii*) Motion with uniform retardation.

(*iii*) Accelerated motion with uniform magnitude of velocity.

(*iv*) Motion in a direction with acceleration in perpendicular direction.

(*v*) Motion in which *v-t* graph is a horizontal line parallel to X-axis.

Sol. (*i*) Object dropped down from a height towards the surface of the earth.

(*ii*) Object thrown up with a velocity, retards uniformly.

(*iii*) Uniform circular motion, say planetary motion.

(*iv*) A bullet fired horizontally from a rifle, has acceleration in downward direction (due to gravity).

(*v*) A car moving with uniform velocity along a straight line.

2 Deduce the following equations of motion.

(i) $s = ut + (1/2)\,at^2$ (ii) $v^2 = u^2 + 2as$

Sol. (i) Consider a body which starts with initial velocity u and due to uniform acceleration a, its final velocity becomes v after time t. Then, its average velocity is given by

$$= \frac{\text{initial velocity} + \text{final velocity}}{2} = \frac{u+v}{2}$$

$\therefore$ The distance covered by the body in time t is given by distance, s = average velocity $\times$ time

or $$s = \frac{u+v}{2} \times t$$

$\Rightarrow$ $$s = \frac{u + (u + at)}{2} \times t \qquad [\because v = u + at]$$

$\therefore$ $$s = \frac{2\,ut + at^2}{2}$$

or $$s = ut + \frac{1}{2}at^2$$

(ii) From second equation of motion,

$$s = ut + \frac{1}{2}at^2 \qquad \text{...(i)}$$

Also, $$a = \frac{v-u}{t}$$

$\Rightarrow$ $$t = \frac{v-u}{a}$$

Substituting the value of t in Eq. (i), we get

$$s = u\left(\frac{v-u}{a}\right) + \frac{1}{2}a\left(\frac{v-u}{a}\right)^2$$

or $$s = \frac{uv - u^2}{a} + \frac{v^2 + u^2 - 2\,uv}{2a}$$

$$[\because (a-b)^2 = a^2 + b^2 - 2ab]$$

or $2\,as = 2\,uv - 2\,u^2 + v^2 + u^2 - 2\,uv$

or $v^2 - u^2 = 2as$

or $v^2 = u^2 + 2as$

3 On a 100 km track, a train travels the first 30 km at a uniform speed of 30 km/h. How fast must the train travel the next 70 km, so as to average 40 km/h for the entire trip?

Sol. Given, total distance, $s = 100$ km

A train travels the first 30 km at a uniform speed of 30 km/h.

Time, $t_1 = \frac{\text{distance}}{\text{speed}} = \frac{30\text{ km}}{30\text{ km/h}}$

Let speed of train is x for next 70 km.

Similarly, time, $t_2 = \frac{70\text{ km}}{x}$

Total time, $t = t_1 + t_2$

$$= \frac{30\text{ km}}{30\text{ km/h}} + \frac{70\text{ km}}{x\text{ (say)}}$$

$$t = 1 + \frac{70}{x} = \left(\frac{x+70}{x}\right)\text{h} \qquad \text{...(i)}$$

Now, average speed, $v = \frac{s}{t} = 40$ km/h ...(ii) (Given)

According to question,

$$\frac{100}{\frac{x+70}{x}} = 40$$

$\Rightarrow$ $$10 = 4\left(\frac{x+70}{x}\right)$$

$\Rightarrow$ $10x = 4x + 280$

$\Rightarrow$ $6x = 280$

$\Rightarrow$ $x = 46.67$ km/h

Speed for next 70 km to maintain average of 40 km/h is 46.67 km/h.

4 The distance-time graph of two trains are shown in figure. The trains start simultaneously in the same direction.

(i) How much A is ahead of B when the motion starts?

(ii) What is the speed of B?

(iii) When and where will A catch B?

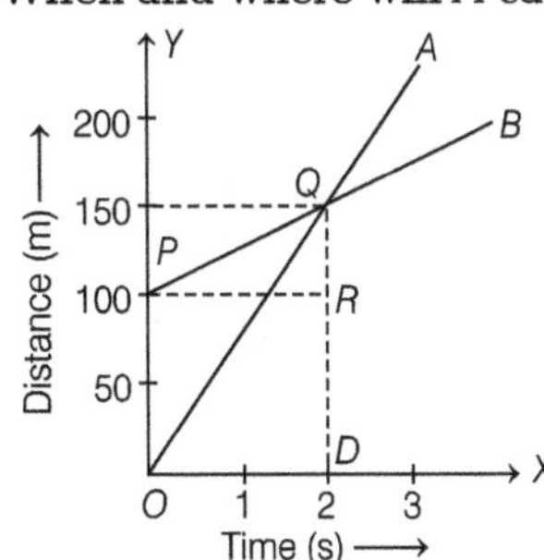

(iv) What is the difference between speeds of A and B?

(v) Is the speed of both the trains uniform or non-uniform? Justify your answer.

Sol. (i) According to given graph, B is 100 m ahead of A.

(ii) Speed of B = Slope of PQ (from given graph)

$$= \frac{150-100}{2-0} = 25\text{ m/s}$$

(iii) A and B meet at Q, i.e. 150 m from origin and 2 s after the starting.

(iv) Speed of A = Slope of OQ (from given graph)

$$= \frac{150}{2} = 75\text{ m/s}$$

Difference between speeds $= 75 - 25 = 50$ m/s

(v) Speed of both the trains is uniform as s-t graph is a straight line.

5 Study the speed-time graph of a body given here and answer the following questions:

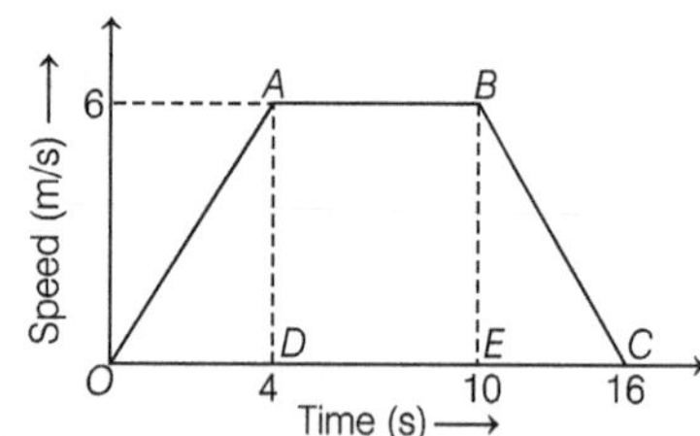

(i) What type of motion is represented by OA?

(ii) What type of motion is represented by AB?

(iii) What type of motion is represented by BC?

(iv) Find out the acceleration of the body.

(v) Calculate the retardation of the body.

(vi) Find out the distance travelled by the body from A to B.

Sol. (i) OA is a straight line graph between speed and time and it is sloping upward from O to A. Here, OA represents uniform acceleration.

(ii) AB is a straight line graph between speed and time which is parallel to the time axis (X-axis). So, AB represents uniform speed. There is no acceleration from A to B.

(iii) BC is a straight line graph between speed and time which is sloping downwards from B to C. Therefore, BC represents uniform retardation or negative acceleration.

(iv) Acceleration of the body as we see from graph line OA represents it. So, the slope of velocity-time graph OA will give the acceleration of the body.

Thus, acceleration = slope of line $OA = \frac{AD}{OD}$

We have, $AD = 6$ m/s and $OD = 4$ s

So, acceleration $= \frac{6\text{ m/s}}{4\text{ s}} = 1.5\text{ m/s}^2$

(v) The slope of line graph BC represents the retardation of the body.

So, retardation = slope of line $BC = \frac{BE}{EC}$

From given graph, we have

$BE = 6$ m/s, $EC = 16 - 10 = 6$ s

Retardation $= \frac{6\text{ m/s}}{6\text{ s}} = 1\text{ m/s}^2$

(vi) The distance travelled by the body is equal to the area enclosed between the speed-time graph and time axis. Distance travelled from A to B = area under the line AB and the time axis = area of rectangle $DABE = DA \times DE$.

Here, $DA = 6$ m/s and $DE = 10 - 4 = 6$ s

Distance travelled from A to $B = 6 \times 6 = 36$ m

6 The v-t graph of an object as shown below:

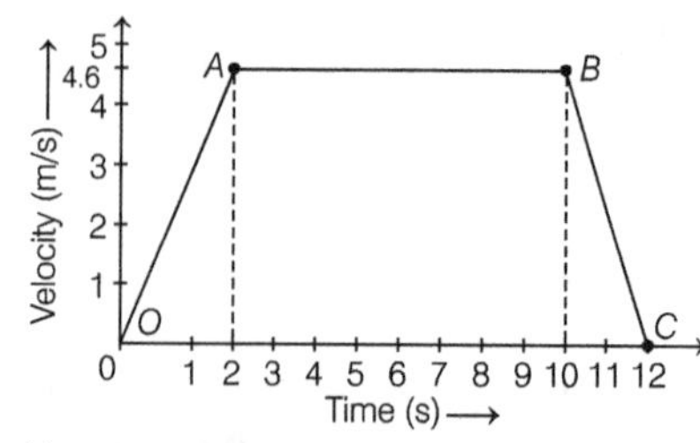

(i) Identify the type of motion by lines OA and BC.

(ii) Velocity at $t = 8$s.

(iii) Calculate acceleration

(a) between 3rd and 10 th second.

(b) last 2s.

Sol. (i) OA represents uniformly accelerated motion, BC represents uniformly retarted motion.

(ii) At $t = 8$ s, velocity of the object is 4.6 m/s.

(iii) (a) Between 3rd and 10 th second, $a = 0$.

(b) During last 2s, (10 to 12s)

acceleration, $a = \frac{\text{change in velocity}}{\text{time interval}}$

From graph, we have values

$= \frac{0 - 4.6}{12 - 10} = \frac{-4.6}{2} = -\frac{4.6}{2} = -2.3\text{ m/s}^2$

7 An insect moves along a circular path of radius 10 cm with a constant speed. It takes 1 min to move from a point on the path to the diametrically opposite point.

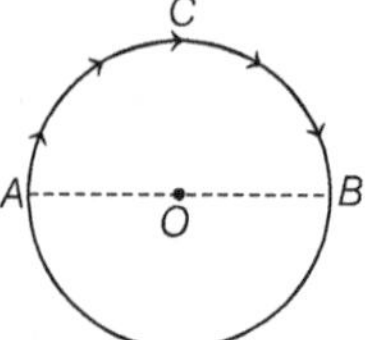

Find (i) the distance covered, (ii) the speed, (iii) the displacement and (iv) the average velocity.

Sol. Suppose the insect was at A initially and it moves along ACB to reach the diametrically opposite point B in 1 min.

(i) $\therefore$ The distance moved in 1 min $= \pi r$

$= 3.14 \times 10 = 31.4$ cm

(ii) $\therefore$ Speed $= \frac{\text{Distance}}{\text{Time}}$

$= \frac{31.4}{1} = 31.4$ cm/min

(iii) $\therefore$ Displacement, $AB = 2r = 2 \times 10 = 20$ cm

(iv) $\therefore$ Average velocity,

$$v_{av} = \frac{\text{Displacement}}{\text{Time}} = \frac{20 \text{ cm}}{1 \text{ min}} = 20 \text{ cm/min}$$

8 The driver of train A travelling at a speed of 54 km/h applies brakes and retards the train uniformly. The train stops in 5 s. Another train B is travelling on the parallel with a speed of 36 km/h.

Its driver applies the brakes and the train retards uniformly, train B stops in 10 s. Plot speed-time graphs for both the trains on the same axis. Which of the trains travelled farther after the brakes were applied?

Sol. For train A, the initial velocity,

$$u = 54 \text{ km/h} = 54 \times \frac{5}{18} = 15 \text{ m/s}$$

Final velocity, $v = 0$ and time, $t = 5$ s

For train B, $u = 36 \text{ km/h} = 36 \times \frac{5}{18} = 10 \text{ m/s}$

$$v = 0, t = 10 \text{ s}$$

Speed-time graph for train A and B are shown in figure below:

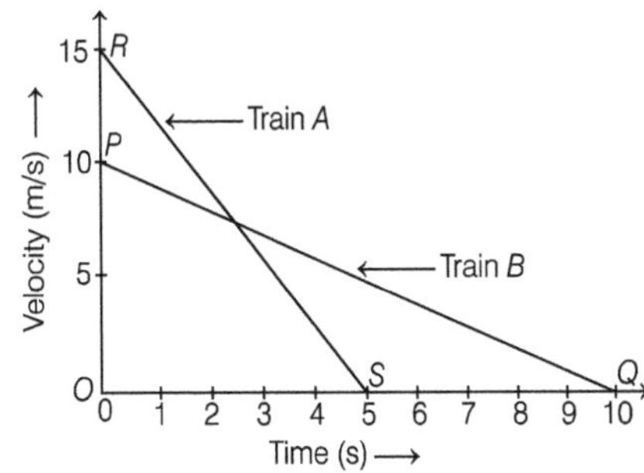

Distance travelled by train A = Area under straight line graph

$$RS = \text{area of } \Delta ORS = \frac{1}{2} \times OR \times OS = \frac{1}{2} \times 15 \times 5 = 37.5 \text{ m}$$

Distance travelled by train B = Area under PQ

$$= \frac{1}{2} \times OP \times OQ = \frac{1}{2} \times 10 \times 10 = 50 \text{ m}$$

Distance travelled by train B is more than train A.

9 Two stones are thrown vertically upwards simultaneously with their initial velocities u_1 and u_2, respectively.

Prove that the heights reached by them would be in the ratio of $u_1^2 : u_2^2$. Assume upward acceleration is $-g$ and downward acceleration is $+g$. **NCERT Exemplar**

Sol. According to the question,

	Stone 1	Stone 2
Initial velocity	u_1	u_2
Acceleration	$-g$	$-g$
Final velocity	$v_1 = 0$	$v_2 = 0$
Height	h_1	h_2

From third equation of motion,

For first stone,

$$v_1^2 = u_1^2 + 2gh_1 \text{ and}$$

For second stone,

$$v_2^2 = u_2^2 + 2gh_2$$

or $$h_1 = \frac{-u_1^2}{-2g} = \frac{u_1^2}{2g}$$

and $$h_2 = \frac{-u_2^2}{-2g} = \frac{u_2^2}{2g}$$

$$\because \quad h_1 : h_2 = \frac{\frac{u_1^2}{2g}}{\frac{u_2^2}{2g}} = u_1^2 : u_2^2$$

Ratio of heights reached by two stone

$$\frac{h_1}{h_2} = \frac{u_1^2}{u_2^2}$$

$$h_1 : h_2$$

$$\Rightarrow \quad u_1^2 : u_2^2$$

CHAPTER EXERCISE

Multiple Type Questions

1 A bridge is 400 m long. A 150 m long train crosses the bridge at a speed of 50 m/s . Time taken by the train to cross it.

(a) 5 s (b) 8 s
(c) 6 s (d) 11 s

2 When two bodies moves uniformly towards each other, then they cross each other at the speed of 10 m/s. If both the bodies move in the same direction, then they cross each other at the speed of 6 m/s. The speed of both bodies are

(a) 8 m/s, 2 m/s (b) 8 m/s, 4 m/s
(c) 6 m/s, 2 m/s (d) 6 m/s, 4 m/s

3 If a body is moving on a circular path of radius 21 cm with velocity of 2 m/s, then time taken by the body to complete half revolution is

(a) 11 s (b) 22 s
(c) 44 s (d) 33 s

4 From the given v-t graph (see figure), it can be inferred that the object is

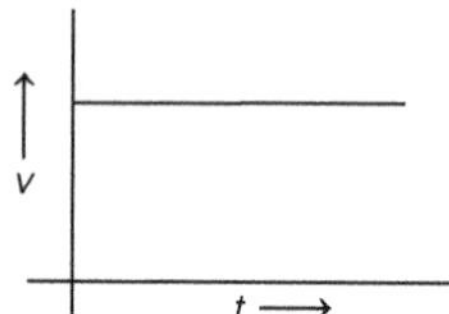

NCERT Exemplar

(a) in uniform motion
(b) at rest
(c) in non-uniform motion
(d) moving with uniform acceleration

5 Suppose a boy is enjoying a ride on a merry-go-round which is moving with a constant speed of $10\ ms^{-1}$. It implies that the boy is **NCERT Exemplar**

(a) at rest
(b) moving with no acceleration
(c) in accelerated motion
(d) moving with uniform velocity

Fill in the Blanks

6 To specify the speed of an object, we require only ....

7 The average speed of an object is obtained by dividing .... by ....

8 The velocity changes due to continuous change in ....

True and False

9 A body having a uniform speed will always have uniform velocity.

10 The acceleration of a moving body can be found from area under velocity-time graph.

11 Area under velocity-time graph gives displacement.

Match the Columns

12 Match the following columns.

	Column I		Column II
A.	Uniform velocity	p.	
B.	Uniform retardation	q.	
C.	Uniform acceleration with initial velocity	r.	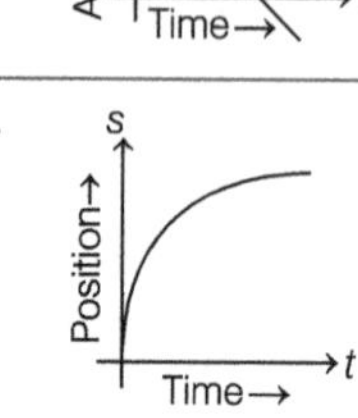
D.	Decreasing acceleration at steady rate	s.	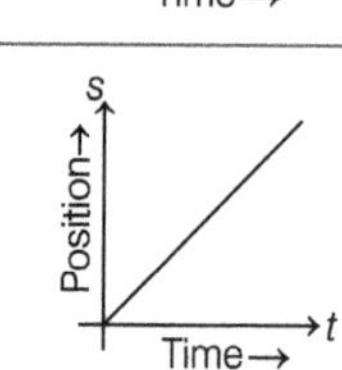

Assertion–Reason

Direction (Q.Nos. 13-15) *In each of the following questions, a statement of Assertion is given by the corresponding statement of Reason. Of the statements, mark the correct answer as*

(a) If both Assertion and Reason are true and Reason is the correct explanation of Assertion.
(b) If both Assertion and Reason are true, but Reason is not the correct explanation of Assertion.
(c) If Assertion is true, but Reason is false.
(d) If Assertion is false, but Reason is true.

13 **Assertion** Distance travelled by a body may be positive, negative or zero.

Reason Shortest distance travelled by the body between two points is called distance.

14 **Assertion** Acceleration of a body can be calculated from velocity-time graph.

Reason Area of velocity-time graph gives displacement of an body.

15 **Assertion** A body performing uniform circular motion with constant speed may have acceleration.

Reason When speed of a body remains constant, then its acceleration is always zero.

Case Based Questions

Direction (Q.Nos. 16-19) *Answer the questions on the basis of your understanding of the following passage and related studied concepts:*

Shikhaj and Sharman went to Mathura through Yamuna - Expressway. Shikhaj started the car and accelerated, so highly that the car was running at 108 km/h within 10 s. Sharman kept a track on the speedometer and stopped him from doing so and told him that overspeeding on road was a straight invitation to life staking situation though, Shikhaj wanted the adventure of speeding but he was convinced by Sharman.

16 Why Sharman kept a track on the speedometer?

17 The numerical ratio of average velocity to average speed of an object when it is moving along a straight path is

(a) 2 : 1 (b) 1 : 2
(c) 1 : 1 (d) 4 : 1

18 What is the acceleration of the car?

19 What advice is given by Sharman to Shikhaj regarding overspeeding on road?

Answers

1. (d) 2. (a) 3. (d) 4. (a) 5. (c)
6. magnitude 7. total distance, total time
8. direction of motion 9. False 10. False 11. True
12. (A) → (s), (B) → (r), (C) → (p), (D) → (q)
13. (d) 14. (d) 15. (c)
16. for tracking the speed of car 17. (c)

Very Short Type Questions

20 If the acceleration of the particle is constant in magnitude but not in direction, then what type of path does the particle follow?

21 What does the path of an object took like when it is in uniform motion?

22 The velocity of a body increases by 10 m/s in every one second. What physical quantity does the body represent and what is its magnitude?

23 Area under the velocity-time graph line is 40 m. What physical quantity does this area represent?

24 Does the motion of second's hand of a watch represent uniform velocity or uniform speed?

Short Answer (SA) Type Questions

25 How can you calculate the following?

(*i*) Speed from distance-time graph.
(*ii*) Acceleration from velocity-time graph.
(*iii*) Displacement from velocity-time graph.

26 How will you show that the slope of displacement-time graph gives velocity of the body?

27 Given below is the velocity-time graph for the motion of the car. What does the nature of the graph show? Also, find the acceleration of the car.

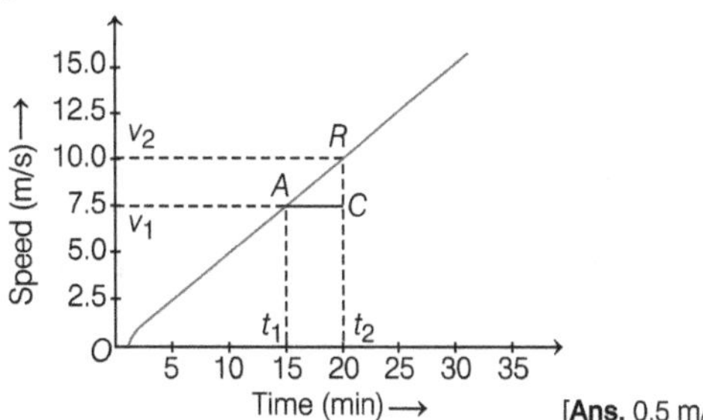

[**Ans.** 0.5 m/s^2]

28 (*i*) If the velocity-time graph of an object is parallel to *X*-axis, then what does it mean? Can it be parallel to *Y*-axis?

(*ii*) What type of motion is represented by each one of the following graphs?

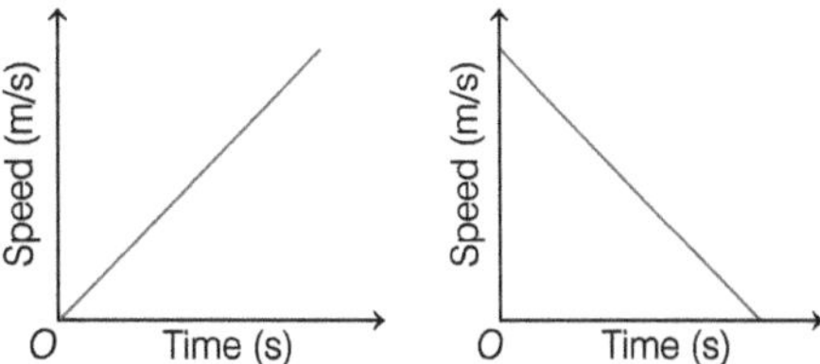

(*iii*) A bus increases its speed from 36 km/h to 54 km/h in 10 s. Find its acceleration. [**Ans.** 0.5 m/s^2]

29 Study the velocity-time graph and calculate

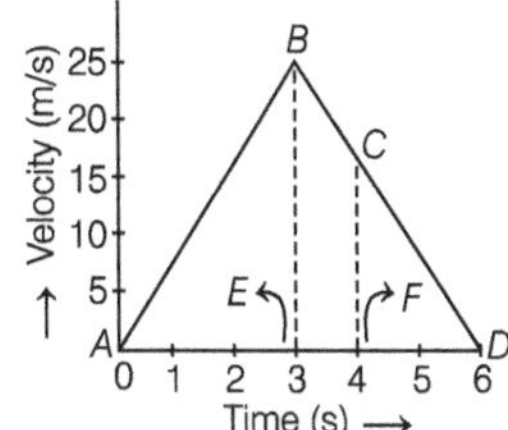

(i) the acceleration from A to B. [Ans. 8.33 m/s^2]
(ii) the acceleration from B to C. [Ans. – 8 m/s^2]
(iii) the distance covered in the region ABE. [Ans. 37.5 m]
(iv) the average velocity from C to D. [Ans. – 8.5 m/s]
(v) the distance covered in the region $BCFE$. [Ans. 21 m]

30 Plot velocity-time graph of a body
(i) moving with a uniform retardation.
(ii) moving with a variable acceleration.

31 A body starts to slide over a horizontal surface with an initial velocity of 0.5 m/s. Due to friction, its velocity decreases at the rate 0.105 m/s^2. How much time will it take for the body to stop? [Ans. 4.8 s]

32 Look at the figure below and answer the following questions:

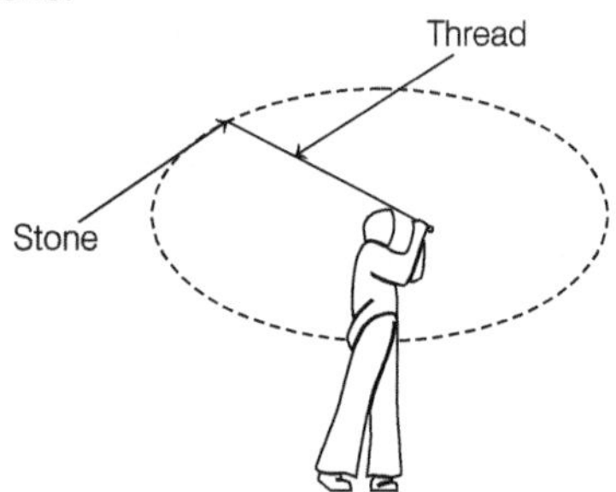

(i) Name the kind of motion of the stone.
(ii) Is this an example of accelerated motion? Why?
(iii) Name the force that keeps the stone in its path.
(iv) What is the direction of this force? Draw it in your answer sheet.

Long Answer (LA) Type Questions]

33 Figure shows x-t graph of a particle moving along a straight line. What is the sign of the acceleration during the intervals OA, AB, BC and CD?

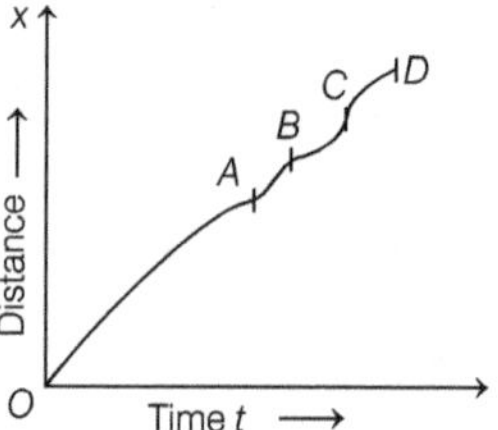

34 Write three equations of uniformly accelerated motion. Also, state the symbols used.

35 An object starting from rest travels 20 m in first 2 s and 160 m in next 4 s. What will be the velocity after 7 s from the start? **NCERT Exemplar**

[Ans. 70 m/s]

36 Obtain a relation for the distance travelled by an object moving with a uniform acceleration in the interval between 4th and 5th second.

NCERT Exemplar

[Ans. $u + 9\frac{a}{2}$]

Challengers*

1 A 100 m sprinter increases her speed from rest uniformly at the rate of 1 m/s^2 upto 40m and covers the remaining distance with a uniform speed. The sprinter covers the first half of the run in t_1s and second half in t_2s, then

(a) $t_1 > t_2$
(b) $t_1 < t_2$
(c) $t_1 = t_2$
(d) information given is incomplete

2 Particles P and Q are undergoing uniform horizontal circular motions along concentric circles of different radii in clockwise sense P completes each round in 2 min while Q does it is 5 min time required by Q to make one revolution around P is

(a) 3 min
(b) 10 min
(c) $\frac{10}{3}$ min
(d) This is not possible as Q is moving slower than P

3 You are sitting in a stationary car. There is a helium balloon tied to its floor. You accelerate and obviously feel like you are being pushed backwards (against the direction of your accelerations). The balloon

(a) will move forward
(b) will move backward
(c) will remain state
(d) None of these

4 A boy begins to walk eastward along a street in front of his house and the graph of his position from have is shown in the following figure. His average speed for whole time interval in equal to

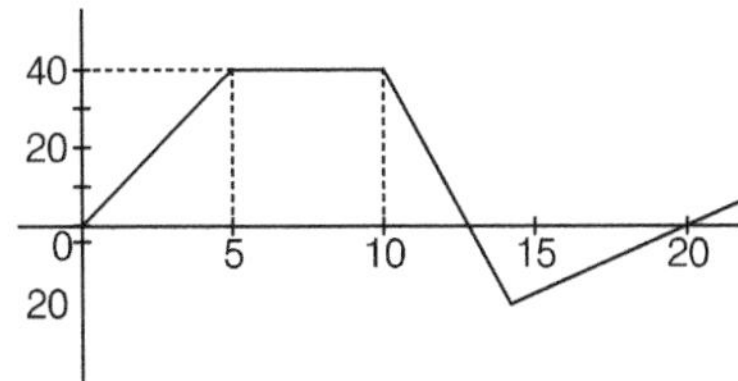

(a) 8 m/min
(b) 6 m/min
(c) $\frac{8}{3}$ m/min
(d) 2 m/min

5 A bus is travelling the first one-third distance at a speed of 10 km/h, the next one-fourth at 20 km/h and the remaining at 40 km/h. What is the average speed of the bus?

(a) 17 km/h
(b) 17.8 km/h
(c) 18 km/h
(d) 20 km/h

6 A car A is travelling on a straight level road with a uniform speed of 60 km/h. It is followed by another car B. which is moving with a speed of 70 km/h. When the distance between them is 2.5 km, the car B is given a deceleration of 20 km/h^2. After how much time will B catch up with A?

(a) 1 h
(b) $\frac{1}{2}$ h
(c) $\frac{1}{4}$ h
(d) $\frac{1}{8}$ h

7 A sprinter has to cover a total run of 100 m. She increases her speed from rest under a uniform acceleration of 1. 0 m/s^2 up to three quarters of the total run and covers the last quarter him uniform speed. The time she takes to cover the first half, and to cover the second half of the run will be

(a) 3.25 s
(b) 4.25 s
(c) 5.25 s
(d) 6.25 s

8 A bus begin to move with an acceleration of 1 m/s^2. A man who is 48 m behind the bus starts running at 10 m/s to catch the bus. The man will be able to catch the bus after

(a) 8 s
(b) 5 s
(c) 6 s
(d) 7 s

9 Which graph represents a state of rest for an object?

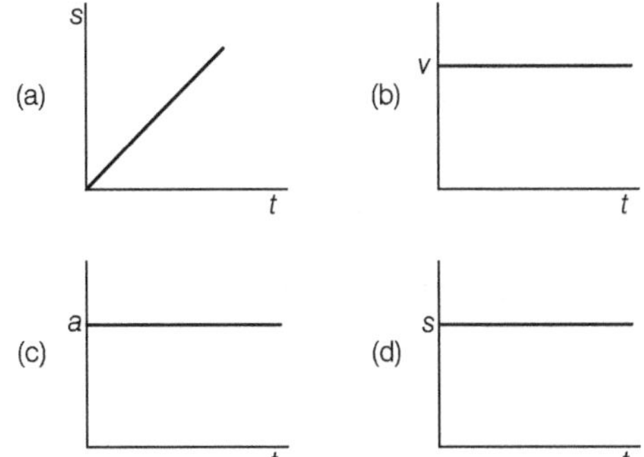

Answer Key

1.	(a)	**2.**	(c)	**3.**	(a)	**4.**	(b)	**5.**	(b)
6.	(b)	**7.**	(b)	**8.**	(a)	**9.**	(c)		

**These questions may or may not be asked in the examination, have been given just for additional practice.*

CHAPTER

08

Force and Laws of Motion

In our everyday life, we observe that some efforts are required to put a stationary object into motion or to stop a moving object. We ordinarily experience this as a muscular effort and say that we must push, hit or pull an object to change its state of motion. The concept of force is based on this push, hit or pull.

Chapter Checklist

- Force
- Newton's Law of Motion

Force

Any action which causes pull, hit or push on a body is called force. Force cannot be seen but it can be judged only by the effects which it produces in various bodies around us. Many effects of force are as given below:

(*i*) A force can move a stationary body.

(*ii*) A force can stop a moving body.

(*iii*) A force can change the direction and speed of a moving body.

(*iv*) A force can change the shape and size of a body.

Balanced and Unbalanced Forces

Forces are of two types such as balanced forces and unbalanced forces which are as given below:

Balanced Forces

When the net effect produced by a number of forces acting on a body is zero, then the forces are said to be balanced forces. Balanced forces can only bring a change in the shape of the body. A block of wood is placed on a horizontal surface and two strings *A* and *B* are connected to it as shown in figure. The block is in a state of rest.

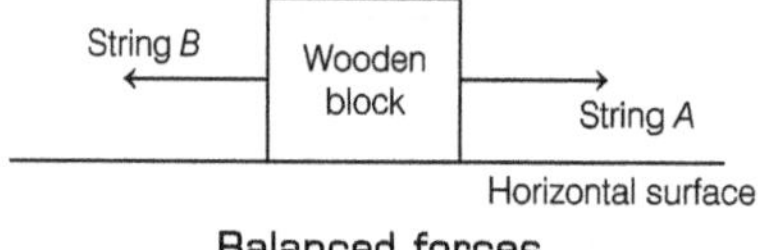

Balanced forces

If we pull A and B strings with equal magnitude of forces, then the block does not change its state of rest. Such type of forces are known as balanced forces.

Balanced forces do not change the following functions:

(*i*) The state of rest (*ii*) The state of motion

e.g. In a tug of war, when both the teams apply similar force from both sides, rope does not move either side, i.e. resultant force is zero. Hence, it is a balanced force.

Unbalanced Forces

When the net effect produced by a number of forces acting on a body is non-zero, then the forces are said to be unbalanced forces.

A boy wants to relocate the refrigerator in his house as shown in the figure.

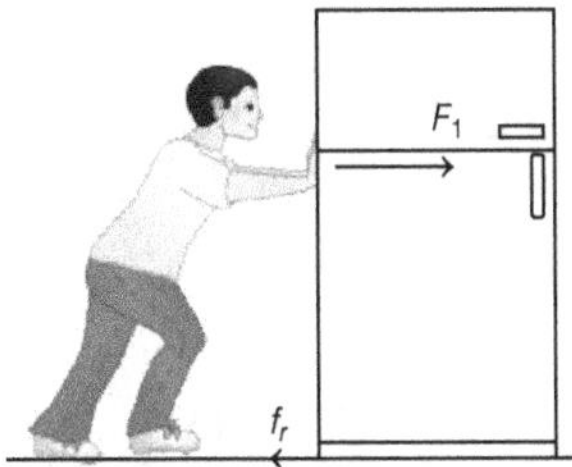

He pushes the refrigerator with a small force, the refrigerator does not move due to frictional force acting in a direction opposite to the push. If he pushes the refrigerator harder, then the pushing force becomes more than the friction and due to this the refrigerator starts moving in the direction of push as shown in the figure.

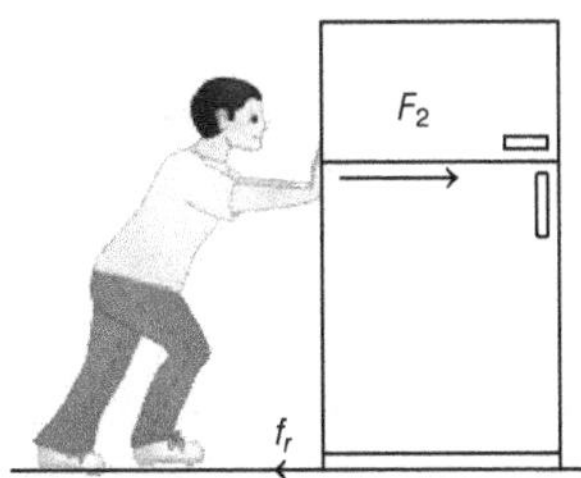

In the above example, there is an unbalanced force which causes motion in the refrigerator. **The unbalanced forces cause a change in the state of rest or of uniform motion of a body.**

e.g. In a tug of war, when one of the teams suddenly releases the rope, then an unbalanced force acts on the other team, due to which it falls backward.

If an unbalanced force is applied on a moving object, there will be a change either in its speed or in the direction of its motion. Thus, to accelerate the motion of an object, an unbalanced force is required.

Newton's Laws of Motion

Newton studied the ideas of Galileo regarding the motion of an object. He formulated three fundamental laws that govern the motion of objects. These three laws are known as Newton's laws of motion, which are as given below:

Newton's First Law of Motion

It states that an object will continue to remain in its state of rest or of uniform motion along a straight line path unless an external force acts on it. This means, all objects resist change in their state.

The state of any object can be changed by applying external forces only.

(*i*) A person standing in a bus falls backward when the bus is started moving suddenly. This happens because the person and bus both are in rest while the person is not moving as bus starts moving. The legs of the person start moving along with bus, but rest portion of his body has tendency to remain in rest. Because of this, person falls backward if he is not alert.

(*ii*) A person standing in a moving bus falls forward, if driver applies brakes suddenly.

Inertia

The natural tendency of an object to resist a change in their state of rest or of uniform motion along a straight line is called inertia of the object.

It is the inherent property of all the objects. Newton's first law of motion is also known as Galileo's law of inertia.

Inertia of an object is measured by its mass. It is directly proportional to the mass. It means that inertia increases with increase in mass and decreases with decrease in mass. A heavy object will have more inertia than lighter one.

Types of Inertia

Inertia is divided into three types as given below:

1. **Inertia of rest** The tendency of a body to resist (oppose) any change in its state of rest is known as inertia of rest.

   e.g.

   (*i*) When a bus suddenly starts moving forward, then the passengers in the bus fall backward.

   (*ii*) The carpet is beaten with a stick to remove the dust particles.

   (*iii*) When a tree is vigorously shaken, then some of the leaves fall from the tree.

2. **Inertia of motion** The tendency of a body to resist (oppose) any change in its state of uniform motion is known as inertia of motion.

   e.g.
   (*i*) The passengers fall forward when a fast moving bus stops suddenly.
   (*ii*) A person falls forward while getting down from a moving bus or train.
   (*iii*) A luggage is usually tied with a rope on the roof of a bus.

3. **Inertia of direction** The tendency of a body to oppose any change in its direction of motion is known as inertia of direction.

   e.g.
   (*i*) When a fast moving bus negotiate a curve on the road, then passengers fall away from the centre of the curved road.
   (*ii*) The sparks produced during sharpening of a knife against a grinding wheel leaves tangentially to its rim.
   (*iii*) A stone tied to string is whirling in a horizontal circle. If the string breaks, then the stone flies away tangentially.

Note Force of friction always opposes motion of objects.

Check Point 01

1. State any three changes that a force brings about on a body with one example each.
2. Write any two differences, between balanced and unbalanced force.
3. In which of the following cases, net force acting is zero? Also, identify the direction of force when
   (*i*) a car drives around a circular race track at a constant speed.
   (*ii*) a person pushes a door to hold it shut.
   (*iii*) a ball, rolling across a grassy field, slowly comes to a stop.
4. Fill in the blanks.
   (*i*) The factor on which the inertia of a body depends, is ....
   (*ii*) When a stationary bus starts suddenly, the passangers fall ....
5. State True or False for the following statement.
   (*i*) The blades of an electric fan continue to rotate for some time after the current is switched off due to inertia of motion.
   (*ii*) When a tree is vigorously shaken, then some of the leaves fall from the tree. [**Ans.** (i) True (ii) True]

Momentum

Momentum measures the quantity of motion possessed by a body. It is defined as the product of mass and velocity of the body. Besides magnitude, momentum also has a direction. At any instant, its direction is the same as the direction of the velocity.

If a body of mass m moves with a velocity v, then momentum p is given by $\boxed{p = mv}$

The SI unit of momentum is kg-m/s.

Note If a body is at rest, its velocity, $v = 0$ and so, momentum, $p = 0$.

Example 1. *A car of mass 1000 kg is moving with a velocity of 72 km/h. Find its momentum.*

Sol. Given, mass, $m = 1000$ kg

Velocity, $v = 72 \text{ km/h} = 72 \times \frac{5}{18} = 20$ m/s

Momentum, $p = ?$

$\therefore$ Momentum $=$ Mass $\times$ Velocity $\Rightarrow p = mv$

$p = 1000 \times 20 = 20000$ kg-m/s

Thus, the momentum of the car is 20000 kg-m/s.

Newton's Second Law of Motion

The second law of motion states that the rate of change of momentum of an object is directly proportional to the applied external force and takes place in the direction in which external force acts.

Mathematical Formulation of Second Law of Motion

If a body of mass m moving at initial velocity u accelerates uniformly with an acceleration a for time t, so that its final velocity changes to v, then

Initial momentum, $p_1 = mu$

Final momentum, $p_2 = mv$

$\therefore$ Change in momentum $= p_2 - p_1 = mv - mu$
$= m(v - u)$

According to the second law of motion,

$$\text{Force, } F \propto \frac{\text{change in momentum}}{\text{time}}$$

$$\Rightarrow \quad F \propto \frac{p_2 - p_1}{t} \Rightarrow F \propto \frac{m(v-u)}{t}$$

$$\Rightarrow \quad F \propto ma \quad \left[\because \frac{v-u}{t} = a\right]$$

$$\therefore \quad F = kma$$

The quantity k is a constant of proportionality.

One unit of force is defined as the amount that produces an acceleration of 1 m/s^2 in an object of 1 kg mass.

i.e. 1 unit of force $= k \times 1\,\text{kg} \times 1\,\text{m/s}^2 \Rightarrow k = 1$

Thus, the force can be written as $\boxed{F = ma}$

The SI unit of force is newton, which is denoted by the symbol N and it is equivalent to kg-m/s^2.

Note
- When the applied force F is zero, then the acceleration a is also zero and the body remains in its state of rest or of a uniform motion.
- 1 dyne $= \frac{1}{10^5}$ N $= 10^{-5}$ N

Applications of Newton's Second Law of Motion

The following applications are based on Newton's second law of motion:

(*i*) A cricket player (or fielder) moves his hands backward while catching a fast cricket ball.

(*ii*) During athletics meet, athletes doing high jump and long jump land on foam or a heap of sand to decrease the force on the body and the landing is comfortable.

Newton's First Law from Mathematical Expression of Second Law

It can be mathematically stated from mathematical expression of second law of motion.

As we know, $F = ma$

$$\Rightarrow \quad F = \frac{m(v-u)}{t} \qquad \left[\because a = \frac{(v-u)}{t}\right]$$

$$\Rightarrow \quad Ft = mv - mu$$

From this equation, if $F = 0$, then $v = u$ for any value of time. This means that, in the absence of an external force, the object will continue moving with uniform velocity u throughout the time t and if u is zero, then v will also be zero, i.e. the object will remain at rest.

Example 2. *Force acts on an object of mass 4 kg and changes its velocity from 10 m/s to 20 m/s in 5 s. Find the magnitude of force.*

Sol. Given, mass of an object, $m = 4$ kg

Initial velocity, $u = 10$ m/s; Final velocity, $v = 20$ m/s

Time taken, $t = 5$ s

We know that, Newton's first law of motion,

$$v = u + at \text{ or } a = \frac{v-u}{t}$$

$$\therefore \quad a = \frac{20-10}{5} = \frac{10}{5} = 2 \text{ m/s}^2$$

$\therefore$ Magnitude of force, F = Mass × Acceleration

$$\Rightarrow \quad F = ma = 4 \text{ kg} \times 2 \text{ m/s}^2 = 8 \text{ N}$$

Hence, magnitude of force is 8 N.

Example 3. *A force of 50 N acts on a stationary body of mass 10 kg for 2 s. Find the acceleration produced in the body and velocity attained by it.*

Sol. Initial velocity, $u = 0$ [since, the body is stationary]

Force, $F = 50$ N, mass, $m = 10$ kg, time, $t = 2$ s

Final velocity, $v = ?$, acceleration, $a = ?$

$$\therefore \text{ Acceleration, } a = \frac{F}{m} \qquad [\because F = ma]$$

$$a = \frac{50}{10} = 5 \text{ m/s}^2.$$

$$\text{Final velocity, } v = \frac{Ft}{m} + u \qquad [\because Ft = m(v-u)]$$

$$\therefore \quad v = \frac{50 \times 2}{10} + 0 = 10 \text{ m/s}$$

Thus, the acceleration produced in the body is 5 m/s^2 and velocity attained by it is 10 m/s.

Example 4. *A bullet train is moving with a velocity of 180 km/h and it takes 5 s to stop after the brakes are applied. Find the force exerted by the brakes on the wheel of train if its mass with the wagan is 2000 kg.*

Sol. Given, initial velocity, $u = 180 \text{ km/h} = 180 \times \frac{5}{18} = 50$ m/s

Final velocity, $v = 0$,

Time, $t = 5$ s, mass, $m = 2000$ kg

As, acceleration is given by

$$a = \frac{(v-u)}{t}$$

$$\Rightarrow \quad a = -\frac{u}{t} = \frac{-50}{5} = -10 \text{ m/s}$$

Now, force exerted by the brakes on the wheel is given by Newton's second law, $F = ma = 2000 \times (-10) = -20000$ N

Negative sign shows that the direction of force is opposite to motion of the body.

Example 5. *A force of 6 N gives a mass m_1 an acceleration of 18 m/s^2 and a mass m_2 an acceleration of 24 m/s^2. What acceleration would it give if both the masses were tied together?*

Sol. Given, force $F = 6$ N

Acceleration of mass m_1, $a_1 = 18$ m/s^2

Acceleration of mass m_2, $a_2 = 24$ m/s^2

Acceleration produced when both masses are tied together $a = ?$

From Newton's second law of motion

$$m_1 = \frac{F}{a_1} = \frac{6}{18} = \frac{1}{3} \text{ kg}$$

$$m_2 = \frac{F}{a_2} = \frac{6}{24} = \frac{1}{4} \text{ kg}$$

$$\text{Total mass, } m = m_1 + m_2 = \frac{1}{3} + \frac{1}{4}$$

$$m = \frac{4+3}{12} = \frac{7}{12} \text{ kg}$$

$$\text{Acceleration produced in combined mass, } a = \frac{F}{m}$$

$$a = \frac{6}{7/12}$$

$$= \frac{12 \times 6}{7} = 10.28 \text{ m/s}^2$$

Example 6. *The velocity-time graph of a ball of mass 30 g moving along a straight line on a long table is given below. How much force does the table exert on the ball to bring it to rest?*

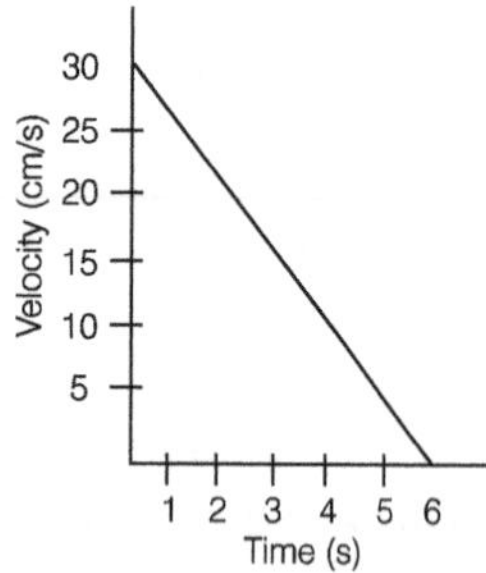

Sol. The initial velocity of the ball, $u = 30$ cm/s

Final velocity, $v = 0$

Time, $t = 6$ s

Acceleration, $a = \dfrac{v-u}{t} = \dfrac{(0-30)}{6}$

$$a = -5 \text{ cm/s}^2$$

$$a = -0.05 \text{ m/s}^2$$

The force exerted on the ball,

$$F = ma = \left(\frac{30}{1000}\right) \times (-0.05) = -1.5 \times 10^{-3} \text{ N}$$

The negative sign show that frictional force exerted by the table is opposite to the direction of motion of the ball.

Impulse

It is termed as the total impact of force. This is equal to the change in momentum of the body. In other words, impulse is defined as the product of force and a small time in which force act.

According to Newton's second law, $F = ma$

$$F = \frac{m(v-u)}{t} \qquad \left[\because a = \frac{v-u}{t}\right]$$

$$\Rightarrow \quad F = \frac{mv - mu}{t}$$

$$\Rightarrow \quad Ft = mv - mu$$

Impulse, $I = Ft = p_2 - p_1$

or Impulse = Change in momentum

The SI unit of impulse is N-s or kg-m/s.

Example 7. *If a force of 1000 N is applied over a vehicle of 500 kg, then for how much time the velocity of the vehicle will increase from 2 m/s to 10 m/s. Also find the impulse.*

Sol. Given, $F = 1000$ N, mass, $m = 500$ kg

Final velocity, $v = 10$ m/s

Initial velocity, $u = 2$ m/s

$$F = \frac{m(v-u)}{t}$$

$$\Rightarrow \quad t = \frac{m(v-u)}{F} = \frac{500 \times (10-2)}{1000} = 4\text{s}$$

$\therefore$ Impulse, $I = Ft = 1000 \times 4 = 4000$ N-s

Thus, the time required by the vehicle is 4s and its impulse is 4000 N-s.

Check Point 02

1 Fill in the blanks.
If a body is at rest, its velocity is equal to ...., so momentum will be ....

2 If the time taken to bring a ball to rest moving with a certain velocity v is reduced to half, then what will be the changes in the values of
(*i*) initial and final momentum?
(*ii*) change of momentum?

3 A car is moving with velocity of 108 km/h. Mass of the car is 300 kg. If driver of the car wants to change its velocity from 108 km/h to 90 km/h in two minutes, what force should be applied by the brakes on the tyres? [**Ans.** – 12.5 N]

4 State True or False for the following statement.
Impulse and momentum have same units.

5 A force of 50 N acts on a body for $\frac{1}{10}$ s. Find the change in the momentum of the body. [**Ans.** 5 kg-m/s]

Newton's Third Law of Motion

It states that, whenever one object exerts a force on another object, then the second object exerts an equal and opposite force on the first object.

Thus, action and reaction forces are equal in magnitude and opposite in direction. They still do not cancel each other's effect because they act on different objects.

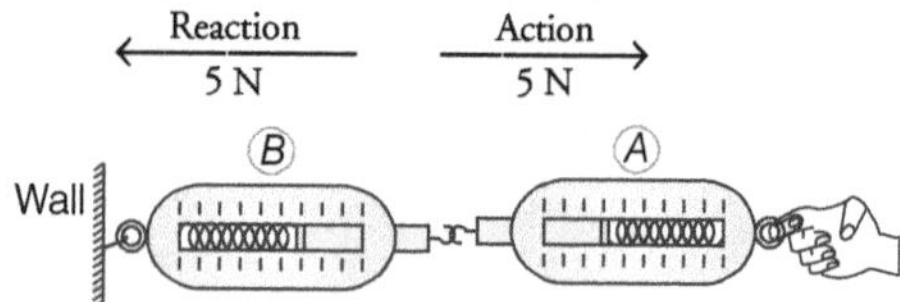

Spring balance action and reaction forces are equal and opposite

Applications of Newton's Third Law of Motion

(*i*) **Collision of two persons** When two persons walking or running in opposite direction collide with each other, then both feel hurt, because they apply force to each other. Two opposing forces are in action and reaction pair.

(ii) **Walking of a person** A person is able to walk because of the Newton's third law of motion. During walking, a person pushes the ground in backward direction and in the reaction, the ground also pushes the person with equal magnitude of force but in opposite direction. This enables him to move in forward direction against the push.

(iii) **Recoil of gun** When bullet is fired from a gun, then the bullet also pushes the gun in opposite direction with equal magnitude of force. Since, the gun has a greater mass than bullet, acceleration of the gun is much less than the acceleration of the bullet.

(iv) **Propulsion of a boat in forward direction** Sailor pushes water with oar in backward direction resulting water to push the oar in forward direction. Consequently, the boat is pushed in forward direction. Force applied by oar and water are of equal magnitude but in opposite directions.

(v) **Rocket propulsion** The propulsion of rocket is based on the principle of **action and reaction**. The rapid burning of fuel produces hot gases which rush out from the nozzle at the rear end at a very high speed. The equal and opposite reaction force moves the rocket upward at a great speed.

Check Point 03

1 Fill in the blank.
A person is able to walk because of the Newton's .... law of motion.

2 State True and False for the following statements:
(i) Third law of Newton is associated with propulsion of rocket.
(ii) If you step ashore from a stationary boat, it tends to leave the shore.
(iii) Momentum is a scalar quantity.

To Study NCERT Activities
Visit https://goo.gl/VgB5uN
OR Scan the Code

NCERT FOLDER

INTEXT QUESTIONS

1 Which of the following has more inertia?
(i) A rubber ball and a stone of same size
(ii) A bicycle and a train
(iii) A five-rupees coin and a one-rupee coin
Give reasons for your answer. **Pg 118**

Sol. Inertia of an object is proportional to its mass.
(i) A stone of same size as that of rubber ball will have greater mass, so the stone will have more inertia.
(ii) A train has much greater mass than that of a bicycle, so the train will have more inertia.
(iii) A five-rupees coin has more mass than a one-rupee coin, so five-rupees coin will have greater inertia.

2 In the following example, try to identify the number of times the velocity of the ball changes.
A football player kicks a football to another player of his team who kicks the football towards the goal. The goalkeeper of opposite team collects the ball and kicks it towards a player of his own team. Also, identify the agent supplying the force in each case. **Pg 118**

Sol. There are a number of times at which the direction and magnitude of velocity of the ball changes, which are as given below:
Whenever a force will be applied on the ball, then the velocity of the ball will change.
(i) When first player kicks the ball towards another player of his team, then the velocity of ball will change, because first player applies some force on the ball.
(ii) When another player kicks the ball towards the goal, then the velocity of ball will change, because here again the force is applied on the ball.
(iii) When goalkeeper of the opposite team collects the ball, then the velocity of ball will be changed, it becomes zero. Here, the goalkeeper applies some force on the ball to stop.
(iv) When the goalkeeper kicks the ball towards his own team, then the velocity of the ball changes, because goalkeeper applies some force on the ball.

3 Explain, why some of the leaves may get detached from a tree, if we vigorously shake its branch? **Pg 118**

Sol. Leaves have inertia of rest. When the branch is shaken, they tend to remain in same state and get detached when the position of branch changes.

4 Why do you fall in the forward direction when a moving bus brakes to a stop and fall backwards when it accelerates from rest? **Pg 118**

Sol. When the moving bus apply brakes to a stop, then our body had inertia of motion, that oppose a change in its state. However, the lower portion of our body in contact with bus comes to rest. So, immediately but the upper part still remains in motion. Hence, to balance our body, we fall forward. When the bus accelerates from rest, then our body had inertia of rest, opposes a change in its state. However, the lower portion of our body starts moving with the bus. Hence, we fall backwards.

5 If action is always equal to the reaction, then explain how a horse can pull a cart? **Pg 126**

Sol. The horse pushes the ground in the backward direction. The ground exerts a reaction force on horse and cart system to push them forward. When the reaction force exceeds the force of friction between the wheels of cart and the ground, then the cart is pushed forward.

6 Explain, why is it difficult for a fireman to hold a hose-pipe, which ejects large amount of water with a high velocity? **Pg 126**

Sol. A fireman finds it difficult to hold a hose-pipe which is ejecting large amount of water at high velocity. Because the stream of water rushing out of the pipe in the forward direction exerts a large force on the pipe. Due to the reaction of the forward force, a (action) or force is applied on the pipe in backward direction as per Newton's third law of motion. Therefore, the fireman struggles to keep the hose-pipe in rest.

EXERCISES
(On Pages 128 and 130)

1 An object experiences a net zero external unbalanced force. Is it possible for the object to be travelling with a non-zero velocity? If yes, state the conditions that must be placed on the magnitude and direction of the velocity. If no, provide a reason.

Sol. As per the Newton's first law of motion, no force is needed to move an object which is already moving with a constant (non-zero) velocity. So, when an object experiences a net zero external unbalanced force, then it can move with a non-zero velocity. When external force is zero then velocity of object remains same both in magnitude and direction.

2 When a carpet is beaten with a stick, dust comes out of it. Explain.

Sol. When a carpet is beaten with a stick, then the fibres of the carpet attain the state of motion while the dust particles remain in rest due to inertia of rest and hence dust particles get detached.

3 Why is it advised to tie any luggage kept on the roof of a bus with a rope?

Sol. When the bus stops suddenly, then bus comes in the state of rest but the luggage remain in the state of motion. So, due to inertia of motion, the luggage move forward and may fall down from the roof of the bus. If the bus starts suddenly, then bus comes in the state of motion but luggage remain in the state of rest. Due to inertia of rest, the luggage does not move in the forward direction and may fall down.

So, it is advised to tie the luggage kept on the roof of the bus with a rope.

4 A batsman hits a cricket ball which then rolls on a level ground. After covering a short distance, the ball comes to rest. Why does the ball slows down to stop?

(a) the batsman did not hit the ball hard enough
(b) velocity is proportional to the force exerted on the ball
(c) there is a force on the ball opposing the motion
(d) there is no unbalanced force on the ball, so the ball would want to come to rest.

Sol. (*c*) The ball slows down to stop because the force of friction acting between the ground and the ball acts as an external force which opposes the motion of the ball.

5 A truck starts from rest and rolls down a hill with a constant acceleration. It travels a distance of 400 m in 20 s. Find its acceleration. Find the force acting on it, if its mass is 7 tonne.
(Hint : 1 tonne = 1000 kg)

Sol. The truck starts from rest, so initial velocity, $u = 0$,

Distance, $s = 400$ m , Time, $t = 20$ s

Mass, $m = 7$ tonne $= 7 \times 1000 = 7000$ kg

From Newton's second law of motion, $s = ut + \frac{1}{2}at^2$

$$\Rightarrow \quad 400 = 0 \times 20 + \frac{1}{2} \times a \times (20)^2$$

$$\Rightarrow \quad 400 = 200\,a \Rightarrow a = 2 \text{ m/s}^2$$

From Newton's second law of motion, force acting on the truck,

$$F = ma = 7000 \times 2$$
$$= 14000 \text{ N}$$
$$= 1.4 \times 10^4 \text{ N}$$

Thus, acceleration of truck is 2 m/s^2 and force acting on it is 1.4×10^4 N.

6 A stone of size 1 kg is thrown with a velocity of 20 m/s across the frozen surface of a lake and comes to rest after travelling a distance of 50 m. What is the force of friction between the stone and the ice?

Sol. Given, mass of stone, $m = 1$ kg, Initial velocity, $u = 20$ m/s

Final velocity, $v = 0$

[since, stone comes to rest]

Distance covered, $s = 50$ m

From Newton's third law of motion, $v^2 = u^2 + 2as$

$$(0)^2 = (20)^2 + 2a(50)$$

$$\Rightarrow \quad 100\, a = -400 \Rightarrow a = -4 \text{ m/s}^2$$

Here, negative sign shows that there is a retardation in the motion of stone.

Force of friction between stone and ice

= Force required to stop the stone

$= ma = 1 \times (-4) = -4$ N

7 A 8000 kg engine pulls a train of 5 wagons, each of 2000 kg along a horizontal track. If the engine exerts a force of 40000 N and the track offers a friction force of 5000 N, then calculate

(*i*) the net accelerating force and

(*ii*) the acceleration of the train.

Sol. (*i*) Net accelerating force = Force exerted by engine − Frictional force

[Here, frictional force is subtracted because it opposes the motion]

$= 40000 - 5000 = 35000 = 3.5 \times 10^4$ N

(*ii*) From Newton's second law of motion,

accelerating force (F) = mass of the train (m) × acceleration of train (a)

$$\Rightarrow \quad a = \frac{F}{m}$$

Mass of train = 5 × Mass of one wagon

= 5 × 2000 = 10000 kg

$$\therefore \text{Acceleration} = \frac{35000}{10000} = 3.5 \text{ m/s}^2$$

8 An automobile vehicle has a mass of 1500 kg. What must be the force between the vehicle and road, if the vehicle is to be stopped with a negative acceleration of 1.7 m/s^2?

Sol. Given, mass, $m = 1500$ kg, acceleration, $a = -1.7$ m/s^2

From Newton's second law of motion,

$$F = ma = 1500 \times (-1.7) = -2550 \text{ N}$$

9 What is the momentum of an object of mass m moving with a velocity v?

(a) m^2v^2 (b) mv^2 (c) $\frac{1}{2}mv^2$ (d) mv

Sol. (*d*) The momentum of an object of mass m moving with a velocity v is given by, $p = mv$.

10 Using a horizontal force of 200 N, we intend to move a wooden cabinet across a floor at a constant velocity. What is the friction force that will be exerted on the cabinet?

Sol. The cabinet will move across the floor with constant velocity, if there is no net external force applied on it. Here, a horizontal force of 200 N is applied on the cabinet, so for the net force to be zero, an external force of 200 N should be applied on the cabinet in opposite direction.

Thus, the frictional force = 200 N

[frictional force always acts in the direction opposite to the direction of motion]

11 According to the third law of motion when we push on an object, the object pushes back on us with an equal and opposite force. If the object is a massive truck parked along the roadside, it will probably not move. A student justifies this by answering that the two opposite and equal forces cancel each other. Comment on this logic and explain why the truck does not move.

Sol. The logic given by the student is not correct because two equal and opposite forces cancel each other only in the case, if they act on the same body. Action and reaction force always act on two different bodies, so they cannot cancel each other.

When a massive truck is pushed, then the truck may not move because the force applied is not sufficient to overcome the force produced by friction acting opposite to applied force to move the truck.

12 A bullet of mass 10 g travelling horizontally with a velocity of 150 m/s strikes a stationary wooden block and comes to rest in 0.03 s. Calculate the distance of penetration of the bullet into the block. Also, calculate the magnitude of the force exerted by the wooden block on the bullet.

Sol. Given, mass of bullet,

$$m = 10 \text{ g} = \frac{10}{1000} \text{ kg} = 0.01 \text{ kg}$$

Initial velocity, $u = 150$ m/s

Final velocity, $v = 0$ [since, bullet comes to rest]

Time, $t = 0.03$ s

From Newton's first law of motion,

$$v = u + at$$

$$0 = 150 + a \times 0.03$$

$$\Rightarrow \quad a = \frac{-150}{0.03} = -5000 \text{ m/s}^2$$

Distance covered by the bullet before coming to rest is given by $v^2 = u^2 + 2as$

$$0 = (150)^2 + 2(-5000)s$$

$$\Rightarrow \quad s = \frac{(150)^2}{10000} = 2.25 \text{ m}$$

Magnitude of the force applied by the bullet on the block,

$$F = ma = 0.01 \times -5000 = -50 \text{ N}$$

13 An object of mass 100 kg is accelerated uniformly from a velocity of 5 m/s to 8 m/s in 6 s. Calculate the initial and final momentum of the object. Also, find the magnitude of the force exerted on the object.

Sol. Given, Mass of the object, $m = 100$ kg

Initial velocity, $u = 5$ m/s

Final velocity, $v = 8$ m/s,

Time, $t = 6$ s

(*i*) $\therefore$ Initial momentum $= mu$

$$= 100 \times 5 = 500 \text{ kg - m / s}$$

and final momentum $= mv$

$$= 100 \times 8 = 800 \text{ kg - m / s}$$

(*ii*) From Newton's second law, force exerted on the object = rate of change of momentum

$$= \frac{\text{Change in momentum}}{\text{Time}}$$

$$= \frac{\text{Final momentum} - \text{Initial momentum}}{\text{Time}}$$

$$= \frac{800 - 500}{6} = \frac{300}{6} = 50 \text{ N}$$

14 How much momentum will a dumb-bell of mass 10 kg transfer to the floor, if it falls from a height of 80 cm? Take, its downward acceleration to be 10 m/s^2.

Sol. Given, Mass of dumb-bell, $m = 10$ kg

Initial velocity, $u = 0$ [because it falls from rest]

Distance covered, $s = 80$ cm $= 0.8$ m

Acceleration, $a = 10$ m/s^2

From Newton's third law of motion, $v^2 = u^2 + 2as$

$$v^2 = 0 + 2 \times 10 \times 0.8 = 16 \Rightarrow v = \sqrt{16} = 4 \text{ m/s}$$

Momentum of dumb-bell just before it touches the floor is given by $p = mv = 10 \times 4 = 40$ kg-m/s

When the dumb-bell touches the floor, then its velocity becomes zero and hence the momentum. Thus, the total momentum of the dumb-bell is transferred to the floor.

So, the momentum transferred to the floor is 40 kg- m/s.

15 The following is the distance-time table of an object in motion:

Time *(in second)*	***Distance*** *(in metre)*
0	0
1	1
2	8
3	27
4	64
5	125
6	216
7	343

(*i*) What conclusion can you draw about the acceleration? Is it constant, increasing and decreasing or zero?

(*ii*) What do you infer about the force acting on the object?

Sol. (*i*) Here, initial velocity, $u = 0$

Using Newton's second law of motion,

$$s = ut + \frac{1}{2}at^2 = \frac{1}{2}at^2 \quad [\because u = 0]$$

We get, $a = \dfrac{2s}{t^2}$

Time *(in second)*	***Distance*** *(in metre)*	$a = 2s/t^2$
0	0	0
1	1	2
2	8	4
3	27	6
4	64	8
5	125	10
6	216	12
7	343	14

Thus, acceleration is increasing.

(*ii*) Since, acceleration is increasing, so net unbalanced force is acting on the object.

16 Two persons manage to push a motorcar of mass 1200 kg at an uniform velocity along a level road. The same motorcar can be pushed by three persons to produce an acceleration of 0.2 m/s^2. With what force does each person push the motorcar? (Assume that all persons push the motorcar with the same muscular effort.)

Sol. Given, mass of motorcar, $m = 1200$ kg

Acceleration produced, $a = 0.2 \text{ m/s}^2$

$\therefore$ Force applied on the car by three persons,

$$F = ma = 1200 \times 0.2 = 240 \text{ N}$$

Force applied on the car by one person $= \dfrac{240}{3} = 80$ N

Each person push the motorcar with a force of 80 N.

17 **A hammer of mass 500 g moving at 50 m/s strikes a nail. The nail stops the hammer in a very short time of 0.01 s. What is the force of the nail on the hammer?**

Sol. Given, Mass of the hammer = 500 g = 0.5 kg

Initial velocity of hammer, $u = 50$ m/s

Final velocity of hammer, $v = 0$

[because the hammer stops]

Time, $t = 0.01$ s

According to Newton's second law of motion,

force of the nail on the hammer

= rate of change of momentum of hammer

$$= \frac{mv - mu}{t} = \frac{0.5 \times 0 - 0.5 \times 50}{0.01} = -\frac{25}{0.01}$$

$$= -2500 \text{ N}$$

The force of the nail on the hammer is equal and opposite to that of hammer on nail.

18 **A motorcar of mass 1200 kg is moving along a straight line with a uniform velocity of 90 km/h. Its velocity is slowed down to 18 km/h in 4 s by an unbalanced external force. Calculate the acceleration and change in momentum. Also, calculate the magnitude of the force required.**

Sol. Given, mass, $m = 1200$ kg

Initial velocity, $u = 90$ km/h

$$= 90 \times \frac{5}{18} = 25 \text{ m/s}$$

Final velocity, $v = 18$ km/h

$$= 18 \times \frac{5}{18} = 5 \text{ m/s}$$

Time, $t = 4$ s

(*i*) $\therefore$ Acceleration, $a = \dfrac{v - u}{t} = \dfrac{5 - 25}{4}$

$$= -\frac{20}{4} = -5 \text{ m/s}^2$$

[here, negative sign indicates that the velocity decreases]

(*ii*) $\therefore$ Change in momentum

= Final momentum − Initial momentum

$= mv - mu = m(v - u) = 1200\,(5 - 25)$

$= 1200 \times (-20) = -24000$ kg-m/s

(*iii*) $\therefore$ Magnitude of the force required

= Rate of change of momentum

$$= \frac{\text{Change in momentum}}{\text{Time}}$$

$$= \frac{-24000}{4} = -6000 \text{ N}$$

SUMMARY

- Any action which causes pull, hit or push on a body is called **force**.
- Types of forces
  (i) **Balanced forces** When the net effect produced by a number of forces acting on a body is zero, then the forces are said to be **balanced forces**.
  (ii) **Unbalanced forces** When the net effect produced by a number of forces acting on a body is non-zero, then the forces are said to be **unbalanced forces.**
- **Newton's first law of motion** States that an object will continue to remain in its state of rest or in a uniform motion along a straight line or path unless an external unbalanced force acts on it.
- The unwillingness (or inability) of an object to change its state of rest or of uniform motion along a straight line is called **inertia** of the object.
- Types of inertia
  (i) **Inertia of Rest** The tendency of a body to oppose any change in its state of rest is known as **inertia of rest.**
  (ii) **Inertia of Motion** The tendency of a body to oppose any change in its state of uniform motion is known as **inertia of motion.**
  (iii) **Inertia of Direction** The tendency of a body to oppose any change in its direction of motion is known as **inertia of direction**.
- **Momentum** Measures the quantity of motion possessed by a body. It is defined as the product of mass and velocity of the body.
  Momentum, $p = mv$
  The SI unit of momentum is kg-m/s.
- **Newton's second law of motion** States that the rate of change of momentum of an object is proportional to the applied external force and takes place in the direction in which external force acts.
- Force applied on an object is equal to the product of mass of the object and acceleration produced in it.
  Force, $F = ma$
  The SI unit of force is **newton** (N).
- **Impulse** is defined as the product of force and a small time in which the force acts.
  Impulse, $I = Ft = p_2 - p_1$
  or Impulse = Change in momentum
  The SI unit of impulse is N-s or kg-m/s.
- **Newton's third law of motion** States that whenever one object exerts a force on another object, then the second object exerts an equal and opposite force on the first object.

For Mind Map
Visit https://goo.gl/nqdJd8
OR Scan the Code

Exam Practice

Objective Type Questions

Multiple Choice Questions

1 A water tanker filled upto $\frac{2}{3}$ of its height is moving with a uniform speed. On sudden application of the brake, the water in the tank would

(a) move backward (b) move forward
(c) be unaffected (d) rise upwards

NCERT Exemplar

Sol. (b) On the sudden application of brake, the tanker will come in the state of rest but the water remains in the state of motion, so the water will move forward.

2 Two forces F_1 and F_2 are acting on a body as shown in the figure, then acceleration in the body is

$F_1 = 50$ N → $m = 5$ kg ← $F_2 = 65$ N

(a) 23 m/s^2 (b) 3 m/s^2 (c) 2 m/s^2 (d) 22 m/s^2

Sol. (b) Resultant force on a body,

$$F = F_2 - F_1 = 65 - 50 = 15\ \text{N}$$

By Newton's second law of motion,

$$F = ma \Rightarrow 15 = 5a \Rightarrow a = 3\ \text{m/s}^2$$

3 Consider two spring balances hooked as shown in the figure below. We pull them in opposite directions. If the reading shown by A is 1.5 N, the reading shown by B will be

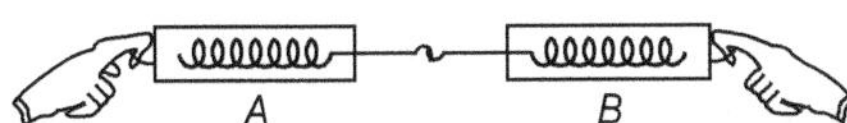

(a) 1.5 N (b) 2.5 N (c) 3.0 N (d) zero

Sol. (a) According to Newton's third law, every action has equal and opposite reaction. Hence, force (action) exerted by A on B and force exerted by B on A reaction are equal and reading shown by B will be 1.5 N in both the spring balance.

4 A bullet of 20 g strikes a sand bag at a speed of 200 m/s and gets embedded after travelling 2 cm, then the resistive force exerted by sand on the bullet is

(a) 2×10^3 N (b) 2×10^4 N
(c) 2×10^6 N (d) 2×10^5 N

Sol. (b) Given, $u = 200$ m/s, $v = 0$, $s = 0.02$ m and $m = 20\ \text{g} = 20 \times 10^{-3}$ kg

From third equation of motion,

$$v^2 = u^2 + 2as \Rightarrow a = \frac{v^2 - u^2}{2s}$$

$$= \frac{(0)^2 - (200)^2}{2 \times 0.02} = -10^6\ \text{m/s}^2$$

Negative sign indicates retardation.

$\therefore$ Resistive force, $F = ma = 20 \times 10^{-3} \times 10^6$

$$= 2 \times 10^4\ \text{N}$$

5 A truck moving with a speed of 54 km/h. Truck driver applied brakes suddenly and brings the truck to rest in 5 s, then the average retarding force on truck, if mass of the truck and driver is 400 kg, will be

(a) 1200 N (b) 600 N
(c) 800 N (d) 500 N

Sol. (a) Given, $u = 54$ km/h $= 54 \times \frac{5}{18}$ m/s $= 15$ m/s, $v = 0$ and $t = 5$s

$\therefore$ Retardation, $a = \frac{v - u}{t} = \frac{0 - 15}{5} = -3\ \text{m/s}^2$

Average retarding force, $F = ma = 400 \times 3 = 1200$ N

6 A bus of mass 500 kg is moving with a velocity of 5 m/s and is acted upon by a forward force of 500 N due to engine and retarding force of 200 N due to friction velocity of bus after 20 s will be

(a) 15 m/s (b) 17 m/s
(c) 19 m/s (d) 21 m/s

Sol. (b) Given, $m = 500$ kg, $u = 5$ m/s and $t = 20$ s

Resultant force, $F = 500 - 200 = 300$ N

$\therefore$ Acceleration, $a = \frac{F}{m} = \frac{300}{500} = 0.6\ \text{m/s}^2$

By equation of motion,

$$v = u + at = 5 + 0.6 \times 20 = 17\ \text{m/s}$$

7 A force acts on a body of mass 5 kg and changes its velocity from 8 m/s to 12 m/s in 4s, then magnitude of force is

(a) 8 N (b) 4 N (c) 5 N (d) 6 N

Sol. (c) According to Newton's second law of motion,

Force = Rate of change in momentum

$$F = \frac{m(v - u)}{t} = \frac{5(12 - 8)}{4} = 5\ \text{N}$$

8 A goalkeeper in a game of football pulls his hands backwards after holding the ball shot at the goal. This enables the goalkeeper to
(a) exert larger force on the ball
(b) reduce the force exerted by the ball on hands
(c) increase the rate of change of momentum
(d) decrease the rate of change of momentum
NCERT Exemplar

Sol. (d) The goalkeeper pulls his hands backwards after holding the ball to decrease the rate of change of momentum by increasing the time. By doing this, less force is exerted on his hands ($\because$ Force is directly proportional to the rate of change of momentum).

9 Impulse is equal to
(a) rate of change in momentum
(b) rate of change in force
(c) change in reaction force
(d) change in momentum

Sol. (d) Impulse, $I = F \times \Delta t = \frac{\Delta p}{\Delta t} \cdot \Delta t = \Delta p$
= Change in momentum.

10 When a person jumps down from a tower into a stretched tarpaulin, then he receives
(a) greater injury (b) less injury
(c) no injury (d) None of these

Sol. (c) When a person jumps, the tarpaulin gets depressed at the place of impact, therefore impact time interval increases, which decreases the impulse or change in momentum. As a result, person experiences a very small force, hence he receives no injury.

11 According to the third law of motion, action and reaction **NCERT Exemplar**
(a) always act on the same body
(b) always act on different bodies in opposite directions
(c) have same magnitude and direction
(d) act on either body at normal to each other

Sol. (b) According to third law of motion, action and reaction always act on different bodies in opposite directions.

Fill in the Blanks

12 The quantity of motion in a body is also known as ....

Sol. Momentum

13 The momentum of a 10 kg car moving with a speed of 36 km/h is .... m/s.

Sol. As, momentum, $p = m \times u$
$$= 10 \times \frac{36 \times 1000}{60 \times 60} = 100 \text{ m/s}$$

14 The linear momentum of a system remains constant if no .... force acts on it.

Sol. net external

15 If an unbalanced force is applied on the moving object there will be a change in its .... or in the .... of its motion.

Sol. speed, direction

16 One Newton is defined as the force which gives a mass of 1 kg an acceleration of ....

Sol. 1 m/s^2 as, $1 \text{ N} = 1 \text{ kg-m/s}^2$

True and False

17 Shock absorbers are provided in the vehicles to smooth out shock impulses which obeys Newton's first law.

Sol. False; Newton's third law.

18 Impulse and momentum have same unit.

Sol. True;
As impulse = $F \times t$, its unit is N-s.
or $\frac{\text{kgm}}{\text{s}^2} \times \text{s}$ i.e. kg-ms^{-1}
and SI unit of momentum = $m \times v$, i.e. kgms^{-1}.

19 A force cannot change the speed of a moving object.

Sol. False

20 A heavy objects will have more inertia than lighter one.

Sol. True; Inertia increases with increase in mass and decreases with decrease in mass.

Match the Columns

21 Match the following columns:

Column I	Column II
A. Recoil of gun	p. Newton's 2nd law of motion
B. Inertia	q. 10^5 g cms^{-1}
C. Momentum	r. Newton's 3rd law of motion
D. 1 kgms^{-1}	s. Newton's 1st law of motion

Sol. (A) $\rightarrow$ (r), (B) $\rightarrow$ (s), (C) $\rightarrow$ (p), (D) $\rightarrow$ (q)

Assertion-Reason

Direction (Q.Nos. 22-25) *In each of the following questions, a statement of Assertion is given by the corresponding statement of Reason. Of the statements, mark the correct answer as*

(a) If both Assertion and Reason are true and Reason is the correct explanation of Assertion.
(b) If both Assertion and Reason are true, but Reason is not the correct explanation of Assertion.
(c) If Assertion is true, but Reason is false.
(d) If Assertion is false, but Reason is true.

22 **Assertion** When various forces are acting on a body, then body may accelerate or remain static.

Reason Acceleration in a body is produced only due to resultant force acting on it.

Sol. (a) When, various forces acting on a body, cause resultant force to zero, then body is in equilibrium. On the other hand, if resultant force is not zero, then body is accelerated because resultant force always produces an acceleration. Hence, Assertion and Reason both are true and Reason is the correct explanation of Assertion.

23 **Assertion** Impulsive force is long range force and acts for a short time.

Reason Change in momentum should be produced by force.

Sol. (a) When a very large force is acting on a body for a very small time interval, then product of force and time interval is called impulse.

Change in momentum is equal to impulse.

Impulse $(I) = F \cdot \Delta t$ but $\left[F = \dfrac{\Delta p}{\Delta t}\right] = \dfrac{\Delta P}{\Delta t} \cdot \Delta t$

$= \Delta p =$ Change in momentum.

Hence, Assertion and Reason both are true and Reason is the correct explanation of Assertion.

24 **Assertion** If two persons walking or running in opposite direction collide with each other, then both feel hurt.

Reason Every action applies equal reaction.

Sol. (a) According to Newton's third law of motion, every action has an equal and opposite reaction, but always act on two different bodies.

Therefore, both persons feel hurt after collision.

Hence, Assertion and Reason both are true and Reason is the correct explanation of Assertion

25 **Assertion** Road accidents occurring due to high speeds are much worse than accidents due to low speeds of vehicles.

Reason Momentum of high speed vehicles is more than that of low speed vehicles.

Sol. (a) Road accidents due to high speeds are much worse than accidents due to low speeds of vehicles. This is because the momentum of high speed vehicles is more than that of the low speed vehicles, as momentum is the product of mass and velocity. Hence, both Assertion and Reason are true and Reason is the correct explanation of Assertion.

Case Based Questions

Direction (Q.Nos. 26-29) *Answer the question on the basis of your understanding of the following passage and related studied concepts:*

A rocket is used for carrying a satellite, etc to a suitable height above the ground. Thrust is generated by the propulsion system of the aircraft. For every action there is an equal and opposite reaction. The fuel in the rocket is burnt and exhaust gases are made to escape in the downward direction through a narrow nozzle. As a reaction, rocket moves upwards. Rocket works on the principle of conservation of momentum.

According to the principle of conservation of linear momentum, the linear momentum of mass of rocket at any instant must be equal to vector sum of linear momentum of rocket and linear momentum of exhaust gases as the exhaust gases escape, the residual mass of rocket decreases with time. Motion of rocket is an accelerated motion.

26 How is mass of rocket related to the mass of gases it expels?

(a) Mass of rocket is greater than mass of gases it expels.
(b) Mass of rocket is less than mass of gases it expels.
(c) Mass of rocket is equal to mass of gases it expels.
(d) Mass of rocket is not related to the mass of gases it expels.

Sol. (a) Mass of rocket is greater than mass of gases as the rocket is used for carrying a satellite etc. to a suitable height above the ground.

27 The fuel in the rocket is burnt and exhaust gases are made to escape in

(a) parallel to rocket (b) upward direction
(c) perpendicular to rocket
(d) downward direction

Sol. (d) The fuel in the rocket is burnt and exhaust gases are made to escape in the downward direction through a narrow nozzle. As a reaction, rocket moves upwards.

28 Newton's which law is associated with rocket propulsion? State the law.

Sol. Newton's 3rd law which states that for every action there is an equal and opposite reaction.

29 What type of motion is described by the rocket uniform or accelerated?

Sol. Accelerated motion

Direction (Q. Nos. 30-33) *Study the following table and graph and anwer the questions based on the table.*

A car was travelling at 30 m/s. The driver applies brakes suddenly by seeing a running dog. The velocity-time (v-t) graph and its corresponding table during the time of applying brakes is shown below.

Time	*Velocity*
0 (s)	30 m/s
1 (s)	23.5 m/s
2 (s)	17 m/s
3 (s)	11 m/s
4 (s)	5 m/s
4.8 (s)	0

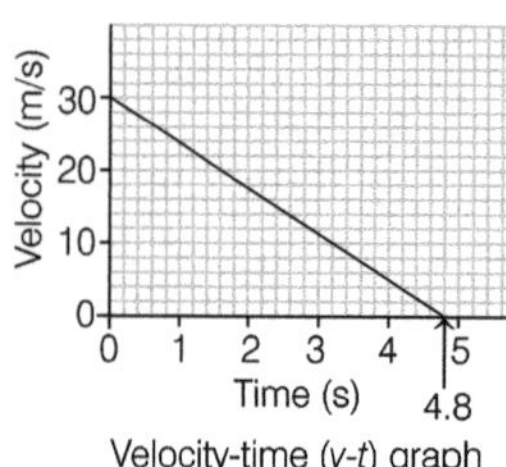

Velocity-time (v-t) graph

30 Calculate the rate at which the velocity of a car decreases (deceleration).

Sol. (b) From given graph, initial velocity, $u = 30$ m/s

Final velocity, $v = 0$ m/s

Time, $t = 4.8$ s

As we know, $v = u + at$

$$\Rightarrow \quad a = \frac{v-u}{t} = \frac{0-30}{4.8} = -6.25 \text{ m/s}^2$$

Thus, deceleration is -6.25 m/s^2.

31 Calculate the braking force, if the mass of the car is 900 kg.

Sol. As, according to Newton's second law,

$$F = ma = 900 \times \left(-\frac{30}{4.8}\right) = -5625 \text{ N}$$

Negative sign shows that the direction of force is opposite to motion of the body.

32 Calculate the braking distance travelled by the car.

Sol. (c) As we know, braking distance, $s = ut - \frac{1}{2}at^2$

$$= 30 \times 4.8 - \frac{1}{2} \times 6.25 \times 4.8 \times 4.8$$
$$= 144 - 72$$
$$= 72 \text{ m}$$

33 Why the driver of car applies brakes suddenly?

Sol. The driver of car applies brakes suddenly by seeing a running dog, to slow down the speed of car.

Very Short Answer Type Questions

34 Give two examples of effects of force.

Sol. (*i*) A toy car starts moving when pushed.
(*ii*) Shape of dough ball changes when rolled.

35 Apart from changing the magnitude of velocity of an object or changing the direction of motion of an object, what other changes can force bring on an object?

Sol. Force can change the state of rest to state of motion and *vice-versa*. It can also change the shape and position of the body.

36 Using a horizontal force of 200 N, we intend to move a wooden cabinet across a floor at a constant velocity. What is the frictional force that will be exerted on the cabinet?

Sol. The frictional force is 200 N but in opposite direction.

37 What do you mean by resultant force?

Sol. When two or more forces act on a body simultaneously, then the single force which produces the same effect as produced by all the other forces acting together is known as the resultant force.

38 While riding on the bicycle, if we stop peddling, why does the bicycle begin to slow down?

Sol. The bicycle begins to slow down because of force of friction acting in opposite direction.

39 What did Galileo conclude on the basis of his experiments on the motion of objects?

Sol. A body continues to move with the same velocity, if no unbalanced force acts on it.

40 Velocity-time graph of a moving particle of mass 1 kg is shown in figure.

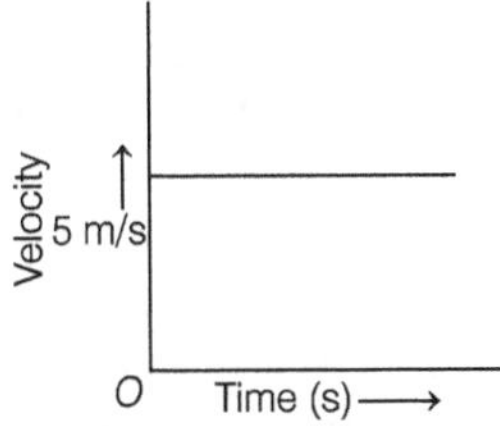

Is any force acting on the body? Justify your answer.

Sol. The velocity of body is uniform, thus acceleration is zero. Hence, no unbalanced force acts on the body.

41 Name the agent which when applied to a body is directly proportional to the rate of change of momentum which it produces in the body.

Sol. Force is the agent, applied to a body which is directly proportional to the rate of change of momentum.

42 A passenger in a moving train tosses a coin which falls behind him. From this incident, what can you predict about the motion of train. **NCERT Exemplar**

Sol. If the coin falls behind the passenger that means the train is accelerated. When the coin is tossed, then it has same velocity as that of train but during the time it is in air its velocity becomes less than that of train (because the train is accelerated), so it falls behind the passenger.

43 Name the physical quantity which corresponds to the rate of change of momentum.

Sol. Force (according to Newton's second law rate of change of momentum is known as force).

44 What is the net momentum of gun and bullet system after firing?

Sol. The net momentum of gun and bullet system after firing is equal to initial momentum, i.e. zero because no external force is acting.

45 If F and F' are balanced forces, then what will be the magnitude of F_2?

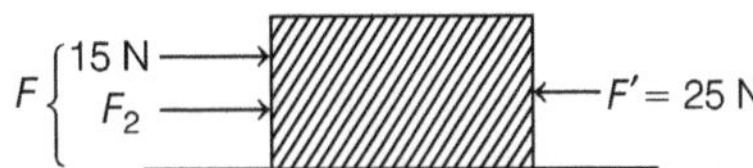

Sol. As per question, F and F' are balanced forces.

So, $F = F' \Rightarrow 15 + F_2 = 25$ N

$\therefore$ $F_2 = 10$ N

Short Answer (SA) Type Questions

1 On what factors do the following physical quantities depend?

(*i*) Inertia (*ii*) Momentum (*iii*) Force

Sol. (*i*) Inertia depends on the mass of a body.

(*ii*) Momentum depends on mass and velocity of the body.

(*iii*) Force depends on mass and acceleration of the body.

2 Give reason for the following questions:

(*i*) Road accidents occurring due to high speeds are much worse than accidents due to low speeds of vehicles.

(*ii*) When a motorcar makes a sharp turn at a high speed passengers tend to get thrown to one side.

Sol. (*i*) Road accidents occurring due to high speeds are worse than accidents due to low speeds of vehicles. This is because the momentum of high speed vehicles is more than that of the low speeds of vehicles.

(*ii*) When a motorcar makes a sharp turn left or right at a high speed, the lower portion, of the passengers turns suddenly along with the motorcar but upper portions do not change its direction due to inertia. So, this portion of passenger moves forward and the passenger tends to get thrown to one side or other side.

3 Glasswares are wrapped in straw during their transportation. Justify giving reason.

Sol. During transportation, the glasswares may break, if they collide with each other in the event of jerks. When they are wrapped in straw, then the force of jerk is transmitted to them through the pieces of straw in a longer period of time. Thus, the change in momentum of the glasswares takes place in a longer period of time. Therefore, a very small force is experienced by them in the event to jerks and hence they do not break.

4 What would happen if a fielder stops the fast moving ball suddenly? Justify your answer.

Sol. The high velocity of the ball decrease to zero in a short time. It means that in a short time, there is a large change in momentum of the ball.

Therefore, to stop the fast moving ball, the fielder have to apply a large force and in the process he may hurt his palm.

5 Give reason for the following:

(i) Water sprinkler used for grass lawns begins to rotate as soon as water is supplied. **NCERT Exemplar**

(ii) Water drops are removed from wet clothes by giving tight jerk to the cloth.

Sol. (i) The working of the rotation of sprinkler is based on Newton's 3rd law of motion, hence when water is pushed out of sprinkler with a force, it exerts reaction force on the sprinkler causing it to rotate.

(ii) Water drops have inertia of rest. They have a tendency to remain in the cloth. By giving jerk to the cloth, its inertia is disturbed which helps in drying.

6 A body of mass m is moving with a velocity u. When a force is applied on it for time t, then its velocity increases to v, write expressions for

(i) initial and final momentum

(ii) change of momentum

(iii) rate of change of momentum. Also, write SI unit for each.

Sol. According to question, mass of the body $= m$

Initial velocity $= u$, Final velocity $= v$

(i) $\therefore$ Initial momentum of the body $= mu$

and final momentum of the body $= mv$

(ii) $\therefore$ Change in momentum $= mv - mu$

(iii) Rate of change of momentum = Applied force

$$= m \cdot a = m\left(\frac{v-u}{t}\right) \quad \left[\because a = \frac{v-u}{t}\right]$$

SI unit of force is newton (N) and SI unit of momentum is kg-m/s.

7 (i) Explain, why is it difficult to walk on sand?

(ii) Why is the recoil of a heavy gun, on firing, not so strong as that of a light gun using the same cartridge?

Sol. (i) While walking on sand, the sand gets pressed down, impacting less reaction force on the person.

(ii) The mass of the heavy gun is more. So, its recoil velocity is less.

8 A bullet fired against a glass window pane makes a hole in it and the glass pane is not cracked. But on the other hand, when a stone strikes the same glass pane, then it gets smashed. Why is it so?

Sol. When the bullet strikes the glass pane, then the part of the glass pane which comes in contact with the bullet immediately shares the large velocity of bullet and makes a hole, while the remaining part of the glass remains at rest and is therefore not smashed due to inertia of rest.

But when a slow moving stone strikes the same glass pane, then the various parts of the glass pane gets enough time to share the velocity of the stone and the glass is smashed, its inertia gets disturbed.

9 What do you understand by momentum? A vehicle is moving with velocity of 5 m/s. If the momentum of the vehicle is 5000 kg-m/s, then what is its mass?

Sol. Momentum is the physical quantity which is the product of mass and velocity of an object. Momentum has both mass as well as direction of motion. Its denoted by p. Its SI unit is kg-m/s.

$\therefore$ Momentum, $p = mv$

Given, $p = 5000$ kg-m/s, $v = 5$ m/s, $m = ?$

$$5000 = m \times 5$$

$$\Rightarrow \quad m = \frac{5000}{5} = 1000 \text{ kg}$$

10 Force of 10 N applied to a mass m_1 produces an acceleration of 5 m/s^2 and when applied to mass m_2, produces an acceleration of 15 m/s^2 in the mass. How much acceleration will the same force produce, if the two masses are tied together?

Sol. We know that, $F = ma$

$$\Rightarrow \quad 10 = m_1 \times 5$$

$$\text{or} \quad m_1 = \frac{10}{5} = 2 \text{ kg}$$

Also, $m_2 = \frac{10}{15} = \frac{2}{3}$ kg

Required acceleration produced when the masses are tied together (i.e. $m = m_1 + m_2$),

$$a = \frac{F}{m} = \frac{10}{m_1 + m_2}$$

$$= \frac{10}{2 + \frac{2}{3}} = \frac{30}{8} = 3.75 \text{ m/s}^2$$

11 A bullet of mass 4 g when fired with a velocity of 50 m/s can enter a wall upto a depth of 10 cm. How much will be the average resistance offered by the wall?

Sol. The hindrance offered by the wall to the motion of bullet is called the resistance offered by the wall.
Given, Mass of the bullet, $m = 4\text{g} = 4 \times 10^{-3}$ kg

Initial velocity, $u = 50$ m/s, Depth, $s = 10 \text{ cm} = \frac{1}{10}$ m

Final velocity, $v = 0$, Force, $F = ?$
Using second equation of motion,

$$v^2 = u^2 + 2as$$

$$\Rightarrow \quad v^2 - u^2 = 2as$$

$$\Rightarrow \quad 0 - (50)^2 = 2a \times \frac{1}{10}$$

$$\Rightarrow \quad -2500 = \frac{a}{5} \Rightarrow a = -12500 \text{ m/s}^2$$

$\therefore$ Force, $F = ma = 4 \times 10^{-3} \times (-12500)$

$$= -50 \text{ N}$$

Thus, the average resistance offered is 50 N.
Negative sign indicates that the force is acting opposite to the motion.

12 For how much time should a force of 200 N acts on an object having mass 5 kg, so as to increase its velocity from 50 m/s to 100 m/s?

Sol. Given, force, $F = 200$ N; Mass of an object, $m = 5$ kg
Initial velocity, $u = 50$ m/s
Final velocity, $v = 100$ m/s
From Newton's second law of motion, we get

$$F = ma = m\left(\frac{v-u}{t}\right) \quad \left[\because a = \frac{v-u}{t}\right]$$

$$200 = 5\left(\frac{100-50}{t}\right)$$

$$\therefore \quad t = 5\left(\frac{100-50}{200}\right) = 1.25 \text{ s}$$

Thus, the time taken is 1.25 s.

13 The motion of a body of mass 5 kg is shown in the velocity-time graph.

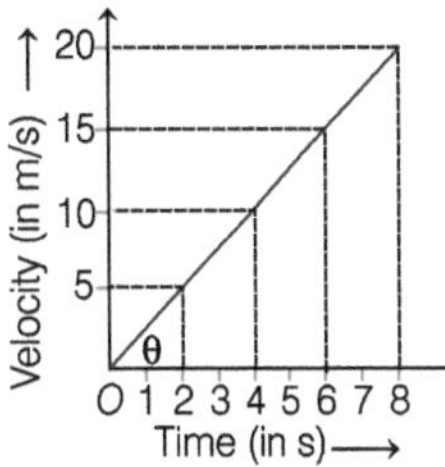

Find from the graph.
(i) Its acceleration.
(ii) The force acting on the body.
(iii) The change in momentum of body in 2 s after start.

Sol. (i) Acceleration = Slope of the line of velocity-time graph

$$a = \frac{v_2 - v_1}{t - t_1} = \frac{5-0}{2-0} = \frac{5}{2} = \frac{10}{4}$$

$$= \frac{15}{6} = 2.5 \text{ m/s}^2$$

(ii) The force acting on the body is given by

$$F = ma = 5 \times 2.5 = 12.5 \text{ N}$$

(iii) $\therefore$ Change in momentum $= mv - mu$

$[\because u = 0 \text{ and } v = 5 \text{ m/s}]$

$$= 5 \times 5 - 5 \times 0$$

$$= 25 \text{ kg-m/s}$$

14 The velocity-time graph of a ball moving on the surface of floor is as shown in figure. Calculate the force acting on the ball, if mass of the ball is 100 g.

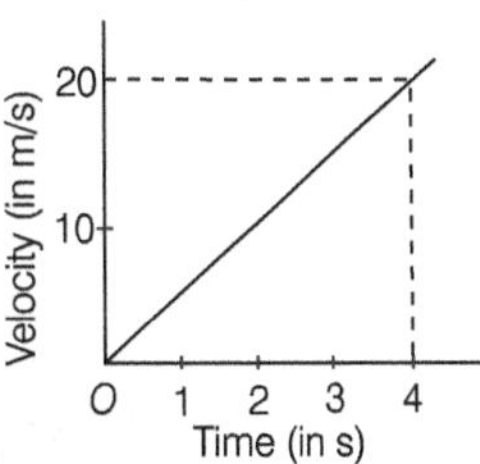

Sol. The velocity-time graph shows that the velocity of the ball at $t = 0$ is zero. So, initial velocity of the ball, $u = 0$.
Velocity of the ball at $t = 4$ s is 20 m/s
i.e. final velocity, $v = 20$ m/s; Time, $t = 4$ s
$\therefore$ Acceleration of the ball,

$$a = \frac{v-u}{t} = \frac{20 \text{ m/s} - 0}{4 \text{ s}} = 5 \text{ m/s}^2$$

Also, mass of the ball,

$$m = 100 \text{ g} = \frac{100}{1000} \text{ kg} = \frac{1}{10} \text{ kg}$$

$\therefore$ Force acting on the ball, $F = ma$

$$= \frac{1}{10} \text{ kg} \times 5 \text{ m/s}^2$$

$= 0.5 \text{ kg-m/s}^2 = 0.5 \text{ N}$ $[\because 1 \text{ kg-m/s}^2 = 1 \text{ N}]$

15 The speed-time graph of a car is given. The car weighs 1000 kg.

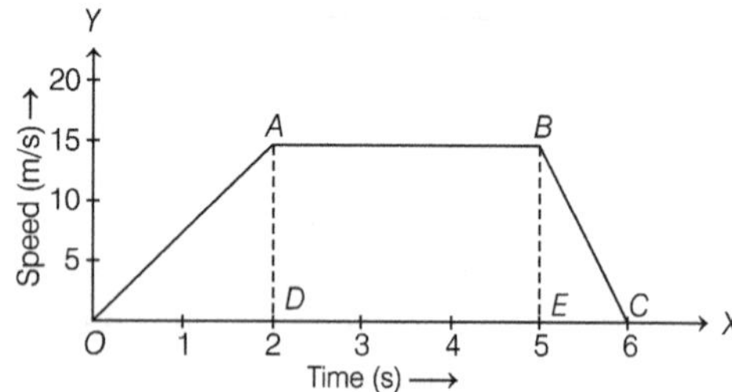

(i) What is the distance travelled by the car in first 2s?

(ii) What is the braking force applied at the end of 5 s to bring the car to stop within one second?

Sol. (i) Distance travelled by the car in first 2 s = Area of $\Delta OAD = \frac{1}{2} \times 2 \times 15 = 15 \text{ m}$

(ii) Braking force, $F = m \times a$

Given, mass of the car, $m = 1000$ kg, initial velocity, $u = 15$ m/s, final velocity, $v = 0$, time, $t = 1$ s

On applying,

$$a = \frac{v-u}{t} \Rightarrow a = \frac{0-15}{1} = -15 \text{ m/s}^2$$

$$\therefore \quad F = m\,a = 1000 \times (-15) = -15000 \text{ N}$$

16 A constant force of friction of 50 N is acting on a body of mass 200 kg moving initially with a speed of 15 m/s. How long does the body take to stop? What distance will it cover before coming to rest?

Sol. Given, $F = 50$ N, $m = 200$ kg, $u = 15$ m/s

The acceleration of the body is obtained from $F = m \cdot a$

or $$a = \frac{F}{m} = \frac{50}{200}$$

$$= -0.25 \text{ m/s}^2$$

Now, from the first equation of motion

$$v = u + at$$

$$\Rightarrow \quad t = \left(\frac{v-u}{a}\right) = \left(\frac{0-15}{-0.25}\right) = 60 \text{ s}$$

Also, distance travelled is obtained from

$$s = ut + \frac{1}{2}at^2$$

$$= 50 \times 60 + 1/2 \times (-0.25) \times (60)^2$$

$$= 450 \text{ m}$$

17 Look at the diagram below and answer the following questions:

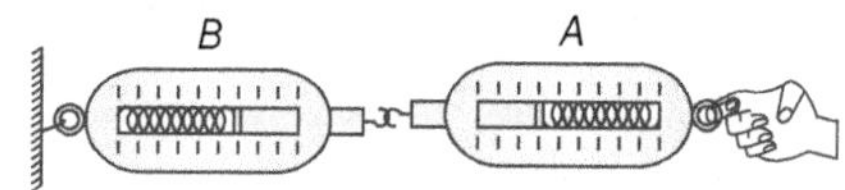

(i) When a force is applied through the free end of the spring balance *A*, then the reading on the spring balance *A* is 15 g-wt. What will be the measure of the reading shown by spring balance *B*?

(ii) Write reasons for your answer.

(iii) Name the forces which balance *A* exerts on balance *B* and of balance *B* on balance *A*.

Sol. (i) 15 g-wt.

(ii) From Newton's third law, the force exerted by *B* on *A* and force exerted by *A* on *B* are equal.

(iii) Force of reaction balance *A* exerts on balance *B* and force of action balance *B* exerts on balance *A*.

Long Answer (LA) Type Questions

1 What is momentum? Write its SI unit. Interpret force in terms of momentum. Represent the following graphically:

(i) Momentum *versus* velocity when mass is fixed.

(ii) Momentum *versus* mass when velocity is constant. **NCERT Exemplar**

Sol. **Momentum** The quantity of motion possessed by a moving body is known as momentum of the body. It is the product of mass and velocity of the body.

Momentum, $p = mv$. Its SI unit is kg-m/s.

Force applied on an object of mass m moving with acceleration a.

$$F = ma = m\frac{\Delta v}{\Delta t}$$

$\left[\because \text{acceleration} = \text{rate of change of velocity} = \frac{\Delta v}{\Delta t}\right]$

$$= \frac{\Delta p}{\Delta t}$$

$\therefore$ Force applied on an object is equal to the rate of change of momentum of the object.

(*i*) Momentum *versus* velocity graph when mass is fixed, $p = mv$.
If m is fixed, then $p \propto v$

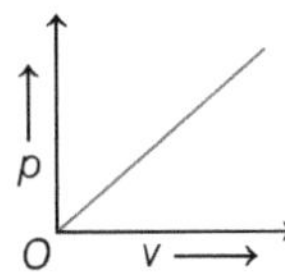

$\therefore$ Momentum *versus* velocity graph will be a straight line passing through the origin (if $v = 0$, then $p = 0$).

(*ii*) Momentum *versus* mass graph when velocity is constant, $p = mv$.

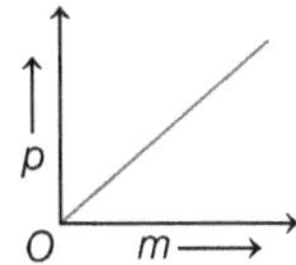

If velocity is constant, then $p \propto m$.
So, the momentum *versus* mass graph will be a straight line passing through the origin (if $m = 0$, then $p = 0$).

2 (*i*) When a carpet is beaten with a stick dust comes out of it. Explain.
(*ii*) Calculate the force required to impart a car with a velocity of 30 m/s in 10 s starting from rest. The mass of the car is 15000 kg.

Sol. (*i*) When we beat the carpet with a strick, then it comes into motion. But the dust particles continue to be at rest due to inertia and get detached from the carpet.
(*ii*) Given, initial velocity, $u = 30$ m/s
Time, $t = 10$ s, final velocity, $v = 0$
Mass, $m = 15000$ kg
From first equation of motion,
$$a = \frac{v-u}{t} = \frac{-30}{10} = -3 \text{ m/s}^2$$
So, retarding force required = ma
$$= 15000 \times (-3) = -45000 \text{ N}$$
Thus, the force required by the car is 45000 N.

3 Derive the mathematical relation of Newton's second law of motion.

Sol. Refer to text on Pg 186.

4 (*i*) Define momentum. State its SI unit.
(*ii*) An object of mass 5 kg is accelerated uniformly from a velocity of 4 m/s to 8 m/s in 8 s. Calculate the initial and final momentum of the object. Also, find the magnitude of the force exerted on the object.

Sol. (*i*) Refer to text on Pg 186.
(*ii*) Given, mass, $m = 5$ kg, initial velocity, $u = 4$ m/s
Final velocity, $v = 8$ m/s, time, $t = 8$ s
$\therefore$ Initial momentum, $p_1 = mu = 5 \times 4 = 20$ kg-m/s
and final momentum, $p_2 = mv = 5 \times 8$
$= 40$ kg-m/s
$$\text{Now, force} = \frac{\Delta p}{t} = \frac{p_2 - p_1}{t} = \frac{40-20}{8} = \frac{20}{8} \text{ N}$$
$= 2.5$ N

5 Using second law of motion, derive the relation between force and acceleration. A bullet of 10 g strikes a sand bag at a speed of 10^3 m/s and gets embedded after travelling 5 cm. Calculate **NCERT Exemplar**
(*i*) the resistive force exerted by sand on the bullet.
(*ii*) the time taken by bullet to come to rest.

Sol. Refer to text on Pg 186.
Given, $m = 10 \text{ g} = 0.01 \text{ kg}, u = 10^3 \text{ m/s}, v = 0,$
$s = 5 \text{ cm} = 0.05 \text{ m}, t = ?, a = ?, F = ?$
(*i*) From third equation of motion,
$$a = \frac{v^2 - u^2}{2s} = \frac{0 - (10^3)^2}{2 \times 0.05} = -10^7 \text{ m/s}^2$$
$\therefore$ Force applied by the bullet,
$$F = ma = 0.01 \times (-10^7) = -10^5 \text{ N}$$
[negative sign shows that force is against the direction of motion]
The resistive force exerted by the sand on the bullet is 10^5 N.
(*ii*) Time taken by bullet to come to rest,
$$t = \frac{v-u}{a} = \frac{0-10^3}{-10^7} = 10^{-4} \text{ s}$$

6 Derive the unit of force using the second law of motion. A force of 5 N produces an acceleration of 8 m/s^2 on a mass m_1 and an acceleration of 24 m/s^2 on a mass m_2. What acceleration would the same provide, if both the masses are tied together? **NCERT Exemplar**

Sol. Refer to text on Pg 186.
Given, $F_1 = 5 \text{ N}, a_1 = 8 \text{ m/s}^2, m_1 = ?$
$F_2 = 5 \text{ N}, a_2 = 24 \text{ m/s}^2, m_2 = ?$
From $F = ma, \quad 5 = m_1 \times 8$

$$\Rightarrow \quad m_1 = \frac{5}{8}\text{ kg}$$

Similarly, $5 = m_2 \times 24 \Rightarrow m_2 = \frac{5}{24}$ kg

$$\therefore \quad m_1 + m_2 = \frac{5}{8} + \frac{5}{24} = \frac{15+5}{24} = \frac{20}{24} = \frac{5}{6}$$

Acceleration produced by the same force provided, if both the masses are tied together is

$$a = \frac{F}{(m_1 + m_2)} = \frac{5}{5/6} = 6 \text{ m/s}^2$$

7 If the engine of a car provides an acceleration of 2 m/s^2 to start it from rest, then assuming the mass to be roughly 1000 kg. Calculate

(*i*) force provided by the engine.

(*ii*) velocity after 10 s.

(*iii*) time after which the car comes to rest, if the engine is turned off after 15 s. (take, frictional force = 15 N)

Sol. Given, initial velocity, $u = 0$ m/s

Acceleration, $a = 2$ m/s^2,

Mass, $m = 1000$ kg

(*i*) From Newton's second law of motion,

force = mass × acceleration

$$F = ma = 1000 \times 2 = 2000 \text{ N}$$

(*ii*) Velocity after 10 s,

from first equation of motion, $v = u + at$

$$v = 0 + 2 \times 10 = 20 \text{ m/s}$$

(*iii*) Final velocity of the car when the engine is on after 15 s.

$v = 0 + 2 \times 15 = 30$ m/s $[\because t = 15\text{ s}]$ ...(i)

So, $p = mv$

$= 1000 \times 20 = 20000$ kg-m/s

After 15 s,

net force = force exerted by engine + friction force = 2000 − 15 = 1985 N

[∵ friction force = 15 N]

[Here, friction force is subtracted because it opposes the motion]

$$\therefore \text{ Acceleration} = \frac{\text{Net force}}{\text{Mass}}$$

$$\Rightarrow \quad a = \frac{1985}{1000}$$

$$a = 1.985 \text{ m/s}^2 \approx 2 \text{ m/s}^2$$

Time taken by the car (comes to rest)

$v = u - at$ [first equation of motion]

[∵ final velocity, $v = 0$]

$\Rightarrow \quad 0 = 30 - 2 \times t$

$\Rightarrow \quad 2t = 30$ [from Eq. (i)]

$\therefore \quad t = 15$ s

CHAPTER EXERCISE

Multiple Type Questions

1 The inertia of an object tends to cause the object **NCERT Exemplar**

(a) to increase its speed
(b) to decrease its speed
(c) to resist any change in its state of motion
(d) to decelerate due to friction

2 Trolley X and trolley Y are joined with stretched spring. Trolley X has twice the mass of trolley Y.

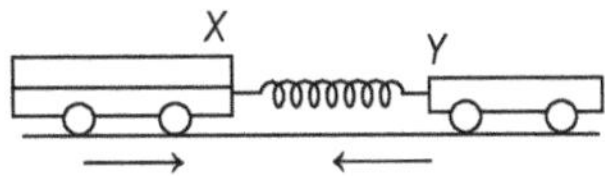

When the trolleys are released, the acceleration of X is $2\ \text{m/s}^2$ to the right.

What is the initial acceleration of trolley Y to the left?

(a) $1\ \text{m/s}^2$ (b) $2\ \text{m/s}^2$
(c) $3\ \text{m/s}^2$ (d) $4\ \text{m/s}^2$

3 The resultant force acting on a body is zero, then a

(a) body is in unequilibrium
(b) body is in equilibrium
(c) body moves with constant acceleration
(d) body moves with retardation

4 Two objects of masses 1 kg and 2 kg are moving with velocities 2 m/s and 4 m/s, respectively. They collide and after collision the first object moves at a velocity 3 m/s, then velocity of second object is

(a) 3.5 m/s (b) 4.5 m/s
(c) 2.5 m/s (d) 0 m/s

Fill in the Blanks

5 The SI unit of momentum is ....

6 If two bodies of different masses have same momentum, the .... body possesses greater velocity.

True and False

7 We cannot see force but we can feel or observe its effect.

8 Newton's third law of motion is applicable only. When bodies are in motion.

Match the Columns

9 Match Column A with Column B.

	Column A	Column B
A.	Impulse	p. kg
B.	Momentum	q. N
C.	Force	r. kg-ms^{-1}
D.	Mass	s. N-s

Assertion–Reason

Direction (Q.Nos. 10-11) *In each of the following questions, a statement of Assertion is given by the corresponding statement of Reason. Of the statements, mark the correct answer as*

(a) If both Assertion and Reason are true and Reason is the correct explanation of Assertion.
(b) If both Assertion and Reason are true, but Reason is not the correct explanation of Assertion.
(c) If Assertion is true, but Reason is false.
(d) If Assertion is false, but Reason is true.

10 **Assertion** Rate of change of momentum of a body is equal to resultant force applied on the body.

Reason Change in momentum is equal to impulse.

11 **Assertion** Newton's third law of motion apply to a system where bodies do not actually touch each other.

Reason Action and reaction forces act on only first body.

Case Based Questions

Direction (Q.Nos. 12-15) *Answer the questions on the basis of your understanding of the following passage and related studied concepts.*

Make a pile of carrom coins. Now, hit the bottom coin hard with a striker. If you do it well, the lowest coin will move away but the rest of the pile will remain at the original position. The lowest coin moves because of the force exerted by the striker on it. However, the rest of the pile remains at its place due to inertia of rest. As the lowest coin moves very fast, any force exerted by it on the coins above it is for a very short time, which is not able to move the upper coins in the horizontal direction.

12 The lowest coin moves because of the force exerted by

(a) rest of pile (b) striker
(c) carrom (d) None of these

13 Rest of the pile remains at its place due to inertia of
(a) momentum (b) direction
(c) motion (d) rest

14 State the factor, which is responsible for not able to move the upper coin.

15 What will happen, when you hit the bottom coin hard with a striker?

Answers

1. (c) 2. (d) 3. (b) 4. (a) 5. kg-ms^{-1}
6. Lighter 7. True 8. False
9. (A) → (s), (B) → (r), (C) → (q), (D) → (p)
10. (b) 11. (c) 12. (b) 13. (d)

Very Short Answer Type Questions

16 Two similar vehicles are moving with the same velocity on the road such that one of them is loaded and the other one is empty. Which of the two vehicles will require larger force to stop it? Give reasons.

17 Name two effects a force can bring about other than moving or stopping a body.

18 State Newton's first law of motion. Why does a rolling football come to rest on its own?

19 A body P has mass $2m$ and velocity $5v$. Another body Q has mass $8m$ and velocity $1.25v$. Which of the P and Q has more momentum?

20 State two factors which determine the momentum of a body.

21 A body of mass 20 kg moves with an acceleration of 2 m/s^2. Calculate change in momentum.

Short Answer (SA) Type Questions

22 A bus starts from the stop and take 50 s to get the speed of 10 m/s. If the mass of the bus alongwith passengers is 10000 kg, then calculate the force applied by the engine of bus to push the bus at the speed of 10 m/s. [Ans. 2000 N]

23 State the action and reaction in the following.
(*i*) Moving rocket
(*ii*) Firing of a bullet from a gun
(*iii*) A person walking on the floor

Long Answer (LA) Type Questions

24 (*i*) State the law that provides the formula for measuring force and the law which provides the definition of force.
(*ii*) Velocity-time graph of a 50 g marble rolling on floor is given below. Find

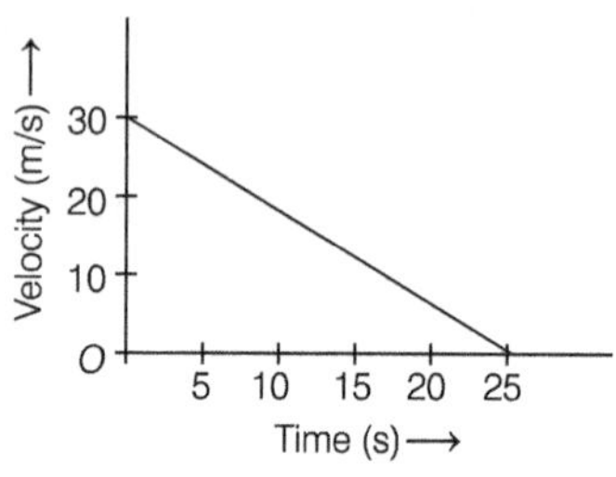

(a) time in which it stops.
(b) negative acceleration produced on it.
(c) positive force acting on the marble.
[Ans. (a) 25 s (b) –12 m/s^2 (c) 0.06 N]

25 (*i*) Explain, why is it difficult to walk on sand?
(*ii*) Why is the recoil of a heavy gun, on firing, not so strong as that of a light gun using the same cartridge?
(*iii*) A constant force acts on an object of 5 kg for a period of 2s. It increases the velocity of an object from 3 m/s to 7 m/s.
(a) Find the magnitude of the applied force.
(b) Now, if the force was applied for a period of 5s, then what would be the final velocity of the object?
[Ans. (a) 10 N (b) 13 m/s]

RELATED ONLINE VIDEOS

Visit https://www.youtube.com/watch?v=21xk6qnfvZc

OR Scan the Code

Challengers*

1 A force-time graph for a linear motion of a body is shown in the figure. The change in linear momentum between 0 and 7 s is

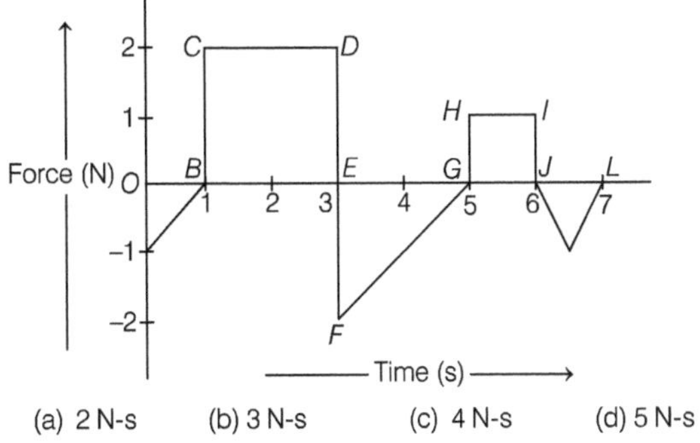

(a) 2 N-s (b) 3 N-s (c) 4 N-s (d) 5 N-s

2 A body of weight 2 kg is suspended as shown in figure.

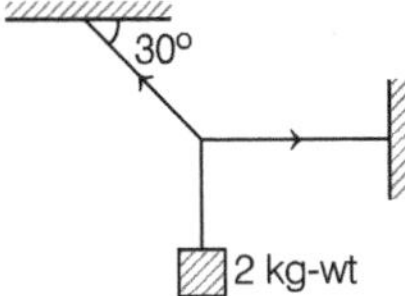

The tension T_1 in the horizontal string (in kg-wt) is

(a) $2/\sqrt{3}$ (b) $\sqrt{3}/2$ (c) $2\sqrt{3}$ (d) 2

3 The pulleys and strings shown in the figure are smooth and of negligible mass.

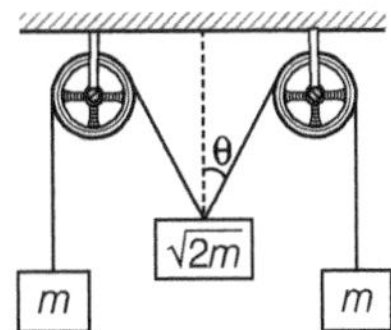

For the system to remain in equilibrium the angle θ should be

(a) 0° (b) 30° (c) 45° (d) 60°

4 A bullet of mass 10g moving with a velocity of 400 m/s gets embedded in a freely suspended wooden block of mass 900 g. What is the velocity acquired by the block?

(a) 4.4 m/s (b) 5.4 m/s (c) 6.4 m/s (d) 3.4 m/s

5 During a football match the ball shot towards the goal struck the defender's foot at the speed of 10 m/s and it bounces back at 20 m/s. If the time of impact was 0.2 s and mass of the ball is 0.5 kg will then the average force exerted by defender on the ball will be

(a) 65 N (b) 75 N (c) 70 N (d) 80 N

6 A mass of 100 g strikes the wall with speed 5 m/s an on angle as shown in figure and it rebounds with the some speed. If the contact time is 2×10^{-3}s, then force applied by the wall is

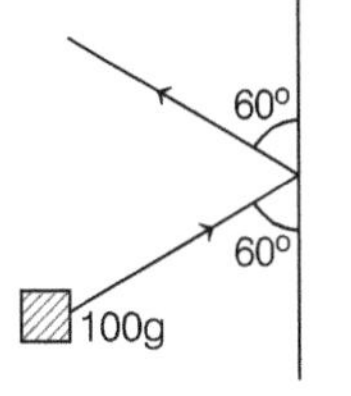

(a) $250\sqrt{3}$ N (b) $550\sqrt{3}$ N
(c) $650\sqrt{3}$ N (d) $200\sqrt{3}$ N

7 Two particles A and B of masses 20 g and 30 g, respectively are at rest at a certain time. Because of the forces exerted by them on each other, the particles start moving. At a given instant, particle A is found to move towards the East with a velocity of 6 cm/s. What is the velocity of particle B at this instant?

(a) 16 cm/s (b) 8 cm/s (c) 4 cm/s (d) 2 cm/s

8 A car is moving with uniform velocity on a rough horizontal road. Therefore, according to Newton's first law of motion.

(a) No force is being applied by its engine
(b) A force is surely being applied by its engine
(c) An acceleration is being produced in the car
(d) The kinetic energy of the car is increasing

9 A ship of mass 3×10^7 kg initially at rest is pulled by a force of 5×10^4 N through a distance of 3m. Assume that the resistance due to water is negligible, the speed of the ship is

(a) 1.5 m/s (b) 60 m/s
(c) 0.1 m/s (d) 5 m/s

Answer Key

1.	(a)	**2.**	(c)	**3.**	(c)	**4.**	(a)	**5.**	(b)
6.	(a)	**7.**	(c)	**8.**	(c)	**9.**	(c)		

*These questions may or may not be asked in the examination, have been given just for additional practice.

CHAPTER

09

Gravitation

It has been observed that an object dropped from a height falls towards the earth. Newton generalised this idea and said that not only the earth but every object in the universe attracts every other object. This force of attraction between two objects is called the **force of gravitation** or **gravitational force.** In this chapter, we shall learn about gravitation and universal law of gravitation.

Chapter Checklist

- Gravitation
- Kepler's Laws of Planetary Motion
- Free Fall
- Mass and Weight
- Thrust and Pressure
- Pressure in Fluids
- Density
- Archimedes' Principle

Gravitation

It is defined as the force of attraction between any two bodies in the universe. The earth attracts (or pulls) all objects lying on or near its surface towards its centre. The force with which the earth pulls the objects towards its centre is called the **gravitational force of the earth** or **gravity of the earth.**

Universal Law of Gravitation

It was given by *Isaac Newton. According to this law, the attractive force between any two bodies in the universe is directly proportional to the product of their masses and inversely proportional to the square of distance between them. The direction of the force is along the line joining the centres of two objects. Consider two bodies A and B having masses m_1 and m_2, whose centres are at a distance d from each other.

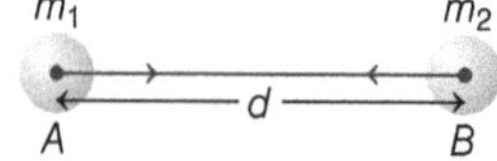

The gravitational force between two bodies is directed along the line joining their centres

Then, the force between two bodies is directly proportional to the product of their masses, i.e.

$$F \propto m_1 m_2 \quad \ldots\text{(i)}$$

* **Isaac Newton** was born in Woolsthorpe near Grantham, England in 1642. In 1665 he observed an apple falling on the ground which prompted Newton to explore the possibility of connecting gravity with the force that kept the moon in its orbit. This led him to the universal law of gravitation.

and the force between two bodies is inversely proportional to the square of the distance between them, i.e.

$$F \propto \frac{1}{d^2} \quad \ldots(ii)$$

Combining Eqs. (i) and (ii), we get

$$F \propto \frac{m_1 m_2}{d^2}$$

or

$$\boxed{F = G\frac{m_1 m_2}{d^2}}$$

where, $G = 6.67 \times 10^{-11} \text{N-m}^2/\text{kg}^2$ is called the **universal gravitational constant.**

Its value does not depend on the medium between the two bodies and the masses of the bodies or the distance between them. Suppose the masses of two bodies are 1 kg each and the distance d between them is 1 m, then

$$F = G \quad [\because m_1 = m_2 = 1 \text{ kg and } d = 1 \text{ m}]$$

Hence, the universal gravitational constant is defined as the gravitational force between two bodies of unit masses and separated by a unit distance from each other placed anywhere in space. The SI unit of G is $\textbf{N-m}^2\ \textbf{kg}^2$.The value of G was found out by Henry Cavendish (1731-1810) by using a sensitive balance.

Importance of Universal Law of Gravitation

The universal law of gravitation successfully explained several phenomena given as below:

(*i*) The force that binds us to the earth.

(*ii*) The motion of the moon around the earth.

(*iii*) The motion of planets around the sun.

(*iv*) The occurrence tides is due to the gravitational force of attraction of moon.

(*v*) The flow of water in rivers is also due to gravitational force of the earth on water.

Motion of Moon Around Earth and Centripetal Force

The force that keeps a body moving along the circular path is acting towards the centre is called **centripetal** (centre seeking) **force.** The motion of the moon around the earth is due to the centripetal force. The centripetal force is provided by the gravitational force of attraction of the earth. If there were no such force, then the moon would pursue a uniform straight line motion.

Example 1. *Find the gravitational force between earth and an object of 2 kg mass placed on its surface. (Given, mass of the earth = 6×10^{24} kg and radius of the earth = 6.4×10^6 m)*

Sol. Given, mass of the earth, $m_e = 6 \times 10^{24}$ kg

Mass of an object, $m_o = 2$ kg

Distance between earth and an object, i.e. radius of the earth, $R = 6.4 \times 10^6$m

Gravitational force, $F = ?$

$$\therefore \quad F = G\frac{m_e m_o}{R^2} \quad \text{[by universal law of gravitation]}$$

$$\therefore \quad F = \frac{6.67 \times 10^{-11} \times 6 \times 10^{24} \times 2}{(6.4 \times 10^6)^2} = 19.5 \text{ N}$$

Example 2. *The mass of the mars is 6.39×10^{23} kg and that of the jupiter is 1.89×10^{27} kg. If the distance between mars and jupiter is 749×10^5 m. Calculate the force exerted by the jupiter on the mars. (G = 6.7×10^{-11} Nm^2 kg^{-2})*

Sol. Given, the mass of the mars, $M_m = 6.39 \times 10^{23}$ kg

The mass of the jupiter, $M_j = 1.89 \times 10^{27}$ kg

The distance between the mars and jupiter,

$$d = 7.49 \times 10^5 \text{ m}$$

Gravitational constant, $G = 6.7 \times 10^{-11}$ Nm^2/kg^2

The force exerted by the jupiter on the mars,

$$F = G\frac{M_m \times M_j}{d^2}$$

$$= \frac{6.7 \times 10^{-11} \times 6.39 \times 10^{23} \times 1.89 \times 10^{27}}{(7.49 \times 10^5)^2}$$

$$= 1.44 \times 10^{29} \text{ N}$$

Thus, the force exerted by the jupiter on the mars is 1.44×10^{29} N.

Check Point 01

1 Why is Newton's law of gravitation called as universal law?

2 Fill in the blanks:
The numerical value of G is .... and its SI unit is ....

3 What is the force of gravity between the earth and mass of 20 kg placed on its surface? **[Ans.** 196 N]

4 Name the source of centripetal force that the moon requires to revolve around the earth.

5 If the distance between masses of two objects is increased by five times, by what factor would the mass of one of them have to be changed to maintain the same gravitational force? Would there be an increase or a decrease in the same? **[Ans.** 25 times, increase]

Kepler's Laws of Planetary Motion

Johannes Kepler proposed three laws of planetary motion in 16th century. The three laws are given as below:

Kepler's First Law

It states that the path of any planet in an orbit around the sun follows the shape of an ellipse with the sun at one of the foci.

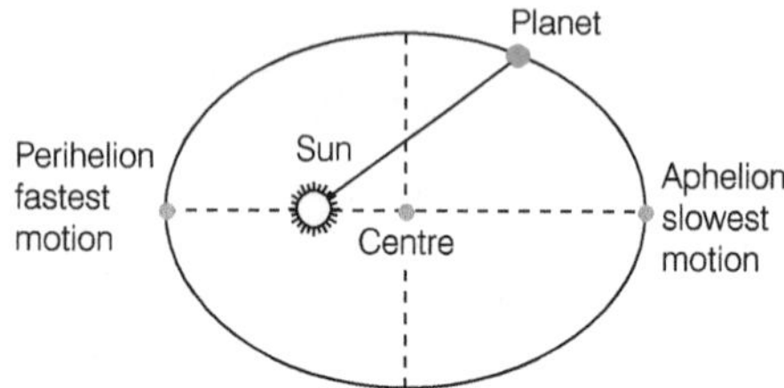

An ellipse showing Kepler's first law

The point in the orbit of a planet nearest to the sun is called **perihelion** and the point farthest from the sun is called **aphelion**.

Kepler's Second Law

It states that an imaginary line from the sun to the planet sweeps out equal areas in equal intervals of time.

Thus, if the time of travelling of a planet from A to B and from C to D is same, then the areas AOB and COD are equal.

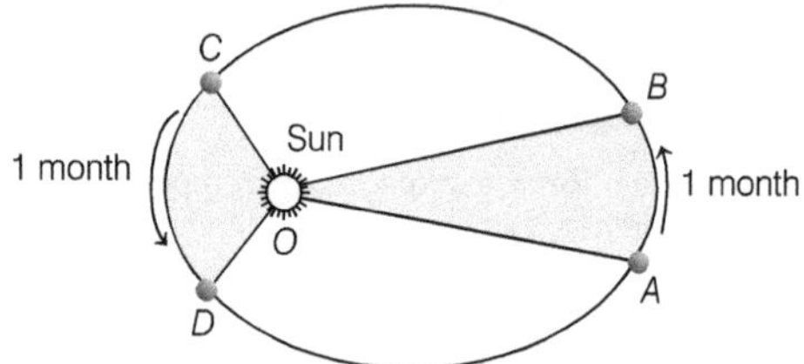

Areas showing Kepler's second law

Kepler's Third Law

It states that the cube of the mean distance of a planet from the sun is directly proportional to the square of its orbital period T. It is expressed as

$$r^3 \propto T^2, \quad r^3 = k \times T^2$$

$$\boxed{k = \frac{r^3}{T^2}}$$

where, T = time period of the planet (around the sun),

r = radius as mean distance of the planet from the sun

and k = Kepler constant.

Kepler could not give a theory to explain the motion of planets. Newton showed that the cause of the planetary motion is the gravitational force that the sun exerts on them.

Newton used Kepler's third law to calculate the gravitational force of attraction. Suppose the orbital velocity is v and the radius of the orbit is r. Then, the force acting on an orbiting planet is given by

$$F = \frac{mv^2}{r} \quad \ldots(i)$$

where, m is the mass of planet.

If T denotes the time period, then

$$T = \frac{2\pi r}{v} \quad \ldots(ii)$$

$$\Rightarrow \quad v = \frac{2\pi r}{T}$$

Substituting the value of v in Eq. (i), we get

$$F = \frac{m}{r}\left(\frac{2\pi r}{T}\right)^2 = 4\pi^2 m \frac{r}{T^2} \quad \ldots(iii)$$

But according to Kepler's third law of planetary motion,

$$r^3 = kT^2$$

$$\therefore \quad T^2 = \frac{r^3}{k}$$

Putting this value into Eq. (iii), we get

$$F = \frac{4\pi^2 m \cdot r}{\left(\frac{r^3}{k}\right)} = \frac{4\pi^2 km}{r^2}$$

Thus, gravitational force between the sun and the planet is inversely proportional to the square of the distance between their centres.

Free Fall

When objects fall towards the earth under the influence of earth's gravitational force alone, then these are called freely falling objects and such a motion is called **free fall.**

Acceleration due to Gravity (g)

Whenever an object falls towards the earth, an acceleration is involved. This acceleration is due to the earth's gravitational pull and is called **acceleration due to gravity.** It is denoted by g.

The SI unit of g is the same as that of acceleration, i.e. $\mathbf{m/s^2}$. Let mass of the earth be M and an object falling freely towards it be m. The distance between centres of the earth and the object is R.

From Newton's law of gravitation,

$$F = \frac{GMm}{R^2} \quad \ldots(i)$$

Also, from second law of motion, force exerted on an object,

$$F = ma$$

Since, $a = g$ (i.e. acceleration due to gravity)

$$F = mg \quad \ldots(ii)$$

Equating RHS of Eqs. (i) and (ii), we get

$$mg = \frac{GMm}{R^2} \quad or \quad \boxed{g = \frac{GM}{R^2}}$$

From the formula, it is clear that acceleration due to gravity does not depend on the mass of a falling object. It depends only on the mass of the earth or celestial bodies.

Note
- As distance of an object from the centre of the celestial body increases, the value of g decreases.
- Earth is flattened at poles. Thus, radius of the earth is less at poles than at equator. Hence, the value of g is less at equator than at poles.

Calculation of the Value of g

To calculate the value of g, we should put the values of G, M and R in above formula, i.e. $g = GM/R^2$.

$\because$ Mass of the earth, $M = 6 \times 10^{24}$ kg

Radius of the earth, $R = 6.4 \times 10^6$ m

Universal gravitational constant, $G = 6.67 \times 10^{-11}$ N-m^2/kg^2

$$g = \frac{GM}{R^2} = \frac{6.67 \times 10^{-11} \times 6 \times 10^{24}}{(6.4 \times 10^6)^2} = 9.8 \text{ m/s}^2$$

$$\boxed{g = 9.8 \text{ m/s}^2}$$

Equations of Motion for Free Fall

The three equations of motion which we have derived earlier is for bodies under uniform acceleration. In case of motion of bodies under free fall, there is a uniform acceleration, i.e. acceleration due to gravity (g) acting downward.

So, the previous three equations of motion can be applied for the motion of bodies under free fall as follows:

General equations of motion	Equations for body under free fall	
1. $v = u + at$	$v = u + gt$	$[\because a = g]$
2. $s = ut + \frac{1}{2}at^2$	$h = ut + \frac{1}{2}gt^2$	$[\because a = g]$
3. $v^2 = u^2 + 2as$	$v^2 = u^2 + 2gh$	$[\because a = g]$

where, h is the height from which the object falls, t is the time of fall, u is the initial velocity and v is the final velocity when the body accelerates at g.

In solving numerical problems, we should remember the following points:

(i) If an object falls vertically downwards, then acceleration due to gravity is taken as **positive,** since its velocity increases while falling.

(ii) If an object is thrown vertically upwards, then acceleration due to gravity is taken as **negative,** since its velocity decreases as it moves upward.

Example 3. *A car falls off a ledge and drops to the ground in 0.6 s. The value of g is 10 m/s^2 (for simplifying the calculation).*

(i) What is its speed on striking the ground?

(ii) What is its average speed during the 0.6 s?

(iii) How high is the ledge from the ground?

Sol. Given, initial velocity, $u = 0$,

Acceleration due to gravity, $g = 10$ m/s^2,

Time, $t = 0.6$ s

(i) Speed, $v = u + gt$

$$v = 0 + 10 \times 0.6$$
$$v = 6 \text{ m/s}$$

(ii) Average speed $= \frac{u+v}{2} = \left(\frac{0+6}{2}\right) = 3.0$ m/s

(iii) Distance travelled, $h = ut + \frac{1}{2}gt^2$

$$h = 0 + \frac{1}{2}gt^2$$
$$h = \frac{1}{2} \times 10 \times (0.6)^2$$
$$= 5 \times 0.36 = 1.80\text{m}$$

Example 4. *An object is thrown vertically upwards and rises to a height of 13.07 m.*

Calculate

(i) the velocity with which the object was thrown upwards.

(ii) the time taken by the object to reach the highest point.

Sol. Distance travelled, $h = 13.07$ m; Final velocity, $v = 0$

Acceleration due to gravity $g = -9.8$ m/s^2 (upward motion)

(i) $v^2 = u^2 + 2gh \Rightarrow 0 = u^2 + 2 \times (-9.8) \times 13.07$

$$u^2 = 256 \Rightarrow u = 16 \text{ m/s}$$

(ii) $v = u + at \Rightarrow 0 = 16 - 9.8 \times t \Rightarrow t = 1.63$ s

Example 5. *A ball is thrown vertically upwards with a velocity of 25 m/s. If g is 10 m/s^2, then calculate*

(i) height it reaches. *(ii) time taken to return back.*

Sol. Given, initial velocity, $u = 25$ m/s, final velocity, $v = 0$

If a body is thrown upwards, then its velocity becomes zero at the highest point, where it reaches, acceleration due to gravity, $g = -10$ m/s^2

(i) $\therefore$ Height, $h = \dfrac{v^2 - u^2}{2g} = \dfrac{0 - (25)^2}{2(-10)} = \dfrac{-625}{-20} = 31.25$ m

(ii) $\therefore$ Time, $t = \dfrac{v - u}{g} = \dfrac{0 - 25}{-10} = 2.5$ s

Time taken to return back,

T = Time of ascent + Time of descent $= 2t$

Time taken to return back, $T = 2 \times 2.5 = 5$ s

Check Point 02

1 State Kepler's first law of planetary motion.

2 What is the difference between perihelion and aphelion?

3 Fill in the blank:
The distance of a planet from the sun is 40 times that of the earth. The ratio of their time periods of revolution around the sun is ....

4 Suppose a planet exists whose mass and radius both are half that of the earth. The acceleration due to gravity on the surface of this planet will be double. Justify.

5 State True and False for the following statements:
(i) Acceleration due to gravity of the earth is less at equator than at poles.
(ii) If an object falls vertically downwards, then acceleration due to gravity is taken as negative. Since, its velocity increases while falling.

6 A body drops down a tower and reaches the ground in 0.6s. If $g = 10$ m/s^2, then find the height of the tower. **[Ans.** 1.8 m]

Mass

It is the total content of the body which measures the inertia of a body. It is a **scalar quantity** and its SI unit is **kilogram.** In other words, mass is the quantity of matter contained in a body.

Irrespective of the position of the body in the universe, mass always remains constant everywhere. The mass of the body cannot be zero.

Weight

The weight of an object is the force with which it is attracted towards the earth.

Weight of an object, $w = mg$

where, m = mass and g = acceleration due to gravity

or $$w = \frac{GMm}{R^2}$$

Here, M = mass of the earth and R = radius of the earth.

Important points regarding weight are as follow:

(i) Weight is a **vector quantity**, it acts in vertically downward direction and its SI unit is **newton** (N). Weight of 1 kg mass is 9.8 N. (i.e. 1 kg-wt = 9.8 N)

(ii) Weight of an object is not constant, it changes from place to place.

(iii) In the space, where $g = 0$, weight of an object is zero.

(iv) At the centre of the earth, weight becomes zero. This is due to the fact that on going down to the earth value of g decreases and at the centre of the earth, $g = 0$.

Note
- From the above formula, it is clear that weight of an object will change on a planet other than the earth.
- Spring balance is used to measure the weight of a body and pan balance is used to measure the mass of a body.

Weight of an Object on the Moon

Let the mass of an object be m and its weight on the moon be w_m. Suppose the mass of the moon is M_m and its radius be R_m. According to universal law of gravitation, the weight of an object on the moon will be

$$w_m = G\frac{M_m \times m}{R_m^2} \quad ...(i)$$

Let the weight of the same object on the earth be w_e. Let the mass of the earth be M_e and the radius of the earth be R_e.

$$\frac{w_m}{w_e} = \frac{\dfrac{GM_m m}{R_m^2}}{\dfrac{GM_e m}{R_e^2}} = \frac{M_m}{M_e} \times \frac{R_e^2}{R_m^2}$$

Now, $M_m = 5.98 \times 10^{24}$ kg; $M_e = 7.36 \times 10^{22}$ kg

$R_m = 1.74 \times 10^6$; $R_e = 6.37 \times 10^6$

$$\therefore \quad \frac{w_m}{w_e} = \frac{5.98 \times 10^{24}}{7.36 \times 10^{22}} \times \frac{(6.37 \times 10^6)^2}{(1.74 \times 10^6)^2} \approx \frac{1}{6}$$

Thus, the weight of an object on the moon is one-sixth of its weight on the earth.

Example 6. *Mass of an object is 12 kg. Calculate*
(i) *its weight on the earth.*
(ii) *its weight on the moon.*

Sol. Given, mass of an object, $m = 12$ kg

(i) Acceleration due to gravity on earth, $g_e = 9.8 \text{ m/s}^2$

Weight on the earth, $w_e = mg_e = 12 \times 9.8 = 117.6$ N

(ii) Acceleration due to gravity on moon, $g_m = \dfrac{g_e}{6}$

$$g_m = \frac{9.8}{6} \text{ m/s}^2$$

Weight on the moon, $w_m = mg_m = 12 \times \dfrac{9.8}{6} = 9.8 \times 2 = 19.6$ N

Example 7. *A man weighs 600 N on the earth. What is his mass, if g is 10 m/s²? On the moon, his weight would be 100 N. What is the acceleration due to gravity on the moon?*

Sol. Given, weight of man on the earth, $w_e = 600$ N

Acceleration due to gravity on the earth, $g_e = 10 \text{ m/s}^2$

Weight of man on the moon, $w_m = 100$ N

Acceleration due to gravity on the moon, $g_m = ?$

As we know, mass of the man, $m = \dfrac{w_e}{g_e} = \dfrac{600}{10} = 60$ kg

$$\Rightarrow \quad g_e = \frac{w_e}{m}$$

Similarly, for the moon, $g_m = \dfrac{w_m}{m}$

$$g_m = \frac{100}{60} = 1.66 \text{ m/s}^2$$

Thus, acceleration due to gravity on the moon is 1.66 m/s^2, i.e. $g_m = \dfrac{g_e}{6}$.

Example 8. *A particle weighs 120 N on the surface of the earth. At what height above the earth's surface will its weight be 30 N? Radius of the earth = 6400 km.*

Sol. Given, weight of particle on the surface of earth, $w = 120$ N

Weight of particle at height h above the earth's surface,

$$w_1 = 30 \text{ N}$$

The weight of a particle on the surface of the earth is

$$w = mg = \frac{mMG}{R^2} \qquad \left[\because g = \frac{GM}{R^2}\right]$$

Let w_1 be the weight of a particle at height h above the earth's surface.

So,
$$\frac{w}{w_1} = \frac{G\dfrac{M}{R^2}}{G\dfrac{M}{(R+h)^2}} = \frac{(R+h)^2}{R^2}$$

Substituting given values, we get

$$\Rightarrow \quad \frac{120}{30} = \left(\frac{R+h}{R}\right)^2 \Rightarrow 4 = \left(\frac{R+h}{R}\right)^2 \Rightarrow 2 = \frac{R+h}{R}$$

$$\Rightarrow \quad 2R = R + h \Rightarrow R = h$$

∴ Height of the particle, h = Radius of the earth,

$$h = 6400 \text{ km}.$$

Check Point 03

1 Fill in the blank:
A body of mass 10 kg is taken to the centre of the earth. Its mass there will be ....

2 How is weight related to mass? Is weight of a body constant?

3 What will the weight of an object of mass 175 kg at the centre of the earth? [**Ans.** Zero]

4 Mitali weighs 750 N on the earth. On the planet mars, the force of gravity is 38% of that of the earth. How much will Mitali weight on the mars? [**Ans.** 285 N]

5 Weight of a girl on the earth's surface is 66 N. Find out her weight on the moon. [**Ans.** 11 N]

Thrust and Pressure

Thrust is the force acting on an object perpendicular to its surface. The effect of thrust depends on the area on which it acts.

The unit of thrust is the same as that of force, i.e. the SI unit of thrust is **newton** (N). It is a **vector quantity.**

Pressure is the force acting perpendicularly on a unit area of an object.

$$\text{Pressure } (p) = \frac{\text{Force}(F)}{\text{Area }(A)} = \frac{\text{Thrust}}{\text{Area}}$$

The SI unit of pressure is **Nm^{-2}**, which is also called **pascal** (Pa) named after the scientist **Blaise Pascal.** It is a **scalar quantity.**

$$1 \text{ Pa} = 1 \text{ Nm}^{-2}$$

From the formula of pressure, it is clear that the same force can produce different pressures depending on the area over which it acts. A force acting on a smaller area exerts a large pressure while the same force acting on a larger area exerts small pressure.

Example 9. *Force of 200 N is applied to an object of area 4 m². Find the pressure.*

Sol. Given, force, $F = 200$ N, area, $A = 4 \text{ m}^2$

Now, Pressure, $p = \dfrac{\text{Force}(F)}{\text{Area}(A)} = \dfrac{200}{4} = 50 \text{ Nm}^{-2}$

Example 10. *A woman is wearing sharp-heeled sandal (stilettos). If the mass of woman is 60 kg and the area of one heel is 1 cm^2, find out the pressure exerted on the ground, when the woman stands on just one heel. (Given, $g = 10 \text{ ms}^{-2}$)*

Sol. In the given case, the force will be the weight of woman which is given by $m \times g$ [where, m is the mass of woman and g is the acceleration due to gravity].

$\therefore$ Force, $F = m \times g$ [weight of woman]

$= 60 \times 10 \text{ N}$ [given, mass of woman, $m = 60$ kg]

$= 600 \text{ N}$

and area, $A = 1 \text{ cm}^2 = \dfrac{1}{10000} \text{m}^2$

$$\therefore \text{ Pressure, } p = \frac{\text{Force }(F)}{\text{Area }(A)} = \frac{600 \times 10000}{1}$$

$= 6000000 \text{ Nm}^{-2}$ (or 6000000 Pa)

Thus, the pressure exerted by the woman (of 60 kg) standing on only one heel of area 1 cm^2 is 6000000 Nm^{-2}.

Example 11. *A block of wood is kept on a table top. The mass of wooden block is 6 kg and its dimensions are $50 \text{ cm} \times 30 \text{ cm} \times 20 \text{ cm}$.*

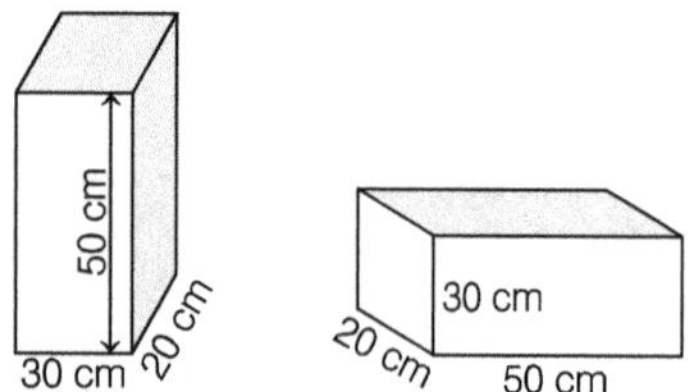

Find the pressure exerted by the wooden block on the table top, if it is made to lie on the table top with its sides of dimensions

(i) $30 \text{ cm} \times 20 \text{ cm}$

(ii) $50 \text{ cm} \times 30 \text{ cm}$

Sol. Given, the mass of the wooden block = 6 kg

The dimensions $= 50 \text{ cm} \times 30 \text{ cm} \times 20 \text{ cm}$

Thrust, $F = mg = 6 \times 9.8 = 58.8 \text{ N}$

(i) Area of a side = Length $\times$ Breadth

Area, $A = 30 \times 20 = 600 \text{ cm}^2 = 0.06 \text{ m}^2$

$$\text{Pressure, } p_1 = \frac{F}{A} = \frac{58.8}{0.06}$$

$= 980 \text{ N/m}^2$

(ii) When the block lies on its side of dimensions $50 \text{ cm} \times 30 \text{ cm}$, it exerts the same thrust

Area = Length $\times$ Breadth

$A = 50 \times 30 = 1500 \text{ cm}^2 = 0.15 \text{ m}^2$

$$\text{Pressure, } p_2 = \frac{F}{A} = \frac{58.8}{0.15} = 392 \text{ N/m}^2$$

Some Daily Life Applications of Pressure

- The handles of bags, suitcases, etc. are made broad, so that less pressure is exerted on the hand.
- Buildings are provided with broad foundations, so that the pressure exerted on the ground becomes less.
- Railway tracks are laid on cement or iron sleepers, so that the pressure exerted by train could spread over the larger area and thus pressure decreases.
- Pins, needles and nails are provided with sharp pointed ends to reduce the area and hence to increase the pressure.
- Cutting tools have sharp edges to reduce the area, so that with lesser force, more pressure could exerted.
- Pressure on ground is more when a man is walking than when he is standing because in case of walking, the effective area is less.
- Depression is much more when a man stands on the cushion than when he lies down on it because in standing case, area is lesser than in case of lying.
- The tractors have broad tyres, to create less pressure on the ground, so that tyres do not sink into comparatively soft ground in the field.

Pressure in Fluids

All liquids and gases are together called **fluids.** Water and air are two most common fluids. Solids exert pressure on a surface due to their weight. Fluids also have weight, therefore fluids also exert pressure on the base and walls of the container in which they are enclosed. Fluids exert pressure in all directions.

Buoyancy

The tendency of a liquid to exert an upward force on an object immersed in it is called **buoyancy.** Gases also exhibit this property of buoyancy.

Buoyant Force is an upward force which acts on an object when it is immersed in a liquid. It is also called **upthrust.**

It is the buoyant force due to which a heavy object seems to be lighter in water. As we lower an object into a liquid, the liquid underneath it, provides an upward force.

e.g. A piece of cork is held below the surface of water. When we apply a force by our thumb, the cork immediately rises to the surface. This is due to the fact that every liquid exerts an upward force on the objects immersed in it.

Note
- An object seems lighter when immersed in liquid. This reduced weight of an object in liquid is called apparent weight of an object.
- The pressure exerted by a liquid increases with depth and acts in all directions.

Factors Affecting Buoyant Force

The magnitude of buoyant force depends on the following factors:

(i) Density of the Fluid

The liquid having higher density exerts more upward buoyant force on an object than another liquid of lower density. This is the reason why it is easier to swim in sea water in comparison to normal water. The sea water has higher density and hence exerts a greater buoyant force on the swimmer than the fresh water having lower density.

(ii) Volume of Object Immersed in the Liquid

As the volume of solid object immersed inside the liquid increases, the upward buoyant force also increases. The magnitude of buoyant force acting on a solid object does not depend on the nature of the solid object. It depends only on its volume.

e.g. When two balls made of different metals having different weights but equal volume are fully immersed in a liquid, they will experience an equal upward buoyant force as both the balls displace equal amount of the liquid due to their equal volumes.

Floating or Sinking of Objects in Liquid

When an object is immersed in a liquid, then following two forces act on it:

- **Weight** of the object which acts in **downward direction**, i.e. it tends to pull down the object.
- **Buoyant force** (upthrust) which acts in **upward direction**, i.e. it tends to push up the object.

Upthrust

Weight

Whether an object will float or sink in a liquid, depends on the relative magnitudes of these two forces which act on the object in opposite directions. There are three conditions of floating and sinking of objects. These are:

(*i*) If the buoyant force or upthrust exerted by the liquid is less than the weight of the object, the **object will sink** in the liquid.

(*ii*) If the buoyant force is equal to the weight of the object, the **object will float** in the liquid.

(*iii*) If the buoyant force is more than the weight of the object, the **object will rise** in the liquid and then float.

Check Point 04

1. Fill in the blank:
   The relation between thrust and pressure is ....
2. What is pascal?
3. Why are buildings provided with broad foundation?
4. A heavy object seems lighter in water. Which force is responsible for this?
5. Name the forces acting on an object while immersed in a liquid.

Density

The density of a substance is defined as mass per unit volume.

$$\text{Density} = \frac{\text{Mass of the substance}}{\text{Volume of the substance}} \text{ or } \rho = \frac{m}{V}$$

The SI unit of density is **kilogram per metre cube** (kg/m^3). It is a **scalar quantity**. The density of a substance under specified conditions always remains same. Hence, the density of a substance is one of its characteristic properties. It can help us to determine its purity. It is different for different substances. The lightness and the heaviness of different substances can be described by using the word density.

Objects having less density than that of a liquid, objects will float on the liquid. Objects having greater density than that of liquid, objects will sink in the liquid. It decreases with increase in temperature.

Note The object having density equal to that of liquid will float on the liquid in such a way that it is totally submerged in the liquid and no part of it remains above the surface of the liquid.

Example 12. *A sealed can of mass* 700 g *has a volume of* 500 cm^3. *Will this can sink in water? (Density of water is* 1 g cm^{-3})

Sol. Given, mass of can, $m = 700$ g

Volume of can, $V = 500 \text{ cm}^3$

$$\therefore \quad \text{Density of can, } \rho = \frac{m}{V} = \frac{700}{500} = 1.4 \text{ g cm}^{-3}$$

Since, density of the can is greater than the density of water, so the can will sink in water.

Archimedes' Principle

It states that, "When an object is fully or partially immersed in a liquid, it experiences a buoyant force or upthrust, which is equal to the weight of liquid displaced by the object", i.e.

Buoyant force or upthrust acting on an object
= Weight of liquid displaced by the object

Note According to this principle, "An object will float in a liquid, if the weight of object is equal to the weight of liquid displaced by it". This is called law of floatation.

Even gases like air, exert an upward force or buoyant force on the objects placed in them. It is buoyant force or upthrust due to displaced air which makes a balloon rise in air.

Applications of Archimedes' Principle

Archimedes' principle is used in:

- designing ships and submarines.
- lactometer (a device used to determine the purity of milk).
- hydrometer (a device used for determining the density of liquid).

How does a Boat Float in Water?

A boat floats in water due to upward force called buoyant force (or upthrust) which is caused by the pressure of water pushing up the bottom of the boat. When boat is gradually lowered into water, it displaces more and more water. Hence, buoyant force on it also increases. When this buoyant force becomes just enough to support the weight of boat, the boat stops sinking down in water. Now, according to Archimedes' principle, "Buoyant force is equal to the weight of liquid displaced by the boat." Hence, during the floating of the boat, the weight of water displaced by the submerged part of the boat is equal to the weight of the boat.

Example 13. *If an iron object is immersed in water, it displaces 8 kg of water. How much is the buoyant force acting on the iron object in newton? (Given, $g = 10\ \text{ms}^{-2}$)*

Sol. According to Archimedes' principle, "The buoyant force acting on this iron object will be equal to the weight of water displaced by this iron object."

We know that, weight,

$$w = m \times g \quad \ldots(i)$$

Given, mass of water,

$$m = 8\ \text{kg}$$

Acceleration due to gravity,

$$g = 10\ \text{ms}^{-2}$$

On putting values in Eq. (i), we get

$$w = 8 \times 10 = 80\ \text{N}$$

Since, the weight of water displaced by the iron object is 80 N, therefore the buoyant force acting on the iron object (due to water) will also be 80 N.

Check Point 05

1 What is the difference between the density and relative density of a substance?
2 Give the reason for the rising of balloons in air.
3 Write any two applications of Archimedes' principle.
4 State True and False for the following statement: Relative density has no units.

To Study NCERT Activities
Visit https://goo.gl/FEVngx
OR Scan the Code

NCERT FOLDER

INTEXT QUESTIONS

1 State the universal law of gravitation. **Pg 134**

Sol. The universal law of gravitation states that, "The force of attraction between any two objects is directly proportional to the product of their masses and inversely proportional to the square of the distance between them". This law is applicable on any two objects anywhere in the universe.

2 Write the formula for magnitude of gravitational force between the earth and an object on the surface of the earth. **Pg 134**

Sol. The formula for magnitude of gravitational force between the earth and an object on the surface of the earth is given by $F = G\dfrac{Mm}{R^2}$

where, M = mass of the earth,
m = mass of an object,
G = gravitational constant
$= 6.67\times10^{-11}\ \text{N-m}^2/\text{kg}^2$

and R = distance between centres of the earth and an object.

3 What do you mean by free fall? **Pg 136**

Sol. The falling of a body from a height towards the earth under the gravitational force of the earth is called free fall. Hence, the motion of a particle falling down or going up under the action of gravity means the body is under free fall.

4 What do you mean by acceleration due to gravity? **Pg 136**

Sol. Acceleration of a body during free fall towards a celestial body is called acceleration due to gravity. Its value is $9.8\ \text{m/s}^2$.

For objects on or near the surface of the earth,

$$mg = G\frac{M\times m}{R^2}$$

where, g = acceleration due to gravity,
M = mass of the earth,
m = mass of an object
and R = radius of the earth.

Hence, $g = \dfrac{GM}{R^2}$.

5 What are the difference between the mass of an object and its weight? **Pg 138**

Sol. Difference between the mass of an object and its weight are as below:

Mass	Weight
Quantity of matter contained in an object.	Force with which an object is attracted towards centre of the earth due to gravity.
Constant everywhere.	Changes from place to place.
It is a scalar quantity.	It is a vector quantity.
Its SI unit is kg.	Its SI unit is N.
Mass is never zero.	Weight is zero at the centre of the earth or free space.

6 Why is the weight of an object on the moon (1/6)th its weight on the earth? **Pg 138**

Sol. Weight of an object, $w = mg$

where, m = mass of an object and g = acceleration due to gravity.

The mass of an object m remains constant at all the places. Acceleration due to gravity changes from place to place. So, we can say that the weight of an object depends on the acceleration due to gravity.

On the moon, the acceleration due to gravity is (1/6)th that of the earth, this is the reason why the weight of an object on the moon is (1/6)th its weight on the earth.

7 Why is it difficult to hold a school bag having a strap made of thin and strong string? **Pg 141**

Sol. It is difficult to hold a school bag having a strap made of a thin and strong string because the area under the strap is small. Hence, large pressure is exerted by the strap on the fingers or shoulders. Due to the large pressure, the strap tends to cut the skin and hence pain is caused.

8 What do you mean by buoyancy? **Pg 141**

Sol. The upward force exerted by a liquid on any object immersed in liquid is called buoyancy or upthrust.

9 Why does an object float or sink when placed on the surface of water? **Pg 141**

Sol. When an object is placed on the surface of water, two forces act on the object.

(*i*) The weight of the object, acting vertically downwards.

(*ii*) The upthrust of the water, acting vertically upwards.

The object will float on the surface of water, if the upthrust is greater than the weight of the object. The object will sink, if the weight of the object is more than the upthrust of the water.

10 You find your mass to be 42 kg on a weighing machine. Is your mass more or less than 42 kg? **Pg 142**

Sol. Mass is more than 42 kg. As the buoyant force due to air is acting on us, the reading of weighing machine will be less than the actual mass of a person.

11 You have a bag of cotton and an iron bar, each indicating a mass of 100 kg when measured on a weighing machine. In reality, one is heavier than other. Can you say which one is heavier and why? **Pg 142**

Sol. Cotton bag is heavier as the buoyant force acting on the cotton bag is more as its surface area is more than that of the iron-piece.

EXERCISES
(On Pages 143 and 144)

1 How does the force of gravitation between two objects change when distance between them is reduced to half?

Sol. Force of gravitation between two objects is given by

$$F = G\frac{m_1 m_2}{r^2}$$

If distance is reduced to half, i.e. $r' = r/2$.
Then, new force of gravitation,

$$F' = \frac{Gm_1 m_2}{r'^2} = \frac{Gm_1 m_2}{(r/2)^2} = 4 \times \frac{Gm_1 m_2}{r^2} = 4F$$

i.e. The force of gravitation becomes 4 times of the original value.

2 Gravitational force acts on all objects in proportion to their masses. Why, a heavy object does not fall faster than a light object?

Sol. Acceleration due to gravity (g) is independent of mass of the falling object and is equal for all objects at a point. So, a heavy object falls with same acceleration as light object.

3 What is the magnitude of the gravitational force between the earth and a 1 kg object on its surface? (Take, mass of the earth is 6×10^{24} kg and radius of the earth is 6.4×10^6 m.)

Sol. Gravitational force between the earth and an object is given by $F = \frac{GMm}{R^2}$.

where, G = gravitational constant $= 6.67 \times 10^{-11}\text{N-m}^2/\text{kg}^2$,

M = mass of the earth $= 6 \times 10^{24}$ kg,

R = radius of the earth $= 6.4 \times 10^6$ m

and m = mass of an object $= 1$ kg

$$\therefore \quad F = \frac{6.67 \times 10^{-11} \times 6 \times 10^{24} \times 1}{(6.4 \times 10^6)^2}$$

$$= 9.77 \approx 9.8 \text{ N}$$

Thus, magnitude of gravitational force between the earth and 1 kg object is 9.8 N.

4 The earth and the moon are attracted to each other by gravitational force. Does the earth attract the moon with a force that is greater than or smaller than or equal to the force with which the moon attracts the earth? Why?

Sol. When two objects attract each other, then gravitational force of attraction applied by first object on the second object is same as the force applied by the second object on the first object. So, both earth and moon attract each other by the same gravitational force of attraction.

5 If the moon attracts the earth, then why does the earth not move towards the moon?

Sol. The earth does not move towards the moon inspite of the attraction by the moon because the mass of earth is much greater than mass of moon and for a given force, acceleration is inversely proportional to mass of the object.

6 What happens to the force between two objects, if

(*i*) the mass of one object is doubled?
(*ii*) the distance between the objects is doubled and tripled?
(*iii*) the masses of both objects are doubled?

Sol. Force of attraction between two objects is given by

$$F = \frac{Gm_1 m_2}{r^2} \quad \ldots\text{(i)}$$

where, m_1 and m_2 = masses of the objects,
r = distance between the objects
and G = gravitational constant.

(*i*) If mass of one object is doubled ($m_1 = 2m_1$), then the new force,

$$F' = \frac{G(2m_1)\, m_2}{r^2} = 2 \times \frac{Gm_1 m_2}{r^2} = 2F$$

i.e. Force becomes double.

(*ii*) If the distance between the objects is doubled $(r)^2 = (2r)^2$, then the new force,

$$F' = \frac{Gm_1 m_2}{(2r)^2} = \frac{Gm_1 m_2}{4r^2} = \frac{1}{4} \cdot \frac{Gm_1 m_2}{r^2} = \frac{F}{4}$$

[substituting Eq. (i)]

i.e. Force becomes one-fourth. If the distance between the objects is tripled, then new force,

$$F' = \frac{Gm_1 m_2}{(3r)^2} = \frac{Gm_1 m_2}{9r^2} = \frac{1}{9}\left(\frac{Gm_1 m_2}{r^2}\right) = \frac{F}{9}$$

[from Eq. (i)]

i.e. Force becomes one-ninth.

(*iii*) If masses of both objects are doubled, then new force,

$$F' = \frac{G(2m_1)(2m_2)}{r^2} = 4 \times \frac{Gm_1 m_2}{r^2} = 4F$$

[from Eq. (i)]

i.e. Force becomes four times.

7 **Calculate the force of gravitation between the earth and the sun, given that the mass of the earth = 6×10^{24} kg and of the sun = 2×10^{30} kg. The average distance between the two is 1.5×10^{11} m.**

Sol. The force of gravitation between the earth and the sun is given by $F = \frac{GM_s M_e}{r^2}$

where, $G = 6.67 \times 10^{-11}$ N-m^2/kg^2

Mass of the sun, $M_s = 2 \times 10^{30}$ kg

Mass of the earth, $M_e = 6 \times 10^{24}$ kg

Average distance between the earth and the sun,

$r = 1.5 \times 10^{11}$ m

$$F = \frac{6.67 \times 10^{-11} \times 2 \times 10^{30} \times 6 \times 10^{24}}{(1.5 \times 10^{11})^2} = 3.6 \times 10^{22} \text{ N}$$

Thus, the force between earth and sun is 3.6×10^{22}N.

8 **What is the importance of universal law of gravitation?**

Sol. The universal law of gravitation successfully explained several phenomena given as below:

(*i*) The force that binds us to the earth.

(*ii*) The motion of the moon around the earth.

(*iii*) The motion of planets around the sun.

(*iv*) The tides due to the moon and the sun.

(*v*) The flow of water in rivers is also due to gravitational force of the earth on water.

9 **What is the acceleration of free fall?**

Sol. The acceleration of free fall is the acceleration produced in the motion of an object when it falls freely towards the earth. It is also called acceleration due to gravity. Its value on the earth surface is 9.8 m/s^2.

10 **What do we call gravitational force between the earth and an object?**

Sol. The gravitational force between the earth and an object is called force of gravity or gravity.

11 **Amit buys few grams of gold at the poles as per the instruction of one of his friends. He hands over the same when he meets him at the equator. Will the friend agree with the weight of gold bought? If not, why?**

[Hint The value of g is greater at the poles than at equator.]

Sol. No, his friend will not agree with the weight of gold.

$$w = mg \quad \text{...(i)}$$

$$w = \frac{GMm}{R^2} \quad \text{...(ii)}$$

From Eqs. (i) and (ii), we get

$$mg = \frac{GMm}{R^2}$$

$$g \propto \frac{1}{(\text{Distance of an object from centre of the earth})^2}$$

or $g \propto \frac{1}{R^2}$

The value of g is greater at poles than at the equator. Therefore, gold at equator weighs less than that at poles. Thus, Amit's friend will not agree with the weight of the gold bought.

12 **Why does a sheet of paper fall slower than one that is crumpled into a ball?**

Sol. The sheet of paper falls slower than one that is crumpled into a ball because in first case, the area of the sheet is more, so it experiences large opposing force due to air. While the sheet crumpled into a ball experience less opposing force due to small area. This opposing force arises due to air resistance or air friction.

13 **Gravitational force on the surface of the moon is only (1/6)th as strong as gravitational force on the earth. What is the weight in Newton of a 10 kg object on the moon and on the earth?**

Sol. Given, mass of the object, $m = 10$ kg

Weight on the earth, $w = mg = 10 \times 9.8 = 98$ N

Weight on the moon $= \frac{1}{6}$ of the weight on the earth

$$= \frac{1}{6} \times 98 = 16.33 \text{ N}$$

14 **A ball is thrown vertically upwards with a velocity of 49 m/s. Calculate**

(*i*) the maximum height to which it rises.

(*ii*) the total time it takes to return to the surface of the earth.

Sol. Given, initial velocity, $u = 49$ m/s

(*i*) At the maximum height velocity becomes zero.

∴ Final velocity, $v = 0$

From the third equation of upward motion,

$$v^2 = u^2 - 2gh$$

$$0 = (49)^2 - 2 \times 9.8 \times h$$

$$\therefore \quad h = \frac{(49)^2}{2 \times 9.8} = 122.5 \text{ m}$$

Maximum height attained = 122.5 m

(ii) Time taken by the ball to reach the maximum height.

From the first equation of motion, $v = u - gt$

or $\quad 0 = 49 - 9.8 \times t$

$$t = \frac{49}{9.8} = 5 \text{ s}$$

For the motion against gravity, the time of descent is same as the time of ascent. So, time taken by the ball to fall from maximum height is 5 s.

$\therefore$ Total time taken by the ball to return to surface of the earth $= 5 + 5 = 10$ s.

15 **A stone is released from the top of a tower of height 19.6 m. Calculate its final velocity just before touching the ground.**

Sol. Given, height, $h = 19.6$ m

Initial velocity, $u = 0$ [$\because$ it starts from rest]

From the third equation of motion, $v^2 = u^2 + 2gh$

$$v^2 = 0 + 2 \times 9.8 \times 19.6 = 19.6 \times 19.6$$

$$\therefore \quad v = \sqrt{19.6 \times 19.6} = 19.6 \text{ m/s}$$

Final velocity of stone just before touching the ground is 19.6 m/s.

16 **A stone is thrown vertically upward with an initial velocity of 40 m/s. Taking $g = 10 \text{ m/s}^2$, find the maximum height reached by the stone. What is the net displacement and the total distance covered by the stone?**

Sol. Given, initial velocity, $u = 40$ m/s

Final velocity becomes zero, i.e. $v = 0$ [at maximum height]

From third equation of upward motion,

$$v^2 = u^2 - 2gh$$

$$(0)^2 = (40)^2 - 2 \times 10 \times h$$

$$0 = 1600 - 20h$$

$$\Rightarrow \quad h = \frac{1600}{20} = 80 \text{ m}$$

$\therefore$ Maximum height reached by the stone = 80 m.

After reaching the maximum height, the stone will fall towards the earth and will reach the earth's surface covering the same distance.

So, distance covered by the stone $= 80 + 80 = 160$ m.

Displacement of the stone = 0.

Because the stone starts from the earth's surface and finally reaches the earth's surface again, i.e. the initial and final positions of the stone are same.

17 **A stone is allowed to fall from the top of a tower 100 m high and at the same time, another stone is projected vertically upwards from the ground with a velocity of 25 m/s. Calculate when and where the two stones will meet.**

Sol. Let after time t both stones meet and s be the distance travelled by the stone dropped from the top of tower at which the stones will meet.

Distance travelled by the stone dropped = s

$\therefore$ Distance travelled by the stone projected upwards $= (100 - s)$ m

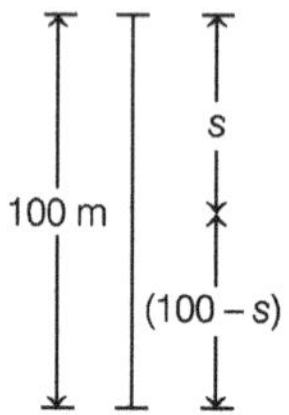

For the stone dropped from the tower,

$$s = ut + \frac{1}{2}gt^2 = 0 + \frac{1}{2}(10)t^2$$

[$u = 0$ because stone is dropped, i.e. it starts from rest]

$$s = 5t^2 \quad \text{...(i)}$$

For the stone projected upwards, $s' = ut - \frac{1}{2}gt^2$

[due to upward motion, negative sign is taken]

$$(100 - s) = 25t - \frac{1}{2} \times 10t^2$$

$$\Rightarrow \quad 100 - s = 25t - 5t^2$$

Substituting value of s from Eq. (i), we get

$$100 - 5t^2 = 25t - 5t^2$$

$$25t = 100$$

$$\Rightarrow \quad t = 4 \text{ s}$$

So, the stones will meet after 4 s.

$$s = 5t^2 = 5 \times (4)^2 = 80 \text{ m}$$

So, the stones will be at a distance of 80 m from the top of tower or 20 m (100 m – 80 m) from the base of the tower.

18 **A ball thrown up vertically returns to the thrower after 6 s, find**

(i) the velocity with which it was thrown up,

(ii) the maximum height it reach

(iii) and its position after 4 s.

Sol. Total time taken = 6 s

$\therefore$ Time taken to reach the maximum height $= \frac{6}{2} = 3$ s

[$\because$ time of ascent = time of descent]

(i) From the first equation of motion, $v = u - gt$

[negative sign is taken due to upward motion]

$$0 = u - 9.8 \times 3$$

[$\because$ at maximum height, $v = 0$]

$\Rightarrow \quad u = 29.4\ \text{m/s}$

(ii) From the third equation of motion,

$$v^2 = u^2 - 2gh$$

[negative sign is taken due to upward motion]

$$0 = (29.4)^2 - 2 \times 9.8 \times h$$

$$\Rightarrow \quad h = \frac{(29.4)^2}{2 \times 9.8} = 44.1\ \text{m}$$

Maximum height attained by the ball is 44.1 m.

(iii) In initial 3 s, the ball will rise, then in next 3 s it falls toward the earth.

$\therefore$ The position after 4 s

= Distance covered in 1s in the downward motion

From the second equation of motion,

$$h = ut + \frac{1}{2}gt^2 = 0 + \frac{1}{2} \times 9.8 \times (1)^2 = 4.9\ \text{m}$$

i.e. The ball will be at 4.9 m below from the top of the tower or the height of ball from the ground will be at $(44.1 - 4.9) = 39.2$

19 **In what direction, does the buoyant force on an object immersed in a liquid act?**

Sol. The buoyant force on an object immersed in a liquid always acts in the vertically upward direction.

20 **Why does a block of plastic released under water, come up to the surface of water?**

Sol. The upthrust or buoyant force acting on the block of plastic by the water is greater than the weight of the plastic block. So, plastic block comes up to the surface of water.

21 **The volume of 50 g of a substance is 20 cm ^{3}. If the density of water is 1 g cm $^{-3}$, will the substance float or sink?**

Sol. Given, mass of substance, $m = 50$ g

Volume of substance, $V = 20\ \text{cm}^3$

$\therefore$ Density of substance,

$$\rho = \frac{\text{Mass}}{\text{Volume}} = \frac{50}{20} = 2.5\ \text{g cm}^{-3}$$

i.e. The density of the substance is greater than the density of water, so it will sink in water.

22 **The volume of a 500 g sealed packet is 350 cm ^{3}. Will the packet float or sink in water, if the density of water is 1 g cm $^{-3}$? What will be the mass of the water displaced by this packet?**

Sol. Given, mass of packet, $m = 500$ g

Volume of packet, $V = 350\ \text{cm}^3$

$\therefore$ Density of packet, $\rho = \frac{\text{Mass}}{\text{Volume}}$

$$= \frac{500\ \text{g}}{350\ \text{cm}^3}$$

$$= 1.43\ \text{g cm}^{-3}$$

i.e. The density of packet is greater than density of water, so it will sink in water.

Mass of water displaced by the packet

= Volume of packet $\times$ Density of water

$= 350 \times 1$

$= 350$ g

SUMMARY

- **Gravitation** is defined as the non-contact force of attraction between any two bodies in the universe.
- According to **universal law of gravitation,** the attractive force between any two bodies in the universe is directly proportional to the product of their masses and inversely proportional to the square of distance between them.
  Mathematically, $F = \frac{GMm}{d^2}$
  where, G is called **universal gravitational constant** and its value is 6.67×10^{-11} N-m^2/kg^2.
- **Kepler's Laws of Planetary Motion**
  (i) The path of any planet in an orbit around the sun follows the shape of an ellipse with the sun at one of the foci.
  (ii) An imaginary line from the sun to the planet sweeps out equal areas in equal intervals of time.
  (iii) The cube of the mean distance of a planet from the sun is directly proportional to the square of its orbital period.
- **Free Fall** Whenever objects falls towards the earth under the earth's gravitational force alone, then such a motion is called free fall.
- The acceleration with which an object falls towards the earth due to earth's gravitational pull is called **acceleration due to gravity.** It is denoted by g.
  At the surface of earth, $g = \frac{GM}{R^2}$
  The SI unit of g is ms^{-2} and its value is 9.8 m/s^2.
- Equations of motion for freely falling bodies,
  $$v = u + gt, \quad h = ut + \frac{1}{2}gt^2, v^2 = u^2 + 2gh$$
  where, h is the height from which the object falls, t is the time of fall, u is the initial velocity and v is the final velocity, when the body accelerates at g.
- The total amount of matter contained in an object is called its **mass.** The SI unit of mass is **kilogram** (kg) and it is a **scalar quantity**.
- The weight of an object is the force with which it is attracted towards the earth, i.e. weight of an object, $w = mg$.
  The SI unit of weight is Newton (N)and it is a vector quantity.
  Weight of an object on the moon is (1/6)th of its weight on the earth.
- Thrust is the force, acting on an object perpendicular to its surface. The SI unit of thrust is **Newton** (N). Thrust is a **vector quantity**.
- **Pressure** is the force acting perpendicularly on a unit area of an object.
  It can be calculated as,
  Pressure $(p) = \frac{\text{Force }(F)}{\text{Area }(A)} = \frac{\text{Thrust}}{\text{Area}}$
  The SI unit of pressure is Nm^{-2} or **pascal**(Pa).
  Pressure is a **scalar quantity.**
- All the liquids and gases are called **fluids.**
- Buoyant force is an upward force, which acts on an object, when it is immersed in a liquid. It is also called **upthrust.**
- **Factors Affecting the Buoyant Force**
  - Density of the fluid.
  - Volume of object immersed in the liquid.
- If the buoyant force exerted by the liquid is less than the weight of the object, the object will sink in the liquid.
- If the buoyant force is equal to the weight of the object, the object will **float** in the liquid.
- If the buoyant force is more than the weight of the object, the object will **rise in the liquid and then float.**
- The density of a substance is defined as mass per unit volume.
  i.e. Density $= \frac{\text{Mass of the substance}}{\text{Volume of the substance}}$
  The SI unit of density is **kilogram per metre cube** (kg/m^3) and it is a **scalar quantity**.
- According to **Archimedes' principle**, 'When an object is fully or partially immersed in a liquid, it experiences a buoyant force or upthrust which is equal to the weight of liquid displaced by the object'.

For Mind Map
Visit https://goo.gl/SHjVJq
OR Scan the Code

Exam Practice

Objective Type Questions

Multiple Choice Questions

1 Law of gravitation gives the gravitational force between

(a) the earth and a point mass only
(b) the earth and the sun only
(c) any two bodies having some mass
(d) two charged bodies only **NCERT Exemplar**

Sol. (c) Law of gravitation is applicable to all bodies having some mass and is given by $F = \frac{Gm_1 m_2}{r^2}$

where, F = Force of attraction between the two bodies, m_1 and m_2 = Masses of two bodies, G = Gravitational constant and r = Distance between the two bodies.

2 The value of quantity G in the law of gravitation

(a) depends on mass of the earth only
(b) depends on radius of earth only
(c) depends on both mass and radius of the earth
(d) is independent of mass and radius of the earth **NCERT Exemplar**

Sol. (d) G is the constant of proportionality and is called the universal gravitational constant. It is independent of mass and radius of the earth.

3 The weakest force in the following is

(a) magnetic force (b) nuclear force
(c) gravitational force (d) electric force

Sol. (c) Gravitational force is the weakest force among given force.

4 A planet is moving around the sun with mean distance r and time period T, then

(a) $T \propto r^3$ (b) $T^2 \propto r^3$
(c) $T^2 \propto r^2$ (d) $T \propto r^2$

Sol. (b) According to Kepler's third law of planetary motion, square of time period (T) is directly proportional to the cube of mean distance (r) between the planet and sun. i.e. $T^2 \propto r^3$

5 The value of gravitational acceleration (g) is

(a) highest at poles (b) highest at equator
(c) lowest at poles (d) lowest at equator

Sol. (a) Gravitational acceleration g is given by $g = \frac{Gm_e}{R_e^2}$

Where, G is gravitational constant, m_e is mass of earth and R_e is radius of earth.

Since, radius of earth at equator is greater than poles, hence value of g at poles is greater than equator.

6 A car falls off a ledge and drops to the ground in 0.9 s. If the value of g is 10 m/s^2, then speed of car on striking the ground is

(a) 6 m/s (b) 8 m/s
(c) 9 m/s (d) 18 m/s

Sol. (c) Initial velocity, $u = 0$

Acceleration due to gravity, $g = 10 \text{ m/s}^2$

$\because$ v be the speed of car on striking the ground, then

$$v = u + gt$$
$$= 0 + 10 \times 0.9 = 9 \text{ m/s}$$

7 An object is thrown vertically upwards and rises to a height of 20 m. Then, the velocity with which the object was thrown upward is [take, $g = 10 \text{ m/s}^2$]

(a) 15 m/s (b) 25 m/s
(c) 10 m/s (d) 20 m/s

Sol. (d) Given, height, $h = 20$ m, $g = 10 \text{ m/s}^2$

At highest point, final velocity, $v = 0$

$\therefore$ From equation, $v^2 = u^2 - 2gh$

$$0 = u^2 - 2 \times 10 \times 20$$

Initial velocity, $u = \sqrt{400} = 20$ m/s

Thus, object was thrown upward with velocity 20 m/s.

8 The atmosphere is held to the earth by

(a) earth's magnetic field
(b) earth's rotation
(c) gravity
(d) earth's electric field

Sol. (c) The atmosphere is held to the earth by gravity.

9 The magnitude of weight of a body at the centre of earth is

(a) zero
(b) equal to mass of the body
(c) greater than g
(d) less than g

Sol. (a) The value of gravitational acceleration (g) at the centre is zero, hence weight, $w = mg = m \times 0 = 0$.

10 A girl stands on a box having 60 cm length, 40 cm breadth and 20 cm width in three ways. In which of the following cases, pressure exerted by the brick will be

(a) maximum when length and breadth form the base
(b) maximum when breadth and width form the base
(c) maximum when width and length form the base
(d) the same in all the above three cases

NCERT Exemplar

Sol. (b) Now, according to question, when base is formed by breadth and width. Area will be minimum. And so, pressure will be maximum.

11 Why the dam of water reservoir is thick at the bottom?

(a) Quantity of water increases with depth
(b) Density of water increases with depth
(c) Pressure of water increases with depth
(d) Temperature of water increases with depth

Sol. (c) The dam of water is made thick at the bottom, because due to maximum depth, the pressure of water is maximum at bottom and to bear this maximum pressure dam should be thick at the bottom.

12 When a ball is fully immersed in a liquid, its weight get decreased. It happens due to

(a) gravitational force
(b) magnetic force
(c) buoyant force
(d) friction force

Sol. (c) When a ball is fully immersed in a liquid, its weight decreases due to buoyant force.

13 An object is put one by one in three liquids having different densities. The object floats with $\frac{1}{9}, \frac{2}{11}$ and $\frac{3}{7}$ parts of their volumes outside the liquid surface in liquids of densities d_1, d_2 and d_3, respectively. Which of the following statement is correct?

(a) $d_1 > d_2 > d_3$ (b) $d_1 > d_2 < d_3$
(c) $d_1 < d_2 > d_3$ (d) $d_1 < d_2 < d_3$

NCERT Exemplar

Sol. (d) In a liquid of higher density, more part of the object remains outside the liquid. Since, the order of part of their volume outside the liquid is given by
part of the body outside the liquid $\propto$ densities of liquid

$$\frac{1}{9} < \frac{2}{11} < \frac{3}{7}$$

Thus, the order of densities in increasing order is

$$d_1 < d_2 < d_3$$

14 A large ship can float, but a steel needle sinks, because of

(a) mass (b) volume
(c) density (d) None of these

Sol. (d) This concept is explained by Archimedes' principle which states that when a body is fully or partly submerged in a fluid, a buoyant force from the surrounding fluid, acts on the body.

Fill in the Blanks

15 Moon does not have strong .... to hold atmospheric gases.

Sol. Gravity

16 Buoyant force acts vertically .... when an object immersed in a liquid.

Sol. Upward direction

17 Pressure is .... proportional to area of contact.

Sol. inversely

18 A coin sinks when placed on the surface of water because its .... is greater than the .... exerted by the liquid.

Sol. weight, upthrust

19 A ...... is used to measure the purity of a given sample of milk.

Sol. Lactometer

True and False

20 An object floats on the surface of water, if an upthrust exerted on it is greater than its weight.

Sol. True

21 Gravitational force exerted between any two objects is directly proportional to square of distance between their centres.

Sol. False

22 Acceleration due to gravity (g) is maximum at poles and minimum at equator on earth surface.

Sol. True

23 Buoyant force depends on the nature of object immersed in the liquid.

Sol. False

24 Objects having greater density than that of liquid, then objects will sink in the liquid.

Sol. True

Match the Columns

25 Match the following columns.

	Column I		Column II
A.	Escape velocity	p.	1.67 ms^{-2}
B.	Gravitational constant, G	q.	9.8 ms^{-2}
C.	Acceleration due to gravity of earth, g_{earth}	r.	6.67×10^{11} Nm^2kg^{-2}
D.	Acceleration due to gravity of moon, g_{moon}	s.	11.2 km/s

Sol. (A) → (s), (B) → (r), (C) → (q), (D) → (p)

Assertion-Reason

Direction (Q.Nos. 26-30) *In each of the following questions, a statement of Assertion is given by the corresponding statement of Reason. Of the statements, mark the correct answer as*

(a) If both Assertion and Reason are true and Reason is the correct explanation of Assertion.
(b) If both Assertion and Reason are true, but Reason is not the correct explanation of Assertion.
(c) If Assertion is true, but Reason is false.
(d) If Assertion is false, but Reason is true.

26 **Assertion** The moon revolves around the earth due to gravitational force between moon and earth.

Reason Gravitational force between moon and earth is calculated by Newton's law of gravitation.

Sol. (b) Moon revolves around the sun and centripetal force is obtained from gravitational force between moon and earth.

i.e. Gravitational force = Centripetal force

Hence, both Assertion and Reason are true but Reason is not the correct explanation of Assertion.

27 **Assertion** The square of the period of revolution of a planet is proportional to the cube of its mean distance from sun.

Reason Sun's gravitational field is directly proportional to the square of its mean distance from the planet.

Sol. (c) According to Kepler's second law, $T^2 \propto r^3$

Sun's gravitational field is inversely proportional to the square of distance from planet.

Hence, Assertion is true, but Reason is false.

28 **Assertion** At the centre of earth, a body has no centre of gravity.

Reason This is because, $g = 0$ at the centre of earth.

Sol. (a) At the centre of earth, acceleration due to gravity, $g = 0$, i.e. a body has no weight and hence no centre of gravity.

Hence, both Assertion and Reason are true and Reason is the correct explanation of Assertion.

29 **Assertion** A hydrogen filled balloon stops rising after it has attained a certain height in the sky.

Reason The atmospheric pressure increases with height.

Sol. (c) When the atmospheric pressure becomes equal to the pressure inside the balloon, the balloon stops rising. The atmospheric pressure decreases with height. Hence, Assertion is true, but Reason is false.

30 **Assertion** When a body is dipped into water, then upthrust force acting on the body is equal to the weight of water displaced by the body.

Reason A body will sink in water, if density of body is less than or equal to density of water.

Sol. (c) According to Archimedes' principle,
Upthrust force = Weight of water displaced

Hence, Assertion is true and Reason is false and the correct statement is, 'A body will sink in a liquid, if its density is more than that of the liquid'.

Case Based Questions

Direction (Q.Nos. 31-34) *Answer the following questions on the basis of your understanding of the passage and related studied concepts:*

Sonia and Rajat went to Kashmir and took a ride on motorboat, on visiting a lake. While taking boat rides they were provided special jackets and were asked to wear the jacket before going to boat. Those jackets were life saving jackets and used for safety.

31 What is the function of air-filled life saving jackets?

Sol. Life saving jackets have air, hence they reduce the density of the person wearing it. This will protect them from drawning as the weight of the person will be equal to weight of the fluid displaced.

32 How does a boat float in water?

Sol. Boat floats in water due to upward force called buoyant force which is caused by the pressure of the water pushing up the bottom of the boat.

33 According to law of floatation, if the weight of the body is equal to weight of the liquid displaced by it, then body will

(a) float in a liquid
(b) partially immersed in liquid
(c) sink in a liquid
(d) Both (a) and (c)

Sol. Option (a) is correct.

34 Sonia and Rajat were asked to wear special jackets because these jackets will
(a) reduce the weight of both persons
(b) increase the density of both the persons
(c) reduce the density of both the persons
(d) None of the above

Sol. Option (c) is correct.

Direction (Q.Nos. 35-38) *Answer the following questions on the basis of your understanding of the table and related studied concepts:*

Consider the earth to be made up of concentric shells and a point mass m situated at a distance r from the centre. The point P lies outside the sphere of radius r and point P lies inside, if the shell's radius is greater than r. The smaller sphere exerts a force on a mass m at P as if its mass m_r is concentrated at the centre.

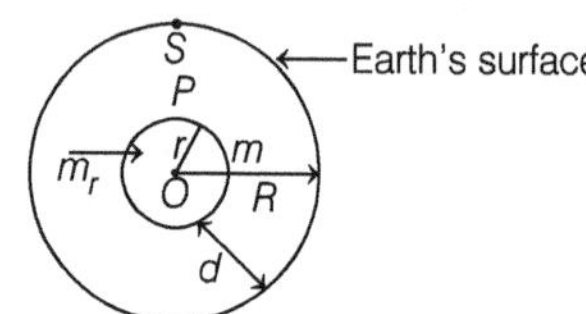

For determination of acceleration due to gravity

Table : Variation in acceleration due to gravity

1.	At the surface of earth	$g = \frac{GM}{R^2}$
2.	Effect of altitude	$g_h = \frac{g}{\left(1 + \frac{h}{R}\right)^2}$
3.	Effect of depth	$g_d = g\left(1 - \frac{d}{R}\right)$

Here, g = acceleration due to gravity,

g_h = acceleration due to gravity at height h above the surface of earth,

g_d = acceleration due to gravity at depth d,

M = mass of earth and R = is radius of earth.

where, $M = 6 \times 10^{24}$ kg and $R = 6.4 \times 10^6$ m

35 From the given table, what conclusion you can derive?

Sol. Given table shows the variation in acceleration due to gravity at the surface of earth, at depth d below from the surface of earth and height h above from the surface of earth. Acceleration due to gravity is different at different points on the earth.

36 Calculate the value of g using formula 1, given in table.

Sol. Given, mass of the earth, $M = 6 \times 10^{24}$ kg

Radius of the earth, $R = 6.4 \times 10^6$ m

Universal gravitational constant,

$$G = 6.67 \times 10^{-11} \text{ N-m}^2/\text{kg}^2$$

$$\because \quad g = \frac{GM}{R^2}$$

$$= \frac{(6.67 \times 10^{-11})(6 \times 10^{24})}{(6.4 \times 10^6)^2}$$

$$g = 9.8 \text{ m/s}^2$$

37 What is the value of acceleration due to gravity at point O (in given figure)?

Sol. Point O is the centre of earth.

At centre O of the earth, $d = R$

From formula (3) given in table, $g_d = g\left(1 - \frac{d}{R}\right) = 0$

Thus, at the centre of earth, acceleration due to gravity is zero.

38 As we increase the value of h in formula 2 given in table, what will be the effect on acceleration due to gravity of earth?

Sol. The value of acceleration due to gravity decreases with increase in height above the surface of earth.

Very Short Answer Type Questions

39 When do we use the term force of gravity rather than force of gravitation?

Sol. We use the term force of gravity rather than force of gravitation for the force of attraction between two bodies in which one body had infinitely large mass.

40 Which force bring tides in the ocean?

Sol. Gravitational force of the moon bring tides in the ocean.

41 Which force keeps the moon in a uniform circular motion around the earth?

Sol. Gravitational force between the moon and the earth keeps the moon in a uniform circular motion around the earth.

42 Suppose gravity of the earth suddenly becomes zero, then which direction will the moon begin to move, if no other celestial body affects it? **NCERT Exemplar**

Sol. The moon will begin to move in a straight line in the direction in which it was moving at that instant because the circular motion of the moon is due to centripetal force provided by the gravitational force of the earth.

43 Two objects kept in a room do not move towards each other as per the universal law of gravitation. Why?

Sol. The size of the bodies are very small, therefore the force of attraction between them is very small. So, both objects do not move towards each other.

44 The earth is acted upon by gravitation of the sun even, then it does not fall into the sun. Why? **NCERT Exemplar**

Sol. The earth does not fall into the sun because the earth remains in its circular orbit due to the gravitational force acting on it.

45 Two objects of masses m_1 and m_2 are dropped in vacuum from a height above the surface of the earth (m_1 is greater than m_2). Which one will reach the ground first and why?

Sol. Both will reach the ground at the same time because acceleration due to gravity is independent of the masses of freely falling bodies.

46 At which place on the earth, the acceleration due to gravity is zero?

Sol. At the centre of the earth, the acceleration due to gravity is zero.

47 Name the place on the earth's surface, where the weight of a body is maximum and minimum?

Sol. Weight is maximum at poles and minimum at equator.

48 The astronauts in space feel weightless. Why?

Sol. They do not exert any force/weight on their spaceship in the absence of gravity in space.

49 Which of the two will double the pressure? Doubling the area or making the area half.

Sol. Making the area half, pressure will be double.

$$\left[\because p = \frac{F}{A}\right]$$

50 A bucket of water weighs less inside the well water. Why?

Sol. Due to the upthrust exerted by the well water on the bottom of bucket in upward direction.

51 Density of glass is 3.5 g cm^{-3}. What does it mean?

Sol. 3.5 g cm^{-3} density of glass means that the volume of 3.5 g glass is 1 cm^3.

52 Name the instrument which is used to determine the density of liquid.

Sol. The instrument which is used to determine the density of liquid is "hydrometer."

53 A stone dropped from a tree takes 2 s to reach the ground. Find its velocity on striking the ground.

Sol. Given, initial velocity, $u = 0$, time, $t = 2$ s,
acceleration due to gravity, $a = g = 9.8 \text{ m/s}^2$
and final velocity, $v = ?$
From the first equation of motion,

$$v = u + at = 0 + 9.8 \times 2 = 19.6 \text{ m/s}$$

Thus, stone with velocity 19.6 m/s strike on the ground.

54 An object weighs 10 N in air. When immersed fully in water, it weighs only 8 N. What will be the weight of the liquid displaced by the object? **NCERT Exemplar**

Sol. Given, weight of an object in air = 10 N
Weight of an object in water = 8 N
Weight of liquid displaced, $F = 10 - 8 = 2$ N

Short Answer (SA) Type Questions

1 State the source of centripetal force that a planet requires to revolve round the sun. On what factors does the force depend? Suppose this force suddenly becomes zero, then in which direction will the planet begin to move, if no other celestial body affects it?

Sol. The source of centripetal force is the gravitation force. It depends upon the following factors:

(*i*) Mass of the planet and the sun.

(*ii*) Distance between the planet and the sun.

If this force suddenly becomes zero, then the planet will begin to move in a straight line in the direction in which it was moving at that instant.

2 (*i*) Seema buys few grains of gold at the poles as per the instruction of one of her friends. She hand over the same when she meets her at the equator. Will the friend agree with the weight of gold bought? If not, why?

(*ii*) If the moon attracts the earth, then why does the earth not move towards the moon?

Sol. (i) No, her friend will not agree with the weight of gold bought because weight at poles is greater than the weight at equator.

(ii) We know that, the gravitational force is always attractive, still the moon does not fall on the earth because the gravitational force between the earth and the moon works as the necessary centripetal force for the moon to make it revolving around the earth.

3 Obtain a relation between the weight of an object on the surface of the earth and that on the moon.

Sol. Refer to text on page 212.

4 (i) Name the SI units of thrust and pressure.

(ii) In which situation, do we exert more pressure on ground when we stand on one foot or on the both feet? Justify your answer.

Sol. (i) The SI unit of thrust is newton (N) and the SI unit of pressure is Nm^{-2}or pascal (Pa).

(ii) We exert more pressure on ground when we stand on one foot than the both feet, as the area of one foot is half than that of two feet as $p \propto \frac{1}{A}$.

5 (i) Explain, why a completely immersed bottle in water bounces back on the surface.

(ii) Why does a bucket of water weighs less inside the well water?

Sol. (i) Since, it is known that a body can sink in water only when its weight is greater than the upthrust act on it by the water. But in this case, the upthrust act on the bottle is greater than its weight, thats why, it bounces back on the water surface.

(ii) A bucket of water weighs less inside the well water, it is because when the bucket immersed in water fully, upthrust act on it by water which reduce its actual weight.

6 When a fresh egg is put into a beaker filled with water, it sinks in water. But when a lot of salt is dissolved in the water, the egg begins to rise and then floats. Why?

Sol. On dissolving a lot of salt in water, the density of salt solution becomes higher than that of pure water. Due to its much higher density, the salt solution exerts much more upward buoyant force on the egg, making the egg rise and then float.

7 Two different bodies are completely immersed in water and undergo the same loss in weight. Is it necessary that their weights in air should also be the same? Justify your answer.

Sol. No, it is not necessary that their weights in air should also be the same. This is because the two bodies have undergone the same loss in weight on completely immersing in water due to their equal volumes, not due to their equal weights. So, they may have different weights in air.

8 (i) Why does a bucket of water feel heavier when taken out of water?

(ii) Lead has greater density than iron and both are denser than water. Is the buoyant force on a lead object greater than, less than or equal to the buoyant force on an iron object of the same volume?

Sol. (i) A bucket of water feels heavier when taken out of water because when immersed in water, an upward force, i.e. buoyant force acts on it which is equal to the weight of water displaced by the bucket.

(ii) The buoyant force on a lead object is lesser than the buoyant force on the iron object because lead has greater density, so it displaces lesser amount of water consequently lesser amount of buoyant force acts on it.

9 Verify Archimedes' principle of buoyancy with an activity. For the activity, you are provided with a piece of stone, a rubber string and a container filled with water.

Sol. First of all, tie up the stone with the rubber string and hold it against a scale fixed on a wall. Put a mark on the elongated rubber string when stone is tied.

Repeat this experiment but this time suspend the stone in a beaker, filled with water. Now, compare the markings.

Explanation As the buoyant force is acting on the stone in upward direction, due to this, gravitational pull decreases and in turn, the stretch of the rubber is lost.

10 State Archimedes' principle. Write its two applications.

Sol. Archimedes' principle states that, "When a body is immersed fully or partially in a liquid, it experiences an upward force that is equal to the weight of the liquid displaced by it."

Applications

(i) It is used in designing ships and submarines.

(ii) It is used in making lactometers, which are used to determine the purity of milk.

11 What happens to the magnitude of the force of gravitation between two objects, if

(i) distance between the objects is tripled?

(ii) mass of both objects is doubled?

(iii) mass of both objects as well as distance between them is doubled?

Sol. As we know,

Force of gravitation, $F = \frac{Gm_1m_2}{r^2}$

[symbols have their usual meanings]

(i) Distance between objects is tripled,

$$r' = 3r \Rightarrow F' = \frac{Gm_1m_2}{9r^2} = \frac{F}{9}$$

[force decreases by 9 times]

(ii) Mass of both objects is doubled,

$$m_1' = 2m_1 \text{ and } m_2' = 2m_2$$

$$\Rightarrow F' = \frac{4Gm_1m_2}{r^2} = 4F$$

[force increases by 4 times]

(iii) Mass of both objects as well as distance between them is doubled, then

$$m_1' = 2m_1,\ m_2' = 2m_2,\ r' = 2r$$

$$\Rightarrow F' = \frac{4Gm_1m_2}{4r^2} = F$$

[force remains unchanged]

12 If the distance between two masses be increased by a factor of 6, by what factor would the mass of one of them have to be altered to maintain the same gravitational force? Would this be an increase or decrease in mass?

Sol. As we know, $F = \frac{Gm_1m_2}{r^2}$ ...(i)

According to question,

Distance between two masses be increased by factor 6, $r' = 6r$

So, $F = \frac{Gm_1m_2}{(6r)^2} = \frac{Gm_1m_2}{36r^2}$ [using Eq. (i)]

$= \frac{F}{36}$

To maintain same force one of the mass is to be increased by 36 times.

13 A body weighs 25 kg on the surface of the earth. If the mass of the earth is 6×10^{24} kg, then the radius of the earth is 6.4×10^6 m and the gravitational constant is 6.67×10^{-11} N-m^2/kg^2.

Calculate

(i) the mutual force of attraction between the body and the earth.

(ii) the acceleration produced in the body.

(iii) the acceleration produced in the earth.

Sol. Given, mass of earth, $M_e = 6 \times 10^{24}$ kg,

Body weighs, $m = 25$ kg,

Radius of earth, $R_e = 6.4 \times 10^6$ m

and gravitational constant,

$$G = 6.67 \times 10^{-11} \text{ N-m}^2/\text{kg}^2$$

(i) ∴ Mutual force, $F = G\frac{M_e}{R_e^2}m$

$$= \frac{6.67 \times 10^{-11} \times 6 \times 10^{24} \times 25}{(6.4 \times 10^6)^2} = 244 \text{ N}$$

(ii) ∴ Acceleration produced in the body,

$$a = \frac{F}{m} = \frac{244}{25} = 9.8 \text{ m/s}^2$$

(iii) ∴ Acceleration produced in the earth,

$$a = \frac{F}{M_e} = \frac{244}{6 \times 10^{24}} = 4.06 \times 10^{-23} \text{ m/s}^2$$

14 Two bodies of masses 3 kg and 12 kg are placed at a distance 12 m. A third body of mass 0.5 kg is to be placed at such a point that the force acting on this body is zero. Find the position of that point.

Sol. Given, mass of first body, $m_1 = 3$ kg

and mass of second body, $m_2 = 12$ kg

Let the mass of third body, $m_3 = 0.5$ kg be placed at a distance of x from m_1 as shown in figure.

m_1 F_{31} m_3 F_{32} m_2

|←x→|← 12 − x →|

|← 12 m →|

Then, force acting on m_3 due to m_1 is equal and opposite to the force acting on m_3 due to m_2.

$$\therefore \quad F_{31} = F_{32}$$

$$\frac{Gm_3m_1}{x^2} = \frac{Gm_3m_2}{(12-x)^2} \Rightarrow \frac{3}{x^2} = \frac{12}{(12-x)^2}$$

$$\Rightarrow \left(\frac{12-x}{x}\right)^2 = \frac{12}{3} = 4 \Rightarrow \frac{12-x}{x} = 2$$

$$\Rightarrow 12 - x = 2x \Rightarrow 12 = 3x$$

$$\Rightarrow x = 4 \text{ m}$$

The position of required point is at a distance 4 m from the mass 3 kg.

15 Calculate the acceleration due to gravity on the surface of satellite having mass 7.4×10^{22} kg and radius 1.74×10^6 cm. (Take, $G = 6.7 \times 10^{-11}$ N-m/kg^2)

Sol. As we know, acceleration due to gravity, $g = \frac{GM}{R^2}$.

For the satellite,

$$R = 1.74 \times 10^6 \text{ cm} = \frac{1.74 \times 10^6}{100}$$

$$= 1.74 \times 10^4 \text{ m}$$

Mass of satellite, $M = 7.4 \times 10^{22}$ kg

$$\therefore \quad g = \frac{6.67 \times 10^{-11} \times 7.4 \times 10^{22}}{1.74 \times 10^4 \times 1.74 \times 10^4}$$

$$= \frac{6.67 \times 7.4}{1.74 \times 1.74} \times 10^3 \quad g = 16.30 \times 10^3 \text{ m/s}^2$$

16 What height above the surface of the earth, the value of g becomes 64% of its value at the surface of the earth? Take, the radius of the earth = 6400 km.

Sol. Let g = acceleration due to gravity at the earth surface.

g_h = acceleration due to gravity at height h

$$= \frac{64}{100} \times g = 0.64\, g$$

$$\because \quad g = \frac{GM}{R_e^2} \quad \text{...(i)}$$

Here, G is gravitational constant, R is radius of earth and M is mass.

$$\text{Similarly,} \quad g_h = \frac{GM}{(R_e + h)^2} \quad \text{...(ii)}$$

From Eqs. (i) and (ii), we get

$$\therefore \quad g_h = \frac{gR_e^2}{(R_e + h)^2}$$

$$\Rightarrow \quad 0.64\, g = \frac{gR_e^2}{(R_e + h)^2}$$

$$\Rightarrow \quad 0.64\,(R_e + h)^2 = R_e^2$$

$$\Rightarrow \quad 0.8\,(R_e + h) = R_e$$

$$\Rightarrow \quad 0.8h = R_e - 0.8\, R_e = 0.2\, R_e$$

$$h = \frac{2 \times 6400}{8} = 1600 \text{ km} \quad [\because R_e = 6400 \text{ km}]$$

Thus, the height above the surface of the earth is 1600 km.

17 Prove that, if a body is thrown vertically upwards, then the time of ascent is equal to the time of descent.

Sol. For the upward motion, equation of motion will be (final velocity, $v = 0$)

$$v = u - gt_1, \quad 0 = u - gt_1, \quad t_1 = \frac{u}{g} \quad \text{...(i)}$$

and the downward motion,

$$v = u + gt_2, \quad v = 0 + gt_2$$

The body falls back to the earth with the same speed as it was thrown vertically upwards.

$$\therefore \quad v = u, \quad u = 0 + gt_2 \Rightarrow t_2 = \frac{u}{g} \quad \text{...(ii)}$$

From Eqs. (i) and (ii), we get

$t_1 = t_2 \Rightarrow$ Time of ascent = Time of descent

18 A ball is dropped from the edge of a roof. It takes 0.1s to cross a window of height 2.0 m. Find the height of the roof above the top of the window.

Sol. Let AB be the window and suppose the roof is at a height y above A. Also, suppose it takes a time t_1, for the ball to reach A. The velocity of the ball at A is

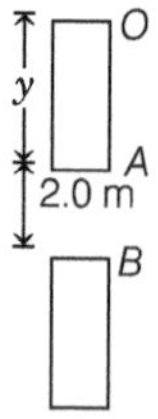

$$v_1 = 0 + gt_1 = 9.8t_1$$

Now, consider the motion of the ball from A to B.

Here, the initial velocity is v_1, the distance covered is 2 m and the time taken is 0.1 s.

From second equation of motion, $s = ut + \frac{1}{2}gt^2$

$$\Rightarrow 2.0 = v_1(0.1) + \frac{1}{2} \times 9.8 \times (0.1)^2 = 9.8t_1(0.1) + 0.049$$

$$\Rightarrow \quad t_1 = 1.99 \approx 2 \text{ s}$$

The height y is $y = \frac{1}{2}gt_1^2 = \frac{1}{2} \times 9.8 \times (2)^2 = 19.6$ m

The roof is at a height 19.6 m above the top of the window.

19 On the earth, a stone is thrown from a height in a direction parallel to the earth's surface while another stone is simultaneously dropped from the same height. Which stone would reach the ground first and why? **NCERT Exemplar**

Sol. For both the stones,

initial velocity, $u = 0$

Acceleration in downward direction $= g$

Now, from second equation of motion,

$$h = ut + \frac{1}{2}gt^2 \Rightarrow h = 0 + \frac{1}{2}gt^2$$

$$\Rightarrow \quad h = \frac{1}{2}gt^2 \quad \Rightarrow \quad t = \sqrt{\frac{2h}{g}}$$

Both stones will take the same time to reach the ground because the two stones fall from the same height.

20 A ball is thrown with some speed u m/s. Show that under the free fall, it will fall on the ground with same speed.

Sol. When the ball is thrown upwards, then it will reach certain height h and starts falling. At maximum height h, the final velocity will be $v = 0$.

Maximum height reached by the ball,

$$v^2 - u^2 = 2gh \quad \text{[using equation]}$$

$$0 - u^2 = -2gh \quad [\because \text{acceleration} = -g]$$

$$\Rightarrow \quad h = \frac{u^2}{2g} \quad \ldots(i)$$

In second case, when the ball starts to fall, then the initial velocity $u = 0$. It will accelerate due to gravity, i.e. $a = g$ and reach ground with speed (say v_2).

Using equation,

$$v_2^2 - u^2 = 2gh$$

$$\Rightarrow \quad v_2^2 - 0 = 2gh$$

$$v_2^2 = 2g\left(\frac{u^2}{2g}\right) = u^2 \quad \text{[from Eq. (i)]}$$

$$\Rightarrow \quad v_2 = u$$

Thus, the ball reach on the ground with same speed.

21 A firecracker is fired and it rises to a height of 1000 m. Find the

(*i*) velocity by which it was released.

(*ii*) time taken by it to reach the highest point. (Take, $g = 9.8 \text{ m/s}^2$)

Sol. Given, height, $H = 1000$ m,

Final velocity, $v = 0$,

Acceleration due to gravity, $g = 9.8 \text{ m/s}^2$

(*i*) From the third equation of motion,

$$v^2 = u^2 + 2gH$$

$$\Rightarrow 0 = u^2 - 2 \times 9.8 \times 1000$$

$$u = \sqrt{2 \times 9.8 \times 1000} = \sqrt{19600} = 140 \text{ m/s}$$

Velocity by which firecracker is released $= 140$ m/s

(*ii*) From the first equation of motion,

$$v = u + gt$$

$$\Rightarrow 0 = 140 - 9.8t$$

$$\Rightarrow t = \frac{140}{9.8} = 14.28 \text{ s}$$

Time taken, $t = 14.28$ s

22 A ball is thrown upwards from the ground of a tower with a speed of 20 m/s. There is a window in the tower at the height of 15 m from the ground. How many times and when will the ball pass the window? (Take, $g = 10 \text{ m/s}^2$)

Sol. Given, initial velocity, $u = 20$ m/s

Maximum height that the ball will reach, $h = ?$

From the third equation of motion, $v^2 = u^2 + 2gh$

[$\because$ at maximum height, $v = 0$]

$$\Rightarrow \quad h = \frac{-u^2}{2g} = \frac{-(20)^2}{2(-10)} = \frac{400}{20} = 20 \text{ m}$$

This means that ball will reach the height of 20 m and comes back. It will pass the window two times.

Now, to calculate the time that ball will take to reach 15 m height.

From the second equation of upward motion,

$$h = ut - \frac{1}{2}gt^2 \quad [\because g \text{ is in the downward direction}]$$

$$15 = 20t - \frac{1}{2}(10)t^2$$

$$\Rightarrow 5t^2 - 20t + 15 = 0$$

$$t^2 - 4t + 3 = 0$$

$$t^2 - 3t - t + 3 = 0$$

$$t(t-3) - 1(t-3) = 0$$

$$(t-1)(t-3) = 0$$

$$\Rightarrow \quad t = 1, 3$$

Thus, ball will pass the window at 1 s and 3 s, respectively.

23 (*i*) According to universal law of gravitation, every object in this universe attracts every other object. Explain, why then a table and a chair lying in the same room do not collide with each other.

(*ii*) An object is thrown vertically upwards to a height of 12 m. Calculate its

(*a*) velocity with which it was thrown upwards.

(*b*) time taken by the object to reach a height of 12 m.

Sol. (*i*) Gravitational force is the weakest force in nature, yet it helps in holding massive bodies in place throughout the universe. Due to this reason, table and chair do not collide.

(*ii*) Given, height, $h = 12$ m,

Final velocity, $v = 0$,

Acceleration due to gravity, $g = -9.8 \text{ m/s}^2$,

Initial velocity, $u = ?$ and time, $t = ?$

(*a*) $\therefore v^2 - u^2 = 2gh$, $0 - u^2 = 2 \times (-9.8) \times 12$

$$\Rightarrow \quad u = 15.33 \text{ m/s}$$

(*b*) $\therefore \quad v = u - gt$

$$\Rightarrow t = \frac{u}{g} = \frac{15.33}{9.8} = 1.56 \text{ s}$$

24 In a hypothetical case, if the diameter of the earth becomes half of its present value and mass becomes four times its present value, then how would the weight of any object on surface of the earth be affected?

NCERT Exemplar

Sol. $\therefore$ Weight, $w = mg$

As mass is a constant, then $w \propto g$

$$g = \frac{GM}{R^2} = 9.8 \text{ m/s}^2$$

Given, diameter of the earth becomes half of its present value, $d = \frac{d}{2}$

Mass becomes four times its present value, $M = 4M$

On bringing modifications,

$$g = \frac{G(4M)}{\left(\frac{R}{2}\right)^2} = 16\frac{GM}{R^2} = 16 \times 9.8$$

w becomes 16 times.

25 A particle weighs 120 N on the surface of the earth. At what height above the earth's surface will its weight be 30 N? Radius of the earth = 6400 km.

Sol. Let the weight of the particle on the surface of the earth,

$$w = 120 = \frac{GMm}{R^2}$$

Hence, $$120 = \frac{GMm}{R^2} \quad \text{...(i)}$$

Let the height h above the earth's surface, where its weight will be 30 N.

Hence, $$30 = \frac{GMm}{(h+R)^2} \quad \text{...(ii)}$$

On dividing Eq. (i) by Eq. (ii), we get

$$\frac{120}{30} = \frac{GMm}{R^2} \times \frac{(h+R)^2}{GMm}$$

$$\frac{4}{1} = \frac{(h+R)^2}{R^2}$$

$$\Rightarrow \quad 2 = \frac{h+R}{R}$$

$$\Rightarrow \quad 2R = h + R$$

$$\Rightarrow \quad h = 2R - R = R = 6400 \text{ km} \quad \text{(given)}$$

$$= 6.4 \times 10^6 \text{ m}$$

26 Shashank placed an iron cuboid of dimensions 4 cm× 7 cm× 10 cm on a tray containing fine sand. He placed the cuboid in such a way that it was made to lie on the sand with its faces of dimensions

(*i*) 4 cm × 7 cm, (*ii*) 7cm × 10 cm

(*iii*) and 4 cm × 10 cm.

If the density of iron is nearly 8 g cm^{-3} and $g = 10 \text{ ms}^{-2}$, find the minimum and maximum pressure as calculated by Shashank.

Sol. $\therefore$ Mass of cuboid = Volume × Density

$$= (4 \text{ cm} \times 7 \text{ cm} \times 10 \text{ cm}) \times 8 \text{ g cm}^{-3}$$

[$\because$ Volume of cuboid $= l \times b \times h$]

$$= 2240 \text{ g} = 2.24 \text{ kg}$$

Force applied by the cuboid on the sand

$$= mg = 2.24 \times 10 = 22.4 \text{ N} \quad [\because g = 10 \text{ ms}^{-2}]$$

Pressure will be minimum when area of the face of cuboid kept on sand is maximum, i.e. in the case of face with 7 cm × 10 cm.

$$\text{Area of the face} = 7 \text{ cm} \times 10 \text{ cm} = \frac{7}{100} \text{ m} \times \frac{10}{100} \text{ m}$$

$$= 0.07 \text{ m} \times 0.1 \text{ m} = 0.007 \text{ m}^2$$

$$\text{Minimum pressure} = \frac{\text{Force}}{\text{Area}} = \frac{22.4}{0.007} = 3200 \text{ N m}^{-2}$$

Pressure will be maximum when area of face of cuboid kept on the sand is minimum, i.e. in the case of face with 4 cm × 7cm.

Area of the face = 4 cm × 7 cm

$$= \frac{4}{100} \text{ m} \times \frac{7}{100} \text{ m} = 0.0028 \text{ m}^2$$

$$\text{Maximum pressure} = \frac{\text{Force}}{\text{Area}} = \frac{22.4}{0.0028} = 8000 \text{ Nm}^{-2}$$

27 A cubical tub of side 2 m is full of water. Calculate the total thrust and pressure at the bottom of tank due to water. (Take, density of water $= 1000 \text{ kg m}^{-3}$ and $g = 10 \text{ m s}^{-2}$)

Sol. $\therefore$ Volume of cubical tub

= Length × Breadth × Height

Here, length = breadth = height = 2 m

$\therefore$ Volume $= 2 \times 2 \times 2 = 8 \text{ m}^3$

Mass of water = Volume × Density of water

$= 8 \times 1000 = 8000$ kg

$\therefore$ Weight of water

= Mass × Acceleration due to gravity

$= 8000 \times 10$

$= 8 \times 10^4$ N

$\therefore$ Total thrust = Weight of water

$= 8 \times 10^4$ N

Area of bottom = Area of square shape of tub

$= 2 \times 2 = 4 \text{ m}^2$

$$\therefore \text{Pressure of water at the bottom} = \frac{\text{Force}}{\text{Area}} = \frac{\text{Weight}}{\text{Area}} = \frac{8 \times 10^4}{4} = 2 \times 10^4 \text{ Pa}$$

28 A ball filled with air has a volume of 500 cm^3. Calculate the minimum force applied by a child to put it completely inside the water. (Take, $g = 10\ ms^{-2}$)

Sol. Given that,

Volume, $V = 500\ cm^3 = 500 \times 10^{-6}\ m^3$,

$g = 10\ ms^{-2}, F = ?$

Force required to put the ball inside the water

= Buoyant force

= Weight of water displaced $= mg$ ...(i)

Now, we know that,

Mass of water = Density of water × Volume

$m = \rho V$

On substituting this value in Eq. (i), we get

Force $= \rho V g$

$= (1000\ kg\ m^{-3}) \times (500 \times 10^{-6}\ m^3) \times (10\ ms^{-2})$

$= 1000 \times 500 \times 10^{-6} \times 10\ N = 5\ N$

∴ Minimum force applied by a child to put the ball completely inside the water is 5 N.

29 A boat of mass 50 kg is floating in the river with $\left(\frac{1}{2}\right)$nd of its volume inside the water. Calculate the buoyant force acting on the boat. (Take, $g = 10\ ms^{-2}$)

Sol. Given that, mass of the boat, $m = 50$ kg

As we know that, when a body floats in river. Its apparent weight is zero.

Therefore, buoyant force = weight of body

$= mg = 50 \times 10$

i.e. Buoyant force = 500 N

30 A cubical object of side 4 cm has fallen in a well. If mass of the cube is 2 kg, then state whether this object will float or sink in water. (Take, density of water 1000 kg m^{-3})

Sol. Given that,

Mass of the object, $m = 2$ kg

Side of cube = 4 cm = 0.04 m [∵ 1 m = 100 cm]

Since, volume of cube = $(\text{side})^3$

∴ Volume of the object, $V = (0.04\ m)^3$

$= 0.000064\ m^3$

As we know that,

$$\text{Density} = \frac{\text{Mass of the object}}{\text{Volume of the object}}$$

$$\Rightarrow \text{Density} = \frac{2}{0.000064}\ kg\,m^{-3}$$

$$= \frac{2000000}{64}\ kg\,m^{-3} = 31250\ kg\,m^{-3}$$

Here, density of the object (i.e. 31250 kg m^{-3}) is greater than the density of water (i.e. 1000 kg m^{-3}). Therefore, the object will sink in water.

Long Answer (LA) Type Questions

1 (*i*) Write the formula to find the magnitude of gravitational force between the earth and an object on the earth's surface.

(*ii*) Derive how does the value of gravitational force F between two objects change when

(a) distance between them is reduced to half

(b) and mass of an object is increased four times.

Sol. (*i*) Formula to find the magnitude of gravitational force, $F = \frac{GMm}{R^2}$.

where, M = mass of the earth,

m = mass of the object,

R = radius of the earth

and universal gravitational constant,

$G = 6.67 \times 10^{-11}\ N\text{-}m^2/kg^2$.

(*ii*) (a) Let gravitational force be F when the distance between them is R,

$$F = \frac{GMm}{R^2} \quad ...(i)$$

Now, when the distance reduces to half,

$$F' = \frac{GMm}{\left(\frac{R}{2}\right)^2} = \frac{4GMm}{R^2} \quad ...(ii)$$

On dividing Eq. (i) by Eq. (ii), we get

$$\frac{F}{F'} = \frac{GMm}{R^2} \times \frac{R^2}{4GMm}$$

$$F' = 4F$$

(b) When the mass becomes 4 times,

$$\frac{F}{F'} = \frac{GMm}{R^2} \times \frac{R^2}{4GMm}$$

$$\Rightarrow F' = 4F$$

2 (i) Prove that, if the earth attracts two bodies placed at the same distance from the centre of the earth with equal force, then their masses will be the same.

(ii) Mathematically express the acceleration due to gravity in terms of mass of the earth and radius of the earth.

(iii) Why is G called a universal constant?

Sol. (i) Let the two bodies have masses m_1 and m_2 and they are placed at the same distance R from the centre of the earth. According to the question, if the same force acts on both of them, then

$$F_1 = \frac{GMm_1}{R^2} \quad \text{...(i)}$$

and $$F_2 = \frac{GMm_2}{R^2} \quad \text{...(ii)}$$

As, $F_1 = F_2$

Hence, $\frac{GMm_1}{R^2} = \frac{GMm_2}{R^2}$

So, $m_1 = m_2$, their masses will be same.

(ii) Mathematically, $g = \frac{GM}{R^2}$.

where, g = acceleration due to gravity,

G = universal gravitational constant,

M = mass of the earth

and R = radius of the earth.

(iii) G is known as the universal gravitational constant because its value remains same all the time everywhere in the universe, applicable to all bodies whether celestial or terrestrial.

3 (i) At some moment, two giant planets jupiter and saturn of the solar system are in the same line as seen from the earth. Find the total gravitational force due to them on a person of mass 50 kg on the earth. Could the force due to the planets be important?

Mass of the jupiter $= 2 \times 10^{27}$ kg

Mass of the saturn $= 6 \times 10^{26}$ kg

Distance of jupiter from the earth $= 6.3 \times 10^{11}$ m

Distance of saturn from the earth $= 1.28 \times 10^{12}$ m

Gravitational constant, $G = 6.67 \times 10^{-11} \text{N-m}^2/\text{kg}^2$

Acceleration due to gravity on the earth $= 9.8 \text{ m/s}^2$

(ii) A bag of sugar weighs w at a certain place on the equator. If this bag is taken to Antarctica, then will it weigh the same or more or less. Give a reason for your answer.

Sol. (i) (a) Gravitational force acting on the 50 kg, $mg = 50 \times 9.8 = 490$ N

(b) Gravitational force acting on the 50 kg mass due to jupiter,

$$F_{\text{jupiter}} = \frac{G \times M_{\text{jupiter}} \times M_{\text{person}}}{(\text{distance of jupiter from the earth})^2}$$

$$F_{\text{jupiter}} = \frac{6.67 \times 10^{-11} \times 2 \times 10^{27} \times 50}{6.3 \times 10^{11} \times 6.3 \times 10^{11}}$$

$$F_{\text{jupiter}} = \frac{6.67 \times 2 \times 50 \times 10^{-11+27-22}}{6.3 \times 6.3}$$

$$F_{\text{jupiter}} = 1.68 \times 10^{-5} \text{ N}$$

(c) Gravitational force acting on the 50 kg mass due to saturn

$$F_{\text{saturn}} = \frac{G \times M_{\text{saturn}} \times M_{\text{person}}}{(\text{distance of saturn from the earth})^2}$$

$$F_{\text{saturn}} = \frac{6.67 \times 10^{-11} \times 6 \times 10^{26} \times 50}{1.28 \times 10^{12} \times 1.28 \times 10^{12}}$$

$$F_{\text{saturn}} = \frac{6.67 \times 6 \times 50}{1.28 \times 1.28} \times 10^{-11+26-24}$$

$$F_{\text{saturn}} = 0.12 \times 10^{-5} \text{N}$$

∴ Total gravitational force due to the jupiter and the saturn $= (1.68 \times 10^{-5} + 0.12 \times 10^{-5})$ N $= 1.8 \times 10^{-5}$ N

Thus, the combined force due to the planets jupiter and saturn (1.8×10^{-5}) N is negligible as compared to the gravitational force due to the earth.

(ii) We know that, g at equator is less than g at poles (Antarctica). Thus, weight at equator is less than weight at pole (Antarctica). A bag of sugar weighs w at a certain place on the equator. If this bag is taken to Antarctica, then it will weigh more due to greater value of g.

4 (i) A person weighs 110.84 N on the moon, whose acceleration due to gravity is 1/6 of that the earth. If the value of g on the earth is 9.8 m/s^2, then calculate

(a) g on the moon

(b) mass of person on the moon

(c) weight of person on the earth

(ii) How does the value of g on the earth is related to the mass of the earth and its radius? Derive it.

Sol. (i) (a) g on the moon is given by

$$g' = \frac{g}{6} = \frac{9.8}{6} = 1.63 \text{ m/s}^2$$

(b) Given, a person weighs on the moon $= 110.84$ N

Mass of the person on the moon,

$$m = \frac{110.84}{1.63} = 68 \text{ kg}$$

(c) Weight of person on the earth $= mg$

$$= 68 \times 9.8 = 666.4 \text{ N-m}^2/\text{kg}^2$$

(ii) Value of g on earth is related to the mass of the earth and its radius.

Derivation

From Newton's law of gravitation,

$$F = \frac{GMm}{R^2} \quad \text{...(i)}$$

Here, M is mass of earth, object having mass m falling towards it and R is the distance between centres of earth and the object.

From second law of motion, force exerted on an object,

$$F = ma$$

Since, $a = g$ (i.e. acceleration due to gravity)

$$F = mg \quad \text{...(ii)}$$

Equating RHS of Eqs. (i) and (ii), we get

$$mg = \frac{GMm}{R^2}$$

$$g = \frac{GM}{R^2}$$

5 Two objects of masses m_1 and m_2 having the same size are dropped simultaneously from heights h_1 and h_2, respectively. Find out the ratio of time they would take in reaching the ground. Will this ratio remain the same, if

(i) one of the objects is hollow and the other one is solid

(ii) and both of them are hollow, size remaining the same in each case? Give reason. **NCERT Exemplar**

Sol. Height of object A, $h_1 = \frac{1}{2} g t_1^2$

Height of object B, $h_2 = \frac{1}{2} g t_2^2$

$\therefore \quad h_1 : h_2 = t_1^2 : t_2^2$ or $t_1 : t_2 = \sqrt{h_1} : \sqrt{h_2}$

(i) Acceleration due to gravity is independent of mass of falling body. So, ratio remains the same.

(ii) If bodies are hollow, then also ratio remains the same, i.e. $t_1 : t_2 = \sqrt{h_1} : \sqrt{h_2}$

6 A stone is dropped from the edge of a roof.

(i) How long does it take to fall 4.9 m?

(ii) How fast does it move at the end of that fall?

(iii) How fast does it move at the end of 7.9 m?

(iv) What is its acceleration after 1s and after 2 s?

Sol. Given, initial velocity, $u = 0$

Acceleration, $g = 9.8 \text{ m/s}^2$

Distance, $s = 4.9$ m

(i) We have, $s = ut + \frac{1}{2} gt^2$

$$4.9 = 0 \times t + \frac{1}{2} \times 9.8 \times t^2$$

$$t^2 = \frac{9.8}{9.8} = 1$$

$$\Rightarrow \quad t = 1 \text{ s}$$

The stone takes 1 s to fall 4.9 m

(ii) We have, $v^2 - u^2 = 2\,as$

$$v^2 - 0^2 = 2 \times 9.8 \times 4.9$$

$$\Rightarrow \quad v = \sqrt{96.04} = 9.8 \text{ m/s}$$

At the end of 4.9 m, stone will be moving at a speed of 9.8 m/s.

(iii) We have, $v^2 - u^2 = 2\,as$

$$v^2 - 0^2 = 2 \times 9.8 \times 7.9 \Rightarrow v = 12.44 \text{ m/s}$$

The stone will be moving with a speed of 12.44 m/s at the end of 7.9 m

(iv) During the free fall, the acceleration produced in a body remains constant.

So, acceleration after 1 s = 9.8 m/s^2

Acceleration after 2 s = 9.8 m/s^2

7 (i) A steel needle sinks in water but a steel ship floats. Explain, how.

(ii) Why do you prefer a broad and thick handle of your suitcase?

Sol. (i) Ship displaces more water than needle as volume of ship is more than that of needle. Since, upthrust depend on volume of object ($U = Vdg$), so more the volume of object, more upthrust act on it and object floats.

(ii) Since, pressure act on the body is inversely proportional to the surface area of contact, i.e.

$$p \propto \frac{1}{A}$$

It means that more the area of contact, less pressure will act on the body. As the broad and the thick handle of our suitcase has large area, due to which less pressure acts on our hand and it is very easy to take from one place to another.

8 The radius of the earth at the poles is 6357 km and the radius at the equator is 6378 km. Calculate the percentage change in the weight of a body when it is taken from the equator to the poles.

Sol. Let acceleration due to gravity at equator,

$$g_e = \frac{GM_e}{R_e^2}$$

and acceleration due to gravity at poles,

$$g_p = \frac{GM_e}{R_p^2}$$

The variation of acceleration due to gravity,

$$\Delta g = g_p - g_e = GM_e\left(\frac{1}{R_p^2} - \frac{1}{R_e^2}\right))$$

$$\text{Percentage variation in } g = \frac{GM_e\left(\frac{1}{R_p^2} - \frac{1}{R_e^2}\right)}{\frac{GM_e}{R_e^2}} \times 100$$

$$= \frac{R_e^2 - R_p^2}{R_e^2 R_p^2} \times 100 \times R_e^2 = \frac{R_e^2 - R_p^2}{R_p^2} \times 100$$

$$= \frac{(6378)^2 - (6357)^2}{(6357)^2} \times 100 \approx 0.7\%$$

∴ % variation in the weight of a body

= % change in g = 0.7%

CHAPTER EXERCISE

Multiple Type Questions

1 Newton's law of gravitation is universal law, because it
(a) acts on all bodies and particles in the universe
(b) acts on all the masses at all distances and not affected by the medium
(c) is always attractive
(d) None of the above

2 Gravitational force between two objects is 10 N. If masses of both objects are doubled without changing distance between them, then the gravitational force would become
(a) 2.5 N (b) 20 N
(c) 40 N (d) 10 N

3 The value of acceleration due to gravity
(a) is same on equator and poles
(b) is least on poles
(c) is least on equator
(d) increases from pole to equator

NCERT Exemplar

4 Three spheres have radii 1 cm, 2 cm and 3 cm, respectively. Which sphere exerts maximum pressure on earth ?
(a) First (b) Second
(c) Third (d) All equal

5 When a body is dipped completly or partially into a liquid, then weight (w) of the liquid displaced by the body and upthrust force on the body into the liquid are related as
(a) $w = F$ (b) $w < F$
(c) $w > F$ (d) None of these

Fill in the Blanks

6 The acceleration due to gravity on the moon is about .... of that on the earth.

7 The weight of an object on the earth is about .... of its weight on the moon.

8 A heavy ship floats in water because its .... density is less than that of water.

9 Archimedes' principle applied to liquids and ....

10 It is the .... force which makes objects appear lighter in water.

True and False

11 The acceleration due to gravity acting on a freely falling body is directly proportional to the mass of the body.

12 The weight of an object is not constant. It changes with the change in acceleration due to gravity (g).

13 The downward force acting on an object immersed in a liquid is called buoyant force.

14 When a body is falling vertically downwards, its acceleration due to gravity g is taken as positive.

Match the Columns

15 Match the following columns.

	Column I		Column II
A.	Fluids	p.	Pressure
B.	Pascal's law	q.	Liquids and gases
C.	Lactometer	r.	Liquids
D.	Hydrometer	s.	Milk

Assertion-Reason

Direction (Q.Nos. 16-18) *In each of the following questions, a statement of Assertion is given by the corresponding statement of Reason. Of the statements, mark the correct answer as*

(a) If both Assertion and Reason are true and Reason is the correct explanation of Assertion.
(b) If both Assertion and Reason are true, but Reason is not the correct explanation of Assertion.
(c) If Assertion is true, but Reason is false.
(d) If Assertion is false, but Reason is true.

16 **Assertion** A planet is heavently body revolving around the sun.

Reason A planet revolving around the sun follows Kepler's law.

17 **Assertion** At the centre of earth, the value of gravitational acceleration is zero.

Reason On going below the earth surface, the value of gravitational acceleration increases.

18 **Assertion** To float, a body must displace liquid whose weight is greater than actual weight of the body.

Reason During floating, the body will experience no net downward force in that case.

Case Based Questions

Direction (Q.Nos. 19-22) *Answer the question on the basis of your understanding of the following paragraph and related studied concepts:*

Weight is the force acting vertically downwards. Here, the force is acting perpendicular to the surface of the contact. The force acting on an object perpendicular to the surface is called thrust. When you stand on loose sand, the force that is the weight of your body is acting on an area equal to area of your feet. When you lie down, the same force acts on an area equal to the contact area of your whole body, which is larger than the area of your feet. Thus, the effects of forces of the same magnitude on different areas are different. The effect of thrust depends on the area on which it acts. The effect of thrust on sand is larger while standing than while lying.

19 When you stand on loose sand, your feet go deep into sand. Why?

20 According to given passage, when will the effect of thrust on sand is larger?

21 When you lie down on loose sand, force acts on an area equal to
(a) contact area of whole body
(b) area of your feet only
(c) weight of sand
(d) None of the above

22 When you stand on loose sand, then the direction of force acting on an area is
(a) horizontal to the surface of contact
(b) perpendicular to the surface of contact
(c) parallel to the surface of contact
(d) Both (a) and (b)

Answers

1. (b) 2. (c) 3. (c) 4. (a) 5. (a)
6. One-sixth 7. Six times 8. Average
9. Gases 10. Buoyant
11. False 12. True 13. False 14. True
15. (A) → (q), (B) → (p), (C) → (s), (D) → (r)
16. (b) 17. (c) 18. (a) 21. (a) 22. (b)

Very Short Answer (VSA) Type Questions

23 Does the force of gravitation exist at all the places of the universe?

24 Is gravitation an attractive or repulsive force?

25 The gravitational force between two objects is F. How will the force change when the distance between them is reduced to (1/4)th?

26 Weight of an object at a given place can be measure of its mass. Comment.

27 Is the volume of liquid displaced always equal to the volume of the body immersed in the liquid?

28 An object is immersed in three different liquids. Will it experience same buoyant force due to all the liquids?

29 Does density vary with temperature?

Short Answer (SA) Type Questions

30 A sphere of mass 40 kg is attracted by a second sphere of mass 15 kg when their centres 320 cm apart with a force of 0.1 milligram weight. Calculate the value of gravitational constant.

[**Ans.** $1.7 \times 10^{-8} \text{N-m}^2/\text{kg}^2$]

31 Does the acceleration of a freely falling object depend to any extent on the location, i.e. whether the object is on top of Mount Everest or in Death Valley, California? Explain.

32 Find the ratio of weights of a body on the earth and jupiter, given g on jupiter is 2.5 times that on the earth.

33 A man is asked to run with a bag containing 20 kg steel block. Will it be easier for him to run with 20 kg cotton replacing the block? Explain with reason.

34 A test tube floats in water with a small coin at its bottom. The mass of this test tube is equal to mass of seven coins and external volume is 16 cm^3. It just sinks when the third coin is added. Calculate the mass of each coin. (Density of water is 1g cm^{-3}) [**Ans.** 1.78 g]

Long Answer (LA) Type Questions

35 A stone is thrown vertically upward with an initial velocity of 50 m/s. Take, g as 10 m/s^2. Find the maximum height reached by the stone. What is the net displacement and the total distance covered by the stone?

[**Ans.** 125 m, zero, 250 m]

36 If a planet existed whose mass was twice that of the earth and whose radius is 3 times greater. How much will a 1 kg mass weigh in the planet? [**Ans.** 2.17 N]

37 What is upthrust? What are the quantities that can vary upthrust? How does it account for the floating of a body? When a partially immersed body is pressed down a little, what will happen to the upthrust?

38 (*i*) How does a boat float in water?

(*ii*) State two factors on which magnitude of buoyant force acting on a body, immersed in a fluid depends.

(*iii*) A block of wood can float while a similar sized block of concrete can be used as an anchor. Why?

39 How does the force of attraction between the two bodies depend upon their masses and distance between them? A student thought that two bricks tied together would fall faster than a single one under the action of gravity. Do you agree with his hypothesis or not? Comment.

Challengers*

1 If a satellite is revolving around a planet of mass M in an elliptical orbit of semi-major axis a, find the orbital speed of the satellite when it is at a distance r from the focus.

(a) $v^2 = GM\left[\frac{2}{r} - \frac{1}{a}\right]$
(b) $v^2 = GM\left[\frac{2}{r^2} - \frac{1}{a}\right]$
(c) $v^2 = GM\left[\frac{2}{r^2} - \frac{1}{a^2}\right]$
(d) $v^2 = G\left[\frac{2}{r} - \frac{1}{a}\right]$

2 Distance between the centres of two stars is $10a$. The masses of these stars are M and $16\,M$ and their radii are a and $2a$, respectively. A body of mass m is fired straight from the surface of the larger star towards the smaller star. The minimum initial speed for the body to reach the surface of smaller star is

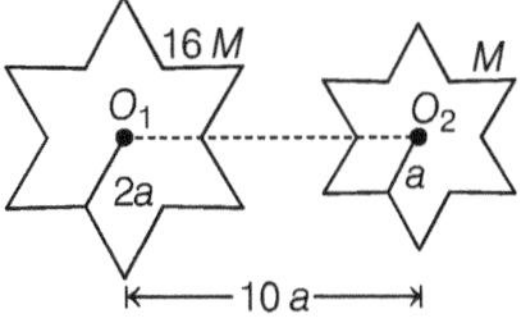

(a) $\frac{2}{3}\sqrt{\frac{GM}{a}}$
(b) $\frac{3}{2}\sqrt{\frac{5GM}{8a}}$
(c) $\frac{2}{3}\sqrt{\frac{5GM}{a}}$
(d) $\frac{3}{2}\sqrt{\frac{GM}{a}}$

3 A satellite is launched in a circular orbit of radius R. Another satellite is also launched in an orbit of radius $1.1\,R$. The period of the second satellite is larger than the first by approximately

(a) 7.5%
(b) 1.5%
(c) 15%
(d) 10%

4 If earth comes closer to sun by (3/4) th of the present distance, then the year of earth consists of how many days?

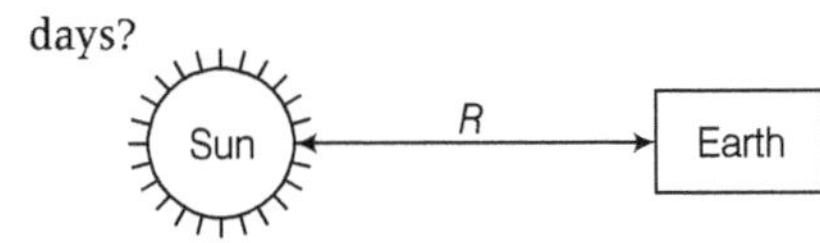

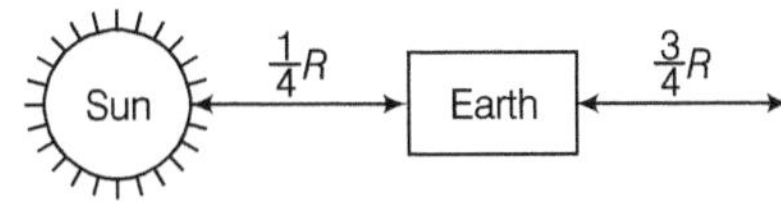

(a) 45.625 days
(b) 25.625 days
(c) 50.625 days
(d) 60.625 days

5 Communication satellites move in orbits of radius 44400 km around the earth. Assume that the only force acting on it is that due to the earth, then what is the acceleration of such a satellite?
(Take, mass of earth $= 6 \times 10^{24}$ kg)

(a) 0.3 m/s^2
(b) 0.2 m/s^2
(c) 0.4 m/s^2
(d) 0.5 m/s^2

6 The mean radius of the earth's orbit round the sun is 1.5×10^{11}. The mean radius of the orbit of mercury round the sun is 6×10^{10} m. The mercury will rotate around the sun in

(a) a year
(b) nearly 4 years
(c) nearly $\frac{1}{4}$ years
(d) 2.5 years

7 A tank 5m is high filled with water and then is filled to the top with oil of density 0.85 g/cm^3. The pressure at the bottom of the tank, due to these liquids is

(a) 1.85 dyne/cm^2
(b) 89.25 dyne/cm^2
(c) 462.5 dyne/cm^2
(d) 500 dyne/cm^2

8 A wooden block of volume 1000 cm^3 is suspended from a spring balance. It weighs 12 N in air. It is suspended in water such that half of the block is below the surface of water. The reading of the spring balance is

(a) 10 N
(b) 9 N
(c) 8 N
(d) 7 N

9 A body is floating in water with $\left(\frac{2}{3}\right)$ rd of its volume below the surface of water. What is the density of body?

(a) 666.7 kg/m^3
(b) 777.6 kg/m^3
(c) 656.7 kg/m^3
(d) 876.6 kg/m^3

10 A body of mass 6kg immerses in water partially. If the body displaces 100 g of water, then the apparent weight of the body is

(a) 59 N
(b) 40 N
(c) 49 N
(d) 60 N

Answer Key

1.	(a)	2.	(b)	3.	(c)	4.	(a)	5.	(b)
6.	(c)	7.	(c)	8.	(d)	9.	(a)	10.	(a)

RELATED ONLINE VIDEOS

Visit https://www.youtube.com/watch?v=P7vc4e8efus
OR Scan the Code

Visit https://www.youtube.com/watch?v=2ReflvqaYg8
OR Scan the Code

Visit https://www.youtube.com/watch?v=QXoQbWoIiRE
OR Scan the Code

These questions may or may not be asked in the examination, have been given just for additional practice.

CHAPTER

10

Work and Energy

In this chapter, we will study about scientific conception of work and its mathematical formula along with it. We will study two scientific which are closely related to work, i.e. energy and power.

Chapter Checklist

- Work
- Energy
  Forms of Energy
  - Kinetic Energy
  - Potential Energy
- Law of Conservation of Energy
- Rate of Doing work : Power

Work

Work is said to be done, if on applying a force on an object, it is displaced from its position in the direction of force.

Scientific Conception of Work

From the point of view of science, following two conditions need to be satisfied for work to be done.

(*i*) A force should act on an object. (*ii*) The object must be displaced.

If any one of the above conditions does not exist, work is not done.

e.g. A girl pulls a trolley and the trolley moves through a distance. In this way, she has exerted a force on the trolley and it is displaced. Hence, work is done.

Work Done by a Constant Force

Work done by a force on an object is equal to the magnitude of the force multiplied by the distance moved in the direction of force.

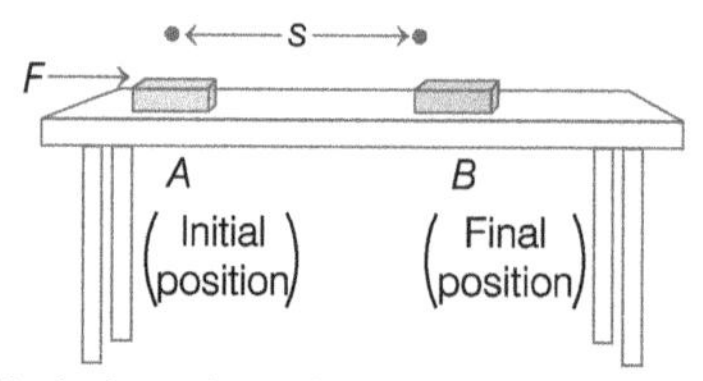

Work done by a force when the body moves in the direction of force

Let us assume, if a constant force F acts on an object at point A (shown in the figure), due to which the object gets displaced through a distance s in the direction of the force and reach at point B, then the work done (W) by force (F) on that object will be equal to the product of the force and displacement.

Work done = Force × Displacement in the direction of force

or $$\boxed{W = F \times s} \quad \ldots(\text{i})$$

SI Unit of Work

In Eq. (i), if $F = 1\text{N}$ and $s = 1\text{m}$, then the work done by the force will be 1 N-m.

The SI unit of work is **newton-metre** (N-m) which is also called **joule** (J).

Thus, 1 J is the amount of work done on an object when a force of 1 N displaces it by 1 m along the line of action of the force.

$$1 \text{ joule} = 1 \text{ newton} \times 1 \text{ metre} \Rightarrow 1\text{J} = 1\text{N-m}$$

Work is a **scalar quantity**, it has only magnitude and no direction.

Example 1. *A force of 10 N is acting on an object. The object is displaced through 5 m in the direction of force. What is the work done in this case?*

5 m

10 N → Initial position   Final position

Sol. Given, force, $F = 10\text{N}$, displacement, $s = 5\text{m}$

$\therefore$ Work done, $W = F \times s = 10 \text{ N} \times 5\text{m}$

$= 50 \text{ N-m or } 50\text{J}$

Positive, Negative and Zero Work

When the force F and displacement s are in the same direction (angle between direction of force and displacement is 0°), work done will be **positive**, i.e. work is done by the force.

e.g. A boy pulls an object towards himself.

$$W = + F \times s$$

When the force F and displacement s are in opposite direction (angle between direction of force and displacement is 180°), work done will be **negative**, i.e. work is done against the force.

e.g. Frictional force acts in the direction opposite to the direction of displacement, so work done by friction will be negative.

$$W = - F \times s$$

When the force and displacement are in perpendicular direction (angle between direction of force and displacement is 90°), work done is **zero.**

e.g. A coolie carrying load on his head. In this case, gravitational force is acting vertically downward (weight of load) and displacement is along horizontal direction, i.e. force and displacement are perpendicular to each other. **So, in this case, work done by gravitational force is zero.**

$$W = 0$$

Example 2. *A crane lifts a crate upwards through a height of 20 m. The lifting force provided by the crane is 5 kN. How much work is done by the force?*

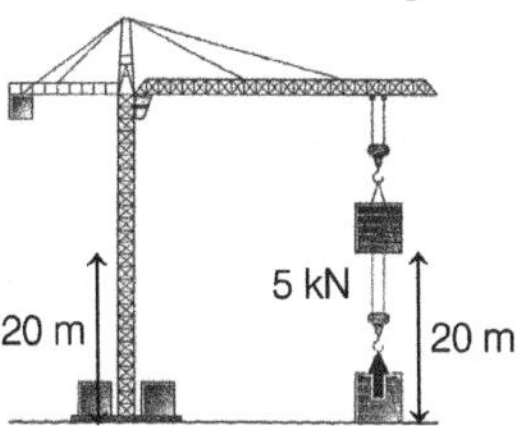

A crane provides the upward force needed to lift a crate

Sol. Given, force, $F = 5 \text{ kN} = 5000 \text{ N}$

Displacement, $s = 20$ m

Work done, $W = ?$

We know that work done, $W = Fs$

Here, force and displacement are in same direction.

So, $W = Fs \Rightarrow W = 5000 \text{ N} \times 20 \text{ m} = 100000 \text{ J}$

So, the work done by the force is 100000 J or 100 kJ.

Check Point 01

1 Give two necessary conditions without which work is not said to be done in science.

2 Fill in the blank:
.... work is done by a coolie to carry load on his head.

3 State True and False for the following statements:
(*i*) The work done by a force will be 1 N-m, if a force of 1N displaces a body by 100 cm.
(*ii*) The SI unit of work is joule-metre.

4 When is the work done said to be negative?

5 Give the formula to calculate work done on an object if force applied and displacement in it, are known.

Energy

It is the ability to do work. It is always essential for performing any mechanical work. An object having the capability to do work is said to possess energy. The object which does the work, losses energy and the object on which work is done, gains energy.

The energy of an object is measured in terms of its capacity of doing work.

The SI unit of energy is same as that of work, i.e. **joule** (J). 1 joule of energy is required to do 1 J of work. A larger unit of energy is kJ.

$$1 \text{kilo joule (kJ)} = 10^3 \text{ J}$$

Work done against a force is therefore stored as energy.

e.g. • When a fast moving cricket ball hits a stationary wicket, the wicket is thrown away.

• When a raised hammer falls on a nail placed on a piece of wood, it drives the nail into the wood.

Sun is the biggest natural source of energy to us. We can also get energy from the nuclei of atoms, the interior of the Earth and the tides in the ocean.

Forms of Energy

Energy exists in various forms like mechanical energy (the sum of potential energy and kinetic energy), heat energy, chemical energy, electrical energy and light energy.

Kinetic Energy

The energy which is possessed by an object due to its motion is called kinetic energy.

Its SI unit is joule (J). Kinetic energy of a body moving with certain velocity is equal to the work done on it to make it acquire that velocity. Kinetic energy of an object increases with its speed.

- Due to kinetic energy, a bullet fired from a gun can pierce a target.
- A moving hammer, drives a nail into the wood. Due to its motion, it has kinetic energy or ability to do work.
- A runing horse has kinetic energy.
- A flowing river passes kinetic energy.

The kinetic energy possessed by an object of mass m, moving with a uniform velocity v is given by,

$$\text{KE (or } E_K) = \frac{1}{2}mv^2$$

Calculation of Kinetic Energy

The kinetic energy of an object moving with a certain velocity is equal to the work done on it to make it acquire that velocity. Consider an object of mass m moving with a uniform velocity u. A force F is applied on it which displaces it through a distance s and it attains a velocity v.

F → [m] u → ... [m] v →
|← s →|

Then, work is done to increase its velocity from u to v.

$$W = Fs \quad \text{...(i)}$$

According to the equation of motion,

$$v^2 - u^2 = 2as$$

$$\therefore \quad s = \frac{v^2 - u^2}{2a} \quad \text{...(ii)}$$

where, a is uniform acceleration, u is initial velocity and v is final velocity.

Also from, $F = ma$ ...(iii)

Substituting the values of F and s from Eqs. (ii) and (iii) in Eq. (i), we have

$$W = ma \cdot \frac{v^2 - u^2}{2a} \quad \text{or} \quad W = \frac{1}{2}m(v^2 - u^2)$$

This is known as **work-energy theorem** (i.e. total work is equal to change in kinetic energy).

If initial velocity, $u = 0$

Then, $W = \frac{1}{2}mv^2$

This work done is equal to the kinetic energy of the object.

$$\therefore \quad \text{KE (or } E_K) = \frac{1}{2}mv^2 \quad \text{...(ii)}$$

Some important results can be derived from the formula $\text{KE} = \frac{1}{2}mv^2$, these are given below :

(*i*) If the mass of an object is doubled, its kinetic energy also gets doubled.

(*ii*) If the mass of an object is halved, its kinetic energy also gets halved.

(*iii*) If the speed of an object is doubled, its kinetic energy becomes four times.

(*iv*) If the speed of an object is halved, its kinetic energy becomes one-fourth.

(*v*) Heavy objects moving with high speed have more kinetic energy than small objects moving with same speed.

Example 3. *A bullet of mass 8 g is fired with a velocity of 80 ms^{-1}. Calculate its kinetic energy.*

Sol. Given, mass, $m = 8\text{ g} = \frac{8}{1000}$ kg and velocity, $v = 80\text{ ms}^{-1}$

$$\text{KE of the bullet} = \frac{1}{2}mv^2 = \frac{1}{2} \times \frac{8}{1000} \times (80)^2$$

$$= \frac{1}{2} \times \frac{8}{1000} \times 80 \times 80 = 25.6\text{ J}$$

Example 4. *If a body of mass 5 kg is moving along a straight line with velocity 10 ms^{-1} and acceleration 20 ms^{-2}. Find its kinetic energy (KE) after 10 s.*

Sol. Given, mass of the body, $m = 5$ kg

Initial velocity, $u = 10\text{ ms}^{-1}$

Acceleration, $a = 20\text{ ms}^{-2}$

Time, $t = 10$ s

Velocity, $v = ?$; KE = ?

First, we use equation of motion, $v = u + at$ to find v.

Then, we use $KE = \frac{1}{2} mv^2$ to find kinetic energy.

So, $v = u + at$

$\Rightarrow \quad v = (u + at)\, ms^{-1} \quad \ldots(i)$

As we know, kinetic energy, $KE = \frac{1}{2} mv^2 \quad \ldots(ii)$

So, $KE = \frac{1}{2} m \times (u + at)^2$ [from Eqs. (i) and (ii)]

$\Rightarrow \quad KE = \frac{1}{2} \times 5 \times (10 + 20 \times 10)^2$

$\Rightarrow \quad KE = \frac{1}{2} \times 5 \times 210 \times 210 = 110250\text{ J}$

Example 5. *What is the work done to increase the velocity of a van from 10 m/s to 20 m/s, if the mass of the is 2000 kg?*

Sol. Given, $m = 2000$ kg, $v_1 = 10\text{ ms}^{-1}$ and $v_2 = 20\text{ ms}^{-1}$

The initial Kinetic energy of the van

$KE_1 = \frac{1}{2} mv_1^2$ $[\because KE = \frac{1}{2} mv^2]$

$= \frac{1}{2} \times 2000\text{ kg} \times (10\text{ ms}^{-1})^2 = 100000\text{ J} = 100\text{ kJ}$

Final kinetic energy of the van

$KE_2 = \frac{1}{2} mv_2^2 = \frac{1}{2} \times 2000\text{ kg} \times (20\text{ ms}^{-1})^2$

$= 400000\text{ J} = 400\text{ kJ}$

The work done = Change in kinetic energy

$= 400\text{ kJ} - 100\text{ kJ} = 300\text{ kJ}$

So, the kinetic energy of van increases by 300 kJ when it speeds up from 10 ms^{-1} to 20 ms^{-1}.

Potential Energy

The energy possessed by a body due to its change in position or shape is called **potential energy.** Its SI unit is **joule** (J).

We can say that, the potential energy possessed by a body is the energy present in it by virtue of its position or configuration, e.g. a stretched rubber band, spring, string on the bow, etc. Now, we can say that a body possesses energy even when it is not in motion.

Examples of potential energy are given below:

- Water stored in dam has potential energy due to its position at the height.
- A stone lying on the roof of the building has potential energy due to its height.
- A wound spring of a watch has potential energy due to change of its shape.

Potential Energy of an Object at a Height

When an object is raised through a certain height above the ground, its energy increases. This is because work is done on it against gravity while it is being raised. The energy present in such an object is the **gravitational potential energy.** The gravitational potential energy of an object at a point above the ground is defined as the work done in raising it from the ground to that point against gravity.

Expression for Potential Energy

Consider an object of mass m, lying at a point A on the Earth's surface. Here, its potential energy is zero and its weight mg acts vertically downwards.

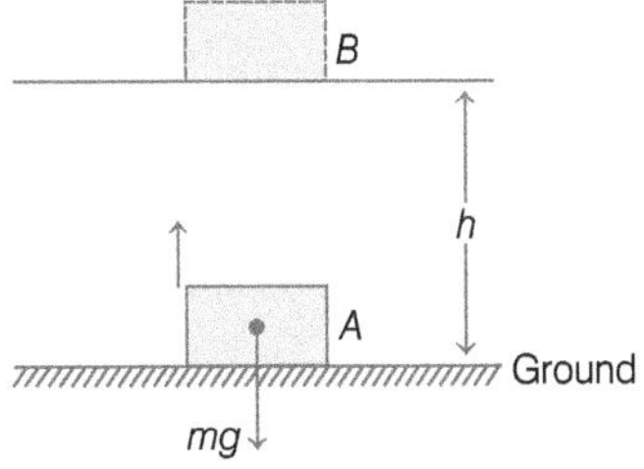

To lift the object to another position B at a height h, we have to apply a minimum force which is equal to mg in the upward direction. So, work is done on the body against the force of gravity. Therefore,

Work done = Force × Displacement

or $W = F \times s$

As, $F = mg$ [weight of the body]

Here, $s = h$

Therefore, $W = mg \times h = mgh$

i.e. $PE = mgh$

This work done is equal to the gain in energy of the body. This is the potential energy (PE) of the body.

$\therefore \quad \boxed{PE\ (\text{or } E_P) = mgh}$

The potential energy of an object at a height depends on the ground level or the zero level we choose.

An object in a given position can have a certain potential energy with respect to one level and a different value of potential energy with respect to another level.

The work done by gravity depends on the difference in vertical heights of the initial and final positions of the objects and not on the path along which the object is moved.

It is clear from the figure given below.

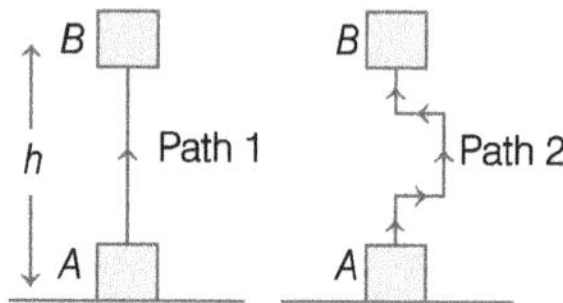

In both the above situations, the work done on the object is mgh.

Example 6. *Suppose you have a body of mass 1 kg in your hand. To what height will you raise it, so that it may acquire a gravitational potential energy of 1 J? (Take, $g = 10 \text{ ms}^{-2}$)*

Sol. Given, PE = 1 J, mass, $m = 1$ kg,

Acceleration due to gravity, $g = 10 \text{ ms}^{-2}$, $h = ?$

We know that, $\text{PE} = mgh$ or $1 = 1 \times 10 \times h$

$\therefore$ Height, $h = \dfrac{1}{1 \times 10} = 0.1 \text{ m} = 10 \text{ cm}$

Example 7. *A boy weighing 40 kg climbs up a vertical height of 200 m. Calculate the amount of work done by him. How much potential energy does he gain? (Take, $g = 9.8 \text{ ms}^{-2}$)*

Sol. Given that, mass, $m = 40$ kg

Acceleration due to gravity, $g = 9.8 \text{ ms}^{-2}$, height, $h = 200$ m

Work done by the body $= mgh = 40 \times 9.8 \times 200$

$= 78400 \text{ J} = 7.84 \times 10^4 \text{ J}$

Gain in PE = Work done $= 7.84 \times 10^4$ J

Example 8. *Suppose two bodies A and B having equal masses are kept at heights of h and 3 h, respectively. Find the ratio of their potential energies.*

Sol. Let the mass of each body be m.

PE of body $A = mgh$; PE of body $B = mg \times 3h$

Ratio of their potential energies $= \dfrac{mgh}{mg \times 3h} = \dfrac{1}{3} = 1:3$

Check Point 02

1. When is an object said to possess energy?
2. Fill in the blank:
   The work done by gravity .... depend on the path along which the object is moved.
3. State True and False for the following statements:
   (i) The kinetic energy of an object becomes one-third, if its speed is halved.
   (ii) When an object is raised through a certain height above the ground, its energy decreases.
4. Name the type of energy possessed by the water stored in a dam.
5. Give the formula to calculate the potential energy of an object of mass M kept at height h.
6. If an engine supplies 100 J of energy to a mass of 200 g, how high it can be lifted? (Given, $g = 9.8 \text{ ms}^{-2}$) **[Ans.** 51.02 m]

Law of Conservation of Energy

Law of conservation of energy states that energy can neither be created nor be destroyed, it can only be transformed from one form to another. The total energy before and after transformation, always remains constant.

Conservation of Energy During the Free Fall of a Body

Consider an object of mass m, lying at position B. It is made to fall freely from a height (h) above the ground as shown in figure.

B
x
A
$(h - x)$
h
C

At point B

At the start, the potential energy is mgh and kinetic energy is zero (as its velocity is zero). i.e. $\text{PE} = mgh$

$\text{KE} = 0$

$\therefore$ Total energy, $\text{TE} = \text{PE} + \text{KE} = mgh$

At point A

As it falls, its potential energy will change into kinetic energy. If v is the velocity of the object at a given instant, its kinetic energy would be $\frac{1}{2}mv^2$.

$$\text{PE} = mg(h - x)$$

From Newton's third equation of motion,

$$v^2 = u^2 + 2gx$$

$$\Rightarrow \quad v^2 = 2gx \qquad [\because u = 0]$$

$$\text{KE} = \frac{1}{2}mv^2 = \frac{1}{2}m \times 2gx = mgx \qquad [\because v^2 = 2gx]$$

$\therefore$ Total energy $= mg(h - x) + mgx = mgh$

Total energy, $\text{TE} = mgh$

At point C

As the fall of the object continues, the potential energy would decrease while the kinetic energy would increase. When the object is about to reach the ground, $h = 0$ and v will be the highest.

$$\text{PE} = 0$$

$$\text{KE} = \frac{1}{2}mv^2 = \frac{1}{2}m(2gh) = mgh \qquad [\because v^2 = 2gh]$$

$\therefore$ Total energy, $\text{TE} = mgh$

Thus, the sum of the potential energy and kinetic energy of the object would be the same at all points, i.e.

$$PE + KE = \text{constant}$$

or $$mgh + \frac{1}{2}mv^2 = \text{constant}$$

This verifies the law of conservation of energy.

Example 9. *An object of mass 10 kg is dropped from a height of 5 m. Fill in the blanks by computing the potential energy and kinetic energy in each case. (Take, $g = 10\ ms^{-2}$)*

Height at which the object is located (m)	Kinetic energy KE(J)	Potential energy PE (J)	Total energy PE + KE (J)
5			
4			
3			
2			
1			
Just above the ground			

Sol. Given, mass, $m = 10$ kg

Height, $h = 5$ m

Acceleration due to gravity, $g = 10\ ms^{-2}$

At height $h = 5$ m,

$KE = 0$, as $v = 0$

$PE = mgh = 10 \times 10 \times 5 = 500\,J$

Total energy (KE + PE) at height 5 m = 500 J

At height $h = 4$ m,

$$KE = \frac{1}{2}mv^2 = \frac{1}{2}m \times 2gs \qquad [\because v^2 = 2gs]$$

Distance covered, $s = 5 - 4 = 1$ m

$$\therefore \quad KE = \frac{1}{2} \times 10 \times 2 \times 10 \times 1 = 100\,J$$

$$PE = mgh = 10 \times 10 \times 4 = 400\,J$$

Total energy (KE + PE) at height 4 m = (100 + 400) = 500 J

At height $h = 3$ m,

$$s = 5 - 3 = 2\text{m}$$

$$\therefore \quad KE = \frac{1}{2}mv^2 = \frac{1}{2}m \times 2gs = mgs = 10 \times 10 \times 2 = 200\,J$$

Therefore, $PE = mgh = 10 \times 10 \times 3 = 300\,J$

Total energy (KE+ PE) at height 3 m =(200+300) = 500 J

At height $h = 2$ m,

$$s = 5 - 2 = 3\text{ m}$$

$$KE = mgs = 10 \times 10 \times 3 = 300\,J$$

$$PE = mgh = 10 \times 10 \times 2 = 200\,J$$

Total energy (KE + PE) at height 2 m = 300 + 200 = 500 J

At height $h = 1$ m,

$$s = 5 - 1 = 4\text{ m}$$

$$KE = \frac{1}{2}mv^2 = \frac{1}{2} \times m \times 2gs$$

$$= mgs = 10 \times 10 \times 4 = 400\,J$$

$$PE = mgh = 10 \times 10 \times 1 = 100\,J$$

Total energy (KE + PE) at height 1m = (400 + 100) = 500 J

At just above the ground, $h = 0$,

$$s = 5 - 0 = 5\text{ m}$$

$$KE = \frac{1}{2}mv^2 = mgs = 10 \times 10 \times 5 = 500\,J$$

$$PE = mgh = 10 \times 10 \times 0 = 0$$

Total energy (KE + PE) at just above the ground

$$= (500 + 0) = 500\,J$$

Therefore, the table will be as follows:

Height at which the object is placed (m)	Kinetic energy KE (J)	Potential energy PE (J)	Total energy KE + PE (J)
5	0	500	500 J
4	100	400	500 J
3	200	300	500 J
2	300	200	500 J
1	400	100	500 J
Just above the ground	500	0	500 J

Thus, total mechanical energy remains constant at each height, which proves that energy is always conserved.

Example 10. *A man is moving with high velocity of $30\ ms^{-1}$. Determine the total mechanical energy of the man weighing 60 kg, if he is on a height of 50 m at this speed. (Take, $g = 10\ ms^{-2}$)*

Sol. Given, mass of man, $m = 60$ kg

Velocity, $v = 30\ ms^{-1}$ and height, $h = 50$ m

Total energy (TE) of the man at a height of 50 m is given by

$$TE = PE + KE \qquad \ldots(i)$$

where, PE = potential energy (= mgh)

and KE = kinetic energy $\left(= \frac{1}{2}mv^2\right)$

$$TE = mgh + \frac{1}{2}mv^2 \qquad \text{[from Eq. (i)]}$$

$$= 60 \times 10 \times 50 + \frac{1}{2} \times 60 \times (30)^2$$

$$= 30000 + 27000$$

$$= 57000\,J$$

Transformation of Energy
(Are Various Energy Forms Interconvertible?)

One form of energy can be converted into other form of energy and this phenomenon is called **transformation of energy**. When an object is dropped from some height, its potential energy continuously converts into kinetic energy. When an object is thrown upwards, its kinetic energy continuously converts into potential energy.

e.g.

(*i*) Green plants prepare their own food (stored in the form of chemical energy) by using solar energy through the process of photosynthesis.

(*ii*) When we throw a ball, the muscular energy which is stored in our body, gets converted into kinetic energy of the ball.

(*iii*) The wound spring in the toy car possesses potential energy. As the spring is released, its potential energy changes into kinetic energy due to which, toy car moves.

(*iv*) In a stretched bow, potential energy is stored. As it is released, the potential energy of the stretched bow gets converted into the kinetic energy of arrow which moves in the forward direction with large velocity.

Some Energy Transformations

S.No.	Instruments	Transformations
1.	Electric motor	Electrical energy into mechanical energy.
2.	Electric generator	Mechanical energy into electrical energy.
3.	Steam engine	Heat energy into kinetic energy.
4.	Electric bulb	Electrical energy into light energy.
5.	Dry cell	Chemical energy into electrical energy.
6.	Solar cell	Light energy into electrical energy.

Check Point 03

1 State law of conservation of energy.

2 Fill in the blank:
.... energy gets converted into kinetic energy, when we throw a ball.

3 State True and False for the following statements:
(*i*) An electric bulb convert electrical energy into mechanical energy.
(*ii*) In a stretched bow, kinetic energy is stored.

4 Name the device which converts chemical energy into electrical energy.

5 A ball is thrown up vertically with a velocity of 20 ms^{-1}. At what height will its kinetic energy be half of its original value?
[**Ans.** 10.20 m]

Rate of Doing Work : Power

The rate of doing work or the rate at which energy is transferred or used or transformed to other form is called **power.**

If work W is done in time t, then

$$\text{Power} = \frac{\text{Work}}{\text{Time}} \Rightarrow \boxed{P = \frac{W}{t}}$$

The unit of power is **watt** (W) in honour of *James Watt.* We express larger rate of energy transfer in kilowatt (kW).

$$1 \text{ W} = 1 \text{ Js}^{-1}$$

or $1 \text{kW} = 1000 \text{ W} = 1000 \text{ Js}^{-1} \Rightarrow 1 \text{ MW} = 10^6 \text{ W},$

$$1 \text{ HP (horse power)} = 746 \text{ W}$$

Average Power

Average power is defined as the ratio of total work done by the total time taken. An agent may perform work at different rates at different intervals of time. In such situation, average power is considered by dividing the total energy consumed by the total time taken.

$$\therefore \boxed{\text{Average power} = \frac{\text{Total energy consumed}}{\text{Total time taken}}}$$

Example 11. *A boy does 400 J of work in 20 s and then he does 100 J of work in 2s. Find the ratio of the power delivered by the boy in two cases.*

Sol. *Case* I Work done by the boy, $W_1 = 400$ J

Time taken, $t_1 = 20$ s,

power, $P_1 = ?$

Case II Work done by the boy, $W_2 = 100$ J

Time taken, $t_2 = 2$ s,

power, $P_2 = ?$

$$\therefore \text{Power, } P = \frac{\text{Work done } (W)}{\text{Time taken } (t)}$$

$$P_1 = \frac{W_1}{t_1} = \frac{400}{20} = 20 \text{ W}$$

and $$P_2 = \frac{W_2}{t_2} = \frac{100}{2} = 50 \text{ W}$$

So, $$\frac{P_1}{P_2} = \frac{20}{50} = 2:5$$

Example 12. *A boy of mass 55 kg runs up a staircase of 50 steps in 10 s. If the height of each step is 10 cm, find his power. (Take g = 10 m/s^2).*

Sol. Weight of the boy = mg

$$= 55 \times 10 = 550 \text{ N}$$

Height of the staircase, $h = \frac{50 \times 10}{100} = 5\text{ m}$

Time taken to clim = 10 s

Thus, power $P = \frac{\text{Work done}}{\text{Time taken}} = \frac{mgh}{t} = \frac{550 \times 5}{10} = 275\text{ W}$

Example 13. *The heart does 1.2 J of work in each heart beat. How many times per minute does it beat, if its power is 2 W?*

Sol. Here, work done in each heart beat = 1.2 J

$t = 1\text{ min} = 60\text{ s}$, power, $P = 2\text{ W} = 2\text{ Js}^{-1}$

Total work done = $P \times t = 2 \times 60 = 120\text{ J}$

Number of times heart beats per minute

$$= \frac{\text{Total work done}}{\text{Work done in each heart beat}} = \frac{120}{1.2} = 100 \text{ times}$$

Example 14. *A horse exerts a pull on a cart of 500 N, so that horse cart system moves with a uniform velocity of 36 kmh^{-1}. What is the power developed by the horse in watt as well as in horse power?*

Sol. Given, Force, $F = 500\text{ N}$

and Velocity, $v = 36\text{ kmh}^{-1} = \frac{36 \times 1000}{3600}\text{ ms}^{-1} = 10\text{ ms}^{-1}$

As, $P = \frac{W}{t} = \frac{Fs}{t}$ [$\because W = Fs$ and $v = s/t$]

$= Fv = 500 \times 10 = 5000\text{ W}$

In horse power, $P = \frac{5000}{746} = 6.70\text{ HP}$

Check Point 04

1 What do you mean by the rate at which energy is transformed to other form?

2 What is the necessity of using term 'Average Power instead of power?

To Study NCERT Activities
Visit https://goo.gl/BGqgX3
OR Scan the Code

NCERT FOLDER

INTEXT QUESTIONS

1 A force of 7 N acts on an object. The displacement is say 8 m, in the direction of the force. Let us take it that the force acts on the object through the displacement. What is the work done in this case? **Pg 148**

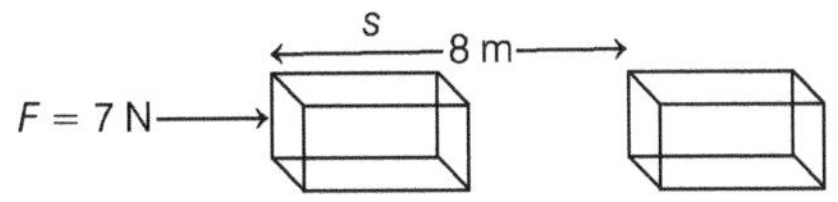

Sol. As work done,

$W = Fs$

[Work done is positive because force and displacement are in same direction]

$\therefore W = 7 \times 8 = 56\text{ J}$

2 When do we say that work is done? **Pg 149**

Sol. If a force acting on a body causes some displacement, then we can say that work is being done by the force on the body which is displaced.

3 Write an expression for the work done when a force is acting on an object in the direction of its displacement. **Pg 149**

Sol. Expression for the work done is given by

Work done, $W = +Fs$ [F and s are in same direction]

where, F = force and s = displacement. So, $W = Fs$

4 Define 1 J of work. **Pg 149**

Sol. 1 J of work is defined as the amount of work done on an object when a force of 1 N displaces it by 1 m along the line of action of the force.

5 A pair of bullocks exerts a force of 140 N on a plough. The field being ploughed is 15 m long. How much work is done in ploughing the length of field? **Pg 149**

Sol. Given, force, $F = 140\text{ N}$, displacement, $s = 15\text{ m}$

$\therefore$ Work done, $W = +Fs$

[F and s are in same direction]

So, $W = Fs = 140 \times 15 = 2100\text{ J}$

6 What is the kinetic energy of an object? **Pg 152**

Sol. Kinetic energy of an object is defined as the energy due to by virtue of its motion.

7 Write an expression for the kinetic energy of an object. **Pg 152**

Sol. The expression for kinetic energy for an object is given by

$$KE = \frac{1}{2} mv^2$$

where, KE = kinetic energy, m = mass of the body and v = velocity of the body.

8 The kinetic energy of an object of mass m moving with a velocity of 5 ms^{-1} is 25 J. What will be its kinetic energy when its velocity is increased three times? **Pg 152**

Sol. As from the question,

Kinetic energy (KE_i) initially is given by $\frac{1}{2} mv_i^2$

where, m = mass of the body, v_i = initial velocity

$$KE_i = \frac{1}{2} mv_i^2 \quad [\text{given, } KE_i = 25\,J, \; v_i = 5\,ms^{-1}]$$

$$\Rightarrow \quad 25\,J = \frac{1}{2} m(5^2)$$

$$\Rightarrow \quad m = \frac{25 \times 2}{5 \times 5}$$

$$\Rightarrow \quad m = 2\,kg$$

Now, as from question, final velocity (v_f) becomes 3 times of its initial velocity, i.e.

$$v_f = 3v_i$$

$$\Rightarrow \quad v_f = 3 \times 5 = 15\,ms^{-1}$$

Now, kinetic energy,

$$KE = \frac{1}{2} mv_f^2 = \frac{1}{2} \times 2 \times 15 \times 15$$

$$= 225\,J$$

9 What is power? **Pg 156**

Sol. Power is defined as the rate of doing work. If the work done by an object in time t is W. Then, power, $P = \frac{W}{t}$

Its unit is Js^{-1} or watt.

10 Define 1 watt of power. **Pg 156**

Sol. $\therefore$ Power, $P = \frac{W}{t}$. If $W = 1\,J, t = 1\,s$

Then, $P = \frac{1\,J}{1\,s} = 1\,W$

Power of an object is said to be 1 watt, if it does 1 J of work in 1 s.

11 A lamp consumes 1000 J of electrical energy in 10 s. What is the power? **Pg 156**

Sol. Given, energy = 1000 J

i.e. work done, $W = 1000\,J$

Time, $t = 10\,s$

$$\therefore \quad \text{Power of lamp, } P = \frac{W}{t} = \frac{1000}{10} = 100\,W$$

12 Define average power. **Pg 149**

Sol. Average power is defined as the ratio of total work done to the total time taken.

EXERCISES

(On Pages 158 and 159)

1 Look at the activities listed below. Reason out whether or not work is done in the light of your understanding of the term 'work.'

(*i*) Seema is swimming in a pond.
(*ii*) A donkey is carrying a load on its back.
(*iii*) A wind mill is lifting water from a well.
(*iv*) A green plant is carrying out photosynthesis.
(*v*) An engine is pulling a train.
(*vi*) Food grains are getting dried in the Sun.
(*vii*) A sail boat is moving due to wind energy.

Sol. (*i*) Work is being done by Seema because she displaces the water by applying the force.

(*ii*) No work is being done by the gravitational force because the direction of force, i.e. load is vertically downward and displacement is along horizontal. If displacement and force are perpendicular, then no work is done.

(*iii*) Work is done because wind mill is lifting the water, i.e. it is changing the position of water.

(*iv*) No work is done because there is no force and displacement.

(*v*) Work is done because engine is changing the position of train.

(*vi*) No work is done because there is no force and no displacement.

(*vii*) Work is done because of the force acting on the boat, it starts moving.

2 An object thrown at a certain angle to the ground moves in a curved path and falls back to the ground. The initial and the final points of the path of the object lie on the same horizontal line. What is the work done by the force of gravity on the object?

Sol. As we know that work done is the product of force and displacement and here in this case, displacement in the direction of gravitational force (change in height) is zero, so work done by the force of gravity on the object is zero.

3 **A battery lights a bulb. Describe the energy changes involved in the process.**

Sol. A battery contains chemicals and supplies electrical energy. So, a battery converts chemical energy into electrical energy. In an electrical bulb, the electrical energy is first converted into heat energy. This heat energy causes the filament of bulb to become white-hot and produce light energy.
Thus, the energy changes are
Chemical energy → Electrical energy → Heat energy → Light energy

4 **Certain force acting on a mass 20 kg mass changes its velocity from 5 ms^{-1} to 2 ms^{-1}. Calculate the work done by the force.**

Sol. Given, mass, $m = 20$ kg

Initial velocity, $u = 5\ ms^{-1}$

Final velocity, $v = 2\ ms^{-1}$

∴ Work done by the force = Change in kinetic energy

= Final kinetic energy − Initial kinetic energy

$$= \frac{1}{2}mv^2 - \frac{1}{2}mu^2$$

$$= \frac{1}{2}m(v^2 - u^2) = \frac{1}{2} \times 20\,[(2)^2 - (5)^2]$$

$$= 10\,(4 - 25) = 10 \times (-21) = -210\ J$$

5 **A mass of 10 kg is at a point *A* on the table. It is moved to a point *B*. If the line joining *A* and *B* is horizontal, what is the work done on the object by the gravitational force? Explain your Solwer.**

Sol. Here, both the initial and final positions are on the same horizontal line. So, there is no difference in height, i.e. $h = 0$. where, h = difference in the heights of initial and final positions of the object.
We know that work done by gravitational force,

$$W = mgh$$

∴ Work done, $W = mg \times 0 = 0$

6 **The potential energy of a freely falling object decreases progressively. Does this violate law of conservation of energy? Why?**

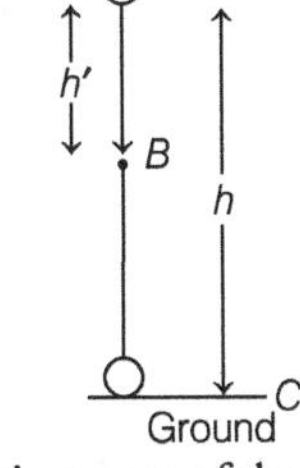

Sol. It is true that the potential energy of freely falling object decreases progressively. But as the object falls down, its speed increases, i.e. the kinetic energy of the object increases progressively (kinetic energy will increase with the increase in speed).
Now, we can say that the law of conservation of energy is not violated, because the decrease in potential energy results in the increase of kinetic energy.

7 **What are the various energy transformations that occur when you are riding a bicycle?**

Sol. In case of riding a bicycle, the muscular energy is converted into the kinetic energy of the bicycle.

8 **Does the transfer of energy take place when you push a huge rock with all your might and fail to move it? Where is the energy you spend going?**

Sol. When we push a huge rock, then the rock also exerts a large force on us (according to Newton's third law of motion). The muscular energy spent by us in the process is used to oppose the huge force acting on us due to the rock.

9 **An object of mass 40 kg is raised to a height of 5 m above the ground. What is its potential energy, if object is allowed to fall. Find its kinetic energy when it is half way down.**

Sol. Given, mass, $m = 40$ kg, height, $h = 5$ m

As potential energy is given by PE = mgh

So, PE = $40 \times 10 \times 5 = 2000$ J [∵ $g = 10\ ms^{-2}$]

When it is allowed to fall, its PE gets converted into kinetic energy KE. So, when it reaches to the half-way, half of its PE gets converted to KE.

So, $mg\frac{h}{2} = \frac{1}{2}mv^2$ [where, v = velocity at the bottom]

So, $KE = mg\frac{h}{2} = 40 \times 10 \times \frac{5}{2}$

$= 1000$ J

10 **What is the work done by the force of gravity on a satellite moving round the Earth? Justify your answer.** **NCERT**

Sol. Work done by the force of gravity on a satellite moving round the Earth is zero. Because the angle between force (centripetal) and displacement in case of circular motion.
So, work done, $W = 0$

11 **Can there be displacement of an object in the absence of any force acting on it? Think, discuss this question with your friends and teacher.**

Sol. Yes, if an object moves with a constant velocity, i.e. there is no acceleration, then no force acts on it. As the object is moving, so it gets displaced from one position to another position.

12 **A person holds a bundle of hay over his head for 30 min and gets tired. Has he done some work or not? Justify your answer.**

Sol. On holding a bundle of hay over the head, work done by the person is zero because there is no displacement.

13 Illustrate the law of conservation of energy by discussing the energy changes which occur when we draw a pendulum bob to one side and allow it to oscillate. Why does the bob eventually come to rest? What happens to its energy eventually? Is it a violation of the law of conservation of energy?

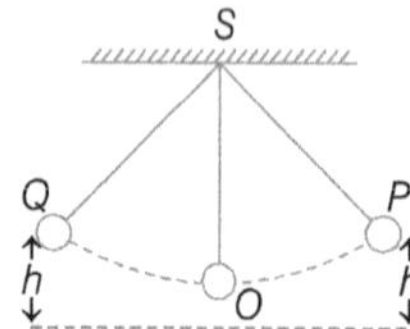

Sol. Let a simple pendulum be suspended from a rigid support S and OS be the equilibrium position of the pendulum. Let the pendulum be displaced to a position P, where it is at rest. At position P, the pendulum has potential energy (mgh). When the pendulum is released from position P, it begins to move towards position O. The speed of the pendulum increases and its height decreases that means the potential energy is converting into kinetic energy.

At position O, whole of the potential energy of the pendulum is converted into its kinetic energy.

Then, the pendulum swings to other side due to inertia of motion. As the pendulum begins to move towards position Q, the speed of pendulum decreases and height increases that means kinetic energy is converting into potential energy. At point Q, whole of the kinetic energy is converted into potential energy.

Thus, we find that the potential energy is converted into kinetic energy and *vice-versa* during the motion of the pendulum. But the total energy remains constant.

When the pendulum oscillates in air, the air friction opposes its motion. So, some part of kinetic energy of pendulum is used to overcome this friction. With the passage of time, energy of the pendulum goes on decreasing and finally becomes zero.

The energy of the pendulum is transferred to the atmosphere. So, energy is being transferred, i.e. is converted from one form to another. So, no violation of law of conservation of energy takes place.

14 An object of mass m is moving with a constant velocity v. How much work should be done on the object in order to bring the object to rest?

Sol. Concept Change in kinetic energy (KE) = Work done

Given, mass = m, initial velocity, $u = v$

Final velocity, $v = 0$

So, $$W = \frac{1}{2}mv^2 - \frac{1}{2}mu^2$$

$$\Rightarrow \quad W = \frac{1}{2}m(0)^2 - \frac{1}{2}mv^2$$

$$\Rightarrow \quad W = -\frac{1}{2}mv^2$$

Hence, the work that should be done in order to bring the object to rest is $\frac{1}{2}mv^2$.

15 Calculate the work required to be done to stop a car of 1500 kg moving at a velocity to 60 kmh^{-1}.

Sol. Concept Change in kinetic energy is equal to the work done W.

Given, initial velocity, $u = 60$ kmh^{-1}

$$= 60 \times \frac{5}{18} = \frac{50}{3} \text{ ms}^{-1}$$

$$[\because 1 \text{ kmh}^{-1} = 5/18 \text{ ms}^{-1}]$$

Final velocity, $v = 0$

So, magnitude of change in kinetic energy = W

$$= \frac{1}{2}mv^2 - \frac{1}{2}mu^2$$

$$\Rightarrow \quad W = \frac{1}{2}m(v^2 - u^2)$$

$$= \frac{1}{2} \times 1500 \times \left(\frac{-50 \times 50}{9}\right)$$

$$= -\frac{1}{2} \times \frac{1500 \times 50 \times 50}{9}$$

$$W = -\frac{625000}{3} = -208333.3 \text{ J}$$

Hence, the work required to be done to stop a car is 208333.3 J.

16 In each of the following, a force F is acting on an object of mass m. The direction of displacement is from West to East shown by the longer arrow. Observe the figure carefully and state whether the work done by the force is negative, positive or zero.

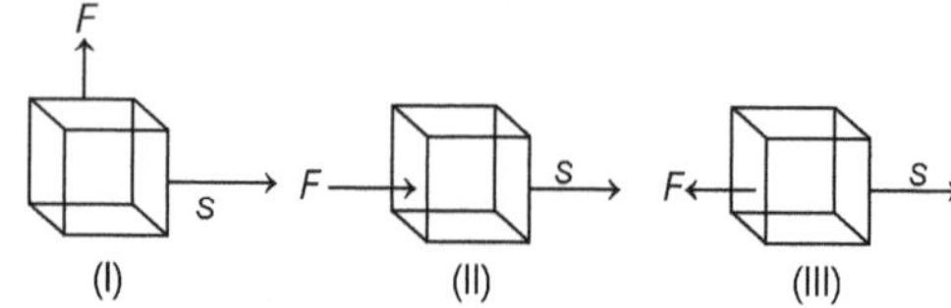

Sol. (*i*) In Fig. (I), angle between F and s is 90°, so work done is zero.

(*ii*) In Fig. (II), angle between F and s is 0°, so work done is positive.

(*iii*) In Fig. (III), angle between F and s is 180°, so work done is negative.

17 Soni says that the acceleration in an object could be zero even when several forces are acting on it. Do you agree with her? Why?

Sol. Yes, I am agree with Soni, the acceleration of an object can be zero even when several forces are acting on it, if the resultant of all the forces acting on object is zero.

18 A freely falling object eventually stops on reaching the ground. What happens to its kinetic energy?

Sol. When freely falling object strikes the Earth, some sound and heat is produced. So, the kinetic energy of the object converts into sound energy and heat energy.

SUMMARY

- **Work** is said to be done in a physical activity involving a force and movement in the direction of force and in the process an equal amount of energy is used up.
  Two conditions which need to be satisfied for work to be done.
  (i) A force should act on the object.
  (ii) The object must be displaced.
- **Work done** by a force on an object is equal to the magnitude of the force multiplied by the distance moved in the direction of force, i.e. $W = F \times s$.
  The SI unit of work is **joule** (J).
  1 J is the amount of work done on an object when a force of 1 N displaces it by 1 m along the line of action of force.
- **Energy** is the ability to do work.
  The SI unit of energy is same as that of work, i.e. **joule.**
  A larger unit of energy is kilojoule (kJ).
- **Relation between Joule and Kilojoule**
  1 kilojoule = 1000 joule.
- The SI unit of work and energy is named after British Physicist, James Prescott Joule.
- Then energy which is possessed by an object due to its motion is called **kinetic energy.**
  The SI unit of kinetic energy is **joule** (J).
  The kinetic energy possessed by an object of mass m, moving with a uniform velocity v is $\text{KE} = \frac{1}{2}mv^2$.
- The **work-energy theorem** is given as $W = \frac{1}{2}m(v^2 - u^2)$.
  If initial velocity $u = 0$, then $W = \frac{1}{2}mv^2$.
- The energy possessed by a body due to its position or change in its configuration (i.e. shape or position) is known as **potential energy**.
  The SI unit of potential energy is **joule** (J).
  The potential energy of an object can be given as PE $= mgh$.
- According to **law of conservation of energy**, energy can neither be created nor be destroyed but it can be transformed from one form to another.
- During the free fall of a body, its energy is always conserved.
- The sum of potential energy and kinetic energy of an object is same at all the points.
- One form of energy can be converted into other forms of energy, this phenomenon is known as **transformation of energy**.

Some Energy Transformations
(i) **Electric Motor** Electrical energy into mechanical energy.
(ii) **Electric Generator** Mechanical energy into electrical energy.
(iii) **Steam Engine** Heat energy into kinetic energy.
(iv) **Electric Bulb** Electrical energy into light energy.
(v) **Dry Cell** Chemical energy into electrical energy.
(vi) **Solar Cell** Light energy into electrical energy.

- The rate of doing work or the rate at which the energy is transformed is known as **power** (P).
  $$\text{Power} = \frac{\text{Work done}}{\text{Time}}$$
  $$\Rightarrow \quad P = \frac{W}{t}$$
  The SI unit of power is **watt** (W).
- The relation between watt and horse power can be given as 1(horse power) HP = 746 W.
- **Average power** is defined as the ratio of total work done by total time taken.

For Mind Map
Visit https://goo.gl/45p5Nb
OR Scan the Code

Exam Practice

Objective Type Questions

Multiple Choice Questions

1 When a horse-pulls a cart, who does the work ?

(a) Cart (b) Wheels (c) Road (d) Horse

Sol. (d) When a horse-pulls a cart, work is being done by horse.

2 If 10 N of force is applied to an object, but the object does not move, then how much work being done by the force ?

(a) Zero (b) 10 J (c) 10 N (d) 20 J

Sol. (a) If there is no displacement due to application of force, then net work done will be zero.

3 The work done on an object does not depend upon the

(a) displacement
(b) force applied
(c) angle between force and displacement
(d) initial velocity of the object

NCERT Exemplar

Sol. (d) We know that, $W = F \cdot d \cos\theta$

Here, $F =$ force applied on the object,
$d =$ displacement and θ is angle between force and displacement. So, the work done on an object does not depend upon the initial velocity of the object.

4 If two stones A and B are dropped from a tower, then which one has maximum kinetic energy ?

(a) Lighter stone (b) Heavier stone
(c) Both have equal (d) None of these

Sol. (b) If two stones are dropped from some height, then the heavier stone has greater kinetic energy w.r.t. lighter stone, because kinetic energy is directly proportional to mass.

5 A monkey weighing 50 kg climbs up a vertical tree of height 300 m. How much potential energy does it gain? [Take, $g = 9.8 \text{ m/s}^2$]

(a) 1.47×10^4 J (b) 14.7×10^3 J
(c) 14.7×10^2 J (d) 14.7×10^4 J

Sol. (d) Given, $m = 50$ kg, $g = 9.8 \text{ ms}^{-2}$, $h = 300$ m

Work done by the body $= mgh$

$$= 50 \times 9.8 \times 300 = 14.7 \times 10^4 \text{ J}$$

Gain in PE = Work done $= 14.7 \times 10^4$ J

6 A ball is allowed to fall freely from a tower. Which energy is possessed at the middle point during the fall ?

(a) Kinetic only
(b) Potential only
(c) Both potential and kinetic
(d) Heat only

Sol. (c) At middle point of fall, the ball has both kinetic and potential energies.

7 Water stored in a dam possesses

(a) no energy (b) electrical energy
(c) kinetic energy (d) potential energy

NCERT Exemplar

Sol. (d) Potential energy is stored energy or the energy of position, so water stored in a dam possesses potential energy.

8 When a body falls freely towards the earth, then its total energy

(a) increases
(b) decreases
(c) remains constant
(d) first increases and then decreases

NCERT Exemplar

Sol. (c) Since, total energy of the system is always conserved, so when a body falls freely towards the earth, then its total energy remains constant, i.e. the sum of the potential energy and kinetic energy of the body would be same at all points.

9 In solar cell, light energy is

(a) converted into chemical energy
(b) converted into mechanical energy
(c) converted into electrical energy
(d) converted into gravitational energy

Sol. (c) In solar cell, light energy is converted into electrical energy.

10 A horse does 5000 J of work in 100 s. What is its power ?

(a) 50 W (b) 50 J
(c) 10 W (d) 10 J

Sol. (a) Given, work done, $W = 5000$ J

Time taken, $t = 100$ s

We know that,

Power, $P = \dfrac{W}{t} = \dfrac{5000}{100} = 50$ J/s

Thus, power, $P = 50$ W

Fill in the Blanks

11 When a force is applied on a body in opposite direction of its displacement, then work done is ....

Sol. Negative

12 The .... energy is possessed by a running horse.

Sol. Kinetic energy

13 Energy can be neither created nor destroyed but it can be converted from one form to another form of energy. This is the ....

Sol. Law of conservation of energy

14 The rate of doing work is called ....

Sol. Power

15 One horse power is equal to ....

Sol. 746 W

True and False

16 When the force and displacement are in perpendicular direction, then work done is said to be positive.

Sol. False; Work done, $W = Fs\cos\theta$

When $\theta = 90°$, $W = Fs\cos 90°$

$W = 0$ $[\because \cos 90° = 0]$

17 If the speed of an object is doubled, then its kinetic energy becomes four times.

Sol. True; Since, kinetic energy of a body is directly proportional to the square of speed, hence if the speed of an object is doubled, then its kinetic energy becomes four times.

18 The energy possessed by a body due to its change in position or shape is called kinetic energy.

Sol. False; The energy possessed by a body due to its change in position or shape is called potential energy.

19 Heavy objects moving with high speed have same kinetic energy of small objects moving with same speed.

Sol. False; Heavy objects moving with high speed have more kinetic energy than small objects moving with more speed because heavy objects have more mass than small objects.

20 The SI unit of power is Js^{-1}.

Sol. True; The SI unit of power is Js^{-1} or watt.

Match the Columns

21 A body is dropped from a height h with zero initial velocity. Match the items of Column I with the items of Column II and choose the correct codes given below.

Column I	Column II
A. At height h, total energy of body remains in the form of	p. Both kinetic and potential energies
B. At height $\frac{h}{2}$, total energy of body remains in the form of	q. Heat energy
C. When body is just about to touch the ground, then its total energy remains in the form of	r. Potential energy
D. When body comes to rest after falling on the ground, then its total energy remains in the form of	s. Kinetic energy

Sol. (A) → (r), (B) → (p), (C) → (s), (D) → (q)

(A) → (r); At maximum height h, body is in rest, so kinetic energy is zero, hence total energy remains in the form of potential energy.

(B) → (p); At height $h/2$, body gains some velocity, hence both kinetic and potential energies are present. Therefore, total energy remains in the form of kinetic and potential energies both.

(C) → (s); When body is just about to reach the ground, then $h = 0$. Velocity of body is maximum, hence total energy of body remains in the form of kinetic energy.

(D) → (q); When body comes to rest, then its total energy is converted into heat energy.

Assertion-Reason

Direction (Q.Nos. 22-25) *In each of the following questions, a statement of Assertion is given by the corresponding statement of Reason. Of the statements, mark the correct answer as*

(a) If both Assertion and Reason are true and Reason is the correct explanation of Assertion.
(b) If both Assertion and Reason are true, but Reason is not the correct explanation of Assertion.
(c) If Assertion is true, but Reason is false.
(d) If Assertion is false, but Reason is true.
(e) If Assertion and Reason both are false.

22 **Assertion** Work done by a force is zero when displacement is in perpendicular direction of applied force.

Reason Work done is given by $W = Fs\cos\theta$, where θ is the angle between force (F) and displacement (s).

Sol. (a) Work done by a force F,

$$W = F\,s\cos\theta$$

when $\theta = 90°$, then $W = Fs\cos 90° = 0$

Hence, both Assertion and Reason are true and Reason is the correct explanation of Assertion.

23 Assertion Work done by friction is always positive.

Reason Work done by a force is given by $W = Fs\cos\theta$, where F, s and θ are force displacement and angle between force and displacement, respectively.

Sol. (d) Friction always acts in opposite direction of displacement, hence $\theta = 180°$.

$\therefore$ Work done by friction,

$$W = Fs\cos 180° = -Fs \quad [\because \cos 180 = -1]$$

Therefore, work done by friction is always negative.

Hence, Assertion is false, but Reason is true.

24 Assertion Total energy of freely falling body is constant at each point.

Reason Kinetic energy of freely falling body is minimum, when it reaches at ground.

Sol. (c) According to law of conservation of energy, total energy of freely falling body remains conserved. Kinetic energy is maximum when body reaches at ground. Hence, Assertion is true, but Reason is false.

25 Assertion Electric motor converts mechanical energy into electrical energy.

Reason Mechanical energy is equal to kinetic energy.

Sol. (e) Electric motor converts electrical energy into mechanical energy. Mechanical energy is equal to sum of kinetic energy and potential energy.

Hence, Assertion and Reason both are false.

Case Based Questions

Direction (Q.Nos. 26-29) *Answer the question on the basis of your understanding of the following table and related studied concepts:*

Following table gives an approximate idea about the energy associated with different phenomena:

Phenomenon	Energy (in J)
Rotational energy of earth	10^{29}
Annual solar energy incident on the earth	5×10^{24}
Annual wind energy dissipated near earth's surface	10^{22}
Energy released of 15 megaton fusion bomb	10^{17}
Energy released in burning 1000 kg of coal	3×10^{10}
Kinetic energy of large jet aircraft	10^{9}
Daily food intake of a human adult	10^{7}
Typical energy of a proton in nucleus	10^{-13}
Typical energy of an electron in an atom	10^{-18}
Energy to break one bond in DNA	10^{-20}

26 The ratio of the phenomenon of maximum energy to the phenomeno of minimum energy is

(a) $10^{39} : 1$ (b) $10^{9} : 1$
(c) $10^{49} : 1$ (d) $10^{19} : 1$

Sol. (c) According to given table, maximum energy is given due to the phenomenon of rotation of earth

$\therefore E_{max} = 10^{29}$ J

Minimum energy is given due to the phenomenon of breaking of one bond in DNA.

i.e. $E_{min} = 10^{-20}$ J

$$\therefore \frac{E_{max}}{E_{min}} = \frac{10^{29}}{10^{-20}} = 10^{49}$$

$$\therefore E_{max} : E_{min} = 10^{49} : 1$$

27 The number of broken bonds in DNA to get 100 J of energy are

(a) 10^{20} (b) 10^{10}
(c) 10^{18} (d) 10^{22}

Sol. (d) $\therefore 10^{-20}$ J energy is obtained due to break of one bond in DNA.

$\therefore$ To obtain energy of 100 J, number of broken bonds is DNA $= \dfrac{100}{10^{-20}} = 10^{22}$

28 Find the calorific value of coal.

Sol. From given table,

Mass of burned coal, $m = 1000$ kg

Energy released, $E = 3 \times 10^{10}$ J

$$\therefore \text{Calorific value of coal} = \frac{E}{m} = \frac{3 \times 10^{10}}{1000} = 3 \times 10^{7} \text{ J/kg}$$

29 If mass of large jet aircraft is 1000 kg, then find the velocity of jet aircraft.

Sol. Given, $m = 1000$ kg

From table, kinetic energy of jet aircraft, $K = 10^9$ J

i.e. $\frac{1}{2}mv^2 = 10^9$

$\Rightarrow \frac{1}{2} \times 1000 \times v^2 = 10^9 \Rightarrow v = \sqrt{2} \times 10^3$

$= 1.414 \times 10^3 = 1414$ m/s

Direction (Q.Nos. 30-33) *Answer the question on the basis of your understanding of the following passage and related studied concepts:*

A ball is thrown vertically upward. When it rises, the gravitational force does negative work on it, decreasing its kinetic energy. As the ball descends, the gravitational force does positive work on it, increasing its kinetic energy. The ball falls back to the point of projection with same velocity and kinetic energy with which it was thrown up. The net work done by the gravitational force on the ball during the round trip is zero because work done by the gravity on displacing a body from one point to another points depends only on the ends positions of the body.

30 Work done by the gravitational force on the ball is

(a) conservative
(b) non-conservative
(c) path independent
(d) Both (a) and (c)

Sol. (d) Work done by the gravitational force on displacing a body from one point to another point does not depend on the path taken, it depends only on the ends positions of the body, hence gravitational force is a conservative force.

31 Net work done by the conservative force during the round trip of a body is always

(a) zero (b) positive
(c) negative (d) None of these

Sol. (a) Work done by the conservative force depends only on initial and final position of the object. During round trip of a body, initial and final position of the body coincides, hence work done by the conservative force is zero.

32 When the ball moves vertically upward, then work done by gravitational force is negative. Why?

Sol. When the ball moves vertically upward, then angle between the direction of gravitational force and displacement remains 180°.

$\therefore$ Work done, $W = Fs \cos 180° = -Fs$

Therefore, work done by gravitational force on the ball during upward movement is negative.

33 Name the energy of the ball which remains same during round trip of the ball.

Sol. Total energy (sum of kinetic and potential energy).

Very Short Answer Type Questions

34 Why do we say work done against gravity is negative?

Sol. It is because force and displacement are in opposite directions to each other.

35 A man is holding a suitcase in his hand at rest. What is the work done by him?

Sol. Zero, as displacement is zero.

36 What will cause greater change in kinetic energy of a body? Changing its mass or changing its velocity.

Sol. Change in velocity will cause greater change in kinetic energy because $KE = \frac{1}{2}mv^2$

37 Name the type of energy stored in spring of a watch.

Sol. Elastic potential energy is stored in spring of a watch.

38 In which situation, the potential energy of a spring be minimum?

Sol. When a spring is at its natural length (i.e. neither stretched nor compressed), the potential energy of a spring will be minimum.

39 If a body is thrown vertically upwards, its velocity goes on decreasing. What happens to its kinetic energy when it reaches at the top?

Sol. The whole of its kinetic energy gets converted into potential energy (mgh), where m is the mass of body, h is the height and g is the acceleration due to gravity.

40 Can any object have mechanical energy even, if its momentum is zero? **NCERT Exemplar**

Sol. Since, mechanical energy is the sum of kinetic energy and potential energy. And as given that, momentum of the body is zero, it means velocity of the body is zero, so it has kinetic energy equals to zero. But it may have potential energy. So, even if the momentum of the body is zero, it may have **mechanical energy**.

41 A car and a truck have the same speed of 60 ms^{-1}. If their masses are in the ratio 1:4. Find the ratio of their KE.

Sol. As, $\frac{KE_1}{KE_2}=\frac{(1/2)m_1v^2}{(1/2)m_2v^2}=\frac{m_1}{m_2}=\frac{1}{4}=1:4$

42 An object of mass 2 kg is dropped from a height of 1m. What will be its kinetic energy as it reaches the ground? (Take, $g = 9.8\ ms^{-2}$)

Sol. Given, mass, $m = 2$ kg and height, $h = 1$ m.
On reaching the ground, the kinetic energy of object is converted into its potential energy such that

$$KE = PE = mgh = 2 \times 9.8 \times 1 = 19.6\ J$$

43 A girl weighing 50 kg runs up a hill raising herself vertically 10 m in 20 s. What is the power expended by girl?

Sol. Power expended by girl $=\frac{\text{Work done by girl}}{\text{Time taken}}$

$$=\frac{F\times s}{t}=\frac{mg\times s}{t}=\frac{50\times 9.8\times 10}{20} \quad [\because F = mg]$$

$= 245$ W

Short Answer (SA) Type Questions

1 A light and a heavy object have the same momentum. Find out the ratio of their kinetic energies. Which one has a larger kinetic energy? **NCERT Exemplar**

Sol. Suppose m_1 and m_2 are masses of a light and a heavy objects, respectively. As we know,

kinetic energy, $K=\frac{1}{2}mv^2$
[where, v = velocity of objects.] ...(i)

and momentum, $p = mv$ ...(ii)

On multiplying and dividing with m in Eq. (i), we get

So, $K=\frac{1}{2}\frac{mv^2\times m}{m}$

$\Rightarrow$ $K=\frac{1}{2}\frac{(mv)^2}{m}$ as from Eq. (ii) $[\because p = mv]$

So, $K=\frac{p^2}{2m}$

We have, kinetic energy, $K=\frac{p^2}{2m}$

$\because$ Momentum is same for light and heavy body.

So, kinetic energy, $K \propto \frac{1}{m}$

Thus, kinetic energy is inversely proportional to the mass.
So, lighter body has larger kinetic energy.

2 When a force retards the motion of a body, what is the nature of work done by force? State reason. List two examples of such a situation.

Sol. The nature of work done in case of retarding motion is negative.
Suppose a force F brings a body moving with velocity v to rest (retards), then work done

$$= \text{change in KE} = (KE)_f - (KE)_i$$

$$W = 0-\frac{1}{2}mu^2$$

$$=-\frac{1}{2}mu^2$$

e.g.
(*i*) When we apply brakes of a car, work done is negative.
(*ii*) Work done by frictional force is negative.

3 A car is moving on a levelled road and gets its velocity doubled. In this process,
(*i*) how would the potential energy of the car change?
(*ii*) how would the kinetic energy of the car change?
(*iii*) how will its momentum change?
Give reasons for your answer.

Sol. (*i*) The potential energy of the car remains same, since PE ($= mgh$) is independent of velocity.
(*ii*) The kinetic energy of the car becomes four times, since KE$\left(=\frac{1}{2}mv^2\right)$ is proportional to square of velocity.
(*iii*) The momentum of the car will also get doubled, since momentum ($p = mv$) is proportional to velocity.

4 A girl sits and stands repeatedly for 6 min. Draw a graph to show the variation of potential energy of her body with time.

Sol.

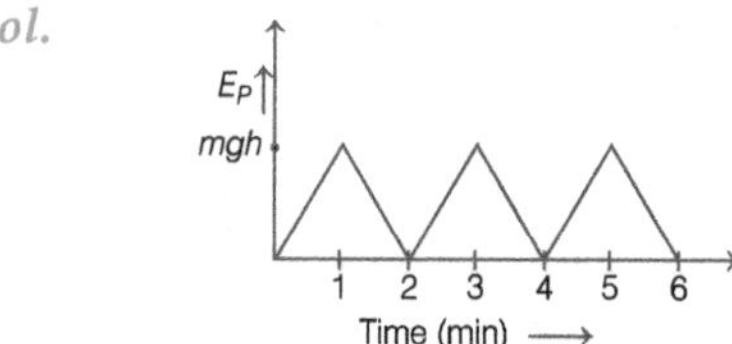

From the graph shown above, we can take the sitting position of the girl as the position of zero potential energy. Let m be the mass of the girl and h be the position of centre of gravity while standing above the sitting position. The PE while standing is + *mgh* and while sitting is zero. We can assume that there is no acceleration or deceleration while standing and sitting, this is repeated after every minute.

5 If a body falls from a height bounces from ground and again goes upwards with loss of a part of its energy.

(*i*) How will its potential energy change?

(*ii*) What are various energy conversions taking place?

(*iii*) What will be its ultimate energy?

Sol. (*i*) When it strikes ground, its PE is zero and after bouncing, its potential energy increases gradually.

(*ii*) At the time it strikes the ground, it has maximum KE and after it bounces, its KE starts changing into potential energy.

(*iii*) The ultimate or total energy remains constant at any point of time during the motion.

6 A labourer whose own mass is 50 kg carries a load of an additional 60 kg on his head to the top of a building 15 m high. Find the total work done by him. Also, find the work done by him, if he carries another additional block of mass 10 kg to the same height. (Take, $g = 10\ \text{ms}^{-2}$)

Sol. Given, total mass, $m = 50 + 60 = 110$ kg

Displacement, $s = 15$ m

Work done by him is given by $W = 0$

[since force and displacement are perpendicular to each other.]

If additional block of mass 10 kg is carried by him to the same height, then also work done by him remains zero because force and displacement are perpendicular to each other.

7 A girl having mass of 35 kg sits on a trolley of mass 5 kg. The trolley is given an initial velocity of $4\ \text{ms}^{-1}$ by applying a force.

The trolley comes to rest after traversing a distance of 16 m. (*i*) How much work is done on the trolley? (*ii*) How much work is done by the girl? **NCERT Exemplar**

Sol. Given, $u = 4\ \text{ms}^{-1}$, $v = 0$ and $s = 16$ m

From the third equation of motion,

[∵ for retardation, the acceleration is negative, i.e. $a = -a$]

$$v^2 = u^2 - 2as$$

$$\Rightarrow\ (0)^2 = (4)^2 - 2a \times 16$$

$$0 = 16 - 32\,a \Rightarrow a = \frac{16}{32} = 0.5\ \text{m s}^{-2}$$

where, u = initial velocity, v = final velocity, a = acceleration and s = displacement.

(*i*) Total mass = 35 + 5 = 40 kg

Work is done on the trolley,

$W = F \cdot d = ma\,s$ [∵ $F = ma$]

$= 40 \times 0.5 \times 16 = 320$ J

(*ii*) Given, mass of girl, $m = 35$ kg

Work done by the girl,

$W = F \cdot d = ma\,s$

$= 35 \times 0.5 \times 16 = 280$ J

8 Calculate the kinetic energy of a car of mass 750 kg moving with a velocity of $54\ \text{kmh}^{-1}$. Find the new kinetic energy of the car, if a passenger of mass 50 kg sits in the car.

Sol. Given, mass, $m = 750$ kg, velocity, $v = 54\ \text{kmh}^{-1}$

$$= 54 \times \frac{5}{18}\ \text{ms}^{-1} = 15\ \text{ms}^{-1}$$

∴ Kinetic energy, $\text{KE} = \frac{1}{2}mv^2$

$$\Rightarrow \quad \text{KE} = \frac{1}{2} \times 750 \times (15)^2 = 84375\ \text{J}$$

If a passenger of mass 50 kg sits in the car, then total mass becomes (750 + 50) kg, i.e. 800 kg

$$\therefore \quad \text{New KE} = \frac{1}{2} \times 800 \times (15)^2 = 90000\ \text{J}$$

9 On a level road, a scooterist applies brakes to slow down from a speed of $54\ \text{kmh}^{-1}$ to $36\ \text{kmh}^{-1}$. What amount of work is done by the brakes? (Assuming, the mass of the empty scooter is 86 kg and that of the scooterist and petrol is 64 kg.)

Sol. Here, total mass, $m = 86 + 64 = 150$ kg

Initial velocity, $u = 54\ \text{kmh}^{-1}$

$$= \frac{54 \times 1000}{3600} = 15\ \text{ms}^{-1}$$

Final velocity, $v = 36\ \text{kmh}^{-1}$

$$= 36 \times \frac{1000}{3600} = 10\ \text{ms}^{-1}$$

Work done by brakes = KE lost by the scooter

= Final KE – Initial KE

$$= \frac{1}{2}mv^2 - \frac{1}{2}mu^2 = \frac{1}{2}m(v^2 - u^2)$$

$$= \frac{1}{2} \times 150\,[(10)^2 - (15)^2]$$
$$= \frac{1}{2} \times 150\,(100 - 225)$$
$$= -75 \times 125 = -9375\text{ J}$$

10 (*i*) Define potential energy.

(*ii*) Give an example where potential energy is acquired by a body due to change in its shape.

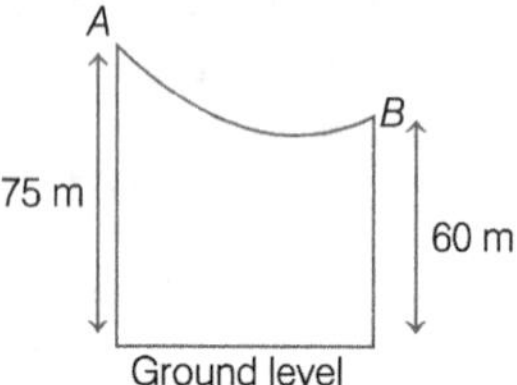

(*iii*) A skier of mass 50 kg stands at *A*, at the top of a ski jump. He takes off from *A* for his jump to *B*. Calculate the change in his gravitational potential energy between *A* and *B*.

Sol. (*i*) **Potential Energy** It is the energy possessed by a body by virtue of its position or shape.

(*ii*) In a toy car, the wound spring possesses potential energy. When spring is released, its potential energy changes into kinetic energy due to which the toy car moves.

(*iii*) Given, $m = 50\text{ kg}, h_1 = 75\text{ m}, h_2 = 60\text{ m}$

At point *A*, $PE_1 = mgh_1 = 50 \times 10 \times 75 = 37500\text{ J}$

At point *B*, $PE_2 = mgh_2 = 50 \times 10 \times 60 = 30000\text{ J}$

Change in PE $= PE_1 - PE_2 = 37500 - 30000 = 7500\text{ J}$

11 A body of mass 5 kg is thrown vertically upwards with an initial velocity of 50 ms^{-1}. What will be its potential energy at the end of 5 s?

Sol. Given, $m = 5\text{ kg},\ u = 50\text{ ms}^{-1},\ t = 5\text{ s}$

and $g = -10\text{ ms}^{-2}$

Height covered by the body in 5 s is $h = ut + \frac{1}{2}gt^2$

$$= 50 \times 5 - \frac{1}{2} \times 10 \times (5)^2$$
$$= 250 - 125$$
$$= 125\text{ m}$$

Therefore, PE of the body after 5 s

$$= mgh = 5 \times 10 \times 125 = 6250\text{ J}$$

12 Four men lift a 250 kg box to a height of 1 m and hold it without raising or lowering it. (*i*) How much work is done by the man in lifting the box? (*ii*) How much work do they do in just holding it? (*iii*) Why do they get tired while holding it? (Given, $g = 10\text{ ms}^{-2}$)

NCERT Exemplar

Sol. Given, mass, $m = 250$ kg, height, $h = 1$ m and acceleration due to gravity, $g = 10\text{ m s}^{-2}$

(*i*) Work done by the man in lifting the box,
W = Potential energy of box
$W = mgh = 250 \times 10 \times 1 = 2500\text{ J}$

(*ii*) Work done is zero in holding a box because displacement is zero.

(*iii*) In holding the box, the energy of each man loses. Due to loss of energy, they felt tired.

13 The weight of a person on a planet *A* is about half that on the Earth. He can jump up to 0.4 m height on the surface of the Earth. How high he can jump on the planet *A*?

NCERT Exemplar

Sol. It is given that, weight of person on the Earth $= w$ (i.e. $w = mg$)

and as he can jump up to height, $h_1 = 0.4$ m

So, potential energy at this point

$$= mgh = mg \times 0.4 \quad \text{...(i)}$$

And it is given that,

weight of the person on the other planet $= \frac{w}{2}$

And if he could jump to height (h_2), its potential energy would be

$$\frac{w}{2}h_2 = \frac{mg}{2}h_2 \quad \text{...(ii)}$$

Since, he applied same amount of effort in both the cases to lift his body, so its potential energy will be same.

From Eqs. (i) and (ii), we get

$$mg \times 0.4 = \frac{mg}{2}h_2$$

$$\Rightarrow \quad h_2 = 0.4 \times 2 = 0.8\text{ m}$$

14 300 J of work is to be done in lifting a bag of mass 5 kg in weight up to height of 4 m from the ground. What will be the acceleration with which the bag was raised? (Take, $g = 10\text{ ms}^{-2}$)

Sol. Given, mass, $m = 5$ kg, work, $W = 300$ J

$h = 4$ m, $g = 10\text{ ms}^{-2}$

If a be the acceleration with which bag is lifted, then

Work done, $W = mgh + mah = m(g + a)h$

$\Rightarrow \quad 300 = 5 \times (10 + a) \times 4$

$\Rightarrow \quad 300 = 20(10 + a)$

$\Rightarrow \quad 10 + a = \frac{300}{20} = 15$

$\Rightarrow \quad a = 15 - 10 = 5 \text{ ms}^{-2}$

15 Shyam drops a ball of 100 g from a building of height 10 m. What will be its kinetic energy at the height of 4 m above the surface of earth? What will happen to its total mechanical energy? Give reasons to justify your answer.

Sol. Given, mass, $m = 100$ g $= 0.1$ kg, height, $h = 10$ m

Potential energy, PE $= mgh = 0.1 \times 10 \times 10$

$= 10$ J $\quad [\because g = 10 \text{ ms}^{-2}]$

At the height of 4 m from the earth's surface, ball falls a distance of $(10 - 4)$ m $= 6$ m,

hence velocity of ball at this height,

$v^2 = u^2 + 2gh$

$\Rightarrow \quad v^2 = 0^2 + 2 \times 10 \times 6 \quad \left[\because h = 10 - 4 \text{ or } h = 6\right]$

$\Rightarrow \quad v = \sqrt{2 \times 10 \times 6} = 2\sqrt{30}$

Now, its kinetic energy at this point is given by

$= \frac{1}{2} mv^2 = \frac{1}{2} \times 0.1 \times 4 \times 30 = 6$J

As, mechanical energy = KE + PE [at highest point]

$\Rightarrow$ Mechanical energy $= (0 + 10)$ J $= 10$ J

Mechanical energy at 4 m height

= KE + PE

$= 6 + 0.1 \times 10 \times 4 = 10$J

Hence, it is seen that total mechanical energy always remains constant during the motion.

16 A mass of 10 kg is dropped from a height of 50 cm. Find its

(*i*) potential energy just before dropping.

(*ii*) kinetic energy just on touching the ground.

(*iii*) velocity with which it hits the ground. (Take, $g = 10 \text{ ms}^{-2}$)

Sol. Given, mass of the object, $m = 10$ kg

Height, $h = 50$ cm $= 0.5$ m

(*i*) As potential energy is given by PE $= mgh$

$= 10 \times 10 \times 0.5$

$= 50$ J

(*ii*) From law of conservation of energy,

total energy of the ball just before dropping

= total energy of the ball just on touching the ground

$\Rightarrow$ KE + PE of ball just before dropping

= KE + PE of ball just on touching the ground

$0 + 50 = (\text{KE} + 0)$ ball just on touching the ground $+ 0$

$\Rightarrow$ KE of ball just touching the ground $= 50$ J

(*iii*) As we know, KE $= 50$ J

If v is the velocity with which it hits the ground, then

$\frac{1}{2} mv^2 = 50 \Rightarrow v^2 = \frac{50 \times 2}{10} = 10$

$\Rightarrow \quad v = \sqrt{10} = 3.16 \text{ ms}^{-1}$

17 A small child tends to mimic his father by lifting a mass of 10 kg on his head. As soon as he succeeds in lifting it, he loses the object that falls back to the ground. If the child has a height of 90 cm, find the kinetic energy (*i*) at half the height of the child, (*ii*) with which the object strikes the ground.

Sol. Given, mass of the object, $m = 10$ kg

Height of the child, $h = 90$ cm $= 0.9$ m

Total energy of the object at head of the child is given by

$= \text{PE} + \text{KE} = mgh + 0 \quad [\because \text{KE} = 0, \text{ as } v = 0]$

$= mgh = 10 \times 9.8 \times 0.9 = 88.2$ J

(*i*) At half the height of child, i.e. at 0.45 m

Total energy, TE = PE + KE $= mgh$ + KE

$= 10 \times 9.8 \times 0.45 + \text{KE}$

Now, from the law of conservation of energy,

$\text{KE} + 10 \times 9.8 \times 0.45 = 88.2$

or $\quad \text{KE} + 44.1 = 88.2$

$\therefore \quad \text{KE} = 88.2 - 44.1 = 44.1$ J

(*ii*) When the object strikes the ground,

Total energy = PE + KE = 0 + KE

$= \text{KE} \quad [\because \text{PE} = 0, \text{ as } h = 0]$

$\therefore$ From the law of conservation of energy,

$\text{KE} = 88.2$ J $\quad [\because \text{TE} = 88.2 \text{ J}]$

18

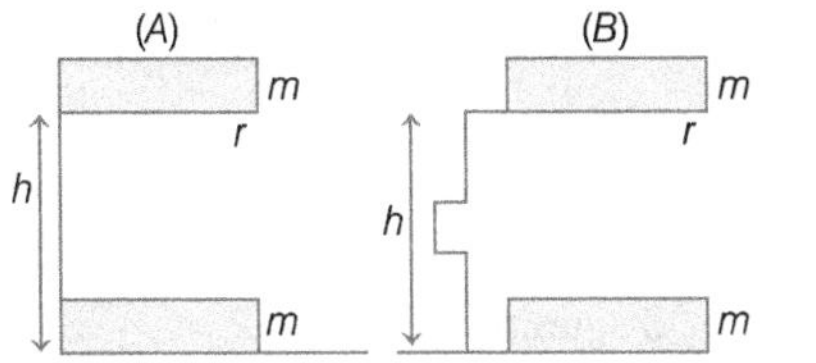

(A) m r h m

(B) m r h m

(*i*) What is meant by potential energy of a body?

(ii) A body of mass m is raised to a vertical height h through two different paths A and B as shown in the figure.

What will be the potential energy of the body in the two cases? Give reason for your answer.

Sol. (i) Energy possessed due to the position of a body is called potential energy.

(ii) The work done against gravity in both the cases is mgh. It is independent of the path along which the body is moved and it depends only on the initial and final positions of the body.

Hence, potential energy of the body is same in both cases.

19 At a height of 20 m above the ground, an object of mass 4 kg is released from rest. It is travelling at a speed of 20 ms^{-1} when it hits the ground. The object does not rebound and the gravitational field strength is 10 Nkg^{-1}.

How much energy is converted into heat and sound on impact?

Sol. Given, height above the ground, $h = 20$ m

Mass of the ball, $m = 4$ kg

Speed of the ball while striking the ground, $v = 20\ ms^{-1}$

Acceleration due to gravity, $g = 10\ Nkg^{-1}$

According to law of conservation of energy, all the energy of the ball will be converted into sound and heat energy because the ball does not rebound.

$$\therefore \text{ Energy of the ball} = \frac{1}{2}mv^2$$

$$= \frac{1}{2} \times 4 \times (20)^2$$

$$= 800\ J$$

Hence, 800 J of energy will be converted into heat and sound.

20 The power of a motor pump is 2 kW. How much water per minute, the pump can raise to a height of 10 m? (Given, $g = 10\ ms^{-2}$)

NCERT Exemplar

Sol. Given, power of a motor

$$= 2\ kW = 2 \times 1000\ W = 2000\ W \quad [\because 1\ kW = 1000\ W]$$

$$\therefore \text{ Power, } P = \frac{\text{Energy}}{\text{Time}}$$

By putting the values, $P = \frac{mgh}{t}$ [where, m = mass of water]

$$2000 = \frac{m \times 10 \times 10}{60}$$

[here, $h = 10$ m and $t = 1$ min $= 60$ s]

$$\Rightarrow \quad m = \frac{2000 \times 60}{10 \times 10} \Rightarrow m = 1200\ kg$$

21 A boy X can run with a speed of 8 ms^{-1} against the frictional force of 10 N and another Y can move with a speed of 3 ms^{-1} against the frictional force of 20 N. Find the ratio of powers of X and Y.

Sol. Given, distance travelled by the boy X in 1 s = 8 m

Distance travelled by the boy Y in 1 s = 3 m

As we know, work done by the boy X to run against the frictional force of 10 N = 10 N× 8 m= 80 J

So, power of 80 J of work done by $X = \frac{W}{t} = \frac{80\ J}{1s} = 80\ W$

Similarly, work done by the boy Y to run against the frictional force of 20 N = 20 N× 3 m= 60J

$$\text{Power of } Y = \frac{60\ J}{1\ s} = 60\ W$$

So, ratio of two values of powers is given by

$$\frac{\text{Power of } X}{\text{Power of } Y} = \frac{80}{60} = \frac{4}{3} = 4 : 3$$

22 (i) State and define SI unit of power.

(ii) A person carrying 10 bricks each of mass 2.5 kg on his head moves to a height 20 m in 50 s. Calculate power spent in carrying bricks of the person. (Given, $g = 10\ ms^{-2}$)

Sol. (i) The SI unit of power is watt.

1 watt is the power of a body which does work at the rate of 1 joule per second.

i.e. $1 \text{ watt} = \frac{1 \text{ joule}}{1 \text{ second}}$

(ii) Given, mass of one brick = 2.5 kg

Mass of 10 bricks = 2.5 × 10 = 25 kg

Height, $h = 20$ m, time, $t = 50$ s, power, $P = ?$

$$\therefore \text{ Power, } P = \frac{mgh}{t} = \frac{25 \times 10 \times 20}{50} = 100\ Js^{-1}$$

23 How much time will a pump of 1 kW power takes to lift 500 kg of water to height of 40 m? (Take, $g = 10\ ms^{-2}$)

Sol. Given, mass, $m = 500$ kg, height, $h = 40$ m

$$P = 1\ kW = 1000\ W,\ t = ?$$

Now, power, $P = \frac{mgh}{t}$

$\Rightarrow \quad 1000 = \dfrac{500 \times 10 \times 40}{t}$

Time, $t = \dfrac{500 \times 10 \times 40}{1000} = 200$ s

$= 3$ min 20 s

24 Mohan lifts his cellphone to a height of 1 m. He takes 1 s to do this. After lowering the phone, he then lifts it 2 m in 2 s. Has he generated more power in doing the second task? Give reason to justify your answer.

Sol. Let, mass of cellphone be m kg

Work done (W) by Mohan $= mgh$

where, h = height at which cellphone is raised

and g = acceleration due to gravity.

$\Rightarrow \quad W = mg \times 1 = mg$

$\therefore$ Power delivered $(P_1) = \dfrac{\text{Work done}(W)}{\text{Time}(T)}$

$= \dfrac{mg}{1} = mg$

Work done to lift cellphone by 2 m $= mg \times 2 = 2mg$

Power delivered $(P_2) = \dfrac{\text{Work done}(W)}{\text{Time}(T)}$

$= \dfrac{2mg}{2} = mg$

So, in both cases power delivered by Mohan is same.

25 A force applied on a body of mass 4 kg for 5 s changes its velocity from 10 ms^{-1} to 20 ms^{-1}. Find the power required.

Sol. Given, $m = 4$ kg, $t = 5$ s, $u = 10\ ms^{-1}$,

$v = 20\ ms^{-1}$, $P = ?$

$\therefore$ Power, $P = \dfrac{W}{t} = \dfrac{\text{Change in KE}}{\text{Time taken}}$

$P = \dfrac{1}{2} \times \dfrac{m(v^2 - u^2)}{t}$

$= \dfrac{1}{2} \times \dfrac{4[(20)^2 - (10)^2]}{5}$

$= \dfrac{1}{2} \times \dfrac{4 \times 300}{5} = 120\ Js^{-1}$

26 A boy of mass 50 kg runs up a staircase of 45 steps in 9 s. If the height of each step of the staircase is 15 cm, find the power of the boy. (Given, g = 10 ms^{-2})

Sol. Given, mass of body, $m = 50$ kg

Height of each step = 15 cm

Total height of staircase,

$h = 45 \times 15 = 675$ cm $= 6.75$ m

$t = 9$ s, $g = 10\ ms^{-2}$

$\therefore$ PE $= mgh = 50 \times 10 \times 6.75 = 3375$ J

So, the energy of the boy is 3375 J.

$\therefore$ Power of the boy,

$P = \dfrac{\text{PE}}{\text{Time}} = \dfrac{\text{Energy}}{\text{Time}}$

$= \dfrac{3375}{9} = 375$ W

27 A machine gun takes 10 s to fire 30 bullets with a velocity of 500 ms^{-1}. Find the power developed by the gun when each bullet has a mass of 100 g.

Sol. Given, mass of 30 bullets $= 30 \times 100 = 3$ kg

Velocity, $v = 500\ ms^{-1}$, time, $t = 10$ s

$\therefore$ Power developed by the gun, $P = \dfrac{W}{t}$

[here, work done by gun will be equal to the kinetic energy of all the bullets.]

$\therefore \quad P = \dfrac{\text{KE}}{t} = \dfrac{\frac{1}{2}mv^2}{t} = \dfrac{mv^2}{2t}$

$= \dfrac{3 \times (500)^2}{2 \times 10}$

$= \dfrac{3 \times 500 \times 500}{20}$

$= 37500$ W

28 What is the output power in watt of a 60 kg sprinter who accelerates from 0 to 10 ms^{-1} in 3 s?

Sol. Given, mass of the sprinter, $m = 60$ kg

Initial velocity, $u = 0$

Final velocity, $v = 10\ ms^{-1}$, time, $t = 3$ s

From equation of motion, $v = u + at$

$\Rightarrow \quad 10 = 0 + a \times 3$

$\Rightarrow$ Acceleration, $a = \dfrac{10}{3}\ ms^{-2}$

As, $\quad s = ut + \dfrac{1}{2}at^2$

$\Rightarrow \quad s = 0 + \dfrac{1}{2} \times \dfrac{10}{3} \times 3 \times 3 = 15$ m

$\therefore$ Work done, (W) = Force $(F) \times$ Displacement (s)

$= 60 \times \dfrac{10}{3} \times 15 \quad [\because F = ma]$

$= 3000$ J

So, power, $P = \dfrac{W}{t} = \dfrac{3000}{3} = 1000$ W

29 Two boys A and B weighing 60 kg and 40 kg respectively, climb on a staircase each carrying a load of 20 kg on their head. The staircase has 10 steps, each of height 50 cm. If A takes 20 s to climb and B takes 10 s to climb, then

(*i*) who possesses greater power?

(*ii*) find the ratio of their powers.

Sol. Given, mass of A, $m_A = 60$ kg

Mass of B, $m_B = 40$ kg

Mass of luggage, $m_L = 20$ kg

Height of staircase, $h = 0.5 \times 10 = 5$ m

So, work done by boy A to climb staircase = mgh

$= (60 + 20) \times 9.8 \times 5 = 3920$ J

So, power of $A = \dfrac{\text{work}}{\text{time}} = \dfrac{3920}{20} = 196$ W

Similarly, power of $B = \dfrac{\text{work}}{\text{time}} = \dfrac{mgh}{t}$

$= \dfrac{[(40 + 20) \times 9.8 \times 5]}{10} = \dfrac{2940}{10} = 294$ W

(*i*) B possesses greater power than A.

(*ii*) So, the ratio is given by

$$\frac{\text{power of } A}{\text{power of } B} = \frac{196}{294} = 2:3$$

So, power, $P = \dfrac{W}{t} = \dfrac{3000}{3} = 1000$ W

30 Define watt. Express kilowatt in terms of joule per second. A 150 kg car engine develops 500 W for each kg. What force does it exert in moving the car at speed of 20 ms^{-1}? **NCERT Exemplar**

Sol. (*i*) One watt is the power of a body which does work at the rate of 1 Js^{-1}.

i.e. $1 \text{ watt} = 1 \dfrac{\text{joule}}{\text{second}}$

(*ii*) 1 kilowatt = 1000 watt = 1000 Js^{-1}.

(*iii*) Given, $m = 150$ kg,

$P = 500$ W and $v = 20 \text{ ms}^{-1}$

A car engine of 150 kg develops 500 watt for each kg.

So, total power = $150 \times 500 = 75000$ W

We have, power = force × speed

$= 75000 = F \times 20$

$\therefore$ Force, $F = \dfrac{75000}{20} = 3750$ N

31 How is the power related to the speed at which a body can be lifted? How many kilograms will a man working at the power of 100 W, be able to lift at constant speed of 1 ms^{-1} vertically? (Take, $g = 10 \text{ ms}^{-2}$) **NCERT Exemplar**

Sol. The power delivered to a body can also expressed in terms of the force F applied to the body and the velocity v of the body

Power, $P = \dfrac{\text{Work}}{\text{Time}} \Rightarrow P = \dfrac{F \cdot s}{t}$

where, F = force, s = displacement and t = time

$P = F \cdot v$ $\quad [\because W = F \cdot s]$

[where, v = velocity of the body] $\quad \left(\because v = \dfrac{s}{t}\right)$

Given, power, $P = 100$ W, $v = 1 \text{ ms}^{-1}$

and $g = 10 \text{ ms}^{-2}$

We know that, power,

$P = F \cdot v \Rightarrow P = mg \cdot v \quad [\because F = mg]$

$100 = mg \cdot v$

$100 = m \times 10 \times 1$

$\Rightarrow m = \dfrac{100}{10} \Rightarrow m = 10$ kg

Therefore, a man working at the power of 100 W can lift 10 kg.

32 Compare the power at which each of the following is moving upwards against the force of gravity? (Given, $g = 10 \text{ ms}^{-2}$)

(*i*) A butterfly of mass 1 g that flies upward at a rate of 0.5 ms^{-1}.

(*ii*) A 250 g squirrel climbing up on a tree at a rate of 0.5 ms^{-1}. **NCERT Exemplar**

Firstly, we find the power by using the formula $P = mg \cdot v$ in both parts and then comparing both powers.

Sol. (*i*) Given, mass of butterfly, $m = 1\text{g} = \dfrac{1}{1000}$ kg, $\quad [\because 1 \text{ kg} = 1000 \text{ g}]$

$g = 10 \text{ ms}^{-2}$

and speed, $v = 0.5 \text{ m s}^{-1}$

$\therefore$ Power = Force × Speed $\quad [\because \text{force}, F = mg]$

$P = mgv$

$\Rightarrow P = \dfrac{1}{1000} \times 10 \times 0.5$

$\Rightarrow P = \dfrac{1}{200}$ W

(*ii*) Given, mass of squirrel = 250 g $= \dfrac{250}{1000}$ kg $\quad [\because 1 \text{ kg} = 1000 \text{ g}]$

and speed = 0.5 m s^{-1}

$\therefore$ Power = Force × Speed [$\because$ force, $F = mg$]

$$P = mg \times v$$

$$\Rightarrow \quad P = \frac{250}{1000} \times 10 \times 0.5 = \frac{250}{200} \text{ W}$$

$$\therefore \quad P = \frac{250}{200} \text{ W}$$

Therefore, a squirrel has more power than butterfly.

33 **Find the ratio of gravitational potential energy, if height of an object is doubled and mass is tripled. Also, find the ratio of work done by gravity in bringing the object to zero height in both cases.**

Sol. Let an object of mass m be placed at height h from the ground level. As we know that, the gravitational potential energy of the object is $PE_1 = mgh$.

When the height of the object is doubled and its mass is tripled, then its gravitational potential energy becomes

$$PE_2 = (3m) \times g \times (2h) = 6\, mgh$$

$$\therefore \quad \frac{PE_2}{PE_1} = 6\frac{mgh}{mgh} = 6:1$$

When the object is at zero height, then its potential energy = 0 [$\because h = 0$]

As, work done by the gravity to bring the object of mass m placed at height h to zero height is given by

$$W_1 = \text{change in energy} = mgh - 0 = mgh$$

So, the work done by gravity to bring the object of mass $3m$ placed at height $2h$ to zero height is

$$W_2 = 6mgh - 0 = 6mgh$$

$$\therefore \quad \frac{W_2}{W_1} = \frac{6}{1} = 6:1$$

Long Answer (LA) Type Questions

1 **The velocity of a body moving in a straight line is increased by applying a constant force F for some distance in the direction of the motion. Prove that the increase in the kinetic energy of the body is equal to the work done by the force on the body.**

NCERT Exemplar

Sol. Consider an object of mass m moving with a uniform velocity u. Let, it now be displaced through a distance s, when a constant force F acts on it in the direction of its displacement.

From the third equation of motion, $v^2 = u^2 + 2as$

$$\Rightarrow \quad v^2 - u^2 = 2as \quad \Rightarrow \quad s = \frac{v^2 - u^2}{2a} \quad \text{...(i)}$$

We know that, work done by F is

$W = Fs\cos\theta = Fs$ [since, force and displacement are in same direction, so $\theta = 0°$]

$$\therefore \quad W = ma \times s \quad [\because F = ma]$$

$$= ma \times \left(\frac{v^2 - u^2}{2a}\right) \quad \text{[from Eq. (i)]}$$

$$W = \frac{1}{2} m (v^2 - u^2) \quad \text{...(ii)}$$

If the object is starting from its stationary position, i.e. $u = 0$, from Eq. (ii), we get

$$W = \frac{1}{2} mv^2$$

It is clear that, the work done is equal to the increase in the kinetic energy of an object.

2 (*i*) **Name two forms of mechanical energy. Define the SI unit of energy.**

(*ii*) **A man of mass 50 kg jumps from a height of 0.5 m. If $g = 10 \text{ ms}^{-2}$, what will be his energy at the highest point?**

(*iii*) **Calculate the energy of a body of mass 20 kg moving with velocity of 0.1 ms^{-1}.**

Sol. (*i*) Two forms of mechanical energy are

(*a*) kinetic energy (*b*) and potential energy

The SI unit of energy is joule (J). 1 J is the amount of work done on an object when a force of 1N displaces it by 1m along the line of action of force.

(*ii*) Given, $m = 50$ kg, $h = 0.5$ m, $g = 10 \text{ ms}^{-2}$

At highest point, kinetic energy is converted into potential energy.

$$\therefore \quad PE = mgh = 50 \times 10 \times 0.5 = 250 \text{ J}$$

(*iii*) Given, $m = 20$ kg, $v = 0.1 \text{ ms}^{-1}$

As we know that, a moving body has kinetic energy.

$$\therefore \quad KE = \frac{1}{2} mv^2 = \frac{1}{2} \times 20 \times (0.1)^2$$

$$= \frac{1}{2} \times 20 \times 0.1 \times 0.1 = 0.1 \text{ J}$$

3 (*i*) **Define kinetic energy of an object. Can kinetic energy of an object be negative? Give reason.**

(*ii*) **A car weighing 1200 kg is uniformly accelerated from rest and covers a distance of 40 m in 5 s. Calculate the work, the car engine had to do during this time.**

Sol. (i) The energy possessed by a body by virtue of its motion is called its kinetic energy.

No, the kinetic energy of an object cannot be negative because both m and v^2 are always positive as $KE = \frac{1}{2}mv^2$

(ii) Given, $m = 1200$ kg, $s = 40$ m, $t = 5$ s, $u = 0$, $W = ?$

We know that, $W = Fs = mas$ ...(i) $[\because F = ma]$

According to second equation of motion,

$$s = ut + \frac{1}{2}at^2$$

$$40 = 0 \times t + \frac{1}{2} \times a \times (5)^2$$

$$a = \frac{40 \times 2}{25} = 3.2 \text{ ms}^{-2}$$

From Eq. (i),

$$\therefore \quad W = Fs = mas$$

$$= 1200 \times 3.2 \times 40 = 153600 \text{ J}$$

4 A vehicle of 1 tonne travelling with a speed of 60 ms^{-1} notices a cow on the road 9 m ahead applies brakes. It stops just infront of the cow.

(i) Find out the KE of the vehicle before applying brakes.

(ii) Calculate the retarding force provided by the brakes.

(iii) How much time did it take to stop after the brakes were applied?

(iv) What is the work done by the braking force?

Sol. Given, mass of the vehicle, $m = 1$ tonne $= 1000$ kg

Initial speed, $u = 60 \text{ ms}^{-1}$

Distance between vehicle and the cow, $s = 9$ m

Final velocity, $v = 0$

(i) KE of vehicle before applying brakes is given by

$$= \frac{1}{2}mu^2 = \frac{1}{2} \times 1000 \times 60 \times 60 = 1800000 \text{ J}$$

(ii) From the third equation of motion,

$$v^2 - u^2 = 2as$$

$$(0)^2 - (60)^2 = 2 \times a \times 9$$

$$\Rightarrow \quad a = -200 \text{ ms}^{-2}$$

So, retarding force provided by the brakes

$$= ma = 1000 \text{ kg} \times (-200) \text{ ms}^{-2}$$

$$= -200000 \text{ N}$$

(iii) Now, again from the second equation of motion,

$$s = ut + \frac{1}{2}at^2$$

$$\Rightarrow \quad 9 = 60t + \frac{1}{2} \times (-200)t^2$$

$$\text{or} \quad 9 = 60t - 100t^2$$

$$\text{or} \quad 100t^2 - 60t + 9 = 0$$

$$\Rightarrow \quad (10t - 3)^2 = 0$$

$$\text{or} \quad 10t - 3 = 0$$

$$\Rightarrow \quad t = \frac{3}{10} = 0.3 \text{ s}$$

(iv) So, work done by the braking force is given by

$$= Fs = -200000 \text{ N} \times 9 \text{ m} = -1800000 \text{ J}$$

5 (i) A battery lights a bulb. Describe the energy changes involved in the process.

(ii) Calculate the amount of work needed to stop a car of 500 kg moving at a speed of 36 kmh^{-1}.

Sol. (i) When a battery lights a bulb, its chemical energy changes into light and heat energies.

(ii) Here, $m = 500$ kg, $v = 0$ and

$$u = 36 \text{ kmh}^{-1} = \frac{36 \times 1000}{3600} = 10 \text{ ms}^{-1}$$

$\therefore$ Work done = Change in kinetic energy

$$= \frac{1}{2}m(v^2 - u^2)$$

$$= \frac{1}{2} \times 500(0 - 10^2)$$

$$= -\frac{1}{2} \times 500 \times 100$$

$$= -25000 \text{ Js}^{-1}$$

So, it is negative because work is done to stop the car.

6 A body of mass 20 kg is raised to the top of a building 15 m high and then dropped freely under gravity.

(i) Find out the work done in raising the body to the top of the building.

(ii) What will be the value of gravitational potential energy at the top of the building?

(iii) By what factor will the gravitational potential energy of the same body increases, if it is raised to the top of a multi-storey building 45 m high?

(iv) When will the kinetic energy of the body be maximum?

Sol. Given, $m = 20$ kg, $h = 15$ m, $g = 10 \text{ ms}^{-2}$

(i) Work done $= mgh = 20 \times 10 \times 15 = 3000$ J

(ii) Gravitational PE = Work done = 3000 J

(iii) Gravitational PE at a height of 45 m

$$= mgh' = 20 \times 10 \times 45 = 9000 \text{ J}$$

Now,

$$\frac{\text{Potential energy at height 45 m}}{\text{Potential energy at height 15 m}} = \frac{9000}{3000} = 3$$

Therefore, PE increases by 3 times.

(iv) KE will be maximum just before the body strikes the ground.

7 A car is moving with uniform velocities; 18 kmh^{-1}, 36 kmh^{-1}, 54 kmh^{-1} and 72 kmh^{-1} at some intervals. Find the KE of the boy of 40 kg sitting in the car at these velocities. Draw a graph between the KE and the velocities. Also, find the nature of the curve.

Sol. At $v_1 = 18 \text{ kmh}^{-1} = \frac{18 \times 1000}{3600} = 5 \text{ ms}^{-1}$,

$$KE_1 = \frac{1}{2} m v_1^2 = \frac{1}{2} \times 40 \times (5)^2 = 500 \text{ J}$$

At $v_2 = 36 \text{ kmh}^{-1} = 10 \text{ ms}^{-1}$,

$$KE_2 = \frac{1}{2} m v_2^2 = \frac{1}{2} \times 40 \times (10)^2 = 2000 \text{ J}$$

At $v_3 = 54 \text{ kmh}^{-1} = 15 \text{ ms}^{-1}$,

$$KE_3 = \frac{1}{2} m v_3^2 = \frac{1}{2} \times 40 \times (15)^2 = 4500 \text{ J}$$

At $v_4 = 72 \text{ kmh}^{-1} = 20 \text{ ms}^{-1}$

$$KE_4 = \frac{1}{2} m v_4^2 = \frac{1}{2} \times 40 \times (20)^2 = 8000 \text{ J}$$

The graph between the KE and the velocities is shown below.

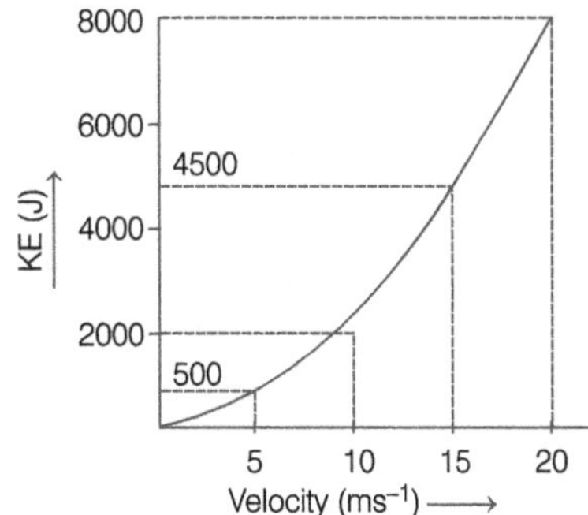

The graph is parabolic curve because $KE \propto v^2$.

CHAPTER EXERCISE

Multiple Type Questions

1 In case of negative work, the angle between the force and displacement is **NCERT Exemplar**

(a) 0 (b) 45°
(c) 90° (d) 180°

2 A girl is carrying a school bag of 3 kg mass on her back and moves 200 m on a levelled road. The work done against the gravitational force will be ($g = 10 \text{ ms}^{-2}$) **NCERT Exemplar**

(a) 6×10^3 J (b) 6 J
(c) 0.6 J (d) zero

3 Mukesh drops a ball of 200 g from a tower of height 20 m. What will be its kinetic energy at the height of 5 m ?

(a) 30 J (b) 50 J
(c) 60 J (d) 65 J

4 Which mathematical relation of energy of a stone of mass m falling freely from height h remains conserved at every point in its downward motion?

(a) $E = mgh$
(b) $E = \frac{1}{2}mv^2$
(c) $E = mgh + \frac{1}{2}mv^2$
(d) None of the above

5 Which of the following is unit of power?

(a) kilowatt-hour
(b) horse power
(c) watt hour
(d) All of the above

Fill in the Blanks

6 The work done by gravity does not depend on the .... along which the object is moved.

7 .... converts electrical energy into mechanical energy.

True and False

8 Solar cell converts electrical energy into light energy.

9 Kilowatt-hour is the unit of energy.

Match the Columns

10 Match the items of Column I with the items of Column II and choose the correct codes given below:

Column I		Column II	
A.	Power	p.	10^{-7} J
B.	Calorie (cal)	q.	1.6×10^{-19} J
C.	erg	r.	4.18 J
D.	Electron-volt (eV)	s.	1 W

Assertion–Reason

Direction (Q.Nos. 11-13) *In each of the following questions, a statement of Assertion is given by the corresponding statement of Reason. Of the statements, mark the correct answer as*

(a) If both Assertion and Reason are true and Reason is the correct explanation of Assertion.
(b) If both Assertion and Reason are true, but Reason is not the correct explanation of Assertion.
(c) If Assertion is true, but Reason is false.
(d) If Assertion is false, but Reason is true.
(e) If Assertion and Reason both are false.

11 **Assertion** Work done by a body is zero only, when displacement produced by the force is zero.

Reason Work done by a force is negative, when displacement occurs in the direction of applied force.

12 **Assertion** In a stretched bow, potential energy is stored.

Reason Mechanical energy of a moving body remains conserved.

13 **Assertion** Steam engine converts heat energy into kinetic energy.

Reason Steam engine works on the principle of conservation of energy.

Case Based Questions

Direction (Q.Nos. 14-17) *Answer the question on the basis of your understanding of the following paragraph and related studied concepts:*

Collision between two billiard balls or between two automobiles on a road are a few examples of collision from everyday life. Even gas atoms and molecules at room temperature keep on colliding against each other. In some collisions, momentum of the system is conserved but the kinetic energy is not conserved while in some collisions, both momentum and kinetic energy of the system are conserved. When two billiard balls collide to each other elastically, then their velocity of separation is equal to velocity of approach. Similarly, in inelastic collision of two bodies, velocity of approach is less than the velocity of separation. In perfectly inelastic collision of two bodies, velocity of separation becomes zero.

14 In elastic collision of two billiard balls,
(a) kinetic energy is conserved
(b) momentum is conserved
(c) total energy is conserved
(d) All of the above

15 When both billiard balls collide inelastically, then coefficient of restitution(e) will be
(a) zero (b) less than one
(c) more than one (d) equal to one

16 In perfectly inelastic collision, the two bodies move with a common velocity. Why?

17 In which type of collision, total energy and momentum both are conserved?

Answers

1. (d) 2. (d) 3. (a) 4. (c) 5. (b)
6. Path 7. Electric motor
8. False 9. True
10. (A) → (s), (B) → (r), (C) → (p), (D) → (q)
11. (e) 12. (b) 13. (a) 14. (d) 15. (b)

Very Short Answer (VSA) Type Questions

18 When is work done by a force zero?

19 Which will have more impact on kinetic energy—doubling mass or velocity?

20 Where does a pendulum have maximum
(*i*) potential energy?
(*ii*) kinetic energy?

21 A man of 50 kg jumps to a height of 3 m. What is the maximum PE that he will have? [**Ans.** 1.5×10^3 J]

Short Answer (SA) Type Questions

22 The velocity of a body moving in a straight line is increased by applying a constant force F, for some distance in the direction of the motion. Prove that the increase in the kinetic energy of the body is equal to the work done by the force on the body.

23 What do you mean by gravitational potential energy? Show that gravitational potential energy is independent of the path followed.

24 How does energy varies in an oscillating pendulum? Express how many times potential energy and kinetic energy attain maximum in an oscillation.

25 (*i*) A mass m is dropped from a height h. At half-way to the ground, what is the total energy?
(*ii*) What happens to the work done by you, as you hit a football?
(*iii*) Write the relation between power, energy and time.

26 When water is flowing through a pipe, then its velocity changes by 5%. Find the percentage change in the power of water. [**Ans.** 5%]

27 A boy of mass 50 kg runs up a staircase of 50 steps in 10 s. If the height of each step is 15 cm, then find the his power. (Take, $g = 10 \text{ ms}^{-2}$) [**Ans.** 375 W]

Long Answer (LA) Type Questions

28 (*i*) What do you understand by the term "transformation of energy?" Explain with an example.
(*ii*) Explain the transformation of energy in the following cases:
(*a*) A ball thrown upwards.
(*b*) A stone dropped from the roof of a building.

29 (*i*) A ball thrown vertically upwards returns to the thrower. How do the kinetic and potential energies of the ball change?
(*ii*) Calculate the power of a pump which lifts 100 kg of water to a water tank placed at a height of 20 m in 10 s. (Take, $g = 10 \text{ ms}^{-2}$) [**Ans.** 2000 W]

Challengers*

1 A horse is running on a playground and comes to a skidding stop. The force applied on the horse due to playground is 500 N, which is directly opposed to the motion of the horse. How much work does the horse do on the playground?

(a) 500 J (b) Zero
(c) 100 J (d) In sufficient data

2 A nuclear power plant operated at 10^{10} kW. How much mass is converted into energy per day?

(a) 9.6 kg (b) 7.6 kg
(c) 7.8 kg (d) 8.6 kg

3 The energy absorbed by a solar panal is used to charge a battery. During the day, the battery stores 1.6 J of energy each second. At night, the battery is used to light a 1.2 W lamp for 18000 s.

What is the minimum time for which the battery must be charged within the day?

(a) 13505 s (b) 13500 s
(c) 15300 s (d) 13050 s

4 A force of 5N acts on a 1.5 kg body initially at rest. The work done by the force during the first second of motion of the body is

(a) 5 J (b) (5/6) J
(c) 6 J (d) 75 J

5 A force is applied by an engine of a train of mass 2.05×10^6 kg changes its velocity from 5 m/s to 25 m/s in 5 min. The power of engine is

(a) 1.025 MW (b) 2.05 MW
(c) 5 MW (d) 6 MW

6 Natural length of a spring is 60 cm and its spring constant is 4000 N/m. A mass of 20 kg is hung from it. The extension produced in the spring is (take, $g = 9.8\,\text{m/s}^2$)

(a) 4.9 cm (b) 0.49 cm
(c) 9.4 cm (d) 0.94 cm

7 A lorry and a car moving with the same KE are brought to rest by applying the same retarding force, then

(a) lorry will come to rest in a shorter distance
(b) car will come to rest in a shorter distance
(c) Both come to rest in a same distance
(d) None of the above

8 Figure shows the variation of force and displacement. The value of work done at the end of the displacement 30 m is

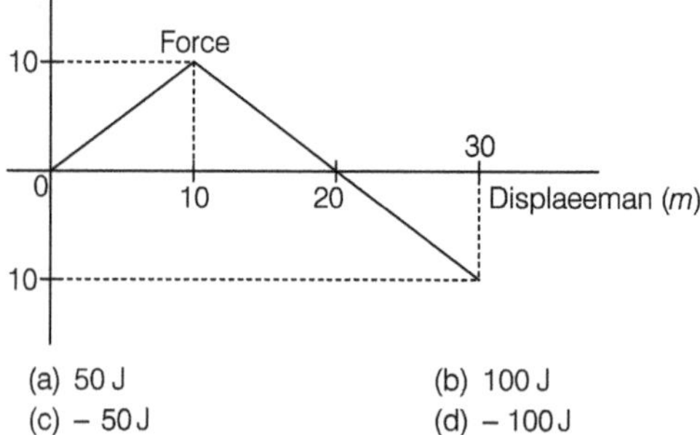

(a) 50 J (b) 100 J
(c) – 50 J (d) – 100 J

9 Water falls from a height of 60 m at the rate of 15 kg/s to operate a turbine. The soosses due to frictional forces are 10% of energy. How much power is generated by the turbine? (Take, $g = 10\,\text{m/s}^2$)

(a) 8.1 kW (b) 10.2 kW
(c) 12.3 kW (d) 7.9 kW

10 A block of mass 10 kg is dropped from a height of 10 m from the earth's surface and it falls onto a vertical helical spring of stiffness 5000 N/m and length 50 cm as shown in the figure. The compression of the springs is (take, $g = 10\,\text{m/s}^2$)

(a) 0.1 m (b) 0.2 m
(c) $\sqrt{0.4}$ m (d) 0.3 m

Answer Key

1.	(b)	2.	(a)	3.	(b)	4.	(b)	5.	(b)
6.	(a)	7.	(c)	8.	(a)	9.	(a)	10.	(c)

These questions may or may not be asked in the examination, have been given just for additional practice.

CHAPTER

11

Sound

We hear sound from various sources, e.g. from humans, birds, machines, vehicles, TV, radio, etc. **Sound** is a form of energy which produces a sensation of hearing in our ears.

Production of Sound

A sound is produced by vibrating objects. **Vibration** means a kind of rapid to and fro motion of an object. The sound of human voice is produced due to vibrations in the vocal cords. We can produce sound by striking the tuning fork, by plucking, scratching, rubbing, blowing or shaking different objects. They all produce sound due to vibrations.

Propagation of Sound

When an object vibrates, it sets the particles of the medium (solid, liquid or gas) around it in vibrations. The particles do not travel all the way from the vibrating object to the ear. A particle of the medium in contact with the vibrating object is first displaced from its **equilibrium position.** It then exerts a force on the adjacent particle. As a result of which, the adjacent particle gets displaced from its position of rest. After displacing the adjacent particle, the first particle comes back to its original position. This process continues in the medium till the sound reaches our ear.

The source of sound creates a disturbance in the medium which travels through the medium. The particles of the medium do not move forward but the disturbance is carried forward. This is propagation of sound in a medium, hence sound can be visualised as a wave. Sound waves require a medium to travel, so they are called **mechanical waves.**

Formation of Compression and Rarefaction in Air

When a vibrating object moves forward in air, it pushes and compresses the air infront of it, creating a **compression** which starts to move away from the vibrating object. When the vibrating object moves backwards, it creates **rarefaction.**

Compression is the part of a longitudinal wave in which the particles of the medium are closer to one another than they normally are and it is the region of high pressure. It is denoted by C in the figure given here.

Chapter Checklist

- Production and Propagation of Sound
- Types of Waves
- Terms to Describe Sound Waves
- Characteristics of Sound
- Reflection of Sound Wave
- Range of Hearing
- Ultrasound and its Applications

Rarefaction is the part of a longitudinal wave in which the particles of the medium are farther apart than they normally are and it is the region of low pressure. It is denoted by *R* in the figure given here.

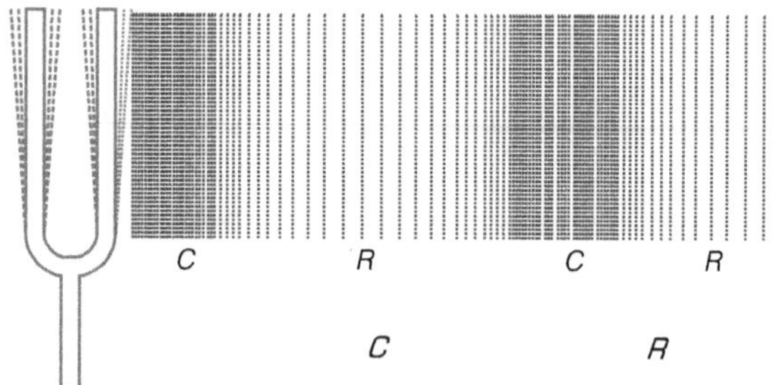

As the object moves back and forth rapidly, a series of compressions and rarefactions is created in air.

Thus, propagation of sound can be visualised as propagation of density variations or pressure variations in the medium as pressure is related to the number of particles of a medium in a given volume. More density of the particles in the medium gives more pressure and *vice-versa.*

Sound Needs a Medium to Travel

The substance through which sound travels is called a medium. It can be solid, liquid or a gas. Sound wave requires a material medium like air, water, steel, etc. for its propagation. Sound wave cannot travel in vacuum.

Types of Waves

There are mainly two types of waves

Longitudinal Waves

In longitudinal waves, the individual particles of the medium move in a direction parallel to the direction of propagation of the disturbance. The particles do not move from one place to another but they simply oscillate back and forth about their positions of rest.

This is exactly how a sound wave propagates, hence **sound waves are longitudinal waves.** Longitudinal waves can be produced in all the three media such as solids, liquids and gases. The waves which travel along a spring when it is pushed and pulled at one end, are the longitudinal waves.

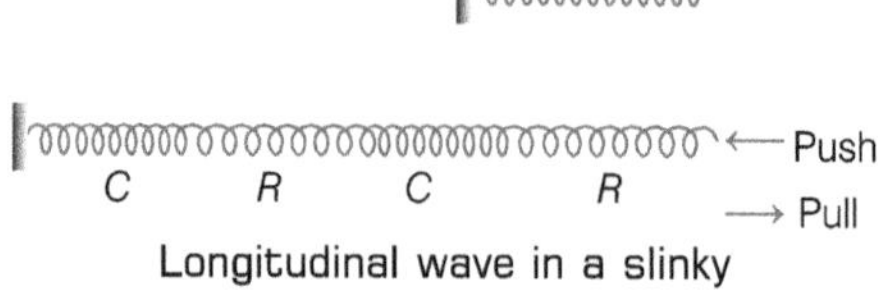

Longitudinal wave in a slinky

When coils are closer together than normal, compressions (*C*) are observed in spring. When coils are farther apart than normal, rarefactions (*R*) are observed. A long flexible spring which can be compressed or extended easily is called **slinky.**

Transverse Waves

In transverse waves, the individual particles of the medium move about its mean position in a direction perpendicular to the direction of wave propagation. e.g. Light is a transverse wave (but it is not a mechanical wave, i.e. it does not require a medium for its propagation).

Transverse waves can be produced only in solids and liquids but not in gases.

The waves produced by moving one end of a long spring or rope, up and down rapidly, whose other end is fixed, are transverse waves.

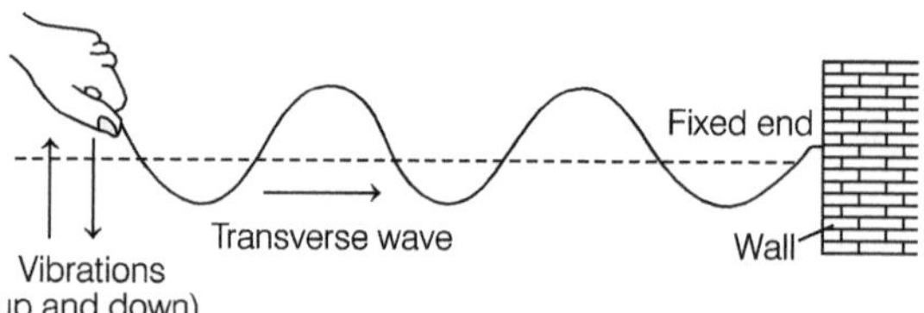

Transverse wave on a long spring or rope

Transverse wave with crest and trough is shown below

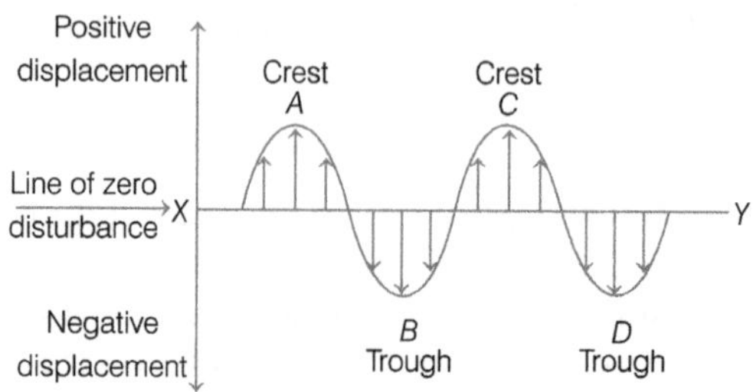

Crest and trough of a transverse wave

Check Point 01

1 State True and False for the following statement:
   (*i*) Sound wave can travel through vacuum.
   (*ii*) The sound of human voice is produced due to vibrations in the vocal chords.
2 Give one difference between longitudinal and transverse waves.
3 Fill in the blanks:
   (*i*) The nature of sound wave is ....
   (*ii*) Transverse waves can be produced only in ...... and ...... but not in ....
4 Give an example for production of transverse wave.

Terms to Describe Sound Waves

Sound waves can be described by its
(*i*) wavelength (*ii*) frequency (*iii*) time period
(*iv*) amplitude (*v*) speed

Wavelength

The distance between the two consecutive compressions (C) or two consecutive rarefactions (R) is called the **wavelength.** Wavelength is the minimum distance in which a sound wave repeats itself.

In other words, it is the combined length of a compression and an adjacent rarefaction. It is represented by a Greek letter **lambda** λ. Its SI unit is **metre** (m).

Frequency

The number of complete waves (or oscillations) produced in one second is called **frequency** of the wave. It is the number of vibrations that occur per second.

Or the number of the compressions or rarefactions that cross a point per unit time.

The frequency of a wave is fixed and does not change even when it passes through different substances. It is denoted by ν (Greek letter, nu). Its SI unit is **hertz** (symbol, Hz) named in honour of **Heinrich Rudolf Hertz** who discovered photoelectric effect.

Time Period

The time taken by two consecutive **compressions** or **rarefactions** to cross a fixed point is called the **time period of the wave.** In other words, the time required to produce one complete wave (or oscillations) is called time period of the wave. It is denoted by symbol T. Its SI unit is **second** (s).

The time period of a wave is the reciprocal of its frequency,

i.e. $$\text{Time period } (T) = \frac{1}{\text{Frequency } (\nu)}$$

Amplitude

The maximum displacement of the particles of the medium from their original mean positions on passing a wave through the medium is called **amplitude** of the wave.

It is used to describe the size of the wave. It is usually denoted by the letter A. Its SI unit is **metre** (m). The amplitude of a wave is same as the amplitude of the vibrating body producing the wave.

Speed

The distance travelled by a wave in one second is called **speed of the wave** or **velocity of the wave.** Under the same physical conditions, the speed of sound remains same for all frequencies. It is represented by letter v. Its SI unit is **metre per second** (m/s or ms^{-1}).

Relationship between speed, frequency and wavelength of a wave

$$\text{Speed} = \frac{\text{Distance travelled}}{\text{Time taken}}$$

Suppose distance travelled by a wave is λ (wavelength), in time T, then the speed is given by $v = \lambda / T$

We know that, frequency, $\nu = 1/T$

Therefore, $v = \lambda \times \nu$ or $v = \nu\lambda$

or $\boxed{\text{Speed (velocity)} = \text{Frequency} \times \text{Wavelength}}$

Graphical Representation of a Sound Wave

When a sound wave passes through air, the density of air changes continuously.

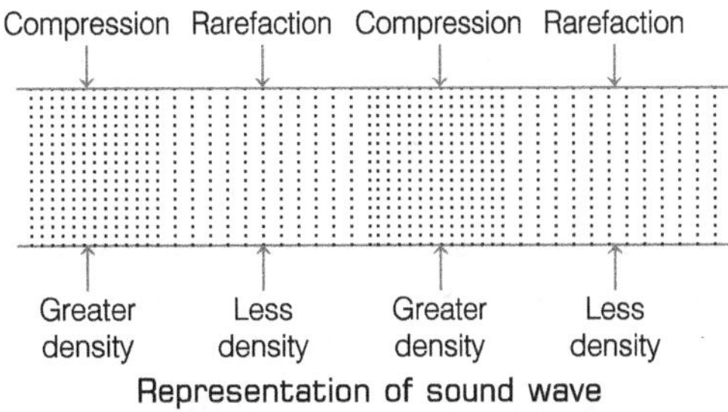

Representation of sound wave

A sound wave in air has been represented by means of a density-distance graph as shown below

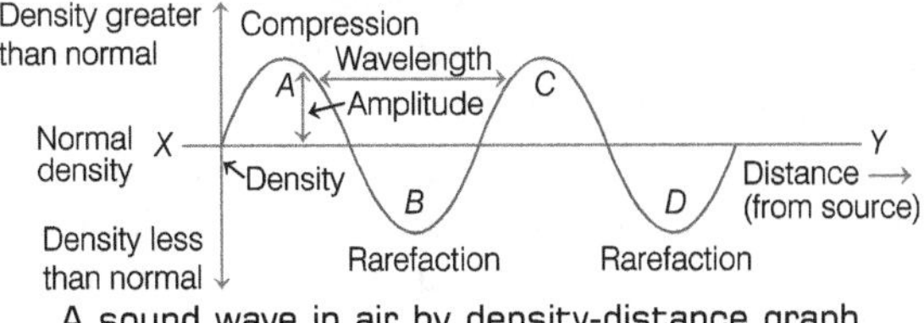

A sound wave in air by density-distance graph

Example 1 *Sound waves travel in air with speed of about 330 ms^{-1}. Calculate the wavelength of sound whose frequency is 550 Hz. Calculate time period of one oscillation.*

Sol. Given, frequency of sound, $\nu = 550$ Hz

Speed of sound wave, $v = 330\ ms^{-1}$

Wavelength of sound wave, $\lambda = ?$

Time period, $T = ?$

We know that, $v = \nu\lambda$ and $T = 1/\nu$

As, $v = \nu\lambda \Rightarrow \lambda = \frac{v}{\nu} = \frac{330}{550} = \frac{3}{5} = 0.6$ m

Again, $T = \frac{1}{\nu} = \frac{1}{550} = 0.001$ s

Characteristics of Sound

A sound has three characteristics. These are loudness, pitch and quality (or timbre).

(i) Loudness

It is the measure of the sound energy reaching the ear per second. Greater the sound energy reaching our ear per second, louder the sound will appear to be.

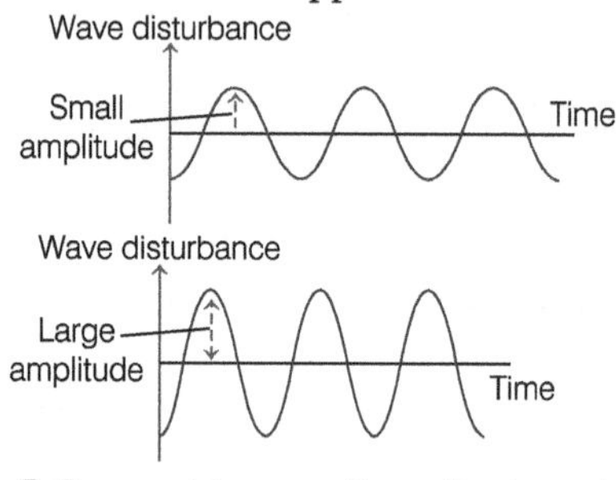

Soft sound has small amplitude and louder sound has large amplitude

If the sound waves have a small amplitude, then sound will be faint or soft but, if waves have a large amplitude, then the sound will be loud. Figure given above shows the wave shapes of a loud and a soft sound of the same frequency.

Since, the amplitude of a sound wave is equal to the amplitude of vibrations of the source producing the sound waves, hence the loudness of sound depends on the amplitude of vibrations of the source producing the sound waves. Loud sound can travel a larger distance as it is associated with higher energy.

A sound wave spreads out from its source, as it moves away from the source, its amplitude as well as its loudness decreases. The loudness of sound is measured in **decibel** (dB). It depends on the sensitivity or the response of our ears.

(ii) Intensity

The amount of sound energy passing each second through unit area is known as the **intensity** of sound. Loudness and intensity are not the same terms. Loudness is a measure of the response of the ear to the sound. Even when two sounds are of equal intensity, we may hear one as louder than the other, simply because our ear detects it in better way.

The SI unit of intensity is **watt per square metre** (W/m^2).

(iii) Pitch or Shrillness

It is that characteristic of sound by which we can distinguish between different sounds of the same loudness. Due to this characteristic, we can distinguish between a man's voice and woman's voice of the same loudness without seeing them.

Pitch of a sound depends on the frequency of vibration. Greater the frequency of a sound, the higher will be its pitch.

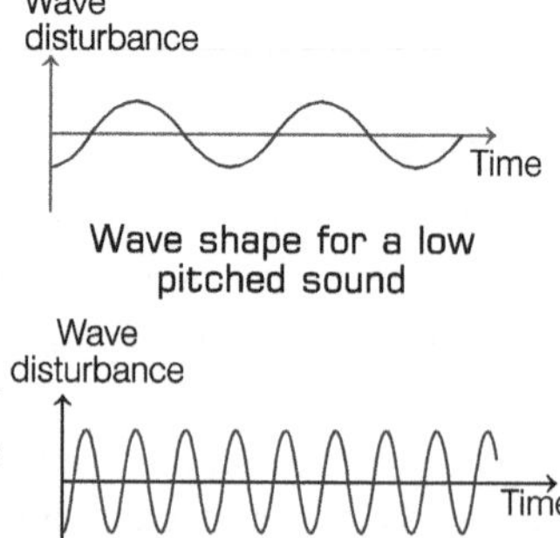

Wave shape for a low pitched sound

Wave shape for a high pitched sound

In other words, the faster the vibration of the source, the higher is the frequency and hence higher is the pitch, as shown in figure. Thus, a high pitch sound corresponds to more number of compressions and rarefactions passing through a fixed point per unit time. Low pitch sound has low frequency and high pitch sound has high frequency.

Objects of different sizes and conditions vibrates at different frequencies to produce sounds of different pitches.

(iv) Quality or Timbre

The quality or timbre of sound enables us to distinguish one sound from another having the same pitch and loudness. A sound of single frequency is called a **tone**. The sound produced due to a mixture of several frequencies is called a **note** and is pleasant in listening too. Noise is unpleasant to ear. Music is pleasant to ear and is of rich quality.

Speed of Sound and Light

The speed of sound in air is about 344 ms^{-1} at 22°C and 331 ms^{-1} at 0°C and the speed of light in air is 300000000 ms^{-1} or 3×10^8 ms^{-1}. Thus, speed of light is very high as compared to the speed of sound.

This is the reason why in the rainy season, the flash of lightning is seen first and the sound of thunder is heard a little later, though both are produced at the same time in clouds.

Speed of Sound in Different Media

The medium through which sound propagates can be a solid substance, a liquid or a gas. The speed of sound depends on the properties of medium through which it travels and the temperature of the medium. The speed of sound decreases when we go from solid to gaseous state. If temperature of the medium increases, then speed of sound also increases.

Sonic Boom

When the speed of any object exceeds the speed of sound, it is said to have supersonic speed. Many objects such as some aircrafts, bullets and rockets, etc. travel at supersonic speeds.When a sound producing source moves with a speed higher than that of sound, it produces shock waves in air, which carry a large amount of energy. The tremendous air pressure variations caused by the shock waves produce a loud burst of sound is known as sonic boom.

It produces untolerable loud noise which causes pain in our ears. The shock waves produced by a supersonic aircraft have enough energy to shatter glass and can even damage buildings.

Check Point 02

1 Wave of frequency 200 Hz is produced in a string as shown in the figure. Find amplitude, wavelength and velocity of the wave.

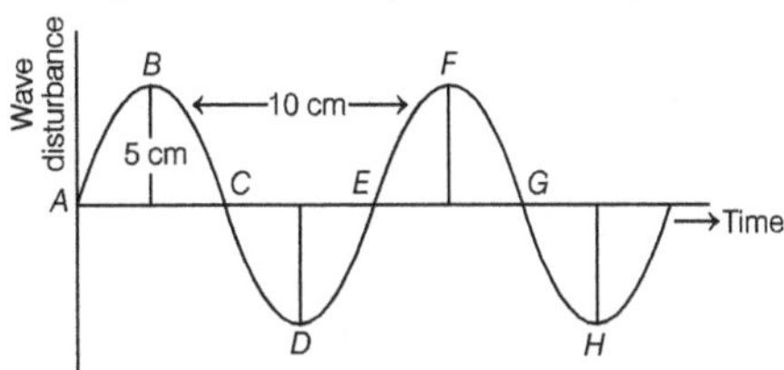

[**Ans.** Amplitude = 5 cm, wavelength = 10 cm and velocity = 20 m/s]

2 Fill in the blank:
A sound wave has a frequency of 2 kHz and wavelength 35 cm. Time taken by this wave to travel 1.5 km is .... [**Ans.** 2.15 s]

3 Define decibel and on what factor does it depend?

4 State True and False for the following statement:
Pitch of sound wave helps us to distinguish between a man's voice and woman's voice without seeing them.

5 What happens to the speed of sound when it goes from solid to gaseous state?

6 How density of particles of compression and rarefaction of a wave different from each other?

Reflection of Sound Wave

The bouncing back of sound when it strikes a hard surface is known as **reflection** of sound. It can be reflected from any surface whether it is smooth or rough. Sound is reflected in the same way as light and follows the same laws of reflection, which are as follows:

1. The incident sound wave (AO), the reflected sound wave (OB) and the normal (ON) at the point of incidence (O), all three lie in the same plane.

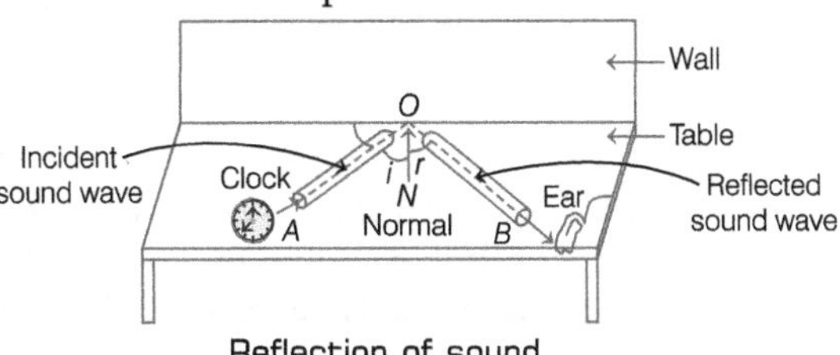

Reflection of sound

2. The angle of incidence ($\angle AON$) of sound is equal to the angle of reflection ($\angle NOB$) of sound.

Echo

When a person shouts in a big empty hall, we first hear his original sound, after that we hear the reflected sound of that shout. So, the repetition of sound caused by reflection of sound waves is called an echo.

The sensation of sound persists in our brain for about 0.1 s. Thus, to hear a distinct echo, the time interval between the original sound and the reflected one must be atleast 0.1 s.

The distance travelled by the sound in 0.1 s

$$= \text{speed} \times \text{time} = 344 \times 0.1 = 34.4 \text{ m}$$

So, echo will be heard, if the minimum distance between the source of sound and the obstacle is $= \frac{34.4}{2} \text{ m} = 17.2 \text{ m}$.

This distance will change with the change in temperature.

Echoes may be heard more than once due to successive multiple reflections. The rolling of thunder is due to successive reflections of sound from a number of reflecting surfaces, such as clouds and the land.

Reverberation

The persistence of a sound in a big hall due to repeated reflections from the walls, ceiling and floor of the wall is known as **reverberation**. This occurs when original sound and reflected sound overlaps. For reverberation to occur, reflection occurs at less than 17 m distance.

A short reverberation is desirable in a concert hall, where music is being played, as it boosts the sound level. But excessive reverberation is highly undesirable because sound becomes blurred, distorted and confusing due to overlapping of different sounds. To reduce reverberation, the roof and walls of the auditorium are generally covered with sound absorbent materials like compressed fibre board, rough plaster or draperies.

Uses of Multiple Reflection of Sound

The reflection of sound is used in the working of devices such as megaphone, horns, stethoscope and sound board. These devices involve multiple reflections of sound waves.

(i) Megaphone and Horn

Megaphone is a large cone shaped device used to amplify and send the voice of a person in particular direction who speaks into it. When a person speaks into the narrow end of the megaphone tube, the sound waves produced are prevented from spreading by successive reflections from the wider end of the megaphone tube, hence sound of his voice can be heard over a longer distance.

(ii) Stethoscope

It is a medical instrument used by doctors to listen to the sound produced within the heart and the lungs in human body. The sound of heartbeats (or lungs) reaches the doctors ears by the multiple reflections of sound waves through the stethoscope tube.

(iii) Sound Board

It is a concave board (curved board) placed behind the stage in big halls, so that sound after reflecting from sound board, spreads evenly across the width of the hall.

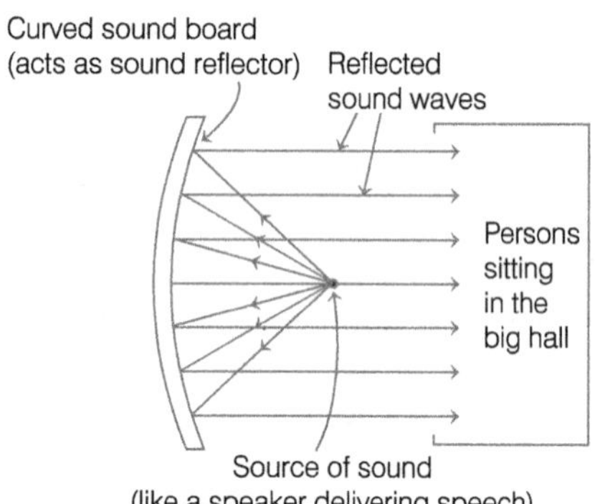

Curved sound board behind the speaker or the stage in big hall

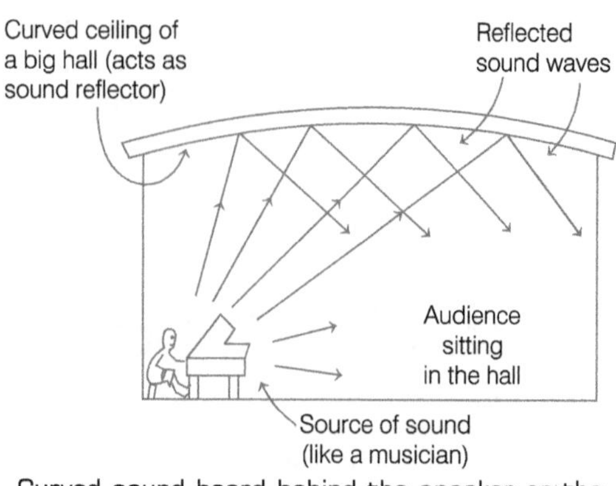

Curved sound board behind the speaker or the stage in big hall

Generally, the ceilings of the concert halls, conference halls and cinema halls are curved, so that sound after reflection reaches all corners of the hall.

Range of Hearing

The average frequency range over which the human ear is sensitive is called **audible range.** The audible range of sound for human beings is from 20 Hz to 20000 Hz (20 kHz).

Children under the age of 5 and some animals such as dogs can hear up to 25000 Hz. As people grow older, their ears become less sensitive to higher and lower frequencies.

Infrasonic Sound

The sound of frequencies lower than 20 Hz are known as **infrasonic sounds** or infrasound, which cannot be heard by human beings. Earthquakes and some animals like whales, elephants and rhinoceroses produce infrasonic sound of frequency 5 Hz. It is observed that some animals get disturbed and start running here and there just before the earthquakes occur. This is because earthquakes produce low frequency infrasound before the main shock waves begin which possibly alert the animals and they get disturbed.

Ultrasonic Sound

The sounds of frequencies higher than 20000 Hz are called **ultrasonic sounds** or ultrasounds which cannot be heard by human beings. Dogs can hear ultrasonic sounds of frequency up to 50000 Hz. This is why dogs are used for detective work by the police. Bats, dolphins, and porpoises can produce ultrasonic sounds.

Hearing Aid

This is a device used by people who are hard of hearing. It is an electronic, battery operated device. It receives sound through a microphone which converts the sound waves to electrical signals.

These electrical signals are amplified by an amplifier. The amplified electrical signals are given to a speaker of the hearing aid. The speaker converts the amplified electrical signals to sound and then sends it to the ear for clear hearing.

Ultrasound and Its Applications

Ultrasounds are high frequency waves. They travel in straight line without bending around the corners. They can penetrate into matter to a large extent. Due to these properties, ultrasound is used in industry and in hospitals for medical purposes.

Some of the important applications of ultrasound are given below

(i) In Cleaning Minute Parts of Machines

Ultrasound is used to clean parts located in hard-to-reach-places, such as spiral tubes, odd-shaped machines and electronic components, etc. Objects to be cleaned are placed in a cleaning solution and ultrasonic waves are sent into the solution.

Due to their high frequency, the ultrasound waves stirr up the solution, hence the particles of dust, grease and dirt vibrate too much, become loose, get detached from the object and fall into the solution. The objects, thus get thoroughly cleaned.

(ii) In Internal Investigation of Human Body

Ultrasound is used to investigate the internal organs of human body such as liver, gall bladder, pancreas, kidneys, uterus and heart, etc.

Ultrasound waves can penetrate the human body and different types of tissues get reflected in different ways from a region where there is a change of tissue density. In this way, ultrasound helps us to see inside the human body and to give pictures of the inner organs by converting into electrical signals. These pictures or images are then displayed on a monitor or printed on a film. This technique is called **ultrasonography.** Ultrasonography is used for the examination of fetus during pregnancy to detect any growth abnormalities, which helps in taking the necessary action to rectify the abnormalities.

Ultrasonic scanner is an instrument that helps the doctor to detect abnormalities, such as stones in the gall bladder and kidney or tumours in different organs and many other ailments. Ultrasound is also used for diagnosing heart diseases by scanning the heart from inside. This technique is **echocardiography.** Ultrasound may be employed to break small stones formed in the kidneys into fine grains which later get flushed out with urine. This way, the patient gets relief from pain.

(iii) In Industries

Ultrasound is used in industry for detecting flaws (cracks, etc.) in metal blocks without damaging them.

Metal blocks are used in the construction of big structures like bridges, machines and scientific equipment, etc. If there are some cracks and flaws in the metal blocks, which are invisible from outside reduces the strength of the structure. These can be detected by using ultrasound. This is based on the fact that an internal crack (or hole) does not allow ultrasound to pass through it.

It reflects the ultrasound. Ultrasound waves are allowed to pass through one face of metal block (to be tested) and detectors are placed on the opposite face of the metal block to detect the transmitted ultrasound waves.

If there is even a small defect, the ultrasound waves gets reflected back indicating the presence of the flaw or defect, as shown in figure.

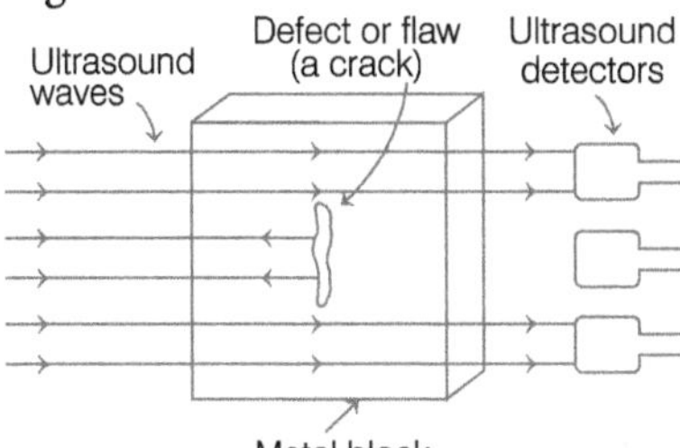

Ultrasound reflected from a part of block, which shows that this metal block has a flaw or defect (like a crack) inside it

Ordinary sound waves cannot be used for detecting the flaws in metal blocks because they will bend around the corners of the defective location and therefore enter the detector.

Use of Ultrasonic Waves by Bats

Bats search out prey and fly in dark night by emitting and detecting reflections of ultrasonic waves. The method used by some animals like bats, tortoises and dolphins to locate the objects by hearing the echoes of their ultrasonic **squeaks** is known as **echolocation.**

Bats emit high frequency or high pitched ultrasonic squeaks while flying and listen to the echoes produced by reflection of their squeaks from the obstacles or prey in their path. From the time taken by the echo to be heard, bats can determine the distance of the obstacle or prey and can avoid the obstacle by changing the direction or catch the prey. However, certain moths can hear the high frequency ultrasonic squeaks of a bat and can know where the bat is flying nearby and are able to escape from being captured.

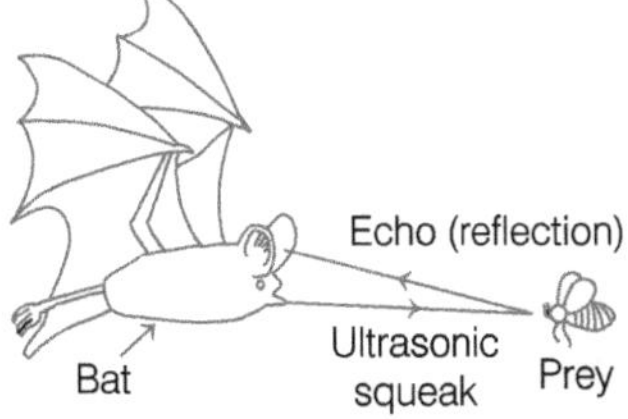

Bats can search their prey in the darkness of night by the method of echolocation

Check Point 03

1 In an experiment on studying the laws of reflection of sound, if the incident wave makes an angle of 35° with the rigid surface (wall), what will be the angle of reflection? [**Ans.** 55°]

2 State True and False for the following statement:
For hearing distant echoes, the minimum distance of the obstacle from the source of sound is 17.2 m.

3 An echo is returned in 6s. What is the distance of reflecting surface from source? [given that speed of sound is 342 m/s] [**Ans.** 1026 m]

4 Fill in the blank:
The sound absorbant materials used in concert hall is ....

5 Give two uses of multiple reflection of sound.

6 Name the sound waves of frequency which are too low to hear for human beings.

7 Give an application of ultrasound for medical purposes. Explain how ultrasound is used to clean spiral tubes and electronic components.

NCERT FOLDER

INTEXT QUESTIONS

1 How does the sound produced by a vibrating object in a medium reach your ear? Pg 162

Sol. Sound is produced by vibrating objects. When an object vibrates, it sets the particles of the medium around it in vibration. There vibrations are passed or transmitted to neighbouring particles in all directions. When vibrations are transmitted by medium particles to our ear, we get sensation of hearing.

2 Explain how sound is produced by your school bell. Pg 163

Sol. The bell produces the sound when gong of the bell is struck by hammer. When the gong is struck by hammer, it starts vibrating. Since, the vibrating objects produce sound, so the bell produces sound.

3 Why are sound waves called mechanical waves? Pg 163

Sol. Sound waves are called mechanical waves because they are produced by the motion of particles of a medium and require material medium for their propagation.

4 Suppose you and your friend are on the Moon. Will you be able to hear any sound produced by your friend? Pg 163

Sol. No, I will not be able to hear any sound produced by my friend because the sound waves require some material medium like air to travel. There is no atmosphere or air on the Moon, so the sound produced by my friend will not reach me and I will not be able to hear.

5 Which wave property determines (*i*) loudness (*ii*) and pitch? Pg 166

Sol. (*i*) Loudness of sound wave is determined by its amplitude.
(*ii*) Pitch of the sound wave is determined by its frequency.

6 Guess which sound has a higher pitch, guitar or car horn. Pg 166

Sol. Pitch of guitar sound is higher because the frequency of sound produced by guitar is higher than that of car horn.

7 What are wavelength, frequency, time period and amplitude of a sound wave? Pg 166

Sol. Refer to text on Pg. 271.

8 How are the wavelength and frequency of a sound wave related to speed? Pg 166

Sol. The relation between wavelength (λ), frequency (ν) and speed of wave (v) is $v = \nu\lambda$.

9 Calculate the wavelength of a sound wave whose frequency is 200Hz and speed is 440 ms^{-1} in a given medium. Pg 166

Sol. Given, frequency, $\nu = 200$ Hz, velocity, $v = 440$ ms^{-1}
According to the relation, $v = \nu\lambda$

$$\Rightarrow \quad \lambda = \frac{v}{\nu} = \frac{440}{200} = 2.2 \text{ m}$$

10 A person is listening to a tone of 500 Hz sitting at a distance of 450 m from the source of the sound, what is the time interval between successive compressions from the source? Pg 166

Sol. The time interval between two successive compressions or rarefactions is equal to the time period of the wave.
$\therefore$ Required time interval = Time period

$$= \frac{1}{\text{Frequency}} = \frac{1}{500} = 0.002 \text{ s}$$

$$= 2 \times 10^{-3} \text{ s} = 2 \text{ ms}$$

11 Distinguish between loudness and intensity of sound. **Pg 166**

Sol. Difference between loudness and intensity

Loudness	*Intensity*
It is a subjective quantity. A sound may be loud for one person but may be feeble for another person.	It is an objective physical quantity which does not change for person to person.
It cannot be measured as it is just a sensation which can be felt only.	It can be measured as a physical quantity.
Loudness of sound is measured by the unit decibel (dB).	Intensity of sound is measured by the unit watt per square metre (W/m^2).
It depends on the sensitivity of ears.	It does not depend on the sensitivity of ears.

12 In which of the three media air, water or iron, does sound travel the fastest at a particular temperature? **Pg 167**

Sol. Sound waves travel fastest in solid medium, i.e. out of the given media, sound wave will travel fastest in iron.

13 An echo returned in 3 s. What is the distance of the reflecting surface from the source, given that the speed of sound is 342 ms^{-1}? **Pg 168**

Sol. Given, speed of sound, $v = 342 \text{ ms}^{-1}$
Time taken, $t = 3$ s
So, distance travelled by sound $= v \times t$

$$= 342 \times 3$$
$$= 1026 \text{ m}$$

Hence, distance between reflecting surface and source should be $\frac{1026}{2} = 513$ m.

14 Why are the ceilings of concert halls curved? **Pg 169**

Sol. The curved ceiling of conference hall focuses reflection of sound from the walls to audience, so that every corner of the hall gets sound equivalently.

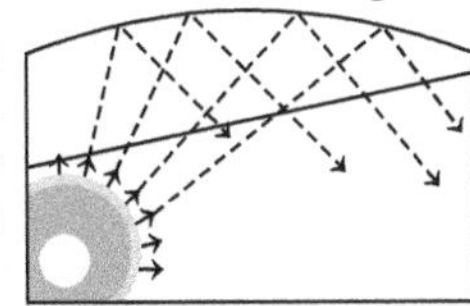

15 What is audible range of the average human ear?

Sol. The audible frequency range for the average human ear is 20 Hz to 20000 Hz.

16 What is the range of frequencies associated with (*i*) infrasound (*ii*) and ultrasound? **Pg 170**

Sol. (*i*) Sound waves having frequencies less than 20 Hz and greater than zero are called **infrasound.**

(*ii*) Sound waves having frequencies more than 20000 Hz are called **ultrasound.**

EXERCISES

(On Pages 174 and 175)

1 What is sound and how is it produced?

Sol. Sound is a form of energy, which produces the sensation of hearing in our ears. It is produced when an object is set to vibrate or we can say that vibrating objects produce sound.

2 Describe with the help of a diagram, how compressions and rarefactions are produced in air near a source of sound.

Sol. When a vibrating object moves forward, it pushes the air infront of it creating a region of high pressure. This region is called **compression.** This compression starts to move away from the vibrating object. When the vibrating object moves backward, it creates a region of low pressure called **rarefaction.** As the object moves back and forth rapidly, a series of compressions and rarefactions is created. These make the sound wave that propagates through the medium.

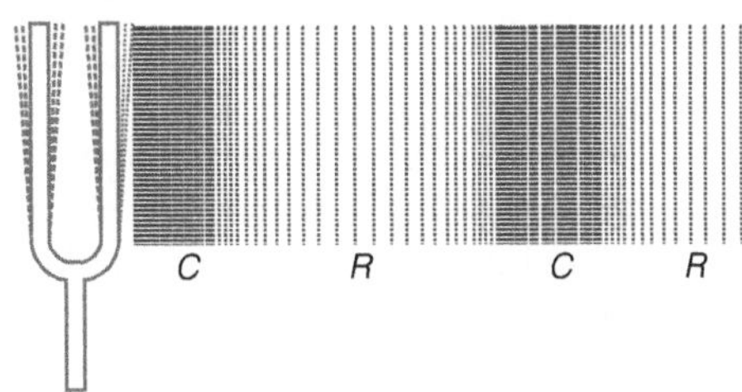

A vibrating object creating a series of compressions (*C*) and rarefactions (*R*) in the medium

3 Cite an experiment to show that sound needs a material medium for its propagation.

Sol. Experiment to show that sound needs a material medium for its propagation is given below

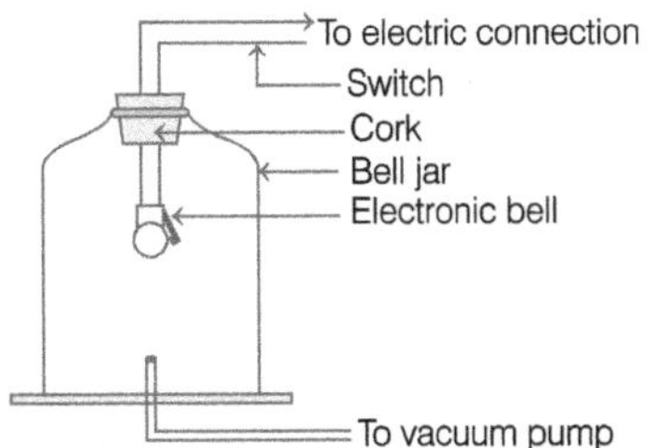

Take an electric bell and an airtight glass bell jar. The electric bell is suspended inside the airtight bell jar. The bell jar is connected to a vacuum pump, as shown in figure. If you press the switch, you will be able to hear the bell. Now, start the vacuum pump. When the air in the jar is pumped out gradually, the sound becomes fainter, although the same current is passing through the bell. After some time when less air is left inside the bell jar, you will hear a very feeble sound. On removal of complete air, no sound is heard.

4 **Why is sound wave called a longitudinal wave?**

Sol. The sound wave is called longitudinal wave because on propagation of sound wave in a medium, the particles of the medium vibrate to and fro about their equilibrium positions and parallel to the direction of propagation of the wave.

5 **Which characteristic of the sound helps you to identify your friend by his voice while sitting with others in a dark room?**

Sol. Timbre, a quality of sound is the characteristic by which we can identify the person by his voice.

6 **Flash and thunder are produced simultaneously. But thunder is heard a few seconds after the flash is seen, why?**

Sol. Thunder is heard few seconds after the flash is seen because speed of light in atmosphere (or air) is $3\times10^8 \text{ms}^{-1}$ which is very high as compared to the speed of sound which is only 330 ms^{-1}. So, sound of thunder reaches us later than the flash.

7 **A person has hearing range from 20 Hz to 20 kHz. What are the typical wavelengths of sound waves in air corresponding to these two frequencies? (Take, the speed of sound in air as 344 ms^{-1})**

Sol. The relation between speed (v), wavelength (λ) and frequency (ν) of a wave is $v = \nu\lambda$

$$\lambda = \frac{v}{\nu}$$

(*i*) Here, $v = 344 \text{ ms}^{-1}$, $\nu = 20$ Hz

$\therefore$ Corresponding wavelength,

$$\lambda = \frac{v}{\nu} = \frac{344}{20} = 17.2 \text{ m}$$

(*ii*) Here, $v = 344 \text{ ms}^{-1}$, $\nu = 20 \text{ kHz} = 20\times10^3$ Hz

$\therefore$ Corresponding wavelength, $\lambda = \frac{v}{\nu} = \frac{344}{20\times10^3}$

$$= 1.72\times10^{-2} \text{ m}$$

8 **Two children are at opposite ends of an aluminium rod. One strikes the end of the rod with a stone. Find the ratio of times taken by the sound wave in air and in aluminium to reach the second child.**

Sol. Let l be length of the rod.

Time taken by the sound to travel through the aluminium rod is given by $t_1 = \frac{\text{distance}}{\text{speed}} = \frac{1}{v_{Al}}$

Similarly, time taken by the sound to travel through the air is given by $t_2 = \frac{\text{distance}}{\text{speed}} = \frac{1}{v_{air}}$

$\therefore$ Required ratio, $t_1 : t_2 = \frac{v_{air}}{v_{Al}}$

9 **The frequency of a source of sound is 100 Hz. How many times does it vibrate in a minute?**

Sol. Given, frequency, $\nu = 100$ Hz

From the definition of frequency, we can say that

Number of oscillations in 1 s = 100

$\therefore$ Number of oscillations in 1 min or 60 s

$$= 100\times60 = 6000$$

Thus, the source of sound vibrates 6000 times in a minute.

10 **Does sound follow the same laws of reflection as light does? Explain.**

Sol. Yes, sound wave follows the same laws as in case of laws of reflection of light.

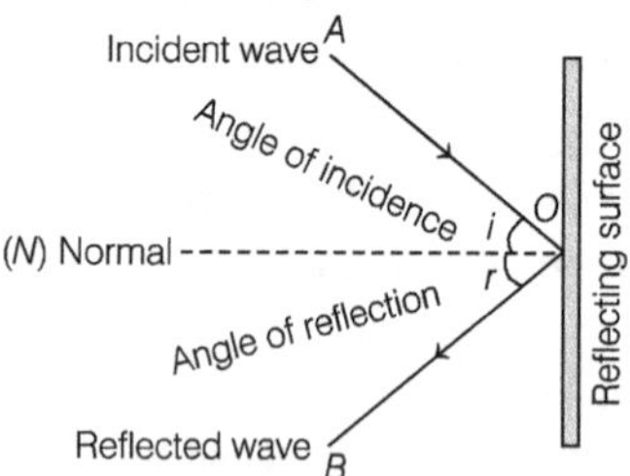

The laws of reflection of sound are as follows:

(*i*) The incident sound wave (*AO*), the reflected sound wave (*OB*) and the normal (*ON*) at the point of incidence, all lie in the same plane.

(*ii*) The angle of incidence ($\angle AON$) of sound is equal to the angle of reflection ($\angle NOB$) of sound.

11 **When a sound is reflected from a distant object, an echo is produced. Let the distance between the reflecting surface and the source of sound production remains the same. Do you hear echo sound on a hotter day?**

Sol. The time taken by echo to be heard, $t = \frac{2d}{v}$

where, d = distance between the reflecting surface and source of sound and v = speed of sound in air.

As we know that, speed of sound increases with increase in temperature, so on a hotter day, speed of sound will be higher, so the time after which echo is heard will decrease. If time taken by the reflected sound is less than 0.1s after the production of original sound, then echo is not heard.

12 A stone is dropped from the top of a tower 500 m high into a pond of water at the base of the tower. When is the splash heard at the top? [Given, $g = 10\ ms^{-2}$ and speed of sound $= 340 ms^{-1}$]

Sol. Time after which the splash is heard = Time taken by the stone to reach the pond + Time taken by splash sound to reach the top of tower.

(*i*) For the time taken by the stone to reach the pond.
Here, $u = 0$ [$\because$ stone is dropped from rest]

From equation of motion, $h = ut + \frac{1}{2} gt^2$

$$500 = 0 \times t + \frac{1}{2} \times 10\,(t)^2$$

$$500 = 5t^2 \Rightarrow t^2 = 100 \Rightarrow t = \sqrt{100} = 10\ s$$

(*ii*) Time taken by splash sound to reach the top of the tower, $t' = \frac{\text{Distance}}{\text{Speed}} = \frac{500}{340} = 1.47\ s$

$\therefore$ Time after which splash is heard
$= 10 + 1.47 = 11.47\ s$

13 A sound wave travels at a speed of $339\ ms^{-1}$. If its wavelength is 1.5 cm, then what is the frequency of the wave? Will it be audible?

Sol. Given, speed, $v = 339\ ms^{-1}$

Wavelength, $\lambda = 1.5\ cm = 1.5 \times 10^{-2}\ m$

$\therefore$ Frequency, $\nu = \frac{v}{\lambda} = \frac{339}{1.5 \times 10^{-2}} = 22600\ Hz$

This frequency is greater than 20000 Hz, so it will not be audible. Audible range for human ear is 20 Hz to 20000 Hz.

14 What is reverberation? How can it be reduced?

Sol. The persistence of a sound in a big hall due to repeated reflections from the walls, ceiling and floor of the wall is known as reverberation. It can be reduced by covering the roofs and walls of the hall by sound absorbing materials.

15 What is loudness of sound? What factors does it depend on?

Sol. Loudness of a sound is a subjective quantity, it is the measure of the sound energy reaching the ear per second.

Loudness depends on
(*i*) the amplitude of the vibrating body
(*ii*) and the sensitivity of human ear.

16 Explain how bats use ultrasound to catch a prey.

Sol. Bats can produce ultrasonic waves by flapping their wings, they can also detect these waves. The ultrasonic waves produced by a bat spread out. These waves after reflecting from a prey like an insect reach the bat. So, the bat can locate its prey.

17 How is ultrasound used for cleaning?

Sol. Refer to text on 275.

18 A SONAR device on a submarine sends out a signal and receives an echo 5 s later. Calculate the speed of sound in water, if the distance of the object from the submarine is 3625 m.

Sol. Time taken by the signal to go from submarine to object,

$$t = \frac{5}{2} = 2.5\ s$$

Distance between submarine and object,
$s = 3625\ m$

$\therefore$ Speed of sound in water,

$$v = \frac{\text{Distance}}{\text{Time}} = \frac{3625}{2.5} = 1450\ ms^{-1}$$

19 Explain how defects in a metal block can be detected using ultrasound.

Sol. Refer to text on Pg. 275.

SUMMARY

- **Sound** is produced by vibrating objects.
- **Vibration** means a kind of rapid to and fro motion of an object.
- Sound waves require a medium to travel, so they are called **mechanical waves.**
- **Compression** is the part of a longitudinal wave in which the particles of a medium are closer to one another than they normally are and it is the region of high pressure.
- **Rarefaction** is the part of a longitudinal wave in which the particles of the medium are farther apart than they normally are and it is the region of low pressure.
- Waves are of two types (*i*) longitudinal waves (*ii*) and transverse waves.
- In **longitudinal waves**, the individual particles of medium move in a direction parallel to the direction of propagation of the disturbance.
- In **transverse waves**, the individual particles of the medium move about its mean position in a direction perpendicular to the direction of wave propagation.
- The distance between the two consecutive compression (C) or two consecutive rarefactions (R) is called the **wavelength**. Its SI unit is **metre** (m).
- The number of vibrations that occur per second is known as **frequency**. Its SI unit is **Hertz** (Hz).
- The time taken by two consecutive compressions or rarefactions to cross a fixed point is called the **time period of the wave**.
- The time period of a wave is reciprocal of its frequency, i.e. $T = \frac{1}{\nu}$.
- The maximum displacement of the particles of medium from their original mean positions on passing a wave through the medium is called the **amplitude** of the wave. Its SI unit is **metre** (m).
- The relationship between speed (v), frequency (ν) and wavelength (λ) of a wave is given by $v = \nu\lambda$.
- The measure of sound energy reaching the ear per second is known as **loudness**. It is measured in **decibel** (dB).
- The amount of sound energy passing each second through unit area is known as **intensity of sound**. Its SI unit is **watt per square metre** (W/m^2).
- **Pitch** is that characteristic of sound by which we can distinguish between the different sounds of the same loudness.
- The **quality or timbre** of sound enables us to distinguish one sound from another having the same pitch and loudness.
- Speed of sound is greatest in solid, then in liquids and least in gases.
- When the speed of any object exceeds the speed of sound, it is said to have **supersonic speed.**
- The bouncing back of sound when it strikes a hard surface is known as **reflection of sound.**
- **Laws of Reflection of Sound**
  (*i*) The incident sound wave, reflected sound wave and the normal at the point of incidence, all lie in the same plane.
  (*ii*) The angle of incidence of sound is equal to the angle of reflection of sound.
- The repitition of sound caused by reflection of sound waves is called an **echo.**
- The persistence of sound in a big hall due to repeated reflections from the walls, ceiling and floor is known as **reverberation.**
- The audible range of sound for human ear is from **20Hz to 20000 Hz.**
- The sound of frequencies lower than 20 Hz are known as **infrasonic sounds**, which cannot be heard by humans.
- The sounds of frequencies higher than 20000 Hz are called **ultrasonic sounds**, which cannot be heard by human beings.
- **Ultrasound** is used to clean parts located in hard to reach places such as spiral tubes, odd-shaped machines.
- **Ultrasound** is also used for diagonosing heart diseases by scanning the heart from inside. This technique is called **echocardiography**.
- The method used by some animals like bats, tortoises and dolphins to locate the objects by hearing the echoes of their ultrasonic squeaks is known as **echolocation.**

For Mind Map
Visit https://goo.gl/MTdMk2
OR Scan the Code

Exam Practice

Objective Type Questions

Multiple Choice Questions

1 A tuning fork produces sound wave, because it creates

(a) heat (b) light
(c) vibration (d) None of these

Sol. (c) If tuning fork is vibrating, it produces sound.

2 Which of the following does not produce sound wave?

(a) Drum (b) Birds
(c) TV (d) Microwave oven

Sol. (d) Microwave oven is used to produce electromagnetic wave.

3 Sound travels in air, if

(a) particles of medium travel from one place to another
(b) there is no moisture in the atmosphere
(c) disturbance moves
(d) both particles as well as disturbance travel from one place to another **NCERT Exemplar**

Sol. (c) When sound travels in air, then only disturbances created by the vibration of particle moves from one place to other.

4 A light string is suspended from a hook which is attached to a 1 kg weight at its lower end. If the string is pulled and then released, the disturbance produced in the spring is

(a) pulse (b) longitudinal wave
(c) transverse wave (d) None of these

Sol. (c) Transverse waves are produced in stretched string.

5 The frequency of a source of sound is 200 Hz. How many times does it vibrate in 2 min ?

(a) 2400 (b) 24000
(c) 24500 (d) 2450

Sol. (b) Given, frequency = 200 Hz

Number of oscillation in 1s = 200

[because frequency represents number of oscillations in 1s]

Number of oscillation in 2 min or 120 s

$= 200 \times 120 = 24000$

6 A guitar of frequency 360 Hz makes 120 vibrations. If the velocity of sound in air is 330 m/s, then how much distance is travelled by the sound in air?

(a) 90 m (b) 100 m
(c) 110 m (d) 140 m

Sol. (c) Given, frequency, $\nu = 360$ Hz

Velocity, $v = 330$ m/s

Wavelength, $\lambda = ?$

As, $\lambda = \frac{v}{\nu} = \frac{330}{360} = \frac{33}{36}$ m

$\therefore$ Distance travelled by the sound wave in 120 vibrations $= 120 \times \frac{33}{36} = 110$ m.

7 When we change feeble sound to loud sound, we increase its

(a) frequency (b) amplitude
(c) velocity (d) wavelength

NCERT Exemplar

Sol. (b) The loudness or softness of a sound is determined by its amplitude. So for a loud sound, it must have higher amplitude.

8 What is the SI unit of loudness ?

(a) Dioptre (b) Metre
(c) Weber (d) Decibel

Sol. (d) The SI unit of loudness is decibel (dB).

9 A man's voice and a woman's voice is differ by its

(a) loudness (b) pitch
(c) intensity (d) amplitude

Sol. (b) Pitch is the characteristic of sound by which we can distinguish between different sounds of the same loudness.

10 Echo is caused by the phenomenon of

(a) reflection (b) rarefaction
(c) refraction (d) reverberation

Sol. (a) An echo is the reflected sound waves.

11 What is the range of audio waves ?

(a) 20 kHz to 200 kHz (b) 20 Hz to 20 kHz
(c) 20 Hz to 20 MHz (d) 20 Hz to 20 MHz

Sol. (b) The range of sound wave is 20 Hz to 20 kHz.

12 Infrasound can be heard by

(a) dog
(b) bat
(c) rhinocerose
(d) human beings **NCERT Exemplar**

Sol. (c) Infrasound are the waves whose frequency is less than 20 Hz. Rhinoceroses communicate using infrasound of frequency as low as 5 Hz.

13 A man beating a drum infront of a cliff hears the echo after 4s. What is the distance of man from the cliff, if velocity of sound in air is 330 m/s?

(a) 660 m (b) 500 m
(c) 1000 m (d) 0.3 km

Sol. (a) Given, speed = 330 m/s and time = 4s

As we know that,
Distance, $s =$ Speed × Time $= 330 \times 4 = 1320$ m

As in 4s, sound has to travel twice distance between man and the cliff.

So, distance between man and cliff is

$$\frac{s}{2} = \frac{1320}{2} = 660 \text{ m}$$

Fill in the Blanks

14 Transverse waves can be produced only in ....

Sol. Solids and liquids

15 The time period of a wave is the reciprocal of its ....

Sol. Frequency

16 Loudness of sound wave is determined by its ....

Sol. Amplitude

17 When the speed of any object exceeds the speed of sound, it is said to have .... speed.

Sol. Supersonic

18 Dogs can hear and detect .... waves.

Sol. Ultrasonic

True and False

19 Wavelength is the minimum distance in which a sound wave repeats itself.

Sol. True

20 The sound produced due to a mixture of several frequencies is called a tone.

Sol. False

21 Infrasound is produced in an earthquake before the main shock wave begins.

Sol. True

22 Quality of sound depends on amplitude.

Sol. False

23 The speed of sound in a solid is greater than in air.

Sol. True

24 The speed of light is very less as compared to the speed of sound.

Sol. False

Match the Columns

25 Match the Column I with Column II.

Column I	Column II
A. Bats	p. Multiple reflection of sound
B. Loudness	q. Sensitivity to ultrasonic
C. Reverberation	r. Human ear
D. Tympanic membrane	s. Amplitude

Sol. (A) → (q), (B) → (s), (C) → (p), (D) → (r)

Assertion-Reason

Direction (Q.Nos. 26-30) *In each of the following questions, a statement of Assertion is given by the corresponding statement of Reason. Of the statements, mark the correct answer as*

(a) If both Assertion and Reason are true and Reason is the correct explanation of Assertion.
(b) If both Assertion and Reason are true, but Reason is not the correct explanation of Assertion.
(c) If Assertion is true, but Reason is false.
(d) If Assertion is false, but Reason is true.

26 **Assertion** Sound wave is a longitudinal wave.

Reason Sound wave can be produced in all the three media such as solids, liquids and gases.

Sol. (b) Sound wave is longitudinal wave which requires a medium (solid, liquid or gas) to travel through them. Hence, Assertion and Reason both are true, but Reason is not the correct explanation of Assertion.

27 **Assertion** Velocity of sound wave of frequency 550 Hz and wavelength 0.6 m is 330 m/s.

Reason Velocity of sound wave is given by Velocity = Frequency × Wavelength

Sol. (a) Velocity of sound wave = Frequency × Wavelength

$= 550 \times 0.6$

$= 330$ m/s

Hence, Assertion and Reason both are true and Reason is the correct explanation of Assertion.

28 **Assertion** Pitch of sound is helpful to distinguish between a man's voice and woman's voice of the same loudness without seeing them.

Reason Greater frequency of sound, the higher will be its pitch.

Sol. (a) Pitch of sound depends on the frequency of vibration. Greater the frequency of a sound, the higher will be its pitch which helps to distinguish between a man's voice and woman's voice of the same loudness.
Hence, Assertion and Reason both are true and Reason is the correct explanation of Assertion.

29 **Assertion** Echo is caused by the phenomenon of reflection.

Reason The persistance of a sound in a big hall is due to echo.

Sol. (c) Echo is caused by the phenomenon of reflection. The persistance of sound in a big hall is due to reverberation.
Hence, Assertion is true, but Reason is false.

30 **Assertion** The audible range of sound for human beings is from 20 Hz to 20000 Hz.

Reason For a human being, it is difficult to hear ultrasonic sound while easy to hear infrasonic sound.

Sol. (c) A human being can hear only audible range of frequency (20 Hz to 20000 Hz) but cannot hear infrasonic and ultrasonic sound.
Hence, Assertion is true, but Reason is false.

Case Based Questions

Direction (Q.Nos. 31-34) *Answer the question on the basis of your understanding of the following passage and related studied concepts:*

Bats search out prey and fly in dark night by emitting and detecting reflections of ultrasonic waves. The method used by some animals like bats, tortoise and dolphins to locate objects by hearing the echoes of their ultrasonic squeaks is known as echolocations.

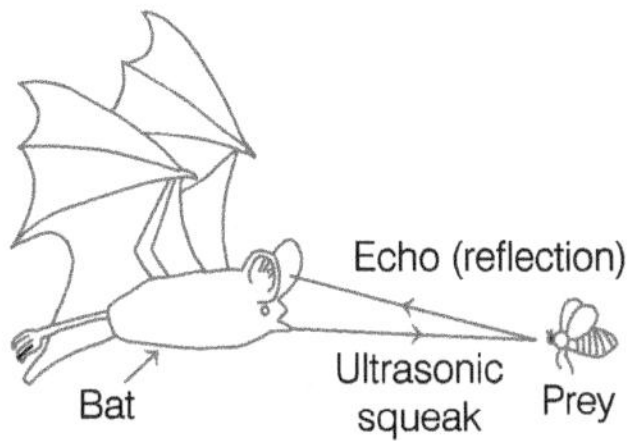

Bats emit high frequency or high pitched ultrasonic squeaks while flying and listen to the echoes produced by reflection of their squeaks from the obstacles or prey in the path. From the time taken by the echo to be heard, bats can determine the distance of the obstacle or prey and can avoid the obstacle by changing the direction or catch the prey. However, certain moths can hear the high frequency ultrasonic squeaks of a bat and can know where the bat is flying nearby and are able to escape from being captured.

31 Define echolocation.

Sol. The methods used by beats, dolphins to locate the objects or prey by hearing the echos of their ultrasonic squeaks is known as echolocations.

32 How bats can determine the distance of the obstacle?

Sol. From the time taken by the echo to be heard, bats can determine the distance of the obstacle.

33 Frequency of ultrasonic waves

(a) less than 20000Hz
(b) equal to 20000Hz
(c) higher than 20000Hz
(d) 2000Hz

Sol. Option (c) is correct.

34 Bats can detects reflection of which type of wave?

(a) Infrasonic waves
(b) Hearing range
(c) Ultrasonic waves
(d) Both (a) and (c)

Sol. Option (c) is correct.

Direction (Q.Nos. 35-38) *Answer the question on the basis of your understanding of the following passage and related studied concepts:*

Hearing range describes the range of frequencies that can be heard by humans or other animals though it can also refer to the range of levels.

Table : Range of frequency of sound

	Frequency
Audible range for human	20Hz to 20000 Hz
Infrasonic sound	less than 20 Hz
Ultrasonic sound	greater than 20 kHz

People with hearing loss need a hearing aid. A hearing aid is an electronic, battery operated device. The hearing aid receives sound through microphone using this hearing aid people able to hear clear sound.

35 In which range, whales and elephants produce frequency of sound?

Sol. Whales and elephants produce sound in the infrasound range, i.e. less than 20 Hz.

36 What do you mean by audible range for human beings?

Sol. The audible range for human beings means the range of frequencies that can be heard by human. Audible range for human is 20 Hz to 2000 Hz.

37 What type of aid used by people suffering from hearing loss?

Sol. People suffering from hearing loss need a hearing aid. A hearing aid is an electronic battery operated device.

38 Name the sound having frequency range less than 20 Hz.

Sol. Infrasonic sound.

Very Short Answer Type Questions

39 Why can't we hear the sound of an explosion on the surface of the Moon?

Sol. There is no atmosphere on Moon and we know that sound waves need a medium to travel. Thus, we do not hear the sound of an explosion on the surface of the Moon.

40 If a freely suspended vertical spring is pulled in downward direction and then released, which type of waves are produced in the spring?

Sol. In this situation, longitudinal waves will produce in spring.

41 Give one example of transverse and longitudinal waves.

Sol. Transverse wave — Light (1/2)
Longitudinal wave — Sound (1/2)

42 On what factor does the quality of the sound depend?

Sol. Quality of the sound depends on the shape of the sound wave.

43 Among air, water and steel, in which medium, the sound wave will travel faster?

Sol. The sound wave will travel faster in steel because speed of sound is the fastest in the solids.

44 A human heartbeats 72 times in a minute. Calculate its frequency.

Sol. Given, number of heartbeats = 72

Time = 1 min = 60 s

$$\therefore \text{Frequency} = \frac{\text{Number of beats}}{\text{Total time (in second)}}$$

$$= \frac{72}{60} = 1.2\ \text{Hz} \qquad [\because 1\ \text{min} = 60\ \text{s}]$$

45 Give the correct picture of reflection of sound marked with the angle of incidence, angle of reflection and the normal.

Sol.

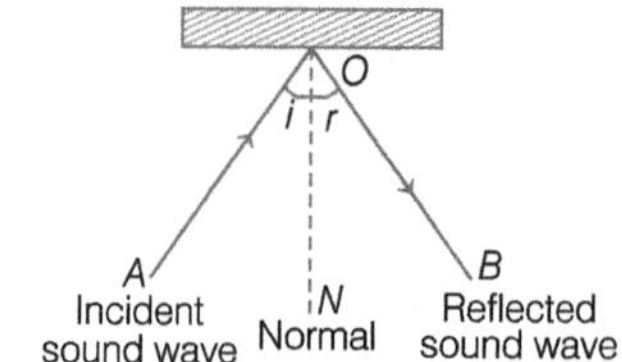

$\angle i$ = angle of incidence

and $\angle r$ = angle of reflection.

46 From which type of surfaces, the reflection of sound is better?

Sol. Hard surface is better reflector of sound.

47 At 20°C, what should be minimum distance of a person from a sound reflecting surface to hear an echo?

Sol. Minimum distance from sound reflecting surface to hear an echo should be atleast 17.2 m.

48 Why are roofs and walls of an auditorium/hall generally covered with sound absorbent materials?

Sol. To reduce reverberation, the roofs and walls of an auditorium or hall are generally covered with sound absorbent materials.

49 What kind of waves are produced in an earthquake before the main shock wave begins?

Sol. Infrasonic waves are produced in an earthquake before the main shock wave begins.

Short Answer (SA) Type Questions

1 (i) Suppose a person whistles standing on the Moon. Will the person standing nearby hear the sound? Explain giving reason.

(ii) What kind of wave needs a material medium to propagate?

Sol. (i) If a person whistles on Moon, nearby person cannot hear the sound because Moon does not have atmosphere. And we know that, sound waves require material medium for their propagation.

(ii) A mechanical wave needs a material medium for its propagation, e.g. sound wave.

2 When the wire of a guitar is plucked, what types of wave are produced in

(i) air

(ii) and wire ?

Give reasons in support of your answer.

Sol. (i) When the wire of a guitar is plucked, a longitudinal wave is produced in air due to the to and fro motion of string of guitar.

(ii) In the wire of guitar, transverse wave is produced as the particle vibrates perpendicular to the direction of motion.

3 Through what type of medium, can

(i) the transverse waves

(ii) and the longitudinal waves be transmitted?

Explain in brief.

Sol. (i) Since, transverse waves travel in the form of crests and troughs, they involve changes in the shape of medium. So, they can be transmitted through a medium having elasticity of shape. As solids and liquids have elasticity of shape, hence transverse waves can be transmitted through solids and liquids.

(ii) Since, longitudinal waves travel in the form of compressions and rarefactions, they involve changes in the volume and density of medium. As all media, i.e. solids, liquids and gases have elasticity of volume. Hence, these waves (longitudinal waves) can be transmitted through all the three types of media.

4 Name the types of waves and two examples associated with

(i) compressions and rarefactions

(ii) crests and troughs.

Sol. (i) The waves which travel along a slinky when it is pushed and pulled at one end, are the longitudinal waves. The following figure shows longitudinal waves

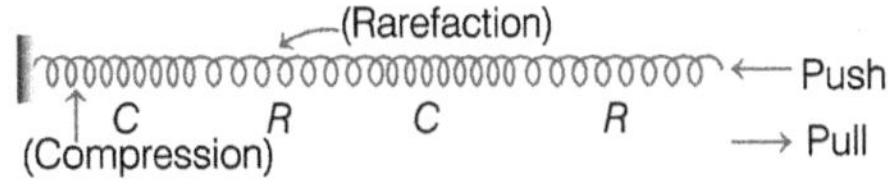

Longitudinal wave in a slinky

(ii) The waves produced by moving one end of a long rope (or spring) up and down rapidly whose other end is fixed, are transverse wave as shown in figure below

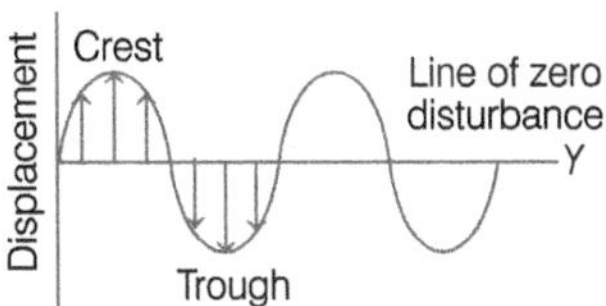

Crest and trough of a transverse wave

5 Waves of frequency 100 Hz are produced in a string as shown in the figure. Give its

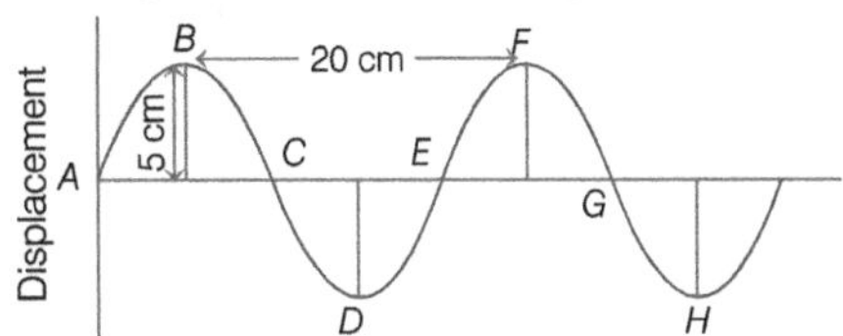

(i) amplitude (ii) wavelength
(iii) velocity (iv) nature

Sol. (i) Amplitude = 5 cm

(ii) Wavelength = 20 cm

(iii) Given, frequency $(\nu) = 100$ Hz

Wavelength = 20 cm

Velocity (v) = Wavelength $(\lambda) \times$ frequency (ν)

$$= 100 \times 20 \times 10^{-2}$$

$$= 20 \text{ ms}^{-1}$$

(iv) Nature It is a transverse wave.

6 What is wave motion? Write any four characteristics of wave motion.

Sol. Wave motion is nothing but a mode of transfer of energy from place to place periodically without material transport.

Four characteristics of wave motion are:

(i) It is the disturbance which travels forward through the medium but not the particles of the medium.

(ii) Each particle receives vibrations a little later than its preceding particle.

(*iii*) The wave velocity is different from the velocity of the particles with which they vibrate about their mean positions.

(*iv*) The wave velocity remains constant in a given medium, whereas particle velocity changes continuously during its vibrations about the mean position.

7 Fig. (A) shows a trace of a sound wave which is produced by a particular tuning fork.

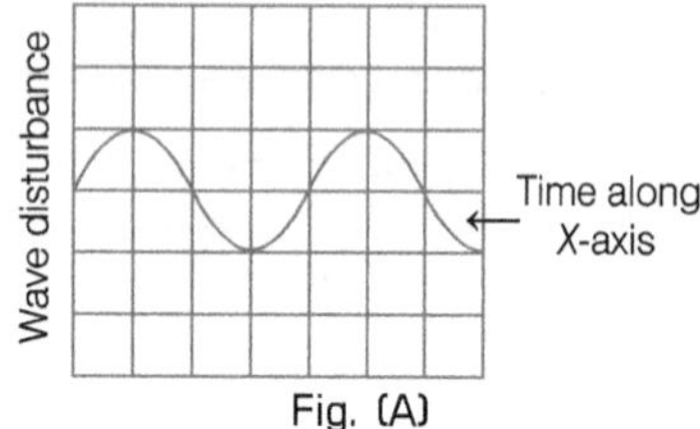

Fig. (A)

(*i*) Draw a trace of the sound wave which has a higher frequency than that shown in Fig. A

(*ii*) Draw a trace of the sound wave which has a larger amplitude than that shown in Fig. A

Sol. (*i*) (*ii*)

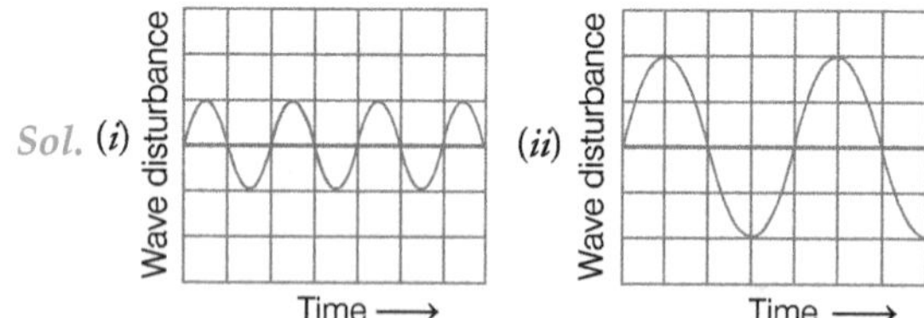

8 What is meant by loudness of sound? State the factor on which it depends. Draw figures to illustrate

(*i*) soft sound

(*ii*) and loud sound.

Sol. **Loudness** It is the measure of sound energy reaching the ear per second. Greater the sound energy reaching our ears per second, louder the sound will appear to be.

It depends on the amplitude of the sound wave, which depends upon the force with which an object is made to vibrate.

(*i*)

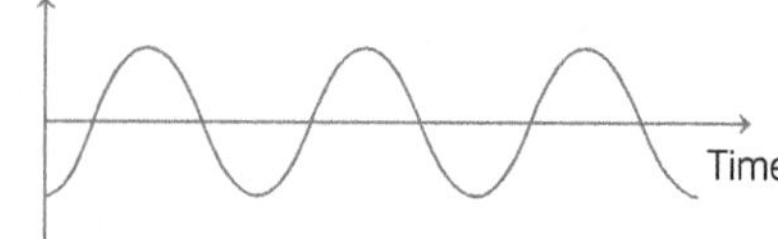

(*ii*)

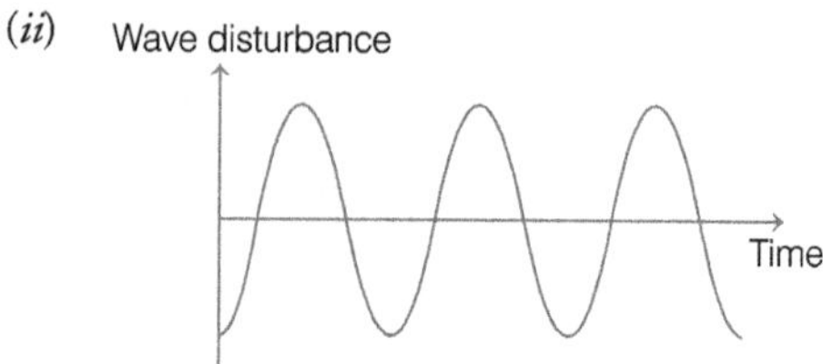

9 A nail was gently touched by the hammer and then was hit harder.

(*i*) When will be the sound created louder?

(*ii*) Which characteristic of sound here is responsible for change in sound?

(*iii*) Give the SI unit of loudness.

Sol. (*i*) Sound will be produced when we beat hard on the nails.

(*ii*) Amplitude of vibrating body is responsible for change in sound.

(*iii*) The SI unit of loudness is decibel (dB).

10 Distinguish between the terms

(*i*) music and noise (*ii*) tone and note.

Sol. (*i*) **Music** The sound which is pleasant to the ears is called music. It is produced by regular periodic vibrations. There is no sudden change in loudness. e.g. Sound produced from a tabla.

Noise The sound which is unpleasant to the ears, is called noise. It is produced at an irregular intervals. There is sudden change in its loudness. e.g. Sound produced in a market and the sound produced by an explosion.

(*ii*) **Tone** The sound of single frequency is called a tone.

Note The sound which is a mixture of several frequencies is called a note.

11 When a workman hammers to one end of the long iron pipeline, an observer places his ear on the other end of pipeline. How he can distinctly hear two sounds? Justify your answer.

Sol. Due to propagation of sound through solids such as iron, the sound of hammering to one end will be heard by the observer in the other end of the pipeline. Also, the sound of hammering will be propagated through air to reach the observer.

As we know that, sound travels faster in iron than in air. So, the observer hear two sounds. The first one, travelling through the iron pipeline and the second travelling through air.

12 (*i*) Define
(*a*) infrasonic wave (*b*) ultrasonic wave.
(*ii*) Name two species each of animals which can produce and detect
(*a*) infrasonic waves
(*b*) ultrasonic waves.

Sol. (*i*) (*a*) **Infrasonic Wave** The sound of frequency lower than 20 Hz are known as infrasonic sound (or wave).
(*b*) **Ultrasonic Wave** The sound of frequency higher than 20000 Hz are called ultrasonic wave.
(*ii*) (*a*) Animals like whales, elephants and rhinoceroses produce infrasonic sound of frequency 5 Hz.
(*b*) Dogs can hear and detect ultrasonic waves of frequency up to 50 Hz.

13 (*i*) Which has shorter wavelength infrasonic or ultrasonic?
(*ii*) Can dolphin detect ultrasonic waves?
(*iii*) Name any one living organism which can detect infrasonic waves.

Sol. (*i*) Ultrasonic wave has shorter wavelength.
(*ii*) Yes, dolphin can detect ultrasonic waves.
(*iii*) Rhinoceros can detect infrasonic waves.

14 How are ultrasonic waves different from ordinary sound waves? State two applications of ultrasound.

Sol. Ultrasonic waves have greater frequency (more than 20000 Hz). Ordinary sound has lower frequency than ultrasonic wave.
Due to their high frequencies,
(*i*) they have high power.
(*ii*) they can penetrate anywhere to a large extent.
(*iii*) they are able to travel along well-defined straight paths, even in the presence of obstacles.
Applications of ultrasound are
(*i*) To detect the flaw or defect in metal.
(*ii*) In the diagnosis of diseases.

15 An echo is heard on a day when temperature is about 22°C. Will echo be heard sooner or later, if the temperature increases to 40°C?

Sol. Echo will be heard sooner than the echo heard when temperature was 22°C. Because speed of sound increases with increase in temperature.
Also, speed of sound in air $= \frac{\text{distance}}{\text{time}}$
i.e. If speed of sound increases, then time after which the echo will be heard decreases.

16 (*i*) Write two main properties of ultrasound.
(*ii*) Mention one application of ultrasound in (*a*) industries (*b*) medical field.

Sol. (*i*) The two main properties of ultrasound are
(*a*) High frequency
(*b*) These travel along well defined path even in presence of obstacles.
(*ii*) (*a*) In industries, ultrasound is used to detect cracks and flaws in metal blocks.
(*b*) In medical field, ultrasound is used to break stones in gall bladder and kidney.

17 How is it that, bats are able to fly at night without colliding with other objects?

Sol. Bats search out prey and fly at night by emitting and detecting reflections of ultrasonic waves.
Bats emit high frequency ultrasonic squeaks while flying and listen to the echoes produced by reflection of their squeaks from the obstacle i.e. prey or object in their path. From the time taken by the echo to be heard, bats can determine the distance of the object and can avoid the object by changing the direction without colliding with it.

18 For hearing the loudest ticking sound heard by the ear, find the angle x in the given figure.

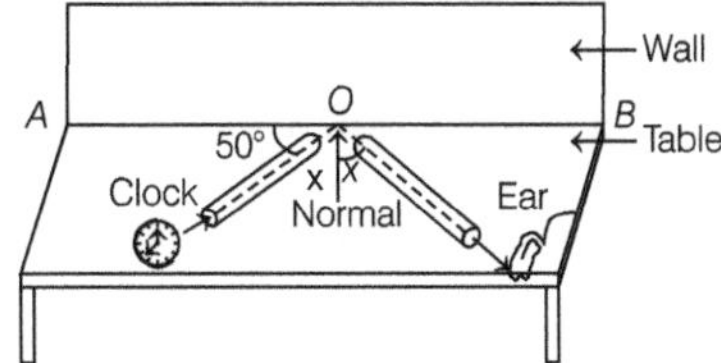

NCERT Exemplar

Sol. We know that in laws of reflection, the angle of incidence (x) is always equal to the angle of reflection (x). Since, AOB is a straight line.

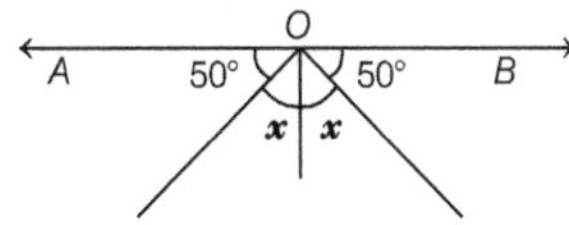

$\therefore \quad \angle AOB = 180°$
$\therefore \quad 50° + x + x + 50° = 180°$
[$\because$ sum of all angles lies on the same side of a line is 180°]

$2x + 100° = 180°$
$\Rightarrow \quad 2x = 180° - 100°$
$\Rightarrow \quad 2x = 80°$
$\Rightarrow \quad x = \frac{80°}{2}$
$\Rightarrow \quad x = 40°$

Hence, the value of x is 40°.

19 A boat is moving with velocity 20 ms^{-1} in a sea is rocked by waves. If its crests are 80 m apart, then at what time the boat bounces up?

Sol. Given that, wavelength, $\lambda = 80$ m

(distance between two consecutive crests and troughs is equal to the wavelength.)

Velocity, $v = 20\ ms^{-1}$, time, $T = ?$

As we know that, $T = \frac{\lambda}{v} = \frac{80}{20} = 4$ s

20 The given graph shows the displacement *versus* time relation for a disturbance travelling with velocity of 1500 ms^{-1}. Calculate the wavelength of the disturbance. **NCERT Exemplar**

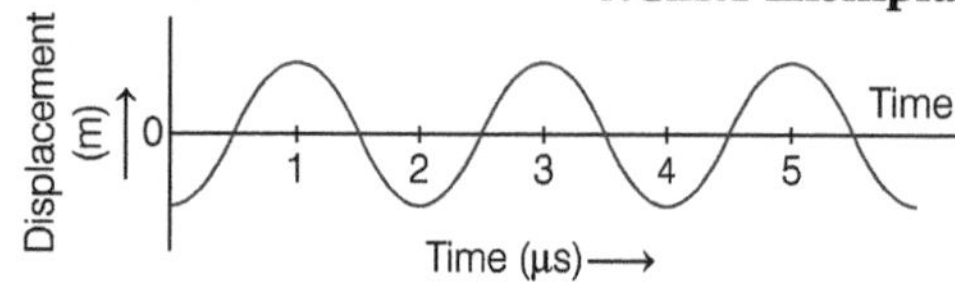

Sol. Given, velocity, $v = 1500\ ms^{-1}$

Time taken in one complete cycle is 2 μs.

Time, $T = 2\ \mu s = 2 \times 10^{-6}$ s $[\because 1\ \mu s = 10^{-6}$ s$]$

We know that, $v = \nu\lambda$ $\left[\because \nu = \frac{1}{T}\right]$

So, $v = \frac{\lambda}{T} \Rightarrow \lambda = vT$

where, λ = wavelength, ν = frequency and T = time period.

So, $\lambda = 1500 \times 2 \times 10^{-6} = 3000 \times 10^{-6}$

$= 3 \times 10^{+3} \times 10^{-6} = 3 \times 10^{-3}$ m

21 A construction worker's helmet slips and falls when he is 78.4 m above the ground. He hears the sound of the helmet hitting the ground 4.23 s after it slipped. Find the speed of sound in air.

Sol. Here, s = distance travelled by the helmet to reach the ground = 78.4 m

and t = total time taken for hearing the sound of the helmet hitting the ground = 4.23 s.

Let t be the time taken by helmet in reaching the ground.

So, we know that, according to equation of motion,

$s = ut + \frac{1}{2}gt^2$ [where, u = initial velocity and g = acceleration due to gravity.]

$\Rightarrow 78.4 = 0 \times t + \frac{1}{2} \times 9.8 \times t^2 \Rightarrow 78.4 = \frac{1}{2} \times 9.8 \times t^2$

$\Rightarrow t^2 = 16 \Rightarrow t = 4$ s

So, time taken by the sound wave to travel distance.

78.4 m = 4.23 s − 4 s = 0.23 s.

So, speed of sound in air $= \frac{78.4\ m}{0.23\ s} = 340.86\ ms^{-1}$

22 A sound wave travels at a speed of 340 ms^{-1}. If its wavelength is 1.5 cm. What is the frequency of the wave? Will it be audible?

Sol. Given that, speed of sound, $v = 340\ ms^{-1}$

Wavelength, $\lambda = 1.5$ cm $= \frac{1.5}{100}$ m. Frequency, $\nu = ?$

Using the formula, $v = \nu\lambda$

$\Rightarrow \nu = \frac{v}{\lambda} = \frac{340}{\left(\frac{1.5}{100}\right)} ms^{-1} = \frac{340 \times 100}{1.5}$

= 22666.6 Hz

We know that, audible range of frequencies is 20 Hz to 20000 Hz.

So, the given frequency (i.e. 22666.6 Hz) is not audible.

23 If the velocity of sound in air is 330 ms^{-1}, then express the audible range of frequencies in terms of time period.

Sol. Audible range of frequencies are $\nu_1 = 20$ Hz, $\nu_2 = 20000$ Hz and the velocity, $v = 330\ ms^{-1}$.

So, time period will become,

$T_1 = \frac{1}{\nu_1} = \frac{1}{20} = 5 \times 10^{-2}$ s

and time period will become,

$T_2 = \frac{1}{\nu_2} = \frac{1}{20000}$

$= 5 \times 10^{-5}$ s

Thus, the audible range in terms of time period is from 5×10^{-2} s to 5×10^{-5} s.

24 A sound wave has a frequency of 2 kHz and a wavelength of 45 cm. It takes 4 s to travel. Calculate the distance it travels.

Sol. Here, frequency of sound wave,

$\nu = 2$ kHz $= 2 \times 10^3$ Hz

Wavelength of the wave, $\lambda = 45$ cm = 0.45 m

Velocity of the wave, $v = \nu\lambda$

$= 2 \times 10^3 \times 0.45 = 900\ ms^{-1}$

Time to travel = 4 s

Distance travelled by the wave

$= vt = 900 \times 4 = 3600$ m

25 A person strikes the end of the iron rod with a stone, a boy places his ear on the other end of the iron rod. What is the ratio of time taken by sound wave in air and in iron rod to reach the boy?

(Given, $v_{iron} = 5950\ ms^{-1}$ and $v_{air} = 346\ ms^{-1}$)

Sol. As we know that, time taken $= \dfrac{\text{distance}}{\text{speed}}$

$$\Rightarrow \quad t = \frac{\lambda}{v} \Rightarrow t \propto \frac{1}{v}$$

$\Rightarrow$ t is inversely proportional to $\dfrac{1}{v}$.

$$\therefore \quad \frac{\text{Speed of sound in iron rod}}{\text{Speed of sound in air}} = \frac{t_{air}}{t_{iron}}$$

$$\Rightarrow \quad \text{Ratio} = \frac{t_{air}}{t_{iron}} = \frac{5950}{346} = 17.2:1$$

26 On a cloudy day, a thunder sound was heard 14 s after the flash of lightning. How far was the cloud? (Given, the speed of sound $340 \, ms^{-1}$.)

Sol. Speed of sound, $v = 340 \text{ ms}^{-1}$

Time taken by thunder to be heard, $t = \dfrac{d}{v} = 14 \text{ s}$

$$d = v \times t = 340 \times 14 = 4760 \text{ m}$$

Therefore, the distance of the cloud is 4760 m.

27 Find the distance of cloud from you when you hear a thunder 3 s after the lightning is seen. Given, speed of light $= 3 \times 10^8 \text{ ms}^{-1}$, speed of sound $= 330 \text{ ms}^{-1}$. Why is lightning before the thunder is heard duirng a thunders storm?

Sol. Given, time, $t = 3$ s

and speed of sound in air $= 330 \text{ ms}^{-1}$

Therefore, the distance from the cloud will be calculated as

Distance = Speed × Time $= 330 \times 3 = 990$ m

As the speed of light in air (i.e. $3 \times 10^8 \text{ ms}^{-1}$) is much greater than the speed of sound in air (i.e. 340 ms^{-1}). So, this is a reason why lightning is seen before the thunder is heard during thunderstorm.

28 Aditi clapped her hands near a cliff and heard the echo after 4 s. What is the distance of the cliff from her, if the speed of sound is taken as 346 ms^{-1}?

Sol. Given, speed of sound, $v = 346 \text{ ms}^{-1}$

Time taken for hearing the echo, $t = 4$ s

$\therefore$ Distance travelled by the sound $= v \times t$

$$= 346 \times 4 = 1384 \text{m}$$

In 4 s, sound has to travel twice the distance between the cliff and Aditi. Therefore, the distance between the cliff and Aditi is $\dfrac{1384}{2} = 692$ m.

29 A ship sends out ultrasound that returns from the sea bed and is detected after 1.71 s. If the speed of ultrasound through sea water is 1531 ms^{-1}, what is the distance of the sea bed from the ship?

Sol. Given, time between transmission and detection,

$t = 1.71$ s

Speed of ultrasound through sea water,

$$v = 1531 \text{ ms}^{-1}$$

Distance travelled by the ultrasound

$= 2 \times$ Depth of the sea $= 2d$

or $\quad 2d = v \times t = 1531 \times 1.71 = 2618.01$ m

$$d = \frac{2618.01}{2} = 1309 \text{ m}$$

Hence, the distance of the sea bed from the ship is 1309 m.

30 A child hears an echo from a cliff, 4 s after the sound from a powerful cracker is produced. How far away is the cliff from the child? (Take, velocity of the sound in air as 330 ms^{-1}.)

Sol. The time taken by echo to be heard, $t = \dfrac{2d}{v} = 4$ s

(In case of echo, sound covers twice the distance between sound source and reflector.)

Velocity of sound in air, $v = 330 \text{ ms}^{-1}$

$$\frac{2d}{v} = 4 \quad \text{or} \quad 2d = 330 \times 4$$

$$\Rightarrow \quad d = \frac{330 \times 4}{2} = 660 \text{ m}$$

Thus, the distance of the cliff from the child is 660 m.

31 A person produced a sound with a siren near a cliff and heard echoes after 6 s. Find the distance of the siren from the cliff, if velocity of sound waves produced is 330 ms^{-1}.

Sol. Time taken by echo to be heard, $t = \dfrac{2d}{v} = 6$ s

Velocity of sound waves, $v = 330 \text{ ms}^{-1}$

$$2d = v \times t$$

$$= 330 \times 6 = 1980 \text{ m}$$

$$d = \frac{1980}{2} = 990 \text{ m}$$

Therefore, the distance of the siren from the cliff is 990 m.

32 A boy is standing in the middle of a big square field. There is a tall building on one side of the field. He explodes a cracker and hears its echo 0.4 s later. What is the size of the square field?
(Given, speed of sound in air is 330 ms^{-1})

Sol. Given, speed of sound in air, $v = 330\ ms^{-1}$

Time taken for hearing the echo, $t = 0.4$ s

As we know, distance travelled by the sound

$$= v \times t = 330\ ms^{-1} \times 0.4\ s = 132\ m$$

As in 0.4 s, sound has to travel twice the distance between the boy and the building.

Hence, the distance between the boy and the building is $= \frac{d}{2} = \frac{132}{2} = 66$ m

Side of the square field = Twice the distance between the boy and the building

Side of the square field $= 2 \times 66\ m = 132$ m

So, size of the square field = (side of the square field)^2

$$= (132\ m)^2 = 132\ m \times 132\ m$$

$$= 17424\ m^2$$

Long Answer (LA) Type Questions

1 (*i*) What is meant by frequency of sound waves?

(*ii*) Give the range of frequencies of sound waves that an average human ear can detect.

(*iii*) A source of wave produces 20 crests and 20 troughs in 0.2 s. The distance between a crest and next trough is 50 cm. Find the

(*a*) wavelength,

(*b*) frequency

(*c*) time period of the wave.

Sol. (*i*) **Frequency** The number of waves produced per second is called the frequency of the wave.

(*ii*) 20 Hz to 20 kHz

(*iii*) (*a*) Since, the distance between a crest and next trough is $\frac{\lambda}{2}$.

Therefore, $\frac{\lambda}{2} = 50$ cm (given)

$$\lambda = 100 \text{ cm or } 1 \text{ m}$$

(*b*) Distance covered in 20 crests $= 20 \times 1 = 20$ m

Velocity of the wave, $v = \nu\lambda = \frac{\lambda}{t}$

$$\nu \times 1 = \frac{20}{0.2} \quad [\because t = 0.2 \text{ s}]$$

$\therefore \nu = 100$ Hz or

$\because$ 1 crest and 1 trough = 1 wave

$\therefore$ 20 crest and 20 trough = 20 waves

$$\therefore \text{Frequency} = \frac{\text{Number of waves}}{\text{Time}} = \frac{20}{0.2}$$

$$= 100 \text{ Hz}$$

(*c*) $\therefore$ Time period, $T = \frac{1}{\nu} = \frac{1}{100} = 0.01$ s

2 Establish the relationship between speed of sound, its wavelength and frequency. If velocity of sound in air is 340 ms^{-1}. Calculate

(*i*) wavelength when frequency is 256 Hz

(*ii*) frequency when wavelength is 0.85 m.

NCERT Exemplar

Sol. The speed of sound is defined as the distance which a point on a wave, such as a compression or a rarefaction, travels per unit time.

We know that, speed,

$$v = \frac{\text{distance}}{\text{time}} = \frac{\lambda}{T}$$

Where, λ is the wavelength of the sound wave.
It is the distance travelled by the sound wave in one time period (T) of the wave.

$$v = \frac{\lambda}{T} = \lambda \times \frac{1}{T}$$

We know that, $\nu = \frac{1}{T}$ [where, ν = frequency]

$$v = \lambda\nu$$

i.e. Speed = Wavelength × Frequency

Given, speed of sound in air, $v = 340\ ms^{-1}$

and frequency, $\nu = 256$ Hz

(*i*) $\therefore$ Speed = Wavelength × Frequency

$\Rightarrow 340 = \lambda \times 256$

$\Rightarrow \lambda = \frac{340}{256} = 1.33$ m

(*ii*) Again, given wavelength, $\lambda = 0.85$ m

Then, frequency of sound in air,

$$\nu = \frac{\text{Speed}}{\text{Wavelength}}$$

[$\because$ Speed = Wavelength × Frequency]

$$\Rightarrow \quad \nu = \frac{340}{0.85} = \frac{340 \times 100}{85} = 400 \text{ Hz}$$

Thus, frequency of sound is 400 Hz.

3 Draw a curve showing density or pressure variations with respect to distance for a disturbance produced by sound. Mark the position of compression and rarefaction on this curve. Also, define wavelengths and time period using this curve. **NCERT Exemplar**

Sol. We have a curve showing density or pressure variations with respect to distance for a disturbance produced by sound.

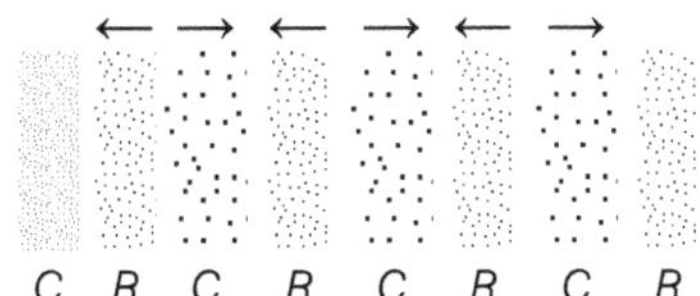

C = Compression, R = Rarefactions

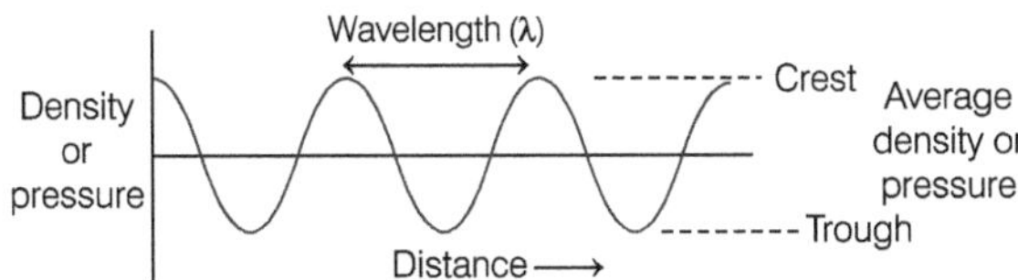

Wavelength can be defined as the distance between two successive compressions or rarefactions. It is denoted by λ. Time taken by the waves to complete one full cycle, so that its particles are in same phase is called time period. It is denoted by T.

4 Represent graphically by two separate diagrams in each case.

(*i*) Two sound waves having the same amplitude but different frequencies.

(*ii*) Two sound waves having the same frequency but different amplitudes.

(*iii*) Two sound waves having different amplitudes and also different wavelengths. **NCERT Exemplar**

Sol. (*i*)

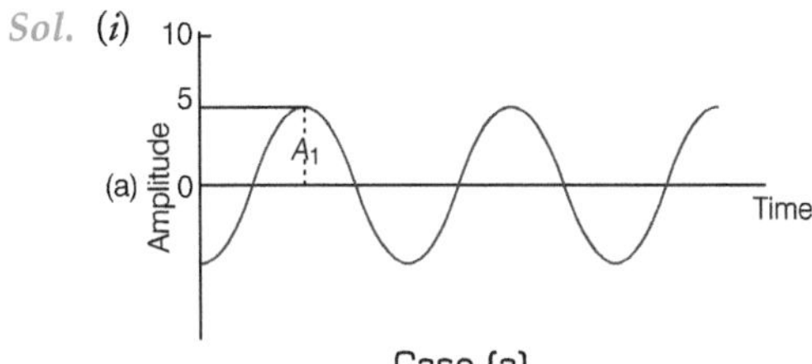

Case (a)

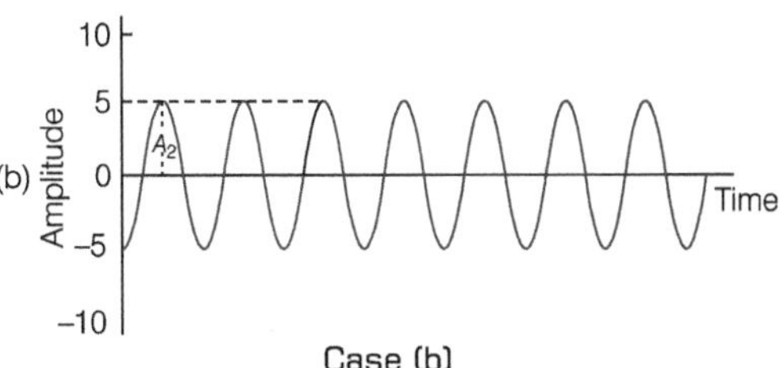

Case (b)

In both cases (a) and (b), same amplitude and different frequencies, i.e. ($A_1 = A_2$).

(*ii*)

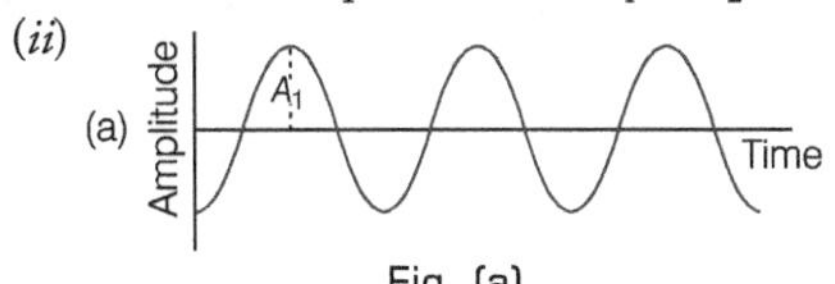

Fig. (a)

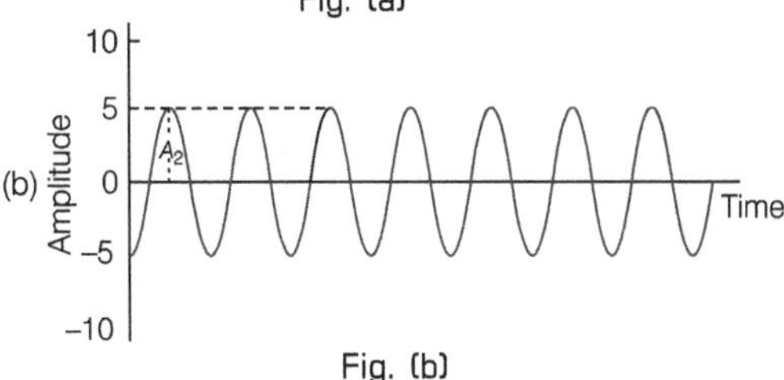

Fig. (b)

In both the Figs. (a) and (b), same frequency and different amplitudes, i.e. ($A_1 \neq A_2$).

(*iii*)

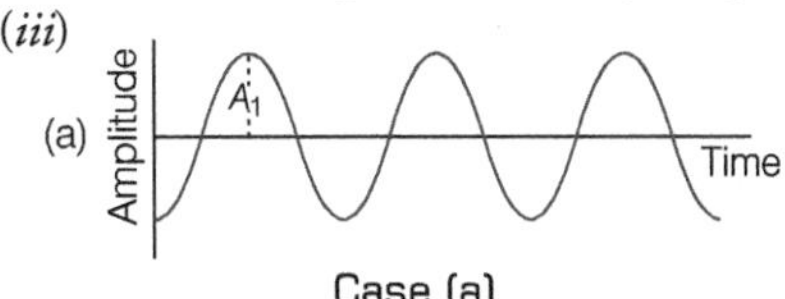

Case (a)

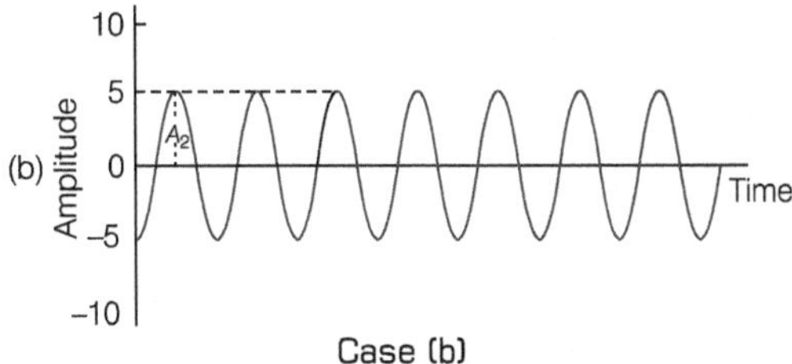

Case (b)

In both cases (a) and (b), different amplitudes and different wavelengths, i.e. $A_1 \neq A_2$, $\lambda_1 \neq \lambda_2$.

CHAPTER EXERCISE

Multiple Type Questions

1 Sound waves transfer
(a) only energy not momentum
(b) energy
(c) momentum
(d) Both (b) and (c)

2 In the given curve, half the wavelength is

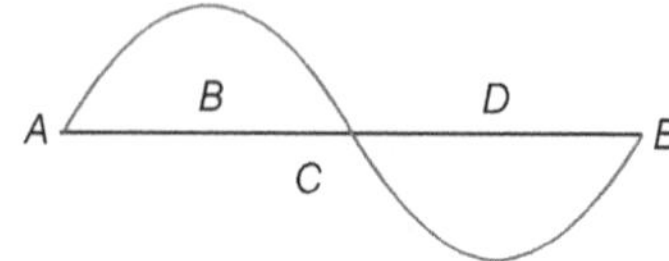

(a) AB (b) BD **NCERT Exemplar**
(c) DE (d) AE

3 Which wave property determines the loudness of sound ?
(a) Frequency (b) Pitch
(c) Speed (d) Amplitude

4 Earthquake produces which kind of sound before the main shock wave begins **NCERT Exemplar**
(a) ultrasound (b) infrasound
(c) audible sound (d) None of these

Fill in the Blanks

5 The substances through which sound travels is called ....

6 An echo is caused by the phenomenon of .... of sound waves.

7 Pitch of sound depends on the .... of the vibration.

8 If the temperature of the medium increases, then speed of sound will ....

True and False

9 Transverse wave is produced when a stone is dropped on the surface of water in a pond.

10 As the humidity of air increases, the speed of sound through it also increases.

11 Sound travels slowest in solids, faster in gases and fastest in liquids.

12 Sound can be heard directly on the surface of Moon.

13 A sound wave can be described completely by amplitude of wave only.

Match the Columns

14 Match the following columns.

	Column I		Column II
A.	String vibration	p.	Tabla
B.	Membrane vibration	q.	Bicycle bell
C.	Vibration of air column	r.	Sitar
D.	Vibration of plate	s.	Flute

Assertion–Reason

Direction (Q.Nos. 15-17) *In each of the following questions, a statement of Assertion is given by the corresponding statement of Reason. Of the statements, mark the correct answer as*

(a) If both Assertion and Reason are true and Reason is the correct explanation of Assertion.
(b) If both Assertion and Reason are true, but Reason is not the correct explanation of Assertion.
(c) If Assertion is true, but Reason is false.
(d) If Assertion is false, but Reason is true.

15 **Assertion** Sound wave is an longitudinal wave.
Reason Speed of sound in solid is less than air.

16 **Assertion** The loudness of sound is measured in decibel.
Reason If sound waves have a large amplitude, then the sound will be loud.

17 **Assertion** Ultrasonic sound is used in industry for detecting flaws (cracks etc) in metal blocks without damaging them.
Reason An internal crack (or hole) does not allow ultrasound to pass through it.

Case Based Questions

Direction (Q.Nos. 18-21) *Answer the question on the basis of your understanding of the following paragraph and related studied concepts:*

Sound travels about 5 times faster in water than in air. The speed of sound in sea water is very large about 1500m/s. Thus, two whales in the sea which are hundreds of kilometres away can talk to each other easily through sea water. Similarly, sound travels about 15 times faster in iron (or steel) than in air.

Since, the speed of sound in steel is very very large (being about 5310 m/s which is more than 1800 km/h), we can hear the sound of an approaching train by putting our ear to the railway line made of steel even when the train is far away. Many objects like aircrafts, rockets travel at speeds greater than speed of sound in air known as supersonic.

18 Give reason, why when we put our ears to a railway line, we can hear the sound of an approaching train even when it is far off.

19 A jet crafts flies at a speed of 410 m/s, what it this speed known as?

20 The distance of a gun from a man, if the flash of a gun is seen by a man 3s before the sound is heard is (speed of sound in air is 332 m/s)

(a) 109 m (b) 996 cm
(c) 996 m (d) 969 m

21 Out of solids, liquids and gases in which medium sound travels slowest?

(a) Liquids (b) Solids
(c) Solids and gases (d) Gases

Answers

1. (d) 2. (b) 3. (d) 4. (b)
5. Medium 6. Reflection 7. Frequency
8. Increases 9. True 10. True
11. False 12. False 13. False
14. (A) $\rightarrow$ (r), (B) $\rightarrow$ (p), (C) $\rightarrow$ (s), (D) $\rightarrow$ (q)
15. (c) 16. (b) 17. (a) 20. (c) 21. (d)

Very Short Answer (VSA) Type Questions

22 What is the nature of the ocean waves in deep water?

23 What will increase, if we change feeble sound to loud sound?

24 Which physical quantity remains unchanged after reflection of a sound wave?

25 Give the principle involved in megaphone.

26 The window panes of houses sometimes crack when a bomb explodes even at a large distance. Why?

27 How do submarines know the depth of a sea?

Short Answer (SA) Type Questions

28 What is compression and rarefaction in longitudinal wave? Explain.

29 Why does the amplitude of oscillation get reduced over a period of time? Explain with diagram.

30 What is the intensity of sound wave? Give its relation with amplitude.

31 A bat can hear sound at frequencies up to 130 kHz. What is the wavelength of sound?

(speed of sound is 344 ms^{-1} in air)

32 Explain how sonic booms are produced.

33 What is the difference between supersonic and ultrasonic?

Long Answer (LA) Type Questions

34 Given below are some examples of wave motion. State in each case, if the wave motion is transverse, longitudinal or a combination of both.

(*i*) Motion of a kink in a long coil spring produced by displacing one end of the string side ways.
(*ii*) Wave produced in a cylinder consisting a liquid by moving its piston back and forth.
(*iii*) Waves produced by a motor boat sailing in water.
(*iv*) Light waves travelling from Sun to Earth.
(*v*) Ultrasonic waves in air produced by a vibrating quartz crystal.

35 Answer the following.

(*i*) Can transverse waves travel in glasses?
(*iii*) At any instant, a compression is formed at a point. After how much time,
(*a*) a rarefaction
(*b*) and a compression will be formed at the same point?

36 State diagrammatically laws of reflections of sound and explain three applications based on these laws.

Challengers*

1 A sound wave of wavelength 0.332 m has a time period of 10^{-3} s. If the time period is decreased to 10^{-4} s, what is wavelength of new wave?

(a) 0.233 m (b) 0.93 m (c) 0.332 m (d) 0.51 m

2 A person standing between two vertical cliffs and 640 m away from the nearest cliff shouted. He heard the first echo after 4 s and the second echo 3 s later. What is the distance between the cliffs?

(a) 1570 m (b) 1760 m (c) 1520 m (d) 1225 m

3 A radar signal is reflected by an aeroplane and is received in 2×10^{-5} s after it was sent. If the speed of these waves is 3×10^{8} m/s, how far is the aeroplane?

(a) 10 km (b) 12 km (c) 3 km (d) 5 km

4 A disused railway line has a length of 300 m. A man puts his ear against one end of the rail and another man hits the other end with a metal hammer. Sound travels at 5000 m/s in steel. The time it takes for the sound to travel along the rail is

(a) 0.03 s (b) 0.05 s
(c) 0.07 s (d) 0.06 s

5 A sound produce in air cannot be heard by a person deep inside the water. This is because,

(a) speed of sound is less in water than in air
(b) sound travels 4 times more in water than in air
(c) most of the sound is reflected from the surface of water
(d) the sound can be heard inside the water

6 A man stands at one end of a long steel pipe hits it with a hammer. Another man standing at the other end of the pipe hear 2 s. This is because,

(a) the pipe is too long
(b) sound undergoes reflection
(c) the second sound is echo
(d) speed of sound is more in steel than in air

7 The value of x in the given figure for hearing the loudest ticking sound is

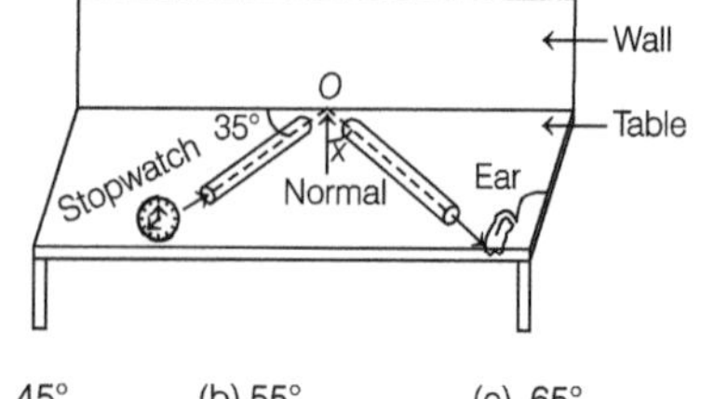

(a) 45° (b) 55° (c) 65° (d) 35°

8 A lighting flash was seen on the sky 10s before the thunder sound. How far was the cloud? (Take, speed of sound = 340ms^{-1})

(a) 2380 m
(b) 3400 m
(c) 1390 m
(d) 2700 m

9 A stone is dropped from the top of a tower 500 m high into a pond of water at the base of the tower. When is the splash heard at the top? (Given, $g = 10\text{m/s}^2$ and speed of sound = 340 m/s.)

(a) 13.65 s
(b) 11.47 s
(c) 15.49 s
(d) 10.96 s

10 A boy hears the echo of his own voice from a distant hill after 0.8 s. If the speed of sound in air is 340 m/s, calculate the distance of hill from the boy.

(a) 96 m
(b) 126 m
(c) 136 m
(d) 156 m

Answer Key

1.	(c)	2.	(b)	3.	(c)	4.	(d)	5.	(c)
6.	(d)	7.	(b)	8.	(b)	9.	(b)	10.	(c)

RELATED ONLINE VIDEOS

Visit https://www.youtube.com/watch?v=rI5BDxWJ_CU
OR Scan the Code

Visit https://www.youtube.com/watch?v=3G5jiXl2LSM
OR Scan the Code

Visit https://www.youtube.com/watch?v=LITxppgVhKA
OR Scan the Code

Visit https://www.youtube.com/watch?v=ZTEjt_m2RLc
OR Scan the Code

These questions may or may not be asked in the examination, have been given just for additional practice.

CHAPTER

12

Natural Resources

Resources provided by nature on Earth are utilised by living organisms to sustain their life. These resources are called natural resources which include air, water, soil, sunlight, minerals, etc.

All these resources are found accumulated in different layers of Earth which are as follows

- **Lithosphere** The outer crust of our planet Earth, which we call as land.
- **Hydrosphere** The Earth's surface is covered with 75% water. This water is found to be present in seas, oceans, rivers, lakes, streams, ponds, underground water, etc. Earth is known as **Blue Planet** because of the presence of plenty of water.
- **Atmosphere** The multi-layered gaseous envelope of air that covers the whole Earth like a blanket.
- **Biosphere** is the life-supporting zone of the Earth. Here, the atmosphere, the hydrosphere and the lithosphere interact and make life possible.

Living things like plants and animals form the **biotic components** of biosphere. Non-living things like air, water and land form the **abiotic components** of biosphere.

Chapter Checklist

- Natural Resources
  - Air the Breath of life
  - Water : A Wonder Liquids
  - Soil
- Biogeochemical Cycles
- Ozone Layer

Natural Resources

Most of the **natural resources** are the non-living (abiotic) components of nature. They are used by human beings in order to meet their basic requirements. The natural resources present on the Earth are mainly air, water and land.

Air : The Breath of Life

It is a mixture of many gases like nitrogen (N_2), oxygen (O_2), carbon dioxide (CO_2) and water vapours. The precise composition of these gases makes life possible on the Earth.

Eukaryotic cells and many prokaryotic cells, need oxygen to breakdown glucose molecules to get energy for their various activities (by the process of respiration). This phenomenon releases carbon dioxide into the atmosphere. The layer of gaseous envelope surrounding the Earth is called atmosphere. It has many significant roles to play, such as protection from ultraviolet rays, helping in mode of communication, etc.

The other sources of CO_2 in the air include

- combustion of fuels by humans and
- forest fires

These sources liberate high amount of CO_2 in the atmosphere, but still the percentage of carbon dioxide in the air is a fraction of a percent. This is because CO_2 is fixed in two ways, which are as follow

(*i*) Green plants convert carbon dioxide into glucose in the presence of sunlight by the process of photosynthesis.

(*ii*) Many marine animals use carbonates (dissolved in sea water) to make their shells.

On planets such as Venus and Mars, no life is known to exist. The major component of the atmosphere on these planets is carbon dioxide (constitutes 95-97% of the atmosphere). The core significance of atmosphere is discussed below

Role of Atmosphere in Climate Control

The atmosphere covers the Earth like a protective blanket. The air is a bad conductor of heat. So, the atmosphere prevents the sudden increase in temperature during the daylight hours. Similarly during night, it slows down the escape of heat into the outer space.

Thus, it keeps the average temperature of Earth fairly steady during the day and even during the course of whole year. The atmosphere therefore, ensures that right amount of heat is received by Earth. It controls and allows the living organisms to survive.

Note Moon has no atmosphere and its temperature ranges from −190°C to 110°C, which is not suitable for existence of life.

Winds : The Movement of Air

Winds result due to changes taking place in our atmosphere like heating of air and formation of water vapours.

Winds occur by the following events in the atmosphere

- When solar radiations fall on the Earth, majority of these radiations are reflected back (re-radiated) by land and waterbodies. Some of them are absorbed. These reflected solar radiations heat the atmosphere from below. Due to this, convection currents are set up in air. Since, land gets heated faster than water, the air over land would also be heated faster than the air over waterbodies.
- In coastal regions during the day, the air above the land gets heated faster and starts rising. As this air rises, a region of low pressure is created. Air over the sea moves to this area of low pressure.

The movement of air from one region to the other creates **winds**. Direction of wind would be from the sea to the land during the day.

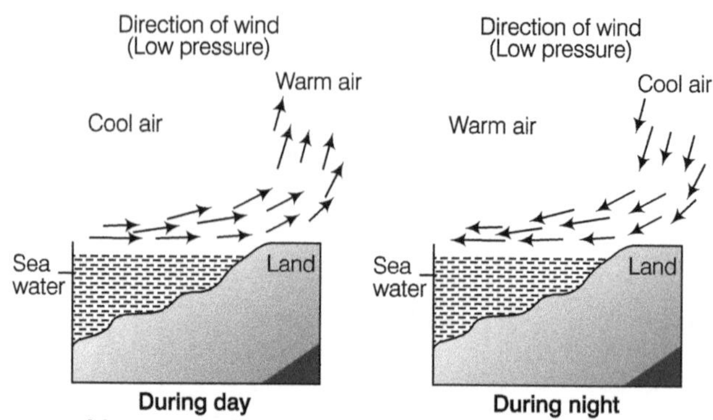

Movement of wind from sea to land during day and from land to sea during night

- At night, both land and sea starts getting cooler. Since, water cools down slowly than land, the air above the water would be warmer than the air above the land. Now, the air above the sea will start rising. Land air moves to low pressure area, i.e. direction of wind would be from land to sea during night.
- Other factors that influence the winds are rotation of Earth and the presence of mountain ranges in the path of winds. Various phenomena occurring in the atmosphere, such as cyclones, thunderstorm, etc., are also due to movements of air caused by uneven heating of atmosphere in different regions.

Rain

Condensation of water vapour in the air causes rain.

Rainfall occurs by the following events in the atmosphere

- Water bodies are heated by solar radiations during the day. Due to this, a large amount of water evaporates. This goes into the air in the form of water vapours. Various biological activities also add some amount of water vapours in the atmosphere.
- Air also becomes much warmer due to sunlight. It starts rising up along with water vapours. As the air rises, it expands and cools. This cooling causes the water vapours in the air to condense in the form of tiny droplets.
- Condensation of water is facilitated by dust and other suspended particles. These act as nucleus for these droplets to adhere around. An excessive collection of tiny droplets of water appears in the form of **clouds**.

- Once the water droplets are formed, they grow bigger in size by their further condensation. When the drops have grown big and heavy, they fall down in the form of rain.
- Sometimes, when the temperature of air is low enough, **precipitation** may occur in the form of snow, sleet or hail.

Rainfall patterns are decided by the prevailing wind patterns. In large parts of our country, rains are mostly brought by the South-West or North-East monsoons. In some areas, these are caused by the depressions in the Bay of Bengal.

Air Pollution

An increase in the composition of harmful or undesirable substances in the air is called air pollution. These undersirable and harmful substances are called air pollutants. Air pollution can also be defined as an undesirable alteration in physical, chemical or biological characteristics of air.

Causes of Air Pollution

Following activities could lead to air pollution

- Excessive burning of fossil fuels (like coal and petroleum) produces large amount of oxides of nitrogen and sulphur (e.g. NO_2 and SO_2). These oxides get mixed with air moisture and cause **acid rain**. It leads to many harmful effects like corrosion of monuments.
  For example, Taj Mahal is facing a great threat due to Mathura refinery. It produces a huge amount of SO_2 and NO_2 that contribute to acid rain. Combustion of fossil fuels also increases the amount of suspended particles in the air. These suspended particles could be unburnt carbon particles or substances, known as **hydrocarbons.**
- Many industries release large amount of poisonous gases like CO into the atmosphere causing air pollution.
- Dust also contributes to pollution and its inhalation causes allergic ailments like asthma, cold etc.

Effects of Air Pollution

These are as follows

- It affects the human respiratory system and causes diseases like asthma, lung cancer, pneumonia, etc.
- Pollutant gases cause allergies, irritation in eyes, lungs, etc.
- Gases like NO_2, SO_2, etc., get dissolved in rain to cause **acid rain.**
- The presence of high levels of pollutants in air reduces the visibility. In cold weather, when water also condenses out of air, forms **smog.** It is a visible indication of air pollution.
- It causes greenhouse effect and leads to global warming.

Note Organisms called lichens are sensitive to pollutants like SO_2 and do not grow near industries and in areas with high air pollution.

Check Point 01

1. Why is Earth called as 'Blue Planet'?
2. What percentage of CO_2 is found on planet Venus?
3. What is the range of temperature found on Moon?
4. State True or False for the following statement.
   The part of Earth where living organisms are found constitute the biosphere.
5. Which among the following diseases can be caused due to air pollution. Lung cancer, Typhoid, Asthma, Hepatitis, AIDS.
6. Fill in the blank.
   On planets like Venus, no life is known to exist because there is no ....

Water : A Wonder Liquid

Water is an inexhaustible natural resource. It occupies very large area of the Earth's surface (both above and under the ground). Some amount of water exists in the form of water vapours in the atmosphere. Most of the water on Earth's surface (found in seas and oceans), is saline. Freshwater is found as frozen ice caps at poles and on snow-covered mountains. The underground water and water in rivers, lakes and ponds is also fresh.

Importance of Water for Living Beings

Water is essential for all living beings because

- It provides a medium for all the cellular processes to take place.
- It is necessary for the transportation of substances from one part of the body to the other part in dissolved or suspended form.
- It helps to maintain body temperature.
- It is required to maintain balance of salts and minerals within the body.
- Terrestrial life forms require freshwater. Their bodies cannot tolerate or get rid of high amount of dissolved salts in saline water.
- All the reactions that take place within our body and within the cells occur between substances that are dissolved in water.

All the organisms need to maintain the adequate level of water within their bodies in order to survive.

Therefore, water is essential for the sustenance of life. The availability of water decides the number of individuals of each species that are able to survive in a particular area and also the diversity of life there.

Note The other factors that decide the sustainability of life in a region are temperature, nature of soil, etc.

Water Pollution

It is defined as an undesirable change in the physical, chemical and biological quality of water. It occurs due to the addition of unwanted and harmful substances called **water pollutants** into water. Water pollution adversely affects living organisms by making the water unsuitable for use.

Causes of Water Pollution

Water pollution is caused due to the following reasons

- Water dissolves fertilisers and pesticides from agricultural fields with surface run off rain water . It takes them to the nearby waterbodies where the aquatic life is affected by the increased concentration of dissolved fertilisers and pesticides.
- Dumping of sewage and other wastes into waterbodies adversely affects the water quality.
- Industries use water for cooling in various operations. Later, this hot water is released into water bodies. This causes sudden changes in the temperature of water body that affects the breeding of aquatic organisms.

Effects of Water Pollution

Polluted water can affect the life forms in various ways as mentioned below:

- **Addition of undesirable substances to waterbodies** Fertilisers, pesticides, dirt, sewage, industrial wastes like heavy metals (mercury and lead) and disease-causing microorganisms get mixed with water, making it unfit for consumption.
- **Death of flora and fauna of waterbodies** As the amount of organic wastes increases in water, bacteria and other organisms multiply very fast by using the dissolved oxygen present in the water. Thus, making the waterbody deficient in oxygen. This lack of oxygen inturn, kills the fishes and other aquatic animals.
- **Thermal pollution or change in temperature** Sudden marked change in the temperature range of waterbody in which the aquatic organisms are living, can be dangerous for them or may affect their breeding. Eggs and larvae are particularly susceptible to any temperature changes.
- **Human diseases** Water provides home to pathogens, which cause infections to humans. These pathogens include viruses, bacteria, fungi, nematodes, protozoans, etc. These cause diseases such as typhoid, cholera, jaundice, etc., in humans.

Minerals Riches in the Soil

It is the portion of the outermost layer of Earth (crust), which provides support for the growth of the plants. The minerals present in the soil, supply a variety of nutrients to life forms. It is an important resource that decides the diversity of life in an area.

Formation of Soil

Soil formation takes long period of time. For thousands and millions of years, the rocks at or near the surface of the Earth are broken down by various physical, chemical and biological processes. The end product of this breaking down is soil.

Following are the factors responsible for the soil formation

1. Sun

It heats up the rocks during the day, so that they expand. During night, these rocks cool down and contract. Since, all parts of rock do not expand and contract at the same rate, this results in the formation of cracks. Ultimately, the huge rocks break up into smaller rocks.

2. Water

It helps in the formation of soil in two ways. First, water could get into the cracks in the rocks formed due to uneven heating by the Sun. Freezing of this water during night would lead to widening up of cracks later.

Second, flowing water wears away even hard rock over long periods of time. Fast flowing water often carries big and small rock pieces downstream.

These rocks rub against other rocks. It results in abrasion that causes the rocks to break into smaller particles. The water then takes these particles along with it and deposits them further down its path. That is why soil is found in distant places from its parent rock.

3. Wind

The action of wind is similar to the action of water. Strong winds erode rocks down. It carries sand from one place to another.

4. Living Organisms

These also influence the process of soil formation. The lichens grow on the surface of rocks. They release certain substances that cause the breaking down of rock constituents and gradually forms a thin layer of soil.

Other small plants like mosses grow on the surface of rocks. They cause further breakdown of rocks. Roots of big trees also break rocks by penetrating deeper into the rock bed (biological weathering).

Constituents of Soil

Soil is a mixture of small particles of rocks, bits of decayed living organisms (**humus**) and partially decomposed plant and animal matter (**detritus**). It also contains various forms of microorganisms. The main constituents of soil are minerals, air, water, organic matter and living organisms.

The type of soil is decided by the average size of particles found in it. Quality of soil is decided by the amount of humus, organic matter, microscopic organisms, etc. For e.g. black soil is rich in Ca, Fe, Mg, Al, whereas red soil is rich in iron oxides.

- **Humus** It is a dark coloured organic substance that plays a major role in deciding the soil structure. It causes soil to become more porous and allows water and air to penetrate deep underground.
- The mineral nutrients that are found in a particular soil depend on the rock from which it was formed.
- The nutrient content of a soil, the amount of humus present in it and depth of the soil are some of the basic factors that decide which plants will grow on a particular soil.
- **Topsoil** is the topmost layer of the soil. It contains humus and living organisms in addition to soil particles. The quality of the topsoil is an important factor that decides the biodiversity of a particular area.

Soil Pollution

Removal of useful components from the soil and addition of hazardous substances (both solid and liquid) into it, is called **soil pollution.** It destroys the soil structure by killing the microorganisms that recycle nutrients in the soil. It also kills the earthworms, which are helpful in making rich humus.

Fertile soil can quickly become unfertile, if sustainable practices are not followed. One of the major cause of soil pollution is modern farming practices. These involve the use of large amount of pesticides and fertilisers. These substances adversely affect the soil fertility.

Soil Erosion

It is the removal of top fertile layer of the soil due to strong winds and flowing water. Vegetation cover helps in the percolation of water into deeper layers. It also helps to prevent the removal of top soil.

In the absence of this cover, topsoil is likely to be removed very quickly. Soil erosion is more likely to occur in hilly or mountain regions. If all the soil gets washed away, the underneath rocks are exposed. These rocks have very low fertility.

Check Point 02

1 Enlist two benefits of water for living beings.
2 Give two human activities that pollute water.
3 State True or False for the following statement.
The composition of top soil in important factor for bring biodiversity in an area.
4 Name the partially decayed organic matter of soil. Mention its functions.
5 What is the composition of red soil?
6 Fill in the blank.
Soil erosion is removal of .... top soil due to strong winds and flowing water.

Biogeochemical Cycles

These refer to the cyclic flow of nutrients between non-living components (soil, rock, air and water) and living organisms, which make the biosphere dynamic, yet a stable system. Such cyclic flow involves transfer of matter and energy between the different components of the biosphere. There are four biogeochemical cycles–water, nitrogen, carbon and oxygen. These are described as follow :

The Water Cycle

There is a constant exchange of water between air, land, ocean and the living organisms. The whole process by which water evaporates and falls on the land as rain and later flows back into sea *via* rivers is called the **water** or **hydrological cycle.**

All the water that falls on the land does not immediately flows back into the sea. Some of it seeps into the soil and becomes a part of the underground reservoir of freshwater. Some of this underground water comes up to the surface through springs. Humans bring it to the surface through wells or tubewells. Water is also used by terrestrial animals and plants for various life processes. The schematic representation of the water cycle is as follows :

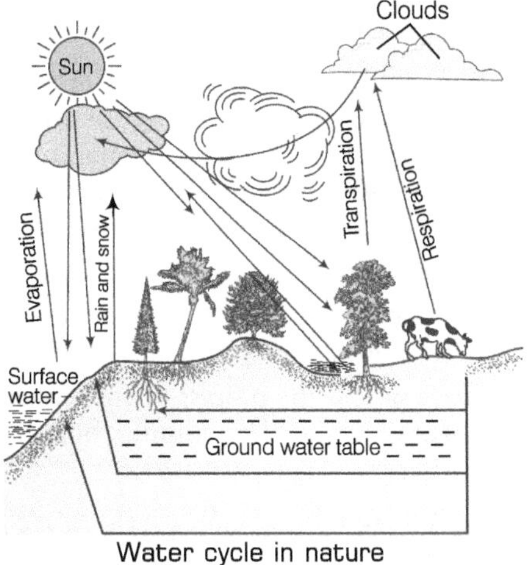

Water cycle in nature

Water, during the water cycle flows through or over rocks containing soluble minerals. Some of these minerals get dissolved in the water. Thus, rivers carry many nutrients from the land to the sea. These nutrients are then used by marine organisms.

The Nitrogen Cycle

It is the cyclic process, by which nitrogen passes from its elemental form present in the atmosphere into simple nitrogenous compounds present in the soil and water that can enter the living beings and forms complex molecules in them. These complex molecules are then broken down again to release nitrogen back into atmosphere.

Our atmosphere contains 78% of nitrogen gas. It is present in all living organisms as structural component in the form of proteins, amino acids, nucleic acids (DNA and RNA) and some vitamins. It is also found as a constituent of other compounds, such as alkaloids and urea. Nitrogen is thus, an essential nutrient for all life-forms.

Nitrogen cycle involves the following important steps

(*i*) **Nitrogen-Fixation** The first step of nitrogen cycle involves nitrogen-fixation. In this process, inert nitrogen molecules are coverted to nitrates or nitrites by nitrogen-fixing bacteria. These bacteria may be free-living or associated with some dicot plants. Most common nitrogen-fixing bacteria are found in the roots of legumes, in their root nodules.

Atmospheric nitrogen can also be converted into soluble nitrates and nitrites by **physical processes** such as **lightning**. During lightning, high temperatures and pressures created in the air convert nitrogen into oxides of nitrogen. These get dissolved in water to give nitric and nitrous acids. These fall on land along with rain. These are then utilised by various life forms.

(*ii*) **Nitrogen Assimilation** It is carried out by plants. Plants absorb nitrate (NO_3^-) and nitrites (NO_2^-) and convert them to amino acids which are used to make proteins. Other complex compounds containing nitrogen are formed in other biochemical pathways. Animals can take organic nitrogen from plants directly or indirectly.

(*iii*) **Ammonification** It is the process of production of ammonia (a compound of nitrogen). It occurs by the decomposition of dead plants and animals.

(*iv*) **Nitrification** It is the process of conversion of ammonia into nitrites and then into nitrates, by nitrifying bacteria (e.g. *Nitrosomonas* and *Nitrobacter*).

$$NH_4^+ \xrightarrow{Nitrosomonas} NO_2^- \xrightarrow{Nitrobacter} NO_3^-$$

(*v*) **Denitrification** It is the process of reducing nitrates or ammonia, present in the soil to molecular nitrogen (N_2) that goes back into the atmosphere.

This is done by microorganisms such as *Pseudomonas.*

The cyclic flow of nitrogen in the nature is diagrammatically shown below

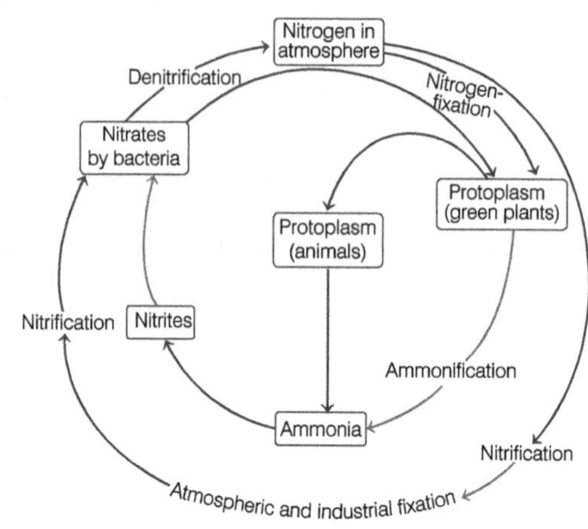

Nitrogen cycle in nature

Check Point 03

1. Define biogeochemical cycle.
2. Name any two biogeochemical cycles.
3. Name the microorganisms that carry out nitrification and denitrification.
4. What is the conversion of NH_3 into NO_3 known as?
5. State True or False for the following statement.
   The process of production of amino acid is called ammonification.
6. Fill in the blank.
   Denitrification process is carried out by bacteria called ....

The Carbon Cycle

Carbon is found in various forms on the Earth. It occurs in the elemental form as diamond and graphite.

In combined state, carbon is found as

- Carbon dioxide in the atmosphere.
- Carbonate and hydrogen-carbonate salts in various minerals.
- Fossil fuels like coal, petroleum and natural gas.
- Carbon-containing molecules like proteins, fats, nucleic acids, vitamins and carbohydrates.
- Endoskeletons and exoskeletons of various animals (carbonate salts).

Carbon is incorporated in life forms through plants by photosynthesis. Green plants perform photosynthesis by utilising CO_2 and H_2O in the presence of sunlight and chlorophyll.

In this process, CO_2 is transformed into simple carbohydrate (glucose). O_2 is liberated as a byproduct. These glucose molecules provide energy for the synthesis of other biologically important molecules or get converted into other substances like starch or cellulose. **Respiration** is the process of obtaining energy from glucose. It releases CO_2 back into the atmosphere. Oxygen may or may not be used in this process.

The other processes that give out CO_2 into atmosphere are

- Decomposition of dead bodies and organic wastes by decomposers.
- Combustion (burning) of fossil fuels like coal and petroleum on large scale.
- Weathering of rocks and volcanic eruptions.

Note The percentage of CO_2 in the atmosphere has doubled, since the industrial revolution.

The cyclic flow of carbon occurs through different forms like water by various physical and biological activities, as given below

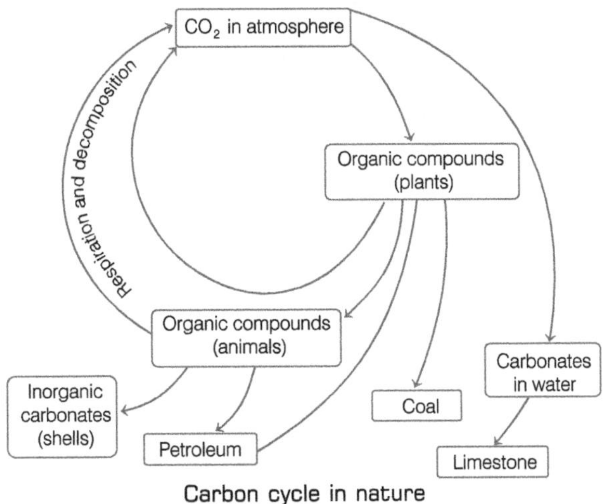

Carbon cycle in nature

Greenhouse Effect and Global Warming

Some gases such as carbon dioxide (CO_2), methane (marsh gas), water vapour, chlorofluorocarbons (CFCs), etc., prevent the escape of heat from the Earth. These gases, present in the atmosphere in correct concentration are responsible for heating of Earth's surface. This is called greenhouse effect. An increase in the percentage of greenhouse gases leads to global warming (the enhanced greenhouse effect).

Note Carbon dioxide is one of the greenhouse gases. Increase in the CO_2 content in atmosphere would cause more heat to be retained by the atmosphere which leads to global warming.

The Oxygen Cycle

Oxygen is an abundant element forming about $20.95\% \approx 21\%$ of the atmospheric gases. It is an essential component of most biological molecules like carbohydrates, proteins, nucleic acids and fats.

In Earth's crust, it is found as oxides of many metals and also as carbonate, sulphate, nitrate and other minerals. It is present in combined form also as in carbon dioxide and in water.

The cyclic flow of oxygen occurs through different forms like water, CO_2, by various processes, as given below

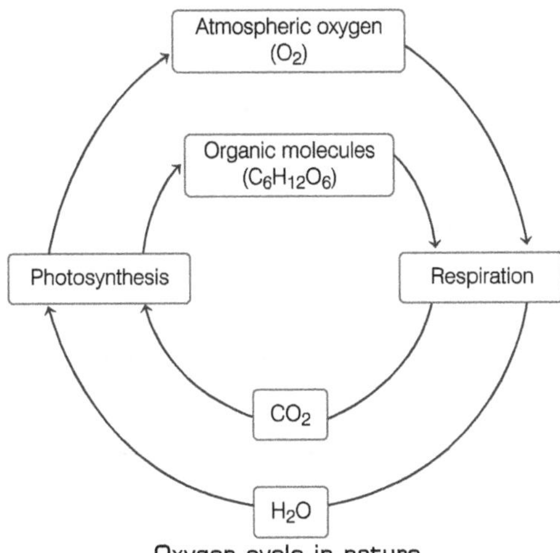

Oxygen cycle in nature

Oxygen cycle maintains the level of oxygen in the atmosphere. Oxygen from the atmosphere is used up in the processes of combustion, respiration and in the formation of oxides of nitrogen.

Photosynthesis is the only major process, by which oxygen is returned to the atmosphere. Therefore, green plants are the major source of oxygen in the atmosphere.

Note Some forms of life especially bacteria are poisoned by elemental oxygen. Even the process of nitrogen-fixation by bacteria does not take place in the presence of oxygen.

Ozone Layer

Ozone is a triatomic molecule of oxygen with the formula O_3. It is found in the upper region of the atmosphere, above the region where elemental oxygen (diatomic molecule) is present. Ozone is poisonous and luckily, it is not stable near Earth's surface.

Importance of Ozone

Ozone forms a thick layer (like a shield) in the upper region of atmosphere and absorbs harmful ultraviolet (UV) radiations from the Sun. Thus, preventing these radiations from reaching the surface of the Earth. It protects life forms the damaging effects of UV-rays.

Threat to Ozone Layer

Various man-made compounds like Chlorofluorocarbons or CFCs (carbon compounds having both fluorine and chlorine), which are very stable and are not degraded by any biological process, reach the ozone layer. They react with ozone layer.

It results in the reduction or thinning of ozone layer. It has already resulted in an ozone hole above Antarctica in 1985.

Check Point 04

1 Write the fate of glucose molecules formed in photosynthesis.

2 Name any two greenhouse gases.

3 In what form, oxygen is found in Earth's crust?

4 How many molecules of oxygen are present in ozone?

5 What is the full form of CFCs?

6 State True or False for the following statement.
Oxygen is an abundant element in atmosphere forming about .... percent of atmospheric gases.

7 Fill in the blank.
Ozone layer is present in......... layer of atmosphere.

To Study NCERT Activities
Visit https://goo.gl/6QKcgP OR **Scan the Code** 

NCERT FOLDER

Intext Questions

1 How is our atmosphere different from the atmosphere on Venus and Mars? **Pg 193**

Sol. The atmosphere of Earth contains a mixture of many gases like nitrogen (78%), oxygen (20.95%), carbon dioxide (0.031%) and water vapours (in varying proportion). The atmosphere on Venus and Mars mainly contains carbon dioxide, that makes about 95-97% of it. This may also be the reason for no life on Venus and Mars.

2 How does the atmosphere act as a blanket? **Pg 193**

Sol. The atmosphere mainly consists of air and covers the Earth like a protective blanket. The air is a bad conductor of heat. So, it keeps the average temperature of Earth fairly steady during the day and even during the course of whole year. In addition, the ozone shield of the atmosphere protects life from harmful ultraviolet radiations of the sun.

3 What causes winds? **Pg 193**

Sol. The uneven heating of the atmosphere in different regions of the Earth causes winds. The rotation of Earth and the presence of mountain ranges, also help in the formation of winds.

4 How are clouds formed? **Pg 193**

Sol. Waterbodies are heated by solar radiations during the day and large amount of water in the form of vapour goes into the air (vaporisation).

Air also gets heated due to sunlight. It starts rising up along with water vapours. As the air rises, it expands and cools. This cooling causes water vapours in the air to condense in the form of tiny droplets.

Condensation of water is facilitated by dust and other suspended particles which act as nuclei. The collection of these tiny droplets of water appears in the form of clouds.

5 List any three human activities that you think would lead to air pollution. **Pg 193**

Sol. The following human activities would lead to air pollution:

(*i*) Excessive burning of fossil fuels like coal and petroleum produces large amount of oxides of nitrogen and sulphur (i.e. NO_2, SO_2). These oxides mix with air and cause acid rain leading to many harmful effects.

(*ii*) Many industries release high amount of poisonous gases like carbon monoxide (CO) into the atmosphere causing air pollution.

(*iii*) Forest fires, excessive use of chlorofluorocarbons (CFCs), excessive mining and ore refining releases harmful gases into the air leading to its pollution.

6 Why do organisms need water? **Pg 194**

Sol. Organisms need water because:

(*i*) It provides a medium for all the cellular processes to take place.

(*ii*) It is necessary for the transportation of substances from one part of the body to the other in dissolved form.

(*iii*) It helps to maintain body temperature.

(*iv*) It is required to maintain balance of salts within the body.

7 What is the major source of fresh water in the city/ town/village where you live? **Pg 194**

Sol. In city/town/village, the major source of water is underground water. It is drawn with the help of handpumps and tube wells. The other nearby fresh water sources are rivers, lakes and ponds.

8 Do you know any activity which may be polluting any water source? **NCERT Intext Pg 194**

Sol. The activities, which may be polluting the waterbodies are:

(*i*) sewage and other wastes being dumped into waterbodies, which deplete water quality.

(*ii*) percolation of dissolved fertilisers, etc., from field into water.

9 How is soil formed? **Pg 196**

Sol. Refer to text on Pg 298 'Formation of soil.'

10 What is soil erosion? **Pg 196**

Sol. The removal and transportation of the top layer of soil that is rich in organic matter, from its original position due to factors, such as strong winds or fast running water is called soil erosion. It normally occurs in barren areas (areas without plant) and get accelerated in hilly or mountainous regions. Soil erosion results in the desertification and reduction in soil fertility.

11 What are the methods of preventing or reducing soil erosion? **Pg 196**

Sol. **Prevention of Soil Erosion** Preventive measures of soil erosion are:

(*i*) **Afforestation** Planting more trees reduces soil erosion.

(*ii*) **Contour ploughing** Ploughing land in furrows across the natural slope of the land helps to trap water and prevents the washing away of topsoil along with it.

(*iii*) **Step farming** (Terrace farming) Farmers form a series of steps by making horizontal strips supported by walls to catch the descending water. It gives the water sufficient time to percolate into the soil and is available to the crop.

(*iv*) **Soil cover** This method involves the removal of excess rainwater through small drainage canal formed around the field.

(*v*) **Controlled grazing** Grasses tend to bind soil particles to prevent their erosion. If overgrazing is allowed, the grasses are uprooted and soil gets eroded. Therefore, excessive grazing should be prevented.

Note
- Step farming is common on hills because it slows down the speed of rainwater run off on slopes, stops soil erosion and increases water absorption by the soil.
- Vegetative cover on the ground plays role in percolation of water into the deeper layers of soil.

12 What are the different states in which water is found during the water cycle? **Pg 201**

Sol. Water can be seen in water cycle in all the different states. These are

(*i*) **Gaseous state** It occurs in the form of water vapours. Water evaporates from the surface of waterbodies and mixes with air.

(*ii*) **Liquid state** Water vapours condense high up in the atmosphere. They fall on the Earth in the form of rain.

(*iii*) **Solid state** It is formed by the freezing of liquid droplets in the upper layer of atmosphere. These droplets fall on the Earth in the form of snow, hail or sleet.

13 Name two biologically important compounds that contain both oxygen and nitrogen. **Pg 201**

Sol. The biologically important compounds that contain both oxygen and nitrogen are proteins and nucleic acids (DNA and RNA).

14 List any three human activities, which would lead to an increase in the carbon dioxide content of air. **Pg 201**

Sol. The human activities, which would lead to an increase in CO_2 content of air are as follows:

(*i*) **Burning of forests** that is associated with agricultural practices, releases CO_2 into the atmosphere.

(*ii*) **Deforestation** also increases the level of CO_2 in the environment. Trees carry out photosynthesis and convert CO_2 into organic compounds, such as glucose, starch, etc. In their absence, CO_2 cannot be utilised.

(*iii*) **Combustion of fuels** leads to increase in CO_2 level in the atmosphere. Fuels are burnt to carry out various activities like cooking, transportation and industrial processes.

15 What is the greenhouse effect? **Pg 201**

Sol. **Greenhouse effect** is a naturally occurring phenomenon that is responsible for the heating of Earth's surface and atmosphere due to the presence of certain gases in the atmosphere. In the absence of greenhouse effect, the average temperature of Earth would have been a chilly (-18°C) rather than the present average temperature of 15°C.

16 What are the two forms of oxygen found in the atmosphere? **Pg 201**

Sol. The two forms of oxygen found in the atmosphere are:

(*i*) **Elemental Oxygen** It is normally found in the form of diatomic molecule (O_2) in the lower part of atmosphere. It constitutes about 20.95% of the atmosphere and is non-poisonous.

(*ii*) **Ozone** It is found in the stratosphere of atmosphere. It contains three atoms of oxygen (O_3). It is the poisonous form of oxygen.

Exercises (On Pages 201 and 202)

1 Why is the atmosphere essential for life?

Sol. Atmosphere is important for life due to following reasons :

(*i*) It keeps the average temperature of the Earth steady during the day and even throughout the year.

(*ii*) It prevents the sudden increase in temperature during the daylight hours.

(*iii*) The gases it contains, are required for sustaining life on the Earth. These gases are
- **Oxygen**, which is required for respiration by all living organisms.
- **Carbon dioxide,** which is used in photosynthesis performed by plants to synthesise food.
- **Nitrogen**, which constitutes about 80% of the atmosphere. It is an important component of proteins, nucleic acids and other cellular constituents.

(*iv*) A thick layer of ozone in stratosphere, filters the harmful UV radiations thus preventing them to reach the Earth.

2 Why is water essential for life?

Sol. Refer to NCERT Folder Intext Q. 6 on Pg. 303.

3 How are living organisms dependent on soil?

Or Are organisms that live in water totally independent of soil as a resource?

Sol. Living organisms depend on soil in the following ways:

(*i*) It provides natural habitat for various living organisms, e.g. bacteria, fungi, algae, earthworms, etc. These help to maintain the fertility of soil.

(*ii*) It provides nutrients to all living organisms.

(*iii*) Earthworm performs all its activities in the soil. It maintains the fertility of soil by releasing nitrogen rich excreta.

(*iv*) Many animals like rats, rabbits, etc., make their home in the soil.

(*v*) Soil helps to bind the roots of plants and provides them anchorage.

(*vi*) The nutrients in soil are absorbed by the plants for their growth and development.

No, all organisms that live in water are not totally independent of soil as a resource because the mineral nutrients are present in water in the dissolved form. But, their recycling depends on the decomposers, which are present in soil beds. Also, the microbes growing on the soil are the primary producers in water which start the food chain.

4 You have seen weather reports on television and in newspapers. How do you think we are able to predict the weather?

Sol. Meteorologists collect information regarding the pattern of temperature, speed of wind, air pressure and all other features which influence weather.

All these informations are collected by remote sensing and weather forecast satellites. This information is then compiled in meteorological departments. They prepare a weather report that is displayed on the maps. The information is further transmitted through radio, television and newspapers.

5 We know that many human activities lead to increasing levels of pollution of the air, waterbodies and soil. Do you think that isolating these activities to specific and limited areas would help in reducing pollution?

Sol. Isolating human activities to specific and limited areas would definitely help in reducing pollution to some extent.

For example,

(*i*) If sewage and garbage generated by homes and industries are collected at an isolated area and treated properly before discharging into water sources, it will reduce water pollution and cause less harm to the aquatic life.

(*ii*) If hot water generated by the industries is collected at a common place, allowed to cool and then discharged into the waterbodies, it will not affect the breeding capacity of aquatic organisms.

(*iii*) If commercial areas, factories and industries are shifted to isolated areas, far away from residential areas, it can reduce the effect of air pollution on people.

6 Write a note on how forests influence the quality of our air, soil and water resources?

Sol. (*i*) **Influence of Forests on Quality of Air**

(*a*) Forests help to maintain oxygen and carbon dioxide balance in the air. They reduce the level of CO_2 in the air and thus, prevent greenhouse effect.

(*b*) They maintain temperature of the environment.

(*c*) Forests increase the rate of photosynthesis in the surrounding region.

(*ii*) **Influence of Forests on Quality of Soil**

(*a*) Trees spread their roots deep inside the Earth and bind the soil particles firmly. This reduces soil erosion.

(*b*) Forests help to maintain nutrient cycles (biogeochemical cycles) in the atmosphere.

(*iii*) **Influence of Forests on Quality of Water**

(*a*) Trees help to maintain water cycle.

(*b*) Forests conserve water and make them available on Earth as water resources, such as rain, underground water, etc.

SUMMARY

- **Biosphere** is the part of Earth in which living organisms are found.
- Life on Earth depends on resources like soil **(lithosphere)**, water **(hydrosphere)** and air **(atmosphere)**.
- **Air** is a mixture of many gases like nitrogen, oxygen, carbon dioxide and water vapours. The precise composition of these gases makes life possible on Earth and plays an important role in climate control, winds (movement of air due to uneven heating of land, rotation of Earth, etc.) and rainfall.
- **Air pollution** is the increase in the content of harmful or undesirable substances in the air. It occurs due to excessive burning of fossil fuels, release of high amount of poisonous gases like CO, forest fires, excessive use of Chlorofluorocarbons (CFCs), dust, etc.
- **The pollution of air** affects the respiratory system and cause diseases like cold, asthma, lung cancer and pneumonia. Pollutant gases cause allergies, irritation in eyes and lungs and acid rain.
- **Water** is necessary for living organisms. It decides the diversity of life in an area.
- **Water pollution** is any undesirable change in the physical, biological or chemical qualities of water due to addition of unwanted and harmful substances.
- The causes of water pollution are fertilisers and pesticides from agricultural fields, dumping of sewage and other wastes into water bodies, sudden change in the temperature of water that affects the breeding of aquatic organisms, etc.
- Addition of undesirable substances and removal of desirable substances from water bodies lead to disturbances in the ecological balance and cause human diseases like typhoid, cholera, jaundice, etc.
- **Soil** is the upper surface of Earth's crust that supports plant life. Factors responsible for soil formation are sun, water, wind, living organisms, etc.
- **Soil pollution** is the removal of useful components from the soil and addition of hazardous substances, both solids and liquids into it.
- The causes for pollution of soil are frequent use of fertilisers and pesticides over a long period of time, strong winds, heavy rains, deforestation, improper cultivation, excessive and extensive farming, etc.
- The preventive measures for soil pollution are afforestation, contour ploughing, step farming, proper vegetation cover on soil surface, controlled grazing, etc.
- **Biogeochemical cycle** is the circulation of nutrients between abiotic and biotic components of environment. Such cyclic flow involves transfer of matter and energy among the different components of the biosphere. Decomposers play a major role in biogeochemical cycles. They decompose the dead plants and excreta of animals.
- **Water cycle** is the whole process in which water evaporates and falls on the land as rain and later flows back into sea *via* rivers.
- In **nitrogen cycle**, nitrogen passes from its elemental form in the atmosphere into simple molecules in the soil and water, which get converted to more complex molecules in living beings and back again to simple nitrogen molecule in the atmosphere.
- In **carbon cycle** carbon tends to cycle from atmosphere to organic compounds (plants and animals, coal, limestone, etc.). It moves from atmospheric CO_2 to biological molecules, then to organic molecules in the soil to geological deposits of fossil fuels. It is returned to atmosphere by respiration and decomposition.
- Disturbance in the carbon cycle can lead to increase in the percentage of CO_2 and other gases like CH_4, CFCs, etc., in the atmosphere. This causes global warming due to retention of heat by these gases.
- **Oxygen cycle** maintains the level of oxygen in the atmosphere. O_2 is used in three processes, i.e. combustion, respiration and formation of oxides of nitrogen. It is returned by only one process, i.e. photosynthesis.
- **Ozone** is a triatomic molecule of oxygen, present in the stratosphere part of atmosphere at the height of 23-25 km as **Ozone layer**. It is depleted by certain chemicals such as CFCs, that cause UV radiations from the sun to reach Earth. It results in harm to life by causing cataract, cancer, damage of immune system, smog formation, decreased crop yield, etc.

For Mind Map

Visit https://goo.gl/ZFiAdb OR **Scan the Code** 

Exam Practice

Objective Type Questions

Multiple Choice Questions

1 The natural resources used by human beings in order to meet their requirements include

(a) all the living components of nature
(b) all the non-living components of nature
(c) all the living and non-living components available in lithosphere
(d) Both (a) and (b)

Sol. (d) Natural resources are both living (plants, animals and microorganisms etc.) and non-living (air, water, etc.) components of nature, used by human beings in order to meet their requirements.

2 Biotic component of biosphere is not constituted by

(a) producers (b) consumers
(c) decomposers (d) air

NCERT Exemplar

Sol. (d) Biotic components are the living things that are essential part of an ecosystem. Biotic components usually include producers, consumers and decomposers.

3 Acid rains are produced by

(a) NO_2 and SO_2 (b) NH_3
(c) CO (d) CO_2

Sol. (a) High amount of oxides of sulphur and nitrogen are released from burning of fossil fuels. These oxides mix with air and mositure causing acid rain.

4 Which of the following is not a point source of water pollution ?

(a) Factories
(b) Nuclear power plants
(c) Oil spills from cargo ships
(d) Oil wells

Sol. (c) The non-point sources of water pollution do not have a specific location for the discharge of water pollutants into the water bodies, e.g. run-off from crop fields, logging areas, oil spills through cargo ships, etc.

5 Select the incorrect statement in context with soil.

(a) Soil supplies a variety of nutrients to life forms
(b) Soil decides the diversity of life in an area
(c) Chemical actions like oxidation do not involve in the formation of soil
(d) Sun, water, wind and living organisms are responsible for the formation of soil

Sol. (c) The chemical actions such as oxidation and reduction, carbonation and solubilisation of rock also lead to the formation of soil. This mode of soil formation is termed as chemical weathering.

6 Among the given options, which one is not correct for the use of large amount of fertilisers and pesticides?

(a) They are eco-friendly
(b) They turn the fields barren after some time
(c) They adversely affect the useful component from the soil
(d) They destroy the soil fertility

NCERT Exemplar

Sol. (a) Use of pesticides and fertilisers over long period of time can destroy soil fertility or soil structure by killing the soil microorganisms that recycle nutrients in the soil. It also kills earthworms which are instrumental in making rich humus.

7 Which one of the following processes is not a step involved in the water cycle operating in nature?

(a) Evaporation (b) Transpiration
(c) Precipitation (d) Photosynthesis

NCERT Exemplar

Sol. (d) Various processes involved in water cycle are evaporation, transpiration and precipitation. Photosynthesis is not important in water cycle.

8 The nitrogen molecules present in air can be converted into nitrates and nitrites by

(a) a biological process of nitrogen-fixing bacteria present in soil
(b) a biological process of carbon-fixing factor present in soil
(c) any of the industries manufacturing nitrogenous compounds
(d) the plants used as cereal crops in field

NCERT Exemplar

Sol. (a) The nitrogen molecules present in air can be converted into nitrates and nitrites by a biological process of nitrogen-fixing bacteria (present in the soil or present in association with plants).

9 An increase in carbon dioxide content in the atmosphere would not cause **NCERT Exemplar**

(a) more heat to be retained by the environment
(b) increase in photosynthesis in plants
(c) global warming
(d) abundance of desert plants

Sol. (d) An increase in carbon dioxide content in the atmosphere would not cause abundance of desert plants. When the temperature rises, their ability to take up carbon dioxide reduces.

10 Oxygen is returned to the atmosphere mainly by

(a) burning of fossil fuel
(b) respiration
(c) photosynthesis
(d) fungi **NCERT Exemplar**

Sol. (c) Photosynthesis is the process by which plants make their food in the presence of CO_2, chlorophyll, water and sunlight, thus returning oxygen as by product to the atmosphere.

11 Depletion of ozone layer leads to ozone hole, which is harmful for life on Earth as it may lead to

(a) snow blindness (cataract)
(b) skin ageing
(c) skin cancer
(d) All of the above

Sol. (d) The depletion or thinning of ozone layer is harmful for life forms on Earth, as the harmful UV-radiations can reach the Earth surface in its absence and cause snow blindness, ageing of skin, mutations in (DNA) genes and cancer.

12 Which of the following is a recently originated problem of environment? **NCERT Exemplar**

(a) Ozone layer depletion (b) Greenhouse effect
(c) Global warming (d) All of these

Sol. (d) Due to the extensive use of vehicles and thermoelectric plants, gaseous emission from industries, use of aerosol propellants, refrigerants, shaving foams, spray agents etc. leads to the emission of various harmful gases.

These gases are major constituents of air pollution and are interlinked in causing ozone layer depletion, greenhouse effect and global warming.

Fill in the Blanks

13 Water covers nearly .... percent of earth's surface.

Sol. 70

14 The green plants use .... gas of atmosphere as source of carbon for photosynthesis.

Sol. carbon dioxide (CO_2)

15 The rainfall patterns of an area are decided by .... patterns.

Sol. wind patterns

16 .... and .... are examples of fossil fuels.

Sol. Coal and petroleum

True and False

17 Burning of organic matter uses O_2 and releases CO_2.

Sol. True

18 Soil plays no role in supplying nutrients to organisms living in water bodies.

Sol. False. Soil plays an important role in suppling nutrienrts to organism living in water bodies.

19 The surface temperature of moon varies from $-140°$ C to $100°$ C.

Sol. False. Surface temperature of moon varies from $-190°$C to $110°$.

20 Earthworm are saprobes which make soil fertile.

Sol. False. The earthworm are detrivores which make soil fertile.

Match the Columns

21 Match the following columns.

Column I		Column II
1. Greenhouse gas	A.	Earth worms
2. Detrivores	B.	SO_2 in atmosphere
3. Acid rain	C.	Ozone depletion
4. CFC	D.	CO_2

Sol. $1 \rightarrow D, 2 \rightarrow A, 3 \rightarrow B, 4 \rightarrow C$

Assertion-Reason

Direction (Q.Nos. 22-26) *In each of the following questions, a statement of Assertion is given by the corresponding statement of Reason. Of the statements, mark the correct answer as*

(a) If both Assertion and Reason are true and reason is the correct explanation of Assertion

(b) If both Assertion and Reason are true, but Reason is not the correct explanation of Assertion
(c) If Assertion is true, but Reason is false
(d) If Assertion is false, but Reason is true

22 **Assertion** Very hot and cold temperature variations exist on the Moon compared to the Earth.

Reason Moon has no atmosphere.

Sol. (a) Moon is at the same distance from the Sun as the Earth. But very cold and hot temperature variations exist on the Moon. This is because Moon has no atmosphere to check the excessive rise or fall of temperature.

23 **Assertion** Dust is a pollutant.

Reason Inhalation of dust particles causes discomfort in organisms.

Sol. (a) Dust contains suspended particles. On inhalation, these particles cause allergy, asthma, bronchitis and other discomforts. Hence, it is considered a pollutant.

24 **Assertion** Lichens are bioindicators of air pollution.

Reason They do not grow in Delhi.

Sol. (b) Lichens are sensitive to SO_2 level in air. Increased release of SO_2 from automobiles and other sources causes their depletion. Delhi has more air plllution due to increased vehicles, thus lichens do not grow here.

25 **Assertion** Aquatic life is adversely affected by polluted water.

Reason Increased use of fertilisers favours microbial growth.

Sol. (b) In polluted water, increased presence of agricultural chemicals like fertilisers increases the amount of organic wastes. As a result, microbes like bacteria multiply very fast using dissolved oxygen in water. The water body becomes deficient in O_2, killing aquatic life.

26 **Assertion** Carbon dioxide is a greenhouse gas.

Reason Increase in CO_2 level leads to global warming.

Sol. (b) Carbon dioxide is one of the greenhouse gases. Increase in CO_2 level causes more heat to be retained by the atmosphere. This leads to global warming.

Case Based Questions

Direction (Q.Nos. 27-30) *Answer the questions on the basis of your understanding of the following passage and related studied concepts:*

It is the presence of acid in rain water. Normal rain is a weak acid with a pH of 6.5 but acid rain has a pH of 5.6-4. Acid rain is a consequence of air pollution and has adverse effects on the crops, health of living organisms, infrastructure, etc. The acid rain formed in the atmosphere gets deposited in followings forms,

Wet Deposition Acidic water received through rain, fog snow, dew, mist, etc.

Dry Deposition of windblown acidic gases and particles on the gorud.

27 How is acid rain a consequence of air pollution?

Sol. Acid rain results from oxides of nitrogen, sulphur and hydrocarbons formed during combustion of fossil fuels. These oxides mix with air and produce acids (H_2SO_4, HNO_3, etc.) and fall as acid rain.

28 It is said in the paragraph that acid rain has a damaging effect on infrastructure. Give an example to show. How?

Sol. Acid rain causes corresion of monuments which are a part of a country's infrastructures, e.g. Taj Mahal faced a great threat of blackening of its white marble due to SO_2 and NO_2 production in from a neighbouring Mathura refinery.

29 Suggest any two effects of air pollution on humans

Sol. (*i*) Respiratory disorders like asthma, bronchitis, etc.
(*ii*) Irritation in eyes

30 What is the pH of normal rain?

Sol. 6.5

Direction (Q.Nos. 31-34) *Answer the questions on the basis of your understanding of the following table and related studied concepts:*

Sizes of Reservoirs of Global water

Reservoir	Quantity (in tetratong 18, 10)
Oceans	1,380,000
Polarice, glacier	29,000
Ground water	4,000
Freshwater lakes	125
Saline lakes	104
Soil moisture	67
Rivers	1.32
Atmosphere water vapour	14

Now answer the questions that follow.

31 All of the water that falls on the land does not immediately flow back into the sea. Justify the statement.

Sol. All of the water that falls on the land does not immediately flow back into the sea. Some of it seeps into the soil and becomes part of the underground reservoir of freshwater. Some of this underground water finds its way to the surface for our use through wells or tube wells.

32 What forms the largest global reservoir and the smallest global reservoir of water?

Sol. The ocean forms the largest global reservoir of water and atmosphere forms the smallest global resevoir of water.

33 There are two overlapping water cycles in nature which are .... and ....

(i) Global water cycle
(ii) Biological water cycle
(iii) Both (i) and (ii)
(iv) None of the above

Sol. (iii) There are two overlapping water cycles in the nature which are global water cycle and biological water cycle.

34 Plants absorb water from the soil or water reservoir and add it to the air by the process called ....

(i) photosynthesis (ii) absorption
(iii) transpiration (iv) translocation

Sol. (iii) Plants absorb water from the soil or water reservoir and addit to the air by the process of transpiration.

Very Short Answer Type Questions

35 What are the resources available on Earth for life to exist?

Sol. The resources available on Earth for life to exist are air, water and land.

36 How is biosphere a dynamic and stable system?

Sol. The constant interaction between the biotic and abiotic components of the biosphere makes it dynamic yet a stable system.

37 State the temperature range on the surface of Moon.

Sol. The temperature range on the surface of moon is – 190°-110°C.

38 What is the direction of air in coastal areas during the day?

Sol. During the day, the direction of air current or wind is from sea to land.

39 Name the stage in the life cycle of aquatic animals, which is affected by change in temperature.

Sol. Hatching (egg stage), larvae and young animals are affected by change in temperature of the water bodies.

40 Name any one method by which water helps in soil formation.

Sol. In physical weathering, water and high temperature cause expansion and contraction of rocks, facilitating their breakdown. As a result soil is formed.

41 Different types of soil have different constituents. Name the main constituent in following soil

(i) Black soil (ii) Red soil

Sol. The main constituents are :

(i) Black soil–Humus, Ca, Fe, Mg, Al.
(ii) Red soil–Iron oxide

42 What happens, when rain falls on the soil that is devoid of vegetation cover?

Sol. Rainwater falling on soil that is without vegetation cover can cause loss of topsoil. The land without vegetation cover is exposed and gets eroded easily thus, causing the topsoil to move-away with water, wind, etc.

43 How can we prevent the loss of topsoil?

Sol. Loss of topsoil can be prevented by increasing the vegetative cover, checking the falling of trees and by preventing excessive grazing by animals.

44 How do forests play an important role in maintaining water cycle?

Sol. Forests play an important role in the hydrological cycle by directly affecting the rate of transpiration and by influencing how water is routed and stored in a watershed and water table.

45 State the role of symbiotic bacteria in nitrogen cycle of nature.

Sol. Plants are unable to take atmospheric nitrogen directly. Symbiotic bacteria convert the atmospheric nitrogen into water soluble nitrates, which are easily utilised by plants.

46 Name two organisms, which play vital role in nitrogen-fixation.

Sol. The organisms, which play vital roles in nitrogen-fixation are :

(i) *Rhizobium* and blue-green algae help in fixation of free atmospheric nitrogen.
(ii) *Nitrosomonas* and *Nitrobacter* are nitrifying bacteria which convert ammonia to nitrite and then to nitrates.

47 Which organisms carry out the process of denitrification?

Sol. The bacterium *Pseudomonas* carries out the process of denitrification. Thus, releasing N_2 into the atmosphere.

48 List two main ways in which oxygen is consumed and carbon dioxide is produced.

Sol. Respiration and combustion.

49 What is the role of respiration in oxygen cycle?

Sol. Oxygen enters in the living world through the process of respiration. It is used to oxidise the food material (glucose molecule) and produce energy and carbon dioxide.

Short Answer (SA) Type Questions

1 State the role of atmosphere in climate control.

Sol. Refer to NCERT Folder Intext Q. 2 on Pg 303.

2 Air pollution has been greatest threat to various form of life in metropolitancities like Delhi, Mumbai, etc. To combat this, Govt. has enforced a law for using CNG instead of petrol. Knowing this answer the following question.

(i) State two gases, which are emitted by burning of petroleum.

(ii) How these gases affect us?

Sol. (i) Oxides of nitrogen and sulphur (i.e. NO_2 and SO_2) are released into the atmosphere by burning of petroleum.

(ii) Inhalation of these gases is dangerous.
When these gases dissolve in rain water, it becomes acidic and results in acid rain. It is harmful to the monuments and crops.

3 Why does Mathura refinery pose problems to the Taj Mahal? **NCERT Exemplar**

Sol. Mathura refinery releases many air pollutants such as sulphur dioxide (SO_2). It reacts with water in the atmosphere to form sulphuric acid. This sulphuric acid is washed away into the soil by rain (acid rain). This acid erodes the stone, surface of buildings and brick works, etc. It can destroy the marble quality and its colour, etc. Thus, posing a great threat to Taj Mahal.

4 (i) 'An increase in temperature of the water bodies would lead to water pollution'. Explain.

(ii) Suggest any two methods to prevent water pollution. **NCERT Exemplar**

Sol. (i) As the temperature of the waterbody increases, aquatic life is disturbed, immature egg and larvae die and this further disturbs the ecological balance.

(ii) Two methods to prevent water pollution are:

(a) Treatment of sewage separately before discharging it into water sources.

(b) Cooling of hot water of industries before discharge.

5 State any two harmful effects of

(i) air pollution, and

(ii) water pollution. **NCERT Exemplar**

Sol. (i) Two harmful effects of air pollution are:

(a) Results in respiratory problems, such as asthma, bronchitis, etc.

(b) **Acid rain** affects monuments, plants and animals adversely.

(ii) Two harmful effects of water pollution are:

(a) Leads to waterborne diseases such as typhoid, cholera, jaundice, etc.

(b) Accumulation of toxins in water causes death of aquatic life.

6 Sun as a natural factor helps in the formation of soil. Explain.

Sol. Sun helps in soil formation as it heats up the rocks during the day so that they expand. At night, these rocks cool down and contract. All parts of the rocks do not expand and contract at the same rate. This results in the formation of cracks and finally breaking of huge rocks into smaller pieces.

7 Fertile soil has lots of humus. Why? **NCERT Exemplar**

Sol. Fertile soil contains sufficient amount of humus because:

(i) Humus is required for binding soil particles into crumbs. Crumb formation helps in both hydration and aeration of soil.

(ii) It makes the soil porous for easy penetration of plant roots.

(iii) It is a source of mineral.

(iv) It contains chemicals that promote growth of plants.

8 How is 'soil formation' different from 'soil erosion'? Write two factors responsible for each one of them.

Sol. **Soil formation** Rocks are broken down by various processes like physical, chemical and biological weathering.

Factors responsible for soil formation are Sun, water, wind, living organisms.

Soil erosion Fine particles of soil may be carried away by the action of wind and water.

Factors responsible for soil erosion are deforestation, overgrazing.

9 (*i*) If decomposers are removed completely from the Earth, what will be the result? Give reasons.

(*ii*) Study the graph alongside and explain how oxygen concentration is affected in the river when sewage is discharged into it.

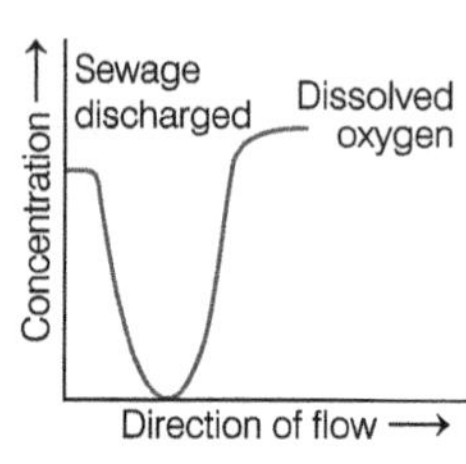

Sol. (*i*) If decomposers are removed completely from the Earth, then dead bodies of plants and animals or other dead organic matter will remain undecomposed. The complex nutrients will not be made available back to atmosphere. After some time, the dead bodies of organisms will acquire the whole space on the Earth. Thus, existence of life will be impossible on the Earth without decomposers.

(*ii*) As per the graph, the concentration of dissolved oxygen gets dropped sharply on the introduction of sewage in waterbody.

A large amount of O_2 is used by microorganisms in river to decompose the organic matter (sewage) thus, reducing its concentration in the highly polluted water.

10 Complete the following cycle by labelling *A-D* and answer the given questions.

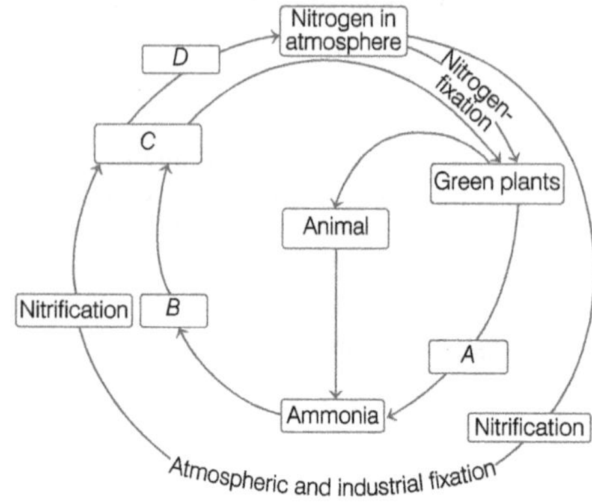

(*i*) What will happen, if step *D* does not occur?

(*ii*) Name two free-living nitrogen-fixing bacteria.

Sol. *A* – Ammonification *B* – Nitrites

C – Nitrates *D* – Denitrification

(*i*) If step *D* does not occur then there will be no replenishment of atmospheric nitrogen.

(*ii*) *Azotobacter* and *Clostridium*.

11 (*i*) Enumerate some differences between nitrification and denitrification processes.

(*ii*) State the importance of nitrogen cycle for living organisms.

Sol. (*i*) Differences between nitrification and denitrification are:

Nitrification	*Denitrification*
It is the process of conversion of ammonia to nitrites and to nitrates.	It is the process of reducing nitrates back into free atmospheric nitrogen.
This is an intermediate step of nitrogen cycle in which nitrogen is converted into another usable form by bacteria, such as *Nitrosomonas*.	This is the last step in which nitrogen is released back into its source, i.e. the atmosphere by *Pseudomonas* (bacteria).

(*ii*) Nitrogen cycle is important to maintain the overall amount of nitrogen content in soil, water and air. Living organisms cannot utilise nitrogen without nitrogen cycle.

12 With the help of a labelled diagram, show the cycling of carbon in nature. What are the two ways in which carbon dioxide is fixed in the environment?

Sol. Refer to Pg 301 for figure.

Fixation of CO_2 occurs through

(*i*) **Photosynthesis** Green plants and other producers fix CO_2 into glucose.

(*ii*) **Formation of Shells and Skeletons**

Marine animals build up their shells and bones from carbonates .

13 (*i*) The circulation of carbon is important in nature. Give reasons for your answer.

(*ii*) Explain any two processes involved in cycling of nitrogen in the environment.

Sol. (*i*) Circulation of carbon is important in nature because it moves carbon, a life sustaining element from the atmosphere, etc., into organisms and vice versa.

If the balance between these two is disturbed, it leads to serious consequences, such as global warming.

(ii) Two processes involved in cycling of nitrogen are

(a) Nitrogen-fixation

(b) Ammonification

For the explanation of these two processes: Refer to text on Pg 300.

14 (i) Name the gas, which is used in the process of photosynthesis.

(ii) Complete the given cycle.

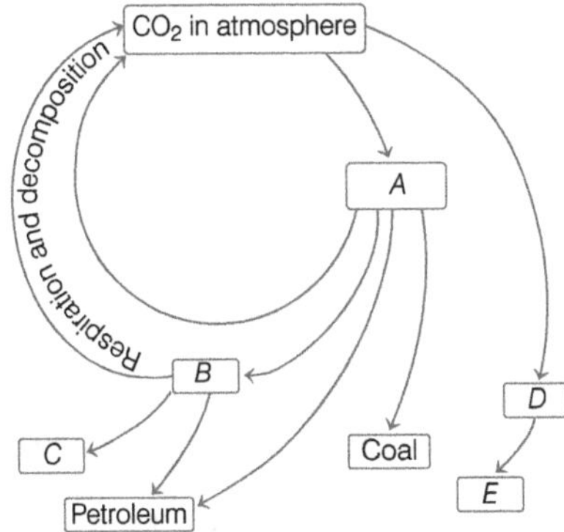

Sol. (i) Carbon dioxide.

(ii) A — Organic compounds (plants)
B — Organic compounds (animals)
C — Inorganic carbonates (shells)
D — Carbonates in water
E — Limestone

15 What is the percentage of oxygen found in the atmosphere? Name two compounds of oxygen found in nature. Name any three processes in which oxygen is used up in atmosphere.

Sol. 20.94% oxygen is found in atmosphere. Diatomic O_2 (oxygen) and triatomic O_3 (ozone) are two compounds of oxygen found in nature.

Processes in which oxygen is used up

(i) **Respiration** in most organisms.

(ii) **Combustion** of fossil fuels.

(iii) **Formation of oxides**, e.g. nitrogen oxides during atmospheric fixation of nitrogen.

(iv) **Decomposition** of organic matter.

16 State in brief the role of photosynthesis and respiration in carbon and oxygen cycle in nature.

Sol. **Photosynthesis** is performed by green plants in the presence of sunlight. It converts carbon dioxide into carbohydrates (glucose). They are utilised by other living organisms through food chain. Oxygen is replenished in nature only through the process of photosynthesis.

Respiration Oxygen enters in the living world through the process of respiration, i.e. it oxidises the food material (glucose molecules) and produces energy and carbon dioxide.

17 Carbon dioxide is necessary for plants. Why do we then consider it as a pollutant? **NCERT Exemplar**

Sol. Carbon dioxide gas is necessary for plants to perform photosynthesis but, it is also a greenhouse gas. Upto a certain concentration (approx. 350 ppm) in atmosphere, it is both a good raw material as well as essential for keeping the Earth warm.

But, when concentration of CO_2 from its specified level rises, it starts acting like a pollutant and causes pollution and global warming. Due to this, temperature of the Earth will increase and polar ice and glaciers will start melting.

18 State the reason for the following:

(i) Excess burning of coal causes greenhouse effect.

(ii) Soil is a mixture.

(iii) Temperature ranges from -190 to 110°C on the surface of the Moon.

Sol. (i) Excess burning of coal adds lot of CO_2 to the atmosphere. Carbon dioxide is a greenhouse gas, which allows the solar radiations to strike the Earth's surface, but prevents the escape of long wave radiations from the Earth's atmosphere. Thus, causing greenhouse effect.

(ii) Soil is a mixture as it consists of particles (sand, silt, clay and humus) of different types which do not get dissolved in water, but settle down in layers, depending on their size.

(iii) The Moon is at the same distance from the Sun as the Earth. But there is very cold and hot temperature variations, from -190°C to 110°C on the Moon. This is because Moon has no atmosphere. The atmosphere plays a very important role in temperature control. It checks excessive rise of temperature during the day and excessive cooling during the night.

19 (i) The temperature inside a glass enclosure is higher than that of the surrounding. Give reason.

(ii) How is the above phenomenon utilised by the cold countries to their advantage?

(iii) Name two greenhouse gases.

Sol. (i) Heat is trapped by glass which leads to rise in temperature.

(ii) The above phenomenon is utilised to create enclosures for keeping tropical plants warm in cold countries.

(iii) Carbon dioxide (CO_2) and methane (CH_4).

20 A motor car with its glass totally closed, is parked directly under the Sun. The temperature inside the car rises very high. Explain. **NCERT Exemplar**

Sol. Sun emits infrared radiations, which pass through the glass and heat the car from inside. The radiations cannot pass out of the glass. So, the heat gets trapped inside, raising the temperature of the interior. This is because glass is transparent to infrared radiations released from the Sun which have smaller wavelength, than that emitted by the interior of the car, which have longer wavelength to which glass is opaque.

Long Answer (LA) Type Questions

1 (i) Air is called as breath of life. Why?

(ii) What are the causes and effects of air pollution?

Sol. (i) Air is called breath of life because it contains oxygen. It is required by all living organisms for respiration.

(ii) For causes of air pollution refer to text on Pg 297.

For effects of air pollution refer to text on Pg 297.

2 State a few causes of water pollution. Discuss some ways of reducing water pollution.

Sol. For causes of water pollution refer to text on Pg 298.

Ways to reduce water pollution The following activities help to control water pollution

(i) Sewage and garbage generated by homes and industries should be treated properly before discharging into water sources. It will reduce water pollution, causing less harm to the aquatic life.

(ii) If hot water generated by the industries is collected at a common place and then cooled before it is discharged into the waterbodies, it will not affect the breeding capacity of aquatic organisms.

(iii) If commercial areas, factories and industries are shifted to isolated areas (i.e. far away from residential areas), it can reduce the effect of water pollution on people.

3 How is life of organisms living in water affected when water gets polluted? **NCERT Exemplar**

Sol. Water gets polluted from domestic wastes (loaded with detergents, faecal matter, etc.), fertilisers and pesticides from crop fields and industrial wastes (heavy metals, heat).

(i) Fertilisers and domestic wastes cause eutrophication or increased organic loading and excessive growth of algae (algal bloom). This ultimately reduces oxygen available to aquatic animals (fish, molluscs) and kill them.

(ii) Domestic wastes also carry pathogens of a number of human diseases. Some of them can cause diseases of animals as well.

(iii) Aquatic organisms can tolerate a certain range of temperature in the waterbody where they live. A sudden marked change in this temperature can be very dangerous for these animals (cold-blooded animals). For e.g. it affects breeding of aquatic animals. The eggs and larvae of various animals are particularly susceptible to temperature changes.

4 There is a mass mortality of fish in a pond. What may be the reasons? **NCERT Exemplar**

Sol. In a pond, a mass mortality of fish may occur due to following reasons:

(i) Passage of pesticide rich water from crop fields.

(ii) Release of toxic industrial waste.

(iii) Pouring of hot water from an industry or thermal power plant into the pond.

(iv) Release of waste rich in heavy metals, such as mercury.

(v) Blockage of gills of fish by some suspended pollutant such as oil.

5 'Soil is formed by water'. If you agree with this statement, then give reasons. **NCERT Exemplar**

Sol. Yes, water helps in the breakdown of bigger rocks into smaller mineral particles, i.e. soil formation. It occurs by following methods:

(i) First, water could enter into cracks in the rocks that are formed due to uneven heating by the sun. If this water freezes, it would cause these cracks to widen.

(*ii*) Second, flowing water wears away even hard rocks over long periods of time. Fast flowing water often carries big and small particles of rocks downstream. These rocks rub against the other rocks and resultant abrasion causes the rock to breakdown into the smaller and smaller particles. The water then takes these particles along with and deposit them further down.

6 Following are a few organisms

(*a*) lichen (*b*) mosses
(*c*) mango tree (*d*) cactus

Which among the above can grow on stones; and also help in formation of soil? Write the mode of their action for making soil.

NCERT Exemplar

Sol. Out of the above given organisms lichens can grow on rocks. During growth, they release certain substances that cause the rock surface to powder down and form a thin layer of soil. Lichens grow on the rock surface and extract minerals from them, thus creating small crevices at places where a thin layer of soil builds up.

Mosses grow over these crevices and cause deepening of the crevices. It results in the build up of more soil inside them. Deeper crevices form cracks and cracks become wider and deeper when the roots of short lived herbs grow into them. With the passage of time, the roots of bigger plants, (e.g. peepal, banyan tree) pass into the cracks. Cracks are gradually widen and cause slow fragmentation and eventually pulverisation of rocks occurs.

7 (*i*) Write a short note on soil erosion.

(*ii*) Name two biologically important compounds that contain both oxygen and nitrogen.

(*iii*) How can you say that water is essential for life?

Sol. (*i*) The removal and transportation of the top layer of soil from its original position to another place, under the effect of strong winds and fast running rain water is called soil erosion.

It can be prevented by planting trees and grasses. Proper drainage canals around the fields can prevent soil erosion.

(*ii*) Amino acid and proteins.

(*iii*) Water is essential for life due to following reasons

(*a*) All cellular processes take place in water medium.

(*b*) Water is required for salt and electrolytes maintenance inside the body.

8 What measures, as an individual, you would take to reduce environmental pollution?

Sol. As an individual, following steps can be taken to reduce environmental pollution:

(*i*) Never use plastic plates/glasses only for once, it generates enormous amount of non-biodegradable waste.

(*ii*) Reuse and recycle plastic, clothes, shoes, bags as much as possible.

(*iii*) Stop wastage of electricity, water, cooking gas, food and any other material.

(*iv*) Walk or use public transport instead of riding in cars, use sunlight instead of electric light, use cloth bags instead of polybags.

(*v*) Use kitchen waste to replenish soil nutrients, use wastewater to water the plants or washing floors/car, etc.

(*vi*) Grow plants and trees in/near our house.

(*vii*) Cut down on wastage of paper, pens, other school supplies.

(*viii*) Never litter around homes or in schools.

(*ix*) Never add to pollution by using fire crackers,etc.

(*x*) Always separate biodegradable and non-biodzegradable wastes.

9 What do you mean by global warming? State the causes and effects of global warming.

Sol. The gradual and continuous rise in average temperature of the Earth's surface is called global warming.

Causes of Global Warming

(*i*) High levels of gases, such as carbon dioxide (CO_2), methane (CH_4), ozone (O_3), nitrogen oxide (N_2O), chlorofluorocarbons (CFCs) are responsible for global warming.

(*ii*) Burning of fossil fuels in homes and industries, deforestation, etc., increase the level of carbon dioxide and methane in atmosphere.

Effects of Global Warming

(*i*) An increase in temperature would lead to melting of polar ice caps and consequent rise in sea levels.

(*ii*) Increase in temperature of Earth can cause changes in weather and precipitation patterns on the Earth.

CHAPTER EXERCISE

Multiple Type Questions

1 Major air pollutant is

(a) CO (b) CO_2 (c) SO_2 (d) All of these

2 If there were no atmosphere around the Earth, the temperature of the Earth will **NCERT Exemplar**

(a) increase

(b) go on decreasing

(c) increase during day and decrease during night

(d) be unaffected

3 Rainfall patterns depend on **NCERT Exemplar**

(a) the underground water table

(b) the number of water bodies in an area

(c) the density pattern of human population in an area

(d) the prevailing season in an area

4 The term used for the cyclic flow of nutrients between biotic and abiotic components of biosphere is

(a) geochemical cycle (b) biogeochemical cycle

(c) geophysical cycle (d) biogeophysical cycle

5 Ozone layer is getting depleted because of

(a) excessive use of automobiles

(b) excessive formation of industrial units

(c) excessive use of man-made compounds containing both fluorine and chlorine

(d) excessive deforestation

Fill in the Blanks

6 .... and .... acids are responsible for acid rain.

7 .... is the example of greenhouse gas.

8 .... is present in all living forms as a structural component of proteins, nucleic acds and some vitamins.

9 The full from of CFC is ....

True and False

10 The acid rain causing gases of atmosphere are CO_2 and CO.

11 Clouds are found in stratosphere.

12 Wind is caused due to uneven heating of Earth's surfaces.

13 Fertiliser and pesticides are main agricultural chemicals causing water pollution.

Match the Columns

14 Match the following columns.

	Column I		Column II
1.	Water pollutnts	A.	Green plants
2.	Antarctica	B.	Agricultural wastes
3.	Photosynthesis	C.	Decomposers
4.	Bacteria Fungi	D.	Ozone hole

Assertion–Reason

Direction (Q.Nos. 15-16) *In each of the following questions, a statement of Assertion is given by the corresponding statement of Reason. Of the statements, mark the correct answer as*

(a) If both Assertion and Reason are true and Reason is the correct explanation of Assertion

(b) If both Assertion and Reason are true, but Reason is not the correct explanation of Assertion

(c) If Assertion is true, but Reason is false

(d) If Assertion is false, but Reason is true

15 **Assertion** A change in the pressure of water bodies is water pollution.

Reason It is one of the most serious environmental problems in the world.

16 **Assertion** Living organisms help in soil formation.

Reason They grow on rocks, release chemicals which aid in weathering process.

Case Based Questions

Direction (Q. Nos. 17-20) *Answer the questions on the basis of your understanding of the following passage and related studied concepts:*

Atmosphere around Earth act as window glass pane that allows solar radiations to enter the surface. It does not alow long Wave Radiation (IR) emitted by Earth to escape in space. These IR radiation are absorbed by greenhouse/radioctively active gases.So the atmosphere radiate part of this energy back to Earth called **Greenhouse flux.** These greenhouse gases keep the atmosphere warm and fit for living called Greenhouse effect. Due to the presence of greenhouse gases, mean annual temperature of Earth is 150° C but in the absence of these gases it would drop sharply to −200°C.

17 What are green house gases?

18 What will be the consequence of an increase in the percentage of green house gases?

19 How will an increase in greenhouse effect the ozone layer?

20 Suggest any ways to advance green house effect.

Answers

1. (d) 2. (c) 3. (b) 4. (b) 5. (c)
6. HNO_3 and H_2SO_4 7. CO_2 8. Nitrogen
9. Chloflouro compounds
10. False 11. False 12. True 13. True
14. 1→(B), 2→(D), 3→(A), 4→(C)
15. (d) 16. (a)

Very Short Answer (VSA) Type Questions

21 What is the functional unit of the environment comprising the living and non-living components called?

22 What are the physical divisions of biosphere called?

23 What would be the direction of air currents coming from Varanasi after it is intercepted by Himalayas in North?

24 Name a few alternative sources of energy other than conventional fossil fuels.

25 Why is water rarely available in pure form?

26 In how many forms, water is available? Mention the names of these forms of water.

27 Give one common pathogen found in polluted water.

28 What is the main cause of floods in rivers?

29 Organisms play a vital role in nitrogen-fixation. Write names of two such organisms.

30 Name the process, which causes a long term withdrawal of carbon from carbon cycle.

31 In which zone of atmosphere, ozone layer is present?

32 Write the harmful effects of the ultraviolet rays.

Short Answer (SA) Type Questions

33 Water needs conservation even though large oceans surround the land masses. Is it true? Justify.

34 Write the composition of soil. On what basis the type of soil is decided?

35 List the factors responsible for soil formation.

36 List the methods of preventing soil erosion.

37 Write a note on nitrogen-fixation.

38 Describe the methods of carbon replenishment in atmosphere.

39 How is nitrogen replenished in atmosphere?

40 What are the possible dangers of global warming?

41 Why is ozone layer called ozone umbrella/shield?

42 What would be the effects of widening of ozone hole?

Long Answer (LA) Type Questions

43 (*i*) What is soil erosion? Give two methods for reducing it.
(*ii*) How is vehicular advancement, a cause of air pollution?
(*iii*) Why is water essential for life?

44 (*i*) With the help of labelled diagram, show oxygen cycle in nature.
(*ii*) Why the process of nitrogen-fixation by bacteria does not take place in presence of oxygen? Give reason.
(*iii*) (*a*) Name a process by which oxygen is utilised from the atmosphere.
(*b*) Name the process by which oxygen is returned to the atmosphere.

45 What is the significance of dissolved oxygen to the aquatic organisms? How does it get depleted?

RELATED ONLINE VIDEOS

Visit https://www.youtube.com/watch?v=Fx8r3o2gsLk
OR **Scan the Code**

Visit https://www.youtube.com/watch?v=rp0b2fEcF_U
OR **Scan the Code**

Visit https://www.youtube.com/watch?v=LbBgPekjiyc
OR **Scan the Code**

Visit https://www.youtube.com/watch?v=d70iDxBtnas
OR **Scan the Code**

Visit https://www.youtube.com/watch?v=mUVX5rg1E0I
OR **Scan the Code**

Challengers*

1. Main deposit of biological carbon is
   (a) atmosphere (b) oceans
   (c) soil (d) All of these

2. What is the correct sequence of occurrence in nitrogen cycle?
   (a) Nitrification, ammonification, nitrogen-fixation, denitrification
   (b) Denitrification, nitrogen-fixation, denitrification, ammonification
   (c) Ammonification, denitrification, nitrogen-fixation, nitrification
   (d) Nitrogen-fixation, ammonification, nitrification, denitrification

3. Which of the following statements is incorrect?
   (a) Rainfall patterns are decided by prevailing wind patterns
   (b) Soil erosion is difficult to reverse in mountainous regions
   (c) Air and water are two biotic components of biosphere
   (d) Excessive amount of CO_2 in atmosphere leads to global warming

4. Soil structure is mainly decided by
   (a) humus (b) particle size
   (c) moisture content (d) exposure to sunlight

5. Choose the odd one out w.r.t. the steps involved in the water cycle operating in nature.
   (a) Evaporation (b) Transpiration
   (c) Precipitation (d) Photosynthesis

6. Which among the following is more likely to get heated maximum due to radiations coming from Sun?
   (a) An open green-field having number of tall trees
   (b) A car parked under sharp sunlight with windows closed
   (c) A barren-land with no greenary around
   (d) Still water bodies like lake, water tanks, etc.

7. Breakdown of $C_6H_{12}O_6$ into CO_2 and H_2O is accomplished by the process of
   (a) photosynthesis
   (b) precipitation
   (c) respiration
   (d) nitrification

8. Percolation of water into deeper layers of soil is aided by
   (a) volcanic eruptions
   (b) soil erosion
   (c) mining
   (d) vegetation cover

9. If there were no atmosphere around the Sun, the temperature of Earth will
   (a) increase
   (b) decrease
   (c) increase during day and decrease during night
   (d) be unaffected

10. Choose the correct statement.
    (a) Soil erosion can be prevented by raising forests
    (b) Oxygen is returned to atmosphere in only one major process, i.e. respiration
    (c) The process of nitrogen-fixing is done by bacteria in the presence of oxygen
    (d) The heating of air causes the water vapours in the air to condense in the form of tiny droplets

Answer Key

1.	(b)	2.	(d)	3.	(c)	4.	(a)	5.	(d)
6.	(b)	7.	(c)	8.	(d)	9.	(c)	10.	(a)

These questions may or may not be asked in the examination, have been given just for additional practice.

CHAPTER

13

Improvement in Food Resources

Chapter Checklist

- Need for Improvement in Food Resources in India
- Improvement in Crop Yield
  - Crop Variety Improvement
  - Crop Production Management
  - Cropping Patterns
  - Crop Protection Management
- Animal Husbandry

Food is an essential organic substance required for the growth and proper functioning of all living organisms. It provides nutrients like carbohydrates, proteins, fats, vitamins and minerals for the growth, development and maintenance of large population present on the Earth. To meet ever increasing demand of food, improvement in food resources is required.

Need for Improvement in Food Resources in India

India is a populous country. Its population is over one billion people and it is still growing. To feed this growing population, we will soon require more than a quarter of a billion tonnes of grain every year. This requirement can be fulfilled by farming on more land, but India is already intensively cultivated. So, we do not have scope of increasing the area of land under cultivation. It is therefore, necessary to increase our production efficiency for both crops and livestock.

To meet these requirements, the **green revolution** has contributed in increasing the food grain production. MS Swaminathan is regarded as the Father of Green Revolution in India. The **white revolution** has led to better availability of milk. Scientific researches have also contributed to these revolutions.

These revolutions mean that our natural resources are getting used more intensively. Due to this, there are more chances of causing damage to our natural resources, environment and disturbing its balance completely.

We should increase our food production without degrading our environment and disturbing its balance. This can be done by incorporating sustainable practices in agriculture and animal husbandry.

High yields from farm can be obtained easily by undertaking scientific management practices. It includes mixed farming, intercropping and integrated farming practices (e.g. combination of agriculture practices with livestock/ poultry/ fisheries/ bee-keeping).

Types of Crops

Crops are cultivated by human beings for their own benefit. The important types of crops are

(*i*) **Cereal crops** These plants are cultivated to provide **carbohydrate** daily energy requirements, e.g. wheat, rice, maize, millets and *Sorghum*.

(*ii*) **Pulses** These are seeds of crops that can be eaten to fulfil **protein** requirement, e.g. gram (chana), pea (matar), black gram (urad), green gram (moong), pigeon pea (arhar), lentil (masoor), etc.

(*iii*) **Oilseed crops** These plants provide necessary fats and oils, e.g. soybean, groundnut, sesame, castor, mustard, linseed and sunflower, etc.

(*iv*) **Vegetables, spices and fruits** These fulfil the requirement of a variety of vitamins and minerals with small quantities of proteins, carbohydrates and fats, e.g. cabbage, onion, pepper, etc.

(*v*) **Fodder crops** These plants are raised as food for the livestock, e.g. berseem, oats or sudan grass, etc.

Each crop requires different climatic conditions, temperature and photoperiods (related to the duration of sunlight) for their growth and completion of life cycle. Growth of plants and flowering depend on the duration of sunlight. Plants manufactures their food in sunlight by the process of photosynthesis.

Classification of Crops

Crops are classified on the basis of seasons are as follows

- **Kharif crops** These crops are grown in hot and rainy season (Kharif season) from the month of June to October, e.g. paddy, soybean, pigeon pea, maize, cotton, green gram, groundnut, black gram, etc.
- **Rabi crops** These crops are grown in dry and winter season (rabi season) from the month of November to April, e.g. wheat, gram, pea, mustard, linseed, barley, etc.

Improvement in Crop Yield

The practices involved in farming to increase crop production can be divided into three stages. The first is the choice of seeds for planting. The second is the nurturing of the crop plants. The third is the protection of the growing and harvested crops from loss.

Accordingly, the major groups of activities for crop yields can be classified as

(*i*) Crop variety improvement

(*ii*) Crop production management

(*iii*) Crop protection management

Note In India, there has been a four times increase in the production of food grains from 1952 to 2010 with only 25% increase in the cultivable land area. It was acheived by the improvement in crop yields.

Crop Variety Improvement

The main aim of this practice is to find a variety of crop, which can withstand different situations like high soil salinity, diverse climatic conditions and water availability (drought and flood).

In order to accept the new varieties of crops, it is necessary that the variety should produce high yields under different conditions found in different areas. For this, farmers should be provided with good quality seeds of a particular variety. The seeds should be of the same variety and germinate under the same conditions.

Varieties or strains of crops can be selected by breeding for various traits such as disease resistance, response to fertilisers, product quality and high yields. A new variety developed with all such features is highly acceptable.

There are two ways to incorporate desirable characteristics into crop varieties. These are as follows

(*i*) **Hybridisation** It is the crossing between genetically dissimilar plants to produce a new type (hybrid) or High Yielding Variety (HYV).

It is further of following types

(*a*) **Intervarietal** The cross is made between two plants belonging to different varieties of crops. It is the most common method used in plant breeding.

(*b*) **Interspecific** The cross is made between two plants belonging to different species of the same genus.

(*c*) **Intergeneric** The cross is made between plants belonging to different genera.

(*ii*) **Genetically modified crops** It involves the manipulation of crop plants for increasing their yield, improving quality, sustainability, etc. Genetic manipulation provides desired characteristics in the crop.

Factors of Crop Variety Improvement

Some of the factors for which crop variety improvement is done are as follows

(*i*) **Higher yield** Variety improvement is done to increase the productivity of the crop per acre.

(*ii*) **Improved quality** The definition of quality is different for different crops. For example, baking quality is important in wheat, protein quality in pulses, oil quality in oilseeds and preserving quality in fruits and vegetables.

(*iii*) **Biotic and abiotic resistance** Biotic stresses (diseases, insects and nematodes) and abiotic stresses (drought, salinity, water logging, heat, cold and frost) affect crop production to a great extent. Varieties resistant to such conditions are always preferred as they help to improve crop production.

(*iv*) **Change in maturity duration** Short duration or period between sowing and harvesting makes a crop more economical. It allows the farmers to grow multiple rounds of crops in a year. It also reduces the cost of crop production. Uniform maturity makes the harvesting process easy. It also reduces losses during the harvesting.

(*v*) **Wider adaptability** Developing varieties that can grow and adapt to different conditions help in stabilising crop production. Thus, a single variety can be grown in different regions with different climatic conditions.

(*vi*) **Desirable agronomic characteristics** These characteristics depict good growth and higher productivity in plants. Plants showing such characteristics are preferred more than others, e.g. tallness and profuse branching are preferred characters for fodder crops. Dwarfness is desired in cereals.

Check Point 01

1 Why India cannot increase the area of cultivable land?

2 How is green revolution different from white revolution?

3 State True or False for the following statement.

Rabi crops are grown in hot and rainy season from the month of June to October.

4 Fill in the blanks.

(*i*) The cross performed between two plants belonging to different species is known as .... cross.

(*ii*) The three factors for which crop variety is improved are .... , ... and ....

Crop Production Management

It involves the control of various aspects of crop production for the best yield. It requires skilful dealing with almost all aspects of crop production.

It is the money or financial condition, which allows farmers to take up different farming practices and agricultural technologies. There is a correlation between higher inputs and yields. The purchasing capacity of farmer for inputs decides cropping system and production practices. Thus, production practices can be grouped at three levels, i.e. 'no cost', 'low cost' and 'high cost' production practices.

Crop production management includes management of nutrients, irrigation and cropping patterns, which are as discussed below

1. Nutrient Management

Like animals, plants also require nutrients for their growth and development. Nutrients are the inorganic elements, which are supplied to plants by air, water and soil. There are sixteen essential nutrients for plants.

Plant Nutrients with their Source

Source	Nutrient
Air	Carbon and oxygen
Water	Hydrogen and oxygen
Soil	Supplies thirteen nutrients to plants

Essential plant nutrients are divided into two categories which are as follows:

(*i*) **Macronutrients** These are utilised by plants in large quantities, hence, known as macronutrients. These include six nutrients. These are nitrogen, phosphorus, potassium, calcium, magnesium and sulphur.

(*ii*) **Micronutrients** These are required by plants in smaller quantities. These include seven nutrients. These are iron, manganese, boron, zinc, copper, molybdenum and chlorine.

Deficiency of any of these nutrients affects physiological processes in plants including reproduction, growth and susceptibility to disease. Nutrients can be supplied to the soil in the form of manure and fertilisers. It helps to increase the yield of crops.

Manure

It is a natural fertiliser. It contains organic substances formed by the decomposition of animal excreta and plant wastes. It also supplies small quantities of nutrients to the soil.

Based on the type of biological material used, manure can be classified as:

(*i*) **Compost and vermicompost** The process in which farm waste materials like livestock excreta (cow dung, etc), vegetable waste, animal refuse, domestic waste, sewage waste, straw, eradicated weeds, etc., are decomposed in pits is known as **composting.**

- The compost is rich in organic matter and nutrients.
- Preparation of compost by using earthworms to hasten the process of decomposition of plant and animal refuse is called **vermicomposting.**

(*ii*) **Green manure** Some plants like sunhemp or guar are grown and mulched by ploughing into the soil before sowing of the crop seeds. These green plants turn into green manure. It helps in increasing **nitrogen** and **phosphorus** content in the soil. It also helps to improve hydration, aeration and crumb structure of the soil.

Advantages of manure are as follows

(*i*) It enriches soil with nutrients and organic matter (called **humus**).

(*ii*) It increases soil fertility and decreases the harmful effects of pesticides and insecticides on soil.

(*iii*) It helps in improving soil structure by increasing the water holding capacity in sandy soils. In clayey soils, large quantity of organic matter helps in drainage and in avoiding waterlogging.

(*iv*) By the use of biological waste material (manure), we can protect the environment from excessive use of fertilisers.

(*v*) It helps in the recycling of farm waste.

Fertilisers

These are commercially produced plant nutrients. These supply Nitrogen, Phosphorus and Potassium (NPK) to the soil.

Advantages of fertilisers are as follows

(*i*) These are easily available, easy to use and store.

(*ii*) These help in the higher yields of high-cost farming.

(*iii*) These are used to ensure good vegetative growth (leaves, branches and flowers) and give rise to healthy plants.

Disadvantages of fertilisers are as follows

(*i*) These need to be applied carefully in terms of proper dose, time and looking after the pre and post-application precautions for their complete utilisation. For example, excessive use of fertilisers can cause water pollution as they get washed away, when they are not absorbed fully by the plants due to excessive irrigation.

(*ii*) Continuous use of fertilisers can destroy soil fertility because the organic matter in the soil does not get replenished. Hence, microorganisms in the soil are harmed by the use of fertilisers.

(*iii*) They provide short-term benefits. Thus, for maintaining soil fertility, short-term benefits of using fertilisers and long-term benefits of using manure must be considered in order to aim optimum yields in crop production.

Organic Farming

It is an environment-friendly farming system.Features of organic farming are:

- Fertilisers, herbicides, pesticides, etc., are used in minimal quantities or not used at all.
- Organic manures, recycled farm-wastes (straw and livestock excreta), etc., are used maximally.
- Biofertilisers formed using bioagents such as culture of blue-green algae, legumes (*Rhizobium*), etc., are used.
- For storage purpose, biopesticides such as neem leaves or turmeric are used.
- The healthy cropping systems (mixed cropping, intercropping and crop rotation) are beneficial in insect, pest and weed control and in providing nutrients.

Check Point 02

1. Name the nutrients provided by air and water.
2. State True or False for the following statement.
   Micronutrients are required by plants in smaller quantities.
3. Why some plants like sunhemp or guar are grown and mulched by ploughing into the soil before sowing of the crop seeds?
4. Fill in the blank.
   The preparation of compost by using earthworms to hasten the process of decomposition of plant and animal refuse is called ....
5. Organic farming is an environment-friendly farming system. Mention one advantage supporting the above claim.

2. Irrigation

The process of supplying water to crop plants in fields by means of canals, reservoirs, wells, tubewells, etc., is called **irrigation.** Agricultural practices in India are mainly rain dependent. The success of a crop mainly depends on timely monsoons and sufficient rainfall during its growing season.

Ensuring that water will be supplied to the crops at right stages and in required amounts, the expected yields of any crop can be increased. Farmers depend on various natural resources like ponds, wells, canals, etc., for the irrigation of their farmlands.

Some commonly used irrigation systems depending on the type of water resources available for agricultural purposes are as follows:

I. Wells

These are constructed wherever groundwater is present for irrigation. These are of two types:

(*i*) **Dug wells** Water is collected from water bearing strata.

(*ii*) **Tube wells** Water can be drawn from deeper strata using pumps.

II. Canals

These are an elaborate and extensive used method of receiving water from reservoirs like dam or rivers. The main canal is further divided into other branches that have distributaries to irrigate fields.

III. River Lift Systems

This method is used in areas, where canal flow is insufficient or irregular due to insufficient reservoir release. Here, water is directly drawn from the rivers for supplementing irrigation in areas close to rivers.

IV. Tanks

These are small storage reservoirs. These catch and store the run-off of smaller catchment areas.

There are fresh initiatives for increasing water availability for agriculture by augmenting groundwater. These include

(*i*) **Rainwater harvesting** Rainwater is collected into ground by digging tunnels, etc. This water percolates into the soil, thus maintaining the water table.

(*ii*) **Watershed development** Small check-dams are built to increase groundwater level. The purpose of check-dams is to stop the rainwater from flowing away and also to reduce soil erosion.

Drought

It is the condition that occurs because of scarcity or irregular distribution of rains. It poses a threat to rain-fed farming areas, where farmers do not use irrigation for crops production and depend only on rain. Hence, poor monsoons in such areas cause crop failure. Light soils have less water retention capacity.

In areas with light soils, crops get adversely affected by drought conditions. Scientists have developed some crop varieties, which can tolerate drought conditions.

3. Cropping Patterns

It involves raising crops so as to obtain maximum benefit from the same piece of land. It reduces the risk of crop failure, diseases, etc. For this purpose, crops can be grown in different ways. Some of these are as follows

I. Mixed Cropping

In this practice, two or more crops are grown simultaneously on the same piece of land. For example, Wheat + Gram, Wheat + Mustard, Groundnut + Sunflower, etc. Some advantages of mixed cropping are:

(*i*) Improves soil fertility.

(*ii*) The risk of total crop failure due to uncertain monsoon is reduced.

(*iii*) Gives some insurance against failure of one of the crops.

II. Intercropping

In this, two or more crops are grown simultaneously on the same field in a definite pattern. A few rows of one crop alternate with a few rows of other crop. The crops are selected be on the basis of their nutrient requirements. Two crops must have different nutrient requirements from each other. For example Soybean + Maize, Finger millet (bajra) + Cowpea (lobia), etc.

Some advantages of intercropping are

(*i*) It ensures maximum utilisation of supplied nutrients and better returns.

(*ii*) It prevents the spread of pests and diseases to all the plants of one crop in a field.

(*iii*) Both crops give better returns in it.

III. Crop Rotation

In this type of practice, different crops are grown on a piece of land in a pre-planned succession. The crop combination depends upon the duration of crops.

One crop is grown on a field and after its harvest, a second crop is grown on the same field. This can also follow a third crop. The crop to be chosen after one harvest depends upon the availability of moisture and irrigation facilities.

Check Point 03

1 Give any one advantage of irrigation.
2 Define drought.
3 Fill in the blanks.
 (i) The type of irrigation system used where canal system is insufficient is ....
 (ii) Two examples of mixed cropping are .... and ....
5 What do you understand by crop rotation?
6 State True or False for the following statement.
If crop rotation is done properly, then two or three crops can be grown in a year with good harvests.

Crop Protection Management

In fields, crops have to be protected from weeds, insects, pests and diseases. Crop protection management includes methods to reduce such kinds of infestation. If not controlled in time, they can cause heavy damage to the crops in a way that most of the crops are lost.

Various threats to crops include:

1. Weeds

These are the unwanted plants in the cultivated field. These compete with the crops for food, space and light.

Weeds take up nutrients and reduce the growth of the crop. Therefore, they should be removed during early stages of crop growth in order to obtain good harvest.

Examples of weeds are:

Xanthium (gokhroo), *Parthenium* (gajar ghas), *Cyperinus rotundus* (motha), *Amaranthus, Chenopodium,* wild oat, etc. Following are the methods to control weeds:

(*i*) **Mechanical methods** Uprooting, weeding with harrow or hand, ploughing, burning and flooding.

(*ii*) **Preventive methods** Proper seed bed preparation, timely sowing of crops, intercropping and crop rotation.

2. Insect Pests

They affect the health of crop and reduce its yield.

Insect pests attack the plants in following ways:

(*i*) They cut the root, stem and leaf, e.g. locusts.

(*ii*) They suck the cell sap from various parts of the plant, e.g. aphids.

(*iii*) They bore into stems and fruits, e.g. shoot borer larvae.

Pests can be controlled in many ways such as:

(*i*) Use of resistant varieties.

(*ii*) **Summer ploughing** In this method, fields are ploughed deep during summers to destroy weeds and pests.

3. Crop Diseases

Diseases in plants are caused by pathogens such as bacteria, fungi and viruses. These pathogens are present in and transmitted through the soil, water and air.

Crop diseases can be controlled by the use of pesticides like herbicides, insecticides and fungicides. They are sprayed on crop plants in limited amounts. Excessive use of these chemicals can be harmful to many species of plants and animals. It also causes environmental pollution.

Storage of Grains

During storage of grains, high losses can occur in agricultural produce. Factors responsible for such losses can be categorised as:

(*i*) **Biotic factors** These include rodents, fungi, insects, mites and bacteria.

(*ii*) **Abiotic factors** These include inappropriate moisture and temperature conditions in the place of storage.

Effects of these factors on grains are as follows:

(*a*) Degradation in quality.

(*b*) Poor germinative capacity.

(*c*) Discolouration of the produce.

(*d*) Loss in weight.

All these lead to poor marketability and heavy economic losses. Some of the preventive and control measures during storage are:

(*i*) The proper storage of grains can be done by proper treatment and systematic management of warehouses.

(*ii*) Strict cleaning of the produce before storage.

(*iii*) Proper drying of the produce in sunlight and then in shade.

(*iv*) Fumigation should be done to kill pests. In fumigation, the insect pests are exposed to fumes of chemicals.

Check Point 04

1 Fill in the blank.
The two factors that can cause heavy damage to crops are ...... and ....
2 State True or False for the following statement.
Xanthium and *Amaranthus* are two examples of weeds.
3 List any two pest control measures.
4 What factors are responsible for the loses during storage of grains?
5 For proper storage of grains what measures can be adopted?

Animal Husbandry

It is the scientific management of animal livestock. It can be defined as the science of rearing, feeding, breeding, disease control and utilisation of animals. Animal based farming includes cattle, goat, sheep, poultry and fish farming.

Need of Animal Husbandry

(*i*) It is required to meet the increasing demands of animal based goods like milk, meat, eggs, leather, etc., according to the size of the population and living standards of the people.

(*ii*) It sets guidelines for proper management and systematic approach to animal rearing.

1. Cattle Farming

In India, cattle husbandry is done for two purposes; milk and draught labour for agricultural work (such as tilling, irrigation and carting).

Cattle in India belong to two different species:

(*i*) *Bos indicus* (cows) (*ii*) *Bos bubalis* (buffaloes).

On the basis of the work done by cattle, they can be divided into two categories:

(*i*) **Milch animals** These are milk producing females or dairy animals.

(*ii*) **Draught animals** These are used to do labour work in farms.

The breeds of cattles are as follows

(*i*) **Indigenous or local breeds** They are selected because of their high resistance to disease, e.g. Redsindhi and Sahiwal.

(*ii*) **Exotic or foreign breeds** They are selected because of their long lactation period, e.g. Jersey and Brown Swiss.

These two breeds can be cross-bred to get both the desirable qualities in animals.

Lactation Period

It is the period of milk production after the birth of a calf. Milk production largely depends on the duration of the lactation period. We can increase the milk production by increasing the lactation period.

Farm Management for Cattle

Efficient farm management is essential for humane farming, better health of animals and production of clean milk.

Various measures for farm management are as follows

(*i*) Proper cleaning and shelter facilities are required for cattles.

(*ii*) Regular brushing of animals should be done to remove dirt and loose hair.

(*iii*) The cattle should be sheltered in well-ventilated roofed sheds in order to protect them from rain, heat and cold.

(*iv*) The floor of the cattle shed should be sloping so as to keep it dry and facilitate cleaning.

Food Requirements of Cattle

Food is required for dairy cattles for following two purposes

(*i*) **For maintenance** Food is required to support the animal to live a healthy life.

(*ii*) **For producing milk** The type of food is required during the lactation period.

Animal feed includes

(*a*) **Roughage** This is largely fibrous and contain low nutrients, e.g. green fodder, silage, hay and legumes.

(*b*) **Concentrates** These are low in fibre. They contain relatively high levels of proteins and other nutrients, e.g. cereals like gram and bajra.

Apart from the above mentioned products, some feed additives containing micronutrients promote the health and milk output of dairy animals. It should also be noted that cattle should be given balanced rations with all the nutrients in proportionate amounts.

Diseases in Cattle

Like other animals, cattle also suffer from a number of diseases. These besides causing death, also reduce milk production. The parasites of cattle can be of following types:

(*i*) **External parasites** They live on the skin and cause skin diseases, e.g. lice, mites, etc.

(*ii*) **Internal parasites** They include worms that affect stomach and intestine and flukes that damage the liver.

Cattle also get infectious diseases from various bacteria and virus. As preventive measure, vaccinations are given to farm animals against many viral and bacterial diseases.

2. Poultry Farming

It involves rearing of domestic fowl for the production of eggs and chicken meat. Therefore, improved poultry breeds are developed and farmed to produce **layers** for eggs and **broilers** for meat.

For the improvement of poultry breeds, cross-breeding is done successfully between Indian or indigenous (e.g. Aseel) and foreign or exotic (e.g. Leghorn) breeds. These cross-breeding programmes focus to develop desirable traits like:

(*i*) Quality and quantity (number) of chicks.

(*ii*) Dwarf broiler parent for commercial chick production.

(*iii*) Summer adaptation capacity/tolerance to high temperature.

(*iv*) Low maintenance requirements.

(*v*) Reduction in the size of egg-laying bird with the ability to utilise more fibrous and cheaper diets. This diet is formulated using agricultural byproducts.

Egg and Broiler Production

Broiler chickens are fed with vitamin-rich supplementary feed for good growth rate and better feed efficiency.

Care is taken to avoid mortality and to maintain feathering and carcass quality. They are produced as broilers and sent to market for meat purposes.

Broilers and egg layers have different housing, nutritional and environmental requirements.

The diet of broilers is rich in protein with adequate fat. In the poultry feed, the level of vitamin-A and K is kept high.

The following practices are required for the maintenance of shelter for poultry birds:

(*i*) Proper cleaning and sanitation of the shelter.

(*ii*) Maintenance of temperature and hygiene in the shelter.

(*iii*) Proper ventilation.

(*iv*) Prevention and control of diseases and pests.

Poultry Diseases and Their Prevention

Poultry fowl suffer from various diseases caused by virus, bacteria, fungi and parasites. They also suffer from nutritional deficiency diseases.

These diseases can be prevented by:

(*i*) Providing nutritional diet to poultry birds.

(*ii*) Proper cleaning and sanitation of shelter.

(*iii*) Vaccination of poultry birds can prevent the occurrence of infectious diseases. Loss of poultry during an outbreak of disease can also be reduced by proper vaccination.

(*iv*) Spraying of disinfectants at regular intervals in the shelter.

Check Point 05

1. What purpose does animal husbandry fulfil?
2. Why are indigenous breeds of cattle selected for cattle farming?
3. Name one external and one internal disease caused due to parasites in cattles.
4. Fill in the blank.
   .... is an Indian and a foreign breed of poultry.
5. How poultry birds are prevented from diseases? Suggest any two.
6. State True or False for the following statement.
   Poultry breeds are developed and formed to produce broilers for eggs.

3. Fish Production

Fish is a cheap source of animal protein for humans. Production of fish includes both finned true fish as well as shellfish like prawns and molluscs.

The two ways of obtaining fish are:

(*i*) **Capture fishing** It is a method of obtaining fish from natural resources. It is undertaken in both inland and marine waters.

(*ii*) **Culture fishery** It is the method of obtaining fish from fish farming or **pisciculture.** It is undertaken mostly inland and near seahores.

Both the methods can be used for fishing in marine and freshwater ecosystems.

Marine Fisheries

Marine fishery resources in India include 7500 km of coastline and the deep seas beyond it. Marine fishes are caught using many kinds of fishing nets from fishing boats.

Popular marine fishes are pomfret, mackerel, tuna, sardines and Bombay duck.

Marine fishes of high economic value that are formed in seawater are:

(*i*) **Finned fishes** Mullets, bhetki and pearl spots.

(*ii*) **Shell fishes** Prawns, mussels, oysters as well as seaweeds. Oysters are also cultivated for the pearls they produce.

Yield of fishes can be increased by locating large schools of fish in the open sea with the use of satellites and echosounders.

Note Mariculture As marine fish stocks get further depleted, the demand for more fish can only be met by culture fisheries. This practice is called mariculture. The marine fishes are cultivated in coastal waters of India on commercial basis. It includes mullets, bhetki, eel, milk fish, etc.

Inland Fisheries

- It includes fishery in freshwater and brackish water. Freshwater resources include canals, ponds, reservoirs and rivers. Brackish water resources are those where seawater and freshwater mix together, e.g. estuaries and lagoons. These are also important fish reservoirs.
- The yield of capture fishing is not high in such inland water bodies. Thus, most fish production from these resources is done through aquaculture. Sometimes fish culture is done in combination with rice crops. In this, paddy crop gets ample of water and fishes get food.

Composite Fish Culture (Polyculture)

Fish production by cultivating a single species (monoculture) gives a low yield and demands higher cost. In composite fish culture, a combination of 5 or 6 fish species is cultivated in a single pond having different food habits. Due to this, they do not compete for food with each other. Thus, it helps in more intensive fish farming.

Advantages of composite fish culture are as follows:

(*i*) Both local and imported fish species are used.

(*ii*) Due to different food habits all the food in pond is consumed by the fishes.

(*iii*) The fish yield from pond is high as their is no competition for food. For example, *catla* is surface feeder, rohu feeds in the middle-zone of the pond, mrigal and common carps are bottom feeders, grass carp feeds on weeds in the pond.

Disadvantages of composite fish culture are as follows:

- Many of the fishes breed only during monsoon. Thus, one of the major problem of fish farming is the lack of availability of good quality seed.
- To overcome this problem, fishes are breed in ponds using hormonal stimulation. It ensures the supply of pure fish seed in desired quantities.

Nutritional Values of Animal Products

Animal Products	Percent (%) Nutrients					
	Fat	Protein	Sugar	Minerals	Water	Vitamins
Milk (Cow)	3.60	4.00	4.50	0.70	87.20	B_1, B_2, C_{12}, D, E
Egg	12.00	13.00	*	1.00	74.00	B_2, D
Meat	3.60	21.10	*	1.10	74.20	B_2, B_{12}
Fish	2.50	19.00	*	1.30	77.20	Niacin, D, A

4. Bee-Keeping

Honey is being widely used for various purposes. Thus, its production has become an agricultural enterprise these days. It is scientifically known as **apiculture.** It is the method of rearing, care and management of honeybees for obtaining bee products like honey, bee wax (used in medicinal preprations) etc. For commercial honey production, apiaries or bee farms are established.

The advantages of bee-keeping are as follows

(*i*) Requires low investment.

(*ii*) Provides varied products like honey (for eating or making other products), wax (used in medicinal and cosmetic preparations), bee venom, etc.

(*iii*) Acts as an additional source of income for farmers.

(*iv*) Helps in increasing crop yield by better pollination.

Varieties of Bees used for Commercial Honey Production

Scientific Name	Common Name
Apis cerana indica	Indian bee
Apis dorsata	Rock bee
Apis florea	Little bee
Apis mellifera	Italian bee

Out of the above mentioned species, *A. mellifera* has been brought in the country in order to increase the yield of honey. This is the main variety used for the commercial honey production.

Advantages of Italian Bees

- They have high honey collection capacity.
- They sting somewhat less.
- They can stay in a given beehive for long periods and breed well.

Honey

It is the major product that is obtained from apiculture.

- **Value of honey** It depends on pasturage or flowers available to bees for nectar and pollen collection.
- **Taste of honey** It depends on adequate quantity of pasturage and kind of flowers available.

Check Point 06

1 Fill in the blank.
The two most popular marine fishes are ..... and ....

2 As a part of fishery industry, why oysters are also cultivated?

3 Why composite fish culture is a preferred method of fish culture? Give one reason.

4 What is the term used for bee farms?

5 Give the scientific name of the following:
(*i*) Little bee (*ii*) Rock bee

6 State True or False for the following statement.
Apis dorsata has been brought in the country in order to increase the yield of honey.

NCERT FOLDER

Intext Questions

1 What do we get from cereals, pulses, fruits and vegetables? **Pg 204**

Sol. Cereals (wheat, rice, maize, etc) are the sources of carbohydrates, which provide energy. Pulses (pea, gram and soybean, etc.) are the source of proteins. Vegetables and fruits provide us vitamins and minerals in addition to small amount of carbohydrates, proteins and fats.

2 How do biotic and abiotic factors affect crop production? **Pg 205**

Sol. Factors which affect crop production are as follows:

(*i*) Biotic factors that cause loss of grains are rodents, pests, insects, etc.

(*ii*) Abiotic factors include drought, salinity, water logging, heat, cold and frost.

Both biotic and abiotic factors cause stresses on crop and affect crop production in the following ways:

(*a*) Poor seed germination (*b*) Infestation of insects
(*c*) Low yield (*d*) Discolouration of leaves

3 What are the desirable agronomic characteristics for crop improvements? **Pg 205**

Sol. Desirable agronomic characteristics in crop plants help to give higher productivity. For example:

(*i*) Tallness and profused branching are desirable characters for fodder crops.

(*ii*) Dwarfness is desired in cereals, because tall crop plants cannot resist strong winds.

4 What are macronutrients and why are they called macronutrients? **Pg 206**

Sol. Macronutrients are essential nutrients required for growth, functioning and survival of plants. They are so called because they are required in large amounts by plants. They are six in number, i.e.

(*i*) nitrogen (*ii*) phosphorus (*iii*) potassium
(*iv*) calcium (*v*) magnesium (*vi*) sulphur

5 How do plants get nutrients? **Pg 206**

Sol. Mostly nutrients to the plants are supplied by soil, which are absorbed by roots of plants. Some nutrients are provided by air and water too (carbon, hydrogen and oxygen).

6 Compare the use of manure and fertilisers in maintaining soil fertility. **Pg 207**

Sol. Effects of the use of manure in maintaining soil fertility are as follows:

(*i*) Manures provide a lot of organic matter (humus) to the soil. Humus helps to restore water retention capacity of sandy soils and drainage in clayey soils.

(*ii*) These are the sources of soil organisms like soil friendly bacteria.

Effects of fertilisers on soil quality are:

(*i*) Use of excess fertilisers leads to dryness of soil and the rate of soil erosion increases.

(*ii*) Due to continuous use of fertilisers, the organic matter decreases. It reduces porosity of the soil and the plant roots do not get sufficient oxygen.

7 Which of the following conditions will give the most benefits? Why? **Pg 208**

(*i*) Farmers use high quality seeds, do not adopt irrigation or use fertilisers.

(*ii*) Farmers use ordinary seeds, adopt irrigation and use fertilisers.

(*iii*) Farmers use quality seeds, adopt irrigation, use fertilisers and use crop protection measures.

Sol. Condition (*iii*) will give most benefits because

(*a*) good quality seeds will give good yield.

(*b*) irrigation methods will overcome drought and flood situation.

(*c*) fertilisers fulfil the nutrient requirement of the soil, providing high yield.

(*d*) crop protection method protects the plants from weeds, pests and pathogens.

Thus, farmers will get maximum benefit of their input in the form of good seeds and agronomic approaches.

8 Why should preventive measures and biological control methods be preferred for protecting crops? **Pg 209**

Sol. Preventive measures and biological control methods should be preferred for protecting crops because :

(*i*) They are simple and target specific.

(*ii*) They are economical as they involve less financial investment.

(*iii*) They minimise pollution and are ecologically safe.

(*iv*) They minimise the adverse effects on soil fertility.

(*v*) They are harmless to other living organisms.

9 What factors may be responsible for losses of grain during storage? **Pg 209**

Sol. The major factors responsible for losses of grain during storage are:

(*i*) **Biotic factors** They include attack from insects, rodents, fungi, mites and bacteria.

(*ii*) **Abiotic factors** They include inappropriate moisture and temperature in the place of storage.

10 Which method is commonly used for improving cattle breeds and why? **Pg 210**

Sol. Cross breeding is a method commonly used for improving cattle breeds. It is the process in which indigenous varieties of cattle are crossed with exotic breeds to get a cross-breed which is of desired qualities.

11 Discuss the implications of the following statement: "It is interesting to note that poultry is India's most efficient converter of low fibre foodstuff (which is unfit for human consumption) into highly nutritious animal protein food". **Pg 211**

Sol. Poultry birds are efficient converters of agricultural byproducts and fibrous wastes into high quality meat. As, the waste which is unfit for human consumption can be formulated into cheaper diets for poultry birds. Also, they help in providing eggs, feather and nutrient rich manure. So, the mentioned statement is implicit for poultry birds.

12 What management practices are common in dairy and poultry farming? **Pg 211**

Sol. The common management practices include:

(*i*) Keeping the shelter well-designed, ventilated and hygienic.

(*ii*) The animals and birds are given healthy feed with balanced nutrition.

(*iii*) Both animals and birds must be protected from various diseases. Regular check-up should be done.

13 What are the differences between broilers and layers and in their management? **Pg 211**

Sol. A broiler is a poultry bird specially kept for obtaining meat. Layer is a poultry bird that gives eggs. There is a difference in their housing, nutrition and environmental requirements.

The daily food requirement of broilers is somewhat different from those of layers. Broilers require protein rich food with adequate fat and high amount of vitamin-A and K. Layers require feed with vitamins, minerals and micronutrients and enough space and proper lighting.

14 How are fish obtained? **Pg 213**

Sol. Fishes are obtained either by capturing them from their natural resources (Capture fishing) or by culturing them by fish farming (Culture fishery).

15 What are the advantages of composite fish culture? **Pg 213**

Sol. Advantages of composite fish culture are as follows:

(*i*) Fishes selected for this culture differ in their feeding habits and thus, avoid competition for food between them.

(*ii*) All these species together use all the food in the pond without competing with each other.

(*iii*) This increases the total fish yield from the pond.

16 What are the desirable characters of bee varieties suitable for honey production? **Pg 213**

Sol. The desirable characters of bee for honey production are as follows:

(*i*) The bee should have good honey production capacity.

(*ii*) They should be stingless and breed very well.

(*iii*) They should be able to stay in a beehive for long periods.

17 What is pasturage and how is it related to honey production? **Pg 213**

Sol. Pasturage includes the flowering plants and trees found around an apiary. From them, nectar and pollen are collected by bees to form honey.

Pasturage plays an important role in determining the quantity and quality of honey.

(*i*) Quality of honey depends upon the pasturage.

(*ii*) Kinds of flowers determine the taste of honey.

Exercises (On Pages 214 and 215)

1 Explain any one method of crop production, which ensures high yield.

Sol. Intercropping is a method of crop production, which ensures high yield. During this, two or more crops having different nutrient requirements are grown simultaneously on the same field in a definite pattern.

2 Why are manures and fertilisers used in fields?

Sol. Manures and fertilisers are used to improve soil fertility and increase crop productivity. They replenish deficient nutrients in the soil.

3 What are the advantages of intercropping and crop rotation?

Sol. Advantages of intercropping are:

(*i*) Crops selected in this method differ in their nutrient requirements. This ensures maximum utilisation of the supplied nutrients.

(*ii*) It prevents pests and diseases from spreading to all the plants belonging to one crop in a field.

Advantages of crop rotation are:

(*i*) It makes the soil fertile and increases the yield from a single field.

(*ii*) It reduces the use of fertilisers. For example, use of nitrogenous fertilisers is not required as leguminous plants that are grown in crop rotation help in biological nitrogen-fixation.

(*iii*) It helps in the replenishment of soil fertility.

4 What is genetic manipulation? How is it useful in agricultural practices?

Sol. Genetic manipulation is the incorporation of desirable characters into an organism by hybridisation, mutation, DNA recombination, etc.

By genetic manipulation, improved varieties of seeds can be obtained having desirable characters like high yield, disease resistance and better adaptability.

5 How do storage grain losses occur?

Sol. Refer to NCERT Intext Q. 9 on Pg 328.

6 How do good animal husbandry practices benefit farmers?

Sol. Animal husbandry involves the scientific management of the farm animals. Its benefits to farmers are:

(*i*) Improvement of the breeds having good desirable characters.

(ii) Better yield in quantity and quality.
(iii) Reduction of input cost.

7 What are the benefits of cattle farming?

Sol. Main benefits of cattle farming are as follows:

(i) We get milk and various milk-based products from cattle.
(ii) Cattle can be employed for labour work in agricultural fields for tilling, irrigation and carting.

8 For increasing production, what is common in poultry, fisheries and bee-keeping?

Sol. Cross-breeding is the most important practice to increase the production and that too of desired characteristics in poultry, fisheries and bee-keeping.

9 How do you differentiate between capture fishing, mariculture and aquaculture?

Sol. Differences between capture fishing, mariculture and aquaculture are as follows:

Capture Fishing	Mariculture	Aquaculture
It is the process of obtaining fish from natural resources like ponds, canals, rivers, etc.	It is a practice of culture of marine fish varieties in the coastal waters.	It is the production of fish from freshwater resources like canals and brackish water resources like estuaries and lagoons.
Fishes can be located easily and then caught using fishing net.	Satellites and echo-sounders are used for locating large fish schools and then caught using many kinds of fishing nets.	Fishes can be located easily and are caught using simple fishing nets.

SUMMARY

- Improvement in food resources is essential to obtain higher yield to fulfil the need of food for continuously increasing population.
- The **green revolution** has contributed in increasing the food grain production, while the **white revolution** has led to better availability of milk.
- High yields from farm can be obtained by undertaking scientific management practices like **mixed cropping, intercropping** and **integrated farming practices.**
- Improvement in crop yield are practices involved in farming to increase crop production. In includes **crop variety improvement, crop production management** and **crop protection management.**
- Crop variety improvement is a practice to find an improved variety of crop, which can withstand different situations like soil quality, different weather conditions, water availability (drought and flood) and can ultimately give good yield.
- **Hybridisation** and **genetic manipulations** are the two ways to incorporate desirable characteristics into crop varieties.
- Factors for which crop variety improvement is done are higher yield, improved quality, resistance against biotic and abiotic factors, change in maturity duration, wider adaptability and desirable agronomic characteristics.
- Crop production management involves the control of various aspects of crop production for the best yield. It includes nutrient management, irrigation and cropping patterns.
- **Nutrient management** includes adopting various methods to increase the nutrient level in the soil. This is done by adding manures and fertilisers in the field.
- **Irrigation** is the process of supplying water to crop plants in fields by means of canals, reservoirs, wells and tube wells.
- **Cropping patterns** involve raising crops so as to obtain maximum benefit from the same piece of land, reducing the risk of crop failure, disease, etc. It can be done by mixed cropping, intercropping and crop rotation.
- **Crop protection management** involves the protection of crops from weeds, insects, pests and disease causing organisms. It includes methods to reduce such kinds of infestation. If not controlled on time, they can cause heavy damage to crops. Grains are affected by biotic and abiotic factors. Thus, proper measures should be adopted for their storage, e.g. fumigation.
- **Animal husbandry** is the scientific management of livestock. It is animal based farming of cattle, goat, sheep, poultry and fish.
- **Cattle farming** is done for milk and drought labour by cattles.
- **Poultry farming** is the method of rearing fowls for the production of meat and egg. It aims to improve poultry breeds.
- **Fish production** refers to capturing and culturing of fishes as a supplement of animal protein for humans. It is a cheap source of animal protein for our food.
- **Beekeeping** is scientifically known as apiculture. It is rearing, care and management of honeybees for obtaining honey, wax, etc. For commercial honey production, apiaries or bee farms are established.

For Mind Map
Visit https://goo.gl/MWD5eD OR **Scan the Code** 

Exam Practice

Objective Type Questions

Multiple Choice Questions

1 The revolution associated with increased food grain production is

(a) white revolution
(b) golden revolution
(c) green revolution
(d) blue revolution

Sol. (c) Green revolution has lead to increase in stocks of food grains, improvement in economic conditions of farmers and increased employment opportunities.

2 Two or more crops are grown simultaneously on same field in a definite pattern is practiced in

(a) mixed cropping (b) intercropping
(c) crop rotation (d) organic farming

Sol. (b) In intercropping, crops selected on the basis of nutritional requirements are grown simultaneously in a definite pattern.

3 Weeds affect the crop plants by

(a) killing of plants in field before they grow
(b) dominating the plants to grow
(c) competing for various resources of crops (plants) causing low availability of nutrients
(d) All of the above **NCERT Exemplar**

Sol. (d) Weeds are unwanted plants, which compete with main crop plants for nutrients and reduce the growth of crops. The seeds of weed germinate easily, their seedlings grow faster, they flower early, their seed production occurs earlier and produce many seeds.

4 Preventive and control measures adopted for the storage of grains include

(a) strict cleaning (b) proper disjoining
(c) fumigation (d) All of these

NCERT Exemplar

Sol. (d) Godown, warehouses and stores should be properly cleaned, dried and repaired. Pathways (alleys) should be provided between the stacks of grain-filled bags, for the periodic inspection, for spraying or for fumigation.

5 Which of the following pairs is not correctly matched?

(a) Calcium and sulphur
(b) Boron and zinc
(c) Phosphorus and molybdenum
(d) Chlorine and copper

Sol. (c) Pair in option (c) is not correctly matched as phosphorus is a macronutrient, whereas molybdenum is a micronutrient. Rest pairs are correct. Calcium and sulphur are macronutrients. Boron, zinc, chlorine and copper are micronutrients.

6 Find out the wrong statement from the following.

(a) White revolution is meant for increase in milk production.
(b) Monoculture is fish production by cultivation of single species
(c) Both (a) and (b)
(d) None of the above

Sol. (d) All the statements are correct. Operation Flood (a project of NDDB) was the world's biggest dairy development programme that made India a milk-sufficient nation. The fish production by cultivation of single species is known as monoculture.

7 The management and production of fishes for commercial use is called

(a) pisciculture (b) apiculture
(c) mariculture (d) monoculture

Sol. (a) Pisciculture is the rearing, management and production of fishes for commercial utilisation.

8 Which of the following are Indian cattle?

(a) *Bos indicus* (b) *Bos bubalis*
(c) *Bos vulgaris* (d) Both (a) and (b)

Sol. (d) *Bos indicus* or zebu or humped cattle and *Bos bubalis* (wild water buffalo) are Indian breeds.

Bos domestica is currently found in Africa, Asia, Eastern and Western Europe, parts of North America and South America.

9 Which one of the following fishes is a surface feeder?

(a) Rohus (b) Mrigals
(c) Common carps (d) Catlas

NCERT Exemplar

Sol. (d) Surface feeder fishes have a back that is perfectly straight, this allows for their upturned mouths to easily get right on the surface and scoop up the food. Catlas possess all these characters, thus is a surface feeder. (1)

Rohus feed in the middle zone of the pond, and mrigals and common carps are bottom feeders.

10 Which type of honeybees are useful for apiary industries in India ?

(a) *Apis florae* (b) *Apis mellifera*
(c) *Apis dorsata* (d) *Apis indica*

Sol. (b) Apiary is the place where bees are cultured and breed to get commercial products. *Apis mellifera* is the best suited in India for apiculture industries. It can be easily domesticated because of gentle nature and have high honey production capacity.

Fill in the Blanks

11 Altogether ...... nutrients are essential to plants.

Sol. sixteen

12 The flowering in plants is affected by ....

Sol. photoperiod

13 Maize, paddy, black gram are the examples of .... crops.

Sol. Kharif

14 At times fish culture is done in combination with .... crops to achieve better yield of both.

Sol. Rice

15 .... helps in increasing the agricultural output from planted crops by enhancing the frequency.

Sol. apiaries

True and False

16 Crops like sun-hemp and guar are commonly grown for green manuring.

Sol. True

17 Fertilisers also provide humus to the soil.

Sol. False; Manure enriches the soil with nutrients and humus.

18 In mixed cropping, usually a cereal crop is grown with a leguminous crop.

Sol. True

19 Jersey Brown Swiss is selected for long lactation period.

Sol. True

20 The housing nutritional and environmental requirements of broilers and those of egg layers are same.

Sol. False; The housing, nutritional and environment requirements of broilers are somewhat different from those of egg layers.

Match the Columns

21 Match the following columns.

	Column A		Column B
1.	Magnesium	A.	Weed
2.	Pathogens	B.	Hybrid
3.	Cross breeding	C.	Macronutrient
4.	Compost	D.	Disease causing organisms
5.	Cyperinus	E.	Animal refuse

Sol. $1 \rightarrow C, 2 \rightarrow D, 3 \rightarrow B, 4 \rightarrow E, 5 \rightarrow A$.

22 Match the following columns.

	Column A		Column B
1.	*Bos indicus*	A.	Marine fishes
2.	*Bos bubalis*	B.	Cow
3.	Leghorn	C.	Buffalo
4.	*Aseel*	D.	Exotic breed
5.	Mullets	E.	Indigenous breed

Sol. $1 \rightarrow B, 2 \rightarrow C, 3 \rightarrow D, 4 \rightarrow E, 5 \rightarrow A$.

Assertion-Reason

Direction (Q.Nos. 23-27) *In each of the following questions, a statement of Assertion is given by the corresponding statement of Reason. Of the statements, mark the correct answer as*

(a) If both Assertion and Reason are true and Reason is the correct explanation of Assertion
(b) If both Assertion and Reason are true, but Reason is not the correct explanation of Assertion
(c) If Assertion is true, but Reason is false
(d) If Assertion is false, but Reason is true

23 **Assertion** Inspite of large population of cattle, milk production is meagre in India.

Reason Poor quality feed is given to cattle.

Sol. (*a*) Milk production is meagre in our country despite a large population of cattle. This is because of poor quality of feed given to them. Also, cattle suffer from many diseases due to lack of proper hygiene in housing. Both Assertion and Reason are true and Reason is the correct explanation of Assertion.

24 **Assertion** Legume crops do not require nitrogenous fertilisers.

Reason Nitrogen-fixing bacterium is present in leguminous roots.

Sol. (a) Nitrogen-fixing bacterium, i.e. *Rhizobium* is present in roots of leguminous plant that fixes atmospheric nitrogen into accessible form (ammonia or nitrates). Therefore, legumes do not require additional application of nitrogenous fertilisers.

Both Assertion and Reason are true and Reason is the correct explanation of Assertion.

25 **Assertion** Cultivation practices and crop yields are related to environmental conditions.

Reason Climatic conditions such as temperature, photoperiod influence a plant's life cycle.

Sol. (a) Different crops and practices employed for their cultivation varies with the climatic conditions, e.g. some crops grow in dry and winter season (Rabi crops) like wheat, gram, etc.

Both Assertion and Reason are true and Reason is the correct explanation of Assertion.

26 **Assertion** Pesticides are poisonous for living organisms and cause environmental pollution.

Reason Organic farming is environment-friendly and does not rely much on agricultural chemicals.

Sol. (b) Pesticides are toxic for target pests other organisms. They also create pollution of natural resources. An alternative practice is organic farming, an environment-friendly practice. It uses fertilisers, pesticides, etc., in minimal amount.

Both Assertion and Reason are true, but Reason is not the correct explanation of Assertion.

27 **Assertion** Manures contain large quantities of organic matter and small quantities of nutrients.

Reason The excessive manure leads to water pollution.

Sol. (c) Manures are bulky source of organic matter which supply nutrients in small quantities to crops. In clayey soils the large quantities of organic matter help in drainage and in avoiding waterlogging. Assertion is true, but Reason is false.

Case Based Questions

Directions (Q. nos. 28-31) *Answer the questions on the basis of your understanding of the following passage and related studied concepts:*

A variety of minerals are required by plants. Macronutrients are required in large quantities, whilst micronutrients are needed in only very small amounts. Harvesting interrupts the normal recycling of nutrients and contributes to nutrient losses. These nutrients can be replaced by the addition of fertilisers.

Some plants form symbiotic associations that aid in their nutrition. Legumes in particular (e.g. peas, beans, clover), are well known for their association with nitrogen-fixing bacteria that share their rich source of fixed nitrogen with their host plants. Legumes have been extensively used to maintain pasture productivity for grazing livestock, as well as in crop rotation of rejuvenate nitrogen-depleted soils.

28 Why production of organic fertilisers is preferred over production of inorganic fertilisers?

Sol. The production of inorganic fertilisers consumes considerable amounts of fossil fuels (e.g. urea may be made from natural gas). In contrast, the use of organic fertilisers reduces waste and has the added benefit of improving soil structure.

29 Based on the text given above, write one or two lines about soil fertility in your own words.

Sol. Soil fertility refers to the condition of the soil relative to the amount and availability to plants of elements required for growth.

30 What will happen, if soils is left unreplenished when nutrients are removed from the land?

Sol. Crop harvesting removes nutrients from the land. If left unreplenished, the soil becomes nutrient deficient and is unable to support the crops planted in it.

31 How can continuous use of fertilisers in an area destroy soil fertility?

Sol. The continuous use of fertilisers in an area can destroy soil fertility because the organic matter in the soil is not replenished and microorganisms in the soil are harmed by the fertilisers used.

Directions (Q. nos. 32-35) *Answer the questions on the basis of your understanding of the following table and related studied concepts:*

Nutritional Values of Animal Products

Animal Products	Fat (%)	Protein (%)	Sugar (%)
Milk (Cow)	3.60	4.00	4.50
Egg	12.00	13.00	Trace amount
Meat	3.60	21.10	Trace amount
Fish	2.50	19.00	Trace amount

32 Why is milk considered better than other food products from animals?

Sol. Milk in comparison to other food products from animals such as egg and meat contain all the major food constituents such as carbohydrates (sugars), proteins, fat, minerals (mainly phosphorus and calcium) and water.

33 Among the given four animal products, which one is best for obtaining quick energy and good protein content ?

Sol. Egg is best in terms of both fat and protein content so its the best option for the individual with quick and large energy requirements.

34 Cattle feed includes roughage and concentrates which are .... and .... , respectively.

(a) largely fibre; high in protein level
(b) largely proteins; high in fibre
(c) low in fibre; low in nutrients
(d) largely proteins ; low in nutrients

Sol. (*a*) Cattle feed includes roughage and concentrates which are largely fibre and high in protein level, respectively.

35 The daily food requirement or the ration for broilers is

(a) carbohydrate rich with adequate minerals
(b) protein rich with adequate fat
(c) fat rich with adequate carbohydrates
(d) Carbohydrate rich with adequate fat

Sol. (*b*) The daily requirement or the ration for broilers is protein rich with adequate fat. The level of vitamin-A and vitamin-K is kept high in the poultry feeds.

Very Short Answer Type Questions

36 Identify two crops from the following, which provide us carbohydrates for energy requirement.

Black gram, wheat, lentil and rice.

Sol. Wheat and rice are cereals which provide us carbohydrates.

37 Name two protein containing Rabi crops.

Sol. Gram and peas are two protein containing Rabi crops.

38 Name the type of nutrient that we get from mustard seeds and linseed.

Sol. Mustard seeds and linseed provide us fats.

39 State one importance of photoperiod in agriculture.

Sol. Photoperiod is important for the growth and flowering of plants.

40 Improved varieties can be produced in both animals and plants. How?

Sol. Hybridisation and genetic modification are two processes used for the production of new and improved species in both animals and plants.

41 What is the advantage of selecting seeds of crops with wider adaptability for agriculture?

Sol. It helps in stabilising the crop production under different environmental conditions.

42 What are exotic breeds in terms of cattle?

Sol. Exotic breeds are not native to that place, e.g. Brown Swiss and Jersey Swiss are the exotic breeds of cow in India.

43 List two desirable traits for fodder crops.

Sol. (*i*) Tall plants
(*ii*) Profuse branching

44 Which type of food is required by dairy animals?

Sol. Dairy animals require two types of food
(*i*) Roughage – Largely fibrous
(*ii*) Concentrates – Low in fibre and contain relatively high level of proteins and other nutrients

45 White leghorn is an exotic breed of an animal. Name the animal.

Sol. It is popular exotic breed of hen that produces long, white eggs and requires less amount of feed.

46 Name the two vitamins, which are added in the poultry feed.

Sol. Vitamin-A and vitamin-K which are added in the poultry feed.

47 What is mariculture?

Sol. Cultivation of marine fishes like mullets, pearl spots, etc., in coastal waters of India on commercial scale is known as mariculture.

48 Why fish culture is done with a combination of rice?

Sol. Fish culture is done with a combination of rice, so that fishes get ample food in the paddy field and the latter can get water.

49 Give two advantages of apiculture.

Sol. Two advantages of apiculture are:
(*i*) It produces honey and wax.
(*ii*) It is a low investment additional income generating activity for farmers.

50 Give one example of each, local variety and foreign variety of bee.

Sol. **Local variety** *Apis cerana indica*
Foreign variety *Apis mellifera*

Short Answer (SA) Type Questions

1 Group the following and tabulate them as energy yielding, protein yielding, oil yielding and fodder crops.

Wheat, rice, berseem, maize, gram, oat, pigeon gram, sudan grass, lentil, soybean, groundnut, castor and mustard.

NCERT Exemplar

Sol. (*i*) **Energy yielding crops** Wheat, rice, maize and oats.

(*ii*) **Protein yielding crops** Gram, lentil and pigeon gram.

(*iii*) **Oil yielding crops** Groundnut, castor, soybean and mustard.

(*iv*) **Fodder crops** Berseem and sudan grass.

2 (*i*) Name the month during which Kharif crop is grown.

(*ii*) List any two factors for which crop variety improvement is done.

Sol. (*i*) Kharif crop is grown during the months from June to October.

(*ii*) Two factors for which crop variety improvement is done are:

(*a*) **Higher yield** To increase productivity of crop per acre.

(*b*) **Improved quality** The definition of quality is different for different crops, e.g. baking quality is important in wheat, protein quality in pulses, etc.

3 Why has improving crop yields become more important these days?

List the major group of activities for improving crop yields. Which one of these activities is the most important and why?

Sol. Due to continuously growing population, requirement of food is also increasing every year to feed this population.

Extra farming land is not available in our country to increase production. Therefore, it is necessary to increase crop yield to meet growing demands for food.

The major activities for improving crop yields include:

(*i*) crop variety improvement

(*ii*) crop production management

(*iii*) crop protection management

Out of these three activities, crop variety improvement is very important. It helps to attain the crops of good yield, improved quality and resistant to various stresses.

4 Discuss the role of hybridisation in crop improvement. **NCERT Exemplar**

Sol. Hybridisation is a method of crossing between genetically dissimilar plants. It is of three types:

(*i*) **Intervarietal cross** between two different varieties.

(*ii*) **Interspecific cross** between two different species of same genus.

(*iii*) **Intergeneric cross** between two different genera.

In plant breeding, intervarietal hybridisation is mostly used to improve the crop variety.

Improved varieties are high yielding and resistant to diseases and pests. They have better quality and various other desirable traits. Thus, they play an important role in crop improvement.

5 In agriculture practices, higher input gives higher yield. Discuss how?

NCERT Exemplar

Sol. In agriculture, higher yield can be obtained by using higher yielding varieties, modern technologies, improved farm practices with latest agricultural machines. All these require high cost and knowledge of new techniques.

Finance thus, plays a very important role as the cost of input decides the outcome of cropping. Therefore, higher input gives higher yield in agricultural practices.

6 What is manure? State two advantages of using manure. How does green manure differ from ordinary manure?

Sol. Manure is an organic substance obtained through the decomposition of plant wastes like straw and animal wastes such as cow dung. The decomposition is brought about by microbes.

Advantages of using manure are:

(*i*) It enriches soil with nutrients without any pollution.

(*ii*) It improves soil texture.

(*iii*) It increases water holding capacity of soil by adding organic matter to it.

Green manure is different as it is obtained by growing green plants such as sun-hemp and guar, which are then mulched by ploughing them into the soil. Later on, it forms green manure.

7 Differentiate between compost and vermicompost. **NCERT Exemplar**

Sol. Differences between compost and vermicompost are as follows:

Compost	*Vermicompost*
It is prepared from all types of organic wastes like sewage, animal refuse, farm waste, etc.	It is prepared from domestic waste, vegetable waste, etc.
It takes 3-6 months to prepare.	It takes 1-2 months to prepare.
Organic remains are decomposed by microbes.	Organic remains are pulverised by earthworms.

8 Define the following:
(*i*) Vermicompost
(*ii*) Green manure
(*iii*) Biofertilisers. **NCERT Exemplar**

Sol. (*i*) **Vermicompost** is a manure rich in pulverised organic matter and nutrients. The compost is prepared by using earthworms to hasten the process of decomposition of plants and animals refuse.

(*ii*) **Green manure** is prepared by growing green plants in the field itself. It helps in enriching the soil in nitrogen and phosphorus content, e.g. sunhemp is grown in fields, mulched by ploughing and allowed to decompose in field for the preparation of green manure.

(*iii*) **Biofertilisers** are living organisms used as fertilisers to supply nutrients to crop plants, e.g. nitrogen-fixing blue-green algae and nitrogen-fixing bacteria, which fix nitrogen in the soil.

9 Give some advantages of mixed cropping.

Sol. Advantages of mixed cropping are as follows:
(*i*) Chances of pest infestation is greatly reduced.
(*ii*) By growing two or more crops simultaneously, soil fertility is improved.
(*iii*) The risk of total crop failure due to uncertain monsoon is reduced.

10 If there is low rainfall in a village throughout the year, what measures will you suggest to the farmers for better cropping? **NCERT Exemplar**

Sol. Suggestions to farmers for better cropping in low rainfall area are:
(*i*) Enrich soil with humus, as it increases water holding capacity of soil.
(*ii*) Reduce tilling.
(*iii*) Use of drought resistant and early maturing varieties of crops.
(*iv*) Better irrigation facilities and methods to conserve water.

11 Observe the following figure and answer the questions that follows.

A – First type of crop

B – Second type of crop

Box represents the agricultural field in which crops are grown.

A	A	A	A	A	A
A	A	A	A	A	A
B	B	B	B	B	B
B	B	B	B	B	B
A	A	A	A	A	A
A	A	A	A	A	A

(*i*) Which type of cropping pattern is seen in picture?
(*ii*) Discuss this cropping pattern.
(*iii*) What should be kept in mind regarding the types of crops, while following this cropping method?

Sol. (*i*) Intercropping is seen in the given picture.
(*ii*) In this cropping pattern, two or more crops are grown simultaneously in a definite pattern on a field.
(*iii*) The nutritional requirements of the selected plants should be different. It ensures maximum utilisation of the nutrients supplied.

12 The food available is decreasing, day by day, both in quantity and in quality. What steps can be employed to improve this condition, when the population is increasing drastically?

Sol. The following steps can be taken to improve the condition of food for present as well as for future generations:
(*i*) By selecting good variety of crops having desirable agronomic traits. Such varieties can be developed using hybridisation technique and by genetic modification of crops.
(*ii*) The field should be kept fertile and nutrient rich by using manure, etc.
(*iii*) By using high yielding variety of seeds for high yield per acre.
(*iv*) By using a beneficial cropping pattern such as mixed cropping, crop rotation, etc.
(*v*) By improving irrigation facilities and bringing more agricultural land under irrigation.
(*vi*) By protecting crops from weeds, diseases, etc.

13 Discuss various methods of weed control. **NCERT Exemplar**

Sol. The various methods of weed control are:

(*i*) **Mechanical method** Uprooting, weeding, ploughing, burying and flooding.

(*ii*) **Cultural method** Proper seed bed preparation, timely sowing of crops, intercropping and crop rotation.

(*iii*) **Chemical method** Spraying of chemicals like herbicides or weedicides.

(*iv*) **Biological control** Use of insects or some organisms, which consume and destroy the weed plants, e.g. prickly-pear cactus (*Opuntia*) is controlled by insects and aquatic weeds are controlled by grass carp.

14 Give one word for the following

(i) Farming without use of chemicals as fertilisers, herbicides and pesticides is known as ....

(ii) Growing of wheat and groundnut on the same field is called ....

(iii) Planting soybean and maize in alternate rows in the same field is called ....

(iv) Growing different crops on a piece of land in pre-planned succession is known as ....

(v) *Xanthium* and *Parthenium* are commonly known as ....

(vi) Causal organism of any disease is called .... **NCERT Exemplar**

Sol. (*i*) organic farming

(*ii*) mixed cropping

(*iii*) intercropping

(*iv*) crop rotation

(*v*) weeds

(*vi*) pathogen

15 Discuss, why pesticides should be used in very accurate concentration and in very appropriate manner. **NCERT Exemplar**

Sol. Pesticides should be used in accurate concentration as they are very harmful to the environment. They are non-biodegradable and can accumulate in organisms (biomagnifiaction).

The environmental impact of pesticides consists of effects on non-target species. Over 98% of sprayed insecticides and 95% of herbicides reach a destination other than their target species, because they are sprayed or spread across entire agricultural fields.

Run-off can carry pesticides into aquatic bodies.

Wind can carry them to other fields, grazing areas, human settlements and undeveloped areas, potentially affecting other species. Other problems emerge from poor production, transport and storage practices.

16 Explain the factors that are to be considered before deciding the nature of feed for cattle.

Sol. Following factors should be considered before deciding the nature of feed for cattle:

(*i*) Food requirements of dairy animals are of two types:

(*a*) **Maintenance requirement** Food required to support the animal to live a healthy life.

(*b*) **Milk producing requirement** Food type required during lactation period.

(*ii*) Animal feed includes

(*a*) **Roughage** Largely fibrous.

(*b*) **Concentrates** High levels of proteins and other nutrients.

(*iii*) The food requirements of cattle are different for every age and type of work they do.

(*iv*) Along with the ration, some feed additives can also be given to add micronutrients. It helps to promote the health and milk output of dairy animals.

17 (*i*) What is poultry farming? How does it help in solving food and nutrition problems?

(*ii*) Name two desirable traits for variety improvement in poultry farming.

Sol. (*i*) Poultry farming is the method to rear domestic fowl for the production of eggs and meat. It helps in solving food and nutrition problem by providing a balanced diet for the human population. It also converts agricultural byproducts into high quality meat.

(*ii*) (a) Quality and quantity (number) of chicks.

(b) Dwarf broiler parents for commercial chick production.

18 Suggest some preventive measures for the diseases of poultry birds. **NCERT Exemplar**

Sol. Poultry fowl suffers from various diseases. These are caused by different agents found in nature and can affect the growth, quality and quantity of chicks.

Fowls also suffer from nutritional deficiencies. These diseases can be prevented by:

(*i*) Providing nutritional diet to poultry birds.

(*ii*) Cleaning and sanitation of shelter.

(*iii*) Appropriate vaccination of poultry birds.

(*iv*) Spraying disinfectant at regular intervals in the shelter.

19 Cross-breeding programme is successfully done in poultry farming for variety improvement. Enlist some desirable traits for which cross-breeding is done in poultry birds.

Sol. The cross-breeding programmes between Indian breeds like Aseel and foreign breeds like Leghorn are carried out for variety improvement. It focusses on developing new varieties for the following desirable traits:

(*i*) **Number and quality of chicks** The cross-bred variety should produce good quality chicks in large quantity.

(*ii*) **Dwarf broiler parent** They help in commercial chick production.

(*iii*) **Summer adaptation capacity** The variety should be adaptable to survive in high temperature and different climatic conditions.

(*iv*) **Low maintenance requirement** It should decrease the investment charges.

(*v*) Reduction in the size of the egg-laying bird with the ability to utilise more fibrous and cheaper diets that is formulated using agricultural byproducts.

20 Differentiate between layers and broilers. What type of food should be given to broilers?

Sol. Differences between layers and broilers are as follows:

Layers	*Broilers*
These are egg-laying birds, managed for the purpose of getting eggs.	These are maintained for getting meat.
These start producing eggs at the age of 20 weeks. So, they are kept for layer periods that depends upon laying period (about 500 days).	These are raised upto 6-7 weeks in poultry farms and then sent to market for meat production.
They require enough space and adequate lighting.	They require conditions to grow fast and low mortality.
They require restricted and calculated feed with vitamins, minerals and micronutrients.	Their daily food requirement is rich in protein and vitamin-A and K. The fat content also should be adequate.

21 Write a short note on marine fisheries.

Sol. India's marine fishery resources area include 7500 km long coastline and deep seas beyond it. Marine fishes are caught using many kinds of fishing nets from fishing boats. The yields are increased by locating large schools of fish in open sea by using satellites, etc.

Popular marine fish varieties are pomfret, mackerel, tuna, sardines and Bombay duck.

High economic value marine fishes are:

(*i*) **Finned fishes** Mullets, bhetki and pearl spots.

(*ii*) **Shellfishes** Prawns, mussels and oysters.

Oysters are also cultivated for the pearls they produce.

22 Differentiate between

(*i*) Inland fishery and Marine Fishery

(*ii*) Apiculture and Aquaculture.

Sol. (*i*) Difference between inland and marine fisheries are as follows:

Inland Fishery	*Marine Fishery*
It consists of fishing in freshwater and brackish water.	It consists of fishing in sea water along the coastline of deep sea beyond it.
Most of the fish production is through aquaculture.	Most of the fish production is through a practice called mariculture.

(*ii*) Difference between apiculture and aquaculture is as follows:

Apiculture	*Aquaculture*
It is the rearing and maintenance of honeybees for obtaining honey, wax and other substances.	It is the production of high economic value aquatic plants and animals under controlled situations by proper utilisation of available water.

23 What is honey? What does the quality of honey depend upon?

Sol. Honey is a dense sweet liquid. It contains 20-40% sugar, small amount of minerals and vitamins. Apart from that, it also contains certain enzymes and pollen. It has medicinal value specially in problems related to digestion and liver. The quality of honey depends upon the pasturage or flowers available to the bees for nectar and pollen collection.

24 What are the advantages of bee-keeping?

Sol. Following are the main advantages of bee-keeping:

(*i*) Along with getting honey on a commercial scale, other products like wax, royal jelly and bee venom are also obtained from bee-keeping.

(*ii*) Bee-keeping requires low investments due to which farmers, along with agriculture also prefer bee-keeping to generate additional income.

(*iii*) It helps in cross-pollination. Pollens are transferred from one flower to another by bees, while collecting nectar.

25 An Italian bee variety *Apis mellifera* has been introduced in India for honey production. Write about its merit over the other varieties. **NCERT Exemplar**

Sol. Merits of Italian bee variety *Apis mellifera* are:

(*i*) It is stingless.

(*ii*) It stays in beehives for long period of time and breeds very well.

(*iii*) It has high honey collection capacity.

26 Differentiate between the following:

(*i*) Capture fishery and culture fishery.

(*ii*) Bee-keeping and poultry farming.

NCERT Exemplar

Sol. (*i*) Differences between capture and culture fisheries are as follows:

Capture Fishery	Culture Fishery
It is a way of obtaining fish from natural resources.	It is a way of obtaining fish from fish farming.
There is no seeding and raising of fish.	The fish is reared.
It is undertaken in both inland and marine waters.	It is undertaken mostly inland and near seashore.

(*ii*) Differences between bee-keeping and poultry farming are as follows:

Bee-Keeping	Poultry Farming
It is a practice of rearing and management of honeybee.	It is the practice of raising domestic fowl.
Bees obtain food (nectar) from flower.	Poultry birds are provided food by the rearers.
It provides honey and wax, etc.	It provides eggs and meat (flesh).

27 Give an example of exotic and indigenous breeds of the following:

(*i*) Poultry

(*ii*) Milk cattle

(*iii*) Bees

Sol.

Animal	Exotic Breed	Indigenous Breed
Poultry	White Leghorn	Aseel
Milk cattle	Jersey	Red Sindhi
Bees	*Apis mellifera*	*Apis cerana indica*

Long Answer (LA) Type Questions

1 How can crop variety improvement methods help farmers facing repeated crop failure? Describe three factors for which they could do crop improvement. Which is the most common method of obtaining improved varieties of crops? Explain briefly.

Sol. Crop variety improvement basically focuses on developing a crop variety that can provide a good yield, resistant to diseases and pests, not responsive to fertilisers and is adaptable. Thus, it can lead to better crop produce. Factors for which crop improvement can be done are:

(*i*) **Higher yield** Every farmer involved in agriculture needs to get a good yield to be economically stable. Crops need to be improved, so that they provide good productivity per acre.

(*ii*) **Improved quality** Both quantity and quality are important for crop improvement. For example, baking quality in wheat, protein quality in pulses and oil quality in oilseeds should be given consideration, while selecting an improved variety.

(*iii*) **Wider adaptability** Varieties having wider adaptability can stabilise their growth in different environmental conditions.

There are two ways of getting a variety with desirable characteristics:

(*i*) **Genetic manipulation** A gene is introduced in plant that provides the desirable characters.

(*ii*) **Hybridisation** The most common method of obtaining improved variety of crops is hybridisation. Hybridisation is the cross between genetically dissimilar plants.

It can be of three types:

(*i*) **Intervarietal** Cross between two different varieties.

(*ii*) **Interspecific** Cross between two different species of the same genus.

(*iii*) **Intergeneric** Cross between two different genera.

2 (*i*) The black and the white dots in the given picture are an indication of two different types of cropping patterns. Identify the cropping patterns.

(*ii*) Mention one advantage of each cropping pattern.

(*iii*) How are the two cropping patterns different from each other?

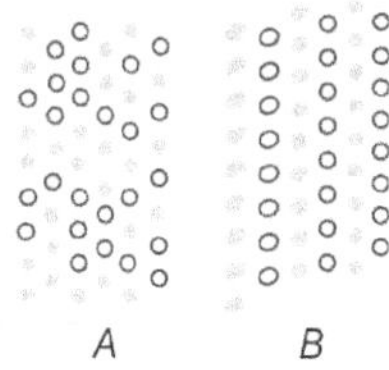

Sol. (*i*) *A*–Mixed cropping
B–Intercropping

(*ii*) *A*–Such cropping pattern gives insurance against failure of one of the crops.
B–It ensures maximum utilisation of nutrients supplied.

(*iii*) Intercropping differs from mixed cropping in several ways, which are as follows:

Intercropping	*Mixed Cropping*
It is a practice of growing two or more crops simultaneously in definite pattern.	It is a practice of growing two or more crops simultaneously on the same piece of land.
Its main target is to increase the productivity per unit area.	Its main target is to minimise the risk of total crop failure.
Seeds of two crops are not mixed before sowing.	Seeds of two crops are mixed before sowing.
Both crops are easily threshed and harvested separately.	Harvesting and threshing of both crops separately is not possible.

3 Match the following columns and write the complete sentences giving one additional information about the sentence.

	Column I		Column II
A.	Black gram	1.	are grown from November-April.
B.	Rabi crops	2.	is a farming system with minimal or no use of chemical and maximum input of organic manure.
C.	Nitrogen, phosphorus, potassium, calcium, magnesium and sulphur	3.	include insecticides, herbicides and fungicides.
D.	Organic farming	4.	is a protein yielding pulse.
E.	Pesticides	5.	are all macronutrients.

Sol. A–4, B–1, C–5, D–2, E–3

Complete sentences are as follows:

(*i*) **Black gram** is a protein yielding pulse. These are the crops that fulfil the protein requirement of our body.

(*ii*) **Rabi crops** are grown from November-April. They are grown in winter season, e.g. wheat, gram, etc.

(*iii*) **Nitrogen, phosphorus, potassium, calcium, magnesium and sulphur** are all macronutrients. They are required in large quantities by the plants.

(*iv*) **Organic farming** is a farming system with minimal or no use of chemicals and maximum input of organic manure. This farming method involves the use of biofertilisers and healthy cropping system.

(*v*) **Pesticides** include insecticides, herbicides and fungicides. These chemicals are sprayed on crop plants to protect them from insect pests.

4 Mention the modern initiatives undertaken in India to supply water to the fields.

Sol. Poor monsoons cause crop failure. The crops should be given water at appropriate stages of life to increase the expected yield of crops. Under such circumstances, different kinds of irrigation systems are developed. It ensures the supply of water to the agricultural lands.

Depending on the type of water resources, the irrigation systems are:

(*i*) **Wells** They are of two types:

(*a*) **Dug wells** In this type of well, water is collected from water bearing strata.

(*b*) **Tube wells** In this type of well, water is lifted by pumps from deeper strata for irrigation.

(*ii*) **Canals** In this system, canal receives water from one or more reservoirs or from rivers. The main branch is divided into branch canals with many distributaries to irrigate fields.

(*iii*) **River lift system** It is most common in those areas, where canal flow is irregular or insufficient due to less number of reservoirs release. In lift system, water is directly drawn from rivers for irrigation in areas near to rivers.

(*iv*) **Tanks** These are small storage reservoirs intercepting and storing the run-off of smaller catchment areas.

5 Figure shows the two crop fields [plots *A* and *B*] that have been treated by manures and chemical fertilisers, respectively, keeping other environmental factors same.

NCERT Exemplar

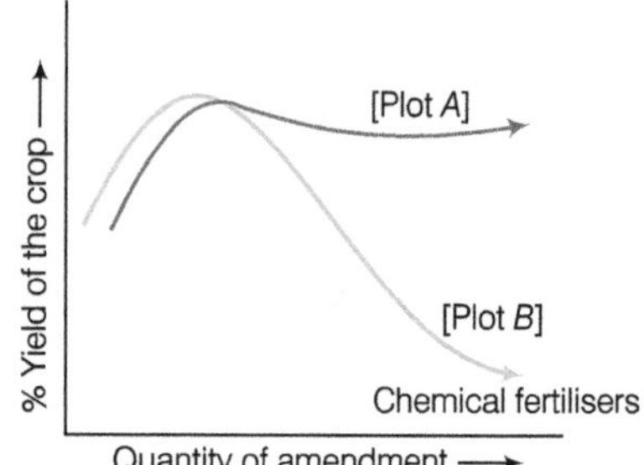

Observe the graph and answer the following questions.

(i) Why does plot B show sudden increase and then gradual decrease in yield?

(ii) Why is the highest peak in plot A graph slightly delayed?

(iii) What is the reason for the different patterns of the two graphs?

Sol. (i) With the addition of chemical fertilisers, there is a sudden increase in yield due to the release of nutrients like N, P, K, etc., in high quantity. The gradual decline in the graph may be due to continuous use of high quantity of chemicals. It has killed microbes useful for replenishing the organic matter in the soil. This results in reduced the soil fertility.

(ii) Manures supply small quantities of nutrients to the soil slowly. It takes time to mix with the soil. It increases water holding capacity and aeration of soil, thereby increasing soil fertility continuously.

(iii) The difference in the two graphs is because of the fact that use of manure is beneficial for longer duration in cropping. The yield gets high when the quantity of manure increases.

In case of plot B, the chemical fertilisers may cause various problems, when used continuously for long time. Loss of microbial activity reduces decomposition of organic matter. As a result, soil fertility is lost that affects the yield.

6 (i) Which factors are responsible for causing loss of storage grains? State some preventive measures for storage of foodgrains.

(ii) What do you mean by animal husbandry? State two advantages of it.

Sol. (i) Factors responsible for the loss during storage of grains are:

(a) **Biotic factors** as insects, rodents, birds, mites and bacteria, etc.

(b) **Abiotic factors** as moisture content, temperature etc.

Preventive measures for storage of foodgrains include:

(i) Drying (ii) Maintenance of hygiene

(iii) Fumigation

(iv) Improved storage structure.

(ii) **Animal husbandry** It is a science of rearing, feeding, caring, breeding and utilisation of animals.

Advantages of animal husbandry are:

(a) It is beneficial for farmers as increased yield brings more income and raises their living standard.

(b) It helps us to undertake proper management of domestic animals.

7 Name two types of animal feed and write their functions. **NCERT Exemplar**

Sol. The dairy cattle is given a balanced ration. It contains all nutrients in proportionate amounts. A ration is the amount of food, which is given to the animal during a twenty-four hour period.

The animal feed includes two types of substances:

(i) **Roughage** It largely contains fibres such as green fodder, silage, hay (straw of cereals) and legumes, (e.g. berseem, cowpea and agathi).

(ii) **Concentrates** The concentrates used in feed of cattle and buffaloes are a mixture of substances. These are rich in one or more nutrients. For e.g., cotton seeds, oil seeds, grains of maize, oats, barley, jowar, bajra and gram. Their byproducts such as wheat bran, rice bran (polish), gram husk, oilseeds, cakes and molasses are also used.

1. Green fodder and dry grasses (roughage) = 15-20 kg
2. Grain mixture (concentrates) = 4-5 kg
3. Water = 30-35 litres.

Besides above mentioned nutritious food material, dairy animals require certain additive feeds. They promote the growth of the animals. They contain antibiotics, minerals and hormones. They facilitate good yield of milk and meat and protect them from diseases.

8 What do you understand by composite fish culture? Describe in detail with its advantages and disadvantages. **NCERT Exemplar**

Sol. Composite fish culture system is adopted for intensive fishing.

Characteristics of composite fish culture These are as follows:

(i) Both local as well as imported fish species can be used in such systems.

(ii) Combination of five or six fish species is used in a single fish pond.

(iii) These species have different feeding habits.

(iv) The species are selected, so that they do not compete for food among them because of their different food habits. Some examples are:

Catla Surface feeders.

Rohu Feeds in the middle zone of the pond.

Mrigal and Common carps Bottom feeders.

Grass carps Weed feeders.

Advantages of composite fish culture are as follow:

(i) All the food available in the pond is utilised.

(ii) There is no competition for food.

(iii) There is an increase in the fish yield from the pond.

One of the disadvantages composite fish. Culture is the lack of availability of good quality fish seeds.

9. (*i*) What is the term used for the scientific management of livestock?

(*ii*) What do you mean by the term apiary and pasturage?

(*iii*) Mention any two desirable traits, for which cross-breeding programmes between Indian and foreign breeds are undertaking in poultry farming.

Sol. (*i*) **Animal husbandry** is the term used for scientific management of livestock.

(*ii*) **Apiary** (Bee farm), which is established for the commercial production of honey, etc., is known as apiary.

Pasturage It is the flora (flowers) present in the surroundings of apiary that provide nectar to bees. Quantity and quality of honey directly depends upon the pasturage.

(*iii*) Two desirable traits for which cross-breeding between Indian and foreign breeds are undertaken in poultry farming are:

(*a*) Number and quality of chicks.

(*b*) Tolerance to high temperature.

10 You are living in an area with abundant greenery and pasturage. A farmer living near your home is not satisfied with the income he gets from his agricultural land. Which additional income generating activity will you suggest him in such a scenario?

Sol. Apiculture is the best suited activity in such a scenario that I would suggest to him. It is a low investment, additional income generating activity.

It is the method of rearing, care and management of honeybees for obtaining honey, wax and other substances.

Utilities of apiculture are:

(*i*) Honey is used for the consumption and manufacturing of other useful products.

(*ii*) Bees wax is used in various medicinal preparations.

(*iii*) Bees help in cross-pollination of crops as bee transfers pollen grain from one flower to another, while collecting nectar.

I will also suggest him to use following varieties of bees in apiculture:

(*i*) ***Apis cerana indica*** Commonly known as Indian bee.

(*ii*) ***Apis dorsata*** Commonly known as rock bee.

(*iii*) ***Apis florea*** Commonly known as little bee.

(*iv*) ***Apis mellifera*** This is the Italian bee that has been brought in to increase the yield of honey.

The advantages of Italian bees are:

(*i*) They have good honey collection capacity.

(*ii*) They are stingless.

(*iii*) They stay in a given beehive for long periods and breed very well.

(*iv*) They are very good for commercial production.

He should also take care of the pasturage around the apiary as the value or quality of honey depends on it.

CHAPTER EXERCISE

Multiple Type Questions

1 Which one is an oil yielding plant among the following? **NCERT Exemplar**

(a) Lentil

(b) Sunflower

(c) Cauliflower

(d) *Hibiscus*

2 To solve the food problem of the country, which among the following is necessary?

(a) Increased production and storage of food grains

(b) Easy access of people to the food grain

(c) People should have money to purchase the grains

(d) All of the above

3 Which one of the following is a breed of cattle?

(a) Jersey

(b) Scampi

(c) Ghagus

(d) Kadaknath

Fill in the Blanks

4 Berseem is the example of an important .... crop.

5 A marine fish is .... and freshwater fist is ....

6 .... is the Indian bee species used in apiculture.

True or False

7 Dwarfness and profuse branching are desirable characters for fodder crops.

8 Neem leaves and turmeric are specifically used as bio fertillsers.

9 Weeds help in providing nutrients to the nearby crops.

Matching the Columns

10 Match the following.

	Column A		Column B
A.	*Parthenium*	(i)	Liver
B.	Flukes	(ii)	Eggs
C.	Layers	(iii)	the rock bee
D.	*A. dorsata*	(iv)	the little bee
E.	A. florae	(v)	Gajar ghas

Assertion–Reason

Direction (Q.Nos. 11-13) *In each of the following questions, a statement of Assertion is given by the corresponding statement of Reason. Of the statements, mark the correct answer as*

(a) If both Assertion and Reason are true and Reason is the correct explanation of Assertion

(b) If both Assertion and Reason are true, but Reason is not the correct explanation of Assertion

(c) If Assertion is true, but Reason is false

(d) If Assertion is false, but Reason is true

11 **Assertion** Dr V. Kurien is known as the Father of White Revolution.

Reason White Revolution is associated with milk production.

12 **Assertion** In intercropping, two or more crops are grown together on same land.

Reason It ensures maximum utilisation of nutrients supplied.

13 **Assertion** *A. mellifera*, an exotic bee species is commercially employed in apiaries.

Reason It produces high yield of honey.

Answers

1. (b) 2. (d) 3. (a)
4. fodder 5. pomfret, catla 6. *Apis indica*
7. True 8. false 9. False
10. A→(v), B→(i), C→(ii), D→(iv), E→(iii)
11. (b) 12. (a) 13. (a)

Case Based Question

Direction (Q. Nos. 14-17) *Answer the questions on the basis of your understanding of the following passage and related studied concepts:*

Cattle farming is one of the most common practice of animal industry in India. Cattle animals includes cow, bull and buffaloes, etc. There are 26 breeds of cattle and 7 breeds of buffaloes in India. They differ in colour, general body build, horns, geographical distribution, etc. The best cattle breeds occur in the drier regions of the country. On the basis of work or their utility cattles are classified into following groups milch draught and general purpose breeds. The exotic or foreign breeds are often mated to obtain new and different offsprings.

14 In India for what purposes cattle forming is done on such a large scale ?

15 Name any two indiginous and exotic breeds of cattle.

16 What is the idea behind mating an indigenous breed of cattle with an exotic breed in cattle forming?

17 In your family is planning to open up a cattle farm, what measures would you advise them to adapt for a successful and financially benefitting practice?

Very Short Answer Type Questions

18 Write the factors on which irrigation requirements depend.

19 Which crop is generally grown between cultivation of two cereal crops to restore the fertility of soil?

20 Why are Jersey and Brown Swiss popular cattle breeds?

21 What is common in poultry, fisheries and bee-keeping with respect to the increase in production of animals?

Short Answer (SA) Type Questions

22 What were the reasons behind the occurrence of the green revolution and the white revolutions

23 Explain the need of irrigation in India.

24 Write the factors for selecting crops for mixed cropping, as well as intercropping.

25 In last few decades, the production of food from animal sources has increased. Justify this statement.

26 What is bee-keeping? Which variety of bee is commonly used for commercial honey production?

27 How can poultry and fish farming help in solving the food and nutrition problem?

Long Answer (LA) Type Questions

28 Differentiate between pathogens and pests. How does an insect-pest attack the plants?

29 Mention any two desirable agronomic characters for crop improvement. Explain how farmers get desired characters incorporated into the new varieties produced. List two conditions necessary for the new varieties to be accepted.

30 A farmer is advised to use manure instead of fertiliser in his fields. List any two advantages that the farmer will get if he accepts this advice. How is the use of manure particularly useful for clayey and sandy soil?

31 There is a water reservoir (river) near a village. Due to insufficient rain, farmers are worried about their crops. Suggest and explain the irrigation practice that can be adopted to supply water to the entire agricultural land in the village.

32 Explain composite fish culture system with examples. State the major problem associated with this system. Can fish culture be done in any type of combination? If yes, explain.

Challengers*

1 Which one of the following is a micronutrient for the crop plants?

(a) Calcium (b) Iron
(c) Magnesium (d) Potassium

2 Pusa Lerma is an improved variety of

(a) rice (b) wheat
(c) maize (d) soyabean

3 Growing two or more crops in definite row pattern is

(a) mixed farming (b) mixed cropping
(c) inter-cropping (d) crop rotation

4 'Organic farming' does not include

(a) green manures
(b) chemical fertilisers
(c) crop rotation
(d) compose and farmyard manures

5 The common biofertilisers used in organic farming are

(a) *Marfosa*
(b) *Pyrethrum*
(c) green manure
(d) nitrogen-fixing bacteria and cyanobacteria

6 Maximum milk yielding breed of buffalo is

(a) Nagpuri (b) Surti
(c) Mehsana (d) Murrah

7 The principal cereal crop of India is

(a) wheat (b) rice
(c) maize (d) *Sorghum*

8 Fill in the blanks by choosing correct option from the following

I. *Puccinia* causes .... disease in wheat.
II. Blast is a .... disease of paddy.
III. Chemical used to kill weeds are called ....
IV. Pesticides are .... chemicals.

Choose the correct option.

(a) rust, fungal, weedicides, toxic
(b) fungal, rust, weedicides, toxic
(c) rust, viral, pesticides, toxic
(d) rust, bacterial, weedicides, toxic

9 Match the following columns and choose the correct option from the codes given below

	Column I		Column II
P.	Ganga-5	1.	Rice
Q.	Kasturi	2.	Maize
R.	Green manure	3.	Brown-swiss
S.	Exotic breed	4.	Guar

Codes

	P	Q	R	S
(a)	1	3	2	4
(b)	2	1	4	3
(c)	4	3	1	2
(d)	4	2	1	3

10 Match the following and choose the correct option from the codes given below.

	Column I		Column II
P.	*Nosema apis*	1.	New castle disease
Q.	*Aspergillus fumigatus*	2.	Nosema disease
R.	*Bererelina virus*	3.	Pebrine
S.	*Nosema bombycis*	4.	Grasserie
T.	*Paramyxovirus*	5.	Stonebrood

Codes

	P	Q	R	S	T
(a)	5	4	3	2	1
(b)	1	2	4	3	5
(c)	2	5	4	3	1
(d)	5	3	4	2	1

Answer Key

1.	(b)	**2.**	(b)	**3.**	(c)	**4.**	(c)	**5.**	(d)
6.	(d)	**7.**	(b)	**8.**	(a)	**9.**	(b)	**10.**	(c)

**These questions may or may not be asked in the examination, have been given just for additional practice.*

EXPERIMENT 1

Experiment 1 (a)

Objective

To prepare a true solution of common salt, sugar and alum.

Materials Required

Powdered samples of common salt (sodium chloride. i.e. NaCl), sugar (sucrose, $C_{12}H_{22}O_{11}$), alum (potassium aluminium sulphate, $KAl(SO_4)_2 \cdot 12H_2O$, distilled water, test tubes (3), pipette, test tube stand and spatula.

Theory

A true solution is obtained when a low molecular mass, soluble substance is dissolved in any solvent.

Procedure

(*i*) Take three clean test tubes. Label these as *A*, *B* and *C* respectively. Place the test tubes on a stand.

(*ii*) Pour 10 mL of distilled water in each of the test tubes *A*, *B* and *C*, with the help of a pipette.

(*iii*) Add about 0.5 g of common salt in test tube *A*, 0.5 g of sugar in test tube *B* and 0.5 g of alum in test tube *C*, with the help of a spatula.

(*iv*) Hold the test tubes one-by-one in your right hand and shake the contents of each tube.

(*v*) Label each test tube with the name of the solution viz, Common salt + Water in test tube *A*

Sugar + Water in test tube *B*

Alum + Water in test tube *C*

(*a*) The solution in test tube *A* is a true solution of common salt.

(*b*) The solution in test tube *B* is a true solution of sugar.

(*c*) The solution in test tube *C* is a true solution of alum.

(*vi*) The process of preparing a true solution is shown below:

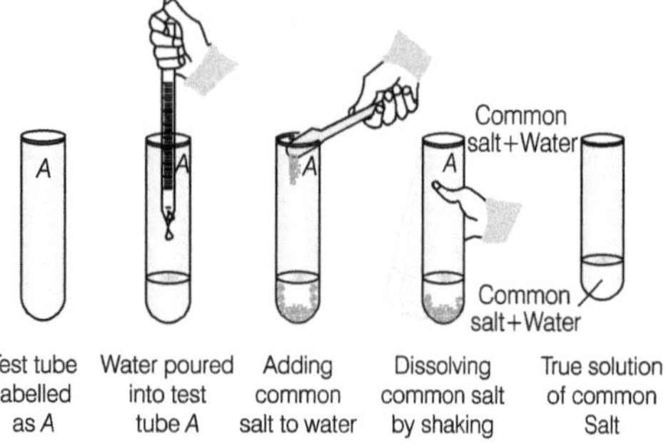

Process of preparing a true solution

Precautions

(*i*) Use powdered sample of the given substance because it dissolves faster than the big crystals/lumps.

(*ii*) Do not take more than 1 g of substance for making a true solution.

(*iii*) Shake the contents thoroughly.

(*iv*) Clean the spatula every time before use.

Experiment 1 (b)

Objective

To prepare the suspension of soil, chalk powder and fine sand in water.

Materials Required

Small samples of soil, powdered chalk, fine sand, test tubes (3), pipette, test tube stand, spatula and distilled water.

Theory

A suspension can be prepared by shaking vigorously a finely powdered and insoluble substance in water.

Procedure

(*i*) Take three clean test tubes. Label them as *A* (soil + water), *B* (chalk powder + water) and *C* (fine sand + water).

(*ii*) Place these test tubes on the test tube stand.

(*iii*) Pour about 10 mL of distilled water in each of these test tubes with the help of a pipette.

(*iv*) Add about 0.5 g of soil in test tube *A*, 0.5 g of powdered chalk in test tube *B* and 0.5 g of fine sand in test tube *C*, with the help of a spatula. Clean the spatula every time before use.

(*v*) Hold the test tubes one-by-one in your right hand and shake the contents of each test tube.

(*vi*) Place these test tubes on the test tube stand.

(*a*) Test tube *A* contains the suspension of soil in water.

(*b*) Test tube *B* contains the suspension of chalk in water.

(*c*) Test tube *C* contains the suspension of fine sand in water.

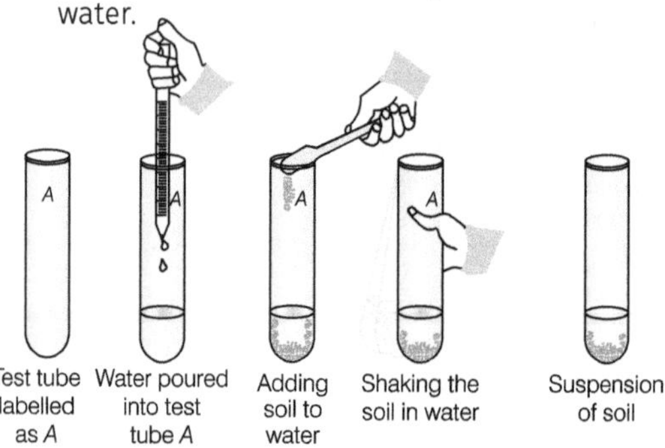

Process of preparing a suspension

Precautions

(i) While measuring a certain volume of solvent, such as water, read the lower meniscus.

(ii) The substance whose suspension in water is to be prepared must be sieved to remove larger particles.

Experiment 1 (c)

Objective

To prepare a colloidal solution of

(i) starch; and (ii) egg albumin in water.

Materials Required

Beakers (100 mL capacity) (2), test tubes (2), glass rod (2), water bath, Bunsen burner, thermometer, funnel, filter paper, starch powder, egg albumin powder (or an egg) and distilled water.

Theory

A material can be brought into colloidal state by dispersion method. In simple dispersion method, the bulk material is shaken vigorously with the solvent.

Procedure

I. Preparation of colloidal solution of starch in water

(i) Take three clean test tubes. Label them as *A*, *B* and *C* respectively. Place the test tubes on a stand.

(ii) Pour about 50 mL of distilled water in a beaker (100 mL capacity) and heat it about 50°C on a water bath.

(iii) Take about 0.5 g of starch in test tube *A* and add a little water to make a thin paste like slurry.

(iv) Pour the starch slurry into hot water (in beaker) and stir it vigorously with a glass rod.

(v) Continue heating and stirring the contents of the beaker for about 10 min.

(vi) Allow it to cool at room temperature.

(vii) Filter the colloidal solution of starch in water to remove any suspended particles/lump and collect the filtrate in a test tube *B*.

(viii) The translucent filtrate in the test tube *B* is the colloidal solution of starch in water.

II. Preparation of a colloidal solution of egg albumin in water

(i) Take about 30 mL of distilled water in a clean beaker (100 mL capacity) and heat it to about 35°C (if required).

(ii) Separate yellow part of the egg from the egg white. The egg white contains egg albumin.

(iii) Add about 0.5 g of egg white (or albumin powder) which is obtained by drying egg white to water in the beaker and stir it vigorously for about 1 min with the help of a glass rod.

(iv) Add another 0.5 g of egg albumin to the solution in the beaker and stir it vigorously for another 1 min.

(v) Filter the turbid solution and collect the filtrate in a clean test tube *C*/beaker.

(vi) This translucent/turbid solution is the colloidal solution of egg albumin in water.

(a) Egg albumin is the major protein constituent of white egg.

(b) Commercially, available egg albumin should be stored at 2-8°C.

Precautions

(i) While adding starch slurry into warm water, stirring must be continued.

(ii) Dry starch should never be added to warm water to prevent lump formation.

(iii) While preparing the colloidal solution of egg albumin, temperature of water should be controlled ($\approx$ 35°C) properly.

(iv) Use a separate glass rod for stirring the contents of the different beakers.

Experiment 1(d)

Objective

To distinguish between a true solution, a suspension and a colloidal solution on the basis of

(i) transparency (ii) filtration criterion

(iii) stability

Materials Required

Test tubes (3), boiling tubes (3), beakers (100 mL capacity), test tube stand , funnels (3) and filter papers.

About 30 mL of each of the following:

(i) True solution of common salt (or sugar) in water.

(ii) Suspension of chalk powder in water.

(iii) Colloidal solution of egg albumin in water.

Theory

Following are the characteristics of the true solution, suspension and a colloidal solution.

True Solution

Transparent, components of a true solution cannot be separated by filtration and stable.

Suspension

Opaque, components of a suspension can be separated by filtration and unstable.

Colloidal Solution

Translucent, component of a colloidal solution cannot be separated by filtration and stable.

Procedure

(i) Take three test tubes and label them as *A*, *B* and *C*.

(ii) Mark each test tube in the lower half with a sign of cross (X).

(iii) Place these test tubes on a test tube stand such that the mark (X) is on your opposite side.
(iv) Perform the experiments and record your observations and conclusions/inferences in the tabular form.

Property	Experiment	Observation	Inference
Transparency	Fill half of the test tube *A* with common salt solution.	The mark (×) is clearly visible when seen through the test tube *A*.	The common salt solution is transparent.
	Fill half of the test tube *B* with the suspension of chalk.	The mark (×) is not visible when seen through the test tube *B*.	The suspension of chalk is opaque.
	Fill half of the test tube *C* with colloidal solution of egg albumin.	The mark (×) is faintly visible when seen through the test tube *C*.	The colloidal solution of egg albumin is translucent.
Filtration criterion	Filter the contents of each test tube separately through a filter paper and collect the filtrate in a boiling tube. (Observe the filtrate and the residue left on the filter paper, if any).	In the case of test tube *A*, a clear filtrate is obtained and no residue is left on the filter paper.	Common salt cannot be separated from its solution in water by filtration.
		In the case of test tube *B*, a clear filtrate is obtained and some residue (chalk powder) is left on the filter paper.	Chalk powder can be separated from its suspension in water by filtration.
		In the case of test tube *C*, a translucent filtrate is obtained and no residue is left on the filter paper.	Egg albumin cannot be separated from its colloidal solution in water by filtration.
Stability	Pour about 10 mL of the true solution of common salt in water into test tube *A* and leave the test tube undisturbed for 5 minutes.	The solute particles in test tube *A* do not settle down.	The solution of common salt in water is stable.
	Pour about 10 mL of the suspension of chalk powder in water into test tube *B* and leave for 5 minutes.	Bigger particles tend to settle down at the bottom of test tube *B*.	The suspension of chalk in water is unstable.
	Pour about 10 mL of the colloidal solution of egg albumin in water into test tube *C* and leave the content undisturbed for 5 minutes.	The contents of test tube *C* remain unchanged and no solid particles settle down.	The colloidal solution of egg albumin in water is stable.
	Pour about 10 mL of the colloidal solution of egg albumin into test tube *C*.	The contents of test tube *C* remain unchanged and no solid particles settle down.	The colloidal solution of egg albumin in water is stable.

Leave these test tubes on a test tube stand undisturbed for about 5 min, and note your observations and inference.

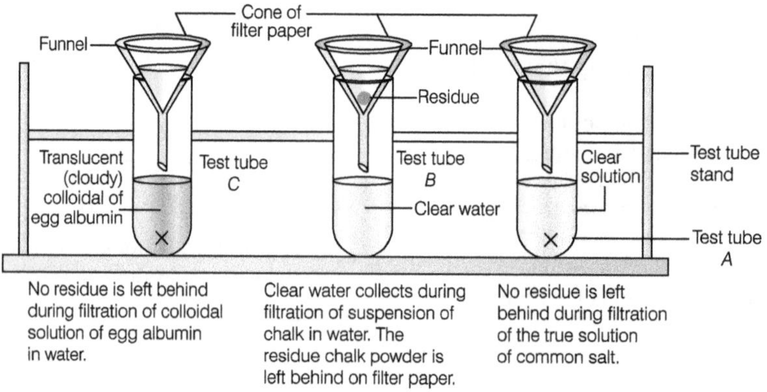

To distinguish between a true solution, a suspension and a colloidal solution on the basis of filtration

Results/Conclusion

(i) Common salt solution is transparent, stable and its components cannot be separated by filtration.
(ii) The suspension of chalk in water is opaque, unstable and its components can be separated by simple filtration.
(iii) The colloidal solution of egg albumin in water is translucent, stable and its components cannot be separated by simple filtration.

QUESTIONS

1. *Give an example of suspension.*

Ans. Copper sulphate in water is a suspension.

2. *Give an example where tyndall effect can be observed?*

Ans. Tyndall effect is observed in colloidal solution. starch + water is a colloidal solution.

3. *If sugar is dissolved in water, which type mixture would be the resulting solution appears?*

Ans. It will appear as a homogeneous mixture.

4. *Three students Avani, Sudesh, Hari were given funnels, filter paper, test tubes, test tube stands, common salt, chalk powder and starch. They prepared true solution, suspension and colloidal solution. Test tubes were arranged as shown in the figure.*

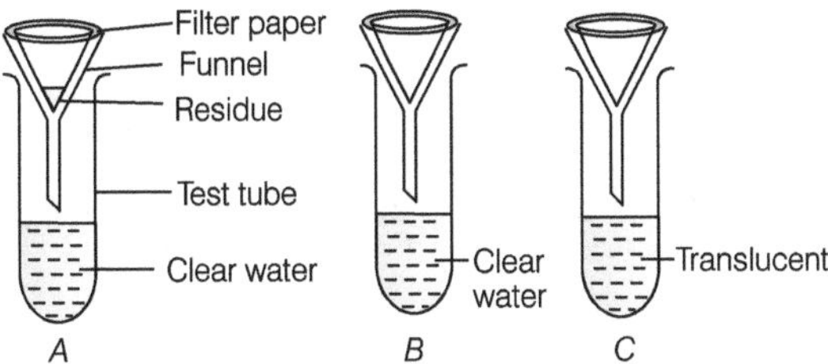

What conclusion he will draw from the above figure?

Ans. *A* is suspension, *B* is true solution and *C* is colloid.

5. *Four students prepared mixtures in water by taking sodium chloride, sand, chalk powder and starch respectively, in four different test tubes. After stirring the mixture, in which solution mixture will appear clear and transparent?*

Ans. Sodium chloride dissolves in water to give clear and transparent solution.

6. *A student mixes white of an egg with water and stirs it well. After some time, what he will observe?*

Ans. Student observed that white of an egg forms a cloudy solution with water.

7. *What is the correct procedure for preparing a colloidal solution of egg albumin in water?*

Ans. The correct procedure is to break the egg shell, take only white portion (egg albumin) and add it to water with constant stirring.

8. *Three unlabelled mixtures of copper sulphate and water, milk and starch, and mud and water are taken. After stirring well were kept for observation and a student was asked to identify. Which solution mixture is opaque translucent and transpaternt, respectively?*

Ans. Copper sulphate and water forms a transparent solution. Milk and starch with water forms a translucent solution and mud with water forms a opaque solution.

9. *What would be the first step to prepare a colloidal solution of starch?*

Ans. To prepare a colloidal solution of starch, one should first add a thin paste of starch powder to boiling water and stir.

10. *What is the particle size of suspension?*

Ans. Suspensions have particles greater than 100 nm (10^{-7} m).

11. *If common salt is added to the unsaturated solution of water and common salt. What will happen?*

Ans. If common salt is added to the unsaturated solution of water and common salt, the solution will remain a true solution.

12. *In an experiment to separate the components of a mixture of sand, common salt and ammonium chloride dissolved in water. Which component will be removed by filtration?*

Ans. Sand dissolved in water is removed by filtration.

13. *How can a suspension of chalk in water be prepared?*

Ans. A suspension of chalk in water can be prepared by placing powdered chalk in water and shaking it vigorously.

14. *Among which of the following is most stable?*

True solution, colloidal, suspension

Ans. True solution is transparent, stable and its components cannot be separated by filtration.

15. *A student was asked to prepare a true solution of sugar in water. By chance, he added sugar in excess. He stirred the solution for quite some time but some sugar settled down. He filtered the contents. What can be the filtrate?*

Ans. The filtrate can be true solution or colloidal solution.

16. *Rohit mixed starch with water, boiled the mixture well and stirred it. What he observed?*

Ans. Starch with water forms a translucent solution.

17. *Give an example of the colloidal solution where both the dispersed phase and the dispersion medium are in liquids state.*

Ans. Milk churned with water forms a colloidal solution i.e., emulsion where both the dispersed phase and the dispersion medium are liquids.

18. *Four students were asked to add water to chalk powder, milk, sand and oil. They were asked in which sample there was no suspension when added to water?*

Ans. Milk and water forms a colloidal solution. Oil and water forms an emulsion. Chalk powder and sand in water form suspension.

19. ***What precautions are to be taken while preparing a true solution, suspension or colloid?***

Ans. (i) Take solute in smaller proportions, not more than one gram every time for making any solution.

(ii) If solute is hard solid, it should be powdered for faster dissolution.

(iii) The contents should be stirred properly after cleaning the glass rod.

(iv) The contents should be shaken thoroughly and given enough time for setting.

20. ***Write the correct order which describes the true solution, colloidal solution and suspension in the order of their increasing stability.***

Ans. The stability depends on the size of solute particles. The order of their increasing stability.

Suspension < Colloidal solution < True solution

21. ***Ramesh took two beakers A and B containing hot water and cold water, respectively. In each beaker, he dropped a crystal of copper sulphate. He kept the beakers undisturbed. After sometime, what did he observe and why?***

Ans. The solutions of both the beakers turned blue after sometime. But the colour change was observed earlier in beaker A containing hot water as compared to beaker B containing cold water. This happened due to the faster rate of diffusion at a higher temperature.

22. ***Four students A, B, C and D were given funnels, filter paper, test tubes, test tube stands, common salt, chalk powder, starch and glucose powder. They prepared the true solution, suspension and colloidal solution. Test tubes were arranged as shown in the figure. Observe the filtrate obtained in the test tubes and residue on filter paper. Conclude about filtrate, residue and type of solution.***

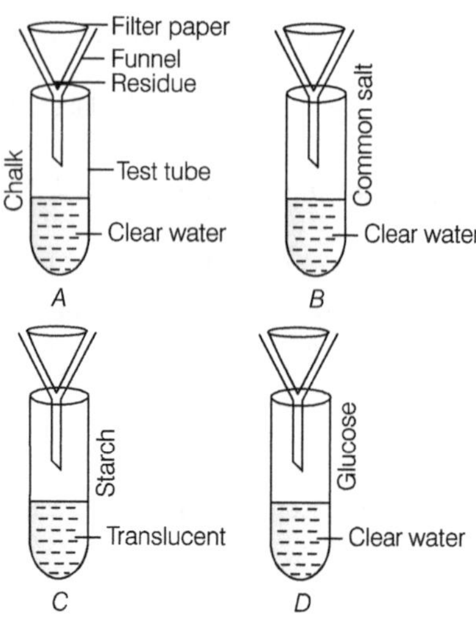

Ans. A – Chalk powder in water forms suspension and leaves residue during filtration.

B – Common salt in water forms a true solution. A true solution is clear and transparent. It leaves no residue on the filter paper.

C – Starch in water forms a colloid which is translucent, leaves no residue on filtration and the particles do not settle at the bottom.

D – Glucose dissolves completely in water and forms true solution. It leaves no residue on filter paper.

EXPERIMENT 2

Objective

To prepare

(*i*) a mixture (*ii*) a compound

using iron filings and sulphur powder and distinguish between these on the basis of

(*a*) appearance, i.e. homogeneity and heterogeneity.

(*b*) behaviour towards a magnet.

(*c*) behaviour towards carbon disulphide as a solvent.

(*d*) effect of heat.

Materials Required

China dish, petri dish, pestle-mortar, watch glass, test tubes, glass rod, Bunsen burner, magnifying glass, bar magnet, funnel, filter paper, iron filings (10 g), sulphur (5 g), carbon disulphide (5 mL), dilute hydrochloric acid or dilute sulphuric acid.

Theory

A mixture is obtained by mixing two or more substances in any proportion. A compound is obtained by the chemical combination of two or more elements in a fixed ratio. Mixtures and compounds differ in their appearance, composition, properties such as behaviour towards magnet, solubility and reaction with dilute acids. The constituents of a compound cannot be separated by physical processes, whereas the constituents of a mixture can be separated by physical means.

Procedure

I. Preparation of a mixture of iron filings and sulphur powder

Take a small amount of fine iron filings and sulphur in a pestle and mortar. Grind them thoroughly. The powder so obtained is a mixture of iron and sulphur. Keep it aside in a petri dish.

II. Preparation of the compound of iron filings and sulphur powder

Take 5.6 g of iron filings and 3.2 g of sulphur in a pestle and mortar. Grind the two components together. Transfer this mixture to a China dish. Heat the China dish on a low flame until the reaction starts. Continue stirring while heating the reaction mixture.

$$\underset{\text{Iron}}{Fe(s)} + \underset{\text{Sulphur}}{S(s)} \xrightarrow{\text{Heat}} \underset{\substack{\text{Iron sulphide} \\ \text{[Fe(II) sulphide]}}}{FeS}$$

When the reaction is over and the whole mass in the China dish turns black, stop heating. Allow it to cool to room temperature. Grind the solid black mass in a clean pestle and mortar to a fine powder. Keep it aside in a petri dish.

III. To distinguish between the mixture and compound containing iron and sulphur

Perform the following experiments and record your observations and inferences in tabular form.

S.No.	Test/Property	Experiment	Observations	Inference
1.	Appearance	Take a small quantity of the mixture prepared on a watch glass. Observe it first with the naked eye and then with a magnifying glass.	Particles of iron and sulphur are seen clearly even with the naked eye.	The mixture is heterogeneous.
		Take a small quantity of the compound of iron and sulphur on a watch glass. Observe it first with the naked eye and then with a magnifying glass.	The whole mass appears uniform in colour.	The compound is homogeneous.
2.	Behaviour towards a magnet	Move a bar magnet over the prepared mixture of iron and sulphur.	Iron particles get attracted towards the magnet and sulphur is left behind.	The components of a mixture can be separated by simple physical methods.
		Move a bar magnet over the prepared compound of iron and sulphur.	The black coloured particles of the compound do not get attracted by the magnet.	The components forming a compound cannot be separated by simple physical methods.
3.	Behaviour towards carbon disulphide	Take a little mixture of iron and sulphur in a test tube. Add 1-2 mL of carbon disulphide. Shake well and filter. Collect the filtrate in a China dish. Let carbon disulphide evaporate.	Carbon disulphide dissolves sulphur and iron particles are left on filter paper. Yellow sulphur crystals can be seen in the China dish after carbon disulphide has evaporated.	In a mixture, each component retains its own properties. Sulphur is soluble in carbon disulphide but iron does not.
		Take a small quantity of the compound of iron and sulphur in a test tube. Add 1-2 mL of carbon disulphide to it and shake well.	The compound of iron and sulphur does not dissolve in carbon disulphide.	In a compound, the constituents lose their characteristic properties and the compound shows altogether different properties.
4.	Effect of heat	Take a small quantity of the prepared mixture in a test tube and heat it.	At higher temperature, iron and sulphur react to form a black substance which does not show the properties of iron and sulphur.	The components of the mixture, iron and sulphur react on heating to give a compound called iron sulphide.
		Take a small quantity of the prepared compound in a test tube and heat it.	No reaction occurs. The substance, on strong heating starts glowing and on cooling, it returns to its original colour.	The compound iron sulphide remains chemically unchanged on heating.

S.No.	Test/Property	Experiment	Observations	Inference
5.	Reaction with dilute sulphuric acid [$H_2SO_4(aq)$]	Take a small quantity of the mixture in a test tube. Add 1-2 mL of dil. H_2SO_4 and heat it.	Bubbles of a colourless and odourless gas are evolved. The gas burns with a blue flame with a pop sound. Yellow powder (sulphur) remains unreacted.	Iron reacts with dil. H_2SO_4 to give hydrogen gas. $2Fe(s) + 3H_2SO_4(aq) \longrightarrow Fe_2(SO_4)_3(aq) + 3H_2(g)$
		Take a small quantity of the compound in a test tube. Add 1-2 mL of dil. H_2SO_4.	A gas having the smell of rotten eggs is evolved.	The liberated gas is hydrogen sulphide. $2FeS(s) + H_2SO_4(aq) \longrightarrow 2FeSO_4(aq) + H_2S(g)$

Conclusion

The following conclusions can be drawn from the experiments performed

(*i*) A mixture can be obtained by just mixing/ grinding the various components together in any ratio.

(*ii*) A chemical compound is formed only when the required components react chemically with each other.

(*iii*) Each component of a mixture retains its properties in a mixture.

(*iv*) The properties of a compound are altogether different from the properties of its constituents.

Precautions

(*i*) Heat the mixture of iron and sulphur in hard glass test tubes only.

(*ii*) Care should be taken while heating iron and sulphur.

(*iii*) Carbon disulphide is inflammable, so keep it away from the flame.

(*iv*) Do not inhale gases evolved directly.

QUESTIONS

1. *Aqueous solutions of zinc sulphate and iron sulphate were taken in test tubes I and II by Mr. Bean. Metal pieces of iron and zinc were dropped in the two solutions. After several hours what observation would be recorded by Mr. Bean?*

Ans. The observation recorded by Mr. Bean

$$Fe + ZnSO_4 \longrightarrow \text{No reaction}$$

It is because iron is less reactive than zinc.

$$\underset{\text{Zinc}}{Zn} + \underset{\text{Green solution}}{FeSO_4} \longrightarrow \underset{\text{Colourless solution}}{ZnSO_4} + \underset{\text{Black}}{Fe}$$

The solution becomes colourless and black iron gets deposited.

2. *In an experiment, carbon disulphide was added to a test tube containing a mixture of iron filings and sulphur powder. Draw the correct figure for this observation.*

Ans. Carbon disulphide dissolves sulphur and iron filings remain in the solution.

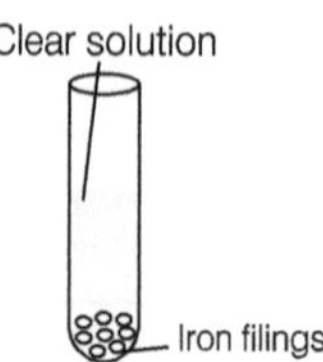

3. *Iron sulphide and a mixture of iron filings and sulphur powder were taken in different China dishes. Which of the following mixtures is heterogeneous and homogeneous?*

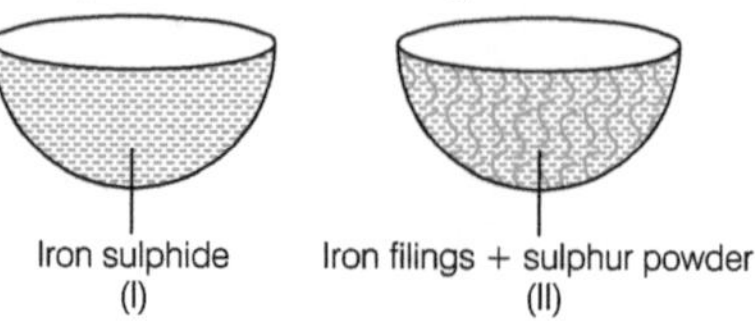

Ans. Iron sulphide is homogeneous but the mixture of iron filings and sulphur is heterogeneous.

4. *Rama heated a mixture of iron filings and sulphur in a hard glass test tube for some time till a grey-black product was formed. He cooled the test tube and then added 2 mL of carbon disulphide in it and stirred the contents of the test tube. In this experiment, what observation had he made?*

Ans. The compound of iron and sulphur, i.e. iron sulphide (FeS) does not dissolve in carbon disulphide.

5. *A student takes a substance A, which is attracted by a magnet and reacts with acids. He takes another substance B, which dissolves in carbon disulphide. He heats A and B together in a test tube to form product AB. What is the substance A and B and the product AB are respectively*

Ans. Iron filings (*A*) are attracted towards a bar magnet and reacts with dilute hydrochloric acid or dilute sulphuric acid to liberate hydrogen. Sulphur (*B*) is soluble in carbon disulphide. Iron filings and sulphur powder react to form iron sulphide (*AB*) which is black in colour.

6. ***China dish A contains mixture of iron filings and sulphur powder. In China dish B, same portion of the mixture is heated till the two components combine together to form a compound. Umesh added carbon disulphide to both the China dishes. What he would observe?***

Ans. In China dish *A*, there is a mixture, so sulphur gets dissolved in carbon disulphide. Iron is insoluble in it. In China dish *B*, compound FeS is formed. Though, sulphur is soluble in carbon disulphide, but the compound FeS is not soluble in it.

7. ***Rahul takes two substances X and Y. X is a mixture of iron filings and sulphur and Y is a product obtained by heating the mixture X and crushing it to a fine powder. On bringing a magnet over both X and Y, What will happen?***

Ans. *X* contains iron filings (magnetic material) while *Y* is a compound of iron and sulphur (FeS, non-magnetic material).

8. ***What is the purpose of separating the components of a mixture?***

Ans. The purpose of separating the components of a mixture is

(i) separation makes it possible to study and use the individual components of a mixture.

(ii) it is helpful in removing any harmful or undesirable constituents.

(iii) it is helpful in obtaining a pure sample of a substance.

9. ***When you mix iron filings with sulphur powder thoroughly and spread the mixture evenly on a white sheet. How do the particles in the mixture appear?***

Ans. In a mixture of iron filings and sulphur powder, sulphur and iron filings are separately visible but are not homogeneous.

10. ***Dil.* HCl *is added separately to***

I. mixture of iron filings and sulphur.

II. iron sulphide.

What would happen?

Ans. In a mixture of iron filings and sulphur, iron reacts with dil. HCl to liberate hydrogen gas.

11. ***What is formed, when iron filings heated with sulphur?***

Ans. Heating iron filings with sulphur forms ferrous sulphide.

12. ***When a mixture of iron filings and sulphur powder is dissolved in carbon disulphide, how do the resulting solution will appear?***

Ans. Here, sulphur powder dissolves in carbon disulphide and iron filings are deposited at the base of the test tube.

13. ***When iron filings and sulphur powder are heated at high temperature in a China dish, what will be the product obtained?***

Ans. When iron filings and sulphur are heated, a black coloured compound, iron sulphide (FeS), is formed which is insoluble in carbon disulphide.

14. ***Give one physical property of a mixture.***

Ans. A mixture does not have a fixed melting or boiling points.

15. ***In the laboratory, what is the major precautions have to be taken with carbon disulphide?***

Ans. Carbon disulphide catches fire easily so, it should be keep away from flame.

16. ***What will happen if iron filings and sulphur are heated in the mass ratio of* 8 : 4?**

Ans. Iron and sulphur form compound only when they are heated in their stoichiometric (relative quantity) ratio, i.e. 56 : 32 or 7 : 4. Here, iron is present more than the stoichiometric (relative quantity) ratio, hence, iron sulphide and iron will be left after the reaction.

17. ***What precautions will you take while handling* H_2S *gas and* CS_2*?***

Ans. (*i*) Do not inhale H_2S (hydrogen sulphide) gas as it is a poisonous gas.

(*ii*) CS_2 (carbon disulphide) is an organic solvent which is inflammable, so it should be kept away from the flame.

18. ***What will happen when dil.* H_2SO_4 *is added to a mixture of iron filings and sulphur?***

Ans. Iron reacts with dil. H_2SO_4 to form H_2 gas and $Fe_2(SO_4)_3$ which is light green in colour whereas sulphur does not react.

$$\underset{\text{Iron}}{2Fe(s)} + \underset{\substack{\text{Sulphuric acid}\\ \text{(dilute)}}}{3H_2SO_4(aq)} \longrightarrow \underset{\text{Ferric sulphate}}{Fe_2(SO_4)_3\, aq} + 3H_2(g)$$

19. ***What is observed when a magnet is moved over***

(i) mixture of iron filings and sulphur?

(ii) compound formed* (FeS) *after heating of iron filings and sulphur?

Ans. Iron filings are only attracted

(i) in a mixture because properties of its constituents are not lost.

(ii) In a compound, the constituents lose their original properties hence, it will not attracted by magnet.

EXPERIMENT 3

Objective

Perform the following reactions and classify them as physical or chemical changes.

(*i*) Iron with copper sulphate solution in water.
(*ii*) Burning of magnesium in air.
(*iii*) Zinc with dilute sulphuric acid.
(*iv*) Heating of copper sulphate crystals.
(*v*) Sodium sulphate with barium chloride in the form of their solutions in water.

Materials Required

Test tubes, test tube holder, test tube stand, China dish, conical flask, beaker dropper, Bunsen burner, iron nails, copper sulphate solution, magnesium ribbon, zinc metal, dilute sulphuric acid, sodium sulphate solution, barium chloride solution and water.

Theory

Substances combine and undergo changes. The changes are classified into two categories:

(i) **Physical changes** Changes in which the original constituents do not change their properties, and there is no formation of new substance or compound, are called physical changes.

(ii) **Chemical changes** Changes in which the original constituents undergo change to form a new substance or compound with different properties, are known as chemical changes.

Chemical Reactions

A chemical reaction in which new substances with new properties are formed. They involve the breaking of bonds in the atoms of reacting substances and making of new bonds between the atoms of products. During chemical reactions, a large number of rearrangements of atoms take place to produce new substances.

(i) Iron is more reactive (or electropositive) than copper. When iron is kept in a solution of copper sulphate, displaces copper from copper sulphate solution and colour of the solution changes from blue to light green.

$$\underset{\substack{\text{Iron}\\\text{(More reactive metal)}}}{Fe(s)} + \underset{\substack{\text{Copper sulphate}\\\text{(Blue coloured)}}}{CuSO_4(aq)} \longrightarrow \underset{\substack{\text{Ferrous sulphate}\\\text{(Light green coloured)}}}{FeSO_4(aq)} + \underset{\substack{\text{Copper}\\\text{Displaced metal}\\\text{(Less reactive)}}}{Cu(s)}$$

In this reaction, iron (Fe) gets oxidised to Fe^{2+} and copper ions (Cu^{2+}) in the solution get reduced to copper metal (Cu).

$$\underset{\text{Copper sulphate}}{CuSO_4(aq)} \longrightarrow \underset{\text{Copper ion}}{Cu^{2+}(aq)} + \underset{\text{Sulphate ion}}{SO_4^{2-}(aq)}$$

$$\underset{\text{Iron metal}}{Fe(s)} \longrightarrow \underset{\substack{\text{Iron (II) ion}\\\text{(goes into the solution)}}}{Fe^{2+}(aq)} + 2e^-\text{(oxidation)}$$

$$Cu^{2+}(aq) + 2e^- \longrightarrow Cu(s) \quad \text{(reduction)}$$

Net ionic reaction,

$$\underset{\substack{\text{Iron metal}\\\text{(Grey)}}}{Fe(s)} + \underset{\substack{\text{Copper (II) ion in solution}\\\text{(Blue)}}}{Cu^{2+}(aq)} \longrightarrow \underset{\substack{\text{Copper metal}\\\text{(Reddish brown)}}}{Cu(s)} + \underset{\substack{\text{Iron (II) ion in solution}\\\text{(Light green)}}}{Fe^{2+}(aq)}$$

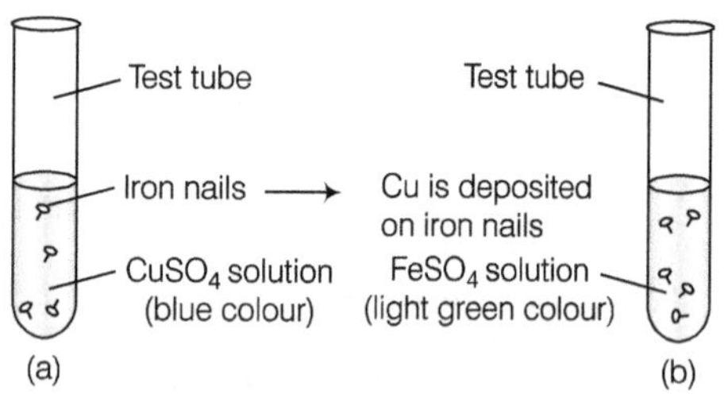

Iron with copper sulphate solution in water

This reaction is classified as displacement reaction and oxidation reduction reaction.

(ii) Magnesium is a silvery-white metal. Magnesium when burnt in air gives magnesium oxide.

This reaction is an example of **chemical combination** (or synthesis reaction) because in this reaction, two elements combine to form a compound.

$$\underset{\text{Magnesium}}{2Mg(s)} + \underset{\text{Oxygen}}{O_2(g)} \xrightarrow[\text{Burns with a dazzling white light}]{\text{Heat}} \underset{\substack{\text{Magnesium oxide}\\\text{(White powder)}}}{2MgO(s)}$$

Magnesium oxide is basic and turns red litmus blue.

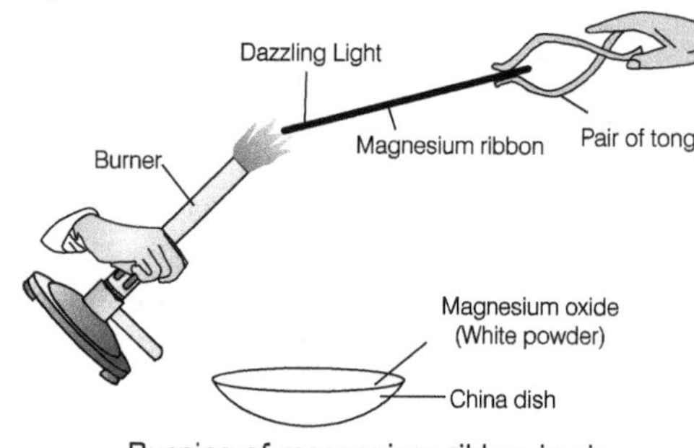

Burning of magnesium ribbon in air

(iii) Zinc reacts with dilute sulphuric acid to form zinc sulphate and hydrogen gas.

$$\underset{\text{Zinc metal}}{Zn(s)} + \underset{\text{Dil. sulphuric acid}}{H_2SO_4(aq)} \longrightarrow \underset{\text{Zinc sulphate}}{ZnSO_4(aq)} + \underset{\text{Hydrogen}}{H_2(g)}$$

In this reaction, zinc displaces hydrogen from acid solution. This reaction can be explained as follows:

Zinc is more electropositive than hydrogen. So, zinc (Zn) has a higher tendency to get oxidised to zinc ion (Zn^{2+}). The electrons so released are then used for reducing H^+ ions present in the acid solution. Thus, the reaction of zinc with an acid solution can be described as follows:

$Zn(s) \longrightarrow Zn^{2+}(aq) + 2e^-$ (Oxidation of Zn) $2H^+(aq) + 2e^- \longrightarrow H_2(g)$ (Reduction of H^+)

or $Zn(s) + 2H^+(aq) \longrightarrow Zn^{2+}(aq) + H_2(g)$

This reaction can be classified as **displacement reaction** and **oxidation-reduction reaction**.

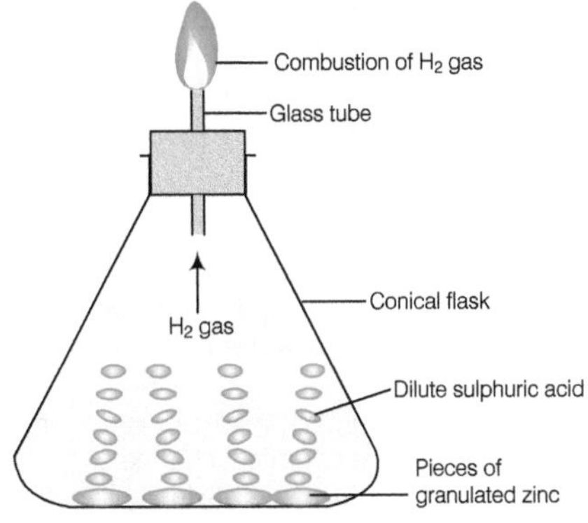

Granulated zinc with dilute sulphuric acid

(iv) On heating, blue copper sulphate pentahydrate changes into white colour.

$$\underset{\substack{\text{Copper sulphate}\\\text{pentahydrate}\\\text{(Blue)}}}{CuSO_4 \cdot 5H_2O} \xrightarrow{110^\circ C} \underset{\substack{\text{Copper sulphate}\\\text{monohydrate}\\\text{(White)}}}{CuSO_4 \cdot H_2O} + 4H_2O$$

$$\underset{\substack{\text{Copper sulphate}\\\text{monohydrate}}}{CuSO_4 \cdot H_2O} \xrightarrow{250^\circ C} \underset{\substack{\text{Copper}\\\text{sulphate}\\\text{(White)}}}{CuSO_4} + H_2O$$

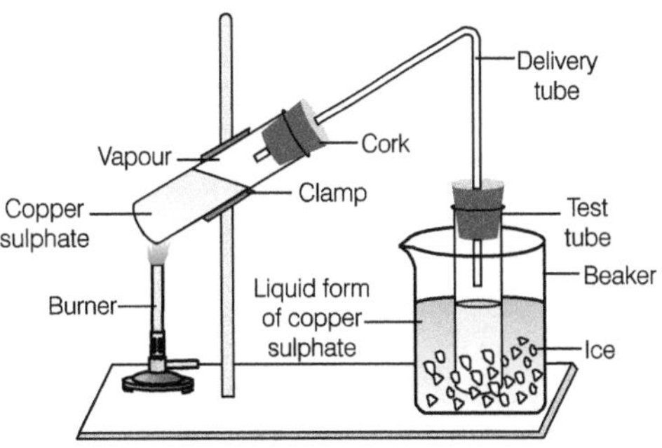

Heating of copper sulphate pentahydrate crystals

On further heating of $CuSO_4$ (720°C), it changes to black CuO and evolve SO_3 gas.

$$\underset{\substack{\text{Copper}\\\text{sulphate}}}{CuSO_4} \xrightarrow{720^\circ C} \underset{\substack{\text{Copper}\\\text{oxide}\\\text{(Black)}}}{CuO} + \underset{\substack{\text{Sulphur}\\\text{trioxide}\\\text{(Gas)}}}{SO_3}$$

It is a **chemical change** since new substance is formed.

(v) Both sodium sulphate and barium chloride are ionic compounds. When dissolved in water, they give colourless solutions containing their ions, i.e. sodium sulphate in aqueous solution gives free $Na^+(aq)$ and $SO_4^{2-}(aq)$ ions, whereas barium chloride in aqueous solution gives $Ba^{2+}(aq)$ and $Cl^-(aq)$ ions. When the solutions of sodium sulphate and barium chloride are mixed, the following reaction takes place

$$\underset{\text{Sodium sulphate}}{Na_2SO_4(aq)} + \underset{\text{Barium chloride}}{BaCl_2(aq)} \longrightarrow \underset{\substack{\text{Barium sulphate}\\\text{(White precipitate)}}}{BaSO_4(s)} + \underset{\text{Sodium chloride}}{2NaCl(aq)}$$

Barium sulphate appears as white precipitate, whereas sodium chloride remains in solution in the form of ions $Na^+(aq)$ and $Cl^-(aq)$. In this reaction, the corresponding ions get exchanged. That is why this reaction is classified as **double displacement reaction**.

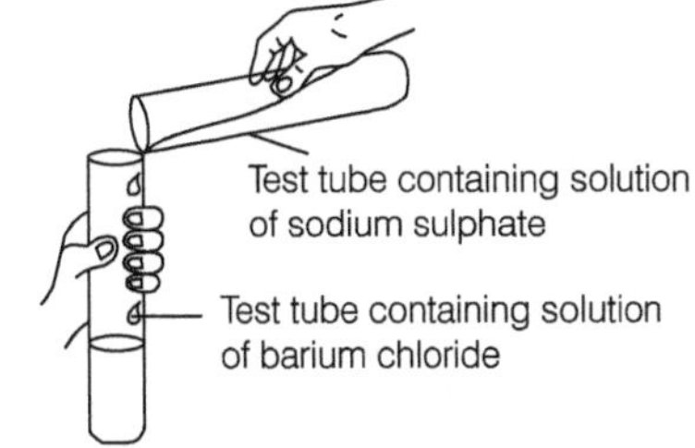

Formation of barium sulphate and sodium chloride

Procedure

S. No.	Experiment	Observation	Inference
1.	Take about 10 mL of $CuSO_4$ solution in a clean, dry test tube and drop iron nails into it. Keep the test tube undisturbed for about 10 min.	The blue coloured solution becomes light green in colour. The iron nails gets coated with a reddish-brown deposit.	On reaction of iron nails with $CuSO_4$ solution, $FeSO_4$, is formed which is light green in colour and free Cu is formed which is deposited over the iron nails as a reddish-brown deposit. It is a *displacement reaction*.
2.	Clean a piece of magnesium ribbon (5 cm) with a sand paper and hold it with a pair of tongs. Keep a China dish below it, burn magnesium ribbon in air with a burner.	The magnesium ribbon on heating with a burner catches fire. It burns with a dazzling white flame to form a white powder which keeps dropping till the ribbon is burning.	Mg burns with O_2 with a dazzling white flame, it forms a new chemical compound MgO, which is a white powder. It is a *combination reaction*.
3. (*i*)	Take a clean and dry conical flask and add small pieces of granulated zinc in it. Put about 5 mL of dil. H_2SO_4 in it. Keep the conical flask undisturbed for about 5 min.	A gas is evolved briskly, the colourless bubbles of which can be seen in the conical flask. It is also seen that the reaction mixture appears to be boiling and the conical flask and its contents become hot.	Zinc reacts with dil. H_2SO_4 briskly. $Zn + H_2SO_4(\text{dil.}) \longrightarrow ZnSO_4 + H_2$
(*ii*)	Bring a burning matchstick near the mouth of the conical flask.	The gas evolved burns with a 'pop' sound (cracking sound).	Gas evolved is H_2. It is a *displacement reaction*.
4.	Take $CuSO_4 \cdot 5H_2O$ in a dry test tube and fix cork with delivery tube and clamp it. Take crushed ice in a beaker and set other end of delivery tube in test tube. Heat the test tube first slowly and then strongly.	On heating at 110°C, $CuSO_4 \cdot 5H_2O$ changes to dirty white. At 150°C, dirty white changes to white. Finally at 250°C, anhydrous copper sulphate changes to black CuO with the evolution of SO_3 gas.	This is a *thermal decomposition reaction*, and also a chemical change. Since, new substance (CuO and SO_3) are formed which have different properties.
5.	Take a clean test tube and add about 5 mL of Na_2SO_4 in it. Now, add about 5 mL of $BaCl_2$ solution in it. Keep the test tube undisturbed for some time.	A white precipitate is formed which gradually settles at the base of the test tube.	Na_2SO_4 reacts with $BaCl_2$ solution to form insoluble $BaSO_4$. It is a *double displacement reaction*.

Chemical Reactions Involved

(*i*) Reaction of iron nails and copper sulphate solution

$$\underset{\text{Iron}}{Fe(s)} + \underset{\substack{\text{Copper sulphate}\\ \text{(Blue solution)}}}{CuSO_4(aq)} \longrightarrow \underset{\substack{\text{Ferrous sulphate}\\ \text{(Light green solution)}}}{FeSO_4(aq)} + \underset{\text{Copper}}{Cu(s)}$$

(Displacement reaction)

(*ii*) Burning of magnesium ribbon in air

$$\underset{\text{Magnesium}}{2\,Mg(s)} + \underset{\text{Oxygen}}{O_2(g)} \longrightarrow \underset{\substack{\text{Magnesium oxide}\\ \text{(White powder)}}}{2MgO(s)}$$

(Combination reaction)

(*iii*) Action of zinc with dilute sulphuric acid

$$\underset{\text{Zinc}}{Zn(s)} + \underset{\text{Sulphuric acid}}{\text{dil.}H_2SO_4(aq)} \longrightarrow \underset{\text{Zinc sulphate}}{ZnSO_4(aq)} + \underset{\text{Hydrogen}}{H_2(g)\uparrow}$$

(Displacement reaction)

(*iv*) Heating of hydrated copper sulphate

$$\underset{\substack{\text{Hydrated copper}\\ \text{sulphate (Blue)}}}{CuSO_4 \cdot 5H_2O} \xrightarrow{\text{Heat}} \underset{\substack{\text{Anhydrous copper}\\ \text{sulphate (White)}}}{CuSO_4} + 5H_2O$$

(Decomposition reaction)

(*v*) Reaction of sodium sulphate solution and barium chloride solution

$$\underset{\substack{\text{Sodium}\\ \text{sulphate}}}{Na_2SO_4(aq)} + \underset{\substack{\text{Barium}\\ \text{chloride}}}{BaCl_2(aq)} \longrightarrow \underset{\substack{\text{Barium}\\ \text{sulphate}\\ \text{(White ppt.)}}}{BaSO_4(s)\downarrow} + \underset{\substack{\text{Sodium}\\ \text{chloride}}}{2NaCl(aq)}$$

(Double displacement reaction)

Result

(*i*) Iron reacts with copper sulphate solution in water is a displacement reaction and is a chemical change.

(*ii*) Burning of magnesium in air is a combination reaction and is a chemical change.

(*iii*) Zinc with dilute sulphuric acid is a displacement reaction and is a chemical change.

(*iv*) Heating of hydrated copper sulphate is a decomposition reaction and is a chemical change.

(*v*) Reaction between sodium sulphate and barium chloride solution is a double displacement reaction and is a chemical change.

Precautions

(*i*) Always take a clean and dry test tube.

(*ii*) The test tube should always be held over the flame with the help of a test tube holder.

(*iii*) Use tongs to hold the magnesium ribbon over the flame.

(*iv*) Do not use excess of chemicals.

(*v*) Clean the iron nails and magnesium ribbon by rubbing with sand paper.

QUESTIONS

1. *When zinc reacts with dilute sulphuric acid, which gas is evolved?*

Ans. Hydrogen gas is evolved, which is colourless, odourless and burns with a pop sound. Reaction involved $\underset{\text{(Dilute)}}{Zn + H_2SO_4} \longrightarrow ZnSO_4 + H_2 \uparrow$

2. *Ankur was doing an experiment to carry out the reaction of zinc granules with dilute sulphuric acid. He observed that a gas is being evolved. Name the gas.*

Ans. Small amount of hydrogen gas escapes from the delivery tube.

3. *An iron nail is placed in a beaker containing copper sulphate solution. In the beaker, a sensitive thermometer is suspended and the temperature of copper sulphate solution is recorded. The nail is taken out after 10 min and the temperature is again recorded. What happen at the end of experiment records.*

Ans. The thermometer records high temperature due to small amount of heat produced in the chemical reaction.

4. *On burning magnesium ribbon in air, a white ash is obtained. What is the product and the type of change are respectively*

Ans. It is a chemical change. A new compound called magnesium oxide is formed on burning of magnesium ribbon in air.

$$\underset{\text{Magnesium}}{2Mg} + O_2 \longrightarrow \underset{\text{Magnesium oxide}}{2MgO}$$

5. *When solution of sodium sulphate is added to the solution of barium chloride. What is the product obtained?*

Ans. When aqueous solutions of sodium sulphate and barium chloride are mixed, a white precipitate of barium sulphate is formed by double displacement.

$$\underset{\text{Sodium sulphate}}{Na_2SO_4(aq)} + \underset{\text{Barium chloride}}{BaCl_2(aq)} \longrightarrow \underset{\text{Barium sulphate}}{BaSO_4(s)} + \underset{\text{Sodium chloride}}{2NaCl\ (aq)}$$

6. *Sketch a diagram for correct way of burning of magnesium ribbon during an experiment.*

Ans. *Magnesium ribbon burns with a dazzling white flame. It should be held with a pair of tongs.*

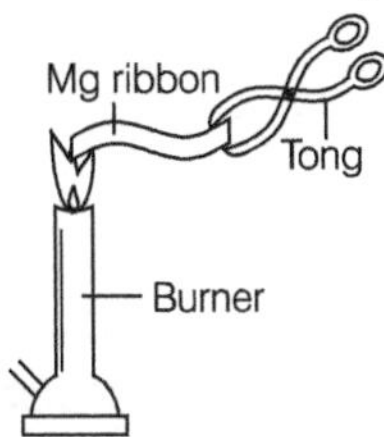

7. *What leads to heating of crystals of copper sulphate?*

Ans. $$\underset{\substack{\text{Hydrated copper sulphate} \\ \text{(Blue)}}}{CuSO_4 \cdot 5H_2O} \xrightarrow{\text{Heat}} \underset{\substack{\text{Anhydrous copper sulphate} \\ \text{(White)}}}{CuSO_4} + \underset{\text{Water}}{5H_2O}$$

8. *Label the diagram.*

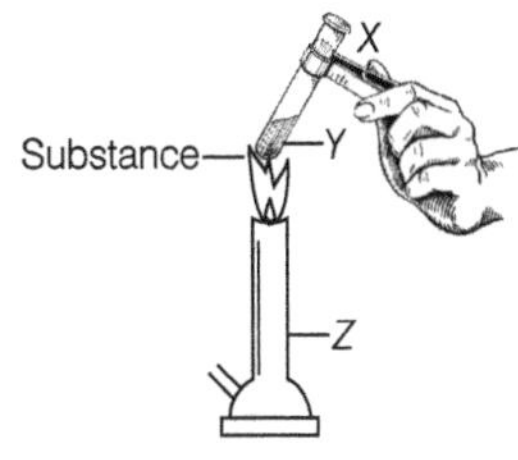

Ans. The labellings are:

X = Test tube holder

Y = Test tube

Z = Burner

9. *Write three points that is observed when zinc granules are added to dilute sulphuric acid in a test tube?*

Ans. (i) Release of bubbles of gas from the test tube.

(ii) Gradual decrease in the size of the granules.

(iii) Heat energy evolved in the reaction.

10. *You are asked to study the reaction between zinc and dilute sulphuric acid. Name the apparatus required for this experiment.*

Ans. Conical flask, delivery tube, rubber stopper, and matchbox.

11. *Which type of the possible changes that may occur on strongly heating of crystals of copper sulphate?*

Ans. It is a chemical and irreversible change.

$$CuSO_4 \xrightarrow{720\,°C} CuO + SO_3$$

12. *Student X puts Fe nails in $CuSO_4$ solution while the other student Y puts Cu pieces in $FeSO_4$ solution. Who made the observation that solution turns green from blue colour is reported?*

Ans. Fe displaces copper (Cu) from $CuSO_4$ solution and the solution turns green from blue colour.

$$\underset{\text{Iron}}{Fe} + \underset{\text{(Blue solution)}}{CuSO_4} \longrightarrow \underset{\text{(Light green)}}{FeSO_4} + \underset{\text{Copper}}{Cu}$$

13. *It is advised to rub magnesium ribbon with sand paper before burning it in air. Why?*

Ans. After rubbing, any layer of its oxide etc., deposited on it is removed and then magnesium comes in direct contact with air.

14. *Aqueous solutions of sodium sulphate and barium chloride are mixed together in a beaker. What would be observed?*

Ans. When aqueous solutions of sodium sulphate and barium chloride are mixed together in a beaker, a white precipitate of barium sulphate is formed.

15. *What is physical or chemical effect on rubbing of magnesium ribbon with sand paper or any other abrasive?*

Ans. After rubbing, magnesium ribbon, any layer of its oxide deposited on it.

16. *When barium chloride solution is added to sodium sulphate solution. What is obtained as precipitate?*

Ans. When barium chloride solution is added to sodium sulphate solution, white precipitate of barium sulphate is formed.

$$Na_2SO_4(aq) + BaCl_2(aq) \rightarrow BaSO_4(s) + 2NaCl(aq)$$

17. *Give three examples of chemical changes.*

Ans. (i) Burning of magnesium ribbon in air.
(ii) Burning of a candle.
(iii) Mixing of zinc and dilute sulphuric acid.

18. *Iron filings were added to a solution of copper sulphate. After 10 min, it was observed that the blue colour of the solution changes and a layer gets deposited on iron filings. What would be the colour of the solution formed and that of coating on iron filings?*

Ans. When iron nails are added to copper sulphate solution, iron displaces copper from copper sulphate forming iron sulphate, which is pale-green in colour and copper is discharged in the solution which is reddish-brown in colour, and gets deposited on the iron nails.

19. *Manav took about 10 mL of $CuSO_4$ in a test tube and added a few iron pieces to it. What did he observe? On the basis of his observations, identify whether the change is physical or chemical.*

Ans. He will observe that the blue colour of copper sulphate solution turns to light green due to the displacement of Cu from $CuSO_4$ by iron and formation of $FeSO_4$ solution will take place. The displaced copper gets deposited on the iron pieces.

Hence, a reddish-brown coating is formed on the pieces. Since a new compound is formed, hence it is a chemical change.

20. *When zinc granules are treated with dil. HCl then it results in the evolution of a gas.*
(i) Identify the gas.
(ii) What type of change is involved in the above reaction?

Ans. (i) The gas evolved, when zinc granules are treated with dil.HCl, is hydrogen (H_2).

$$Zn + 2HCl \longrightarrow ZnCl_2 + H_2 \uparrow$$

(ii) Zinc displaces hydrogen from hydrochloric acid and a salt is formed. It is an irreversible chemical change.

21. *What precautions should be taken while studying the chemical reaction of burning of magnesium ribbon in air?*

Ans. (i) Clean the magnesium ribbon carefully to remove the deposited oxide layer on it.
(ii) Do not look at the dazzling light emitted during burning of magnesium.
(iii) Keep the Mg ribbon away from your eyes and use dark coloured goggles during this experiment.
(iv) Collect magnesium oxide powder carefully.

22. *(i) What will be your immediate observation on adding barium chloride solution to sodium sulphate solution?*
(ii) When an iron nail rubbed with sand paper, is dipped in copper sulphate solution, then whereon the nail, copper will get deposited first?

Ans. (i) A white precipitate is formed instantaneously.
(ii) Copper will get deposited evenly on the entire surface of the nail, because iron nail was rubbed before doing the experiment so that the entire surface becomes smooth for deposition of copper metal.

EXPERIMENT 4

Experiment 4 (a)

Objective

To prepare stained, temporary mount of onion peel and to study its cells.

Materials Required

An onion bulb, slide, cover slip, two watch glasses, needle, brush, forceps, razor blade, compound microscope, blotting paper, methylene blue (or safranin) solution, glycerine and water.

Theory

All living organisms are composed of cells. New cells arise by the division of pre-existing cells. Cell is the structural and functional unit of life. In plants, cells have an outermost rigid cell wall beneath which is a cell membrane. The cell membrane encloses cytoplasm, cell organelles and a nucleus.

Procedure

(i) Take a fleshy scaly leaf of an onion. Using a pair of forceps, pull out a thin membranous peel adhering to the inner surface of the leaf. This is the epidermal peel.

(ii) Place the peel in a watch glass containing water and cut it into small rectangular pieces.
(iii) Mix 1 or 2 drops of methylene blue or safranin in a small quantity of water taken in another watch glass and transfer the peel into it. Leave the peel for about 3 minutes. Dip the peel in water to remove excess stain.
(iv) Take a clean slide with a drop of glycerine in the middle and using a brush, transfer the washed and stained peel on to it.
(v) Place a cover slip over it by slowly lowering it with a needle. Avoid entry of air bubbles.
(vi) Remove excess glycerine from the edges of cover slip with the help of a piece of blotting paper.
(vii) Observe the slide under the microscope, first in low power (10x) and then in high power (45x).
(viii) Draw a labelled diagram of the cells as seen under microscope.
(ix) Observe and record its features.

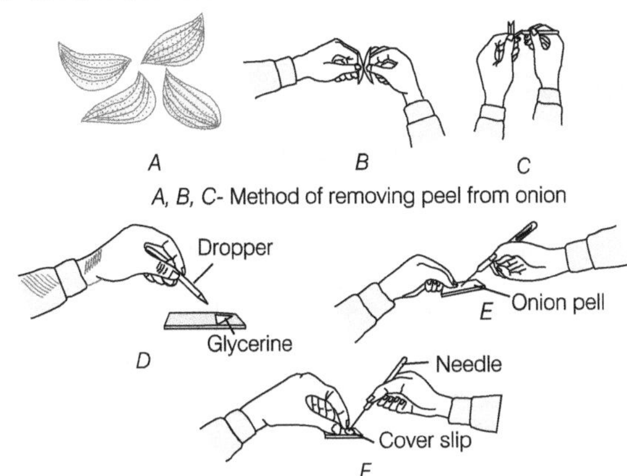

Observations

- There are a large number of brick-shaped (rectangular) epidermal cells lying side by side (compactly arranged).
- Each cell has a distinct cell wall and there are no intercellular spaces.
- A distinct darkly stained nucleus is present in each cell.
- A prominent vacuole is seen in the centre and cytoplasm is present in the periphery of every cell.

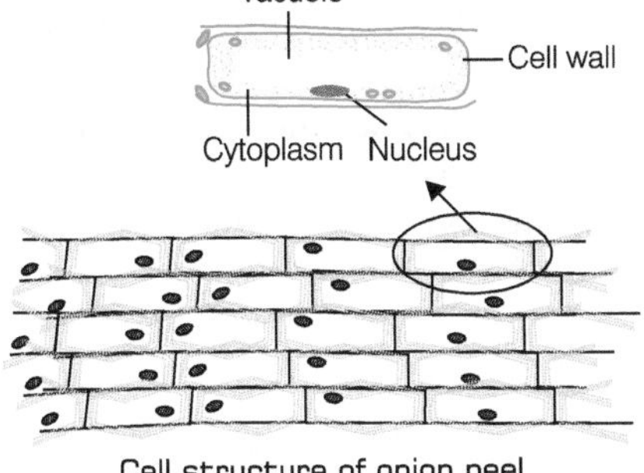

Cell structure of onion peel

Conclusion

The cells observed under microscope are plant cells as each cell has a distinct cell wall and a large vacuole in the centre. The cells form the outer layer of the leaf known as epidermis.

Precautions

(i) Always hold the slide from its edges.
(ii) The slide and cover slip should be cleaned before use.
(iii) Staining of peel should be appropriate. Avoid understaining or excessive staining of the peel.
(iv) Keep the cover slip gently so as to avoid the entry of air bubbles.
(v) Extra glycerine from the edges of the cover slip should be soaked with blotting paper.
(vi) Use a brush to transfer the peel on the slide.

Experiment 4 (b)

Objective

To prepare a temporary mount of human cheek cells and to study their characteristics.

Materials Required

Methylene blue stain, glycerine, a compound microscope, slide, cover slip, a clean spatula or a toothpick, a brush, a needle and a piece of blotting paper.

Theory

Like plants, the body of all animals including humans is composed of cells. Unlike plant cells, animal cells do not have cell wall. The outermost covering of an animal cell is a cell membrane. The cytoplasm, nucleus and other cell organelles are enclosed in it. Epithelial tissue is the outermost covering of most organs and cavities of an animal body.

Procedure

(i) Rinse your mouth with freshwater.
(ii) With the help of a clean spatula or a toothpick, gently scrape the inner side of your cheek.
(iii) Transfer the scrapped material into a drop of water taken on a clean slide.
(iv) With the help of a needle, spread the material uniformly.
(v) Add a drop of methylene blue stain. After about 3 minutes put a drop of glycerine over it.
(vi) Place a clean cover slip over the glycerine. Remove the excess glycerine from the edges of cover slip with the help of a piece of blotting paper.
(vii) Examine the slide under microscope, first under low power (10x) and then under high power (45x).

(viii) Draw diagrams of cells as seen under the microscope. Observe and record the features.

Observations

(i) A large number of flat polygonal cells arranged compactly are observed under the microscopic field.
(ii) Each cell is bounded by a thin cell membrane.
(iii) A darkly stained distinct nucleus is observed in each cell.
(iv) Cytoplasm is granular.
(v) Cells lack cell wall and large vacuoles.

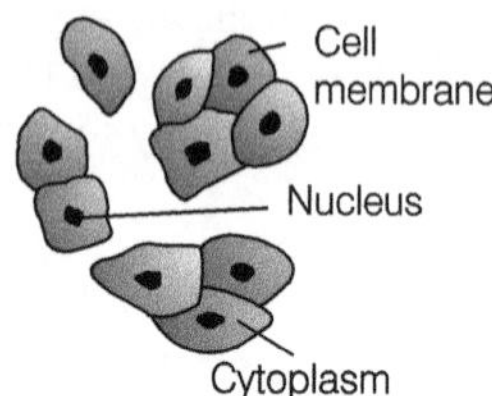

Conclusion

The cells observed under microscope are animal cells as each cell has a cell membrane as outer boundary enclosing a distinct nucleus and dense cytoplasm. Cell wall and central prominent vacuoles are absent.

Precautions

(i) Clean your mouth cavity with warm water before scraping the cheek.
(ii) Scrape the cheek gently to avoid bleeding.
(iii) Scraping should be properly spread so that the cells are widely separated.
(iv) The cover slip should be kept gently to avoid entry of air bubbles.
(v) Always hold the slide by its edges to avoid fingerprints.
(vi) Avoid overstaining or understaining of the material.

QUESTIONS

1. *Which scientist discovered 'cell'?*

Ans. Robert Hooke discovered 'cell' in 1665. It is the basic unit of life.

2. *Which is the largest known cell?*

Ans. Ostrich egg is the largest known cell.

3. *Write the name of the smallest human cell.*

Ans. Sperms are the smallest known human cells whereas neuron is the largest cell in a human body.

4. *Which is called as the 'powerhouse of the cell'?*

Ans. Mitochondria are known as the 'powerhouse of the cell'. They possess enzymes necessary for oxidation of carbohydrates. This process releases energy in the form of ATP and hence, they are referred to as powerhouse.

5. *Draw the diagram of the cells of an onion peel.*

Ans.

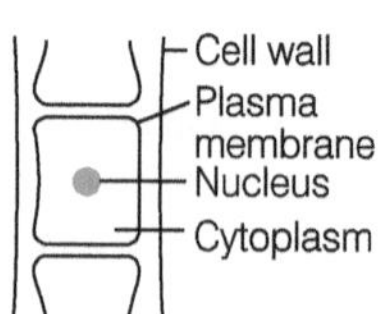

6. *Which cell organelle is known as protein factory of the cell?*

Ans. Ribosome is known as protein factory of the cell, as it is involved in the synthesis of proteins.

7. *How many type of plastids are found in plant cells?*

Ans. Plastids are of three types, i.e. leucoplasts, chloroplasts and chromoplasts. Leucoplasts are colourless plastids, chloroplasts are green plastids and chromoplasts are variously coloured plastids.

8. *Give the name of a single membranous organelle?*

Ans. Lysosome is a single membranous organelle. It is also known as suicide bag of the cell.

9. *Which part of a typical plant cell is non-living?*

Ans. The only non-living part of a plant cell is a cell wall. It is rigid, permeable, composed of cellulose and provides strength and rigidity to the cell.

10. *How a human cheek cell is different from a plant cell?*

Ans. Unlike plant cell, animal cell (i.e. human cheek cell) does not have a cell wall and chloroplast.

11. *Which organelle helps in photosynthesis in plant cells?*

Ans. Plastids present in plant cells help in photosynthesis. The green plastids, i.e. chloroplasts are the main site of photosynthesis in plants.

12. *Name the two cell organelles which are not found in animal cell?*

Ans. Cell wall and plastids are absent in an animal cell. These are found in plant cells.

13. ***The teacher asked a student to draw the diagram of human cheek cell. The student draw the following diagram. Identify the part wrongly labelled by him.***

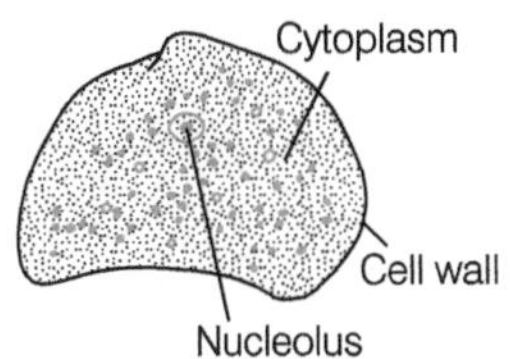

Ans. Cell wall is wrongly labelled. It is the plasma membrane. An animal cell such as human cheek cell does not have a cell wall. It is present only in plant cells.

14. ***Centrioles are found in which cells?***

Ans. Centrioles are found in all animal cells, (e.g. human cheek cells).

15. ***Which membrane of mitochondria forms cristae?***

Ans. The inner membrane of mitochondria forms folds called cristae. They increase the surface area for respiration.

16. ***Which cell organelle regulates the growth of a cell?***

Ans. The growth of the cells is regulated by nucleus.

17. ***Name the outer membrane of an animal cell?***

Ans. The outer membrane found in an animal cell is called as cell membrane. Animal cells lack a cell wall.

18. ***What is nucleoplasm?***

Ans. Nucleoplasm is the colourless dense fluid-like substance present inside the nuclear membrane.

19. ***Which cells have true nucleus and membrane-bound organelles?***

Ans. Eukaryotic cells have true nucleus and membrane-bound organelles.

20. ***Give the name of two single celled eukaryotes who can change their shape?***

Ans. Eukaryotic, single cell animals like *Euglena* and *Amoeba* can change their shape.

21. ***(i) Which stain will you prefer to prepare a temporary mount of onion peel?***

(ii) Why glycerine is used for mounting material?

Ans. (i) Safranin.

(ii) Glycerine being hygroscopic does not allow the mounted material to lose water and become dry.

22. ***(i) Which cell components can be seen clearly in a temporary mount of onion peel under compound microscope?***

(ii) What is the name given to outermost covering in case of a, (a) plant cell (b) animal cell?

Ans. (i) Cell wall, cytoplasm, vacuole and nucleus.

(ii) (a) Cell wall

(b) Plasma membrane.

23. ***Pick the odd one out from Golgi apparatus, cytoplasm, endoplasmic reticulum, lysosomes. Explain.***

Ans. Cytoplasm form the structural part of the cell, while ER, lysosomes and Golgi apparatus are the organelles present in cytoplasm.

24. ***Can a single cell live independently on its own? Explain with example.***

Ans. Yes, the unicellular organisms can live independently as they are devoid of organelles and perform all the living processes themselves, e.g. *Amoeba, Paramecium*.

EXPERIMENT 5

Experiment 5 (a)

Objective

To identify parenchyma collenchyma and sclerenchyma tissues in plants from prepared slides and draw their labelled diagrams.

Materials Required

Permanent slides of parenchyma, sclerenchyma tissues and compound microscope.

Theory

Plant tissues are broadly classified into meristematic and permanent tissues. Permanent tissues may be, simple tissues like parenchyma, collenchyma and sclerenchyma or complex tissues like xylem and phloem. The structural features of tissues like wall characteristics, cell size, lumen size and cytoplasmic contents vary in different types of permanent tissues.

Procedure

Focus the prepared slides of parenchyma and sclerenchyma tissues one by one, under the compound microscope. Observe their characteristic features. Draw labelled diagrams and note down your observations.

Observations

1. Parenchyma Tissue

Identifying Features

- Parenchyma cells are isodiametric, oval or round in shape.
- Each cell has a prominent nucleus, a large vacuole, thin cell wall and peripheral cytoplasm.

- Intercellular spaces are present in between the parenchyma cells.

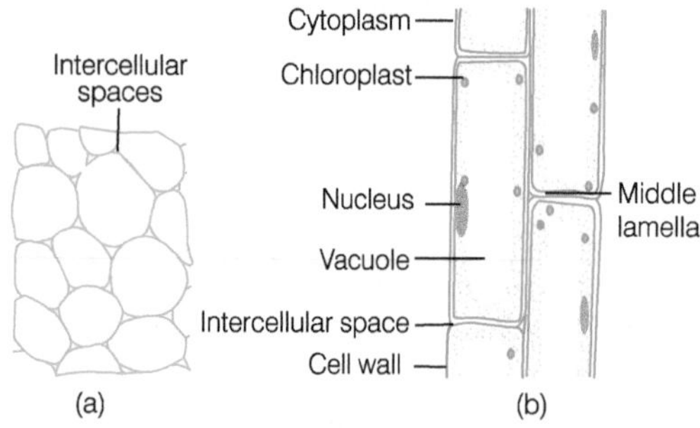

Parenchyma tissue; (a) Transverse section and (b) Longitudinal section

Functions

- Keeping the cells turgid they provide rigidity to the plant.
- It stores food materials in the form of proteins, starch, oil and fats.
- Chlorophyll containing parenchyma (chlorenchyma) helps in photosynthesis.

Conclusion

As cells are thin-walled, isodiametric and have intercellular spaces, the given slide is of parenchyma tissue. It is a simple and permanent plant tissue.

2. Collenchyma Tissue

Identifying Features

- Cells appear oval, spherical or polygonal.
- Cells are elastic, living and mechanical tissue.
- Cells are closely packed hence, there is no intercellular space.
- Cell walls of these cells possess thickenings at the corners.

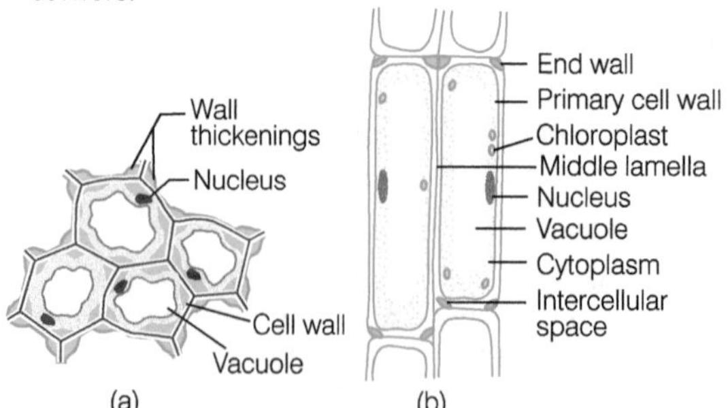

Collenchyma tissue : (a) Transverse section and (b) Longitudinal section

Functions

- This tissue gives mechanical strength to young plant parts.
- It prevents tearing of leaves and resists bending of stems.

Conclusion

Since, the cells of the tissue are living, oval or spherical in shape and not have intercellular spaces, the given slide is of Collenchyma tissue. It is a simple and permanent plant tissue.

3. Sclerenchyma Tissue

Identifying Features

- Cells appear polygonal, oval or circular in transverse section.
- Cells are dead and devoid of protoplasm.
- Cells have a thick lignified cell wall perforated with pits.
- Cells are closely packed hence, there is no intercellular space.
- The sclerenchyma tissue has two types of cells, i.e. fibres and sclereids. Fibres are long, narrow and pointed at both ends. Sclereids are short, isodiametric and are also called grit or stone cells.

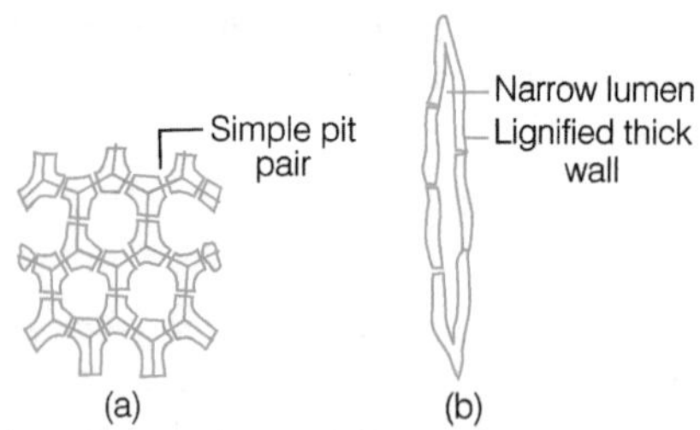

Sclerenchyma tissue; (a) Transverse section and (b) Longitudinal section

Function

This tissue provides mechanical strength to the plant.

Conclusion

Since, the cells of the tissue are thick-walled and highly lignified, it is sclerenchyma tissue. It is a simple permanent plant tissue.

Experiment 5 (b)

Objective

To identify striated muscle fibre and nerve cells from prepared slides and draw their labelled diagrams.

Materials Required

Prepared slides of striated muscle fibre, nerve fibre and compound microscope.

Theory

Animal body is made up of groups of similar cells which perform specific functions. Such groups of identical cells are called tissues. There are four basic types of tissues, i.e. epithelial, connective, muscular and nervous. These tissues vary from each other not only in their structure but also in their functions.

Procedure

Focus the given slides first under the low power of microscope and then under high power. Observe their characteristic features, draw labelled diagrams and note down your observations.

Observations

1. Striated Muscle Fibre

Identifying Features

- The muscle cells are long, cylindrical and unbranched.
- These fibres show alternate light and dark bands or transverse striations.
- Each muscle cell is multinucleated and nuclei lie at the periphery.
- The cytoplasm of muscle cell is known as sarcoplasm and the plasma membrane is called sarcolemma.
- These muscles are attached to the bones hence, are also called skeletal muscles.
- Striated muscles are controlled by our will. Therefore, they are called voluntary muscles.
- These muscles are found in arms, legs, tongue, pharynx etc.

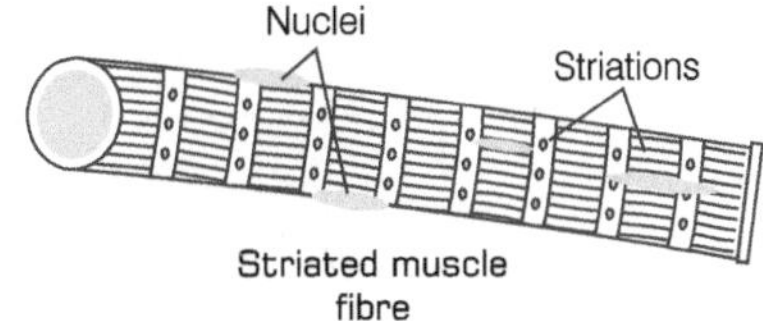

Striated muscle fibre

Conclusion

The observed slide is of striated muscles as muscle fibres are long, cylindrical, multinucleated and show transverse striations.

2. Nerve Fibres

Identifying Features

- Each typical nerve cell or neuron has three main parts:
  (*i*) Cell body or cyton (*ii*) Axon (*iii*) Dendrites.
- Cyton or cell body has a prominent nucleus and cytoplasm.
- In the cytoplasm, granules are present, which are called Nissl's granules.
- The cell body gives out several branches called dendrons, which further divide and form dendrites.
- Axon is a single elongated branch given out from the cell body. Its ends are called axon endings.
- Axon is covered with a myelin sheath or medullary sheath in some cells. It is interrupted at places. There are gaps called node of Ranvier. Such nerve fibres are called myelinated nerve fibres.
- The loose connection between the axon endings of one nerve cell and dendrons and cell body of other nerve cell is called synapse.

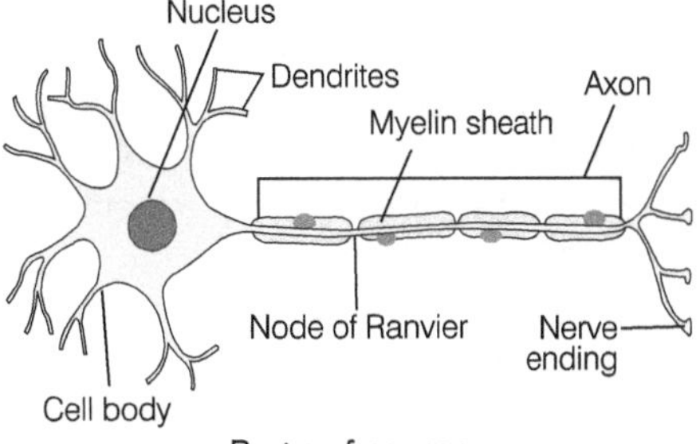

Parts of neuron

Conclusion

The elongated thread-like shape, division of cell into cyton, axon and dendrons and the presence of myelin sheath shows that the given slide is of a nerve cell or neuron.

QUESTIONS

1. ***A student was observing a slide. He observed long unbranched cells with striations and many nuclei. Identify the slide.***

Ans. The given features are of striated muscle fibres, i.e. multinucleated cells that are long and unbranched and show striations.

2. ***Give the name of a simple, permanent living tissue of plants, which has wall thickenings.***

Ans. Collenchyma is a living tissue. It consists of living cells with wall thickenings at the corners.

3. ***Name the tissue which provide mechanical strength as well as elasticity to the plants.***

Ans. Collenchyma provide mechanical strength as well as elasticity to the plants.

4. ***Identify the part labelled as 'C' in the given diagram.***

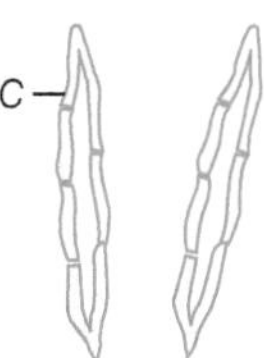

Ans. The given figure is of a sclerenchyma fibre. In the given diagram 'C' is narrow lumen.

5. *Identify the tissue (A) and (B).*

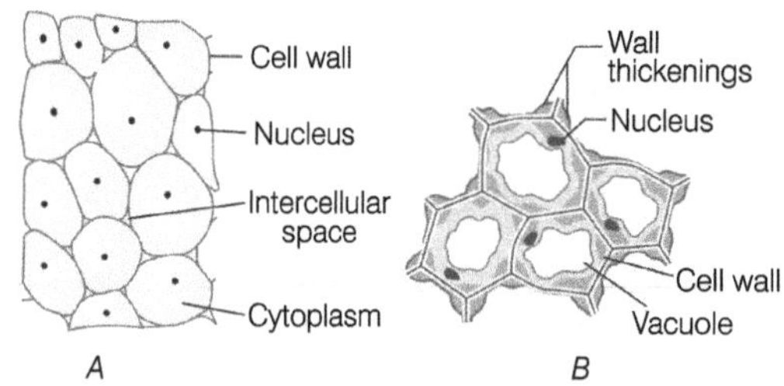

Ans. In the given diagram,

A – Parenchyma tissue, *B* – Collenchyma tissue.

6. *Which chemical substances are deposited in the walls of collenchyma cell/tissue?*

Ans. Pectin and cellulose are deposited in the walls of collenchyma.

7. *Name the branch of biology which deals with the study of tissues.*

Ans. The branch of biology which deals with the study of tissues is called histology.

8. *Which muscles are involved in the movement of arms?*

Ans. The muscles involved in the movement of arms are striated muscles.

9. *Which plant tissue is present in seed coat of almond?*

Ans. Sclerenchyma, mainly sclereids (stone cells) are present in seed coat of almond and makes it very hard.

10. *Which plant cells have perforated cell wall?*

Ans. Vessels have perforated cell walls.

11. *Give the diagram of the striated muscle fibre as seen under the microscope? Give reason supporting your answer.*

Ans. Under microscope, striated muscles show alternate light and dark bands on striations when stained appropriately. Also, the nucleus in them lies at periphery.

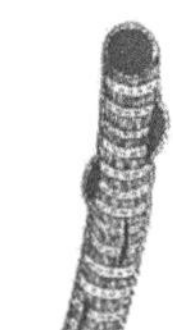

Straited muscle fibre

12. *The figure shows the longitudinal section of a plant tissue. Which cell type is represented by this figure?*

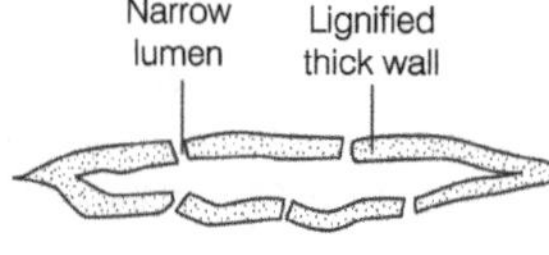

Ans. The cell is of sclerenchyma tissue as the walls are long and narrow and are thickened due to lignin. The cell walls are so thick that there is very little internal space inside the cell.

13. *Identify the type of tissue based on characteristics given.*

(i) *Attached to bones, help in body movements. Alternate light and dark bands are present in them.*

(ii) *Involved in rhythmic contraction and relaxation of the heart.*

Ans. (i) Skeletal or striated muscle tissue.

(ii) Cardiac muscle tissue.

14. *Differentiate the following components of blood, which viewed under microscope appears.*

(i) *Enucleated irregular shaped*

(ii) *Kidney-shaped nucleus in cell*

(iii) *Multinucleated cells*

Ans. (i) Red Blood Cells (RBCs)

(ii) Monocyte-Largest white blood cell

(iii) Neutrophil-Granulocyte (WBC) present in maximum amount in blood.

15. *Observe the given figures and answer the questions that follow.*

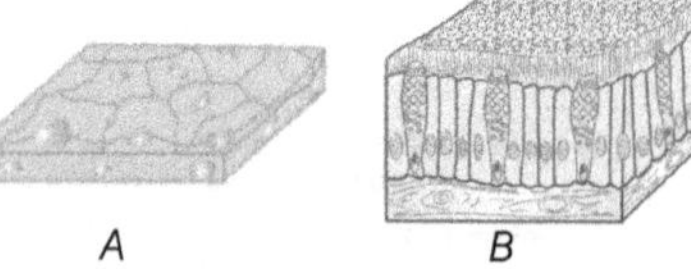

(i) *Identify figures A and B.*

(ii) *Which is called tessellated and pavement epithelium?*

(iii) *Which one lines the gastrointestinal tract and epiglottis?*

(iv) *Which one allows diffusion of substances?*

Ans. (i) Figure *A* is squamous epithelium.
Figure *B* is columnar epithelium.

(ii) Tessellated and pavement epithelium is another name for the squamous epithelium (*A*).

(iii) Gastrointestinal tract and epiglottis both are lined by simple columnar epithelium (*B*).

(iv) Simple epithelium such as squamous epithelium (*A*) allows diffusion of substances through it.

16. *Identify the given two slides A and B as a parenchyma or sclerenchyma. Sclerenchyma can be identified by which characteristic?*

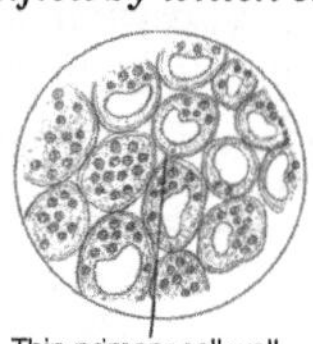

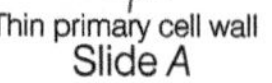

Slide *A*

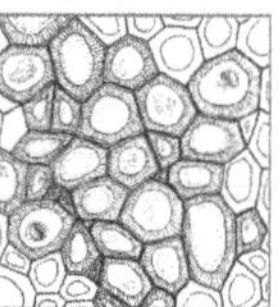

Slide *B*

Ans. Slide *A* represents the parenchyma cells and slide *B* represents the sclerenchyma cells.

Sclerenchyma can be identified by the presence of thick cell walls, closely packed cells without intercellular spaces and presence of conspicuous middle lamella between two sclerenchymatous cells.

17. ***A horse and a mango tree both are complex living organisms with specialised different tissue systems to perform the basic life processes. Give two reasons as to why both possess different tissues to perform similar function.***

Ans. Horse is an animal, whereas mango tree is a plant. Plants and animals have different types of tissues because:

(i) plants do not show locomotion, while most of the animals move from one place to another in search of food, water and shelter.

(ii) they have different patterns of growth. Plant's growth is limited to certain regions and continues throughout the life, whereas animal's growth is more or less uniform.

EXPERIMENT 6

Experiment 6 (a)

Objective

To determine the melting point of ice.

Materials Required

Ice (crushed), beaker, thermometer, iron stand, water bath burner, tripod stand and stopwatch.

Theory

During a change of state, temperature of the substance remains constant. Thus,

(*i*) during melting of ice, temperature of ice will remain constant at its melting point until the entire solid converts into liquid.

(*ii*) the constant temperature during melting gives the melting point of ice.

Procedure

(*i*) Take a small quantity of crushed ice in a beaker.

(*ii*) Place a thermometer in the ice.

(*iii*) Place this ice containing beaker in a water bath.

(*iv*) Note down the temperature of ice and at the same time, start the stopwatch.

(*v*) Now, start heating the water bath on a low flame.

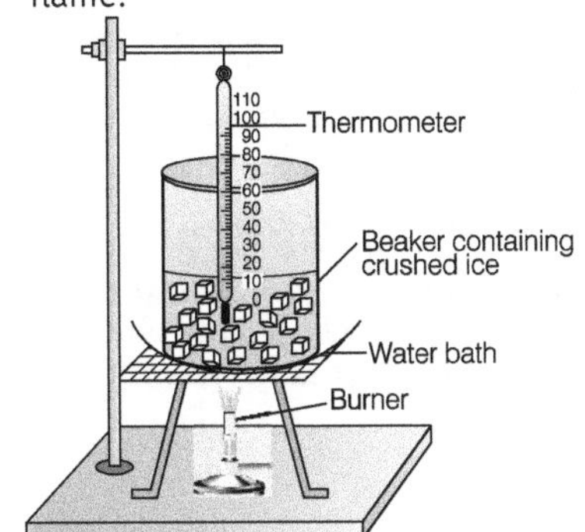

Determination of the melting point of ice

(*vi*) Note down the temperature of ice after every half minute and record it in a tabular form.

(*vii*) Continue until the whole ice gets melted.

Observations

S. No.	*Time* (min)	*Temperature* (°C)
1.	0.0	....
2.	0.5	....
3.	1.0	....
4.	1.5	....
5.	2.0	....
6.	2.5	....
7.	3.0	....
8.	3.5	....
9.	4.0	....
10.	4.5	....
11.	5.0	....
12.	5.5	....
13.	6.0	....
14.	6.5	....
15.	7.0	....

Result

Since, during the melting of ice, the temperature of ice remains constant at its melting point. Therefore, from the values given in the table

Melting point of ice = ... °C or .... K

Precautions

(*i*) Immersed only the bulb of the thermometer in the crushed ice.

(*ii*) While taking the reading on the thermometer, keep your eye at the level of mercury thread.

(*iii*) The thermometer should not touch the wall of the beaker.

Experiment 6 (b)

Objective

To determine the boiling point of water.

Materials Required

Distilled water, round bottom flask, thermometer, iron stand, sand bath, tripod stand, burner, stopwatch and bent tube.

Theory

During a change of state, temperature of the substance remains constant. Thus,

(*i*) during boiling of water, temperature of water will remain constant at its boiling point.

(*ii*) the constant temperature during boiling gives the boiling point of water.

Procedure

(*i*) Take about 50 mL of water in a round bottom distillation flask.

(*ii*) Fix up a thermometer and a bent tube in the cork of the flask as shown in the figure.

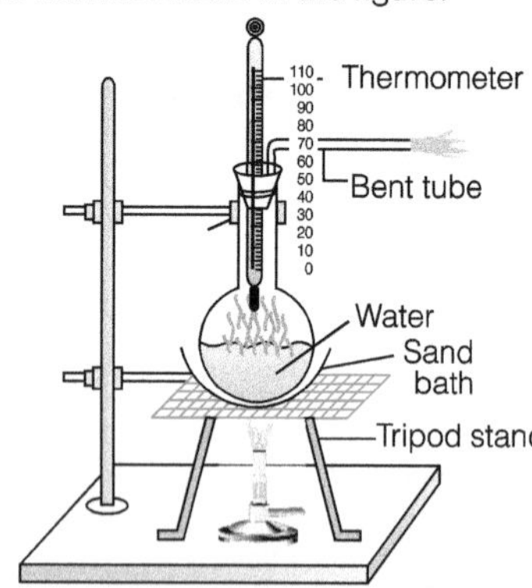

(*iii*) Heat the flask on a sand bath kept on a tripod stand.

(*iv*) Start the stopwatch and read temperature on the thermometer.

(*v*) Keep recording the temperature after every one minute until water starts boiling.

(*vi*) Continue recording the temperature on the thermometer for few more minutes.

(*vii*) Record all observations in a tabular form.

Observations

S. No.	*Time* (min)	*Temperature* (°C)
1.	0	....
2.	1	....
3.	2	....
4.	3	....
5.	4	....
6.	5	....
7.	6	....
8.	7	....
9.	8	....
10.	9	....
11.	10	....
12.	11	....
13.	12	....
14.	13	....
15.	14	....

Result

Since, during the boiling of water, the temperature of water remains constant at its boiling point. Therefore, from the values given in the table

Boiling point of water = ... °C or .... K

Precautions

(*i*) The bulb of the thermometer should be kept outside the water.

(*ii*) While taking the reading on the thermometer, keep your eye at the level of mercury thread.

QUESTIONS

1. ***Sketch a diagram representing is the correct method of finding the melting point of ice?***

Ans.

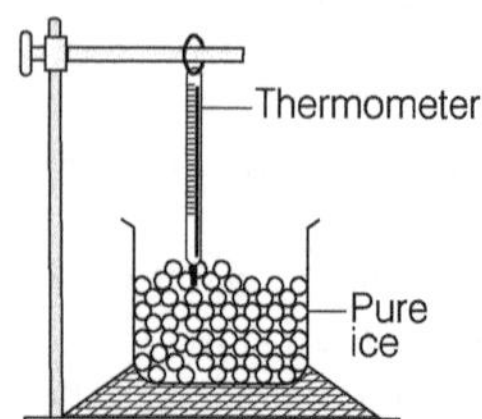

The bulb of the thermometer should be dipped completely inside the crushed ice.

2. ***In an experiment to determine the boiling point of water, the stopwatch used to note down the temperature of water at different intervals of time has 20 divisions between 0 to 10 s marks. Find the least count of the stopwatch.***

Ans. 20 divisions indicate 10 s of time.

So, least count $= \frac{10}{20} = 0.5\,s$

3. ***You are given ice at −10° C. It is supplied with heat at a constant rate. The temperature of ice changes with the heat supplied. Represent this observation in graph.***

Ans.

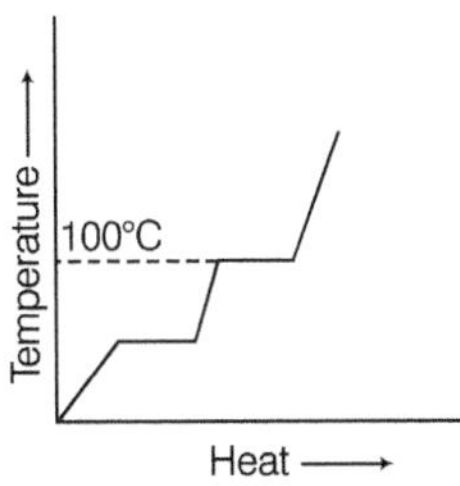

4. *What do you mean by melting of a substance?*

Ans. Melting point of a substance is that constant temperature at which the melting of substance starts and remain same until the entire solid converts into liquid.

5. *Liquid A boils at 60°C, while liquid B boils at 80° C. Which is more volatile?*

Ans. Low boiling point refers to high volatility. Hence, liquid *A* is more volatile.

6. *Draw a set up representing the determination of boiling point of water.*

Ans.

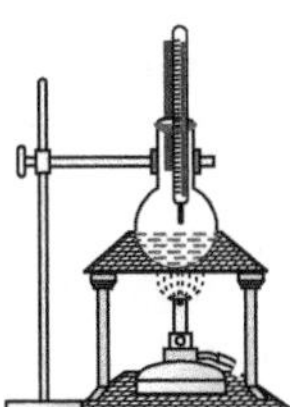

The bulb of the thermometer should be just above the surface of water and delivery tube should be above in space.

7. *Consider the following graph*

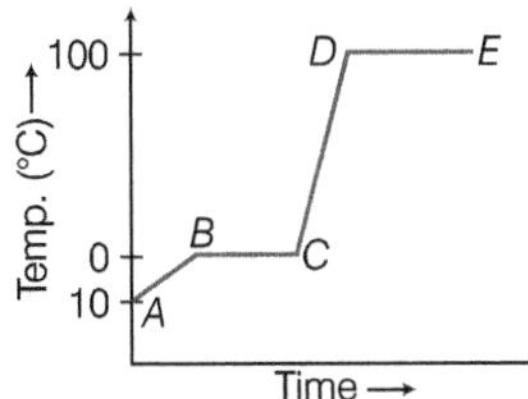

Which portion of temperature-time graph showing heating of ice at −10° C to water at 100° C represent the change of state on heating?

Ans. *BC* represents the change of state of ice from solid to liquid and *DE* represents the change of state of water from liquid to steam (gas).

8. *In an experiment to determine the melting point of ice, Rakshita observes no change in the temperature, when she heats the ice till the whole ice melts. What could be the reason of no rise in temperature.*

Ans. During melting, the temperature remains constant until the entire ice changes into water as the heat supplied to ice is used to change the ice from its solid to liquid state.

9. *Name the set of apparatus required to determine the boiling point of water.*

Ans. Round bottom flask, burner, thermometer, wire gauze, stand with clamp, cork with two holes and glass tube.

10. *At room temperature, a student sets up an apparatus to determine the melting point of ice. He takes a beaker half-filled with crushed ice and dips a mercury thermometer in it. After this, what would he observed?*

Ans. Once a solid attains its melting temperature, the temperature remains same until entire solid converts into liquid.

11. *A student sets up an apparatus for the determination of boiling point of a sample of water supplied to him in his laboratory. He recorded the boiling point as 102°C. Assuming that the thermometer is accurate. What is reason for the error in the determined value of boiling point?*

Ans. Distilled water should be selected for determining the boiling point of water more accurately.

12. *During melting of ice, cooling effect is produced. Why?*

Ans. Ice absorbs heat from the surroundings, resulting in a cooling effect.

13. *In the determination of melting point of ice, when will the correct reading of melting point is noted in the thermometer?*

Ans. Melting point is the constant temperature at which the ice converts into water.

14. *Mohan used a thermometer having 20 divisions between 30°C mark and 40°C mark.*
While determining the boiling point of water using this thermometer, he observed that the level of mercury becomes constant just three divisions below the 100°C mark. What should be the least count and boiling point recorded by Mohan?

Ans. 20 divisions indicate 10° C range of temperature, so, least count $= \frac{10}{20} = 0.5°$ C and the level of mercury just three divisions below 100° C will be

$$100°C - 3 \times 0.5°C = 98.5°C$$

15. *Water in a container is heated uniformly from 0° C to 100° C. Its temperature decreases up to 4°C and increases further. Why?*

Ans. Due to latent heat of vapourisation, its temperature decreases upto 4° C and increases further.

16. *Prakhar sets up an apparatus for the determination of boiling point of distilled water at Shimla. He recorded the boiling point as 97°C, instead of 100° C. Assuming that the thermometer is accurate. What is the reason for this lesser boiling point?*

Ans. Shimla is a hilly region, so here pressure is less than atmospheric pressure, hence boiling point of water is less than 100°C.

17. ***While heating a liquid, it has to be stirred properly. Why?***

Ans. During heating, if it is stirred properly, the liquid gets uniform temperature throughout.

18. ***What would be the reading of a thermometer, when it is kept in the ice?***

Ans. The temperature of ice decreases gradually and after reaching at 0°C (melting point), it becomes constant.

19. ***In an experiment to determine the boiling point of water, mention two important precautions that should be taken.***

Ans. (i) Constant stirring must be done so that heating may be uniform.

(ii) Bulb of the thermometer must not dip in water.

20. ***If in the determination of melting point of ice, ice is contaminated with some non-volatile impurity like common salt, how the melting point of ice is affected?***

Ans. Melting point of ice get lowered. Impurities always lower than melting point of solid.

21. ***In an experiment to determine the boiling point of water, state the reason for the following precautions:***

(i) The bulb of thermometer should not touch the sides of beaker.

(ii) While boiling water, pumice stones should be added.

Ans. (i) The sides of the glass beaker are at higher temperature than the contents present inside the beaker. Therefore, the reading given by the thermometer touching the sides of the beaker does not give correct result.

(ii) Pieces of pumice stone are added to boiling water in order to avoid any bumping.

22. ***Write melting point of ice and boiling point of water in degree Celsius and Kelvin scale.***

Ans. (i) Melting point of ice = 0°C = 0 + 273 = 273

(ii) Boiling point of water = 100°C = 100 + 273 = 373 K

23. ***Three students A, B and C used distilled water at 0°C, distilled water at room temperature and lukewarm distilled water respectively. Compare the boiling point of water observed by the three students and also give reason.***

Ans. All the students will record the boiling point of water as same, i.e. 100°C because distilled water, no matter what its initial state is, boils at 100°C only.

24. ***A sample of water under study was found to boil at 102°C, at normal temperature and pressure. Is the water pure? Will this water freeze at 0°C? Comment.***

Ans. The boiling point of pure water is 100°C. The given sample boils at 102°C, indicates that it contains dissolved impurities. Thus, it is not pure. No, the water will not freeze at 0°C. Instead, it will freeze below 0°C.

EXPERIMENT 7

Objective

To verify the laws of reflection of sound.

Materials Required

(*i*) Two glass tubes of 3 ft in length and 2 inches in diameter.

(*ii*) Vertical reflector (polished wooden drawing board).

(*iii*) Sounding body (Gallon's whistle or clock).

Theory

(*i*) **Reflection of Sound** When sound travels in a given medium, it strikes the surface of another medium and bounces back in some other direction, this phenomenon is called reflection of sound.

(*ii*) **First Law of Reflection of Sound** It states that incident sound wave, the reflected sound wave and the normal at the point of incidence, all lie in the same plane.

(*iii*) **Second Law of Reflection of Sound** The angle of incidence of sound is equal to the angle of reflection of sound.

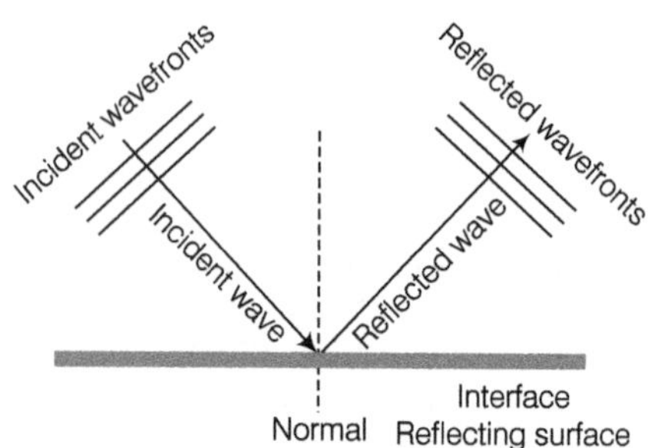

(*iv*) **Speed of Sound** It depends upon the nature of the medium through which the waves pass.

Presence of moisture increases the velocity of sound in air because density of dry air is greater than the density of moisture.

Procedure

(*i*) Arrange two glass tubes *AB* and *CD* horizontally at same angle in front of a vertical reflector R_1R_2.

(ii) At the mouth A, of tube AB, place a sounding body (a tuning fork or a clock).

(iii) Adjust the inclination of the tube CD with respect to the reflector R_1R_2, so that sound is distinctly and loudly heard when the ear is placed at D.

(iv) Mark the position of tubes AB and CD.

(v) Draw a dotted line from the centre of diameter of tube AB and CD and extend upto reflector board. Draw normal.

(vi) Measure the angle between the sound waves coming from the tube AB and the normal (i.e. the angle of incidence of sound waves).

(vii) $\angle AON$ is called angle of incidence ($\angle i$).

(viii) Then, measure the angle of reflection ($\angle r$), i.e. angle between normal and the central line drawn from the tube CD, when sound is distinctly and loudly audible. This is the angle of reflection of sound wave ($\angle r$), i.e. $\angle DON$.

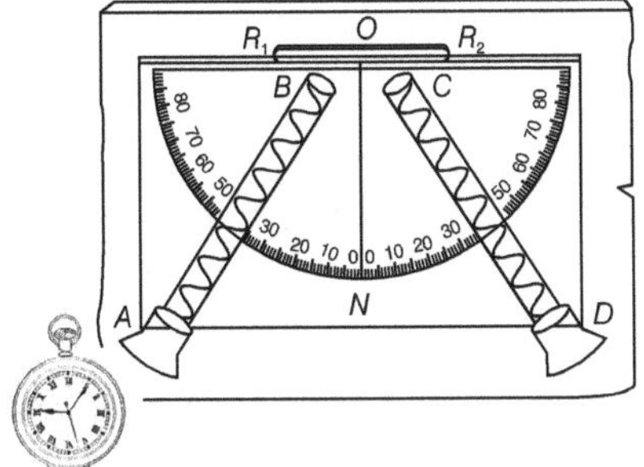

Observation Table

S. No.	Angle of incidence ($\angle i = \angle AON$)	Angle of reflection ($\angle r = \angle DON$)
1.		
2.		
3.		

Inference (Result)

(i) When glass tube CD (through which sound is heard) is lifted vertically or obliquely, then the sound of clock either weakens or diminishes completely. It shows that the reflected wave should lie in the same plane of incidence, which verifies first law of reflection of sound.

(ii) The angle of incidence and the angle of reflection of sound are found to be equal, which verifies second law of reflection of sound.

Precautions

(i) The inner surface of metallic tube should be highly polished.

(ii) Metal plate should be polished.

(iii) Tuning fork or clock should be closed to the tube, but it should not touch the tube.

(iv) There should be complete silence in the laboratory, so that sounds from other sources do not interfere.

QUESTIONS

1. ***What is the value of difference between the angle of reflection and angle of incidence?***

Ans. We know that,

Angle of incidence = Angle of reflection

or $\angle i = \angle r$

Now, difference between angle of reflection and angle of incidence $= \angle r - \angle i = \angle r - \angle r = 0$

2. ***Suppose the whole experimental set up of this experiment is submerged in water. What changes do you expect in your observation?***

Ans. The speed of sound in water at 20 °C is 1482 m/s while in air it is 343 m/s at 20 °C. Therefore, when the whole experimental set up is submerged in water, the reflected sound will be heard faster as compared to air.

3. ***How does bats search out prey and fly in dark night?***

Ans. Bats emit ultrasonic squeaks while flying and listen to the echoes produced by reflection of their squeaks from the obstacles or prey in their path. From time taken by echo to be heard, bats can determine the distance of obstacle or prey and can avoid the obstacles or can catch the prey.

4. ***What will be the direction of sound, while performing the experiment on reflection of sound?***

Ans. It is a precaution to keep the position of the ticking clock (source of sound) through which incident sound is coming, along the axis of tube which specifies that ear, ticking clock (source of sound) and reflecting surface all lie in the same plane.

5. ***Ramjeet, while verifying the laws of reflection of sound measured the angle between the incident sound wave and reflected sound wave to be 130°. Find the angle of incidence?***

Ans. Since, angle of incidence = angle of reflection

or $\angle i = \angle r$

$\therefore \quad \angle i = \dfrac{\angle i + \angle r}{2} = \dfrac{130°}{2} = 65°$

6. ***In which medium, the reflection of sound does not occur?***

Ans. Since, propagation of sound requires medium. So, reflection of sound does not occur in vacuum.

7. *If the reflecting surface and the source of sound both are in the plane of the table, the position of the ear of the observer should be where?*

Ans. From first law of reflection of sound, source of sound through which incident sound wave is coming, reflecting surface through which normal is drawn and position of the ear of an observer at which reflected sound wave reaches, all lie in the same plane.

8. *When the sound wave propagates, which physical quantity changes in the medium?*

Ans. Propagation of sound can be visualised as propagation of density variations or pressure variations in the medium as pressure is related to number of particles in the medium in a given volume. More density of particles in the medium gives more pressure and *vice-versa*.

9. *While doing experiment on verifying the law of reflection of sound, four students measured the angles ∠i and ∠r as shown in the diagram below. Sketch the correct measurements of angle of incidence and angle of reflection done by student.*

Ans. The angle of incidence is the angle, which the incident wave makes with the normal to the surface. Also, the angle of reflection is the angle, which reflected wave makes with the normal to the surface.

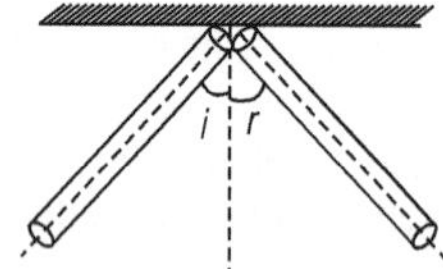

10. *Sound wave is also known as longitudinal wave. Why?*

Ans. Sound travels in the form of longitudinal wave. In longitudinal wave, the individual particles of the medium move in a direction parallel to the direction of propagation of disturbance. The particles do not move from one place to another but they simply oscillate back and forth about their mean position. Hence, it is longitudinal wave.

11. *Which physical phenomenon or phenomena is/are also based on reflection of sound waves?*

Ans. Echo is the phenomenon which is repetition of sound caused by reflection of sound waves.

12. *On which physical quantity, the speed of sound depends?*

Ans. Speed of sound in a medium depends upon the temperature and pressure of the medium.

13. *The given figure represents the graph between the angle of incidence and angle of reflection for a sound wave. What conclusion can be drawn from it?*

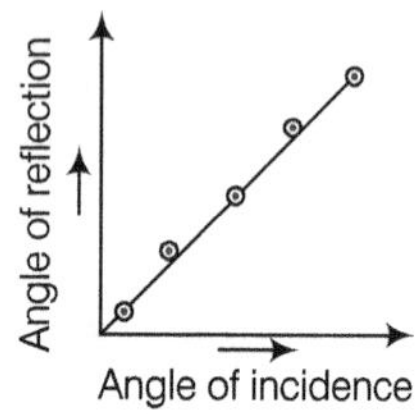

Ans. The conclusion is that angle of incidence is always equal to angle of reflection, i.e. ∠i = ∠r, which is second law of reflection of sound.

14. *A student does the experiment on verifying the law of reflection of sound. He records the following values of the angle of incidence (∠i) and angle of reflection (∠r).*

S.No.	1	2	3	4	5
Angle of incidence	30°	40°	45°	50°	60°
Angle of reflection	60°	50°	45°	40°	30°

Which reading/s among 1, 2, 3, 4 and 5 is/are correct?

Ans. Only 3 is correct, as ∠i = ∠r.

EXPERIMENT 8

Objective

To determine the density of a solid (denser than water) by using a spring balance and a measuring cylinder.

Materials Required

(*i*) A solid block (whose density is to be measured).
(*ii*) Spring balance (0–100 g-f)
(*iii*) Measuring cylinder (100 mL)
(*iv*) Iron stand
(*v*) Glass stopper
(*vi*) Fine cotton thread
(*vii*) Beaker containing water

Theory

(*i*) **Density** It is defined as mass per unit volume of a substance.

$$\text{Density} = \frac{\text{Mass of a substance}}{\text{Volume of a substance}}$$

SI unit of density is $kg\,m^{-3}$ or kg/m^3.

(*ii*) **Principle of spring balance** It states that the extension produced in a spring is directly proportional to the stretching force applied, provided the elastic limit of the spring is not exceeded.

(*iii*) **Graduated measuring cylinder** It is made from hard glass, so that it can withstand variations in temperature. Its side is marked in mL or cc. The volume of a liquid in mL or cc can be read directly by pouring the liquid in it.

Procedure

This experiment can be completed in two steps

I. To determine the mass of the solid block by using a spring balance.
   (*i*) Take spring balance capable of weighing upto 100 g.
   (*ii*) Suspend the spring balance vertically on an iron stand and note down the position of its pointer on the scale. Record its zero error.
   (*iii*) Suspend the given solid block from the lower hook of the spring balance and note down the position of the pointer on the scale. Record the reading on the scale.
   (*iv*) Calculate the corrected mass of solid block.
   (*v*) Remove solid block from the spring balance and reload it. Note down the reading again.
   (*vi*) Repeat this atleast three times.
   (*vii*) Record your observations in tabular form.

II. To determine the volume of the solid block using measuring cylinder.
   (*i*) Note down the least count of the measuring cylinder.
   For a 100 mL capacity cylinder, usually the least count is 1 mL.
   (*ii*) Pour some water into measuring cylinder and place it on a table.
   (*iii*) Note the level of water in the cylinder by reading the lower meniscus.
   (*iv*) Attach the solid block with a few cm long thread and lower it gently into the water, so that it is completely immersed in water.
   (*v*) Note down the new reading.
   (*vi*) Take difference between the two readings that give the volume of the solid block.

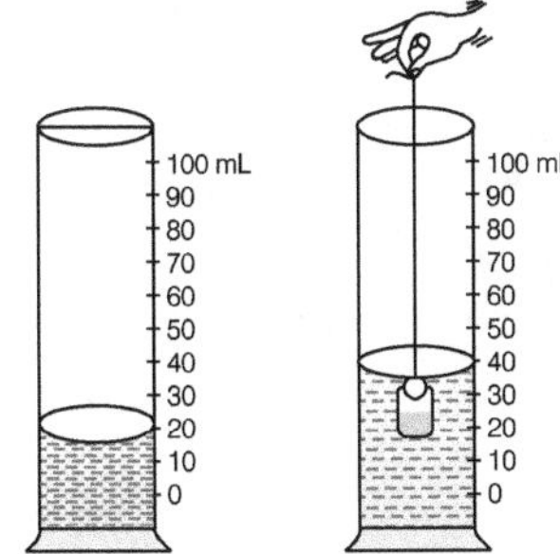

   (*vii*) Repeat this experiment atleast three times.
   (*viii*) Record your observations in tabular form.

Observations

(*i*) Least count of spring balance = ... g-f.
(*ii*) Zero error of the spring balance = ... g-f.

Observation Table

(A) Weight of the given solid block

S. No.	Weight of the given solid block		Mean value of the corrected weight of the solid block
	Observed	Corrected	
1			
2			
3			

(*iii*) Mean mass of solid block = m g.
(*iv*) Least count of measuring cylinder = ... mL.

(B) Reading of water level in measuring cylinder

S. No.	Initial level of water (V_1)	Final level of water (V_2)	Volume of solid block ($V_2 - V_1$)	Mean volume of solid block (mL)
1				
2				
3				

Calculations

(*i*) Mean volume of solid block = V mL.
(*ii*) Density of solid block

$$= \frac{\text{Mean mass of solid block}}{\text{Mean volume of solid block}} = \frac{m}{V} \text{ g/mL}$$

Result

Density of the given solid block at .... °C
= .... g/mL
= .... kg/m^3

Precautions

(*i*) The pointer of spring balance should move freely on the scale.
(*ii*) The solid block should be fully immersed in water and should not touch the sides and bottom of measuring cylinder.
(*iii*) While reading the level of water in the measuring cylinder, keep your eye at the level of the lower meniscus and read the lower meniscus.
(*iv*) The pointer on the scale should be read only after it becomes steady.

Sources of Error

Mass and volume of solid block can be measured only upto the least counts of spring balance and measuring cylinder. So, the result obtained in the experiment may not be absolutely correct.

QUESTIONS

1. *What will be the density of water with respect to its density at 4°C with the fall in temperature?*

Ans. Density of water will decrease with fall in temperature.

2. *Density of glass is 2.5 g/cm^3. What does it mean?*

Ans. It means that 1 cm^3 of glass will weigh 2.5 g or volume of 2.5 g glass is 1 cm^3.

3. *A stone of mass 50 g is tied to a fine cotton thread and then immersed in water contained in measuring cylinder. Find the density of stone.*

Ans. We know that density $= \frac{M}{V}$

Volume of water displaced $= (V_2 - V_1)$cc

$= (40 - 25)$ cc $= 15$ cc

$\therefore \quad D = \frac{50}{15} = 3.33$ g/cc $\quad [\because M = 50 \text{ g}]$

4. *Mass of the body = 62.4 g*

   (i) Reading of water level in measuring cylinder without solid body (V_1) = 16.4 mL

   (ii) V_2 (with solid body) = 24.4 mL

   Based on the above observation, what is the density of material in g/cc?

Ans. We know that, $D = \frac{M}{V}$

$V = V_2 - V_1 = (24.4 - 16.4)$ cc $= 8$ cc

$\therefore \; D = \frac{62.4}{8}$ g/cc $= 7.8$ g/cc

5. *Spring balance is based on which principle?*

Ans. As the scale of spring balance is linear.

$\therefore$ Extension of spring $\propto$ stretching force.

6. *A metal cylinder is melted and the whole mass is cast in the shape of cube. What will happen to its density?*

Ans. In both the cases, the volume displaced by metallic cylinder and cube will be same. So, mass per unit volume does not change. Hence, the density of both cube and metallic cylinder will be same.

7. *In a spring balance, the space between 0 and 25 g marking is divided into 10 equal parts. What will be the least count of spring balance?*

Ans. Least count of spring balance $= \frac{25}{10}$

$= 2.5$ g-wt.

8. *If we want to determine the volume of a solid by immersing it in water, what should be the nature of solid?*

Ans. To determine the volume of a solid by immersing it in water, the solid should be heavier than water and insoluble in it.

9. *While determining the density of a solid, a student is provided with four different combinations*

Measuring cylinder

S. No.	Range	LC
1.	0-100 mL	1 mL
2.	0-200 mL	5 mL
3.	0-100 mL	2 mL
4.	0-200 mL	2 mL

Spring balance

S. No.	Range	LC
1.	0-100 g-wt	1 g-wt
2.	0-200 g-wt	5 g-wt
3.	0-100 g-wt	2 g-wt
4.	0-200 g-wt	2 g-wt

The student should choose which combination?

Ans. The student should choose 1-1,

i.e. Measuring cylinder 0-100 mL and LC = 1 mL

Spring balance 0-100 g-wt and LC = 1 g-wt

10. *Density of gold is 19600 kg/m^3. What will be its density in CGS system?*

Ans. Density of gold in CGS system

$= \frac{\text{Density of gold in SI system}}{1000}$

$= \frac{19600}{1000} = 19.6 \text{ g cm}^{-3}$ (or g/cm^3)

11. *What is the relation between density D, mass M and volume V of the body?*

Ans. The correct relation between density (D), mass (M) and volume (V) of the body is

$D = \frac{M}{V}$.

12. *Which instrument is used to measure mass of the body in the experiment of density?*

Ans. Spring balance is used to measure the mass of the body in the experiment of density.

13. *Four measuring cylinders with different least counts are shown in figures A, B, C and D. Which of the following cylinders is the most suitable cylinder for determining the volume of a cube of side nearly 1 cm?*

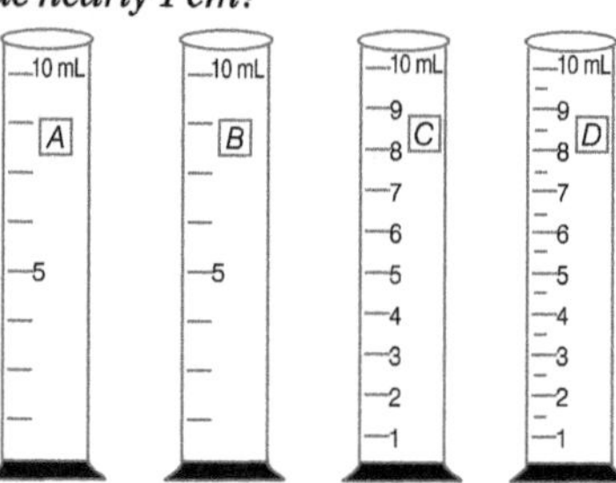

Ans. Figure D, as cylinder D has the smallest least count.

EXPERIMENT 9

Objective

To establish the relation between the loss in weight of a solid when fully immersed in

(i) tap water (ii) strongly salty water, with the weight of water displaced by it, by taking atleast two different solids.

Materials Required

(*i*) A spring balance (0-100 g-f).
(*ii*) A glass stopper (about 50 g).
(*iii*) A brass weight (50 g).
(*iv*) Thin cotton thread.
(*v*) An overflow jar.
(*vi*) A wooden block.
(*vii*) A pre-weighed beaker, showing its weight on the label affixed to it, 250 cc beaker containing tap water, 250 cc beaker containing strong salty water and a common compression balance.

Theory

(*i*) **Archimedes' Principle** It states that when a body is partly or wholly immersed in a fluid (i.e. liquid or gas), it experiences an apparent loss in weight, which is equal to the weight of the fluid displaced by it.
(*ii*) The apparent loss in weight can be calculated by weighing the body, firstly in air and then completely immersing it in water, with the help of a spring balance. The difference in weights, gives the apparent loss of weight of the body in water.
(*iii*) The water displaced can be calculated as under weight of water displaced is found by collecting it in a pre-weighed beaker, then reweighing it.
(*iv*) It is found that weight of water displaced by the solid is always equal to the apparent loss of weight of the solid in water. This verifies Archimedes' principle.
(*v*) **Buoyant force** An upward force experienced by a solid, when partly or wholly immersed in a fluid.

Procedure (A)

(*i*) Take a clean glass stopper and tie it with a fine thread. Make a loop on the other end of the cotton thread.
(*ii*) Check the spring balance for zero error and record it. Let, the zero error be x g-f.
(*iii*) Suspend the glass stopper from the hook of the spring balance. Read and record its weight in air. Let, the weight be w g-f.
(*iv*) Calculate the true weight of the glass stopper in air, by subtracting the zero error from the observed weight of the glass stopper in air.
(*v*) Place the overflow jar on the wooden block and slowly pour tap water in it, till the water just starts overflowing through its spout. At this moment, stop pouring water. In a few moments, the water from the spout stops overflowing. In this situation, the water in the overflow jar is at the verge of overflowing.
(*vi*) Place the clean and dry pre-weighed beaker (say its weight is P g-f) under the spout of the overflow jar.
(*vii*) Now, gently lower the glass stopper (which is suspended from the hook of the spring balance) into the water in the overflow jar till it gets completely immersed. Also, at the same time, the water overflows through the spout and gets collected in the measuring pre-weighed beaker.
(*viii*) Read and record the weight of the glass stopper when fully immersed in water by subtracting the zero error from the observed weight.
(*ix*) Weigh the pre-weighed beaker alongwith the displaced water on the common compression balance. Let, the weight be P_1 g-f.
(*x*) Calculate the loss of weight of water displaced by the glass stopper when fully immersed in water.
(*xi*) Calculate the weight of water displaced by the glass stopper.
(*xii*) It is noticed that
  (*a*) Loss of weight of the glass stopper in water = Weight of water displaced by glass stopper
  (*b*) Repeat the above experiment by immersing the glass stopper in salty water. It is noticed that;
  Loss of weight of glass stopper in salty water = Weight of salty water displaced by the glass stopper
  (*c*) Repeat the experiment by using brass weight and immersing it fully in tap water. It is noticed that;
  Loss of weight of brass weight in water = Weight of water displaced by brass weight
  (*d*) Repeat the experiment by using brass weight and immersing it fully in salty water. It is noticed

that; Loss of weight of brass weight in salty water = Weight of salty water displaced by brass weight.

Observation Table

(*i*) Least count of the spring balance = ... g-f. (*ii*) Zero error of spring balance = ± x.

(A) Weight of the solid block in air and in tap water

S. No.	Weight of solid in air		Weight of solid in tap water		Apparent loss in weight of solid $(w'_1 - w'_2)$ (g-f)
	Observed weight w_1 (g-f)	Corrected weight $w'_1 = [w_1 - (\pm x)]$ (g-f)	Observed weight w_2 (g-f)	Corrected weight $w'_2 = [w_2 - (\pm x)]$ (g-f)	
1.					
2.					
3.					

(B) Volume of tap water displaced by solid block

S. No.	Initial level of water, V_1 (mL)	Final level of water, V_2 (mL)	Volume of tap water displaced, $(V_2 - V_1)$ (mL)
1.			
2.			
3.			

Mean volume of water displaced = ... mL.

(C) Weight of solid block in air and in salty water

S. No.	Weight of solid block in air		Weight of solid block in salty water		Apparent loss in weight of solid block $(w'_1 - w'_2)$ (g-f)
	Observed weight w_1 (g-f)	Corrected weight $w'_1 = [w_1 - (\pm x)]$ (g-f)	Observed weight w_2 (g-f)	Corrected weight $w'_2 = [w_2 - (\pm x)]$ (g-f)	
1.					
2.					
3.					

(D) Volume of the common salt solution displaced by solid block

S. No.	Initial level of salt in water, V_1 (mL)	Final level of salt solution, V_2 (mL)	Volume of the displaced salt solution, $(V_2 - V_1)$ mL
1.			
2.			
3.			

Mean volume of salty solution displaced = ...

(E) To determine density of salt solution

- Weigh accurately a dry beaker (100 mL) on a physical balance.
- Pipette out 50 mL of salt water and weigh it again.
- Mass of 50 mL of salt solution can be obtained from the above weighing.

Then, $D = \frac{\text{Mass of salt solution (g)}}{50 \text{ mL}}$

S. No.	Mass of empty beaker m_1(g)	Mass of beaker +50 mL of salty water m_2 (g)	Mass of salt solution $= (m_2 - m_1)$ (g)	$D = \frac{(m_2 - m_1)}{50}$ (g/mL)
1.				
2.				
3.				

Mean value of density = ... g/mL.

Calculations (From Tables A and B)

(i) Apparent loss in weight of solid block in tap water = ... g-f.

(ii) Volume of tap water displaced by the solid block = ... mL.

(iii) Density of tap water = 1 g/mL.

(iv) Mass of tap water displaced by the solid block = Mean volume × Density = $(V_2 - V_1) \times 1$ g/mL.

(v) Weight of tap water displaced by solid block = ... g-f.

(vi) (From tables *C* and *D*) Apparent loss in weight of solid block in salt solution = ... g-f.

(vii) Mean volume of salt solution displaced by solid block = ... mL.

(viii) Density of salt solution, (as obtained experimentally), ρ = ... g/mL.

(ix) Mass of salt solution displaced by the solid block = mean volume × density = ... g.

(x) Weight of salt solution displaced by solid block = ... g-f.

Result

(i) Apparent loss in weight of solid block in tap water = Weight of tap water displaced by the solid block

(ii) Apparent loss in weight of solid block in salty water = Weight of salty water displaced by solid block

(iii) Apparent loss in weight of solid block when dipped in salt solution > Apparent loss in weight of solid block when dipped in tap water.

Conclusion

(i) The apparent loss in weight of a body when placed in a liquid is equal to the weight of liquid displaced by the body.

(ii) If the same body is immersed completely in two different liquids, the apparent loss in its weight is more in denser liquid. The liquid having higher density is called denser.

Precautions

(i) Use a sensitive spring balance.

(ii) Read and record zero error.

(iii) The water/salty water in the overflow jar should be at the verge of overflowing.

Sources of Error

(i) The spring balance can generally measure weight upto 1 g. Any change in weight less than 1 g will not be measured by it. Thus, there can be an error of ± 1 g in the weight of the glass stopper/brass weight.

(ii) While using pre-weighed beaker in subsequent experiments, if it is not thoroughly cleaned and dried, it can give wrong weight of water/salty water displaced.

QUESTIONS

1. *When an object is immersed in different fluids, what will be the buoyant force acting on it.*

Ans. This is so because different fluids have different densities.

2. *What will be the effect on density, when a man adds salt in water present in a bucket?*

Ans. Density of salt is greater than that of water. When salt is mixed in water, its density will increase.

3. *What will be the level of water in a beaker, when a piece of ice is floating on water surface in a beaker?*

Ans. Level of the water in a beaker will remain same because while floating, ice displaces water equal to its own weight. Hence, there is no rise in level of water.

4. *When a body is immersed in a liquid, in which direction the buoyant force acts on the body?*

Ans. Buoyant force exerted by the fluids always acts in vertically upward direction.

5. *An object weighing 5 N in air, weighs 4.5 N in liquid. What will be the buoyant force experienced by the object?*

Ans. Buoyant force = Weight in air – Weight in liquid

$$= (5 - 4.5) \text{ N}$$
$$= 0.5 \text{ N}$$

6. *Name the physical quantity in which apparent loss is observed when a solid object is immersed in a liquid.*

Ans. Apparent loss is observed in a force and is measured in terms of weight.

7. *While performing the experiment 'Archimedes principle' Rama took a glass stopper of 10 cm^3 volume and observed its weight as 40 g-wt. using a spring balance. Then, she immersed the glass stopper completely in tap water. What will be the weight of glass stopper?*

Ans. We know that,

Apparent loss in weight = Weight of water displaced $= 10 \text{ cm}^3$

$\therefore$ Upthrust = 10 g

$\therefore$ Apparent weight in water $= (40 - 10) = 30$ g-wt.

8. *The weight of body in air is 1500 N, when the body is immersed completely in a liquid of density d_1 it weighs 1000 N, while in another liquid of density d_2, it weighs 800 N. What will be the ratio of d_1 and d_2?*

Ans. $$\frac{\text{Density of liquid } A}{\text{Density of liquid } B} = \frac{d_1}{d_2} = \frac{\text{Upthrust due to } A}{\text{Upthrust due to } B} = \frac{500}{700} = \frac{5}{7}$$

$\therefore$ Ratio of $d_1 : d_2 = 5 : 7$

9. *A boat floats in water with $\frac{2}{5}$th of its volume outside water. If density of water is 10^3 kg/m^3, what will be the density of the material of this boat?*

Ans. Volume of boat inside water $= 1 - \frac{2}{5} = \frac{3}{5}$

$\therefore$ Density of material of boat

$$= \frac{\text{Volume of boat inside water}}{\text{Total volume of boat}}$$
$$= \frac{3}{5 \times 1} = 0.6 \text{ g/cm}^3$$

Density of material of boat in SI system

$$= 1000 \times 0.6 \text{ kg/m}^3$$

$\therefore$ Density of material of boat is $0.6 \times 10^3 \text{ kg/m}^3$.

10. *If the density of the object placed in a liquid is equal to the density of the liquid. Wheather the object float or not?*

Ans. As the density of object and liquid is same, it will float.

11. *In what factor, the buoyant force on an object submerged in a fluid depends on?*

Ans. As we know that,

Buoyant force $= V\rho g$

where, ρ = density of fluid

g = acceleration due to gravity

V = volume of fluid displaced

So, buoyant force depends on density of fluid, volume of fluid displaced and acceleration due to gravity.

12. *What is the density of a block of wood which floats with 0.2 of its volume above water?*

Ans. Volume of wood inside water $= (1 - 0.2) = 0.8 \text{ cm}^3$

$\therefore$ Density of wood

$$= \frac{\text{Volume of wood inside water}}{\text{Total volume of wood}}$$
$$= \frac{0.8}{1} = 0.8 \text{ g/cm}^3$$

13. *Who discovered that the weight of the water displaced by a body is equal to the apparent loss of weight of a body in water?*

Ans. Archimedes' discovered that the weight of the water (liquid) displaced by a body is equal to apparent loss of weight of a body in water.

14. *Why is it more difficult to swim in the river water compared to sea water?*

Ans. The density of sea water is more than river water. Thus, the swimmer experiences more upthrust in sea water than in the river water as the upthrust is directly proportional to the density of the liquid. Thus, it is easier to swim in the sea water as compared to the river water.

15. *Four students have taken readings to verify Archimedes' principle. Which of the following students has taken the correct reading?*

	Weight of the object in air	Weight lost by the object	Buoyant force	Weight of the water displaced
Student 1	100 N	30 N	70 N	30 N
Student 2	100 N	30 N	30 N	70 N
Student 3	80 N	30 N	30 N	30 N
Student 4	80 N	30 N	50 N	50 N

Ans. Student 3.

As, weight lost by the object = buoyant force

= weight of water displaced.

EXPERIMENT 10

Objective

To determine the speed of a pulse propagated through a stretched helical spring.

Materials Required

(i) Flat wire helical spring of copper.
(ii) A metre rod.
(iii) A stopwatch.
(iv) A small wooden board.

Theory

(i) **Pulse** It is defined as the wave produced by a small disturbance in a medium.
(ii) **Helical spring** Long flexible spring is called slinky.
(iii) **Velocity of a pulse** It is defined as total distance travelled by the pulse from point *A* to *B* and back from *B* to *A* with respect to time.

i.e. $v = \frac{\text{Total distance travelled by pulse}}{\text{Time taken}} = \frac{2d}{t}$

Procedure

(i) Mark a line on the floor. From this line, measure a distance of 6 m with the help of metre rod and mark another line *AB* on the floor.
(ii) Let, one of the students (say S_1) hold the helical spring at point *A*.
(iii) Let, the other student (say S_2) stretch the helical spring to point *B*.
(iv) At point *A*, let student S_1 place a wooden block or a hard bound book parallel to the end of helical spring. This wooden block or hard bound book acts as a stopper.
(v) Let, the student S_1 pull the helical spring to position *C*, which is 10 cm from *A* and then give it a sharp push towards *A*, such that the motion of his hand stops at *A*, because of the wooden block. A pulse is produced in the helical spring, which travels towards *B*. It is then reflected towards *A* and again towards *B*. Practice it 5-10 times, till you are sure that you can generate a pulse and see it moving forward and backward.
(vi) Student S_2 will hold the stopwatch. When S_1 generates a pulse, student S_2 will watch the pulse to travel towards him. When the pulse reaches *B*, the student S_2 will start the stopwatch. This pulse on reflection will move towards point *A* and again towards *B*. As soon as the pulse again reaches *B*, the student S_2 will stop the stopwatch and will record the time for the pulse to travel from *B* to *A* and then back to *B*.
(vii) Repeat the experiment three more times.
(viii) Calculate the velocity of the pulse.

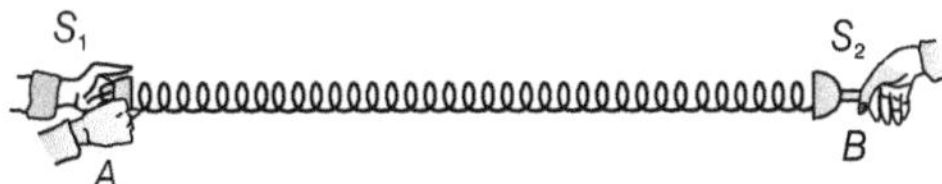

Observation Table

S. No.	Length between points A and B	Total distance travelled by pulse from B to A and back to B	Time taken	Velocity of pulse = $\frac{\text{Total distance}}{\text{Total time}}$
1.	...... m	2 × ...... m = ... m	...... s	v_1 = ... m/s
2.	...... m	2 × ...... m = ... m	...... s	v_2 = ... m/s
3.	...... m	2 × ...... m = ... m	...... s	v_3 = ... m/s
4.	...... m	2 × ...... m = ... m	...... s	v_4 = ... m/s

Calculation

Average velocity of pulse $= \dfrac{V_1 + V_2 + V_3 + V_4}{4}$

$= ......m/s$

Result

Velocity of pulse = ... m/s

Precautions

(i) Helical spring should be made of flat wire of copper.

(ii) Measure distance between points *A* and *B* very accurately.

(iii) Give a very sharp push to generate a pulse. Practice for atleast 5 to 10 times till you are sure that a pulse can be generated.

(iv) Make sure to arrest the push by a wooden block or a hard bound book, so that it does not overshoot point *A*.

(v) Experiment should be performed on a smooth floor or on a smooth table.

Sources of Error

(i) The student who starts and stops the stopwatch can be slow or fast and hence may record wrong time.

(ii) The push should not exceed the limit of 10 cm as it will reduce the distances between points *A* and *B*.

QUESTIONS

1. ***When a pulse is formed on a helical spring, how medium oscillate?***

Ans. When a pulse is formed on a helical spring, the medium oscillates for a short while and then returns to its original position.

2. ***If the air in the room cools down, what will be effect on the speed of sound?***

Ans. Speed of sound decreases with the fall in temperature.

3. ***How can we sense a compression in a spring?***

Ans. When turns in a slinky are close to one another, it signifies compressions.

4. ***While performing experiment to determine the velocity of pulse through helical spring, four students A, B, C and D did it by stretching the slinky given to each of them of length 4 m, 10 m, 3.5 m, 2.8 m, respectively. Which student will get the most correct result?***

Ans. Student *B* will get the most correct result because time can be measured more accurately in larger helical spring.

5. ***The stopwatch used by a student to measure velocity of a pulse in a slinky was of least count 0.1s. He stops the stopwatch, when a pulse has made 3 journeys from one end to the other of the slinky. He finds seconds hand to be at 47th division. What will be correct time?***

Ans. Time = Number of divisions × Least count = 47 × 0.1

∴ Time = 4.7 s

6. ***Following figure shows a pulse generated in a string which moves through it and strikes a rigid pole.***

What will be the direction of reflected pulse?

Ans. The reflected pulse after striking the rigid pole will be as follows:

7. ***If a stopwatch makes 't' second, when pulse moves 'n' times to and fro, what will be the time period of the motion of pulse?***

Ans. Time period = Total time ÷ number of oscillations

$= \dfrac{t}{n}$

8. ***A weight suspended from a spring is pulled downward and then released. Which type of wave is produced in the spring?***

Ans. A periodic wave is produced.

9. ***A pulse was created in a stretched string of length 5 m by four students A, B, C and D. They observed that the pulse returned after reflection at the point of creation 5 times in 10 s and calculated the speed as given below.***

Student	A	B	C	D
Speed m/s	0.5	2.5	5	10

Which student's observation is correct?

Ans. We know that velocity of pulse $= \dfrac{2d}{t} = \dfrac{2 \times 5 \times 5}{10}$

$= 5\ m/s$

∴ Student *C*'s observation is correct.

10. ***Write the factor in which the speed of propagation of a pulse in a helical spring depends on?***

Ans. It depends on

(i) dimensions of helical spring

(ii) material of helical spring

(iii) length of helical spring

11. ***To find the velocity of the pulse produced in a string. What will be needed?***

Ans. To find the velocity of the pulse produced in a string, we need (i) measuring scale and (ii) stopwatch.

12. *Two slinkies A and B of same length are made up of two different materials. The time taken by 20 pulses to travel through both of them and then come back are 70 s and 90 s, respectively. What does it conclude?*

Ans. From the above statement, it can be concluded that in slinky B, pulse takes larger time to travel than in A and hence moves slower.

13. *While determining the velocity of propagation of pulse, which type of pulse is generated on the helical spring in the experiment?*

Ans. Longitudinal pulse is produced as the pulse and the particles of medium travel in the same direction.

14. *In the experiment for determining the velocity of a pulse propagating along the length of string. We prefer a long thick cotton string. Why?*

Ans. We prefer long thick cotton string, because longer the string, more accurately we can measure the time.

15. *A weight is suspended from a flexible spring which is tied rigidly to a wall. It is released and then left. What will be the disturbance produced to the spring called?*

Ans. The disturbance produced in the spring will be called pulse.

16. *What is the velocity of a pulse for the slinky when it takes 5 s to travel from point A to B and back to A. The distance between A and B is 5 m.*

Ans. $v = \frac{2d}{t} = \frac{2 \times 5}{5} = 2$ m/s

17. *When a stone is dropped in water, what is produced at the point of impact?*

Ans. A pulse is produced at the point of impact on dropping a stone in water.

18. *The distance between compression and rarefaction of a sound is 7 cm. So, what will be its wavelength?*

Ans. Wavelength is the distance between two compressions or two rarefactions. In other words, wavelength is a combined length of a compression and an adjacent rarefaction, i.e. 2×7 cm = 14 cm.

19. *Shyam was calculating the velocity of wave using a slinky. What should be the features of spring to be used?*

Ans. It should be long, soft and flexible. With more elastic and lengthier spring, velocity of the wave can be studied better.

20. *A student sets up a slinky on a smooth table top in the manner shown below. If he gives a jerk to its free end, then in what direction, he can produce a pulse in the helical spring?*

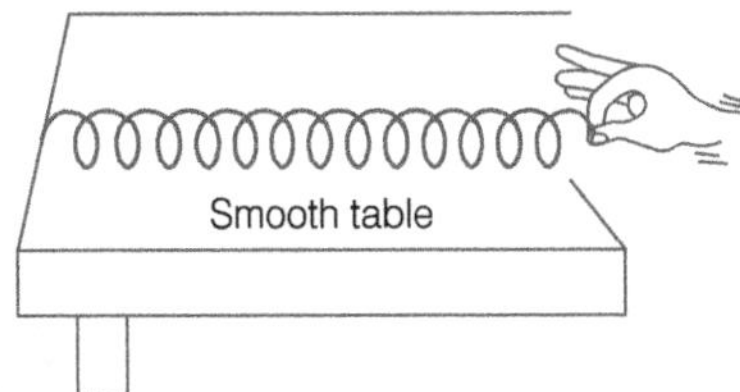

Ans. Backward and forward along the length of the helical spring.

EXPERIMENT 11

Objective

To verify the law of conservation of mass in a chemical reaction.

Materials Required

Barium chloride ($BaCl_2 \cdot 2H_2O$), sodium sulphate ($Na_2SO_4 \cdot 10H_2O$), distilled water, two beakers (150 mL), one beaker (250 mL), physical balance, spring balance (0–500 g) and a polythene bag, two watch glasses of known masses and a glass stirrer.

Theory

- Law of conservation of mass is also known as **law of indestructibility of mass**.
- It states that during a chemical reaction, matter is neither created nor destroyed.
- Thus, in a chemical reaction, total mass of the reactants is equal to the total mass of the products or we can say that mass remains conserved during a chemical reaction.

Procedure

(*i*) Pour 100 mL distilled water in two beakers (150 mL).

(*ii*) Using the physical balance and a watch glass of known mass, weigh 7.2 g of $BaCl_2 \cdot 2H_2O$ and dissolve it in a beaker (150 mL) containing 100 mL distilled water.

(*iii*) Similarly, weigh 16.1 g of $Na_2SO_4 \cdot 10H_2O$ in another watch glass of known mass and dissolve it in another beaker (150 mL) containing 100 mL distilled water.

(*iv*) Take the third beaker (250 mL) and weigh it using a spring balance and polythene bag.

(*v*) Both solutions are mixed in the third beaker and contents are stirred using a glass stirrer.

(*vi*) The beaker containing the reaction mixture is weighed again for determining the mass of reaction products.

(*vii*) Compare the masses of reactants and products before and after the chemical reaction.

Observations

(i) Mass of 100 mL distilled water = 100.0 g
(The density of distilled water is 1 g/mL)

(ii) Mass of $BaCl_2 \cdot 2H_2O$ = 7.2 g

(iii) Mass of $BaCl_2$ solution = 107.2 g

(iv) Mass of $Na_2SO_4 \cdot 10H_2O$ = 16.1 g

(v) Mass of Na_2SO_4 solution = 116.1 g

(vi) Total mass of reactants (solutions of $BaCl_2$ and Na_2SO_4) = 223.3 g

(vii) Mass of empty 250 mL beaker, m_1 = _____ g

(viii) Initial mass of reaction mixture and empty beaker (before the precipitation), $m_2 = (m_1 + 223.3\text{ g})$ = _____ g

(ix) Final mass of reaction mixture in the beaker after the precipitation, m_3 = _____ g

Observation Table

Experiment	Observation	Inference
Dissolve separately solid $BaCl_2 \cdot 2H_2O$ and $Na_2SO_4 \cdot 10H_2O$ in distilled water taken in separate beakers.	A clear solution is formed in both the beakers.	
Mix the above two solutions in a separate beaker.	A white precipitate of $BaSO_4$ is formed.	$BaCl_2(aq) + Na_2SO_4(aq) \longrightarrow BaSO_4(s) + 2NaCl(aq)$ (white ppt.)

Result

On comparison of the masses of the reaction mixture before and after the reaction, it is found that,

Total mass before reaction = Total mass after reaction

Conclusion

Above results verifies the law of conservation of mass.

Precautions

(i) The spring balance should be held vertically while taking measurements.

(ii) Before using the spring balance, ensure that the pointer is at zero mark.

(iii) The readings of the spring balance should be noted only when its pointer comes to rest.

(iv) Mixing of barium chloride and sodium sulphate solutions should be done slowly with constant stirring.

QUESTIONS

1. *4 g of calcium completely react with 1.6 g of oxygen. What will be the mass of calcium oxide formed?*

Ans. $2Ca + O_2 \longrightarrow 2CaO$
Calcium 4 g; Oxygen 1.6 g; Calcium oxide x

According to the law of conservation of mass,

Mass of reactants = Mass of product

$\therefore \quad 4\text{g} + 1.6\text{ g} = x \Rightarrow x = 5.6\text{g}$

2. *"The mass can neither be created nor destroyed in a chemical reaction". Which law is described by this statement?*

Ans. Law of conservation of mass states that "mass can neither be created nor destroyed in a chemical reaction". Law of constant proportion deals about the ratio by which atoms are combined. Dalton's atomic theory deals about indivisibility of atom.
Avogadro's law say, one mole of any substance have equal number of constituent particles.

3. *1.25 g of copper carbonate was added to a beaker containing 20 g of HCl. After completion of chemical reaction, the mass of the beaker and its contents were less than 21.25 g. Why does this happen?*

Ans. Chemical equation for the above reaction can be written as

$CuCO_3 + 2HCl \longrightarrow CuCl_2 + CO_2 + H_2O$
Copper carbonate; Dil. hydrochloric acid; Copper chloride; Carbon dioxide; Water

Since, CO_2 gas escapes in air and hence, its mass goes unrecorded. This explains, why the recorded mass is less than 21.25 g.

4. *3 g of magnesium ribbon burns completely in 2 g of oxygen to form magnesium oxide. What is the mass of magnesium oxide thus formed?*

Ans. $2Mg + O_2 \longrightarrow 2MgO$

$3\text{g} + 2\text{g} \longrightarrow x$

According to the law of conservation of mass, we can write

$x = 3 + 2 = 5\text{g}$

$\therefore$ Mass of MgO = 5 g

5. *2 g of zinc metal is completely burned in air to form zinc oxide. It was found that mass of zinc oxide is 2.5 g. Find the mass of oxygen used to form zinc oxide.*

Ans. $2Zn + O_2 \longrightarrow 2ZnO$
$\underset{2\,g}{}\quad \underset{x\,g}{}\quad \underset{2.5\,g}{}$

∴ From law of conservation of mass

$$2 + x = 2.5$$

$$\Rightarrow \quad x = (2.5 - 2)\,g = 0.5\,g$$

6. *10 g of $CaCO_3$ on complete decomposition gives 4.4 g of CO_2. What will be the mass of the residue left behind?*

Ans. The chemical equation for the above reaction can be written as

$$CaCO_3(s) \xrightarrow{\Delta} CaO(s) + CO_2(g)$$

Mass of residue = Mass of $CaCO_3$ – mass of CO_2
$= (10 - 4.4)\,g = 5.6\,g$

7. *To verify the law of conservation of mass in the case of a chemical change, in which form of sodium sulphate and barium chloride should be used?*

Ans. Aqueous solutions are used because precipitation reactions take place only when reactants are in aqueous states.

8. *For which types of changes law of conservation of mass is applicable?*

Ans. Law of conservation of mass is applicable to all physical and chemical changes.

9. *To verify law of conservation of mass, name the type of reaction which is commonly preferred?*

Ans. In precipitation reaction, one product precipitates and other one is soluble in solution hence, it is convenient to measure weight before and after the reaction. In other reactions, there is a possibility of the formation of one or more gaseous product which might escape out, thus making comparison of masses inconvenient.

10. *4.0 g of hydrogen completely reacts with 32 g of oxygen. What will be the mass of water thus formed?*

Ans. Equation for formation of water is as follows:

$$\underset{4\,g}{2H_2} + \underset{32\,g}{O_2} \longrightarrow \underset{x}{2H_2O}$$

According to the law of conservation of mass,

Mass of reactants = Mass of products

Amount of water formed is

$$x = (4 + 32)\,g = 36\,g$$

11. *4.90 g of $KClO_3$, when heated produced 1.94 g of oxygen. What will be the mass of residue left?*

Ans. $\underset{4.90\,g}{2KClO_3} \xrightarrow{\Delta} \underset{x}{2KCl} + \underset{1.94\,g}{3O_2}$

According to the law of conservation of mass,

Mass of reactants = Mass of products

$$4.9 = x + 1.94$$

∴ $x = (4.9 - 1.94)\,g = 2.96\,g$

∴ Mass of residue left is 2.96 g

12. *Two reactants kept in beaker as aqueous solution, weighs 200 g altogether. If beaker weighs 100 g, then find the total mass of product formed.*

Ans. From law of conservation of mass,

Mass of (2 reactants + beaker) = Mass of product + mass of beaker

200 g = Mass of product + 100 g

Mass of product = 100 g

13. $\underset{10\,g}{AgNO_3(aq)} + \underset{5\,g}{NaCl(aq)} \longrightarrow \underset{7\,g}{AgCl(s)} + \underset{x}{NaNO_3(aq)}$

In the above reaction, find the amount of $NaNO_3$?

Ans. According to the law of conservation of mass,

Mass of ($AgNO_3$ + NaCl) = Mass of (AgCl + $NaNO_3$)

∴ $(10 + 5)\,g = (7 + x)\,g$

∴ $x = 15 - 7 = 8\,g$

∴ Mass of $NaNO_3$ is 8 g.

14. *170 g of silver nitrate ($AgNO_3$) reacts with 58 g of sodium chloride (NaCl) to produce 143 g of silver chloride precipitate and 85 g of sodium nitrate. Verify that the reaction is in agreement with the law of conservation of mass.*

Ans. The chemical equation for the above reaction is as follows:

$$\underset{170\,g}{AgNO_3(aq)} + \underset{58\,g}{NaCl(aq)} \longrightarrow \underset{143\,g}{AgCl(s)} + \underset{85\,g}{NaNO_3(aq)}$$

Total mass of reactants = 170 + 58 = 228 g

Total mass of products = 143 + 85 = 228 g

∵ The total mass of the reactants are equal to the total mass of the product, therefore, the given reaction is in accordance with the law of conservation of mass.

15. *Give two precautions which should be taken while performing the experiment to verify the law of conservation of mass.*

Ans. (*i*) The spring balance should be held vertically while taking measurements.

(*ii*) Before using the spring balance, ensure that the pointer is at zero mark.

16. *To verify the law of conservation of mass in a chemical reaction a student takes a known amount of solution of $BaCl_2$ in a small test tube and hanged it in a sealed conical flask, containing Na_2SO_4 solution. The flask is slightly tilted, so that the two solutions mix with each other and a chemical reaction occurs. What is the relation between the masses of the chemical involved?*

Ans. Barium chloride ($BaCl_2$) solution reacts with the solution of sodium sulphate (Na_2SO_4) to give the precipitate of barium sulphate ($BaSO_4$)and a solution of sodium chloride (NaCl).

The reaction involved is as follows:

$$BaCl_2(aq) + Na_2SO_4\,(aq) \longrightarrow BaSO_4\,(s) + 2NaCl(aq)$$

$$\therefore \text{Mass of } (BaCl_2 + Na_2SO_4) = \text{Mass of } (BaSO_4 + NaCl)$$

17. ***On complete combustion of a hydrocarbon in 0.22g oxygen, 0.9g of water and 0.44g of CO_2 is produced. Calculate the mass of hydrocarbon used.***

Ans. The chemical equation for the above reaction is as follows:

$$\underset{\substack{\text{(Hydrocarbon)}\\ x}}{C_nH_{2n+2}} + \underset{\substack{\text{(Oxygen)}\\ 0.22\text{ g}}}{O_2} \longrightarrow \underset{\substack{\text{(Water)}\\ 0.9\text{ g}}}{H_2O} + \underset{\substack{\text{(Carbon}\\ \text{dioxide)}\\ 0.44\text{ g}}}{CO_2}$$

From law of conservation of mass, we have

$$x + 0.22 = 0.9 + 0.44$$
$$x = 1.34 - 0.22$$
$$= 1.12\text{ g}$$

18. ***If law of conservation of mass holds good, predict how much the residue would weigh when 96 g of $CaCO_3$ is heated and 12.2 g of CO_2 is released?***

Ans. Mass of reactant = 96 g

Total mass of products = (x + 12.2)g

$\because$ Mass of reactant = Mass of product

(law of conservation of mass)

$\therefore \quad 96 = x + 12.2$

$\Rightarrow \quad x = 83.8\text{ g}$

Pre-Mid Term Tests

{Chapters covered—Chemistry (1, 2), Physics (7, 8), Biology (5, 6) }

10 MARKS

TEST 1

1. 16 g of a solute is dissolved in 100 mL of water to form a saturated solution at 25°C. The strength of the solution (in $g\,L^{-1}$), will be equal to

(a) $16\ g\ L^{-1}$ (b) $13.79\ g\ L^{-1}$
(c) $160\ g\ L^{-1}$ (d) $7.25\ g\ L^{-1}$ (1/2)

2. Which one of the following organelles is the site for ATP synthesis?

(a) Chloroplast (b) Mitochondria
(c) Ribosomes (d) Cytoplasm (1/2)

3. Which instrument is used to measured the distance travelled by vehicle?

(a) Odometer (b) Speedometer
(c) Meter scale (d) None of these (1/2)

4. Name the physical quantity which corresponds to the rate of change of momentum. (1/2)

5. Differentiate between chloroplast and leucoplast by function. (1)

6. Give an example of

(i) gas in liquid solution
(ii) gas in gas solution (1)

7. For how much time should a force of 200 N acts on an object having mass 5 kg, so as to increase its velocity from 50 m/s to 100 m/s ?
[**Ans.** $t = 1.25\,s$] (2)

8. Water as ice has a cooling effect, whereas water as steam may cause severe burns. Explain, these observations. (2)

9. Give reasons for the following

(i) Meristematic cells have prominent nucleus and dense cytoplasm but they lack vacoule.
(ii) Intercellular spaces are absent in sclerenchymatous tissue. (2)

Test 2

1. When a particle moves with a uniform velocity, then

(a) the particle must be at rest
(b) the particle moves along a curved path
(c) the particle moves along a circle
(d) the particle moves along a straight line (1/2)

2. The boiling point of water is 100°C under normal atmospheric pressure. The value of this temperature on Kelvin scale would be

(a) 273
(b) 373
(c) 300
(d) 298 (1/2)

3. Xylem and phloem are called as complex tissues

(a) as they are complex in their cellular activities
(b) as they are made up of more than one type of cells
(c) as they are made up of one type of highly specialised cells
(d) as they are found in plants which are morphologically complex (1/2)

4. Name the dye used for preparing the temporary slide of plant cell. (1/2)

5. Which characteristic of a gas is used in supplying oxygen cylinders to hospitals? (1)

6. Why should we wear safety belts in a car? (1)

7. Give reasons:

(i) Path of beam of light is not visible through a true solution.
(ii) Particles of suspension can be seen with naked eyes. (2)

8. (i) Why lysosomes are known as 'scavengers of the cell'?
(ii) Justify that lysosomes are self-destructive. (2)

9. Differentiate between distance and displacement. (2)

Test 3

1. .... takes part in the formation of lysosome.
   (a) Nucleus
   (b) Golgi bodies
   (c) Chloroplast
   (d) Endoplasmic reticulum (1/2)
2. A quantity has a value of – 9.0 m/s. It may be the
   (a) speed of a particle
   (b) position of a particle
   (c) velocity of a particle
   (d) acceleration of a particle (1/2)
3. Which of the following statement is correct?
   (a) When a solid melts into a liquid, its temperature increases on heating
   (b) When a solid melts into a liquid, its temperature decreases on heating
   (c) When a solid melts into a liquid, its temperature first decreases and then increases on heating
   (d) When a solid melts into a liquid, its temperature does not increase even on heating (1/2)
4. Salt can be recovered from its solution by evaporation. Suggest some other technique for the same. (1/2)
5. Why is a person hurt less when he falls on a spongy surface? (1)
6. Differentiate between bone and cartilage functionally. (1)
7. In desert, plants have thick waxy epidermis. Why? (2)
8. A bullet of mass 20 g is fired from a pistol of mass 2 kg with a horizontal velocity of 150 m/s. Calculate the recoil velocity of the pistol.
   [Ans. $v = -1.5$ m/s] (2)
9. Distinguish between physical and chemical changes in a tabular from giving examples. (2)

Mid Term Tests

{Chapters covered—Chemistry (1, 2 and 3), Physics (7, 8, 9 and 10), Biology (5, 6) }

10 MARKS

Test 1

1. A man is standing on a boat in still water. If he walks towards the shore the boat will
   (a) move towards the shore
   (b) sink
   (c) move away from shore
   (d) remain stationary (1/2)
2. Which of the following molecule is octa-atomic?
   (a) Sulphur (b) Water
   (c) Ozone (d) Both (b) and (c) (1/2)
3. Which of the following organelles is called as 'factory of ribosomes'?
   (a) Nucleus
   (b) Endoplosmic reticulum
   (c) Golgi bodies
   (d) Mitochondria (1/2)
4. What is the rate at which energy is transformed to other form called? (1/2)
5. Give one example of two miscible liquids, where distillation can be used for separating them. (1)
6. Define the term "Dendrites". (1)
7. Define atomic mass unit. State how do atoms exist? (2)
8. What is the intensity of sound wave? (2)
9. Write two important functions of mitochondria. (2)

Test 2

1. Evaporation causes cooling. This is because
   (a) it is a surface phenomenon
   (b) it is a bulk phenomenon
   (c) liquid takes away the heat from the surroundings
   (d) temperature decreases as the rate of evaporation increases (1/2)

2. A graph is plotted showing the velocity of a bus as a function of time. If the graph is a straight lines means that
   (a) the bus started at rest.
   (b) velocity was constant.
   (c) acceleration was constant.
   (d) acceleration was increasing. (1/2)

3. The tissue, which is responsible for growth of plant is ....
   (a) meristematic tissue
   (b) secretory tissue
   (c) permanent tissue
   (d) connective tissue (1/2)

4. Two kidney-shaped cells that enclose stomata are called ____________ . (1/2)

5. Why do we say work done against gravity is negative? (1)

6. What is the formula unit mass of H_3PO_4? (1)

7. Differentiate between prokaryotic and eukaryotic cell with one example of each. (2)

8. How do sol and gel differ from each other? Give an example for each. (2)

9. Calculate the average density of the earth in terms of g, G and R. (2)

Test 3

1. Which of the following plastid occurs most widely?
   (a) Chromoplast (b) Leucoplast
   (c) Amyloplast (d) Chloroplast (1/2)

2. The correct formula of magnesium phosphate is
   (a) $MgPO_4$ (b) $Mg_3(PO_4)_2$
   (c) Mg_2PO_4 (d) $Mg(PO_4)_2$ (1/2)

3. Two bodies of equal mass(m) moving with equal speed (v) in opposite directions collide. The resultant velocity of the combination is
   (a) zero (b) $2v$
   (c) v (d) $-v$ (1/2)

4. What is meant by latent heat of vaporisation? (1/2)

5. Write two functions of Golgi Apparatus. (1)

6. How is weight related to mass? Is weight of a body constant? (1)

7. A coolie lifts a box of 15 kg from the ground to a height of 2m. Calculate the work done by coolie on the box. (Given, $g = 9.8 ms^{-2}$)
   [Ans. w = 294N] (2)

8. Write any four characteristics of sclerenchyma. (2)

9. If 12g of C is burnt in the presence of 32g of O_2. How much CO_2 will be formed? **[Ans. 44g]** (2)

Post-Mid Term Tests

{Chapters covered—Chemistry (1, 2, 3 and 4), Physics (7, 8, 9, 10 and 11), Biology (5, 6 and 13)}

10 MARKS

Test 1

1. When the speed of object is doubled, then the ratio of its kinetic energy to its momentum
   (a) get doubled (b) becomes half
   (c) becomes four times (d) None of these (1/2)
2. Ticture of iodine is a solution of
   (a) sodium chloride in water
   (b) iodine in water
   (c) sodium chloride in alcohol
   (d) iodine in alcohol (1/2)
3. Which of the following is present in plant cell?
   (a) Cell wall (b) Plastids
   (c) Vacuole (d) All of these (1/2)
4. State whether displacement is scalar of vector quantity. (1/2)
5. State the law of constant proportion. (1)
6. Give one word
   (i) Farming without chemicals as fertilisers, herbicides and pesticides.
   (ii) Growing of wheat and groundnut in the same field. (1)
7. Why the waves produced by a motorboat sailing in the sea, are longitudinal and transverse? (2)
8. Differentiate between meristematic and permanent tissues. (2)
9. Write one pair of isobars. Why the chemical properties of isobars are not similar? (2)

Test 2

1. Which of the following pair contains a pure substance and a mixture?
   (a) copper and oxygen.
   (b) water and sulphur in carbon disulphide.
   (c) sugar in water and water in oil
   (d) methane and sugar (1/2)
2. Which wave property determines loudness of sound?
   (a) Frequency (b) Pitch
   (c) Speed (d) Amplitude (1/2)
3. WBCs are also known as
   (a) Thrombocytes (b) Leucocytes
   (c) Plasma (d) Basophil (1/2)
4. Differentiate between osmosis and diffusion on the basis of medium. (1/2)
5. Name two factors which act on a body immersed in a liquid. (1)
6. What happens to the melting point of ice when pressure is increased? (1)
7. (i) What do you mean by irrigation?
   (ii) Give two examples of weeds. (2)
8. An atom of an element has two electrons in the *K*-shell, four electron in *L*-shell. What is the atomic number of the element? Identify the element. (2)
9. Find the wavelength of the sound for frequencies upto 120 kHz at which a bat can hear it. [Take, the speed of sound in air is $344 ms^{-1}$]
   [Ans. 2.8×10^{-3} m] (2)

Test 3

1. The distance-time graph of a body is a straight line inclined to time axis. The body is in
   (a) uniform motion
   (b) uniform accelerated motion
   (c) uniform retarded motion
   (d) rest position (1/2)

2. What is the chemical formula of calcium oxide?
   (a) Ca_2O (b) CaO_2
   (c) Ca_2O_3 (d) CaO (1/2)

3. Which of the following is not a type of connective tissue?
   (a) Blood
   (b) Tendons
   (c) Squamous epithelium
   (d) Cartilage (1/2)

4. Name any one element whose symbol do not start with the same letter as that of the name of the element. (1/2)

5. Can any object have mechanical energy even if its momentum is zero ? Give reason. (1)

6. Differentiate between unicellular and multicellular organisms. (1)

7. An atom contains 3 protons, 3 electrons and 4 neutrons. Find its atomic number, mass number and valency. (2)

8. State the conditions required to hear an echo. (2)

9. Define the following
   (i) Green manure (ii) Biofertilisers (2)

SAMPLE QUESTION PAPER 1

A Highly Simulated Sample Question Paper for CBSE Class IXth Examination

SCIENCE

UNSOLVED

General Instructions

- The question paper comprises four Sections A, B, C and D. There are 36 questions in the question paper. All questions are compulsory.
- **Section A** Qns. 1 to 20 all questions and parts there of are of one mark each. These questions contain multiple choice questions (MCQs), very short answer type questions and Assertion-Reason type questions. Answers to these should be given in one word or one sentence.
- **Section B** Qns. 21 to 26 are short answer type questions, carrying 2 marks each. Answers to these questions should be in the range of 30 to 50 words.
- **Section C** Qns. 27 to 33 are short answer type questions, carrying 3 marks each. Answers to these questions should be in the range of 50 to 80 words.
- **Section D** Qns. 34 to 36 are long answer type questions carrying 5 marks each. Answer to these questions should be in the range of 80 to 120 words.
- There is no overall choice. However, internal choices have been provided in some questions. A student has to attempt only one of the alternatives in such questions.
- Wherever necessary, neat and properly labelled diagrams should be drawn.

Time : 3 hours　　　　Max. Marks : 80

Section A

1. What do you understand by inertia?
2. In which medium, speed of sound is maximum?

Or Why we cannot hear an echo in a small room?

3. What are leucoplasts?
4. What does the symbol μ represent?
5. An object of mass 2 kg is dropped from a height of 1m. What will be its kinetic energy as it reaches the ground?
6. Which of the following are considered to be a pure substance and mixture?

   Granite, Sodium chloride, Muddy water, Milk of magnesia
7. The formula of chloride of metal M is MCl_3, then the formula of the phosphate of metal M will be

   MPO_4 or M_2PO_4

   Or

   Which of the following statement(s) about ions, is/are correct?

   (i) Carbonate is triatomic ion.

   (ii) Chloride is cation.

   (iii) Sulphide ion carries –2 charge.
8. Which kind of cells can secrete substances at the epithelial surface?

   Or

   Which body cell provide resistance against infection?
9. What do you mean by free fall?
10. On which principle do the mud guards over the wheels of a car work?

Or What is the total momentum of a bullet and a gun before firing?

11. Why epidermis of plants living in dry habitat is thicker?

Or

Which feature of meristimatic tissue helps aquatic plants to maintain buoyancy in water?

12. The symbol of an element is ${}^{4}_{2}He$. It suggests that

I. an atom of helium contains two electrons.

II. an atom of helium has two protons and four neutrons in its nucleus.

III. helium has a proton (atomic) number of 4.

IV. helium occurs as a diatomic molecule.

Which is/are incorrect statement(s)?

13. In which cell organelle, the complete breakdown of glucose in the presence of oxygen takes place?

Direction (Q.Nos. 14-16) *In each of the following questions, a statement of Assertion is given by the corresponding statement of Reason. Out of the given statements, choose the correct one.*

(a) If both Assertion and Reason are true and Reason is the correct explanation of Assertion.
(b) If both Assertion and Reason are true but Reason is not the correct explanation of Assertion.
(c) If Assertion is true but Reason is false.
(d) If Assertion is false but Reason is true.

14. **Assertion** Hybridisation is a way to obtain new and improved varieties of plants and animals.

Reason Crossing may be done between two different varieties, two different species of same genus or different genus.

15. **Assertion** Pure substances in which molecules are make up of only one kind of atoms are known as elements.

Reason Hydrogen, oxygen and nitrogen are elements.

16. **Assertion** A body can float only if it displaces liquid whose weight is equal to the actual weight.

Reason The body will experience zero downward force in that case.

Answer *Q. Nos. 17-20 Contain five sub-parts each. You are expected to answer any four sub-parts in these questions.*

17. *Read the following and answer any four questions from 17 (i) to 17 (v).*

Newton studied the ideas of Galileo regarding the motion of an object. He formulated three fundamental laws that govern the motion of objects. These three laws are known as Newton's laws of motion.

The first law of motion states that an object will continue to remain in its state of rest or of uniform motion along a straight line path unless an external force acts on it. This means, all objects resist change in their state.

The second law of motion states that the rate of change of momentum of an object is directly proportional to the applied external force and takes place in the direction in which external force acts.

The third law of motion states that whenever an object exerts a force on another object, then the second object exerts an equal and opposite force on the first object.

(i) A goalkeeper in a game of football pulls his hands backwards after holding the ball shot at the goal. This enables the goalkeeper to

(a) exert larger force on the ball
(b) reduce the force exerted by the ball on hands
(c) increase the rate of change of momentum
(d) decrease the rate of change of momentum

(ii) According to the third law of motion, action and reaction

(a) always act on the same body
(b) always act on different bodies in opposite directions
(c) have same magnitude and direction
(d) act on either body at normal to each other

UNSOLVED

(iii) The given graph represents

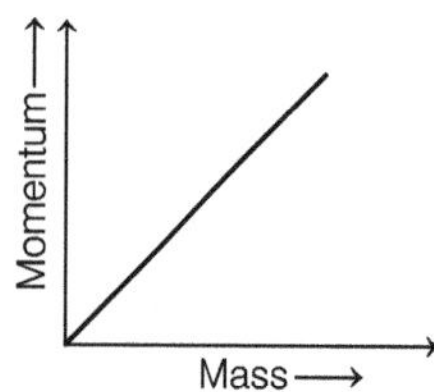

(a) the velocity of the body is variable
(b) the velocity of the body is constant
(c) the mass of the body is constant
(d) None of the above

(iv) Velocity-time graph of a moving particle of mass 1 kg is shown below. The force acting on the particle is

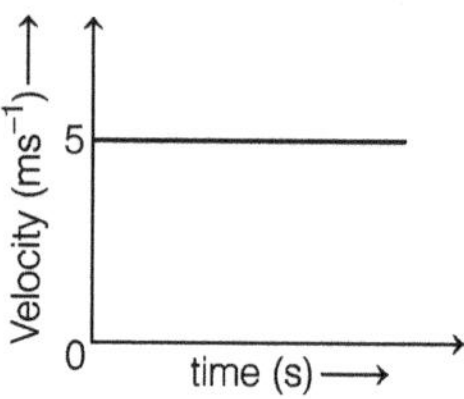

(a) 0 (b) 4 N
(c) 8 N (d) 10 N

(v) How much momentum will a dumb bell of mass 10 kg transfer to the floor, if it falls from a height of 80 cm ? [Take, its downward acceleration to be 10 ms^{-2}]
(a) 10 kg ms^{-1} (b) 20 kg ms^{-1}
(c) 30 kg ms^{-1} (d) 40 kg ms^{-1}

18. *Read the following and answer any four questions from 18(i) to 18(v).*

Two miscible liquids *A* and *B* are present in a solution. The boiling point of *A* is 50°C while that of *B* is 85°C.

(i) Which method is used to separate the liquids *A* and *B*?
(a) Filteration (b) Centrifugation
(c) Distillation (d) None of these

(ii) Which describe the method of separation?
(a) Mixture heated in the distillation flask.
(b) First liquid evaporates at its boiling point, then pass it through a condenser.
(c) Vapour of first liquid condenses to liquid droplets and collected in a reciever, then do same with second liquid.
(d) All of the above

(iii) Which one of the following is an essential condition for the separation of *A* and *B*?
(a) The difference in boiling point should be more than 25°C.
(b) The difference in boiling points should be less than 25°C.
(c) In the apparatus, a fractionating column must be fitted between the distillation flask and the condenser.
(d) None of the above

(iv) Which of the following methods must be used to separate *A* and *B*, if their boiling points were 60°C and 70°C, respectively?
(a) Simple distillation
(b) Fractional distillation
(c) Centrifugation
(d) Evaporation

(v) Three liquids *A*, *B* and *C*, they have boiling points 100, 112 and 102, respectively. In which sequence, they will come in condenser?
(a) *A*, *B*, *C* (b) *C*, *B*, *A*
(c) *A*, *C* *B* (d) *B*, *C* *A*

19. *Read the following and answer any four questions from 19 (i) to 19 (v).*

Elements	Protons	Neutrons	Electrons
P	19	21	19
Q	20	20	20
R	17	18	17
S	17	20	17

(i) The element *R* is a
(a) metal (b) non-metal
(c) metalloid (d) None of these

(ii) What is the electronic configuration of element *P*?
(a) 2, 8, 7 (b) 2, 8, 8, 1
(c) 2, 8, 9 (d) 1, 8, 8, 1

(iii) Which two elements form a pair of isobars?
(a) *R* and *S* (b) *R* and *P*
(c) *S* and *Q* (d) *P* and *Q*

(iv) Which of the following statement is correct?
(a) The sum of number of electrons and protons is equal to the mass number.
(b) The sum of number of electrons and protons is equal to the atomic number.

UNSOLVED

(c) The sum of number of neutrons and electrons is equal to the atomic number.

(d) The sum of number of neutrons and protons is equal to the mass number.

(v) Which is the correct increasing order of atomic number?

(a) $R = S < P < Q$ (b) $P + Q < R < S$

(c) $R < Q = S < P$ (d) $R < P = Q < S$

20. *Read the following and answer any four questions from 20 (i) to 20 (v).*

Plant cells, in addition to the plasma membrane, have another rigid outer covering called the cell wall. The cell wall lies outside the plasma membrane. An extensive compartmentalisation of cytoplasm is seen through the presence of membrane-bound organelles. Cell-organelles like plastids, vacuoles are present in plant cell but absent in animal cell.

(i) Which of the following is main constituent of cell wall?

(a) Proteins (b) Lipids

(c) Lipoproteins (d) Cellulose

(ii) Cell wall is differentiated into how many parts?

(a) Two (b) Four

(c) Three (d) Seven

(iii) Fluid Mosaic Model was given by

(a) Singer and Nicolson

(b) Robert Hooke

(c) Robert Brown

(d) Scleiden

(iv) Which of the following are very rare in plant cells?

(a) Microtubules (b) Cilia

(c) Nucleus (d) Ribosomes

(v) Active transports requires

(a) carrier proteins (b) energy

(c) Both (a) and (b) (d) None of these

Section B

21. Can a body have constant speed and still be accelerating? Give an example.

Or

Draw a velocity *versus* time graph of a stone thrown vertically upwards and then coming downwards after attaining the maximum height.

22. (a) Helium atom has an atomic mass of 4 u and two protons in its nucleus. How many neutrons does it have?

(b) Write the distribution of electrons in carbon and sodium atoms.

23. (a) Name the following :

(i) Tissue present in the brain.

(ii) Tissue that forms inner lining of mouth.

(iii) Tissue present in skin.

(iv) Tissue that transports food in plants.

(b) What happens to the cells formed by meristematic tissue?

24. (a) Define

(i) infrasonic wave and

(ii) ultrasonic wave.

(b) Name two species of animals each of which can produce and detect

(i) infrasonic waves and

(ii) ultrasonic waves.

25. (a) What is plasmolysis?

(b) Write two functions of cytoplasm.

Or Differentiate between simple permanent tissue and complex permanent tissue.

26. Draw the diagram of a neuron. Also, define the term synapse.

Section C

27. An object of mass 5 kg is accelerated uniformly from a velocity of 4 m/s to 8m/s in 0.8s, when a large force is applied. The impulse applied on the body is calculated as

From, $v = u + at$

$8 = 4 + a \times 0.8$

$a = 5 \text{ m/s}^2$

$\because$ Force, $F = m \cdot a$

$= 5 \times 5 = 25 \text{ N}$

Impulse $= F \cdot \Delta t = 25 \times 0.8 = 20$ N-s

Calculate the impulse on the object by alternate method.

28. Name the type of colloids in each of the following in which the dispersed phase and the dispersion medium are respectively.

(a) Liquid and gas

(b) Liquid and liquid

(c) Liquid and solid

Also, give one example of each.

UNSOLVED

Or (a) What is meant by concentration of a solution? How will you prepare a 10% solution of sugar ?

(b) Explain, why particles of colloidal solution do not settle down when lift undisturbed, while in case of a suspension they do.

(c) Tincture of iodine has antiseptic properties. How it is prepared ?

29. (a) The temperature inside a glass enclosure is higher than that of the surrounding. Give reason.

(b) How is the above phenomenon utilised by cold countries to their advantage?

(c) Name two greenhouse gases.

30. When dried raisins are placed in plain water, raisins swell up. Also, when same swelled raisins are placed in concentrated salt solution, raisins shrunk.

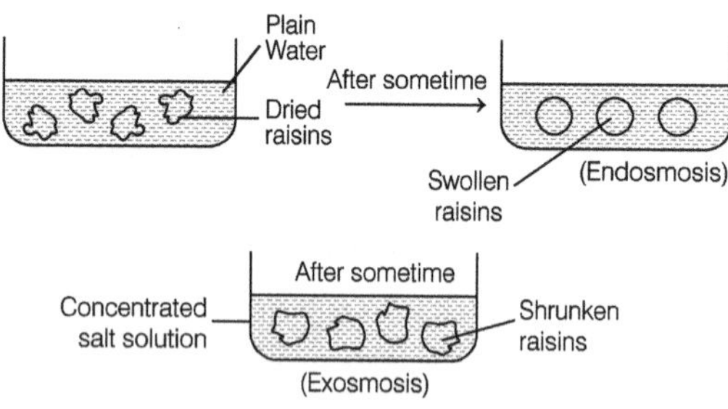

Analyse and compile the facts for the above experiment and write the whole process in your own words.

31. Calculate the kinetic energy of a car of mass 400 kg moving with a velocity of 72 km/h. What is new kinetic energy, if a passenger of mass 50 kg sits in the car ?

32. Write the formulae for the following and calculate the molecular mass for each one of them

(a) Caustic potash

(b) Lime stone

(c) Common salt

33. (a) Differentiate between electrovalency and covalency.

(b) What do you understand by the ground state and excited state of the atom ?

UNSOLVED

Section D

34. (a) What is the need of animal husbandry?

(b) What is cattle farming? What are different breeds of cattle?

Or

(a) Classify the crops on the basis of season in which grow. Give example of each classification.

(b) Differentiate between manure and fertiliser.

35. An insect moves along a circular path of radius 10 cm with a constant speed. It takes 1 min to move from a point on the path to the diametrically opposite point, find (a) the distance covered, (b) the speed, (c) the displacement and (d) the average velocity.

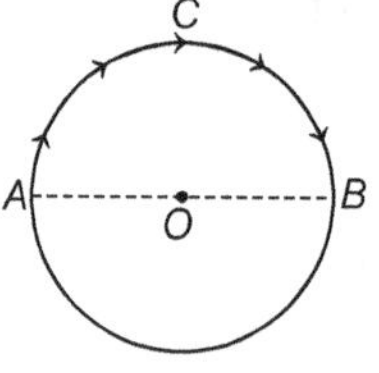

Or

The distance-time graph of two trains are shown in figure. The trains start simultaneously in the same direction.

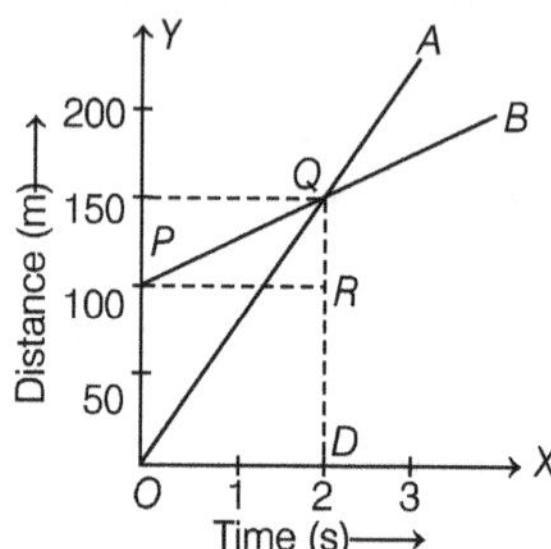

(a) How much *A* is ahead of *B* when the motion starts?

(b) What is the speed of *B*?

(c) When and where will *A* catch *B*?

(d) What is the difference between speeds of *A* and *B*?

(e) Is the speed of both the trains uniform or non-uniform ? Justify your answer.

36. Given below is a diagrammatic sketch of certain generalised cell.

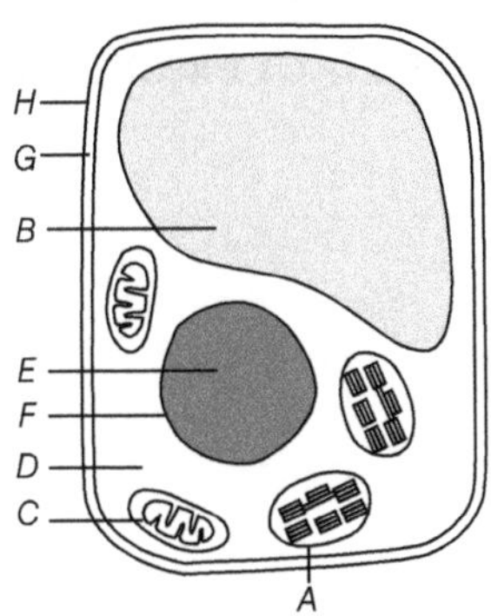

(a) Name the parts labelled as *A*-*H*.

(b) Is it a plant cell or an animal cell? Give two reasons to support your answer.

(c) Give one function of parts marked as *A*, *F* and *H*.

Answers

5. 19.6 J **14.** (a)

15. (b) *Or* (b) **16.** (b)

17. (i) (d) (ii) (b) (iii) (b) (iv) (a) (v) (d)

18. (i) (b) (ii) (d) (iii) (a) (iv) (b) (v) (c)

19. (i) (b) (ii) (b) (iii) (d) (iv) (d) (v) (a)

20. (i) (d) (ii) (c) (iii) (a) (iv) (b) (v) (c)

31. 8×10^4 J, 9×10^4 J

32. (a) 56 u
(b) 100 u
(c) 58.5 u

35. (a) 31.4 cm (b) 31.4 cm/min
(c) 20 cm and (d) 20 cm/min

Or (a) 100 m (b) 25 ms^{-1}
(c) 2s, 150 m (d) 50 ms^{-1}

SAMPLE QUESTION PAPER 2

A Highly Simulated Sample Question Paper for CBSE Class IXth Examination

SCIENCE

UNSOLVED

General Instructions

See Sample Paper 1

Section A

1. What is audible range of frequency?

Or

Define echo.

2. What effects occur on the gravitational acceleration when we are moving from equator to pole?

3. While preparing a temporary mount of onion peel, the peel taken from onion bulb is placed immediately into the petridish containing water, because
   (a) it is an experimental procedure
   (b) it brings out plasmolysis due to osmosis of water into the cell
   (c) it prevents peel from getting folded and dehydrated
   (d) it removes the impurities from the peel

4. Ramesh was given a mixture of common salt and sand. He was asked by his teacher to separate both the components from it. Which technique will be used by him to separate the components?

5. Goldstein's experiment which involved passing high voltage electricity through gases at very low pressure resulted in the discovery of which atomic species?

6. State Newton's third law of motion.

Or

A car is travelling at 20 m/s along a road. The driver suddenly applies brakes when he saw a child running out into the road 50 m ahead. Determine the car's deceleration to stop before it reaches the child.

7. How does the prokaryotic cell differs from the eukaryotic cell?

Or Who discovered free-living cells?

8. The atomic mass of the lead is 208 and its atomic number is 82. The atomic mass of bismuth is 209 and its atomic number is 83. Compare the ratio of the neutrons/protons.

9. A stone is thrown vertically upwards with an initial velocity of 40 m/s. Determine the maximum height reached by the stone. (Take, $g = 10\ \text{m/s}^2$)

10. State any two conditions essential for good health.

11. A mixture is prepared by mixing two liquids *A* and *B*. Which property will be used to separate them by the process of distillation?

Or

Name the process used for separating the components of a mixture containing sand, salt and ammonium chloride.

12. Which technique is used to separate the components of fountain pen ink?

Or

Pure $CuSO_4$ can be obtained from an impure sample by which process?

13. What do you mean by capture fishery?

Direction (Q.Nos. 14-16) *In each of the following questions, a statement of Assertion is given by the corresponding statement of Reason. Out of the given statements, choose the correct one.*

(a) If both Assertion and Reason are true and Reason is the correct explanation of Assertion.

(b) If both Assertion and Reason are true but Reason is not the correct explanation of Assertion.
(c) If Assertion is true but Reason is false.
(d) If Assertion is false but Reason is true.

14. **Assertion** Circular motion is an example of uniform accelerated motion.

Reason A uniform circular motion, there is no acceleration.

15. **Assertion** Air is a mixture of gases.

Reason The composition of air includes gases like N_2, O_2, CO_2 and water vapour.

16. **Assertion** Chromosomes are composed of DNA and protein.

Reason These are thread-like structures present in nucleus.

Or

Assertion Axon and dendrites are special feature of neurons.

Reason They help in rapid conduction of nerve impulses.

Answer *Q. Nos. 17-20 Contain five sub-parts each. You are expected to answer any four sub-parts in these questions.*

17. *Read the following and answer any four questions from 17 (i) to 17 (v).*

The symptoms of acidity are controlled by an antacid. Commercially available antacids consist of magnesium hydroxide, sugar and flavouring agents. The hydrochloric acid in the stomach is neutralised by the magnesium hydroxide to form salt and water. The mass of salt and water formed is equal to combined mass of base and acid reacted.

(i) Which law of chemical combination is mentioned in the above passage?
(a) Law of conservation of energy
(b) Law of conservation of mass
(c) Law of definite proportions
(d) All of these

(ii) Choose the correct match.

(A)	Polyatomic ion	(i) H
(B)	Monoatomic molecule	(ii) Cl_2
(C)	Diatomic molecule	(iii) $\bar{O}H$

(a) A-i, B-iii, C-iii (b) A-ii, B-i, C-iii
(c) A-iii, B-i, C-ii (d) A-ii, C-i, B-iii

(iii) Which salt is formed in the neutralisation reaction given in the passage?
(a) $Mg(OH)_2$
(b) $MgCl_2$
(c) $MgCO_3$
(d) $AlCl_3$

(iv) What is the combined mass of acid and antacid reacted to produce 9.5 g of salt and 3.6 g of water?
(a) 13.31 g (b) 12.6 g
(c) 13.1 g (d) 10.9 g

(v) Which of the following correctly state the law mentioned above?
(a) Energy can neither be created nor be destroyed.
(b) Mass can neither be created nor be destroyed.
(c) Energy can be created and can be vanish.
(d) Mass can be created and can be vary and vanish.

18. *Read the following and answer any four questions from 18 (i) to 18 (v).*

All living organisms present on the Earth are classified into non-cellular (e.g. virus) and cellular organisms. Cellular organisms can be prokaryotes and eukaryotes.

These two types of forms are very much different from one another, which can be learned from the table given below :

Differences between Prokaryotic and Eukaryotic Cells

Feature	Prokaryotic Cell	Eukaryotic Cell
Size	Generally small (1-10 μm)	Generally large (5-100 μm)
Nuclear region	Poorly developed, no nuclear membrane	Well-defined, surrounded by nuclear membrane.
Chromosome	Single	More than one
Nucleolus	Absent	Present
Membrane-bound cell organelles	Absent	Present, e.g. mitochondria, plastids, endoplasmic reticulum, etc.
Centriole	Absent	Present in animal cells.

UNSOLVED

(i) Which structure are present in animal cells?

	Cell membrane	Cell wall	Chloroplast	Cytoplasm
(a)	×	✓	✓	✓
(b)	✓	×	×	✓
(c)	✓	×	✓	×
(d)	✓	✓	×	✓

(ii) How permeable are the cell wall and the cell membrane?

	Cell wall	Cell membrane
(a)	Fully	Fully
(b)	Fully	Partially
(c)	Partially	Fully
(d)	Partially	Partially

(iii) Correct sequence of true/false for the given statement can be

(I) Cell wall of prokaryotic cell is made up of cellulose, chitin and hemicellulose

(II) Spindle fibres are present in prokaryotic cells

(III) Prokaryotic cell have 80S ribosome

(IV) Flagella have 9-12 arrangement in eukaryotic cells.

(a) TTFT (b) FTTT
(c) TTTT (d) FFFF

(iv) Which statement is incorrect about prokaryotic cell?

(a) Ribosomes are associated with the plasma membrane of the cell.

(b) Size of ribosome is about 15 nm by 20 nm.

(c) Ribosomes are made up of two subunit 60S and 40S.

(d) The ribosomes of a polysome translate the *m*RNA into protiens.

(v) What is the nuclear region of prokaryotic cells called?

(a) Pro-nucleus (b) Nucleoid
(c) Nucleus (d) None of these

UNSOLVED

19. *Read the following and answer any four questions from 19 (i) to 19 (v).*

The distance travelled by a body is the actual length of the path covered by it, irrespective of the direction in which body travels. It is a scalar quantity.

The displacement of a body is the change in the position of the object when it moves from a given position to another position. It is equal to the length of the shortest path measured in the direction from the initial position to the final position of the object. It is a vector quantity.

(i) Choose the correct statement.

(a) The displacement can be greater than distance when the path of motion is circular.

(b) The displacement can never be greater than distance. It can either be less than or equal to distance.

(c) The displacement can be greater than distance when the path of motion is parabolic.

(d) The displacement of an object is always equal to the distance travelled by it.

(ii) Displacement of a body can be

(a) positive (b) negative
(c) zero (d) All of these

(iii) The velocity *versus* time graph of a body in motion is shown below. The displacement of the body will be

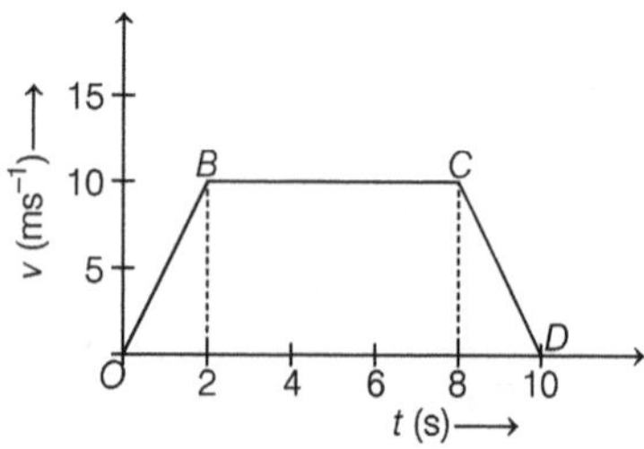

(a) 20 m (b) 60 m
(c) 80 m (d) 110 m

(iv) A particle starting from origin, moves 3 m North, 4 m East, 5 m South and then returns back to its initial position. Which of the following figures represents the path travelled by the particle?

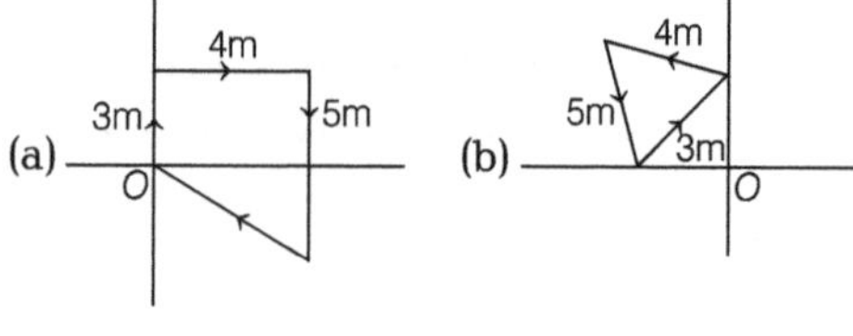

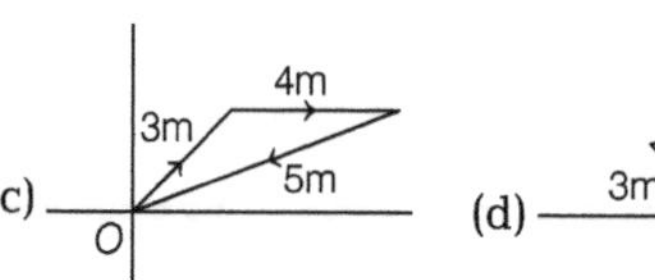

(v) A body travels a distance of 15 m from *A* to *B* and then moves a distance of 20 m at right angle to AB. The displacement of the body will be

(a) 15 m (b) 25 m
(c) 35 m (d) 40 m

20. *Read the following and answer any four questions from 20 (i) to 20 (v).*

A water solution that contanis nutrients, wastes, gases, salts and other substances surround cells. This the external environment of a cell. The cell's outer surface of the plasma membrane is in constant with this external environment, while the inner surface is in contact with the cytoplasm. Thus, the plasma membrane control what is loss and will leave the cell with the help of various process, e.g. Osmosis, diffusion imbibition, etc.

(i) Select the odd one out.

(a) The movement of water across a semipermeable membrane is affected by the amount of substances dissolved in it
(b) Membrane are made up of organic molecules such as proteins and lipids
(c) Molecules soluble in organic solvents can easily pass through the membrane
(d) Plasma membrane contain chitin sugar in plants

(ii) Following are a few difinations of osmosis. Select the correct one.

(a) Movement of water molecules from a region of higher concentration to a region of lower concentration through a semipermeable membrane
(b) Movement of solvent molecules from its higher concentration to lower concentration
(c) Movement of solvent molecules from higher concentration to lower concentration of solution through permeable membrane
(d) Movement of solute molecules from lower concentration to higher concentration of solution through semipermeable membrane

(iii) Root hairs absorbs water from soil through

(a) diffusion (b) imbibition
(c) osmosis (d) All of these

(iv) Two solutions of different concentrations (A and B) are separated by means of a membrane (C). Which of the following option is correct? (Take, X = solute and Y = water)

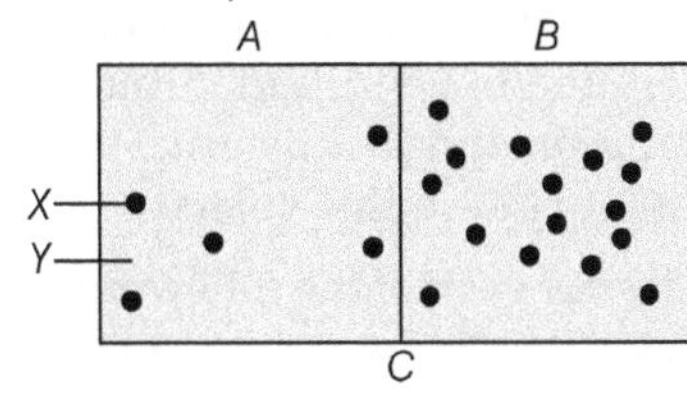

	Nature of membrane (R)	Net movement	Direction of movement
(a)	Permeable	X	$A \to B$
(b)	Permeable	Y	$A \to B$
(c)	Semi-permeable	Y	$B \to A$
(d)	Semi-permeable	Y	$A \to B$

(v) Dry wooden stakes driven in cracks of a rock and soaked will develop pressure that will split the rock. The phenomenon is

(a) osmotic pressure
(b) imbibition
(c) turgor pressure
(d) deplasmolysis

Section B

21. A sound wave has a frequency of 3 kHz and wavelength 30 cm. How long will it take to travel 500 m?

22. The average atomic mass of a sample of an element X is 16.2 u. What are the percentages of isotopes ${}^{16}_{8}X$ and ${}^{18}_{8}X$ in the sample?

Or

Give example of two atoms

(a) having same number of neutrons but different atomic numbers.
(b) having same valency but different valence electrons.

23. (a) Write three differences between epithelial tissue and connective tissue.

(b) Draw the diagram of areolar tissue and label the following parts

(i) Reticular fibre (ii) Fibroblast
(iii) Collagen fibre

24. A player throws a ball upwards with an initial speed of 19.6 m/s.

(a) What is the direction of acceleration of the ball during the upward motion?
(b) What are the velocity and acceleration of the ball at highest point of its motion?

UNSOLVED

Or

A train starting from rest attains a velocity of 72 km/h in 20 min. Assuming, the acceleration to be uniform, find the acceleration and the distance travelled by the train to attain this velocity.

25. (a) Classify each of the following as a homogeneous or heterogeneous mixture : soda water, wood, air, soil, vinegar.
(b) How would you confirm that a colour liquid given to you is pure water?

26. Differentiate between the following :
(a) Capture fishery and culture fishery
(b) Bee keeping and poultry farming

Section C

27. A ball is thrown up with a velocity of 19.6 m/s. The time taken by the ball to reach at maximum height is calculated below.
At maximum height, final velocity of ball, $v = 0$
From equation of vertical motion,

$$v^2 = u^2 - 2gh \quad [\because g = 9.8\,\text{m/s}^2]$$
$$0 = (19.6)^2 - 2 \times 9.8 \times h$$
$$\Rightarrow \quad h = 19.6\text{ m}$$

From equation of upward motion,

$$h = ut - \frac{1}{2}gt^2$$
$$19.6 = 19.6t - \frac{1}{2} \times 9.8t^2$$
$$4 = 4t - t^2$$
$$(t-2)^2 = 0 \Rightarrow t = 2\text{s}$$

Calculate the time taken by the ball to reach at maximum height by alternate method.

28. (a) Distinguish between mass and weight of an object.
(b) Give reason why objects with different masses take same time to fall from a fixed height.

29. Dheeraj has been cultivating wheat crop year after next. However, he observed a steady decline in crop yield for past few years. Agriculture inspector then advised him to cultivate soybean or chick pea crop for next year before planting wheat crop. Comment on the logic and validity of this suggestion.

Or Crop protection management aims at reducing the kind of infestations caused by weeds, insect pests, crop diseases, etc. Explain how.

30. (a) Differentiate between collenchyma and sclerenchyma.
(b) Which tissues are referred as conducting tissue?

31. Waves of higher frequencies are used for cleaning hard to reach the places. These are also used to detect and find the distance of object underwater.
(a) Name the type of waves.
(b) Mention the frequency of these waves.
(c) Write another important use of this wave.

32. (a) Many substances are said to be actively transported across cell membrane. Elaborate how.
(b) Present any two reasons supporting the fact that transport across cell membrane is vital to a cell.

33. Give reasons for the following observations.
(i) When a boy jumps out of a boat, the boat moves backwards.
(ii) The passengers sitting in a bus fall backward when the bus starts to move suddenly.

Section D

34. (a) Explain the three states of matter on the basis of the following properties.
(i) Intermolecular force
(ii) Arrangement of molecule
(b) Liquids generally have lower density as compared to solids but ice floats on water, why? Explain in brief.

Or When 3.0 g of carbon is burnt is 8.00 g oxygen, 11.00 g of carbon dioxide is produced. What mass of carbon dioxide will be formed when 3.00 g of carbon is burnt in 50.00 g of oxygen? Which law of combination will govern your answer?

35.

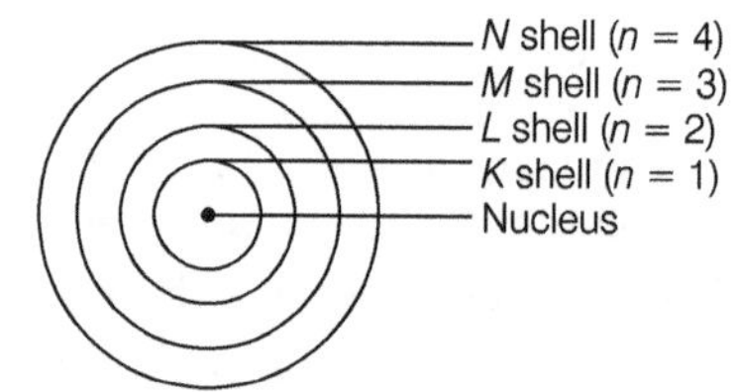

(a) Name the scientist who proposed this model of atom.
(b) Write the three postulates of this model.

UNSOLVED

(c) How many maximum electrons can be accommodated in M-orbit?

(d) What are canal rays? Give the characteristics of canal rays.

36. (a) Flash and thunder are produced simultaneously but thunder is heard a few seconds after the flash is seen, why?

(b) Does sound follow the same law of reflection as light does? Explain.

Or

(a) How can reverberation be reduced?

(b) A submarine emits an SONAR pulse, which returns from an underwater cliff in 2 s. If the speed of sound in sea water is 1530 m/s, then how far away is the cliff?

Answers

14. (c) **15.** (c) **16.** (b) *Or* (a)

17. (i) (b) (ii) (c) (iii) (b) (iv) (c) (v) (b)

18. (i) (b) (ii) (b) (iii) (d) (iv) (a) (v) (b)

19. (i) (b) (ii) (d) (iii) (c) (iv) (a) (v) (b)

20. (i) (d) (ii) (d) (iii) (c) (iv) (b) (v) (b)

21. $\frac{5}{9}$ s

22. Isotope $^{16}_{8}X = 90\%$, Isotope $^{18}_{8}X = 10\%$

24. (b)0 m/s, 9.8 ms^{-2} *Or* $\frac{1}{60}$ m/s^2, 12 km

36. *Or* (b) 1530 *n*

UNSOLVED

SAMPLE QUESTION PAPER 3

A Highly Simulated Sample Question Paper for CBSE Class IXth Examination

SCIENCE

UNSOLVED

General Instructions

See Sample Paper 1

Section A

1. Define valency.

Or Consider the following elements.

Elements	Electronic configuration
X	2, 8
Y	2, 8, 6

Which of them have high atomic radius and why?

2. What are oilseed crops? Give examples.

3. Golgi apparatus is involved in the formation of which organelle?

Or

What is the difference between columnar and glandular epithelium?

4. What are striated muscles?

Or Involuntary muscles present only in heart are called?

5. What is the function of cellulose in plant cell?

Or Why nucleus is called brain of the cell?

6. Alloys are example of which of the following, mixture or compound?

7. Atomic models have been improved over the years. Arrange the following atomic models in the order of their chronological order.

I. Rutherford's atomic model
II. Thomson's atomic model
III. Bohr's atomic model

8. How are ribosomes related to the endoplasmic reticulum?

9. An object is thrown vertically upwards with a velocity u, find the greatest height h to which it will rise before falling back.

Or What is the force of attraction between two unit point masses separated by a unit distance called?

10. How does pigments of natural colours can be separated?

Or Which of the following is a homogeneous mixture?

Solution of sugar in water or chalk powder in water

11. Which tissue is found in hypodermis of herbaceous stem?

12. The motion of a body of mass 5 kg is shown in the velocity-time graph.

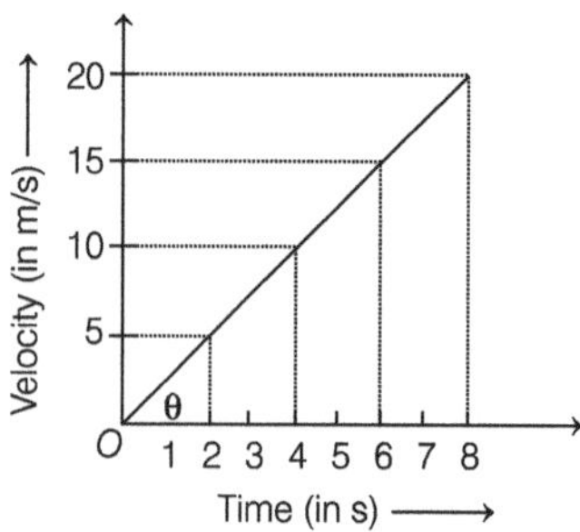

From the graph, find the acceleration of the body.

13. List any two properties of solution.

Direction (Q.Nos. 14-16) *In each of the following questions, a statement of Assertion is given by the corresponding statement of Reason. Out of the given statements, choose the correct one.*

(a) If both Assertion and Reason are true and Reason is the correct explanation of Assertion.

(b) If both Assertion and Reason are true, but Reason is not the correct explanation of Assertion.
(c) If Assertion is true, but Reason is false.
(d) If Assertion is false, but Reason is true.

14. **Assertion** Work done by a force on a body is positive when displacement is in the direction of applied force.

Reason Work done W on a body is calculated by $W = Fs\cos\theta$, where θ is the angle between force F and displacement s.

15. **Assertion** If the dispersed phase is liquid and dispersion medium is solid, then colloid is known as gel.

Reason Whipped cream is an example of gel.

16. **Assertion** The presence of genetic material as nucleoid is the characteristic of a prokaryotic cell.

Reason The genetic material in these cells is not present in nucleus.

Answer *Q. Nos. 17-20 Contain five sub-parts each. You are expected to answer any four sub-parts in these questions.*

17. *Read the following and answer any four questions from 17 (i) to 17 (v).*

Energy exists in many different forms. The change of one form of energy into another form of energy is known as transformation of energy. When a body is released from a height, then the potential energy of the body is gradually transformed (or changed) into kinetic energy. When a body is thrown upwards, the kinetic energy of body is gradually transformed into potential energy.

Some examples of the energy converters which make our life more comfortable are: electric motor, electric generator, electric iron, electric bulb and solar cell.

When energy changes from one form to another, there is no loss or gain of energy. The total energy before and after transformation remains the same, i.e. energy can neither be created nor be destroyed.

(i) In case of riding a bicycle,
(a) the muscular energy is converted into the kinetic energy of the bicycle
(b) the kinetic energy is converted into the muscular energy
(c) the potential energy is converted into mechanical energy
(d) None of the above

(ii) The potential energy of a freely falling object decreases progressively, then
(a) total mechanical energy will decrease
(b) total mechanical energy will increase
(c) total mechanical energy will remain constant
(d) None of the above

(iii) The velocity of a body of mass 100 g having a kinetic energy of 20 J is
(a) $10\ ms^{-1}$ (b) $15\ ms^{-1}$
(c) $20\ ms^{-1}$ (d) $25\ ms^{-1}$

(iv) Figure shows the frictional force *versus* displacement for a particle in motion. The loss of kinetic energy (work done against friction) in travelling over $s = 0$ to $s = 20$ m will be

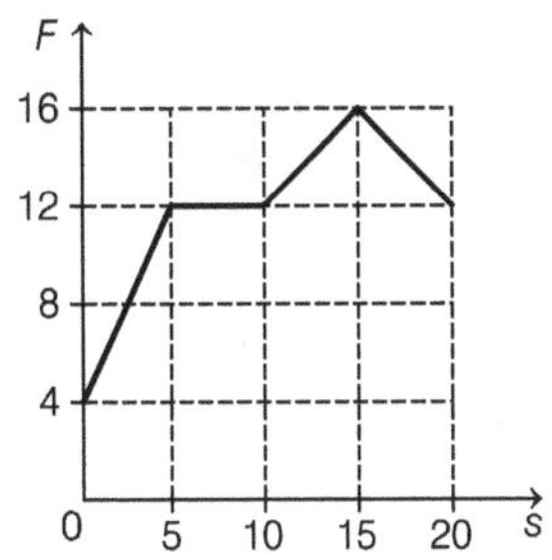

(a) 80 J (b) 160 J
(c) 240 J (d) 24 J

(v) The work done in lifting 200 kg of a mass through a vertical distance of 6 m is
(a) 10000 J (b) 12000 J
(c) 15000 J (d) 19000 J

18. *Read the following and answer any four questions from 18 (i) to 18 (v).*

Lysosomes are membrane bound sac that are filled with digestive enzymes. The enzymes are made by rough endoplasmic reticulum. Lysosomes are also called the suicidal bags of a cell because during the disturbance in cellular metabolism or when the cell gets damaged, lysosomes may burst and the enzymes can digest their own cell. They are absent in RBC.

(i) How do lysosomes originate?
(a) From the cytoplasm
(b) Phospholipid bilayer
(c) By budding off from the membrane of the trans-Golgi network
(d) None of the above

(ii) Refer to the given diagram of lysosome and choose the correct label of *A*, *B* and *C*.

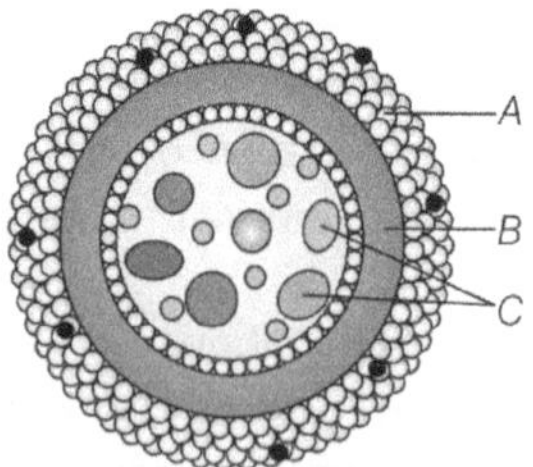

(a) *A*-Membrane, *B*-Lipid layer, *C*- Hydrolytic and digestive enzymes
(b) *A*-Lipid layer, *B*-Membrane, *C*- Hydrolytic and digestive enzymes
(c) *A*-Membrane, *B*-Lipid layer, *C*- Secretory vesicle
(d) None of the above

(iii) Why are lysosomes considered the 'garbage trucks' of a cell?
(a) Because they transport materials between two cell organelles
(b) Because they pump materials from outside to inside of a cell
(c) Because they remove all unwanted cellular materials
(d) Because they transport materials from one cell to another

(iv) The lysosomal membrane is rich in
(a) Sterols (b) Cardiolipin
(c) Sialic acid (d) All of these

(v) What is the pH of a lysosome?
(a) Acidic
(b) Basic
(c) Neutral
(d) Depends on the cell type

19. *Read the following and answer any four questions from 19 (i) to 19 (v).*

Manu went to watch a movie with his parents. In the dark, he found a small beam of light within which millions of tiny particles were dancing. He thought, when there was light, no such beam appears. He was very surprised.
He asked about this from his science teacher who told him that it, was due to scattering of light.

(i) What were the tiny particles?
(a) Dust (b) Smoke
(c) Fog (d) Both (a) and (b)

(ii) Why these particles do not appear in the presence of light?
(a) Because these only seen in the dark
(b) Because these are too small
(c) Because these are invisible
(d) None of the above

(iii) What is the name of the process of scattering of light?
(a) Dispersion effect
(b) Centrifugation
(c) Tyndall effect
(d) None of the above

(iv) Which type of mixtures scatter light?
(a) Colloid (b) Suspension
(b) True solution (d) Both (a) and (b)

(v) Choose the correct match

A.	Element	(i) Soap
B.	Compound	(ii) Silicon
C.	Mixture	(iii) Coal

Codes

	A	B	C		A	B	C
(a)	(ii)	(iii)	(i)	(b)	(iii)	(i)	(ii)
(c)	(i)	(ii)	(iii)	(d)	(ii)	(i)	(iii)

20. *Read the following and answer any four questions from 20 (i) to 20 (v).*

Sunil while playing football with his friends got injured suddenly. His friends took him to the hospital and the doctor told that he was suffering from a sprain and advised bed rest. Every afternoon, his friends visited him to enquire about his health.

(i) During a sprain, which type of tissues are stressed?
(a) Tendons (b) Ligaments
(c) Nervous (d) Connective

(ii) Which tissue connects muscles to bones?
(a) Cartilage (b) Tendons
(c) Areolar tissue (d) Blood

(iii) What is the composition of a bone?
(a) Calcium and phosphorus salts
(b) Calcium and magnesium salts
(c) Magnesium salts only
(d) Calcium salts only

(iv) Where is cartilage found in human body?
(a) Nose (b) Ear
(c) Trachea (d) All of these

UNSOLVED

(v) What is present in harvesian canals?
(a) Blood vessels (b) Nerve fibres
(c) Tendons (d) Both (a) and (c)

Section B

21. A train accelerates uniformly from 36 km/h to 72 km/h in 10s. Find the distance travelled.

Or An object is moving with a uniform speed in a circle of radius *r*. Calculate the distance and displacement
(a) when it completes half the circle.
(b) when it completes full the circle.

22. Two elements are represented as ${}_{17}X^{35}$ and ${}_{12}Y^{24}$.
(a) Write the electronic configurations of X and Y.
(b) Which of these elements will lose and gain electrons?

23. Comment on the following statements.
(a) Evaporation produces cooling.
(b) Sponge though compressible is a solid.

Or Why does the temperature of a substance remain constant during its melting point or boiling point?

24. Sucrose (sugar) crystals obtained from sugarcane and beetroot are mixed together. Will it be a pure substance or a mixture? Give reasons for the same.

25. Account for the following
(a) Name two properties of a substance to check its purity.
(b) Alloys cannot be separated by physical means, though it is considered mixture, why?

26. Spraying or fumigation?
Can you suggest which is an effective method for destruction of pest infestation occurring in stored food grain?

27. A force applied on a body of mass 4kg for 5s changes its velocity from 10 m/s to 20 m/s. Find the power required.

Section C

28. The velocity-time graph of a ball moving on the surface of floor is as shown in figure.

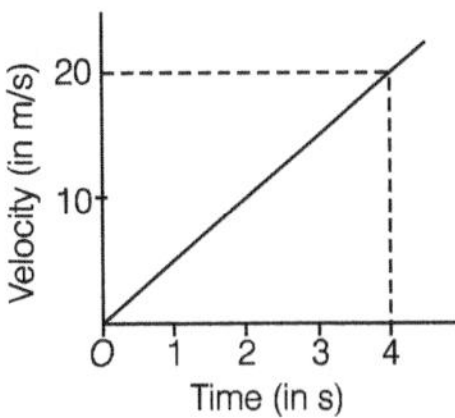

Distance travelled by the ball in 4 s is calculated as

At $t = 4$ s, $v = 20$ m/s; at $t = 0$ s, $u = 0$

Acceleration, $a = \dfrac{v-u}{t} = \dfrac{20-0}{4} = 5 \text{ m/s}^2$

Since, $s = ut + \dfrac{1}{2}at^2 = 0 \times 4 + \dfrac{1}{2} \times 5 \times (4)^2$

$= 40$ m

Calculate the distance travelled by ball is 4s, by alternate method.

29. (a) Define atomic mass unit.
(b) Give the difference between a cation and an anion.
(c) Calculate the formula unit mass of $Al_2(CO_3)_3$.

Or

(a) Define isotopes. Give any two uses of isotopes in the field of medicine.
(b) Chlorine occurs in nature in two isotopic forms with masses 35u and 37u. The percentage of ^{35}Cl is 75%. Find the average atomic mass of chlorine atom.

30. (a) Excessive use of fertilisers is detrimental for the environment. What inference (any one) do you draw from the above statement?
(b) How does the top soil present in an area determine its biodiversity.

31. (a) List two differences between thrust and pressure.
(b) What is meant by one Pascal and one Newton? How will the pressure change, if area of contact is doubled?

UNSOLVED

32. (a) Differentiate between isotopes and isobars giving suitable examples.
(b) Write the uses of I-131, C-14, Co-60 and P-32.

33. List any five characteristics of parenchyma.

Section D

34. (a) Write the formula to find the magnitude of gravitational force between the earth and an object on the earth's surface.
(b) Derive how does the value of gravitational force F between two objects change, when
(i) distance between them is reduced to half and
(ii) mass of an object is increased four times.

35. (a) Differentiate between hypotonic and hypertonic solution.
(b) With the help of a diagram, explain the structure of nucleus.

Or

(a) What are the various types of animal tissues?
(b) Mention briefly the location and one main function of each class of tissues.
(c) Draw the diagram of epithelium present in the oesophagus of our body.

36. (a) Deduce the following equation of motion.

$$s = ut + (1/2)at^2$$

(b) The following graph shows part of a journey made by a cyclist.

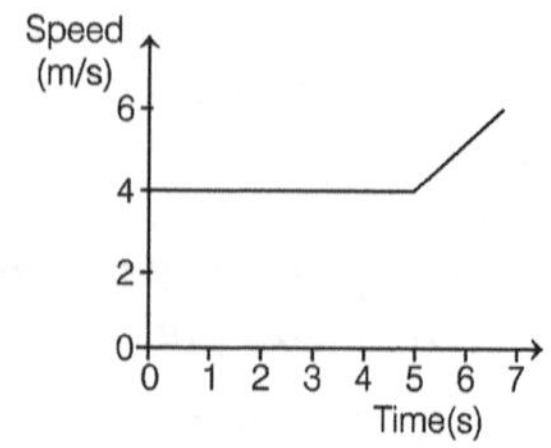

How far did the cyclist travel in 7 s?

Or

(a) How much water should be added to 15g of salt to obtain 15% salt solution?
(b) Write the difference between aqueous and non-aqueous solution.
(c) Why does solution of common salt in water not show Tyndall effect whereas the mixture of water and milk shows?

UNSOLVED

Answers

15. (c)
16. (a)
17. (i) (a) (ii) (c) (iii) (c) (iv) (c) (v) (b)
18. (i) (c) (ii) (a) (iii) (c) (iv) (c) (v) (a)
19. (i) (d) (ii) (b) (iii) (c) (iv) (d) (v) (d)
20. (i) (b) (ii) (b) (iii) (a) (iv) (d) (v) (d)
21. 150 m

Or

(a) For half circle distance $= \pi r$
displacement $= 2r$
(b) For complete circle, distance $= 2\pi r$
displacement $= 0$

27. 120 W
36. (b) 30 m *Or* (a) 85 g

STATEWISE

NTSE QUESTIONS

FULLY SOLVED

Matter in Our Surroundings

1. Dry ice is **(UP)**
   (a) freon (b) liquid chlorine
   (c) solid carbon dioxide (d) plaster of Paris

2. The melting point of ice is .... **(Gujarat)**
   (a) 273.15 K (b) 173.15 K
   (c) 373.5 K (d) 100 K

3. Arrange the following is the increasing order of forces of attraction **(Tamil Nadu)**
   (a) water, air, sugar (b) O_2, H_2O, sugar
   (c) salt, air, fruit juice (d) sugar, oil, air

4. Change of solid into vapour without changing into liquid is known as **(Telangana)**
   (a) evaporation (b) vapourisation
   (c) sublimation (d) boiling

5. If water turns into ice at a pressure of atmosphere at 0°C, then the temperature of this system in this process **(Telangana)**
   (a) decreases (b) increases
   (c) remains same (d) None of these

6. Physical state of water at 0°C is **(MP)**
   (a) solid (b) liquid
   (c) gas (d) None of these

Is Matter Around us Pure?

7. The method used to extract oils which give fragrance to flowers is **(Kerala)**
   (a) fractional distillation (b) steam distillation
   (c) sublimation (d) crystallisation

8. Which of the following is an aerosol? **(Kerala)**
   (a) Automobile exhaust (b) Shaving cream
   (c) Milk (d) Rubber

9. Which method is used to separate cream from milk? **(Uttarakhand)**
   (a) Crystallisation (b) Distillation
   (c) Centrifugation (d) Vapourisation

10. Who give the definition of an element? **(Gujarat)**
    (a) Robert Boyle (b) John Dalton
    (c) Lavoisier (d) Thomson

11. Which of these shows Tyndall effect? **(Chandigarh)**
    (a) Common salt solution
    (b) Lemon juice
    (c) Milk
    (d) Copper sulphate solution

12. The physical mixtures of two substances is called **(Telangana)**
    (a) mixture (b) compound
    (c) colloid (d) suspension

13. The phenomenon of scattering of a visible light by the particle of a colloid is known as **(Telangana)**
    (a) tyndall effect (b) chromatography
    (c) sublimation (d) reflection

14. Homogeneous mixture among the following is **(Rajasthan)**
    (a) milk (b) cloud
    (c) smoke (d) air

15. The substance showing sublimation property among the following is **(Rajasthan)**
    (a) common salt (b) copper sulphate
    (c) potassium nitrate (d) camphor

Atoms and Molecules

16. The formulae of an oxide of an element M is MO. The formulae of its phosphate is **(UP)**
    (a) $M_3(PO_4)_2$ (b) MPO_4
    (c) $M_2(PO_4)_3$ (d) M_3PO_4

17. What is the mass of the oxygen required to react completely with 15 g of H_2 gas to form water? **(Uttarakhand)**
    (a) 140 g (b) 115 g (c) 107.5 g (d) 120

18. What is the formula of carbon tetrachloride? **(Gujarat)**
    (a) CCl_4 (b) CCl_3
    (c) CCl_2 (d) CCl

19. What mass of oxygen is required to react completely with 15g of hydrogen gas to form water? **(Chandigarh)**
    (a) 120g (b) 107.5g
    (c) 132.5g (d) 112g

20. Chemical formula of lime stone is (Maharashtra)
(a) $Ca(OH)_2$ (b) $CaCO_3$ (c) $CaCl_2$ (d) CCl_4

21. An example of a homo atomic molecule is (Tamil Nadu)
(a) ozone (b) ammonia
(c) methane (d) sulphur dioxide

22. Common hydrogen is also called as (Tamil Nadu)
(a) protium atom (b) deuterium atom
(c) tritium atom (d) None of these

23. The other name of tungsten is (Telangana)
(a) natrium (b) kalium
(c) wolfram (d) cuprum

Structure of an Atom

24. The isotope of which element is used for treatment of cancer disease? (Odisha)
(a) Uranium (b) Cobalt
(c) Iodine (d) Chlorine

25. Hydrogen contains three types of atoms ($_1H^1$ protium, $_1H^2$ deuterium and $_1H^3$ tritium) these atoms are (Uttarakhand)
(a) isotopic (b) isobaric
(c) isotopic and isobaric (d) None of these

26. What is the maximum number of electrons that an be accommodated in the outermost orbit? (Gujarat)
(a) 2 (b) 8
(c) 3 (d) 18

27. Which of the following radioactive isotope is used in the treatment of cancer? (Punjab)
(a) Iodine-131 (b) Uranium-235
(c) Sodium-24 (d) Cobalt-60

28. The ion of an element has 3 positive charge, 27 mass number and 14 neutrons. Which of the number of electrons in this ion? (Chandigarh)
(a) 13 (b) 10 (c) 14 (d) 16

29. Which of the following elements does not consist isotopes? (Maharashtra)
(a) Carbon (b) Neon
(c) Chlorine (d) Iodine

30. Pick out the isobar pair (Tamil Nadu)
(a) $_1H^1$, $_1H^2$, (b) $_6Cl^{13}$, $_7N^{14}$
(c) $_{17}Cl^{35}$, $_{17}H^{37}$ (d) $_{18}Ar^{40}$, $_{20}Ca^{40}$

31. Number of neutrons in isotope of hydrogen, tritium is (Rajasthan)
(a) 0 (b) 1 (c) 2 (d) 3

32. Isotopes of an element contains (MP)
(a) similar physical properties
(b) different chemical properties
(c) different number of neutrons
(d) different atomic number

33. Valency electron in Cl^- ion is (MP)
(a) 16 (b) 8
(c) 17 (d) 18

34. Which one of the following is correct electronic configuration of sodium? (MP)
(a) 2, 8 (b) 8, 2, 1
(c) 2, 1, 8 (d) 2, 8, 1

35. Electron is invented by (MP)
(a) J.J. Thomson (b) Dalton
(c) Niels Bohr (d) None of these

36. Distribution of electrons in carbon is as follow (MP)
(a) 2, 4 (b) 2, 2, 2
(c) 4, 2 (d) None of these

The Fundamental Unit of Life

37. .... is also known as the 'suicidal bags' of a cell. (Gujarat)
(a) Mitochondria (b) Lysosomes
(c) Plastids (d) Golgi apparatus

38. DNA is not present in (Delhi)
(a) chloroplast (b) mitochondria
(c) nucleus (d) ribosome

39. An exception to cell theory is (MP)
(a) bacteria (b) virus
(c) algae (d) All of these

40. Cristae are associated with (MP)
(a) nucleus (b) chloroplast
(c) cell wall (d) mitochondria

41. Lipoprotein is found in (MP)
(a) cell membrane (b) nucleus
(c) cytoplasm (d) cell wall

42. A cell is having two boundaries, the outer being cell wall and the inner being plasma membrane. The inherent property of this pair moving from outside to inside is (Chandigarh)
(a) semipermeable and permeable
(b) semipermeable and semipermeable
(c) permeable and semipermeable
(d) permeable and permeable

43. The process of osmosis is the movement across the cell membrane of (Chandigarh)
(a) salts from a hypotonic solution to hypertonic solution

FULLY SOLVED

(b) salts from a hypertonic solution to hypotonic solution
(c) water from a hypotonic solution to hypertonic solution
(d) water from a hypertonic solution to hypotonic solution

44. A poorly developed zone in the centre of a cell that has DNA molecule is called as **(Chandigarh)**

(a) nucleolus of prokaryote
(b) nucleoid of prokaryote
(c) nucleus of prokaryote
(d) nucleus of eukaryote

45. Granular structures present on the rough endoplasmic reticulum are **(AP)**

(a) lipids (b) plastids
(c) ribosomes (d) lysosomes

Tissues

46. .... is not an example of simple tissues. **(Gujarat)**

(a) Parenchyma (b) Collenchyma
(c) Sclerenchyma (d) Phloem

47. Skeletal muscles are **(Rajasthan)**

(a) striated and voluntary
(b) unstriated and voluntary
(c) striated and involuntary
(d) unstriated and involuntary

48. A tissue which makes up the husk of coconut and whose cells are dead, elongated and lignified is **(Punjab)**

(a) chlorenchyma (b) collenchyma
(c) parenchyma (d) sclerenchyma

49. In a practical laboratory, a student while observing the slide of tissue with the help of a microscope, found a bunch of cylindrical-shaped cells having interconnections belong to the category of **(Chandigarh)**

(a) adipose tissue (b) heart muscle
(c) smooth muscle (d) skeletal muscle

50. Name the connecting tissue that connects a muscle to the bone. **(AP)**

(a) Areolar tissue (b) Cartilage
(c) Ligament (d) Tendon

51. Identify the function of columnar epithelium. **(Maharashtra)**

(a) Selective transport of substances
(b) Prevention of wearing of organs
(c) Secretion of digestive juice
(d) Reabsorption of useful materials from urine

52. Tendons and ligaments are the types of **(Haryana)**

(a) muscular tissue (b) epithelial tissue
(c) nervous tissue (d) fibrous tissue

Motion

53. A body starts from rest is accelerated uniformly for 30s. If x_1, x_2 and x_3 are the distances travelled in first 10s, next 10s and last 10s respectively, then $x_1 : x_2 : x_3$ is **(Delhi)**

(a) 1 : 2 : 3 (b) 1:1:1 (c) 1:3 :5 (d) 1 : 3 :9

54. The velocity-time graph of a moving body is shown in the figure.

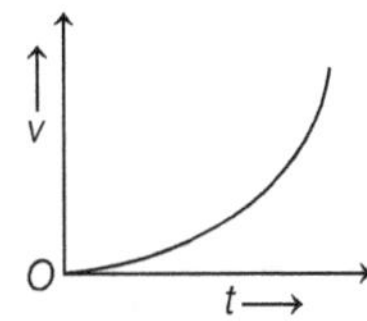

Which of the following statement is true? **(Delhi)**

(a) The acceleration is constant and positive
(b) The acceleration is constant and negative
(c) The acceleration is increasing and positive
(d) The acceleration is decreasing and negative

55. A woman is wearing her seat belt, while driving at 60 km/h. She finds it necessary to slam on her brakes and she slows uniformly to a stop in 1.6 s. What is the average acceleration experienced by her? **(Goa)**

(a) -10.4 m/s^2 (b) 10.4 m/s^2
(c) 1.04 m/s^2 (d) -1.04 m/s^2

56. Velocity-time graph of a body moving with a uniform acceleration is shown in the figure. The distance travelled by the body in 3 s is **(Rajasthan)**

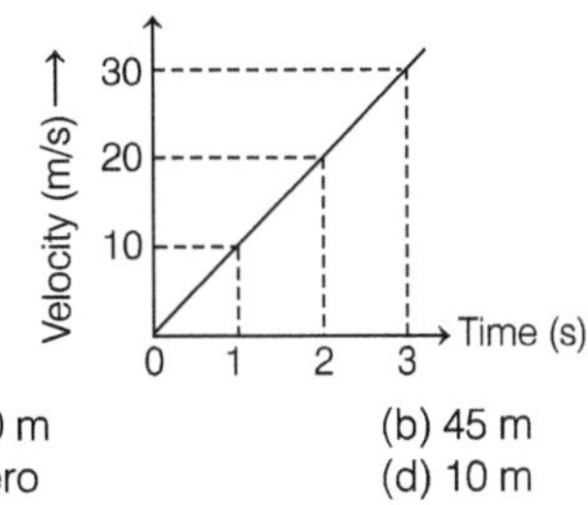

(a) 90 m (b) 45 m
(c) zero (d) 10 m

57. A car accelerates uniformly from 18 km/h to 36 km/h in 5 s. What is the value of acceleration? **(Gujarat)**

(a) 1 ms^{-2} (b) 3.6 ms^{-2}
(c) 2 ms^{-2} (d) 2.6 ms^{-2}

58. A body is thrown vertically upwards against gravity alone with velocity u. The greatest height h to which it will rise and time taken t to attain this height is given by **(Punjab)**

(a) $\frac{u}{2g}, \frac{2u}{g}$
(b) $\frac{u}{g}, \frac{u}{g}$
(c) $\frac{u^2}{g}, \frac{2u}{g}$
(d) $\frac{u^2}{2g}, \frac{u}{g}$

59. In which of the following situations, the distance moved and the magnitude of displacement are equal? **(Punjab)**

(a) A pendulum is moving to and fro
(b) Moon is revolving around the earth
(c) A boy is sitting in moving merry-go-round
(d) A bus is moving on a straight road

60. Two trains with v_1, v_2 speeds take 3 s to pass one another when going in opposite direction, but takes only 2.5 s, if the speed of any one of it is increased by (its speed) 50%. The time one would take to pass the other when going in the same direction with v_1, v_2 speed in .... s. **(AP)**

(a) 10
(b) 18
(c) 15
(d) 12

61. An athlete completes one round of a circular track of radius R in 40 s. The displacement at the end of 2 min 20 s will be **(Karnataka)**

(a) zero
(b) $2R$
(c) πR
(d) $7\pi R$

62. A boy moving along a circular path of radius 10 m completes 3/4th of the circle in 10 s. The magnitude of speed and velocity are **(Kerala)**

(a) 4.71 m/s and 47.1 m/s
(b) 4.71 m/s and 1.41 m/s
(c) 1.41 m/s and 4.71 m/s
(d) 1.41 m/s and 1.41 m/s

63. The velocity-time graph of an object thrown vertically up is **(Kerala)**

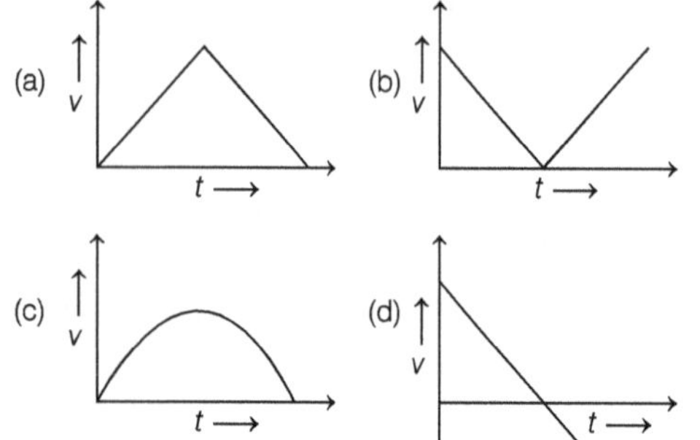

64. The displacement-time graph for two particles are shown in the figure. The ratio of velocity of A to velocity of B is **(Tamil Nadu)**

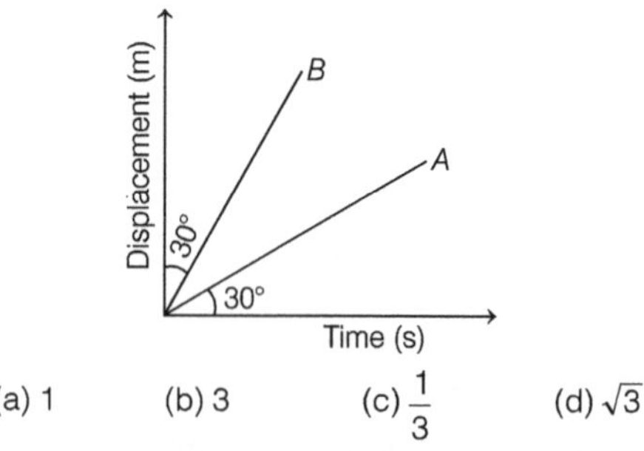

(a) 1
(b) 3
(c) $\frac{1}{3}$
(d) $\sqrt{3}$

65. The velocity-time graph of a body moving along a straight line is shown below. The acceleration of the body along OA, AB and BC is **(Tamil Nadu)**

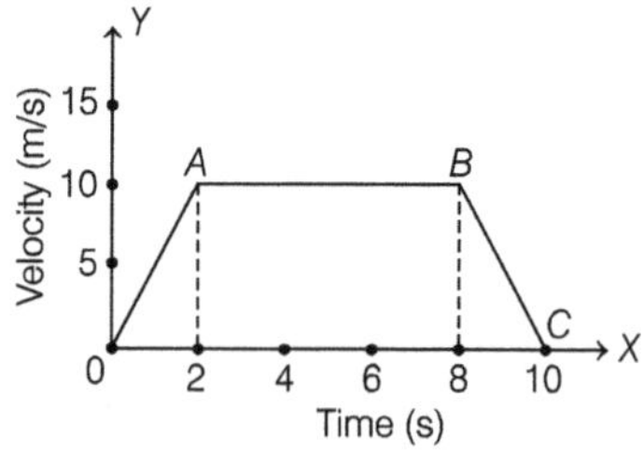

(a) 5 m/s^2, 0, – 5 m/s^2
(b) – 5 m/s^2, 0, + 5 m/s^2
(c) 5 m/s^2, 1.6 m/s^2, – 5 m/s^2
(d) – 5 m/s^2, 1.6 m/s^2, 5 m/s^2

66. If an object is moving with constant velocity, then the motion is **(Telangana)**

(a) speed
(b) uniform acceleration
(c) uniform motion
(d) non-uniform motion

Force and Laws of Motion

67. The inertia of a body depends upon **(Rajasthan)**

(a) gravitational acceleration
(b) centre of gravity of body
(c) shape of body
(d) mass of body

68. A bird is in a wire cage hanging from a spring balance. The reading of the balance is taken when the bird is flying inside the cage and when the bird is at rest in the cage. The first reading will be **(Chandigarh)**

(a) much greater than the second
(b) greater than the second
(c) less than the second
(d) same as the second

FULLY SOLVED

69. What is the SI unit of momentum? **(Gujarat)**
(a) g-ms^{-1} (b) g-m^2s^{-1}
(c) kg-ms^{-1} (d) kg-ms^{-2}

70. Action and reaction force, according to Newton's third law act on **(Punjab)**
(a) same body in opposite direction
(b) different bodies in same direction
(c) different bodies in opposite direction
(d) same body in same direction

71. A passenger in a moving bus tosses a coin which falls behind him. It means that, motion of the bus is **(Punjab)**
(a) uniform (b) accelerated
(c) retarded (d) circular motion

72. Two objects have masses in the ratio 1 : 2. If the forces acting on them are in the ratio 2 : 1, then the ratio of their accelerations is **(Kerala)**
(a) 1:1 (b) 1:2 (c) 2:1 (d) 4:1

73. The net force acting on a book placed on a table is **(Kerala)**
(a) force of gravity
(b) force exerted by table on the book
(c) frictional force
(d) zero

74. What will be the percentage change in momentum of a body when both its mass and velocity are doubled? **(Tamil Nadu)**
(a) 400 (b) 75
(c) 500 (d) 300

75. A ship of mass 3×10^7 kg initially at rest is pulled by force of 5×10^4 N through a distance of 3 m. Assuming that the resistance due to water is negligible, then the speed of the ship is **(Tamil Nadu)**
(a) 1.5 m/s (b) 60 m/s
(c) 0.1 m/s (d) 5 m/s

Gravitation

76. The mass of a planet is twice and its radius is three times that of the earth. The weight of a body, which has a mass of 5 kg on that planet will be **(Delhi)**
(a) 11.95 N (b) 10.88 N
(c) 9.88 N (d) 20.99 N

77. The buoyancy depends on **(Goa)**
(a) mass of liquid displaced
(b) viscosity of the liquid
(c) pressure of the liquid displaced
(d) depth of immersion

78. The distance between two masses is to be halved. The gravitational force between them will be **(Rajasthan)**
(a) double (b) one-fourth
(c) quadruple (d) half

79. On a planet whose size (including radii) is the same and mass is 4 times as that of our earth. Then, the amount of work done to lift 3 kg mass vertically upwards through 3 m distance on that planet is
(Take, g on the surface of earth is 10 m/s^2) **(AP)**
(a) 40 J (b) 360 kg
(c) 360 J (d) 40 kg

80. Two bodies A and B having masses 2 kg and 4 kg respectively are separated by 2 m. Where should a body of mass 1 kg be placed, so that the gravitational force on this body due to A and B is zero? **(Tamil Nadu)**
(a) 8.3 m (b) 0.83 m
(c) 3.8 m (d) 0.38 m

81. Among the statements which is/are correct?
Acceleration due to gravity
(i) decreases from equator to poles
(ii) decreases from poles to equator
(iii) is maximum at the centre of the earth **(Tamil Nadu)**
(a) (i) only (b) (ii) and (iii) only
(c) (iii) only (d) (ii) only

Work and Energy

82. A bomb of mass $3m$ kg explodes into two pieces of mass m kg and $2m$ kg. If the velocity of m kg mass is 16 ms^{-1}, then the total kinetic energy released in the explosion is **(Delhi)**
(a) 192 mJ (b) 96 mJ
(c) 384 mJ (d) 768 mJ

83. If two bodies one light and other heavy have equal kinetic energies, then which one has a greater momentum? **(Goa)**
(a) Heavy body
(b) Light body
(c) Both have equal momentum
(d) It depends on the actual velocities

84. A boy of mass 50 kg runs up a staircase of 45 steps in 9 s. If the height of each step is 15 cm, then what is his power?
(Take, $g = 10\ ms^{-2}$) **(Gujarat)**
(a) 275 W (b) 350 W
(c) 325 W (d) 375 W

85. An object is dropped from a height h, find the height from the ground at which the kinetic energy and potential energy are in the ratio 3 : 4. **(Kerala)**

(a) $\frac{3h}{4}$ (b) $\frac{4h}{3}$ (c) $\frac{4h}{7}$ (d) $\frac{3h}{7}$

86. How fast should a man weighing 600 N run to achieve a kinetic energy of 750 J? (Take, $g = 10 \text{ m/s}^2$) **(Uttarakhand)**

(a) 5 m/s (b) 7 m/s
(c) 10 m/s (d) 7.5 m/s

87. Which of the following graphs shows correct relation of kinetic energy (E), potential energy (U) and height (h) from the ground of a particle **(Uttarakhand)**

(a)
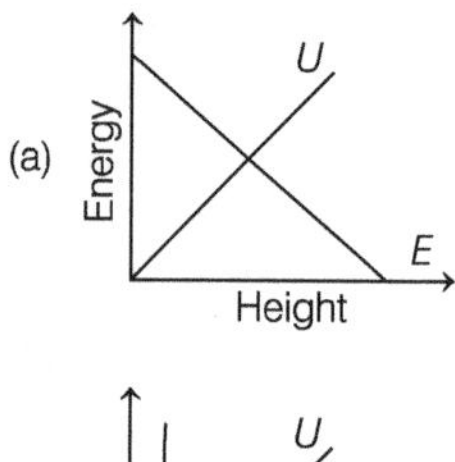

(b)
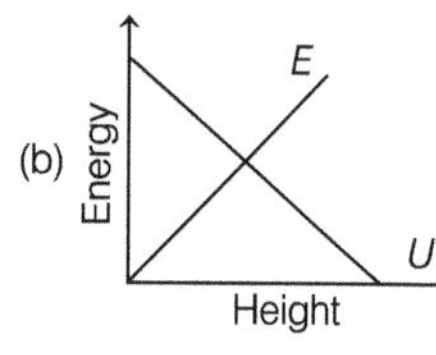

(c)
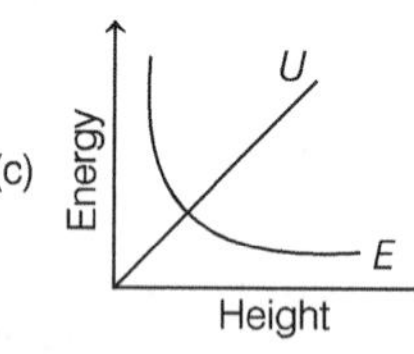

(d)
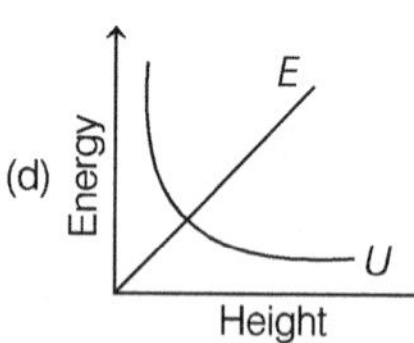

Sound

88. The linear distance between a consecutive compression and a rarefaction in longitudinal wave is **(Delhi)**

(a) γ (b) $\frac{\gamma}{2}$ (c) $\frac{\gamma}{4}$ (d) $\frac{3\gamma}{4}$

89. The speed of a wave is 350 m/s and wavelength is 70 cm. The frequency of wave is **(Rajasthan)**

(a) 500 Hz (b) 700 Hz
(c) 50 Hz (d) 200 Hz

90. When we go from solid to gaseous state, then the speed of sound **(Gujarat)**

(a) increases (b) increases or decreases
(c) decreases (d) constant

91. A stone is dropped from the top of a tower 490 m high into a pond of water at the base of the tower. The splash is heard after (given $g = 9.8 \text{ m/s}^2$, speed of sound = 350 m/s) **(Tamil Nadu)**

(a) 11.4 s (b) 10 s (c) 22.8 s (d) 20 s

92. Infrasound can be heard by **(Tamil Nadu)**

(a) dog (b) bat
(c) rhinoceros (d) tiger

93. A person has a hearing range from 20 Hz to 20 kHz. The typical wavelengths of sound waves in air corresponding to these two frequencies are
(Take, speed of sound in air = 344 m/s). **(Uttarakhand)**

(a) 1.72 m, 1.72 mm (b) 17.2 m, 17.2 mm
(c) 17.2 m, 1.72 mm (d) None of these

Natural Resources

94. How many of the following are involved in nitrogen-fixation?

Nostoc, Anabaena, Rhizobium, Azotobacter **(Goa)**

(a) 1 (b) 2 (c) 3 (d) 4

95. Soil contains decomposed matter. Plants that grow from the soil absorb nutrient elements. When we eat the plants, the nutrients enter into our body. After our death, when our body is buried into the soil, our body will become decomposed matter. This cyclic process refers to **(Tamil Nadu)**

(a) life cycle (b) biogeochemical cycle
(c) biological cycle (d) geological cycle

96. Identify the macronutrient obtained by plants from the soil. **(Kerala)**

(a) Molybdenum (b) Zinc
(c) Boron (d) Phosphorus

Improvement in Food Resources

97. Jaya and Ratna are the varieties of **(Delhi)**

(a) maize (b) rice
(c) wheat (d) bajra

98. Honeybee culture is known as **(Rajasthan)**

(a) silviculture (b) apiculture
(c) sericulture (d) pisciculture

99. High yielding varieties of wheat were initially developed by an Indian scientist by cross-breeding the traditional varieties with **(Haryana)**

(a) Mexican varieties
(b) Europian varieties
(c) American varieties
(d) African varieties

100. ILS-82 and B-77 are the breeds of **(Haryana)**

(a) cow (b) fowl
(c) pig (d) buffalo

Answers

1. (c) Dry ice is solid CO_2.

2. (a) $0°C = 273.15$ K

3. (b) Increasing order of forces of attraction of states of matter is
gases < liquids < solids, i.e. $O_2 < H_2O <$ sugar.

4. (c) The process of transformation of solid directly to gas is sublimation.

5. (c) Phase transformation take place at constant temperature. So, temperature remains same.

6. (a, b, c) At 0°C, water exists as are solid, liquid or gas depending upon the conditions.

7. (b) The method used to extract oils which give fragrance to flowers is steam distillation. As the steam rises through the flowers, it captures the scent bearing components which are then cooled.

8. (a) Automobile exhaust is an aerosol. Aerosol is a colloidal solution in which both dispersed phase and dispersion medium are present in gaseous state.

9. (c) Centrifugation

10. (c) Antoine Lavoisier

11. (c) Milk is a colloidal solution.

12. (a) The physical mixtures of two substances is called mixture. In a mixture, the substances are present in any proportion, while in compound the substance are present in definite proportion.

13. (a) The phenomenon of scattering of visible light by a particle of colloid is called Tyndall effect. The particles of solution do not show Tyndall effect, while suspension particle also show Tyndall effect.

14. (d) Air is a homogenous mixture of gases like N_2, O_2, Ar etc.

15. (d) Camphor is a substance that sublimes i.e. directly changes from solid to vapour state.

16. (a) Formula of oxide = MO
Valency of M will be 2.
So formula of phosphate
$$M^{2+} \times PO_4^{3-} \longrightarrow M_3\ (PO_4)_2$$

17. (d) $2H_2 + O_2 \longrightarrow 2H_2O$
4 g hydrogen combine with 32 g oxygen
$\therefore$ 15 g hydrogen combine with $\left(\frac{15 \times 32}{4}\right)$ g oxygen
$$= 120 \text{ g}$$

18. (a) Carbon tetrachloride :
$$C^{4+} \times Cl^{-1} \longrightarrow CCl_4$$

19. (a) $\underset{4g}{2H_2} + \underset{32g}{O_2} \longrightarrow \underset{36g}{2H_2O}$
To forms one mole of water (18g), hydrogen gas and oxygen gas are combining in the ratio of 1 : 8.
$\therefore$ To react completely with 15g of hydrogen gas, oxygen required is 120g.
[$\because H : O = 15 : 120$ or $1 : 8$]

20. (b) $CaCO_3$ is lime stone.

21. (a) Ozone is made up of oxygen atoms only.

22. (a) Common hydrogen is also called as protium. It contains only one proton and no neutron.

23. (c) The other name of tungsten of wolfram. The name wolfram comes from mineral wolframite in which it was discovered.

24. (b) The isotope of cobalt (Co – 60) is used for the treatment of cancer diseases.

25. (a) Atoms having same atomic number but different mass numbers are termed as isotopes.

26. (b) 8

27. (d) Fact (based)

28. (b) Mass number = Number of protons + Number of neutron
$$27 + P + N$$
$$27 - 14 = P$$
$$P = 13$$
In an neutral atom, number of proton = number of electrons. The ion of this element has three positive charge.
Thus, number of electrons present in ion $= 13 - 3 = 10$.
The element is Al and ion is Al^{3+}.

29. (b) Neon is an inert gas and has no isotope.

30. (d) The elements having different atomic number but same mass number are called isobars.

31. (c) Tritium is ${}_1^3H$
Mass number option : (A)
$$= \text{Number of neutron} + \text{proton} = 3$$
Atomic number option : (Z) = Number of proton = 1
Number of neutron $= A - Z = 3 - 1 = 2$

32. (c) Isotopes have same number of protons and different number of neutrons or mass number is different.

33. (b) Cl^- ion = $\begin{matrix} K & L & M \\ 2 & 8 & 8 \end{matrix}$ so, valence electrons are 8.

34. (d) Na $\Rightarrow (Z = 11)$; $\begin{matrix} K & L & M \\ 2 & 8 & 1 \end{matrix}$

35. (a) Electron is invented by J.J. Thomson by plum pudding model.

FULLY SOLVED

FULLY SOLVED

36. (a) $C(Z=6)$ has electronic configuration $= \begin{matrix} K & L \\ 2 & 4 \end{matrix}$

37. (b) Lysosomes contain hydrolytic enzymes in vesicles that burst, if cell gets damaged or stops working. The released enzymes then digest their own cell and ultimately cell dies. Hence, lysosomes are also called as suicidal bags of cell.

38. (d) Ribosome is made up of proteins and *r*RNA. DNA is absent in ribosome.

39. (b) Virus is acellular structure made up of protein and nucleic acid. It cannot replicate unless it is inside a host cell.

40. (d) Inner membrane of mitochondria have finger-like projections called cristae. These create large surface area for ATP generating chemical reactions.

41. (a) Cell membrane or plasma membrane is made up of protein and lipid (lipoprotein).

42. (c) The outer boundary of cell is cell wall, which is fully permeable and inner boundary is plasma membrane which is semipermeable.

43. (c) Osmosis is the movement of solvent from high concentration to low concentration through semipermeable membrane, so water movement from a hypotonic solution (contains more solvent) to hypertonic solution (contains less solvent) will take place.

44. (b) Undefined, poorly developed zone in the centre of prokaryotic cell is nucleoid.

45. (c) Rough endoplasmic reticulum is rough in appearance due to the ribosomes present on its surface, which are the sites of synthesis of proteins.

46. (d) Phloem is a complex tissue.

47. (a) Skeletal muscles are attached to bones. They are striated and voluntary.

48. (d) Sclerenchyma are dead tissues because of lignin deposition and are present in husk of coconut.

49. (b) Cylindrical-shaped, found in network (bunch) of branched interconnections are heart muscles.

50. (d) Tendon is a flexible but inelastic cord of strong fibrous collagen tissue attaching a muscle to a bone.

51. (c) Glands secreting digestive juices consist of columnar epithelium.

52. (d) Tendons and ligaments are the dense regular connective tissues which contain more fibres and less matrix.

53. (c) From second equation of motion, $s = ut + \frac{1}{2}at^2$

$$x_1 = \frac{1}{2}a(10)^2 = 50a$$

$$x_2 = \frac{1}{2}a[(20)^2 - (10)^2] = 150a$$

and $x_3 = \frac{1}{2}a[(30)^2 - (20)^2] = 250a$

$\therefore \quad x_1 : x_2 : x_3 = 1:3:5$

54. (c) Slope of velocity-time curve is increasing with time.

55. (a) Given, $u = 60 \text{ km/h} = 60 \times \frac{5}{18} \text{ m/s} = \frac{50}{3} \text{ m/s}$,

$t = 1.6, v = 0$

$\therefore$ Average acceleration,

$$a = \frac{v-u}{t} = \frac{0 - \frac{50}{3}}{1.6} = \frac{-50}{3 \times 1.6} = \frac{-100}{3 \times 3.2} = \frac{-1000}{96}$$

$$= -10.4 \text{ m/s}^2$$

56. (b) Area under velocity-time graph gives displacement. Since, the motion of the object is in straight line and in same direction, so displacement will be equal to distance.

Area under graph = Area of triangle

$$\text{Distance} = \frac{1}{2} \times B \times H = \frac{1}{2} \times 3 \times 30 = 45 \text{ m}$$

57. (a) According to first equation of motion,

$$v = u + at$$

$$\Rightarrow \quad a = \frac{v-u}{t} = \frac{10-5}{5} = 1 \text{ ms}^{-2}$$

[$\because$ 36 km/h = 10 m/s and 18 km/h = 5 m/s]

58. (d) From third equation of motion,

$$v^2 - u^2 = 2as$$

Given, $a = -g$ and $v = 0$

So, $u^2 = 2gs$

$$\Rightarrow \quad s = \frac{u^2}{2g}$$

From first equation of motion, $v = u + at$

Given, $a = -g$ and $v = 0$

So, $u = gt \Rightarrow t = \frac{u}{g}$

59. (d) (a) Distance > Displacement

(b) Distance > Displacement

(c) Distance > Displacement

(d) Distance = Displacement

So, option (d) is correct.

60. (c) **In first case**

$$\frac{2x}{v_1 + v_2} = 3$$

In second case

$$\frac{2x}{v_1 + \frac{3v_2}{2}} = 2.5$$

On solving, $v_1 = \frac{2x}{5}, v_2 = \frac{4x}{15}$

In third case $t = \dfrac{2x}{\dfrac{2x}{5} - \dfrac{4x}{15}}$

$t = 15$ s

61. (b) 1 round completes in 40 s.

$2\pi r = 40$ s

2 min 20 s = 140 s

$\therefore \quad t = 3 \times 40 + 20$

He completed 3 round and $\frac{1}{2}$ revolution.

So, displacement is $2R$.

62. (b) $\therefore$ Distance $= \frac{3}{4} \times 2\pi r$

$= \frac{3}{4} \times 2 \times \frac{22}{7} \times 10 = 47.10$

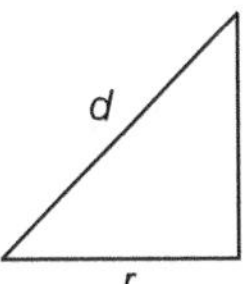

Displacement $(d) = \sqrt{2}r = 10\sqrt{2}$

$\therefore$ Speed $= \dfrac{\text{Distance}}{\text{Time}} = \dfrac{47.10}{10} = 4.71 \text{ ms}^{-1}$

$\therefore$ Velocity $= \dfrac{\text{Displacement}}{\text{Time}} = \dfrac{10\sqrt{2}}{10} = 1.41 \text{ ms}^{-1}$

63. (d) When an object is thrown vertically upwards, then it has some initial velocity. As the object goes up its velocity decreases, because it is moving against the gravity. At the highest point, its velocity becomes zero. After that object begins to fall and its velocity goes on increasing, but its sign would be negative, as it is now moving with the gravity.

64. (c) $\therefore$ Velocity $= \dfrac{\text{Displacement}}{\text{Time}} \propto \tan\theta$

So, $\dfrac{v_A}{v_B} = \dfrac{\tan\theta_A}{\tan\theta_B} = \dfrac{\tan 30°}{\tan 60°} = \dfrac{1}{3}$

65. (a) We know that, $a = \dfrac{\Delta v}{\Delta t}$

So, $a(O \text{ to } A) = 5 \text{ m/s}^2$

$a(A \text{ to } B) = 0$

$a(B \text{ to } C) = -5 \text{ m/s}^2$

66. (c) As velocity is constant, so it travels equal distance in equal interval of time. Hence, object is in uniform motion.

67. (d) Inertia depends on mass of body.

68. (c) Flying bird exert no weight on wire cage, so the first reading will be less than the second.

69. (c) As we know, momentum, $p = mv$ = kg-ms^{-1}

So, unit = kg-ms^{-1}

70. (c) Action and reaction force work on different bodies in opposite direction.

71. (b) Motion of the bus is accelerated.

$\because$ Final velocity of passenger is higher than the coin.

72. (d) $\therefore$ Force (F) = Mass (m) × Acceleration (a)

$\Rightarrow \quad \dfrac{F_1}{F_2} = \dfrac{m_1 a_1}{m_2 a_2}$

$\dfrac{2}{1} = \dfrac{1}{2} \times \dfrac{a_1}{a_2} \Rightarrow \dfrac{a_1}{a_2} = \dfrac{4}{1}$ or $4:1$

73. (d) When a book is placed on a table, then there will be two forces acting on it, such that first would be in downward direction due to force of gravity. Secondly would be the force exerted by the table on the book in the upward direction, that would balance the force of gravity. Thus, the net force acting on it would be zero.

74. (d) % change $= \dfrac{\Delta \mathbf{p}}{\mathbf{p}} \times 100 = \dfrac{4\mathbf{p} - \mathbf{p}}{\mathbf{p}} \times 100$

$= 300\%$ $\quad (\because 2m \cdot 2v = 4\,mv = 4\mathbf{p})$

75. (c) Retardation of ship $= \dfrac{F}{M} = \dfrac{5 \times 10^4}{3 \times 10^7}$

$= \dfrac{5}{3} \times 10^{-3} \text{ m/s}^2$

As, $v^2 - u^2 = 2as$

$\Rightarrow \quad v = \sqrt{2 \times \frac{5}{3} \times 10^{-3} \times 3}$ $\quad [\because u = 0]$

$= 0.1$ m/s

76. (b) $\therefore M_p = 2M_e$ and $r_p = 3r_e$

$\therefore \quad g_p = \dfrac{GM_p}{r_p^2}$

$g_p = \dfrac{G(2M_e)}{(3r_e)^2} = \dfrac{2}{9} g_e$

$\therefore \quad w_p = 5 \times \dfrac{2}{9} \times 9.8 = \dfrac{98}{9} = 10.88$ N

77. (a) $\therefore$ Buoyancy $= V_c \rho_c g = Mg$

Buoyancy depends on mass.

78. (c) $\therefore F = \dfrac{Gm_1 m_2}{r^2}$ $\quad \ldots$(i)

$\because \quad r' = \dfrac{r}{2}$

So, $F' = \dfrac{Gm_1 m_2}{\left(\frac{r}{2}\right)^2} = \dfrac{4Gm_1 m_2}{r^2} = 4F$ $\quad$ [from Eq. (i)]

79. (c) $\because g' = 4g$

$\therefore W = mg'h = 3 \times 4g \times 3 = 36 \times 10 = 360$ J

FULLY SOLVED

80. (b) 2 kg 1 kg 4 kg

A x C (2 − x) B

$$F_{AC} = F_{BC}$$

$$\frac{Gm_A m_C}{x^2} = \frac{Gm_B m_C}{(2-x)^2}$$

$$\Rightarrow \quad \left(\frac{2-x}{x}\right)^2 = \frac{4}{2}$$

$$\Rightarrow \quad 2 - x = \sqrt{2}x$$

$$\Rightarrow \quad x = \frac{2}{1+\sqrt{2}} = 0.83 \text{ m}$$

81. (d) Gravitational acceleration decreases from poles to equator.

There is weightlessness at the centre of earth.

82. (a) From law of conservation of momentum,

$$0 = m \times 16 + 2m \times v$$

$$v = -8 \text{ ms}^{-1}$$

$$\text{Total kinetic energy} = \frac{1}{2} m_1 v_1^2 + \frac{1}{2} m_2 v_2^2$$

$$= \frac{1}{2} \times m \times (16)^2 + \frac{1}{2} \times 2m \times (8)^2$$

$$= \frac{1}{2}[256 + 128] \times m = 192 \text{ mJ}$$

83. (a) $\therefore$ $\text{KE} = \frac{p^2}{2m} \Rightarrow p = \sqrt{2 \text{ KE } m}$

If $\frac{p_1}{p_2} = \frac{\sqrt{m_1}}{\sqrt{m_2}}$, when KE is same.

$$p \propto \sqrt{m}$$

84. (d) As, $\text{power} = \frac{\text{work}}{\text{time}}$

$$= \frac{mgh}{t} = \frac{50 \times 10 \times 15 \times 10^{-2} \times 45}{9}$$

$$= 375 \text{ W}$$

85. (c) Given, $\frac{\text{kinetic energy (KE)}}{\text{potential energy (PE)}} = \frac{3}{4} \Rightarrow \text{KE} = \frac{3}{4}\text{PE}$

As, from the law of conservation of energy,

$$\text{KE} + \text{PE} = mgh \Rightarrow \frac{7}{4}\text{PE} = mgh$$

So, for height (h') from the ground, PE = mgh'

$$\Rightarrow \quad \frac{7}{4} mgh' = mgh \quad \text{or} \quad h' = \frac{4}{7}h$$

86. (a) Given, $w = 600$ N, $m = 60$ kg

$$\therefore \quad \text{KE} = \frac{1}{2} m \times v^2$$

$$\Rightarrow \quad v = \sqrt{\frac{2\text{KE}}{m}} = \sqrt{\frac{2 \times 750}{60}}$$

$$v = 5 \text{ m/s}$$

87. (a) From the point of projection, velocity is maximum, so that kinetic energy is maximum after attending a height h, velocity becomes zero, so kinetic energy also become zero.

Potential energy is directly proportional to height.

So, correct graph is (a).

88. (b)

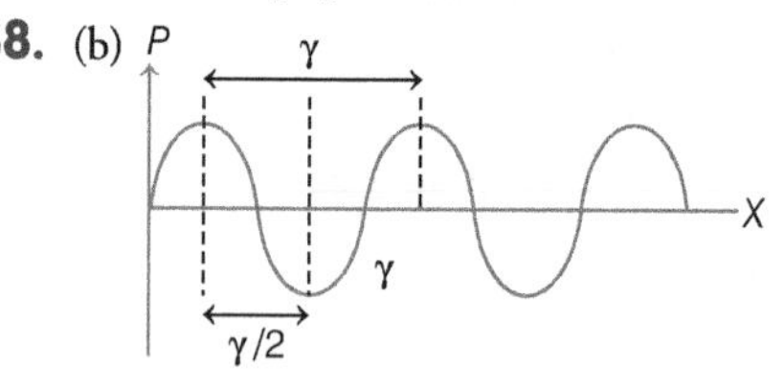

89. (a) Given, speed of wave (v) = 350 m/s

Wavelength (λ) = 70 cm or 0.7 m

$$\therefore \quad v = \lambda \times f$$

$$\Rightarrow \quad f = \frac{v}{\lambda} = \frac{350}{0.7} = 500 \text{ Hz}$$

90. (c) Speed of sound is decreases, as we go from solid to gaseous state.

91. (a) Time to the ground, $t_1 = \sqrt{\frac{2h}{g}} = \sqrt{\frac{2 \times 490}{9.8}} = 10$ s

Time for sound wave to reach 490 m,

$$t_2 = \frac{h}{v} = \frac{490}{350} = 1.4 \text{ s}$$

So, $T_{\text{total}} = t_1 + t_2 = 10 + 1.4$

$= 11.4$ s

92. (c) Rhinoceros can hear infrasound waves.

93. (b) $\therefore \lambda_1 = \frac{344}{20} = \frac{172}{10} = 17.2$ m $\quad \left[\because \lambda = \frac{v}{f}\right]$

and $\lambda_2 = \frac{344}{20 \times 10^3} = 17.2 \times 10^{-3}$ m

$= 17.2$ mm

94. (d) *Rhizobium* is a symbiotic nitrogen-fixing bacterium. *Nostoc*, *Anabaena* and *Azotobacter* are also involved in nitrogen-fixation.

95. (b) Biogeochemical cycles involve the cyclic flow of nutrients and energy among the biotic and abiotic components of ecosystem.

96. (d) Nutrients that are required in large amount by plants for their growth are called as macronutrients, e.g. calcium, nitrogen, phosphorus, etc.

97. (b) Jaya and Ratna are hybrid varieties of rice.

98. (b) Beekeeping is scientifically termed as apiculture.

99. (a) High yielding varieties of wheat were developed by Indian scientist by cross-breeding traditional varieties with varieties of Mexico. Sonora-64 and Lerma Rojo-64 were modified through gamma mutations.

100. (b) ILS-82 and B-77 are the breeds of present day chickens (fowl) for egg and meat production.

Junior Science Olympiad

Chapterwise Questions

Atoms and Molecules

1. An astronaut has to burn 40g of glucose in his body per hour to get the required energy. Find the amount of oxygen that would need to be carried in space to meet his energy requirement for thirty days **(2018)**
(a) 10.2 kg (b) 28.8 kg
(c) 30.7 kg (d) 96.1 kg

2. A sample of clay was partially dried and then found to contain 60% silica and 8% water. The original sample of clay contained 15% water. Find the percentage of silica in the original sample **(2018)**
(a) 52.3% (b) 47.8%
(c) 55.5% (d) 51.7%

3. A solution of pure ferric sulphate containing 0.140 g of ferric ions is treated with excess of barium hydroxide solution. Total weight of the precipitate will be **(2017)**
(a) 0.87 g (b) 1.14 g
(c) 0.25 g (d) 0.56 g

The Fundamental Unit of Life

4. Many proteins of the chloroplast are encoded by genes in the nucleus. In these cases, the RNA is transcribed in the nucleus, translated by the cytoplasmic ribosomes and the protein transported to the chloroplast. For such a protein how many membrane(s) does the protein cross to reach the thylakoid space (lumen) of the chloroplast? **(2018)**
(a) One (b) Two
(c) Three (d) Four

5. In a hypothetical situation, a cell was found to lack rough endoplasmic reticulum. Which one of the following activities was all likely absent in this cell? **(2017)**
(a) Transcription
(b) Translation
(c) Synthesis of secretory proteins
(d) Manufacture of fat molecules or lipids

Motion

6. While driving on a level road at 72 km/h, Vinayak observes the traffic signal turning red, the (white) stopping line being 52 m away from the front end of his car. Immediately he applies the brakes that decelerate his car at 4 m/s^2. How far from the stopping line will the front end of Vinayak's car be after 6 s? **(2017)**
(a) Zero (b) 2 m (c) 4 m (d) 6 m

Gravitation

7. A piece of ice with a stone (denser than water) embedded inside, is kept in a vessel containing water. Size and mass of the stone is such that the stone-ice combination is floating on water. When the ice melts, what will happen to the level of water in the breaker? **(2016)**
(a) Water level will rise
(b) Water level will fall
(c) Water level will remain unchanged
(d) Final level of water will depend upon actual density of the stone

8. Figure given below shows a small boat, containing some iron balls, floating on a still lake. These iron blocks are now dropped into the lake. Select the ***WRONG*** statement. **(2015)**

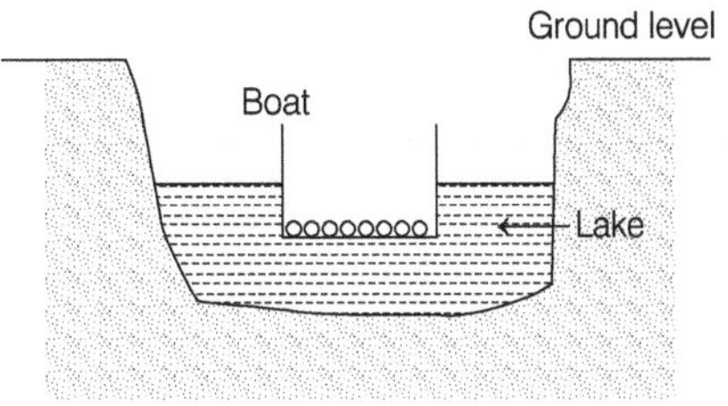

(a) Level of the lake will fall with ground reference
(b) The boat will rise with water reference
(c) Level of the boat will rise with ground reference
(d) Water level will not change from the ground reference

FULLY SOLVED

9. A satellite is launched in a circular orbit of radius R. Another satellite is also launched in an orbit of radius $1.1R$. The period of the second satellite is larger than the first by approximately **(2014)**
(a) 7.5% (b) 1.5% (c) 15% (d) 10%

Answers

FULLY SOLVED

1. (c) One molecule (180 g) of glucose requires 6 oxygen molecules to burn and release energy.
180g of glucose requires $= 6\ O_2$ or 12 oxygen atom
$= 12 \times 16 = 192$g of oxygen
40g of glucose requires $= \frac{192}{180} \times 40$
$\therefore$ 40 g of glucose requires 42.66 g of oxygen per hour.
For 24×30 hours (30 days) requires oxygen
$= 42.66 \times 720$
$= 30722.4$ g
$= 30.7$ kg
Therefore, 30.7 kg of oxygen would be required by astronaut to be carried with him to meet his energy requirement for thirty day.

2. (c) Let 100 g of the partially dried clay sample contains 8% water and 60% silica.
Therefore, non water component present in partially dried sample =92 g.
Original clay sample contained = 15 g water
Total non-water components = 85 g
$\therefore$ Mass % age of silica $= \frac{60}{92} \times 85$
$= 55.42\%$

3. (b) Balanced reaction for the reaction between ferric sulphate and excess of barium hydroxide solution is given as,
$$Fe_2(SO_4)_3 + \underset{\text{Excess}}{3Ba(OH)_2} \longrightarrow \underset{\text{pecipitate}}{2Fe(OH)_3} + 3BaSO_4$$
or $$2Fe^{3+} + \underset{\text{Excess}}{OH^-} \longrightarrow 2Fe(OH)_3$$
From the above equation, it is clear that,
55.845 g of Fe^{3+} produces
$= (55.845 + 51)\ g$ of precipitates of $Fe(OH)_3$
1 g of Fe^{3+} produces $= \frac{(55.845 + 51)}{55.845}$ g of precipitates
$\therefore$ 0.140 g of Fe^{3+} produces $= \frac{(55.845 + 51 \times 0.140)}{55.845}$
$= 1.14$ g

4. (c) Chloroplast is a double membranous cell organelle with an inner and an outer membrane. It encloses single membranous thylakoids.
Thus, for a protein present in cytoplasm has to cross three membranes to reach the lumen of thylakoid.

5. (c) Rough endoplasmic reticulum is involved in the manufacturing of proteins secreted by a cell, thus a cell lacking it would not exhibit synthesis of secretory proteins.

6. (b) Given, speed = 72 km/h = 20 m/s,
retardation = 4 m/s^2
$\therefore$ Distance of stop, $v^2 - u^2 = 2as$
$\Rightarrow$ $400 = 2 \times 4 \times s$
$\therefore$ $s = 50$ m
So, distance of stopping line from the car
$= 52 - 50 = 2$ m

7. (b) As the stone-ice combination is floating in water, the volume of ice is greater than that of water, so when the ice melts, it occupies less volume than that occupied by the ice in water. Hence, water level will fall.

8. (d) By dropping the iron block, the level of boat rises and the level of lake water also decreases, because iron blocks are linked now.
So, option (d) is incorrect.

9. (c) According to Kepler's law, the period of a planetary motion is given by
$$T \propto r^{3/2}$$
$$\Rightarrow \quad \frac{T_1}{T_2} = \frac{R^{3/2}}{(1.1R)^{3/2}} = \frac{1}{1.15}$$
$\therefore$ Percentage increase in period $= \frac{1.15 - 1}{1} \times 100 = 15\%$

Lightning Source UK Ltd.
Milton Keynes UK
UKHW051929131022
410412UK00003B/7